W9-DHX-125

Scandinavia

Fodor's 90

Scandinavia

FODOR'S TRAVEL PUBLICATIONS, INC.
New York

Copyright © 1990 by Fodor's Travel Publications, Inc.

Fodor's is a trademark of Fodor's Travel Publications, Inc.

All rights reserved under International and Pan-American Copyright Conventions.
Published in the United States by Fodor's Travel Publications, Inc., a subsidiary of
Random House, Inc., New York, and simultaneously in Canada by Random House of
Canada Limited, Toronto. Distributed by Random House, Inc., New York.

*No maps, illustrations, or other portions of this book may be reproduced in any form without
written permission from the publisher.*

ISBN 0–679–01822–0

Fodor's Scandinavia

Executive Editor: Richard Moore
Associate Editor: Sean Connolly
Assistant Editors: Caz Philcox, Judy Tither
Area Editors: Asgeir Fridgeirsson, Sylvie
     Nickels, Anita Peltonen, Carla Power, Philip Ray
Editorial Contributor: Andrew Brown

Drawings: Elizabeth Haines
Maps and Plans: Swanston Graphics, Bryan Woodfield
Cover Photograph: Adam Woolfitt/Wes Light

Cover Design: Vignelli Associates

Special Sales

Fodor's Travel Publications are available at special discounts for bulk purchases
(100 copies or more) for sales promotions or premiums. Special editions,
including personalized covers, excerpts of existing guides, and corporate
imprints, can be created in large quantities for special needs. For more
information, write to Special Marketing, Fodor's Travel Publications, 201 East
50th Street, New York, NY 10022. Inquiries from the United Kingdom should
be sent to Fodor's Travel Publications, 30–32 Bedford Square, London WC1B
3SG.

MANUFACTURED IN THE UNITED STATES OF AMERICA
10 9 8 7 6 5 4 3 2 1

CONTENTS

ICELAND

NORWAY

FOREWORD

Scandinavia is an unusual part of Europe. It is a small group of nations, with interdependent histories, many elements of society and background in common, and yet each fiercely proud of its own national identity; a sort of mini United Nations. It is also a region which offers perhaps the widest variety of holiday opportunities in Europe, ranging from the sophistication of such capitals as Copenhagen and Stockholm, through the calm serenity of clear, ice-blue waters, unpopulated forests and unspoiled countryside to the adventure of the far northern tracts of the Arctic Circle. All this with the genuine friendliness and hospitality of the people themselves into the bargain.

But perhaps "bargain" is not quite the right word. If Scandinavia does have a drawback as a vacation destination, it is that it is an expensive region. This in itself can be taken as a compliment to the industriousness and consequent prosperity of the Scandinavians. Their countries are among the most affluent in the world, and living standards, and therefore of course the cost of living, are correspondingly high. Moreover, the Scandinavians all enjoy remarkably comprehensive welfare benefits, and this in turn—admirable though it is—pushes up the cost of living still further by dint of very much higher-than-average taxes on almost all services and goods.

But all need not be gloom. The particular pleasures of Scandinavia are nearly all—with the exception of her capital cities—to be found in the great outdoors. The opportunities for open-air holidays—farm vacations (raised to a fine art here), riding, camping, fishing, sailing, canoeing—are absolutely second to none; and all, by their very nature, are of course essentially inexpensive. Moreover, the very industriousness that has raised Scandinavia to her present lofty place on the world's pecking order, also ensures that all these activities are excellently-organized and superbly-run.

There are other plus marks too. Scandinavia is easy to reach and easy to travel around in. The quality of hotels, even those in the depths of the country, is almost always high. For those who do want to spend time in one or more of the capital cities—and there are compelling reasons for doing so—there are a whole host of travel bargains, museum entry cards and inexpensive hotel and restaurant deals. And of course, the cities themselves, as well as being among Europe's most orderly, are uniformly elegant, urbane and charming. And wherever you go in Scandinavia, there is the added bonus of knowing that English will not only be spoken—it will be spoken excellently, no small relief when you consider the tortuosities of Finnish. All in all, it's hard to think of reasons not to go.

* * * *

We are indebted once again to the Directors of the Scandinavian National Tourist Offices in London for their generous cooperation; specifically to Boris Taimitarha and Marjatta Haapio of the Finnish Tourist Board; to Barbro Hunter of the Swedish National Tourist Office; to Poul Christensen of the Danish Tourist Board; and to Ivar Hauff of the Norwegian Tourist Board.

We would especially like to acknowledge the hard work and helpful interest of our team of Area Editors without whom this edition would not have been possible.

FOREWORD

* * * *

While every care has been taken to assure the accuracy of the information in this guide, the passage of time will always bring change, and consequently the publisher cannot accept responsibility for errors that may occur.

All prices and opening times quoted in this guide are based on information available to us at press time. Hours and admission fees may change, however, and the prudent traveler will avoid inconvenience by calling ahead.

Fodor's wants to hear about your travel experiences, both pleasant and unpleasant. When a hotel or restaurant fails to live up to its billing, let us know and we will investigate the complaint and revise our entries where the facts warrant it.

Send your letters to the editors of Fodor's Travel Publications, 201 East 50th Street, New York, NY 10022.

PLANNING YOUR TRIP

SOURCES OF INFORMATION. The major sources of information for anyone planning a vacation in Scandinavia are the National Tourist Offices of the five Scandinavian countries. They will be able to supply information on all aspects of travel to and around Scandinavia—from which type of vacation is best suited to your needs and purse to the best and most economical ways of getting to Scandinavia, as well as information on hotels, restaurants, excursions, museums, travel discounts and so on. They produce copious amounts of information, much of it free and all of it useful. Anyone planning a vacation in Scandinavia would be well advised to make the National Tourist Offices their starting point.

In the U.S., all five Scandinavian countries operate from one principal office in New York. In the U.K., each country has its own office.

Their addresses are:

In the U.S.: *Scandinavian National Tourist Office,* 655 Third Ave., New York, NY 10017 (212–370–5540). *Finnish Tourist Board,* 1900 Avenue of the Stars, Suite 1025, Los Angeles CA 90067 (213–277–5226).

In Canada: *Danish Tourist Board,* Box 115, Station N, Toronto, Ontario M8V 3S4 (416–823–9620). *Finnish Tourist Board,* 1200 Bay St., Suite 604, Toronto, Ontario M5R 2A5 (416–964–9159).

In the U.K.: *Danish Tourist Board,* 169–173 Regent St., London W.1 (01–734 2637). *Finnish Tourist Board,* 66–68 Haymarket, London S.W.1 (01–839 4048). *Iceland Tourist Information Bureau,* 73 Grosvenor St., London W.1 (01–499 9971). *Norwegian Tourist Board,* 20 Pall Mall, London S.W.1 (01–839 6255). *Swedish National Tourist Office,* 3 Cork St., London W.1 (01–437 5816).

In addition, within Scandinavia each country has a network of highly efficient local tourist offices (some open summer only) which can supply specific information on where to stay and eat, what's on and where, local travel discounts and sightseeing trips. We give addresses and telephone numbers of all the major local offices at the beginning of every *Practical Information* section.

PACKAGE TOURS OR INDEPENDENT TRAVEL? The best and most economical way to visit Scandinavia, especially from the States and Canada, is on a package tour. The number and variety of these is immense and most offer excellent value for money. The principal advantage of any package tour is that the two single most expensive components of any vacation—getting there and accommodations—will generally be very competitively priced and will be arranged for you.

At the same time, most packages offer considerable flexibility. You can, for example, buy an all-inclusive, pre-paid package, which gives you flight, accommodations, meals and excursions—all at a fixed price—leaving only incidental expenditure (drinks, shopping, mail etc.) for you to pay for during your trip. For those making a first visit and unsure of where to visit or how to get around, this is frequently an excellent introduction to a country. Many, however, find this type of trip too stifling or regimented. There is also the drawback that you might find your fellow packagees—from whom there is no escape—dull, though of course at the same time you might get on fine.

Alternatively, therefore, there are packages which give you flight and accommodations only, with optional pre-paid meals and excursions. To a large extent, this sort of semi-independent package gives you the best of both worlds. Accordingly, it tends to be the most popular.

Other options available include fly-drive, which is particularly suitable for those who want the maximum independence, though here costs tend to be steeper, or a rail-air combination. Similarly, special interest packages, again offering varying degrees of flexibility and independence, are also available. Popular themes include sailing, bird-watching, castle touring, painting, photography, art tours, gourmet tours, sporting activities of all kinds, farm vacations, and much else besides.

However, if you do plump for a package, be very sure to find out in advance exactly what is included in the price and how much you will have to pay for once in Scandinavia. For example, how many meals are included? How tied to the tour are you? If it is a bus tour, do you have to stay with the tour city by city or can you leave and rejoin it at will? If you have a car, is the rate included in the package or is there an additional fee per mile? Is the car exactly what you want? Airconditioning is certainly unnecessary at any time of year in Scandinavia, and there is a substantial difference between the charge for standard and automatic shifts. Can you drive a standard? What is the tour operator's responsibility for getting you home on time?

In other words, be absolutely certain you know what you are paying for, *and read the fine print very carefully.*

Independent travel, on the other hand, has the great advantage of allowing you to do precisely as you please, but it also has the drawback of almost always being more expensive than a comparable package tour. That is not to say it can't be better value for money. For instance, while dinner and meals on a package tour may generally be very inexpensive, this is normally because the tour operator has struck a cut-price rate with your hotel or restaurant. Accordingly, you will tend to get cut-price food and service, while anyone traveling on their own will almost certainly get both better food and better service. Is this better value for money? Possibly, but individual preference is clearly the dominant factor in choosing any vacation and it is up to you to decide.

TRAVEL AGENTS. Regardless of whether you plan to visit Scandinavia independently or take a package, it is advisable to consult a reputable travel agent. If you are only after an inexpensive flight, at the very least he will be able to guide you through the impenetrable maze of trans-Atlantic air fares. But if you want to buy a complete package, or even have an entire itinerary devised (which will prove expensive) he will be able to recommend the most appropriate for your particular needs. He will also be able to arrange insurance and passports. A good travel agent can save you time, money and a good deal of inconvenience, and is an invaluable extra source of information.

If you are in any doubt which agent to contact, consult the American Society of Travel Agents, 1101 King St., Alexandria, VA 22314, or the Association of British Travel Agents, 55–57 Newman St., London W.1. Both will point you in the right direction.

TOUR OPERATORS. Full details of the many operators offering trips to Scandinavia are available from the Scandinavia National Tourist Office, Scandinavian Airlines (SAS) and of course your travel agent. But such is the range of tours and vacations on offer from both North America and the U.K., that a summary of some of the more typical should provide you with a handy pointer to availability. Bear in mind, however, that the few we list here are only the tip of the iceberg and that many, many more are available. All details quoted below are for 1988 only—check latest information with your travel agent.

From the U.S.: *Crownline Tours,* 3300 S. Gessner Rd., Suite 100, Houston, TX 77063 (800–556–8747 or 800–722–6737), offers various escorted tours ranging from three to 16 days. The "Scandinavian Gem" priced from $998 per person, double, is a 12-day fully escorted tour with hotels representing outstanding value. Both tours go to Sweden, Norway, and Denmark. Crownline also offers a Fly-Drive Program based on an affordable rent-a-car, plus hotel checks (from $37 per person, double). One-week hotel packages are available in Copenhagen from $396 and in Stockholm from $179 per person, double. *Bennett,* 270 Madison Ave., New York, NY 10016 (212–532–5060) runs a 15-day "Scandinavian Vikinglands" tour taking in Oslo, Stockholm and Copenhagen and including a short fjord cruise. Accommodations are all in first-class hotels and cost is about $1,890 per person excluding airfare.

A similar 15-day tour is offered by *Four Winds,* 175 Fifth Ave., New York, NY 10010 (212–777–0260 or 800–248–4444). Its "Scandinavian Highlights" is a bus tour that also takes in two overnight cruises. Accommodations are all first-class and cost is around $2,498 per person excluding airfare. For those in search of more rugged landscapes who don't want to give up creature comforts, *Four Winds*'s "Scandinavian Explorer" is a 21-day tour of Norway, Denmark, Sweden, and Finland, with an overnight on a Baltic Sea cruise. Cost is around $3,798 per person, not including airfare.

From the U.K.: The *Norwegian State Railways Travel Bureau,* Norway House, 21–24 Cockspur St., London SW1Y 5DA, offers an impressive range of vacations in the four main Scandinavian countries, though the bulk of their tours are Norwegian based. They also have city tours of varying lengths, most in deluxe or first-class hotels. *Fred Olsen Lines,* Victoria Plaza, 111 Buckingham Palace Rd., London SW1W OSP, have all-inclusive holidays in Norway and Denmark including self-catering, farmhouse holidays, touring, cruises and mini-breaks in cities. *Scanscape Holidays,* 197–199 City Rd., London EC1V 1JN, operated by the Danish-owned Maersk Air group, offers a wide range of inclusive holidays in all the Nordic countries, including Finland and Iceland. Those after a little more in the way of culture could do worse than head in the direction of *Serenissima,* 21 Dorset Sq., London NW1 5PG, the experts in art and archeology tours, who offer a cruise, "Baltic with Music," for £845 to £1,525.

Finally, for vacations in Iceland, contact *Icelandair,* 360 W. 31 St., New York, NY 10001 (800–223–5500, ext. 71) for details on camping, fishing, fly-drive, city and safari vacations in Scandinavia's Atlantic outpost.

WHEN TO GO. By far and away the best time to visit any of the Scandinavian countries is in the summer. The Scandinavian winter is not only very long and very cold, with shorter and shorter days the further north you go (and correspondingly lower and lower temperatures), but almost all the major tourist facilities—museums, sightseeing excursions, ferries, even many museums—are scaled right down or in some cases, the Tivoli Gardens in Copenhagen, for example, closed completely. More to the point, however, is the fact that most of the real fun to be had in Scandinavia takes place outdoors, and with the exception of winter sports, of which more in a moment, there is very little you are liable to want to do, or will even be able to do, outside during the Scandinavian winter. That said, however, clear, crisp and sunny days are by no means uncommon in the winter, and though short they can be delightful.

Nonetheless, it is from mid-May to mid-September that Scandinavia is at its best. Summer temperatures are surprisingly high—certainly comparable to Maine or Vermont, for example—while the sea is generally much warmer than you might expect, largely as a result of the Gulf Stream and the shallowness of the Baltic. You may accordingly consider visiting in April or late September, but bear in mind that the weather can be unpredictable.

For devotees of the midnight sun, Norway, Sweden, Finland, and Iceland are the countries to visit; Denmark being too far south for the full effect. June is the best month for the midnight sun in Iceland, when the sun touches the sea and rises again. It is light enough to read through the night, and even at midnight there is always a certain luminosity in the night sky. But in the far north of Scandinavia—Norway's North Cape or Utsjoki in Finland for example—the sun does not sink below the horizon from the second week in May until the last week in July. (At the same time of course, during the corresponding period in the winter, the sun never rises.)

Winter sports last from mid-December to mid-April. Denmark's lack of mountains limits the sports available. Iceland has been improving its winter sports facilities over the last few years. Both Sweden and Finland have well developed winter resorts, offering cross-country skiing, skating and curling, though little in the way of Alpine, or downhill, skiing. Norway, while it has equally good facilities for all forms of Nordic skiing, also has some good downhill skiing. Winter sports facilities are now generally good throughout these four countries, but bear in mind that the winter weather here is not always equally accommodating.

TIME. Iceland operates on Greenwich Mean Time, which is five hours ahead of Eastern Standard Time, while Denmark, Norway and Sweden are all one hour ahead of Greenwich Mean Time and six hours ahead of Eastern Standard Time (two hours ahead during summer). Finland is two hours ahead of Greenwich Mean Time and seven hours ahead of Eastern Standard Time.

WHAT TO PACK. The golden rule is to travel light; generally, try not to take more than you can carry yourself. Not only are porters more or less wholly extinct in Europe these days (where you can find them they're very expensive anyway), the less luggage you take the easier checking in and out of hotels becomes, similarly airports (increasingly the number one nightmare of all modern travel) become much easier to get through and, if you only take one piece of luggage, the less risk there is of your luggage being lost en route, and, in theory anyway, the less time you need to wait for it to appear when you get off the plane. It's an excellent idea also to make sure that your luggage is sturdy; there's no worse way to start or finish your vacation than by discovering that your clothes are generously distributing themselves along a station platform or, even worse, have already scattered themselves around the hold of a 747. It can also be a good idea to pack the bulk of your things in one large bag and put everything you need for overnight, or for two or three nights, in a smaller one, to obviate packing and repacking at brief stops.

Bear in mind that on trans-Atlantic flights there is, in any case, a size limit to the amount of luggage you may take with you. Charges for excess baggage are high. On most flights you may check in no more than two pieces of luggage, neither more than 62 inches overall (that is, height plus length plus width) and both together no more than 106 inches. Hand baggage is restricted to one piece no more than 65 inches overall.

Having said all this, however, don't forget to leave room for shopping. Though at the same time remember that almost all Scandinavian stores can have goods sent directly to your home.

Clothes. Informality is the key word throughout Scandinavia, even in relatively more upright and old fashioned Norway. So at even the smartest restaurants or at the theater—and this applies to the opera and ballet as well—you are not likely to have to dress up. Those few restaurants that do expect men to wear a tie will always lend you one if necessary. Thus normal summer clothes, with a generous sprinkling of sports clothes, will happily suffice, but also take along sweaters and stout shoes if you are going into the mountains. And don't forget a light topcoat or raincoat. The summer weather is generally fine, but rain is by no means uncommon. If you are going to Scandinavia in the winter, it will be very cold, so take along plenty of warm clothing. Be prepared to shed it once indoors, however; Scandinavian central heating is nothing if not efficient.

Finally, mosquitoes, especially in the far north, can be a real nuisance from the end of June to early August. Take some repellent with you.

TAKING MONEY ABROAD. Traveler's checks are still the standard and best way to safeguard your travel funds; and you will usually get a better exchange rate in Europe for traveler's checks than for cash. In the U.S., Bank of America and Republic Bank of Dallas issue checks only in U.S. dollars; Thomas Cook issues checks in U.S., British and Australian currencies; Barclays Bank in dollars and pounds; and American Express in U.S., Canadian, French, German, British, Swiss and Japanese currencies. Your choice of branch will depend on several factors. American Express checks are widely known, Bank of America has some 28,000 correspondents throughout the world, Thomas Cook about 20,000. The best-known British checks are Cook's and those of Barclays, Lloyds, Midland and National Westminster banks.

Britons holding a Uniform Eurocheque card and cheque book—apply for them at your bank—can cash cheques for up to £100 a day at banks participating in the scheme and write cheques for goods and services—in hotels, restaurants, shops, etc.—again up to £100.

Details of currency within each Scandinavian country, changing money and exchange rates are given at the beginning of the *Facts at Your Fingertips* for each country later in this guide.

Credit Cards. Most major credit cards are generally, but by no means universally, accepted in larger Scandinavian hotels, restaurants and shops. Accordingly, you would be well advised to check carefully which cards *are* accepted, particularly in hotels and restaurants, before checking in or ordering a meal.

Our hotel and restaurant listings in the *Practical Information* sections at the end of every chapter give details of each of the four major cards—American Express, Diner's Club, MasterCard (incorporating Access and EuroCard) and Visa, which are listed under the abbreviations AE, DC, MC and V—accepted in each hotel and restaurant we carry. But as we say, double check. As a general rule, you will find that Visa is the most commonly accepted.

PASSPORTS. Americans. All U.S. citizens require a valid passport to enter any Scandinavian country. Visas are not required. If you do not have a passport, apply in person at U.S. Passport Agency Offices, local county courthouses or selected Post Offices. Renewals can be handled by mail (Form DSP-82) provided that your previous passport is not more than 12 years old. In addition to the completed application (Form DSP-11), new applicants will need:

—Proof of citizenship, such as a birth certificate.

—Two identical photographs, in either black and white or color, on nonglossy paper and taken within the past six months.

—$35 for the passport itself plus a $7 processing fee if you are applying in person (no processing fee when renewing your passport by mail) for those 18 years and older, or if you are under 18, $20 for the passport plus a $7 processing fee if you are applying in person (again, no extra fee when applying by mail).

—Proof of identity that includes a photograph and signature, such as a driver's license, previous passport, any governmental ID card.

Adult passports are valid for 10 years, others for five years; they are not renewable. Allow four to six weeks for your application to be processed, but in an emergency, Passport Agency offices can have a passport readied within 24–48 hours, and even the postal authorities can indicate "Rush" when necessary.

If you expect to travel extensively, request a 48- or 96-page passport rather than the usual 24-page one. There is no extra charge. When you receive your passport, write down its number, date and place of issue in a separate, secure place. The loss of a valid passport should be reported immediately to the local police and to the Passport Office, Dept. of State, 1425 K. St., NW, Washington, DC 20524. If your passport is lost or stolen while abroad, report it immediately to the local authorities and apply for a replacement at the nearest U.S. Embassy or consular office.

Canadians. Canadian citizens should apply in person at regional passport offices and Post Offices, or by mail to Bureau of Passports, External Affairs, Ottawa, Ont. K1A OG3. A $25 fee, two photographs, a guarantor, and evidence of citizenship are required. Canadian passports are valid for five years and are non-renewable.

Britons. You should apply for passports on special forms obtainable from main post offices or a travel agent. The application should be sent or taken to the Passport Office according to residential area (as indicated on the guidance form) or lodged with them through a travel agent. It is best to apply for the passport 4–5 weeks before it is required, although in some cases it will be issued sooner. The regional Passport Offices are located in London, Liverpool, Peterborough, Glasgow and Newport. The application must be countersigned by your bank manager or by a solicitor, barrister, doctor, clergyman or justice of the peace who knows you personally. You will need two full-face photos. The fee is £15; passport valid for 10 years.

British Visitor's Passport. This simplified form of passport has advantages for the once-in-a-while tourist to most European countries, including Scandinavia. Valid for one year and not renewable, it costs £7.50. Application may be made at main post office in England, Scotland and Wales, and in Northern Ireland at the Passport Office in Belfast. Birth certificate or medical card for identification and two passport photographs are required—no other formalities.

HEALTH AND INSURANCE. The different varieties of travel insurance cover everything from health and accident costs, to lost baggage and trip cancelation. Sometimes they can all be obtained with one blanket policy; other times they overlap with existing coverage you might have for health and/or home; still other times it is best to buy policies that are tailored to very specific needs. Insurance is available from many sources, however, and many travelers unwittingly end up with duplicate coverage. Before purchasing separate travel insurance of any kind, be sure to check your regular policies carefully.

Generally, it is best to take care of your insurance needs before embarking on your trip. You'll pay more for less coverage—and have less chance to read the fine print—if you wait until the last minute and make your purchases from, say, an airport vending machine or insurance company counter. If you have a regular insurance agent, he or she is the person to consult first.

Flight insurance, which is often included in the price of the ticket when the fare is paid via American Express, Visa or certain other major credit cards, is also often included in package policies providing accident coverage as well. These policies are available from most tour operators and insurance companies. But while it is a good idea to have health and accident insurance when traveling, be careful not to spend money to duplicate coverage you may already have . . . or to neglect some eventuality which could end up costing a small fortune.

For example, basic Blue Cross-Blue Shield policies do cover health costs incurred while traveling. They will not, however, cover the cost of emergency transportation, which can often add up to several thousand dollars. Emergency transportation *is* covered, in part at least, by many major medical policies such as those underwritten by Prudential and Metropolitan. Again, we can't urge you too strongly that in order to be sure you are getting the coverage you need, check any policy carefully before buying. And bear in mind also that most insurance issued specifically for travel will not cover pre-existing conditions, such as a heart condition.

Several organizations offer coverage designed to supplement existing health insurance and to help defray costs not covered by many standard policies, such as emergency transportation. Some of the more prominent are:

Carefree Travel Insurance, c/o ARM Coverage, Inc., 120 Mineola Blvd., Box 310, Mineola, NY 11501, underwritten by the Hartford Accident and Indemnity Co., offers a comprehensive benefits package that includes trip cancelation and interruption, medical, and accidental death/dismemberment coverage, as well as medical, legal, and economic assistance. Trip cancelation and interruption insurance can be purchased separately. Call 800–654–2424 for additional information.

International SOS Assistance Inc., Box 11568, Philadelphia, PA 19116, has fees from $15 a person for seven days, to $195 for a year (800–523–8930).

IAMAT (International Association for Medical Assistance to Travelers), 417 Center St., Lewiston, NY 14092 (716–754–4883) in the U.S.; or 40 Regal Rd., Guelph, Ontario, N1K 1B5 (519–836–0102), makes available a free list of English-speaking doctors throughout Europe who adhere to the following fee schedule: office calls, $20; hotel calls, $30; night and holiday calls, $40.

Travel Assistance International, the American arm of Europ Assistance, offers a comprehensive program providing medical and personal emergency services and offering immediate, on-the-spot medical, personal and financial help. Trip protection ranges from $40 for an individual for up to eight days to $600 for an entire family for a year. Full details from travel agents or insurance brokers, or from Europ Assistance Worldwide Services, Inc., 1133 15th St. NW, Washington, DC (800–821–2828). In the U.K., contact Europ Assistance Ltd., 252 High St. Croydon, Surrey (01–680 1234).

The British Insurance Association, Aldermary House, Queen St., London E.C.4 (01–248 4477), will give comprehensive advice on all aspects of vacation travel insurance from the U.K.

Another frequent inconvenience to travelers is the loss of baggage. It is possible, though often a complicated affair, to insure your luggage against loss through theft or negligence. Insurance companies are reluctant to sell such coverage alone, however, since it is often a losing proposition for them. Instead, this type of coverage is usually included as part of a package that also covers accidents or health. Should you lose your luggage or some other personal possession, it is essential to report it to the local police immediately. Without documentation of such a report, your insurance company might be very stingy. Also, before buying baggage insurance, check your homeowner's policy. Some such policies offer "off-premises theft" coverage, including the loss of luggage while traveling.

Trip cancellation coverage is especially important to travelers on APEX or charter flights. Should you be unable to continue your trip during your vacation, you may be stuck having to buy a new one-way fare home, plus paying for the charter you're not using. You can guard against this with "trip cancellation insurance." Most of these policies will also cover last-minute cancellations.

STUDENT AND YOUTH TRAVEL. All student travelers should obtain an *International Student Identity Card,* which is generally needed to get student discounts, youth rail passes, and travel insurance. Apply to *Council On International Educational Exchange (CIEE),* 205 E. 42 St., New York, NY 10017 (212–661–1414). Canadian students should apply to the *Canadian Federation of Students-Services,* 187 College St., Toronto, Ontario M5T 1P7 (416–979–2406).

The following organizations can also be helpful in finding student flights, educational opportunities and other information. Most deal with international student travel generally, but those listed cover Scandinavia.

American Youth Hostels, Box 37613, Washington, DC 20013 (202–783–6161). Members are eligible to use the worldwide network of youth hostels. The organization publishes an extensive directory on same.

CIEE provides information on study, travel, and work abroad and travel programs, and services for college and high school students and other budget travelers. Write for a free copy of CIEE's annual *Student Travel Catalog.* Another CIEE publication, *Work, Study, Travel Abroad: The Whole World Handbook* ($8.95 plus $1 postage for the 1989–1990 edition) is the best listing for such possibilities.

Institute of International Education, 809 United Nations Plaza, New York, NY 10017 (212–883–8200), is primarily concerned with study opportunities and administers scholarships and fellowships for international study and training. It publishes *Vacation Study Abroad,* ($22.95), an annual guide to over 1,100 courses offered by both foreign and American colleges and universities, and *Academic Year Abroad,* ($24.95), which details foreign study programs offered by American schools for academic credit during the academic year.

Also worth contacting is *Educational Travel Center,* 438 N. Frances, Madison, WI 53703 (608–256–5551).

Specific information on rail and other discounts is listed in the *Facts at Your Fingertips* sections for each Scandinavian country.

HINTS FOR HANDICAPPED TRAVELERS. Facilities for the handicapped in Scandinavia are generally good, if somewhat variable. Most of the major tourist offices produce information detailing facilities. The Danish Tourist Board have an *Access in Denmark—A Tourist Guide for the Disabled* booklet; alternatively, write *Bolig-, Motor- og Hjaelpemiddeludvalget* (Committee for Housing, Transportation and Technical Aids), Hans Knudsens Plads 1A, DK-2100 Copenhagen. The Norwegian Tourist Board produces a *Travel Guide for the Disabled,* available only from the Tourist Board in Oslo (H Heyerdahlsgate 1, Oslo 1, Norway), and a leaflet detailing all hotels with facilities for handicapped visitors.

In Finland, Area Travel Agency, Kaisaniemenkatu 13A, 00100 Helsinki (90–18 551) runs a seven-day Triangle Tour for handicapped persons (minimum of 10 per group) year-round; itinerary is Helsinki–Turku–Tampere–Hämeenlinna–Helsinki.

The Swedish Tourist Board has published a comprehensive 150-page guide in English on all aspects of travel for the disabled within Sweden. The guide lists suitable accommodations with an indication of the special facilities provided. Holiday sporting activities and sightseeing attractions suitable for disabled travelers are also listed.

Otherwise, the major sources of information are: *Access to the World: A Travel Guide for the Handicapped,* by Louise Weiss, a helpful but dated book covering all aspects of travel for anyone with health or medical problems; it features extensive listings and suggestions on everything from availability of special diets to wheelchair accessibility. The book is out of print but can be ordered from *Facts On File,* 460 Park Ave. South, New York, NY 10016. The Travel Information Service at the *Moss Rehabilitation Hospital,* 12th St. and Tabor Rd., Philadelphia, PA 19141 (215–329–5715), gives information on facilities for the handicapped in many countries and also provides toll-free numbers of airlines with special lines for the hearing impaired; they can also provide listings of tour operators who arrange vacations for the handicapped. But for a complete list of tour operators, write to the *Society for the Advancement of Travel for the Handicapped (SATH),* 26 Court St., Penthouse Suite, Brooklyn, NY 11242.

In the U.K., contact *Mobility International,* 43 Dorset St., London W.1; the *National Society for Mentally Handicapped Children,* 117 Golden Lane, London E.C.1; the *Across Trust,* Crown House, Morden, Surrey (they have an amazing series of "Jumbulances," huge articulated ambulances, staffed by volunteer doctors and nurses, that can whisk even the most seriously handicapped across Europe in comfort and safety). But the main sources in Britain for all advice on handicapped travel are *The Royal Association for Disability and Rehabilitation,* (RADAR), 25 Mortimer St., London W.1, and the *Holiday Care Service,* 2 Old Bank Chambers, Station Road, Horley, Surrey.

Getting to Scandinavia

FROM THE U.S. By Air. Flights from major departure points in the U.S. and Canada to the Scandinavian capitals, and some other major Scandinavian cities, are frequent and generally easy to arrange. And, given the perpetual battle for customers among airlines flying the Atlantic, even to relatively less important destinations such as Scandinavia, fares are generally inexpensive. We give details of sample fares and of the principal carriers operating from North America to Scandinavia below.

However, be warned that though fares may be low and flights numerous, long-distance flying today is no bed of roses. Lines and delays at ever-more-crowded airports, perfunctory in-flight service and shrinking leg-room on board a giant jet with some 400 other people, followed by interminable waits for your luggage when you arrive, are the clearest possible signals that the glamour of air travel—if it ever existed—is very much a thing of the past.

Unfortunately, these problems are compounded when flying to Europe by the fact that most flights from the States are scheduled to arrive first thing in the morning. Not only are you in for a night's discomfort on the plane, but you arrive at the start of a new day to be greeted by the confusion (some would say chaos) of a modern airport. To make life even more difficult for the weary traveler, many hotels will not allow you to check in before noon or even 1 P.M. giving you as much as six hours with nothing to do and nowhere to go.

There are a number of steps you can take, however, in order to lessen the traumas of long-distance flying. The first and possibly most important of all is to harbor no illusions about the supposed luxury. If you approach your flight knowing that you are going to be cooped up for a long time and will have to face delays and discomforts of all kinds, the odds are that you will get through it without doing terrible things to your blood pressure or being disillusioned—but there's no point expecting comfort, good service and efficiency because you won't get them.

The right attitude is half the battle, but there are a number of other practical points to follow. Wear comfortable, loose-fitting clothes and take off your shoes.

Try to sleep as much as possible, especially on night flights; this can very often mean not watching the movie (they are invariably dull anyway) as it will probably be shown during the only period when meals are not being served and you can sleep. If you have difficulty sleeping, or think you might, take along a light sedative and try to get a window seat in order to avoid being woken up to let the person next to you get to the toilet or being bashed by people walking down the aisle. Above all, avoid alcohol, or at least drink only a little. The dry air of a pressurized airplane causes rapid dehydration, exaggerating the effects of drink and jet lag. Similarly, drink as much water as possible. Finally, once you arrive, try to take things easily for a day or so. In the excitement of being in a new place, especially for the first time, you can very often not realize how tired you are and optimistically set out sightseeing, only to come down to earth with a bump. Whatever you do, don't have any business meetings for at least 24 hours after arriving.

Fares. With air fares in a constant state of flux, the best advice for anyone planning to fly to Scandinavia independently (rather than as part of a package tour, in which case your flight will have been arranged for you) is to check with a travel agent and let him make your reservations for you. Nonetheless, there are a number of points to bear in mind.

The best bet is to buy either an APEX or Super APEX ticket. First Class, Business and even the misleadingly-named Economy, though giving maximum flexibility on flying dates and cancellations, as well as permitting stopovers, are extremely expensive. APEX and Super APEX, by contrast, are reasonably priced and offer the all-important security of fixed return dates (all APEX tickets are round trip). In addition, you get exactly the same service as flying Economy. However, there are a number of restrictions: you must book, and pay for, your ticket 21 days or more in advance; you can stay in Scandinavia no less than and no longer than a stated period (usually seven days to three months); if you miss your flight, you forfeit the fare. But from the point of view of price and convenience, these tickets certainly represent the best value for money.

If your plans are sufficiently flexible and tighter budgeting is important, you can sometimes benefit from the last-minute bargains offered by tour operators otherwise unable to fill their plane or quota of seats. A number of brokers specializing in these discount sales have sprung up who can book seats of this type. All charge an annual membership fee, usually around $35–50.

Among them are: *Stand-Buys Ltd.,* 311 W. Superior, Ste. 404, Chicago, IL 60610 (800–255–1488); *Moments Notice,* 40 East 49th St., New York, NY 10017 (212–486–0503); *Discount Travel Intl.,* 114 Forest Ave., Suite 205, Narberth, PA 19072 (215–668–2182); and *Worldwide Discount Travel Club,* 1674 Meridian Ave., Miami Beach, FL 33139 (305–534–2082).

Charter flights are also available to Scandinavia, though their number has decreased in recent years. Again, a travel agent will be able to recommend the most reliable. You might also consider, though this too should be done via a travel agent, buying a package tour to Scandinavia but using only the plane ticket. As packagers are able to get substantial discounts on fares through block booking seats, the price of the total package can sometimes be less than an ordinary air fare alone.

Typical round-trip fares as of mid-1989 for New York to Copenhagen: First Class, $3,621; Business, $1,503; Economy, $1,291; APEX, from $909.

The principal airlines serving Scandinavia from the U.S. (generally flying via New York) are *Finnair,* 10 E. 40th, New York, NY 10016 (212–889–7070); *Icelandair,* 360 W. 31 St., New York, NY 10001 (212–967–8888); *Northwest,* International Airport, Minneapolis/St. Paul, MN 55111 (800–225–2525); *SAS,* 138–02 Queens Blvd., Jamaica, NY 11435 (718–657–7700); and *TWA,* 100 S. Bedford Rd., Mt. Kisco, NY 10549 (800–892–4141).

By Boat. There are very few direct sailings from either the U.S. or Canada to Scandinavia on passenger or cruise ships, though *Royal Viking,* 750 Battery St., San Francisco, CA 94111, sometimes schedules a handful of sailings from New York. Prices, however, are high. Sailing time is around five or six days.

Alternatively, some freighter lines have a limited number of cabins for paying passengers to Scandinavia, though you may find you will have to wait for up to a year for a berth.

FROM THE U.K. By Air. All the Scandinavian capitals are well served by regular flights from the U.K., principally from London's Heathrow and Gatwick airports, but there are also flights from a limited number of other U.K. airports. The greatest frequency of flights is to Copenhagen—with several flights a day from various U.K. airports, as well as flights to provincial airports in Denmark. Maersk Air fly daily from Southend, near London, to Billund in Jutland. There are at least four flights a day to both Oslo and Stockholm. Helsinki has only two flights daily, while Reykjavik has only one flight daily, though *Finnair* also operate flights from Glasgow three times a week with connections from London. *British Airways* and *SAS* are the principal carriers to all other Scandinavian destinations.

Fares. European air fares are high, disproportionately so in many cases, and unfortunately flights to Scandinavia are no exception. The return Club Class fare to Copenhagen is about £355, and an APEX is £160 in high season. Charters tend to cost more than the APEX fares. If you only intend taking a short holiday it's worth considering an inclusive break.

Accordingly, you can check the bucket shop ads in the Sunday papers and magazines such as *Time Out* and *Business Traveler* (the latter an excellent source of information on budget fares). Bucket shops—some more reliable than others, so don't hand over all your money until you have the ticket—offer tickets at rates significantly below the so-called official ones, and can often prove very good value. But they do often operate at rather short notice and so may not be suitable for anyone hoping to book their flight some time in advance.

By Train. If you are in a hurry, go by air! The Scandinavian countries, with the exception of Denmark, are relatively isolated from the U.K. and the rail/ferry trek can occupy up to two full days. Approximate journey times from London are: Copenhagen 24 hours, Stockholm 31 hours, Oslo 34 hours, Helsinki 46 hours.

This having been said, getting to Scandinavia by train and ferry is great fun! The classic route is from London (Liverpool Street) to Harwich by rail, then by ferry to the Hook of Holland. From the Hook of Holland you go by train on to Hamburg, then by way of the Vogelfluglinie and the Puttgarden to Rødby train ferry to the Danish capital, Copenhagen. From Copenhagen the routes fan out to the other Nordic countries.

You can travel on to Helsingør for the train ferry to Helsingborg in Sweden and then on to Stockholm. From Helsingborg you can also go direct by train to Oslo, though the Norwegian capital can also be reached direct by ferry from Copenhagen. From Stockholm there are ferry services to Helsinki. Incidentally, it is possible to travel by train from Stockholm to Helsinki—but more of this mini-marathon later!

To Denmark. The "Nord West Express" is a useful service, with a morning departure (day 1) from London, giving a daytime crossing of the North Sea to Holland. The main train leaves the Hook at 8 in the evening and then runs overnight to arrive in Copenhagen just after 8 the following morning (day 2). Second-class couchettes are available from the Hook to Helsingør and there are also ordinary seats. Alternatively use the "Holland-Scandinavia Express." This departs from London (Liverpool Street) in the evening (7.35) and the North Sea crossing is made overnight. Departure from the Hook is at 8.58 A.M. on day 2 and Copenhagen is reached at 8.50 P.M. The great advantage of this service is that it gives you a more comfortable overnight crossing on the ferry. You also travel over the beautiful Vogelfluglinie with its spectacular Fehmarn bridge and enjoy the Puttgarden to Rødby crossing all in daylight. One note: at Puttgarden the whole train goes on board the ship so there's no need to change.

There are also other rail routes to Copenhagen involving much shorter train journeys if you don't like the idea of the long overland haul. *Scandinavian* ferries for example operate from Harwich and Newcastle to Esbjerg in Jutland. (See ferry chart.) For real comfort and personal service try their *Commodore Class* cabins.

FERRY SERVICES SUITABLE FOR TRAVEL TO SCANDINAVIA FROM BRITAIN

	Services operate	Sailings per week	SCANDI-NAVIAN	BRITISH FERRIES/SEALINK	THORESEN JETFOIL	FRED OLSEN	OLAU	NORWAY LINE
NEWCASTLE								
— Esbjerg	May-Sep	3	●					
— Bergen	May-Oct	2-3						●
— Gothenburg	Jun-Aug	2	●					
HARWICH								
— Esbjerg	All Year	Daily	◆					
— Hamburg	"	3-4	◆					
— Hook of Holland	"	Daily		◆				
— Gothenburg	"	3-4	●					
— Kristiansand¹	Jun-Aug	1				◆		
— Hirtshals/Oslo	All Year	1				◆		
SHEERNESS								
— Vlissingen	All Year	Daily					●	
DOVER								
— Ostend	All Year	Daily			◆			

Note: It is essential to check the dates of Operation of each service.

◆ Recommended for Rail travellers – easy rail/ship interchange. Through trains for Copenhagen operate from Ostend and the Hook of Holland. (Reservation is essential.)

● Only really suitable for car-borne travellers. Several of the Operators provide bus services between the local railway stations and the port terminal buildings. They are only suitable for passengers with light luggage.

1) Also serves Hirstals

(There are connecting rail services from London to Harwich and from Esbjerg to Copenhagen by the aptly named "Englanderen".) On this route, by leaving London in the early afternoon of day 1 you will be in Copenhagen at 7 P.M. the following day. It is essential to book seats on this train, in either direction: Dkr. 10 booking fee on top of fare (this is sometimes cheaper mid-week, always worth checking at station booking offices). Overnight crossings can also be made on the *Fred Olsen Line* from Harwich to Hirtshals in Jutland, which is a stop-over on the Harwich–Oslo route.

Alternatively, if you wish to minimize the sea crossing make use of the Jetfoil service (*(P&O/RTM)* from Dover to Oostende and there join the "Nord Express" for the overnight run to Copenhagen. This train has the advantage of having first- and second-class sleeping cars as well as couchettes. Reservation is obligatory on this service.

To Sweden. For travel to Sweden read the section on getting to Denmark; this explains the initial part of the journey. The "Nord-West Express" during the summer has through carriages from the Hook of Holland to Stockholm and this makes things very simple! The train re-starts from Copenhagen at 8.15 A.M. (day 2 from London) and arrives in Stockholm at 4.45 P.M. During winter you change trains at Copenhagen, departing at 9.45 A.M., arriving Stockholm 5.29 P.M. A restaurant car is available from Helsingborg to Stockholm.

The "Holland-Scandinavia Express" doesn't have any through coaches for Stockholm, but there is a conveniently timed connecting service which leaves Copenhagen at 10.20 P.M., running overnight to Stockholm, arriving at 7.17 A.M. (day 3 from London). There are first- and second-class sleeping cars, second-class couchettes and day coaches. Alternatively, use the summer-only relief train which leaves Copenhagen at 11.20 P.M.

Alternatively you can reach Stockholm by using the *Scandinavian* service from Harwich to Gothenburg and then continue by train and bus across Sweden. The ferry service runs on three or four days a week and the sea crossing takes about 24 hours. *British Rail* runs a connecting boat-train service to Harwich from London's Liverpool Street Station, and there is an hourly train service from Gothenburg to Stockholm. Buses to and from Stockholm connect at the Gothenburg quayside terminal with all the Scandinavian Harwich sailings. The journey takes seven hours and stops are made at a number of important centers en route, including Borås and Norrköping. On this route schedules vary from sailing to sailing so check carefully with *Scandinavian.*

To Norway. For rail travel to Norway first read the sections on getting to Denmark. The "Nord-West Express" reaches Copenhagen in good time (8.09 A.M.) to catch a through train to Oslo. This departs at 10.15 and runs via the Helsingør–Helsingborg ferry and Gothenburg. Oslo is reached at 7.58 P.M.—day 3 from London. There is also a good (summer only) overnight service from Copenhagen to Oslo which dovetails nicely into the "Holland-Scandinavia Express." This train leaves at 9.15 P.M. and gets you into Oslo at 7.01 in the morning (day 3 from London). It has first-class sleepers and second-class couchettes as well as ordinary day coaches.

To Finland. First of all read the section on rail travel to Denmark and Sweden using the "Nord West Express," or the 10.55 P.M. overnight sleeping car train connecting with the "Holland-Scandinavia Express." This will have taken you as far as Stockholm. Rail travelers have three choices for onward travel to Helsinki. First, one can abandon the rails and sail by one of the superb *Silja Line* ferries direct to Helsinki. There is one sailing a day leaving Stockholm at 6 P.M. and berthing in the Finnish capital at 9 the next morning. The sailing is very conveniently timed for passengers using the "Nord-West Express" as this arrives in Stockholm at 4.46 P.M. allowing ample time to transfer to the ferry terminal at Värtan. Secondly, there is the sea/rail route via Turku. There are two sailings a day on this route, with the morning departure 8.15 reaching Turku at 8 P.M. where there is a connecting train at 8.30 to Helsinki arriving at 11.20 P.M. The overnight sailing leaves at 9.30 with the connecting train leaving Turku at 8.30 the following morning and arriving in Helsinki at 11.35. Thirdly, for the real railway/travel buff there is the overland "all rail" route taking you up around the head of the Gulf of Bothnia to Helsinki via Haparanda/Tornio (change to Finnish broad gauge) and then down the other side. This mini-marathon will take the best part of three days to complete.

Finally less dedicated rail travelers (or their families!) may prefer to use the long sea crossing to Helsinki from Travemünde in north Germany. This is operated by the *Silja Line's* Finnjet. First of all travel to Hamburg by rail, from where there is a bus connection to the ferry terminal at Skaninavienkai.

By Bus. There are few bus services to Scandinavia from the U.K., but in summer a four-times-weekly service is operated from London to Malmö, Gothenburg and Stockholm—as part of the *National Express–Eurolines* network—by Grey Green Coaches of London in conjunction with Bovo Tours of the Netherlands and GDG Continentbus of Sweden. During the winter the service runs twice weekly. It is routed across the Channel from Dover to Oostende, then through Belgium, the Netherlands and Germany to Travemünde on the Baltic, where you board the ferry to the Swedish port of Trelleborg. Journey time from London to Malmö is about 37 hours, 41 hours to Gothenburg and 47 hours to Stockholm. Bookings can be made through *National Express–Eurolines,* The Coach Travel Center, 13 Regent Street, London, SW1Y 4LR (01–730 0202). There is also a twice weekly summer only service from London Victoria Coach Station to Copenhagen, Stockholm, Turku and Helsinki. Details from *National Express–Eurolines.*

By Car. This can be a delightful journey, especially if you enjoy sea trips, as many of the ships sailing to Scandinavian ports are really mini-liners. Alternatively, if you wish to keep the sea crossings to a minimum, use one of the shorter North Sea or English Channel crossings and then drive up through Holland and Germany to Denmark and the rest of Scandinavia. However, remember that all this takes time, and you should carefully consider one of the numerous fly-drive packages, either with or without hotel accommodations.

To Denmark. This is the easiest of the Scandinavian countries to get to, with one region—Jutland—being a part of mainland Europe. The capital, Copenhagen, is situated on the island of Zealand. There are three direct ferry services to Denmark from the U.K., two run by *Scandinavian* and one by *Fred Olsen Lines.* The crossing time from Harwich to Esbjerg is around 19 hours. Fares are relatively high, for a car, driver and passenger allow £280 each way (including cabin). Demand is particularly heavy during the summer, especially on weekends, so book well in advance.

Scandinavian —under the banner of *Longship Holidays*—also offer a wide range of inclusive arrangements, including go-as-you-please holidays which are excellent value for money. It is well worth checking them out.

If you drive through Holland and Germany to Denmark it's no problem either, as the train ferries from Puttgarden to Rødby carry cars as well. Coupled with the excellent roads in north Germany and Denmark itself, this means that things couldn't be easier for the motorist.

To Sweden. There are two direct ferry services to Sweden from the U.K., both operated by *Scandinavian* and both running to Gothenburg (see ferry chart). One, from Harwich, operates three or four times weekly and takes 24 hours. The second is a twice weekly sailing from Newcastle and runs summer only; this takes slightly longer. In 1988, high-season fares worked out at around £290 one-way for a car, driver and one passenger, with a cabin.

If you decide to drive up through Germany there are several ferry services to Sweden. A *Stena Line* ferry makes the crossing from Kiel to Gothenburg daily, contact *P & O* for details. *TT Line* have two services daily from Travemünde to Trelleborg on the southernmost tip of Sweden. On this route *Olau Line* offer a special low fare when combined with their services from Sheerness to Vlissingen. The crossing takes seven hours.

There is no problem reaching Sweden if you want to drive through Denmark first. A regular ferry shuttle operated by *Scandinavian Ferry Lines* runs from Dragør (just south of Copenhagen) to Limhamn, near Malmö, while farther north a ser-

vice is operated every 15 minutes on the short crossing from Helsingør to Helsingborg by Scandinavian Ferry Lines in conjunction with Danish State Railways.
There is also a service between Grenå in northern Jutland and Varberg on Sweden's
west coast, operated by Lion Ferry, which also has a service from Grenå to Helsingborg. The most northerly crossing is from Frederikshavn to Gothenburg, run by
Stena Line. Many of these services can be booked in advance through *DFDS,* 199
Regent Street, London W1R 8HG (for central reservations, 0255–240240).

To Norway. There are three direct routes to Norway. *Fred Olsen* run a weekly
service all year from Harwich to Oslo taking 36 hours, and a summer service only
to Kristiansand. Details from Fred Olsen Lines. *Norway Line* sail from Newcastle
to Stavanger and Bergen during the summer. Alternatively you can travel via Denmark, driving north through Jutland and then taking the ferry from Hirstals to
Kristiansand, or from Frederikshavn to Larvik by *Larvik Line. DFDS* offer up to
50% discount on this latter route if the passage is booked at the same time as their
crossing to Esbjerg in Denmark from Harwich/Newcastle.

To Finland. There are no direct ferry services to Finland from the U.K., though
there is a weekly cargo service by *United Baltic Corporation/Finncarriers* with limited, though high quality, passenger accommodations; duration three days. The least
complicated route is to use one of the convenient North Sea crossings and then
to sail direct to Helsinki from Travemünde on the Baltic coast of Germany by the
Silja Line's Finnjet. Alternatively, drive to Stockholm (see section on Sweden) and
then use one of the shorter sea crossings to Helsinki/Turku. Both *Viking* and *Silja*
lines sail to these two ports from Stockholm. Book through *DFDS.*

To Iceland—By sea. The journey to Iceland is frankly rather complicated and
difficult, not least because it is necessary to sail via the Shetland Islands and the
Faroes. For the first part of the journey use one of the thrice weekly *P & O* sailings
from Aberdeen to Lerwick. From Lerwick there is a weekly sailing by the *Smyril
Line* to Torshavn in the Faroe Islands and from there on to Seydisfjordur in Iceland.

The *Smyril Line* services are marketed by *P & O;* details from *P & O Ferries
Ltd,* PO Box 5, Jamieson's Quay, Aberdeen AB9 8DL (0224–572615).

Getting Around Scandinavia

The following section gives general travel facts for the whole of Scandinavia. For
specific and more detailed information on traveling within individual Scandinavian
countries, see *Facts at Your Fingertips* for each country.

BY AIR. SAS and Finnair operate an extensive air network between all the major
Scandinavian cities, as well as flying to many more remote points within the region.
Services between the capitals are the most frequent and journey times are short;
no more than 90 minutes between Oslo and Helsinki, for example, the two Scandinavian capitals most widely separated. Between Oslo, Copenhagen and Stockholm,
journey times are around one hour.

BY TRAIN. Rail travel in Scandinavia is to be recommended, not only for the
comfort of the majority of the rolling stock, but also for its cleanliness and general
efficiency of the systems. Speeds may not always match those in France or Germany, but the majority of the routes are scenic or have considerable interest. Fares
are based on a sliding scale, the farther you travel the cheaper per kilometer it gets.
Seats on inter-city express trains in Denmark must be booked ahead to be sure of
a place on the train.

Iceland is the only Scandinavian country that is without any rail system at all.
The problems created by the nature of its terrain and severe climate make the building of railroads impossible.

Discount tickets. As well as the discount tickets available in each Scandinavian
country (see the relevant *Facts at Your Fingertips* sections for details), the following
rail discount tickets are good for the whole of Scandinavia.

Eurailpass. Visitors from outside Europe should take advantage of the Eurailpass which covers all the European railways (except Britain) including Denmark, Sweden, Norway and Finland. The Eurailpass is first-class only and can be bought for periods of 15 days ($320), 21 days ($398), one month ($498), two months ($698), and three months ($860). The card is excellent value especially if you intend to tour widely. You might also consider adding on a Scandinavian Bonus Pass to obtain reduced rates at first-class hotels (see below) for £10 (1989 price). Younger travelers (under 26) should purchase the Eurail Youth pass—second-class only—for either one month ($360) or two months ($470).

Nordturist Ticket. For Europeans the best bargain for getting around the whole of Scandinavia is the Nordturist ticket (note: this ticket is also promoted as the *Scanrail* card). The Nordturist gives unlimited travel in Denmark, Sweden, Norway and Finland for 21 days for $328 in first class and $220 in second (mid-1989 figure). Extra cost for first class is well worth it as trains can get very full with Inter-Railers (see below) in the peak summer months. Included with the Nordturist ticket is the *Scandinavian Bonus Pass.* This gives discounts of up to 40% for accommodations in over 95 first-class hotels throughout the region. Details and bookings from *Norwegian State Railways Travel Bureau,* Norway House, 21–24 Cockspur St., London SW1Y 5DA.

Nordturist (Scanrail Card) is also valid for passage on certain ferry crossings in Denmark and allows a 50% reduction on the price of sailings between Denmark and Sweden, Denmark and Norway, and Sweden and Finland. The pass can be purchased at any railway station in Scandinavia.

Inter-Rail Card. Youthful travelers (under 26) should consider the Inter-Rail Card which gives the freedom of Europe for one month for around £150, especially as this will cover large parts of the rail journey to Scandinavia (and also half fare in the country of purchase and on some cross channel routes). The Inter-Rail card is only available to those residing in Europe for six months prior to purchase. There are close associations between Inter-Rail and the Youth Hostel Association giving inexpensive accommodations when you arrive. Details from *YHA,* 14, Southampton St., London WC2E 7HY.

Rail Europ Senior Card. More elderly travelers who hold a British Rail Senior Citizens Railcard can buy an add-on Rail Europ Senior Card which gives discounts of up to 50% on rail travel throughout Scandinavia.

BY FERRY. The major boat routes within Scandinavia are operated by car-carrying (as well as passenger) ferries. Services between Sweden and Finland run from Stockholm or nearby ports to Helsinki, Turku and Mariehamn (Åland); Kapellskär (near Stockholm) to Mariehamn and Naantali; also Skellefteå–Pietarsaari, Umeå–Vaasa, Sundsvall–Vaasa, and Örnsköldsvik–Vassa. *Silja Line* operates an excellent car ferry service from Travemünde (northern Germany) to Helsinki, offering top facilities aboard the ultramodern Finnjet.

There are daily sailings between Copenhagen and Oslo. From Jutland in Denmark it is possible to cross directly into Norway and Sweden. Various companies operate from North Jutland to Norway, namely from Frederikshavn to Oslo, Frederikshavn–Larvik, Hanstholm–Arendal, Hanstholm–Kristiansand, and Hirtshals to Kristiansand. From Copenhagen to Sweden only passenger ferries (hydrofoils) leave the city center, but car ferries connect Dragør outside Copenhagen with Limhamn in the south of Sweden. The Elsinore (Helsingør)–Helsingborg route with frequent departures takes both cars and passengers and is the shortest connection available. Other car ferries provide regular services between Denmark and Sweden, running from Grenå to Varberg or Helsingborg and from Frederikshavn to Gothenburg.

Scandinavian operates between Copenhagen and Oslo and the Faroe Islands. *Smyril* links the Faroes, Bergen (Norway) and Hanstholm (Denmark) with Iceland and Scotland during the summer. Advance booking recommended to ensure passage on ferries at a definite time, and to avoid waiting during the busy season.

Cruises. The most famous of Scandinavian coastal voyages is the 11-day trip from Bergen via North Cape to Kirkenes and return, leaving Bergen daily. A similar round-Iceland voyage takes about a week.

In Norway summer cruises along the fabulous coastline to North Cape and even to Spitsbergen are offered by *Chandris, Cunard, North Star Line, Norwegian American Line* and *Royal Viking Line.* The Telemark Canal, a famous inland waterway, runs from Skien on the Oslo fjord to Dalen among the mountains of Telemark. Also during the summer, the world's oldest paddle steamer, the *Skibladner,* plods its way from Eidsvoll to Lillehammer on Lake Mjøsa, the largest lake in Norway.

In Finland you can cruise for up to a week—over some 700 miles—on Europe's largest lake area, the Saimaa lake region, eating and sleeping on board. There are also interesting trips across the Gulf of Finland from Helsinki to Tallinn in Estonia, Riga in Latvia, and Gdansk in Poland (visa essential). In addition, weekly "no visa" cruises from Helsinki to Leningrad have been resumed throughout summer, but must be booked 10 days in advance.

In Sweden, there is the delightful trip on the Göta Canal from Gothenburg to Stockholm, through the country's lovely Lake District. The trip takes 3 days and there are several sailings weekly.

Silja Line and Viking Line ships, sailing between Helsinki and Stockholm and Turku and Stockholm, offer a 50% reduction on regular passenger fares for senior citizens. These are car-carrying cruise liners, with excellent facilities on board. The 14-hour cruise can be combined with a package to include a tour of Helsinki or Stockholm, depending on which city you start from.

Hydrofoils. There are frequent daily services between Copenhagen and Malmö (35-minute crossing).

Hydrofoil boats are widely used in Norway. Stavanger, Haugesund and Bergen on the west coast are linked by hydrofoil services, as are the Ryfylke fjords from Stavanger, the Hardangerfjord from Bergen. Speed boat services, too, from Bergen to the Sognefjord and Nordfjord areas.

BY CAR. Scandinavia is an excellent area to visit by car, not least because its great size and small population mean that many very beautiful areas are easily accessible in a car. However, though roads in Denmark and most of southern Norway, Sweden and Finland are generally very good, in more remote regions they can be both narrow and twisting, and badly surfaced. Even the affluent Scandinavians have not yet found a way of protecting their roads from the destructive effects of their long and bitter winters.

Iceland's roads, on the other hand, are almost all poor. The only stretch of highway is between Keflavik and Reykjavik and is a toll road. Roads on the outskirts of towns are surfaced, but elsewhere they consist of scraped lava, occasionally disappearing altogether when a riverbed changes course, though there is usually a crossing place. In consequence, though distances are not very great, journeys by road can be slow.

Regulations. You drive on the *right* in all Scandinavian countries. In all Scandinavian towns the speed limit is 31 m.p.h. (50 km.p.h.), except in Iceland, where it is 27 m.p.h. (45 km.p.h.). Denmark has a general limit of 50 m.p.h. (80 km.p.h.), but 60 m.p.h. (100 km.p.h.) on motorways. (Maximum speed for trailers on motorways is 70 km.p.h.) In Iceland, the general limit is 45 m.p.h. (70 km.p.h.), in Norway 50 m.p.h. (80 km.p.h.), in Sweden 56 m.p.h. (90 km.p.h.) and in Finland 50 m.p.h. (80 km.p.h.) in non built-up areas.

As the liquor regulations might lead you to suspect, Scandinavians are strict about drinking. When it comes to driving a car, they are absolutely inflexible. If you are involved in an accident, a blood test is taken as a matter of course, and if you have had more than a mild whisky and soda, you will spend up to three weeks in jail. No exceptions are made for anyone, so you'd better take a taxi if you've been out on the town. In Sweden, incorrectly parked cars are towed away and dipped headlights used all day.

Documents. For Denmark, Norway, Sweden, and Finland, you need only your national driving license. In Sweden, unless your driving license is issued in English, French, Dutch, Italian, Spanish or German, you must produce a special certificate confirming the authenticity and validity of the license, written in Swedish, English or French. For Iceland, an international license is necessary. Internationally valid third-party insurance (Green Card) is not required but is recommended.

Maps. The Scandinavian touring and automobile clubs will supply you with maps and itineraries. All publish excellent touring books and have branch offices in the larger towns in addition to the following headquarters.

Denmark: *De Forenede Danske Motorejere* (FDM), Blegdamsvej 124, in Copenhagen. The official Geodaetisk Institut maps, available in most bookshops, are among the world's best.

Finland: *The Automobile and Touring Club,* Kansakoulunkatu 10, Helsinki. Excellent maps of Finland on various scales are published by that country's Map Service of the National Board of Survey. They can be obtained from main bookshops in Finland or from the Map Service shop at Eteläesplanadi 10, Helsinki 13.

Iceland: excellent maps are available from the Iceland tourist bureau.

Norway: *Kongelig Norsk Automobilklub* (KNA), Parkveien 68, and *Norges Automobil-Forbund,* Storgate 2, both in Oslo.

Sweden: *Kungliga Automobil Klubben* (KAK), and *Motormännens Riksförbund* (M), Sturegatan 32, in Stockholm.

Car hire. All leading car hire firms offer self-drive cars throughout Scandinavia ranging from Volkswagens to Land-Rovers. Chauffeur-driven cars are also available.

Addresses are given in the *Practical Information* after each chapter. Package fly-drive arrangements with unlimited mileage are also available offering flexibility and advantageous rates.

In Sweden low rental rates are sometimes offered as part of rail and air packages.

In Iceland, Land-Rovers and minibuses are especially suitable; they cost more and must be booked well in advance. Rental rates are higher than elsewhere here and a sales tax of 20% does nothing to help, but fly-drive arrangements bring costs down.

CONVERSION TABLES. One of the most confusing experiences for many motorists is their first encounter with the metric system. The following quick conversion table may help to speed you on your way.

Kilometers into Miles. This simple chart will help you to convert to both miles and kilometers. If you want to convert from miles into kilometers read from the center column to the right, if from kilometers into miles, from the center column to the left. Example: 5 miles = 8 km., 5 km. = 3.1 miles.

Miles		Kilometers	Miles		Kilometers
0.6	1	1.6	37.3	60	96.6
1.2	2	3.2	43.5	70	112.3
1.9	3	4.8	49.7	80	128.7
2.5	4	6.3	55.9	90	144.8
3.1	5	8.0	62.1	100	160.9
3.7	6	9.6	124.3	200	321.9
4.3	7	11.3	186.4	300	482.8
5.0	8	12.9	248.5	400	643.7
5.6	9	14.5	310.7	500	804.7
6.2	10	16.1	372.8	600	965.6
12.4	20	32.2	434.9	700	1,126.5
18.6	30	48.3	497.1	800	1,287.5
24.8	40	64.4	559.2	900	1,448.4
31.0	50	80.5	621.4	1,000	1,609.3

Motor fuel. Imperial gallon is approximately 4½ liters; a U.S. gallon about 3¾ liters.

Liters	Imp. gals.	U.S. gals.
1	0.22	0.26
5	1.10	1.32
10	2.20	2.64
20	4.40	5.28

40	8.80	10.56
100	22.01	26.42

Tire pressure. Measured in kilograms per square centimeter instead of pounds per square inch; the ratio is approximately 14.2 lbs. to 1 kg.

Lbs per sq. in.	Kg per sq. cm	Lbs per sq. in.	Kg per sq. cm
20	1.406	26	1.828
22	1.547	28	1.969
24	1.687	30	2.109

Returning Home

CUSTOMS. If you propose to take on your holiday any *foreign-made* articles, such as cameras, binoculars, expensive timepieces and the like, it is wise to put with your travel documents the receipt from the retailer or some other evidence that the item was bought in your home country. If you bought the article on a previous holiday abroad and have already paid duty on it, carry with you the receipt for this. Otherwise, on returning home, you may be charged duty (for British residents, Value Added Tax as well). In other words, unless you can prove prior possession, foreign-made articles are dutiable *each time* they enter the U.S. The details below are correct as we go to press. It would be wise to check in case of change.

American residents who have been out of the country for at least 48 hours and have claimed no exemption during the previous 30 days are entitled to bring in duty-free up to $400 worth of bona fide gifts or items for personal use. If you buy clothing abroad and wear it during your travels it will nonetheless be dutiable when you reenter the U.S.

The $400 figure is based on the fair retail value of the goods in the country where acquired. Included for travelers over the age of 21 are one liter of alcohol, 100 cigars (non-Cuban) and 200 cigarettes. Any amount in excess of those limits will be taxed at the port of entry, and may additionally be taxed in the traveler's home state. Only one bottle of perfume trademarked in the U.S. may be brought in. Write to the U.S. Customs Service, Box 7407, Washington, DC 20044 for information regarding importation of automobiles and/or motorcycles. You may not bring home meats, fruits, plants, soil, or other agricultural items.

Gifts valued at under $50 may be mailed to friends or relatives at home duty-free, but not more than one per day (or receipt) to any one addressee. These gifts must not include perfumes costing more than $5, tobacco, or liquor.

If you are traveling with such foreign-made articles as cameras, watches, or binoculars that were purchased at home, it is best either to carry the receipt for them with you or to register them with U.S. Customs prior to departing. This will save much time (and potential aggravation) upon your return.

Military personnel returning from abroad should check with the nearest American Embassy for special regulations.

Canadian residents may, in addition to personal effects, bring in the following duty-free: a maximum of 50 cigars, 200 cigarettes, 2 pounds of tobacco and 40 ounces of liquor, provided these are declared in writing to customs on arrival and accompany the traveler in hand or checked-through baggage. These are included in the basic exemption of $300 a year or $100 per quarter. Personal gifts should be mailed as "Unsolicited Gift—Value Under $40." Canadian customs regulations are strictly enforced; you are recommended to check what your allowances are and to make sure you have kept receipts for whatever you have bought abroad. For details ask for the Canada Customs brochure, "I Declare."

British residents face two levels of duty-free allowance entering the U.K.; one, for goods bought outside the EEC or for goods bought in a duty-free shop within the EEC; two, for goods bought in an EEC country but not in a duty-free shop.

In the first category you may import duty-free: 200 cigarettes or 100 cigarillos or 50 cigars or 250 grammes of tobacco (*Note* if you live outside Europe, these allowances are doubled); plus one liter of alcoholic drinks over 22% vol. (38.8% proof) or two liters of alcoholic drinks not over 22% vol. or fortified, still or sparkling wine; plus two liters of still table wine; plus 50 grammes of perfume; plus nine fluid ounces of toilet water; plus other goods to the value of £32.

In the second category you may import duty-free: 300 cigarettes or 150 cigarillos or 75 cigars or 400 grammes of tobacco; plus 1½ liters of alcoholic drinks over 22% vol. (38.8% proof) or three liters of alcoholic drinks not over 22% vol. or fortified, still or sparkling wine; plus five liters of still table wine; plus 75 grammes of perfume; plus 13 fluid ounces of toilet water; plus other goods to the value of £250 (*Note* though it is not classified as an alcoholic drink by EEC countries for Customs' purposes and is thus considered part of the "other goods" allowance, you may not import more than 50 liters of beer).

In addition, no animals or pets of any kind may be brought into the U.K. The penalties for doing so are severe and are strictly enforced; there are *no* exceptions. Similarly, fresh meats, plants and vegetables, controlled drugs and firearms and ammunition may not be brought into the U.K. There are no restrictions on the import or export of British and foreign currencies.

Anyone planning to stay in the U.K. for more than six months should contact H.M. Customs and Excise, Kent House, Upper Ground, London S.E.1 (tel. 01–928 0533) for further information.

AN INTRODUCTION TO
SCANDINAVIA

Variety within Harmony

by
SYLVIE NICKELS

Space—vast quantities of it—is one of the first qualities you're likely to associate with Scandinavia. Between them, the five Scandinavian nations cover an area of some 500,000 square miles, give or take a few (and that doesn't include the huge and largely autonomous Danish territory of Greenland). You could fit the U.K. five times into that, or Texas twice, and still have acreage to spare. What's more, all this is shared out among some 20 million souls—rather less than three Londons or New Yorks. So if plenty of elbow room makes you feel nervous, you had better keep away!

If you have any pre-conceived ideas that one Scandinavian country is much like another, you can also begin by forgetting these. Of course, they all share a broadly similar cultural background, have strong historical and economic ties, and enjoy many similarities in political and social structure. But that said, the individual components of the Scandinavian scene are just that—highly individual. The special qualities of each are no more comparable than are the tidy, well-husbanded landscapes and long sandy beaches of Denmark with the wild tawny fjords and fells of Norway; which in turn are quite different from the huge lake-and-forestscapes that so characterize Sweden and Finland, and the bizarre volcanic majesty of much of Iceland.

So, space and magnificent scenery are among the great (and free) trump cards of the region. To these you can add several natural phenomena which, in European terms, are unique to Scandinavia: long golden summer evenings stretching right into next day's dawn as you travel into the northern latitudes of the midnight sun; and, in winter, the rippling veils of the Northern Lights that weave magical curtains across the sky. The fall colors, too, have a special brilliance as you progress northwards, and spring, though relatively late, banishes the long winter with a welcome speed and vigor.

With so much unadulterated nature around, you won't find it too surprising that in large areas people—and all the paraphernalia that goes with them—can be rather thin on the ground. In fact, their numbers work out more or less in direct ratio to their latitude; from relatively (but only relatively) crowded little Denmark to the almost (but only almost) empty far north of Lapland up there beyond the Arctic Circle. Which brings us to another Scandinavian certainty, one that may at first sight seem somewhat paradoxical given the harsh climate: wherever there are people, there are good living conditions. These nordic folk learned long ago how to make themselves at home in conditions that range from the temperately comfortable to the downright inhospitable. The result is that, however remote a community may be, you can expect it to have all the amenities that the traveler of the 1980s is likely to need. They won't be lacking in finesse either. The Scandinavians like things to be not only practical, but aesthetic as well.

Transports of Delight

As far as you, the visitor, is concerned, the combination of human and natural history has tailor-made these countries for three particular types of holiday. The first is touring. Though you won't find historical monuments and art treasures in such multiplicity as in some other parts of Europe, there is nevertheless an enormous amount to see: prehistoric and Viking burial grounds, runic stones, Viking ships, medieval wooden or stone churches, Hanseatic merchants' houses, Renaissance castles and manors, the occasional Gothic cathedral, the graciously neo-Classical 19th-century buildings of Stockholm and Helsinki, and a great deal of spectacular modern architecture, to name but some of the region's specialties.

With the exception of Denmark and the more urban areas of Norway, Sweden and Finland, however, the serious culture vulture may need to cover quite a lot of territory to get his fill, though most of it is, happily, very travel-worthy terrritory, well serviced by varied means of communication. Outside urban areas, roads are blessedly uncrowded, in addition to being well maintained—if occasionally bumpy—and, if you haven't a car, you can fall back on northern Europe's finest public transport systems—air, rail, bus, ferry, lake steamer, hydrofoil—often interlinked to meet the needs of widely differing terrain.

For those intent on seeing as much as possible, there are good transport bargains to be investigated. Some depend on your age—both ends of the age-scale benefit, but the minimums and maximums vary from country to country, as do the types of transport to which they apply. Others depend on the composition of your group—families with one child or more get good concessions on air and rail throughout much of the region. Yet others depend on nothing more than careful advance planning, as in the case of the Scanrail Pass and the comparable facilities that give unlimited rail travel in individual countries for fixed periods, such as the Finnrail Pass, or good reductions in Norway or Sweden for travel on several days of the week. But check these *before* you arrive in Scandinavia, and remember that many of them are also marketed as part of reasonably priced packages from your home country.

Hand-in-hand with flexible travel facilities go flexible accommodation systems. A variety of "hotel check" schemes—hotel vouchers essentially—operate in each of the countries, except Iceland, the greatest choice being in Sweden. Some, such as Scandic hotel checks, extend across borders and are valid in specified hotels in Sweden, Norway and Denmark. The Danes also have an attractive scheme concentrating on the *kro* or country inn, nearly all in rural settings, most of them family run and many contained in fine old half-timbered buildings of considerable vintage. Similarly, summer hotels are a feature of all five countries. These act as student accommodation during the rest of the year, offer good value for money and are often enthusiastically run by the students themselves.

Catering to the Self

There are ways, though, of getting to even closer grips with the way of life of your chosen country; and this brings us to the second type of vacation in which Scandinavia excels: self-catering. One of its most popular forms is the farm vacation, which the Danes in particular have developed to a fine art. Usually these vacations are on a half- or full-board basis, but in most cases the great attraction is that you will be staying on a working farm with the option of participating in the way of life of a working family. The potential benefits hardly need stressing, especially if you have youngsters in tow. The rural settings are likely to be idyllic, if remote, so it's an advantage to have your own transport.

But if you want to savor the northern summer as only the Scandinavians know how, you should give serious thought to that quite indispensable feature of their way of life: the summer cottage. It probably isn't too much of an exaggeration to say that most families in all five nations own, rent, borrow or otherwise have access to four walls and a roof somewhere in the great beyond of the countryside. It can be anything from a simple shack to a minor mansion, but is likely to be somewhere in between with an almost guaranteed tranquillity—except perhaps on a few popular coastal stretches of Denmark and Sweden—on some lake, river or sea shore.

To such havens, families will retire for the entire summer, working members joining them at every opportunity, spending their time swimming, fishing, boating, walking in woods or over hills and fells, or simply watching the ever changing interplay of light and color as reflections are flung from water to sky and back again, or the surrealistic sunsets that linger far into the nordic night. You, the visitor, would do well to follow suit.

The best-equipped (and most expensive) summer cottages usually form part of a holiday village, often featuring a restaurant, shop, some sports facilities and perhaps entertainment. Centers of this kind tend to reach a higher degree of sophistication in Denmark and Sweden than in Norway and Finland (you won't find them in Iceland), and it is this type of holiday property that is mainly marketed overseas. Rentals for individually sited cottages, for which there are many agencies in Scandinavia, can be very much lower—even downright cheap if you are content to "get back to nature" as so many Scandinavians are (whatever they like to say). This, at its most basic, may mean drawing water from a well, hewing your own firewood or accepting the sufficiency of an outdoor privy. Whatever the standard, though, the setting will certainly be memorable.

Nature, Naturally

So we come to the third and final type of holiday for which these lands are especially well suited: holidays in which the emphasis is, quite simply, on nature itself and the various ways of savoring it to the full. The most obvious way is on foot; Scandinavia, after all, is the home of orienteering. But never fear—you won't need to go armed with a compass. Marked trails cater for those whose energies are geared only to a short stroll through fragrant pinewoods along a lake shore all the way up to those more rugged types whose idea of fun is many days back-packing through terrain as isolated as any that Europe can offer. Punctuating the latter, overnight shelter is available in strategically-sited wilderness refuges or well-equipped hostels and mountain cabins. In Norway they have taken things a stage further with a unique system of mountain huts where basic essentials (blankets, food, fuel, etc.) can be purchased or hired on a self-service basis, offering a welcome economy in muscle power. Not to be outdone, the Danes, whose greatest claim to a mountain touches the sky at around 500 feet in Jutland, have evolved their own specialty: organized "marches" or, better, rambles of various duration, one of the most popular being along the old Military Road, a historic track through Jutland. Hundreds of people take part in these but, of course, the trails are available at any time if you're not the gregarious type.

Cycling is another activity that the Danes have got well organized, though the lack of hills does give them a substantial headstart. Packages include a detailed itinerary, accommodations of various grades and, of course, the bike itself, though you can also bring your own, transported free on most North Sea ferries. Similar packages have spread to Sweden and, to a lesser extent, Norway and Finland. In Iceland, the sturdy little horses directly descended from Viking-era ancestry are rather better adapted to the rugged terrain.

With so many lakes and so much sea around, messing about in boats is an activity more or less built-in to the Scandinavian summer scene. You'll find that a rowing boat comes almost, as it were, as part of the furniture with a lot of self-catering accommodations, and there will be something that floats available, either free or at nominal cost, at many hotels and most campsites. The Finns and Swedes are great canoeists, with a whole range of rallies weaving across the blue and green landscapes. On one Swedish river, you can even build your own log raft for a leisurely float of several days, borne by the current at a mile per hour. Sailing is immensely popular—after all, some of the most famous windjammers from the great era of sail were built and had their home ports in Baltic waters, and a number of them are now museum ships. Today, the vessels may be more modest, but the flutter of sails is pretty well a constant feature of any coastal scene and the spectacle provided by the major regattas that punctuate the Danish calendar especially are sights to remember. Chartering a yacht isn't quite so easy (the best chances are in Denmark and Sweden), but if you want to get a good grounding in what every budding yachtsman ought to know, a number of sailing schools are ready to oblige.

The Scandinavians are also inveterate swimmers. Don't be put off by the latitudes. Water temperatures won't, of course, match those of the Mediterranean, but in summer you'll find them surprisingly acceptable and, at worst, refreshing! The best sands are on the west coast of Denmark's Jutland, where they're so firm and extensive that you can drive a car along them for miles on end; other good sands are on the west coast of Finland. Almost anywhere else, whether by lake or sea, the bathing is off rocks, usually long, smooth shoulders of granite comfortably shaped for soaking in the sun, which happens to be another favorite occupation in these parts.

If you get the opportunity to take a sauna bath—and you almost certainly will—you'll never have a better one, especially if you are in Finland, the home of the sauna, where for many people, it is still almost as intrinsic a part of life as eating and sleeping. A true country sauna poised on lake- or sea-shore bears little resemblance to its urbanized descendant, even less to most exported versions. For the Finn, the sauna is a social as well as a cleansing experience—for some almost a spiritual one, too; and when you relax afterwards looking out across quiet waters under the huge northern sky, you may begin to understand why. The Icelanders have their own specialty: an abundance of natural warm water piped from the bowels of the earth into swimming pools in which you can bathe in the open air even in the depths of winter.

And this brings us to that entirely different part of the Scandinavian scene: the Nordic winter. Skiing as a sport was born in Norway: to be precise in the village of Morgedal, in the province of Telemark. As far as large numbers of Norwegians, Swedes and Finns are concerned, skiing was—and for some still is—an essential part of everyday life for several months of the year. For most, however, the element of necessity has been entirely removed, though this does not prevent them donning their skis at any excuse, or even without one, for it's a quite common sight to see city dwellers skiing to work across their parks. Though there are quite a few resorts, many of them well-known, offering good downhill facilities, especially in Norway, those accustomed to the more vertical type of skiing will find things a bit different here. The terrain varies enormously from the considerable mountains of Norway to the smooth treeless slopes of the northern Swedish and Finnish fells, and the great white expanses of lowland lake-and-forestscapes. But generally speaking, the Scandinavian preference remains for cross-country skiing—or the other extreme of hurling themselves into the void from the top of a sky-scraping ski jump. In both, their successes in Olympic and World Championship events speak for themselves.

Of Nansen and Nobel

Maybe these preferences reflect certain traits of the northern temperament, so what of the Scandinavians themselves? There is little argument that the extrovert Danes are the easiest to get to know. Norwegians and Finns have a self-sufficiency and reserve which you might even interpret as indifference, though you'd be quite wrong; you may have to make the first move, but the results will probably be overwhelming. In between are the Swedes, a little more solemn, still a bit sensitive about their long neutrality and material well-being, but responsive to a friendly interest in their affairs.

That said, they all share common characteristics, most of them rooted in the pioneer spirit which has led them to develop one of the highest standards of living anywhere, despite a predominantly harsh climate. One is a fine, dry sense of humor allied to an endearing ability to laugh at themselves. Another is more paradoxical, for the very pioneer spirit which has produced some exceptional explorers, from Viking times onwards, is matched by a rare compassion and concern for the more wretched affairs of the world. Thus 20th century Scandinavia has been in the vanguard in helping the under-privileged and in striving to inject peace into a humanity sometimes seemingly bent upon self-destruction.

Just one example is the Norwegian, Fridtjof Nansen, who achieved majestic feats of human endurance as an Arctic explorer and then, with equal single-mindedness, applied his energies to the seemingly intractable problems of the world at the League of Nations, concerning himself especially with the agonies of the world's refugees. In 1923, he won the cherished Peace Prize instituted by yet another Scandinavian, Alfred Bernhard Nobel, the Swedish inventor of dynamite. Since those days, international forums seeking disarmament accords have regularly taken place on Scandinavian soil, while young Scandinavians participate in peace-keeping forces and medical missions in various troubled parts of the globe.

Design As Art

We've already established that the Scandinavians know how to make themselves comfortable under almost any circumstance. But they are also very insistent that things should be beautiful as well as practical. Scandinavian architects have established reputations that are world-wide, Scandinavian designers regularly carry off prizes at international contests. And this is probably largely because the "average" citizen cares to a degree that is rare elsewhere about the design and craftsmanship that has gone into the bowl which decorates his table, the ceramics or glass from which he eats and drinks, the textiles that hang at his windows, even the pots and pans he cooks in or the tools with which he will further endeavour to improve the quality of life. This intrinsic preference for the aesthetic, and the talents with which to satisfy it, have visible repercussions on the holiday scene. A less obvious, but nonetheless pleasing side effect is the number of crafts centers or studios to be stumbled upon, often in the most unexpected backwoods areas, where talented artists—many of them escapees from city life—are producing beautiful items in wood, ceramics, textiles, precious or semi-precious metals and stones, either for practical use or pure adornment.

When it comes to the fine arts, interestingly (and with a few obvious exceptions), the Scandinavians are more successful as sculptors than as painters, though there are probably proportionately more of both than in most other parts of the world. Open-air art exhibitions are a strong feature of the Scandinavian summer, some of them so remotely tucked away among the woods and lakes that you wonder how anyone ever gets to hear of them, let alone make the effort to go there. But they do. They're also prolific writers and avid readers not only of their own literature, but everyone else's too. To a degree you'll probably find shaming, they will almost certainly know more about you than you know about them.

Markets and Midsummer Madness

Open-air exhibitions are only one small aspect of the al fresco activities that characterize the long days of the Scandinavian summer. Most symbolic of all is the great festival common to the whole region which celebrates Midsummer, usually at the weekend closest to the longest day. Focal points of the festivities are the huge bonfires lit on Midsummer's Eve pretty well everywhere; except, that is, in Sweden and western Finland where these are replaced by decorated maypoles. Music and dancing is the order of the day—or rather night, for few people will see their beds on this occasion.

During the light summer evenings, open-air theaters take over when most regular theaters are closed for the season. Street entertainment is particularly popular, especially in the cities and towns of Denmark and Sweden. The main ones will probably attract a few protest marches, too, with the Scandinavian young passionately recording their assent or (more likely) dissent on issues ranging from local laws to distant wars. Sporting activities confined for so many months of the year to indoor sports complexes are smartly transferred to the great outdoors. This sporting exodus to the great outdoors is by no means confined solely to more obviously athletic pursuits. One of the sights of Sweden's urban parks are the open-air chess games, played with giant-size chessmen and great solemnity to the accompaniment of murmured advice from the audience of enthusiasts which invariably gathers round.

The open-air museum, reconstructing the living conditions and way-of-life long past, was born in Scandinavia: in Stockholm, to be precise, where you can visit the original Skansen whose name has been adopted by a proliferation of "skansens" the world over. And, of course, there are open-air markets filling the squares and narrow streets of many of the pretty provincial towns and, incidentally, providing a good hunting ground for less expensive handicrafts. In fact in larger cities, some of these markets flourish year-round, and there's nothing that quite matches the atmosphere of a mid-winter market with be-furred and heavily-booted stall holders stamping their feet in the snow, the sun low on the horizon.

Festivals of a more cultural nature—of all kinds and at all levels—now pack the Scandinavian summer calendar. Some cover just about every cultural activity you can think of, others are more specialized, ranging from jazz to chamber or organ music and folklore to historic pageantry. The top events attract top international performers from the world of theater, ballet, opera and music; among the leading festivals are those at Bergen, Helsinki and Århus. But if you've made opera your scene, you want to head for the gorgeous Rococo theater of Drottningholm, Stockholm, or the splendid medieval castle that provides the setting for the Savonlinna Opera Festival in Finland. For lovers of jazz, the choice includes Copenhagen, Molde in Norway, Pori in Finland, while the Roskilde Festival in Denmark tops the lot in northern Europe for a feast of rock, jazz and folk music. Allegorical plays are a specialty of Dalarna province in Sweden; the Swedish island of Gotland focuses on a moving mystery pageant; the Danes of southern Jutland have a nostalgia for medieval times with tilting at the ring tournaments; and their compatriots in Frederikssund grow beards (or at least the men do!) and recreate the life and times of the Vikings at their annual Viking Festival.

Some events will never make the international calendar and are just pure fun, like the Sleepyhead Day of Naantali in Finland when, if you're a late riser, you might just qualify for being thrown into the sea! Folkloric custom and culture are strong favorites, whether as part of an organized festival (Kaustinen in Finland, Skagen in Denmark) or perpetuating such deep-rooted traditions as church boat processions, again in Dalarna where this was once the only way of traveling to worship, or the peasant-style weddings of western Norway.

With a bit of careful planning, you could fill the months from late spring to early fall moving from one event to another. For the rest of the year, the theater, opera and concert season takes over in the towns and cities, and out in the country districts workaday activities, geared to the rhythm of the seasons, provide some of the most colorful events of all. Up around the Arctic Circle and beyond, for example, the reindeer round-ups of northern Norway, Sweden and Finland provide a memorably boisterous scene of whirling lassos and thundering hooves, strongly reminiscent of the Wild West, yet muted by deep-freeze temperatures and a thick blanket of snow. And still way beyond the Arctic Circle, thousands of fishermen in hundreds of vessels converge during the early months of the year on the icy seas around Norway's spectacular Lofoten Islands for the annual harvest of the Lofotens Fisheries. This scene of extraordinary activity, which depends on nothing more or less than the life cycle of the cod, goes back to the Middle Ages, and such is its importance that the whole procedure comes under the jurisdiction of its own special Fisheries "government."

Of the People . . .

But what of the broader canvas of the Scandinavian social and political scene? Certainly, the flame of democracy burns steadily here and with historic continuity. Here the world's first parliament saw the light of day (in Iceland around A.D. 930). Here originated the post of Ombudsman to investigate complaints against government departments (in Sweden in 1809). Here the first women in Europe—the second in the world—won the franchise (in Finland in 1906). And here the first woman ever was freely elected as head of state (presently, the President of Iceland). Yet traditions die hard and few Scandinavians have any inclination to tamper with their aristocratic and royal heritage where it exists. Three of the countries can produce a royal family apiece, two of them a plethora of counts and barons.

That said, the Scandinavian royals are as much "of the people" as you are likely to find anywhere, as you'll discover when you brush elbows with the Swedish king in a Stockholm theater lobby, or meet the Danish royal family cycling along a rural lane, or learn that the Norwegian Crown Prince underwent all the same hardships of a military winter exercise as his contemporaries. The fact of the matter is that these monarchs provide the stabilizing influence, above and beyond political considerations, and the continuity so necessary to the continued well-being of the countries. It's probably no exaggeration to say that if the monarchy were abolished in any of the three countries where it exists, the king would be a strong contender for president!

Politically, the emphasis is on moderation. If you are accustomed to a two-party system, you may find the number of parties from which Scandinavian electors need to choose their representatives a little excessive (10 in Denmark, for example, and nine in Finland), and it's true that coalitions are often a necessary by-product. In parts of the region, too, the Communist party is rather more in evidence than most of us are used to, though its steady decline is equally apparent, its position in Finland (one of its former strongholds) having dropped from a close second in 1945 to a lagging fourth in 1987. It is also important to realise that Scandinavia's brand of Eurocommunism has moved some distance from the Soviet variety with which it is often in conflict.

But for the most part, it's the Social Democrats—broadly comparable to the Democrats—who constitute the overall political makeup of Scandinavia, at the expense of such other major groups as the the Center, Conservative and Liberal parties.

Economy and Enterprise

In any survey of the contemporary Scandinavian scene, the question arises sooner or later, on what have the Scandinavians based their current considerable prosperity? Fortuitously, most of the natural features that contribute so much to their countries' attractions can be translated one way or another into hard cash. Thus, timber, fish, iron and steel, dairy farming, hydro-electric energy, shipping and, in more recent years, oil, all constitute a major part of the region's economy, along with their by-products and the specialized equipment with which to process them. But in modern times, overspecialization has revealed its own hazards, as became evident to the Finns once dangerously dependent on timber and paper exports, and Icelanders whose economy was almost entirely based on fishing.

But like the rest of us, the Scandinavians have recognized the vital need to diversify and are now applying their special talents to a much broader range of goods. The latest in electronic equipment and medical supplies, complex machinery of all kinds, fashions and furniture, sports equipment and household appliances, all swell the selection of items that now appear on their order books. To such exports an all-important addition can be made, albeit an invisible one: know-how. All over the world, you'll come across Scandinavians bringing their expertise to the development of new enterprise, whether it's a tractor factory in Brazil, a telex-data installation in Saudi Arabia, a smelting furnace in India, a paper mill in Canada, or a hotel in the Balkans.

You could almost call it a new Viking era.

Detail from Picture-stone. Gotland, 8th century.

SCANDINAVIAN HISTORY

Prosperity Out of Conflict

Scandinavia today presents a picture of harmonious unity: five countries, linked by a common culture, geography and history, politically and technologically sophisticated, at peace with themselves and the world. There are, to be sure, differences between them. Finland, for example, has a language that owes nothing to the other Scandinavian tongues. Norway, Sweden and Denmark are monarchies, Finland and Iceland are republics. Denmark is the only Scandinavian member of the EEC, the Common Market. Sweden and Finland have long been politically non-aligned, Norway, Denmark and Iceland are all active members of NATO. But what unites Scandinavia is ultimately of greater significance than what divides her, and it is difficult to think of any other grouping of countries in the modern world more happily or naturally united.

But it was not always so. Her present enviable prosperity and stability are a striking tribute to the new maturity of once rival and warring lands, with little more than a common tongue—Finland excepted—and their harsh climate and isolation on the northern fringes of Europe to unite them.

Bog People and Berserkers

More than anything else, it is the fact of her isolation that provides the key note of much early Scandinavian history. With the exception of Denmark and parts of southern Sweden, Scandinavia is a vast and frequently inhospitable land, underpopulated even today; a land of endless forests and mountain fastnesses, laced by rivers and lakes and buffeted by the long northern winter. This combination of remoteness and vast scale long conspired to ensure that she remained in the backwaters of early European history.

Not surprisingly, Scandinavia's earliest inhabitants seem naturally to have gravitated towards its most fertile and temperate regions. Though relics dating back six or seven thousand years—in particular primitive skis—have been found in the empty wastes of Finland and northern Sweden, it was in the south of Scandinavia, in present day Denmark and southern Sweden, that the first sizeable settlements existed. There is considerable evidence to suggest that by the Bronze Age (c. 1500 B.C.–500 B.C.) the early Scandinavians had become successful farmers and hunters, skilled also at pottery and weaving. A number of Scandinavian museums—the Nordic Museum in Stockholm pre-eminently—contain sizeable collections of jewelry, pottery and other artefacts from burial mounds which attest to the relative sophistication of these early inhabitants. Remarkably, two of the men themselves, pickled by the peat bogs in which they were buried, have also been found. The severed heads of these grisly remains—Graubolle man and Tollund man—are today on view, for those with strong stomachs, at the Århus and Silkeborg museums in Denmark.

Yet despite this evidence of a not inconsiderable population, Scandinavia remained isolated from the main centers of Europe. Even the Romans baulked at her trackless forests and vast unpopulated expanses, no doubt discouraged also by her brutal winters, and the northernmost limits of their empire stopped far to the south of the Scandinavian lands. Nonetheless, it seems clear that merchants from the south were happy to barter with the mysterious northern tribes. The pieces of amber that could be picked up on Denmark's beaches were particularly prized by the Romans, who traded ivory, silver and gold for them. Roman coins have even been found in remote and rugged Iceland—*Ultima Thule* indeed.

By about A.D. 700 much of coastal southern Scandinavia had been settled, though vast areas of the interior remained uninhabited. Interestingly, though perhaps not surprisingly, the most densely populated areas, at the heart of the most important agricultural lands and strategically placed for trade, were subsequently to grow into modern Scandinavia's capitals. But in addition, Trondheim, on the northwest coast of Norway, also developed as an important center.

As well as being successful hunters and farmers, the Scandinavians also traded extensively. The Swedes, for example, controlled the fur trade between north and south Scandinavia, while the Norwegians of the Atlantic coast had trade links with both southern Sweden and Denmark and the Frisian islands on the west coast of Germany. However, the inhospitable interior meant that most trade was dependent on sea travel, and it is evident that despite their primitive navigational know-how the early Scandinavians were skilled shipwrights and routinely undertook long and arduous sea voyages. At the same time, increasingly persistent warring between rival tribes also made the possession of sea-going vessels necessary.

Around A.D. 800 something very strange happened to these somewhat primitive hunters and farmers, relegated to the outer fringes of Europe. Without warning, and for reasons that still remain the subject of speculation, they exploded onto the European scene, sallying forth from Scandinavia in their long ships and wreaking havoc—pillaging, looting and terrorizing—over the length and breadth of Europe. The Vikings had arrived.

"From the fury of the Norsemen, Good Lord deliver us," was to become a deeply-felt and oft-uttered prayer in many parts of Europe.

Whatever the reasons for the sudden appearance of the Vikings—whether economic pressure created by population increases in their homelands, changes in the climate, or just a simple-minded taste for a wandering life of excitement and exploration (the ultimate test of Viking manhood was to enter battle bare-chested or "berserk")—one thing is clear. The Vikings were successful because the disintegration of the Roman empire had created a power vacuum in Europe, leaving the continent weak and disordered, a prey to any who chanced upon her. Thus the Vikings remorselessly swept through Europe, as though a cannon loaded with grapeshot had been suddenly fired.

Swedes thrust southeastwards across the Baltic, founding Russia some say (*rus* means Swede), and reaching the Black Sea by means of the Dnieper river, and Persia by the Volga river and Caspian sea. In Constantinople they enrolled as Varangian (or Viking) guards, elite bodyguards to the Byzantine emperor. The Norwegians sailed west and north, overtaking Orkney and Shetland, which remained Scandinavian until 1468 when they were mortgaged to the Scottish crown. Step by step, they then bridged the Atlantic, reaching the Faroes (850), Iceland (874), Greenland (984) and finally Vinland—North America—(1000). The Atlantic leap itself was achieved in just two generations. Eric the Red left Norway to farm in Iceland, and then moved on to found the Greenland colony. It was his son, Leif, who discovered America.

The Norwegians also swept down the west coast of Britain, to the Isle of Man, the Lake District and Ireland. The Danes meanwhile landed in eastern England, establishing York as their major center. In the south of England, the Danish king Canute eventually reigned (1016–1035) over a combined English, Danish and Norwegian domain. At the same time Northern France became Normandy, the land of the northmen, soon to emerge as an independent country and, under Duke William, to begin the conquest of Britain in 1066.

The Coming of Christianity

Though the impact of the Vikings was great, the Viking age itself was relatively short lived, lasting from about 800 to 1050. Perhaps its very vividness was such as to ensure that it exhausted itself quickly. At all events, by the middle of the 11th century, the Viking period was rapidly being superceded by a new and much more stable economic and political order that was to last right up to the Renaissance. And at the heart of this new medieval society was Christianity, slowly but inevitably dispersing the seemingly endless night of the Dark Ages.

The Vikings themselves yielded to the forces of the "pale Galilean." Some indeed appeared positively to welcome the new religion and proved themselves enthusiastic converts and, later, missionaries, happy to despatch those whose interest was more tepid to the Viking Valhalla. Nonetheless, the old beliefs and religions of the Vikings lingered on—their Gods Tyr, Wodon, Thor and Frey are still with us, disguised as Tuesday, Wednesday, Thursday and Friday. For a time, Christianity fused with the Viking religions to create curious hybrids, nowhere better illustrated than by the 12th-century stave churches of Norway, a number of which have survived to the present day at Fantoft, Borgund and Lom. These tall,

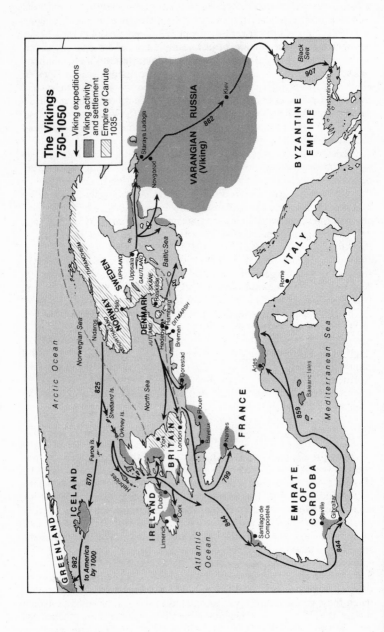

The Vikings
750–1050

→ Viking expeditions
▨ Viking activity and settlement
▨ Empire of Canute 1035

BYZANTINE EMPIRE

Black Sea
907
Constantinople

VARANGIAN RUSSIA
(Viking)

Kiev
982
Staraya Ladoga
Novgorod

ITALY
Rome

Baltic Sea

SWEDEN
NORWAY
Uppsala
GAUTLAND
Oslo
SKÅNE
THRANDHEIM
Nidaros
NORTHLAND

DENMARK
JUTLAND
Hedeby
Roskilde
Hamburg
DITMARSH
Bremen

Arctic Ocean

Norwegian Sea

North Sea

825

Shetland Is.
Orkney Is.
Faroe Is.
870

ICELAND

GREENLAND

982
to America by 1000

Hebrides

BRITAIN
York
London

IRELAND
Dublin
Limerick
Cork

Atlantic Ocean

Borestad
Rouen
Bayeux
Nantes

FRANCE

844
799

Santiago de Compostela

EMIRATE OF CORDOBA
Seville
Gibraltar
844

Mediterranean Sea

Balearic Isles

Arles
859

pagoda-like structures, whose tiered wooden roofs rise delicately sky-wards, are always surmounted by a cross, but on their eaves and along the door jambs dragons and other pagan symbols are carved. Even today there are clear traces of the old Scandinavian religions in the far north among the Lapps and in Finnmark.

But Christianity proved itself an irresistable force and by 1300 had established itself throughout Scandinavia. Sweden even produced a saint, Bridget, born in 1303. She subsequently moved to Rome where she wrote a series of widely influential mystic *Revelations* and founded an order of nuns, the Bridgettines.

The Middle Ages

For all that Christianity underpinned Scandinavian society in the Middle Ages, Scandinavian history in this period nonetheless presents a confused picture of succeeding dynasties, recalcitrant nobles and scheming bishops. And for much of the period, that is until the beginning of the 17th century, Scandinavia remained essentially remote from developments on the wider European stage, a minor player in an increasingly important game. Even Denmark, for example, long the most developed and prosperous of the Scandinavian countries, largely by virtue of its proximity to the European mainland, was reduced to bit part status, falling under the sway of the Hanseatic League, the predatory merchants of Hamburg and Lübeck in north Germany who negotiated for themselves lucrative trading monopolies among the hapless Scandinavians. The Hansa quays in Bergen, Norway, have survived as potent evidence of Hanseatic power.

At the same time that Scandinavia was groaning under the Hanseatic yoke in the 13th and 14th centuries, another catastrophe struck in the form of the Black Death. Norway alone lost a third of her population between 1349 and 1350. Essential reading for an idea of the impact of the Black Death on the infant Scandinavian states is Sigrid Undset's sprawling novel *Kristin Lavransdatter.*

Literature of another sort was actually being produced during this period, in Iceland, by the aristocratic and cultured Snorri Sturlson (1179–1241). He it was who committed to writing the achievements and adventures of the Viking age, and celebrated early Iceland's turmoil and warring, in the Sagas and Eddas, the greatest monuments of early Scandinavian literature and an invaluable treasure house of historic myths and tales. Ironically perhaps, he did so at a moment when not only had the Vikings all but faded from the scene but when Iceland itself, until the 13th century a considerable political force in Scandinavian affairs and a proudly independent land—it is Iceland's happy boast that she is the site of the oldest republic north of the Alps—was fast fading herself, a decline continued in 1264 when Iceland succumbed to Norwegian rule, as had Greenland three years earlier.

However, this period of Norwegian expansion in the 13th century was to prove brief and, the Hanseatic League notwithstanding, by the 14th century it was Denmark that had emerged as the dominant voice in Scandinavian affairs, consolidating her hold on the whole of the region in 1389 in the shape of the Kalmar Union by which Sweden, Finland and Norway were united under Danish rule. The Kalmar Union, which lasted until 1521, was essentially the work of the remarkable Queen Margrethe of Denmark. She was, however, Regent only and in 1397 handed the reigns of power to her incompetent nephew, Eric of Pomerania. The combination of his maladministration and the greed of his henchmen was more than sufficient to cause a seemingly endless series of revolts among his subject peoples, especially in Sweden. The Danish rulers that followed Eric were hardly less inept, but nonetheless the Union struggled precariously through the 15th century. By the end of the century, following the ascendency of the energetic and authoritarian Christian II of Denmark, it appeared set for greater things, however. Determined to stamp out dissent among the Swedes once and for all, in 1520 Christian initiated a massacre of the leading members of the so-called Freedom Party in Stockholm. But his efforts were to prove entirely counter-productive, and only sparked greater demands for Swedish independence. This the Swedes were dramatically and violently to achieve, principally under the imaginative and forceful leadership of Gustavus Vasa. Capitalizing on a popular uprising in the province of Dalecarlia, Gustavus fanned the flame of revolt and by 1523 had established himself as undisputed ruler of a newly-independent and aggressive Sweden. Thus the stage was set for Sweden's greatest moment of glory and expansion.

The Reformation and Sweden's Rise

The Sweden now ruled by the indomitable Gustavus Vasa was still an essentially impoverished and downtrodden land following almost two centuries of Danish domination. Similarly, though the Danes had been ousted from Sweden, their military intentions toward her were by no means exhausted and they remained in control of parts of southern Sweden, a permanent threat to Gustavus. Thus much of Gustavus's reign was characterized by an urgent need to consolidate Sweden's independence from Denmark and to build up trade as rapidly as possible in order to finance his increasingly ambitious military goals.

In this, Gustavus shrewdly and pragmatically took advantage of the slow spread of the Reformation into Scandinavia. Like his contemporary Henry VIII in England, Gustavus, guided largely by political rather than spiritual considerations, took advantage of the split with Rome to support and eventually to establish as the new national church the Reformed—that is, the Protestant—religion. Simultaneously, he systematically confiscated much of the considerable wealth of the old Catholic church in Sweden, using it to finance his armies.

As Sweden grew in strength, in the process ridding herself of the remaining monopolies enjoyed by the waning Hanseatic League, so Gustavus began to interest himself more and more in foreign affairs. And it was under Gustavus that for the first time since the Vikings a Scandinavian country began to enjoy influence and status on the wider European stage. An alliance with Francis I of France against the future emperor of the Holy Roman Empire, Charles V, represented only the first stirrings of Sweden's ambitions toward, and influence over, the affairs of the Holy Roman Empire on the European mainland.

The Reformation enjoyed equal success in the rest of Scandinavia, spreading throughout the joint kingdom of Denmark and Norway and into Swedish controlled Finland, and finally to Iceland. To some extent, the Reformed Church acted as a new focus of nationalism for the Danes, still smarting from their defeat at the hands of Gustavus Vasa. Sweden's position by the end of the 16th century was still somewhat precarious. Her

only outlet to the North Sea, for example, was a narrow strip at the mouth
of the Göta river between hostile Denmark and Norway, and her ambitions in the Baltic were permanently under threat from Russia and Poland
as well as Denmark herself. Moreover, by the beginning of the 17th century Denmark had acquired a new ruler in Christian IV (1588–1648) whose
dynamism and ambition were formidable. As well as being an indefatigable builder—Copenhagen's fairy-tale summer palace of Rosenborg and the
Borsen (Stock Exchange) with its barley-sugar-twist spire both owe their
existence to the energetic Christian; similarly, he rebuilt Oslo, moving it
nearer to its present location and renaming it Christiania in the process—
Christian made strident efforts to regain the dominance Denmark had enjoyed during the heyday of the Kalmar Union. Denmark still controlled
all shipping passing through the narrow sound between Copenhagen and
southern Sweden—the Sound of Sounds, as it came to be known, and the
principal link between the Baltic and the North Sea. Similarly, her maritime prowess in the Baltic remained impressive.

Under Christian the Danes embarked on an extended series of military
campaigns against the Swedes. However, while the Danes were fortunate
to have so outstanding a ruler in Christian, the Swedes were even more
blessed. And in Gustavus II Adolphus, the Lion of the North who roared
his way to the throne in 1611, they found themselves a ruler of outstanding
military abilities, more than the equal of even one as apparently awesome
as Christian IV.

Under Gustavus, Sweden swept confidently into the 17th century and
her age of greatness, during which she defeated the Danes, driving them
out of southern Sweden, and turned the Baltic into what was to amount
to her own private preserve. In addition, the brilliant military campaigns
waged by Gustavus were to ensure Sweden a decisive role in the complex
entanglements of the Thirty Years War (1618–1648), in which the Catholic forces of the Holy Roman Empire, ruled by the Habsburgs, grappled
brutally and somewhat pointlessly with the Protestant forces of northern
Europe, represented principally by Sweden. By 1632, in fact, the Swedes
under Gustavus had swept through the whole of present day Germany
and were poised to take Austria, the heart of the Holy Roman Empire,
when Gustavus was killed at the battle of Lutzen in 1632. The Swedes
were victorious at Lutzen, but the death of their charismatic general and
king broke the momentum of their campaign, and the battle was to mark
the high point of the European adventures.

Gustavus Adolphus was succeded by his young daughter, the enigmatic
and ambivalent Christina. In the early part of her reign, however, when
Christina was still a child, the country was governed by a Council headed
by the able statesman Axel Oxenstierna. Though Sweden under Oxenstierna remained a major military influence in the Thirty Years War, which,
as it neared its climax, was to turn Germany into one vast and chaotic
battlefield, Oxenstierna himself turned his attentions increasingly towards
developments in the Baltic, seeking to establish Sweden as the pre-eminent
power there. In this, as in other matters of foreign policy, Christina played
no very significant role once she had come of age. Though a woman of
striking intelligence (but of less-than-lovely appearance), Christina devoted herself almost exclusively to establishing luxury, elegance and learning
in her court. Her reckless extravagance and neglect of matters of state,
despite the warnings of Oxenstierna, were eventually to prove her undoing
and in 1654 she was forced to abdicate. Her disgrace in the eyes of her

The Swedish Empire, 1523 to 1721

- Sweden in the reign of Gustavus Vasa (1523-60)
- Swedish gains, 1561-1645
- Swedish gains, 1645-58
- greatest extent of Swedish Empire, 1658
- fortress
- 1617 dates refer to Swedish acquisition

Arctic Ocean

JOINT RUSSIAN-
NORWEGIAN-
SWEDISH LANDS

LAPLAND

Arctic Circle

RUSSIA

VARDÖHUS

Norwegian Sea

VÄSTERBOTTEN

Steinviksholm

Luleå

TRONDHJEM
1658-60
Trondhjem

ÅNGERMAN
LAND

Gulf of Bothnia

ÖSTERBOTTEN

Kajana

JÄMTLAND
1645

KEX
HOLM
1617

IDRE
SÄRNA

Vasa

FINLAND

Sundsvall

DALARNA

Tavastehus

Lake
Ladoga

Åbo

Viborg

AREA

Bergen

Akershus

Christiania
(Oslo)

BERGS-
LADEN

Åland

Helsingfors
(Helsinki)

Noteborg

INGRIA
1617

Stavern

Karlstad

Uppsala

Gulf of Finland

KINGDOM
OF
DENMARK
AND
NORWAY

Fredrikshald

Stockholm

Reval

ESTONIA
1561

Novgorod

BOHUSLÄN
1658

Norrköping

Dorpat

Lake
Peipus

Lake
Ilmen

Gothenburg

HALLAND
1645

SMÅLAND

Gotland
1645

Öland

LIVONIA
1629

RUSSIA

JUTLAND

Viborg

Kalmar

Karlskrona

Riga

COUR-
LAND

Kronborg

BLEKINGE
1658

Baltic Sea

Fredericia

Copenhagen

Malmö

Zealand

SCANIA

Swedish
1626-35

Memel
R. Niemen

LITHUANIA

SCHLESWIG

Gottorp

Bornholm
1658-60

Pillau

HOLSTEIN

Kiel

Wismar

1648

WEST
POMERANIA
1648

Elbing

PRUSSIA

1648

Stettin

BREMEN
VERDEN

MECKLENBURG

BRANDENBURG

R. Vistula

KINGDOM OF

POLAND

HOLY ROMAN EMPIRE

N

countrymen, who by now she affected to despise for their ignorance and crudity, was compounded by her subsequent conversion to Catholicism in Paris. She thereafter settled in Rome, living in the same house that St. Bridget had used, where she died in 1689.

However, the combined efforts of Oxenstierna and Christina's successors Charles X Gustavus and Charles XI Gustavus were equal to the task of ensuring that Sweden's dominant role in Scandinavia and the Baltic was continued. Indeed it was under Charles X in the Danish-Swedish war of 1657–60 that Sweden eventually reclaimed the remaining Danish territories in southern Sweden, confining Denmark once and for all to the areas west of the Sound.

By the end of the 17th century Sweden was again ruled by a man of outstanding military ability, the romantic soldier-king Charles XII Gustavus. He needed to be, too, for in 1700 Sweden was attacked simultaneously by the combined armies of Poland, Denmark and Russia. Despite the overwhelming numerical superiority of his enemies, Charles achieved a remarkable victory over the Russians at Narva in 1700, which effectively destroyed the enemy alliance. He subsequently marched on Moscow but was defeated—as much by the Russian winter as by the Russian army—at Poltava in 1709. Charles sought refuge in Turkey from where, extraordinarily, he continued to rule over distant Sweden. By now, however, Sweden faced an even larger alliance, made up of Russia, Poland, Denmark, Britain and two of the north German states, Hanover and Prussia. Hopelessly outnumbered, Charles then attempted to disrupt the alliance between Russia and Britain, to which end he returned, incognito, to Scandinavia in 1718. In the middle of these clandestine negotiations, Charles was mysteriously murdered in Norway, ending all hope of disrupting the powerful forces ranged against him. The Swedes were forced to capitulate.

Much of Sweden's Baltic empire was ceded to the Russians, including large parts of Finland, and by 1721 the once indomitable Swedes found that their empire had all but vanished leaving the way clear for the Russians, who soon after emerged as the dominant power in the Baltic.

Rococo and Revolution

Though Sweden remained the dominant power in the 18th century among the Scandinavian nations, the period as a whole witnessed the gradual decline of Scandinavian influence. For example, while Denmark continued to enjoy considerable maritime prestige, she was also to fall increasingly under the influence of Prussia in northern Germany, a trend that continued into the 19th century. Similarly, Norway and Finland, the one still ruled by Denmark, the other partitioned between Sweden and Russia, remained obscure and generally insignificant lands. And Sweden herself was forced to watch the gradual erosion of what remained of her Baltic empire.

Nonetheless, it was in Sweden that the most interesting developments occurred, especially during the reign of Gustavus III, who came to the throne in 1771. He was responsible both for a radical reshaping of Swedish government—a vital early step in the development of democracy in Sweden—and for a great upsurge in the importance of Swedish arts. His marvelous palace at Drottningholm, just outside Stockholm, with its delightful Rococo theater, is eloquent proof of the artistic revolution that occurred under this most enlightened of Swedish kings. The period also saw Sweden step into the intellectual and scientific limelight. Carl von Linée—we know him as Linnaeus—was the leading botanist of his day, whose revolutionary *Systems of Nature* pioneered the same essential system of classification for plants as that used today. Gustavus—a great admirer of all things French—also founded the Swedish Academy, modeled on its famous French cousin.

But in 1792 Gustavus was assassinated, a victim of the violent political opposition his far-reaching reforms had stirred up among the Swedish aristocracy. Yet to some extent even his death amounted to little more than a sideshow, for by the end of the 18th century, internal events in Scandinavia were being more and more overshadowed by the turmoil engulfing Europe as a whole following the French Revolution. As Napoleon and his revolutionary armies marched across the Continent, the Scandinavians found themselves inexorably drawn into the greater European conflict, with consequences that were to influence decisively the further development of Scandinavian history.

Thus in 1801, for example, Nelson attacked Copenhagen to prevent Napoleon obtaining the Danish navy for his intended invasion of Britain. Six years later, Wellington bombarded the capital again and seized the fleet himself. Similarly, Sweden under Gustavus IV Adolphus, having declared herself for Britain largely on the strength of her trading links, was attacked by the Russians in 1807 following a recent alliance forged between Napoleon and Russia. The Swedish–Russian conflict was in fact to have a number of very important consequences. Not only did Sweden lose her remaining Finnish territories to the Russians, she also found herself with a new, and very unexpected ruler. This was one of Napoleon's marshalls, one Bernadotte, who, with the active collusion of Napoleon (who saw Bernadotte as a swift means of obtaining control over Sweden), was elected king of Sweden in 1809. However, the French emperor's hopes were quickly dashed when Bernadotte revealed himself as both profoundly opposed to Napoleon's scheming and shrewd in the extreme. At the Congress of Vienna in 1815, which settled the fate of post-Napoleonic Europe, Bernadotte was able to obtain considerable compensation for the loss of Sweden's Finnish lands, and even more spectacularly confirmed the transfer of Norway, which had been ruled by Denmark since the 14th century, from Denmark to Sweden. Denmark meanwhile was left only with the politically and economically insignificant North Atlantic islands of Iceland, Greenland and the Faroes.

Industrialization and Independence

More than the political map of Scandinavia was changed by the events of the first decades of the 19th century, however. By about 1820, it was evident that Scandinavia was economically crippled, unable to keep pace with the ever more rapid developments of the Industrial Revolution or to exploit the growing opportunities for trade created by the opening of new markets outside Europe by the leading European nations, among whom the Scandinavians emphatically no longer numbered.

The 19th century was in fact a generally dismal time for the Scandinavians. Lacking the capital to develop their own modern industries, their trade was gradually taken over by foreign concerns, causing a decline in home markets that made only all the more remote the likelihood of the industrialization that by 1850 had become long overdue. Simultaneously,

Scandinavian agriculture also declined, giving rise to wide-spread rural poverty which in turn led to massive emigration, particularly to America. This reached a peak between 1880 and the turn of the century.

But bankruptcy was in some senses the mother of Scandinavian invention, and from the middle years of the 19th century, a slow industrialization spread throughout the region. Such breakthroughs as Ørsted's in electro-magnetism helped the Nordic lands, lavishly endowed with water for electricity, to industrialize efficiently. Nobel's invention of dynamite changed the nature of war and mining. Similar inventive genius assisted in the growth of Danish dairying, Norwegian nitrates and Swedish ball-bearing factories. Developments in steamships helped found an expanding Norwegian merchant navy for fishing, world trade and, at home, provided the coastal services from Bergen to Kirkenes and back, forerunner of today's Coastal Express. Railways opened up vast interior tracts and serviced mines in Sweden and Finland, while canals bypassed the Baltic, linking Stockholm with Gothenburg through the great lakes. The Danes established Esbjerg in 1868 especially for trade with Britain, while the United Steamship Company was created two years earlier to link the nation's scattered areas, and is still with us as DFDS.

Scandinavians, with their small populations, were also among the first to realize the importance of an educated, fully participatory majority. Here the chief figure was the Dane Gruntvig (1783–1872), whose deep reading in the Sagas, widely-based religious views, boundless energy and patriotism led him to create the highly influential Folk High School movement. These schools, somewhat misnamed in English, offered "Education for Life"—culture, history and poetry, moral and practical subjects and economics for all.

While the latter half of the 19th century saw a slow rise in prosperity in Scandinavia and the political foundation of the modern Scandinavian states, it also saw the only serious foreign entanglement to befall Scandinavia since the end of the Napoleonic wars. This occurred on Denmark's southern border with Prussia in Germany, long a source of friction between Danes and Germans. By the 1860s, the Prussians, guided by their wily Chancellor Bismarck, had begun to cast covetous eyes on Denmark's border provinces, the acquisition of which they saw as the first step in the unification of Germany under Prussia. When war came in 1864 the military might of the Prussians was rapidly decisive and Denmark, having lost Norway only 50 years earlier, now found herself stripped of one sixth of her remaining lands. That the Danish monarchy survived such a crushing national humiliation spoke volumes for its stability and popularity. (Denmark's southern provinces were eventually restored to her in 1920).

The latter part of the 19th century was also marked by the growing spread of democratic and nationalistic ideals, culminating in 1905 with the dissolution of the joint kingdom of Sweden and Norway and the granting of full independence to Norway. Finland's independence from Russia in 1917, however, was achieved at much greater cost. All the Scandinavian nations had managed to remain neutral in World War I (though all, especially Norway, suffered considerable disruption of their trade). The Finns were thus well placed to take advantage of the Russian Revolution in 1917, which plunged an already war-torn Russia into terrible chaos, and declare themselves independent. Though the new Russian regime under Lenin soon recognized this independent Finland, a large body of opinion in Finland did not and civil war broke out; the "whites" favoring independence, the "reds" continued union with Russia, or the Soviet Union as it had now become. The whites were quickly victorious, however, and in 1920 the borders of modern Finland were established.

The Modern States

The Scandinavian nations continued on their peaceful course until the late '30s, all by now determinedly neutral and essentially removed from the growing tensions in Europe caused by the rapid rise of Nazism and the Soviet Union. But in 1939, despite their professed neutrality, the Finns were invaded by the Soviet Union, with whom they had signed a pact of non-aggression in 1932. Remarkably, Finland resisted the vast but disorganized Soviet army for over 100 days before capitulating in March 1940. Under the terms of the subsequent peace treaty the Finns were obliged to cede large parts of their eastern lands to Russia.

This, however, was only the beginning of Scandinavia's troubles. As in World War I, all the Scandinavian nations attempted to remain neutral following the outbreak of World War II. The Swedes alone succeeded in doing so. Both Norway and Denmark were invaded by Nazi Germany in April 1940, while Iceland was occupied by Britain and, later, by the Americans who used it as a vital staging post for ferrying men and supplies across the Atlantic. Finland, meanwhile, then sided with the Nazis; not, as they are quick to point out, for any ideological reasons but because they saw the Nazi invasion of Russia in 1941 as an ideal opportunity to regain the territories lost in 1940. In this they were singularly unsuccessful, and ended the war by fighting the Russians *and* the Germans. Though noncombatants, the Danes and, even more particularly, the Norwegians, had suffered almost equally grave destruction by the end of the war. To some extent the very effectiveness of the Resistance movements both spawned was responsible, provoking the occupying Nazis into terrible acts of reprisal.

By 1945 Norway, Denmark and Finland were all seriously weakened, the Finns in addition having lost again to the Russians all the territory they had regained following their initial invasion with the Germans. Even neutral Sweden ended the war with severe economic problems caused by the disruption of her trade and the expense of the rapid armaments program she had been forced into in order to maintain her neutrality.

Thus it is really only in the immediate post-war period that Scandinavia has grown into the plenty and excellence that so distinguishes her today. Politically, the major developments of this period were the granting of full independence to Iceland in 1944, followed by the granting of full autonomy to Greenland in 1979. 1956 saw the formation of the Nordic Council, a loose grouping of all the Scandinavian states designed to further cooperation and development. Still a thriving organization today, it expresses eloquently the new and happy unity of this much-troubled region.

Yet even in today's affluent society—and Scandinavia seems to have weathered the recessions of the '70s and early '80s better than most—there are many reminders that the Scandinavia of the past, the vast and trackless land that even the Romans failed to penetrate, lingers on, a permanent reminder of an ancient people. In the far north Eskimos still hunt seal and polar bear where best they can be found, and Lapps still wander in search of fresh pastures for their reindeer. They may have walkie-talkies and central heating, but their lives are otherwise little changed from those of their ancestors two thousand years ago.

himself. Edgar rapes Signhild, to symbolize the triumph of religious repression, but in the process her back is broken on a nearby cartwheel. Their child has many problems."

I should add that this plot is quite genuine, and such a book really has been published. I have even attempted to read another novel by X. In chapter one the characters stood around exchanging significant silences in a frozen potato patch. In chapter two they were doing the same thing a month later in the same potato patch. I cannot really comment on the following chapters.

Anyway, there you are, reviewing this sort of thing week after week, and fighting off the mounting temptation to follow Thorbjörn's example and drown yourself, when you come across a book that is both literate and interesting, if not very remarkable. Naturally, you overpraise it grotesquely: in order to show off your learning, you compare it with foreign models; and the poor author believes you. Why shouldn't he? No one else is likely to read his book and tell him otherwise; and so another promising young author is ruined.

Only Finland is free of this sort of thing, saved by the innate flamboyance of the Finnish character. And the Finnish author Henrik Tikkannen, many of whose books have been translated into English, is one of the real delights of modern Scandinavian writing.

A Chronicle of Need

What came before 1950 will not enrich your experience of modern, Americanized Scandinavia, but it is well worth reading anyway. The plays of Ibsen and Strindberg should really be seen rather than read: which means that they should be seen before you travel, since they are seldom performed in English in Scandinavia, for obvious reasons. But the novels of Selma Lagerlöf, Hjalmar Söderberg, and Knut Hamsun can be read with pleasure and profit anywhere. They are three very different writers, and the differences between them make plain the difficulty of discussing "Scandinavian Culture." Quite apart from the fact that Hamsun wrote in Norwegian, and the other two in Swedish—this hardly matters in translation—the tones they adapt could hardly be further apart. What they do have in common is that they all wrote about the same sort of carefully stratified society, where you might not like your place but you knew it well. There, if you like, was a common Scandinavian culture.

Quality is always extraordinary, so perhaps one should regard Selma Lagerlöf as the strangest author of the three; but Knut Hamsun is the one who least resembles any other author (with the possible exception of the early George Orwell, which is odd, for Hamsun died a Nazi).

The book that made his name was *Hunger,* published in 1892. The title is not to be taken metaphorically: the book is a study of the effects of starvation on a young author in Oslo over a period of three months. It is, when you think of it, a subject so obvious that it is astonishing that no-one else before or since has dealt with it. Orwell tried to in his early work, but there was always a flavor of pity in Orwell's work: the sense that this was happening to other people too. Hamsun is truer to life in that his hero is intensely selfish: you cannot imagine Orwell's narrator in *Down and Out in London and Paris* fighting over a garbage can, yet this is the sort of thing that really hungry people do.

A mere chronicle of need would not be terribly interesting: what gives *Hunger* its peculiar power is the sense of personal outrage. Appetite eats at the narrator like a cancer. "Erst kommt das Fressen, dann die Moral," wrote Brecht, (First you must pig yourself; then think of morality). With Hamsun you can see it happening. And just as the narrator's own body rebels against him, demanding food when he would rather consider morality, so he rebels against the social organism surrounding him. The society of Hamsun's day was still extremely formal: you will find traces of this in modern Finland, but nowhere else in Scandinavia nowadays. The pressures of good, or respectable behavior are as great as the demands of hunger, and together they grind at the narrator like the jaws of a pike.

A little of this crushing movement tends to be lost in translation, for a technical reason that must also be borne in mind when reading Selma Lagerlöf: Swedes, and Scandinavians generally, swear religiously, rather than sexually, as Anglo-Saxons do. So when characters in these books go around exclaiming: "The Devil!", as they are prone to do, this should be understood as something a great deal ruder and more shocking in English. It is anything but quaint in the original.

Tale against Saga

Geographically speaking, the nearest great novelist to Hamsun was Selma Lagerlöf, whose stories are set in Värmland, a hilly, forested, and exceptionally beautiful province of Sweden along the southern edge of the border with Norway. Värmland remains an untamed place to this day: the last thriving family of wild wolves in Sweden lives on elk and sheep in the forests there now. It is the sort of place where children walked seven or eight miles to school every day through the forests, with their coats turned inside out as a charm against trolls. The towns and settlements are isolated and hierarchical places, almost like ships in the unfriendly wilderness. The likeness is deliberate, since from this unpromising countryside, Lagerlöf was able to extract much the same lessons as Joseph Conrad drew from the Far East. Both writers are concerned with courage more than anything: not the histrionic, mannered courage of Hemingway, where the hero can always expect an opportunity to be brave, even if no one (except five million readers) is watching him, but the more difficult exercise of bravery when there seems no reason or opportunity for it. Gösta Berling, the alcoholic priest in *Gösta Berling's Saga,* has much in common with Lord Jim. I can see them together drinking in a bar in Penang, though they would not need to say much to each other. Berling, a priest and an educated man, was at least as strange to his parishioners as "Tuan Jim" was to his Malay tribesmen.

The likeness between Selma Lagerlöf and Conrad should not be driven too far. Lagerlöf has a much less involuted style, for one thing; then there is a difference in the time their stories cover: Gösta Berling's *Saga* as against *A Tale of the Islands*. Selma Lagerlöf's characters have children, which Conrad's seldom do, and this gives a quite different significance to their actions.

Conrad, too, had a political understanding and interest that you would not find in any Scandinavian (or native English) writer: only someone born in Central Europe could have written *Under Western Eyes*. But the comparison is still worth making, if only because it may suggest just how good Selma Lagerlöf can be.

An Urban Miniaturist

Hjalmar Söderberg is an altogether more delicate writer; almost a min-
iaturist. He is the most urban and civilized of the three: equable, detatched,
and clear. His effects are gained by exact concentration on small things,
like a masterless dog wandering loose in the streets. All through the story
in which the dog appears, its master has been a brutal boor, cowing and
beating the animal whenever he gets the chance. The narrator is refined
and disdainful as he watches this. Then the master dies, unmourned and
the dog runs howling through the streets all night, not because he was
happy with his treatment, but because any master is better than none at
all: nothing could be more terrible than to be a dog for whom no one cares.
If one considers the English writer who could have written such a story
without sentimentality, it becomes clear that Kipling or Jack London
would have made it a story about the dog, about suffering and loyalty,
and living up to your alloted fate. Graham Greene would have made it
a story about the boorish master—in fact this situation does appear in one
of his short stories, set on the Mexican border. Söderberg makes it a story
about the narrator, or you and I, who so dislike the squalor of other people's lives. The dog's ridiculous and humiliating longing is no more incon-
gruous or avoidable than any of our aspirations; and they are just as likely
to be arbitrarily crushed as the dog's was.

This sounds a very "Scandinavian" plot. It doesn't read like that at all.
Söderberg's style is far too poised for melodrama or vulgarity. You don't
notice the barb until it cannot be extracted, just as the beautiful color of
the blood in a Renaissance painting disguises the fact that its subject is
a crucifixion.

Another point in Söderberg's favour is that he wrote short stories, which
make ideal reading on journeys. Perhaps *A Masterless Dog* would be a little
overpowering in an airport departure lounge, which makes most people
feel like that anyway; but even the best-planned journeys involve a certain
amount of waiting in pointless places, and a volume of Söderberg's short
stories makes a splendid charm against such horrors.

Visual Delights

There are of course other Scandinavian authors worth reading than the
five I have discussed, but those you will have to discover for yourself. It's
easy enough when once you've started, but the difficulty is beginning. All
that a guide book can achieve is to point out things that are known to
be good, without pretending to give a comprehensive coverage. Besides,
few visitors will spend more than a month in Scandinavia, and there's a
limit to what anyone can read in a month.

Language forms another limiting factor. The rhythms of Scandinavian
languages are sufficiently strong to make the accurate translation of poetry
into English extremely difficult. Similarly, the language barrier cuts one
off from the theater. Swedish and Finnish drama is very good indeed: the
production and the acting can be as good as anything you could see in
London or New York. And the theater—and films—give great scope to
the Swedish talent for collective belief.

Fortunately, there are theatrical experiences that are not dependent on
language. Both opera and ballet thrive in Scandinavia. The best—and most

expensive—performances, are to be seen in Copenhagen. You must book in advance for them, but it is well worth doing so. The Swedish equivalent would be the little theater at Drottningholm, a perfectly restored 18th-century Court theater, set in a palace on an island just outside Stockholm. This is where Ingmar Bergman's production of *The Magic Flute* was filmed, and it's hard to think of a more perfect setting for Mozart than Drottningholm. It is another place that can be difficult to get into because it seats so few people, but if you have any feeling for the theater at all, it is worth making very strenuous efforts to get to Drottningholm.

Finland presents a more difficult case. This is not because it is an uncultured country—on the contrary, the arts are in a better condition there than anywhere else in Scandinavia. But the Finns *will* speak Finnish, which makes their culture difficult of access. What is the point of knowing that there are five good theaters in Helsinki when you cannot understand a word that is said in any of them?

But there is hope for the traveler in music and architecture. Musically—obviously—there is Sibelius, though other Finnish composers well repay attention. There is also a considerable tradition of Russian music in Finland, and this can take unexpected forms. The Finnish equivalent of the Drottningholm theater—in as much as it is the perfect marriage of what you see with what you hear—is a high mass sung in the Russian Orthodox cathedral in Helsinki.

But in addition, the old town of Helsinki is itself a considerable aesthetic experience. Whether it is "Scandinavian" is another matter—it was built by German architects for a Russian Tsar: but it would be worth traveling to see even if it had been built on the moon by Martian trilobites. Those looking for a specifically Finnish cultural experience should try for the annual Arts Festival at Jyväskylä in the forests of Central Finland. The town of Jyväskylä is perhaps the best showplace for modern Finnish architecture, while the festival itself is famous, among other things, for the performance of that traditional Finnish music—jazz.

The Richest Scandinavians

The point behind these observations is a serious one: there is no longer any such thing as a specifically Scandinavian high culture. Such experiences are available, and I have tried to suggest some. But they are not greatly different from things you can find elsewhere in Europe. Yet if culture is taken in its broadest sense—as all organized human activities that tend to make life more worth living—then there does exist a specifically Scandinavian culture, and one which is very enjoyable. That is why children's books are important: they suggest the sort of areas where Scandinavian culture should be sought.

It is a cliché that the culture of any society tends to reflect the interests and concerns of the most powerful groups in the society, but it is an instructive cliché; and, by comparison with the rest of the world, it is women and children who are the most powerful and the richest Scandinavians. In consequence, you will find what the Scandinavians do best in the sort of places where women and children spend their money. The effort that in other countries is devoted to the arts is in Scandinavia used to make homes. What flourishes here is not so much culture as taste, and Scandinavian taste is easily acquired. Anything woven, sewn, or crotcheted that can be used to brighten up a home will be done beautifully in Scandinavia.

Glass, tableware, even the most humble piece of kitchen equipment, all show a perfect balance between form and function. Such things may not seem terribly important, but they do make a tremendous difference to one's day-to-day mood, and they are the things that Scandinavians make excellently.

It is significant that the most popular museum in Scandinavia is the openair adjunct of the Anthropological Museum at Skansen in Stockholm. What Skansen commemorates is the lives and homes of ordinary people through the ages. Whole houses from all over Sweden have been moved and rebuilt there, so that visitors can peek around and see how other people made their homes. This is the culture that the Scandinavians really care about, and there is more to be seen in the Anthropological Museum itself.

Here—in a neat touch—you can buy the patterns to weave or sew the clothes you see; while tucked away in the basement are the exhibitions about the the Lapps. They are really another story, stemming from a quite different tradition, but their artefacts are the strangest and most beautiful to be found in all Scandinavia.

FOOD AND DRINK

How to Skal and Survive

Although the Viking custom of drinking toasts out of somebody else's skull went out of fashion quite some time ago, it's only fair to warn you, as a visitor to Scandinavia, that you're still in danger of losing your head. But the threat to the visitor is more subtle these days, as you'll discover when you first slide your feet under a Scandinavian table.

When Do We Eat?

The first thing which will puzzle you as you edge uncertainly towards the *spisesal* (dining room) is the question of mealtimes. Breakfast, of course, is a natural, and is consumed sometime between the early morning bath and a glance at the newspaper. But now the difficulty begins. The next meal of the day defies definition. Some Anglo-Saxons are tempted to call it dinner, counting the sandwiches and glass of milk that many businessmen eat at their desks around noon as lunch. There are even those who stick by this theory doggedly, refusing to notice that the clatter of silverware against china, which starts up around 4.30 P.M. and becomes deafening towards 6.00 P.M. has completely disappeared, in Norway at least, by the dinner hour. The Scandinavians, being practical people, avoid the dispute by calling it *middag*. We advise you to do the same, thereby working for peace in a troubled world.

Instead of sowing discord, the Scandinavians are interested merely in making maximum use of the long and bright summer evenings. Accordingly, families sit down to the main meal of the day as soon as father comes home from work, somewhere towards the tag end of the afternoon. The great advantage of this arrangement is that, once *middag* is over, everyone is free for the rest of the day. If you come hotfoot from South Dakota or South Kensington with a hatful of introductions to near relations or business acquaintances, you can turn this custom into a game. Don't refuse three or four dinner invitations you received for the same day. Just fix a different hour for each.

While you have your napkin unfolded and are wondering who's going to eat all that food, we should urge you to save some room for *aftens* or supper, the final meal of the day, not counting incidental snacks. This may be no more than cakes and coffee or it may consist of no less than a complete cold buffet, depending on the circumstances and whether or not your eyes have the socially-accepted glaze. No one is looked down upon for starting this as early as 7.00 P.M. although, at a formal party, it might well not appear until midnight.

With this overall timetable in mind, let's get down to particular dishes. The typically Scandinavian breakfast is more varied than the typical English or American one. The larger hotels, accustomed to catering to visitors from abroad, will be able to offer you bacon and eggs, though this honorable combination is not indigenous to the Scandinavian ménage. Instead, eggs, cheese, cold meats, herrings in a number of guises, jams, and fruit are all likely to make their appearance, in addition to less usual items such as cereals, porridge, hot meatballs, and salad. These you'll discover together with a great variety of bread, many kinds rarely found in other countries. One of them, *Knekkebrød,* is of the hard, unleavened type which you've undoubtedly seen elsewhere under the proprietary name of Ry King. Unless you specify otherwise, your egg will normally be served softboiled and still in its shell.

By the time you've tried everything, chances are you'll have a solid foundation which will carry you through to mid-afternoon. But if you find your fancy gradually turning towards thoughts of food around about noon, you have a number of choices. In most of the bigger cities there are sidewalk stands displaying signs reading *Pølser* or *Varm Korv.* At these you will be able to buy hot dogs, often wrapped in what looks like a pancake instead of a roll. They are smaller than what you're used to, and you will probably agree that they taste better.

If all you want is something cool, look for another kind of sidewalk stand, marked *Is* or *Glass.* The name has nothing to do with the verb "to be" or with windowpanes, but informs you that here you can have ice cream. The Finns, incidentally, call it *jäätelö.*

The Mysterious Open Sandwich

Failing both of these (and still assuming you're interested), make for the nearest restaurant. If you see the word *smørbrød,* you're in luck, for this is Scandinavia's most typical dish (the Swedish spelling is *smörgasbørd).* The word means simply, "butter-bread," but there's nothing simple about it, as you'll discover when the waiter hands you a menu listing dozens of varieties.

Smørbrød is the rich uncle of its English or American nephew, the sandwich. Unlike the anonymous sort of thing served at garden parties or railway stations, it is a single-decker, and presents its offering naked and unashamed. Lobster, smoked salmon, prawns, shrimps, smoked herrings, all appropriately and artistically garnished, cold turkey, chicken, roast beef, pork, a host of sausages, cheeses, eggs, and salads, all tastefully and appetizingly arranged. Variously called *smörgås* by the Swedes and *voileipä* by the Finns, three of them taken with a cool lager are generally considered an excellent lunch, whether or not you abandon all caution and succumb to a piece of pastry for dessert. Hot food is available too, if you are still hungry.

Wherever you may be in Scandinavia, the sea is never far off, and this is a good thing to remember when you sit down to *middag*. Perhaps because the fish served in restaurants and hotels is invariably fresh, the Scandinavians are all great fish-eaters. Whatever the reason, their seafood dishes are justly renowned for their variety and excellence. Lobster, salmon, and trout are great favorites, but you will also have your choice of cured herrings, crayfish, crab, oysters, shrimps, prawns, hake, eel, and other seaborne morsels. Boiled cod may sound unromantic, yet you'll find it transformed when served *à la Scandinave* with melted butter and parsley. In the summer the Swedes and Finns indulge in traditional crayfish weeks when you can go on eating these succulent little creatures until your conscience begins to bother you. In Denmark you'll compare the Limfjord oysters to the best that Baltimore or Colchester has to offer.

Then there are a number of fish dishes which only the bolder spirits are advised to try. The first of these is *rakørret,* which is trout that, like Keats' wine, has "lain long years in the deep-delved earth." There is actually much more to the preparation of this highly odiferous *spécialité de la maison* than burying it in the backyard, but it is undoubtedly an acquired taste. Next comes *surströmming,* another form of man's inhumanity to fish, except that this time it's a herring who suffers. As the name suggests, the taste is distinctly sour; that is, if you get that far. The third of our "don'ts" for cautious gourmets is *lutefisk,* which is codfish steeped in a lye of potash. The finished product has the consistency of frog spawn and a taste which can only be experienced and not described. The Norwegians who eat this "delicacy" anesthetize themselves with such copious drams of *akvavit* one might suspect that the *lutefisk* is only an excuse.

While we are on the subject of dishes which should be approached circumspectly, we may as well complete the story with a mention of *geitost* or goat's cheese, which has the hue of scrubbing soap or milk chocolate and the texture of plastic wood. Give it a try anyhow; you'll be called on for your own opinion sooner or later. And if you are too disappointed, all the Scandinavian countries produce excellent imitations of such well-known favorites as Roquefort, Camembert, Gruyère, and even England's Stilton. Danish Blue is another local variety with which no cheese-lover could possibly quarrel.

Scandinavian cooks use margarine or butter for their cooking, and not oil as the Latins do. Game and roasts are usually served with a cream sauce which is delicious. In some cases, sour cream is used, and *ryper* (a variety of grouse or ptarmigan) prepared with this sauce and accompanied by cranberry jam is a rare treat.

By now you are doubtless wondering what has happened to the renowned Swedish *smörgåsbord.* It's doing fine, thank you. But let me first explain to the uninitiated that the *smörgåsbord* (called *voileipäpöytä* by the Finns) is a very special *hors d'oeuvre,* offering the diner a stupendous number of small dishes, each more calculated than the last to whet his appetite and make him forget all rash resolutions to respect his waistline. The beauty of this institution is that it contains no *pièce de résistance* to dominate the table. You roam at will like the honey bee, savoring here a morsel of smoked eel, there a little lobster, and roving through the delicacies of the animal kingdom, with regular rounds of *akvavit* and beer to give you fresh incentive. These days, the *smörgåsbord* is seldom the prelude to a four-course dinner in private homes, but some restaurants feature it as a specialty, maybe on a certain day in the week.

Desserts do not run to the English or American pattern. Neither the English pudding nor the American ice cream desserts are as prevalent as soufflés, large, tiered cream cakes, and berries in season. Strawberries reach the table somewhere around the end of June and manage to survive for a commendable number of weeks. Later on in the year, Finland, Norway and Sweden offer a delicious wild berry which is hardly known elsewhere, the cloudberry, called *suomuurain* or *lakka* in Finnish, *hjortron* in Sweden, and *multer* in Norway. In appearance rather like an overgrown unripe raspberry, it has a delicate aroma which is unique. Incidentally, the Finns make a delicious liqueur from the juice of this berry.

Speaking of liquid refreshments, we should note that the Scandinavians are coffee-drinkers rather than tea-drinkers, and they make their coffee good and strong, in the best Continental tradition. In Denmark and Norway, coffee is somewhat expensive, and families who drink a lot have to make up for it with some sort of substitute. This trend has, of course, resulted in an increase in tea-drinking, but on the whole the Scandinavians have not yet acquired the English touch. So be sure to emphasize that you want your tea strong. Don't expect to find that the cult of tea has made the Scandinavians tea-conscious. The buttered toast, crumpets and muffins of Belgravia have no afternoon counterpart in Bergen or Bornholm. Instead, look for a restaurant-type of place with the sign *"Konditori"* over the door. The waitress will bring cakes to your table along with tea, coffee, milk or a soft drink. You'll be hard put to choose among the several delicious varieties.

Skål

Scandinavia's local brand of firewater is known as *akvavit,* and a glass of this is known in Denmark, Sweden and Finland as *snaps,* whereas the Norwegians call it a *dram.* Served at the beginning of the main meal of the day—at the *hors d'oeuvre* stage, or occasionally with the first course—it is invariably taken with a beer chaser. *Akvavit* emphatically is not a drink for the tyro toper and you'll find it takes a little practice to attain proficiency in the local ritual of gulping it down without falling off your chair. The mysteries of the *skål* or toast, apart from regional variations, are too complicated to explain here, but you won't go far wrong if you stick to the following procedure.

First, at the start of any meal, wait for someone to give the signal. At a formal party, the host, after clearing his throat ominously or belaboring the nearest piece of china or crystal with a soup spoon, will seize his glass and launch into a *velkommen til bords* speech. All this means is "welcome to the table" and you may even find it a gracious gesture of hospitality. Anyhow, the crucial thing is to listen intently for the word *skål.* This is your cue. Seizing your own glass, you hold it firmly in a position of tantalizing proximity to your parched lips, though preferably far enough away from your nose to avoid asphyxiation. Then you nod your head north, south, east, and west as you echo *"skål."* Now, and not a moment sooner, your *akvavit* starts its downward journey. This is the supreme test. As all hell breaks loose somewhere in your gullet, you may be tempted to reach convulsively for the beaker of cool beer that beckons by your plate. Not so the trained snapser. He returns his glass to its original position just south of his chin, nods blandly to the four points of the compass while simulating an air of complete indifference to the fires consuming within, and then sends a mouthful of malt brew in pursuit of the *akvavit.*

When the urge to wet your whistle descends on you, don't try a surreptitious drink on your own, but pick up your glass boldly, fix a fellow diner with a purposeful stare, pronounce the word *"skål,"* and proceed as above. Anyone is fair game for this except your hostess; after all, someone has to keep track of the time. Apart from achieving a drink, you will undoubtedly have won the undying gratitude of your friend across the table, who was almost certainly contemplating a similar move. Remember that husbands are expected to *skål* their wives, who, if slighted, are entitled to collect a pair of stockings by way of damages.

Although there are so many striking points of similarity between the food and drink of each of the Scandinavian countries, it is surprising that in a few unimportant details, which only indirectly affect the table, there should be some startling discrepancies. For example, one may say without any risk of offending the Swedes and the Danes, that the Finns and Norwegians make infinitely better dessert and eating chocolate. On the other hand, the Danish Aalborg akvavit and the Swedish Norrland akvavit can be said to be the best of its kind—but the Norwegians have gone one step further by producing their *linje akevitt,* which is stored in huge sherry vats of American white oak, and then sent on Norwegian cargo liners to Australia and back. It is said that the rolling of the ship, combined with the change of climate when crossing the Equator—the "Linje"—adds an unusual flavor to the "scalplifter." Lager beer in Scandinavia is of top quality, whether you drink Danish Carlsberg or Tuborg or Norwegian Ringnes or Schou, all of which are exported around the world.

There is, unfortunately, one more essential piece of advice to impart while on the subject of liquor in Scandinavia—namely, that it is very expensive. The Danes get away quite lightly in this respect, but in all the other Scandinavian countries, alcohol, especially the imported variety, is very, very pricey. And just to add insult to injury, you'll also discover that, except for the carefree Danes, the Scandinavians, like the British, have strict and inflexible licensing hours, outside which it is not possible to buy so much as the humblest glass of beer. Don't say you haven't been warned.

A Final Word

You will find that the Scandinavians have elevated the culinary arts to a high place among the graces which add flavor to life. Wherever you dine you will discover that the serving is on a par with the cuisine. Helpings are generous, dishes and drinks which are supposed to be hot really are hot, and iced drinks never arrive in a semitepid state. This is only natural where hospitality is regarded as one of the supreme virtues.

After finishing a meal in Scandinavia, it is a time-honored custom for the hostess to stand near the door of the dining room. The guests, one by one, shake her hand on their way into the living room and pronounce the words, *"takk for maten."* Badly translated, this means "thank you for the food." A phrase well-worn by usage, perhaps, but nonetheless welcome from those who have dined well in congenial company.

DENMARK

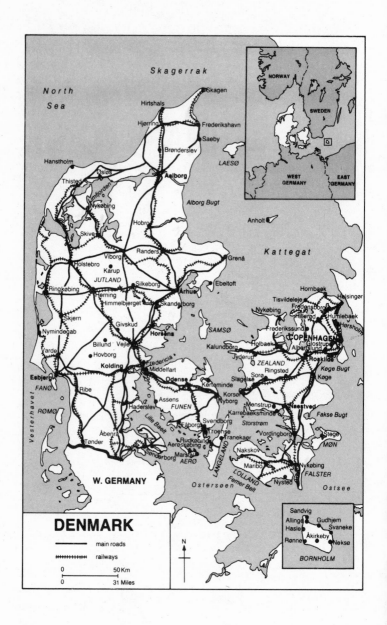

Skagerrak

North Sea

Skagen
Hirtshals
Hjørring
Frederikshavn
Saeby
Brønderslev
Hanstholm
Oslos
Aalborg
Thisted
Limfjorden
Nykøbing
Alborg Bugt
Hobro
Skive
Anholt
Viborg
Randers
Grenå
Holstebro
Karup
JUTLAND
Silkeborg
Ringkøbing
Herning
Himmelbjerget
Skjern
Givskud
Nymindegab
Billund
Vejle
Hovborg
Varde
Kolding
Esbjerg
Fredericia
FANØ
Middelfart
RØMØ
Ribe
Haderslev
Assens
FUNEN
Åbenrå
Tønder
Sønderborg
Vesterhavet
W. GERMANY
Ostersøen

North Sea

LAESØ

Kattegat
Hornbaek
Tisvildeleje
Helsingør
Nykøbing
Fredensborg
Humlebaek
Hillerød
Hørsholm
Frederikssund
COPENHAGEN
Holbaek
Glostrup
Kalundborg
Albertslund
Jyderup
Roskilde
ZEALAND
Ringsted
Køge Bugt
Sorø
Køge
Slagelse
Odense
Kerteminde
Korsør
Nyborg
Mønstrup
Naestved
Fakse Bugt
Svendborg
Karrebaeksminde
Faaborg
Troense
Storstrøm
Vordingborg
Stege
Rudkøbing
Tranekaer
MØN
Aerøskøbing
Nakskov
Marstal
Nykøbing
AERØ
Maribo
FALSTER
LOLLAND
Nysted
Femer Belt
Ostsee

SAMSØ
Århus
Ebeltoft
Skanderborg
Horsens

LANGELAND

DENMARK

—— main roads

+++++ railways

0 ———— 50 Km
0 ———— 31 Miles

N

NORWAY
SWEDEN
WEST GERMANY
EAST GERMANY

Sandvig
Allinge
Gudhjem
Hasle
Svaneke
Rønne
Åkirkeby
Neksø
BORNHOLM

DENMARK—FACTS AT YOUR FINGERTIPS

NATIONAL TOURIST OFFICE. In the U.S.: Danish Tourist Board, 655 Third Avenue, New York, NY 10017 (212–949–2333).

In Canada: Danish Tourist Board, Box 115, Station "N," Toronto, Ontario M8V 3S4 (416–823–9620).

In the U.K.: Danish Tourist Board, 169–173 Regent St., London W1R 8PY (01–734 2637).

Within Denmark, there are some 172 local tourist offices, all of which can supply information on their own areas and can also make reservations for you in local hotels, boarding houses and the like. Not all are open all year, but those that are display the international "i" sign. We list all the major Danish tourist offices at the beginning of each *Practical Information* section.

CURRENCY. The unit of currency in Denmark is the *krone,* written as Dkr. It is divided into 100 *øre,* but as the smallest coin is 25 øre, all prices are rounded the nearest 25 øre. Note that as the coinage is being changed, several coins come in two different forms.

The rate of exchange at the time of writing (mid-1989) was 6.53 Dkr. to the U.S. dollar and 11.40 Dkr. to the pound sterling. However, these rates will certainly change during 1990, so be sure to keep a careful check on them while planning and during your trip.

COSTS IN DENMARK. Like all the Scandinavian countries, Denmark has a high standard of living and costs are correspondingly high. At the same time, however, while it cannot easily be considered a budget destination, Denmark is definitely less expensive to visit than either Norway or Sweden, for example. The reasonably low rate of inflation has helped keep costs manageable. Nonetheless, certain items, especially alcohol, are very expensive, and it is as well to keep a watchful eye on your budget, and take in your full supply of duty frees.

Sample costs. A cinema seat for one, Dkr. 25.–55; visit to a museum or castle, Dkr. 10 (but may be more, though many are open free of charge). The following sample costs of drinks are about the minimum in Copenhagen, they cost more depending on venue. Costs in Jutland are slightly less. Bottle of beer in a restaurant, Dkr. 15; house wine, by the glass in a cafe, Dkr. 18, by the bottle in a restaurant, Dkr. 90; a Coke, Dkr. 8; taxi ride in Copenhagen, Dkr. 12 plus Dkr. 8–10 per kilometer; bus ride in Copenhagen, Dkr. 8.

SEASONAL EVENTS. Almost all Denmark's special events take place in the summer. The Danish Tourist Board produces a comprehensive list of events in Denmark twice a year, but among the more famous and popular are the following.

April Opening of Bakken, reputedly the world's oldest amusement park, in Klampenborg Forest, north of Copenhagen. Numus Festival in Århus at the end of the month is one of the biggest festivals of contemporary music in Europe.

May 1 traditionally sees the opening of the Tivoli Gardens in Copenhagen, while toward the end of the month thousands of Copenhageners dance through the streets in fancy dress during the Copenhagen Carnival. The "Wonderful Copenhagen" marathon is also at the end of the month.

June A number of important cultural events, some lasting to the end of the summer, take place now. Among them are the Egeskov Summer Festival Matinees, held every Sunday to the end of August at Egeskov Castle in Funen. The 19th International Organ Festival, lasting through to September and held at Søro church, consists of a series of concerts on Wednesdays featuring a wide range of works, both old and new. The Copenhagen Municipal Summer Entertainment also starts in June and lasts till September. At locations throughout the city, music, theater, dance, drama and the like are presented every day. Hans Christian Andersen Festival mid-June to early August, open-air plays performed in the writer's native town, Odense. Mid-June sees the Zealand sailing race, one of the world's largest yacht races with upwards of 1,600 competitors. The end of the month brings the Frederikssund Viking plays, with audience participation and traditional feasts.

July 4th celebrations of American Independence Day at Rebild near Aalborg (in 1912 Americans of Danish descent presented an area of land to the Danish nation to be a national park and thousands gather here every year). More Viking plays, this time at Jels in south Jutland. The Copenhagen Summer Festival also gets under way in July, and lasts until the middle of August; young Danish and foreign singers and musicians perform at Charlottenborg's Grand Hall and in the Christianborg chapel. Among numerous music festivals, the Roskilde and Copenhagen Jazz Festivals are the two most important; the former presenting music of all types. In the middle of the month another music festival takes place in Bornholm, featuring music from all ages, played in churches throughout the island every Monday and Thursday.

August kicks off with the festival at Lerchenborg Castle in Kalundborg where classical and contemporary music is performed. The month ends with jazz, at the Tønder Jazz and Folk Festival in south Jutland.

September sees the largest cultural festival in Scandinavia, the Århus Festival Week at the very beginning of the month. Ballet, theater, opera, jazz, classical and folk music, street parties and sports abound.

NATIONAL HOLIDAYS. Jan. 1 (New Year's Day); Apr. 12–16 (Easter, shops open Apr. 14); May 11 (Common Prayer); May 24 (Ascension); June 4 (Whit. Mon.); June 5 (Constitution Day, shops close at noon); Dec. 25 and 26 (Christmas).

LANGUAGE. English-speaking visitors will have very few language difficulties in Denmark. Nearly all younger Danes speak excellent English, while most older people are almost equally fluent. In fact in larger cities, you'll have a job finding people who don't speak English. And you can rest assured that in hotels, restaurants, tourist offices, museums, bars and so on, English will practically be as common as Danish.

CUSTOMS. Duty-free allowances are the same for both U.S. and U.K. residents *except* with regard to tobacco. Otherwise duty-free allowances depend on from which country you enter Denmark.

Coming from an EEC country people of all nationalities may import duty-free: 1.5 liters of alcoholic beverages or 3 liters of strong wine (under 22%) plus 4 liters of other wine. U.S. residents may import 300 cigarettes or 75 cigars or 400 grams of tobacco; U.K. residents may import 300 cigarettes or 75 cigars or 400 grams of tobacco. Other articles up to a maximum of 2,800 Dkr.

Entering from all other countries, all nationalities may import duty-free: 1 liter of spirits or 2 liters of strong wine plus 2 liters of other wine. U.S. residents may import 300 cigarettes or 75 cigars or 400 grams of tobacco; U.K. residents may import 200 cigarettes or 50 cigars or 250 grams of tobacco. Other articles (including beer) up to a maximum of 375 Dkr; 50 grams of perfume allowed (75 grams when coming from EEC countries).

Import allowances for tobacco and alcohol are only for those aged 17 or over.

You may also import and export any amount of foreign currency, provided you declare it on arrival. You may also export any amount of Danish krone, provided you can prove they were legally imported or obtained by converting declared foreign currency.

HOTELS. Danish hotels are the equal of those anywhere in Scandinavia, or anywhere else in Europe come to that. Indeed, standards are very high throughout the country, and, with the exception of certain rather seedy city hotels which are best avoided, even the smallest and most modest hotels will be clean, comfortable and welcoming. We give prices below, but bear in mind that for the most part high season prices (generally early-May to late-September) are quite a bit higher than in the rest of the year. As a rule, breakfast and taxes are always included in the price, but be sure to check before booking that this is the case. Hotels designated (BE) charge for breakfast.

Inns—'kro'. The old stagecoach inns, scattered throughout Denmark, are considerably less expensive than hotels. Though well modernized, they have the charm of the past, and have sometimes been expanded by motel rooms, which again are of a high standard, often with nice touches, such as wild flowers growing outside the window. The 'kro' meals, eaten in the original inn, are also good, homey, and less expensive than in a hotel. The cost for two in a double room for one night is from Dkr. 200 to Dkr. 400, without private bath/shower, and from Dkr. 250 to Dkr. 500 with bath/shower. You can also buy a book of Inn Checks valid at 66 different inns, for Dkr. 195 per person, per night. Vouchers are available from travel agents; alternatively, contact *Dansk Kroferie,* Horsens Tourist Office, Søndergade 26, DK-8700 Horsens (tel. 75–62 38 22).

All local tourist offices will be able to help with finding places to stay and making reservations.

Prices. We have divided all the hotels we list into four categories—Deluxe (L), Expensive (E), Moderate (M) and Inexpensive (I). These grades are determined solely by price.

Two people in a double room can expect to pay (prices in Dkr.)

	Copenhagen	Elsewhere
Deluxe	1,100 and up	——
Expensive	800–1,100	600 and up
Moderate	670–800	400–600
Inexpensive	under 670	under 400

All prices are inclusive of service and taxes. We indicate which of the major credit cards—American Express, Diner's Club, MasterCard (incorporating Access and EuroCard) or Visa—a hotel or restaurant accepts by the abbreviations AE, DC, MC and V.

SELF-CATERING. If you want to spend more than a few days in the countryside, you might consider one of Denmark's country vacations. Summer chalets rent for a minimum of one week and it is important to book early as they are very popular. Peak season prices: Dkr. 1,400–3,200 per week. A good substitute for these chalets are the *Danish Country Holidays.* You have two choices:

1. *Farm holidays* are a good way to find out how country Danes live. Many families welcome visitors, not just to make money but as a way of meeting people. You usually live as a family, share meal times, and share the sitting room. This is a popular holiday choice, particularly for those with children and, if you choose, you get a chance to help around the farm. You book and pay through the local tourist office—a tactful idea that means you don't have to hand over money as you shake hands with your host or hostess. The only thing you will be asked to pay for are extras like beer, which the farm may provide. Prices range from Dkr. 200 per person per day, half-board, to Dkr. 230 per person per day full-board, with reductions for children under 12. Minimum stay is 3–5 days, or sometimes, one week.

2. *Country Holidays* offer self-catering in a house or flat for four to six people. You are supposed to bring your own linen and bedclothes. Prices are Dkr. 1,500 June–Aug., rest of year Dkr. 1,100.

Minimum stay for this program is 7 days. These holidays are especially recommended for families with children.

The Danish Tourist Board are keen to promote holiday packages which emphasize active, outdoor family vacations in rural areas, and there are many variations on the basic Country Holiday scheme. It should not be difficult to find the one that suits you. We suggest careful research into the options on offer. *Holiday Centers/Holiday Apartment Hotels* have accommodations and facilities (often a pool, a game room, always a restaurant and a cafeteria). From two to eight people will pay Dkr. 1,500–5,000 in the high season (June–September, Easter, and Christmas), but there are good out-of-season offers. It is worth remembering that local tourist offices will probably be able to furnish you with more detailed pamphlets and information, and will be happy to make your reservations for you. A list of their addresses is available from the Danish Tourist Board.

CAMPING. Denmark has more than 500 approved camp sites, about 60 of which are open all year round. All are rated from one to three stars. You can be sure that those with three stars will be of very high quality, with many facilities, but even the more lowly sites will be well-maintained and clean. Lists of all sites are available from the Danish Tourist Board and from local tourist offices. Note, however, that camping is not permitted outside official sites without the landowner's permission.

An International Camping Carnet or Danish camping pass—available at any campsite and valid one year—is required to stay at any camp. Details from *Campingradet,* Olof Palmes Gade 10, DK-2100, Copenhagen (31–42 32 22). Cost at a 3-star site is about Dkr. 28 per person per night. Children half price.

YOUTH HOSTELS. There are 95 Youth Hostels in Denmark, all comfortable, clean and well-run. Hostels are open to all, regardless of age, but you must have an International Youth Hostels Association card. These are available from the Youth Hostels Association in the U.S., Canada and U.K., otherwise there's a guest fee of Dkr. 18 per night. A guest card valid for 1 year costs Dkr. 90. Family rooms (for families *only*) with four beds are available at most hostels. A small supplement in addition to the normal nightly fee is charged for these, and only families with children under 18 may use them. Overnight stays cost, on average, 50 Dkr.

The Danish Tourist Board produces a list of all Youth Hostels. This is also available from *Danmarks Vandrerhjem,* Vesterbrogade 39, DK-1620, Copenhagen V. Price Dkr. 20 plus postage.

RESTAURANTS. Though a little on the expensive side, for the most part Danish restaurants are excellent. The Danes take their food very seriously, and you'll find that even the most humble meal will be carefully prepared and served, so you need feel no qualms about eating in more modest establishments. But of course, if you do splurge, you can be very sure it will be well worth it.

Many Danish restaurants, even the most expensive, also offer fixed price menus, so always check the menu displayed in the window. But in addition, look out for the *DanMenu* sign. Around 700 restaurants have joined this scheme whereby you get a two-course meal, either lunch or dinner, for Dkr. 75 per person including service. Another good budget bet are the restaurants at rail stations. This may not sound too tempting a prospect, but in fact you can be sure of very good value. Similarly, you'll find that many department stores and supermarkets have good cafeterias. Where you see a blue-and-white striped sign at a cafeteria, you can be sure of getting a hot, inexpensive two-course meal.

Be sure also to try one—or more!—of Denmark's famous open sandwiches. You can buy packaged sandwiches more or less anywhere in towns and cities. Some can be huge meals in themselves, and costs vary according to the filling you choose. Alternatively, you can also buy a packet of three or four sandwiches for around Dkr. 25 to 35. Many country inns cater for guests who bring their own sandwiches. These usually have a notice saying *Madkurve kan medbringes* or *Medbragt mad kan spises her.* All you have to do is order a bottle of beer and ask for "service."

of Copenhagen," it was not a very glorious chapter in British history. You can find the scars if you look hard enough, but no one walking around Copenhagen today would suppose that anything very terrible had ever happened to the city. Poverty and misfortune have left few traces on the city, whereas the evidence of successive ages of prosperity has been lovingly preserved. Public buildings in other countries tend to be ostentatious, proclaiming the power and wealth of the people who built them. The public buildings of Copenhagen boast only of the solid comforts that their owners could afford. They are not awe-inspiring: the only emotion they arouse is envy for the people who can look at them every day.

Scandinavia's Best Joke

History is a misleading guide to the other Scandinavian countries because they have had so little of it for so long, and then changed so rapidly in the last 100 years. In 1885 two of them did not even exist: Finland was a Russian province and Norway was a part of Sweden. But history is a misleading guide to Denmark because the country has had so much of it. 100 years ago it was very poor. Now it is very rich. But this has happened to the Danes before. Everything has happened to the Danes before. They have had empires and lost them. For the last 200 years, their role in the world has been largely to provide target practice for aggressive neighbors (though they did manage to stay out of World War I). What this experience seems to have taught the Danes is that you should not take seriously anything you cannot eat.

This is just as well, since the Danes are not good at taking things seriously. They will do it if they have to—they dealt very well with a German occupation in World War II—but the effort does not really suit their character. The philosopher Kierkegaard tried it in the 19th century with unhappy results—he invented existentialism. Danish politicians have tried it, and the result of that was Mogens Glistrup, the best joke ever to come out of Scandinavia.

Glistrup was a very successful tax lawyer in the '60s. The field was a profitable one because Denmark has the most comprehensive Welfare State, and had then the highest taxes, of anywhere in the world. Though it is Sweden that is famous in America for socialism, the Danes can actually get far more goodies from the state than the Swedes can. They just think less about it: or they did, until Glistrup came along. By 1972, Glistrup was a recognized authority on tax law. He had graduated from University with the highest marks ever attained by a legal student, and had only just failed to be appointed as Denmark's first professor of tax law. So he was a natural choice to give a talk on nationwide television on the consequences of the budget for 1972. This was not an exciting subject, however important, and Glistrup's script duly fell to the occasion. In fact, it was so boring that the producer begged him to think of something even slightly more interesting to say.

Glistrup replied that the only really interesting thing about income tax was that a clever man need pay none at all. Of course, it would have been grossly irresponsible to allow him to say as much on television, but the producer was a Dane, and it was more interesting than taking the budget seriously, so Glistrup went right ahead and said it. There he was, on nationwide television, a fat man with an even fatter man inside him struggling to get out, explaining that everyone could beat the system, if only their tax lawyer was good enough.

The Ministry of Finance disagreed. Glistrup's office and home were raided, and the investigators settled down to the long job of discovering how he did it, and what he could be charged with. Glistrup responded by forming a political party, dedicated to the total abolition of income tax. The government's books would be balanced by such reforms as replacing the Armed Forces with a tape recorder in the Ministry of Defence that would repeat to curious visitors the message "We surrender," in Russian.

This programme won 20% of the votes in the first election the party contested. Overnight, Glistrup became the leader of the second-largest party in Denmark. Unfortunately, he remained a crook. The Danes could have tolerated this, though their politicians could not; but it slowly became apparent that, though Glistrup took nothing else seriously, he did believe in himself, and this was intolerable. In 1983 he was returned to parliament from a prison cell, where he was serving a four year sentence for Gross Tax Fraud. Going to prison was for him the equivalent of death for a rock star—an admittedly drastic, but very effective way of prolonging a career that would otherwise have come to an end.

On Being Balanced

The moral of the Glistrup story is not that the Danes detest income tax, but that they will not stand for pomposity. Balance, not moderation, is the Danish virtue. The National Anthem should really consist of a recording of a fat man chuckling at the world after a very good meal indeed. The Danes are an extremely stable people, but the price they pay for this is a rather low center of gravity—in the stomach perhaps, or some inches lower.

There is a children's toy, a sort of egg-shaped doll, heavily weighted on the bottom, so that however you tip it over it will always come back to an upright position. The Danes are a lot like that.

They can recover from anything: in World War II they fought less than anyone when the Germans invaded them, yet they developed an effective resistance movement. When the Nazis ordered that all Jews should wear a yellow star, the King set an example to his people by declaring that he too would wear a yellow star. It was a brilliantly Danish solution: if everyone in the country pretended to be a Jew, there was really not very much that the Germans could do about it; meanwhile almost all the real Jews were smuggled across the Sound to neutral Sweden.

But, just as typically, this was a counterpunch. Left to themselves, the Danes would have left everyone else alone. The finest monument to Danish foreign policy this century is, fittingly enough, in Copenhagen, where the world's first specialized hospital for the rehabilitation of torture victims has been set up. It's a very simple and very necessary idea. Only the Danes of all the Scandinavians, are sufficiently rich, practical, and thoughtful to have done anything about it.

Everyday Excellence

Given the Danish center of gravity, it should not be surprising that Danish food is so very good. Nonetheless, it is surprising, if only because all of it is good. In the rest of Scandinavia you can eat well, but you must make an effort to do so. In Denmark you must make an effort to eat badly: it is characteristic that the Danes should have raised the sandwich to an art-form. Everywhere else in the world, it is an everyday and unromantic food, but it is in the perfection of everything that is everyday and unromantic that the Danes excell. This may not sound exciting, but it is very enjoyable.

None of this sounds very "Scandinavian"; nor is it. If the Swedes can believe in anything, the Danes find great difficulty—until they are disturbed—in supposing that anything is worth believing in. They are as realistic as the Finns, but quite without the Finnish habit of drama. The only thing about the Danes that corresponds to the Scandinavian stereotype is their attitude to sex. They rather enjoy it.

Nor do they mind other people enjoying it, each in his or her own way, provided that no one who does not want to gets hurt. So Copenhagen has become the pornographic capital of Europe. This need not bother the visitor—all the unsavory things happen in a very small portion of the city, and you can walk for hours through the more beautiful parts of Copenhagen without seeing or suspecting anything untoward. But it is worth a warning, since the cheapest hotels in the city are clustered on the fringes of the red light area. It would be a pity if the unprepared visitor were to take one look, get a frightful shock, and then run screaming into the night—in either direction.

The Danes do not really approve of this sort of thing; but the paradigm of all Danish pleasures is eating, which is not an activity about which one can moralize, so they tend not to moralize about anything else. I suppose that the final Danish comment on commercial sex has been made by the evening paper that runs columns and columns of ads from willing girls and boys, who display all the persistence of an aardvaark in their efforts to get to the front of the alphabet, and so attract the casual reader. Yet these advertisements are sandwiched undramatically between the flats for sale and the used cars.

The Danes enjoy drink in much the same way. It is not cheap but it is very freely available. This means that if you see a drunk in Denmark, you can be almost certain that he is a Swede. It is another example of the Danish capacity for balance. Not that Denmark is a statically perfect place. The Danish press is the liveliest and best in Scandinavia largely because it has so much bad news—or so many good stories—to report. Such things happen all over Scandinavia; only the Danes can whole-heartedly regard them as amusing.

And this is really the point of going to Denmark. There is, of course, a great deal to see and do, but what one remembers most of all is the way the Danes live together. In an unspectacular way, they have addressed themselves to the task of making life more comfortable and amusing; and they have had great success. The rest of Scandinavia is attractive because it is exotic; Denmark may seem exotic, but what you remember afterwards is how well the Danes do the things that everybody has to do. It is a very civilized country indeed.

COPENHAGEN

Scandinavia's Fun Capital

The center of Danish fun is Copenhagen, biggest and happiest of the Scandinavian capitals and by almost unanimous agreement one of the liveliest cities of Europe. More than a million Danes, a quarter of the country's population, live and let live here. The city, on the island of Zealand, is just as flat as the sea that embraces it, as flat as the rest of Denmark, which averages only 98 feet above sea level. (This is why every second inhabitant has a bicycle.)

When is the best time to come? Denmark is lovely in summer, fall and spring. In winter, well, let's just say that while Copenhagen is as welcoming as ever, it can be a little chilly. However, there is a special atmosphere in Copenhagen in winter, which the Danes call *hyggelig*—the nearest translation they can give is "warm and cozy." There is an intimate and welcoming ambience in the warm, candle-lit cellar bars and restaurants, and with far fewer visitors shopping is much easier—hotel prices are often lower too. The first sign of the approach of spring is the opening of the oldest amusement park in the world, Bakken in the Klampenborg forest just outside Copenhagen.

By May, however, Denmark has escaped from the bonds of the long Nordic winter, a fact neatly underlined by the opening of the world-famous Tivoli Gardens on May 1. Celebratory candles flicker in the windows of every home too, in commemoration of Denmark's liberation on May 4, 1945, while the next day there are celebrations in every Danish town from southern Jutland to the far reaches of Bornholm. The circus arrives in May. At the end of June, the world's largest yacht race, known as "Round Zealand" attracts between 1,500 and 2,000 participants annually. The Royal Danish Ballet end their season, and June comes to a climax on 23 June with Midsummer's Eve, a night of outdoor dancing, singing, feasting, bonfires and fireworks, transforming the whole nation into one big carnival. Try to celebrate this night along the Sound. You'll never forget the unreal summer twilight, streaked with rockets edged with a thousand fires along the shores of Sweden and Denmark.

With the end of June, everyone enjoys the long, sunflooded days and short balmy nights in Denmark. Make your reservations early; the Danes will do the rest.

The Lie of the Land

Many visitors find it odd that Denmark's capital should be on the extreme eastern edge of one of the country's larger islands, only a few miles from Sweden. But the reason is simple. Historically, Copenhagen was the capital not only of Denmark in its modern form, but also of Norway and southern Sweden and other Baltic territories. As a well-sheltered port with immediate access to the high seas—large ships still sail from the city center—Copenhagen in days gone by was an ideally situated capital.

Being on the coast, Copenhagen is a cleaner capital than most. Though it lacks a background of mountains to set it off, viewpoints from which it can be admired, hills to which its houses can cling, and though much of it has had to be rebuilt, Copenhagen remains a charming city.

Exploring Copenhagen

If you suggest to someone that, although Copenhagen has a history stretching back to the 11th century, the city really doesn't look very old, you are likely to get the reply, "Considering it's been bashed about by the Swedes a few times, ravaged by a number of fires and bombarded by the British, that's hardly surprising." Strategically located on the Sound connecting the Baltic with the Kattegat and the North Sea, Copenhagen was just a small village ceaselessly harassed by Wendian pirates until the middle of the 12th century. But in 1167 Bishop Absalon, warrior and politician as well as priest, like many contemporary clerics, decided to protect the infant village by building a castle on the small central island known as Slotsholmen, today the very heart of the old city.

Shortly thereafter the town adopted the name of Køpmannaehafn (Merchants' Haven), and proceeded to grow apace within its protecting walls. In the 15th century, the king came to live in Copenhagen and a university was started. Increasing in both size and importance little by little, the prosperous city entered upon a great period of expansion with the accession of King Christian IV (1588–1648) to the throne. This man of extraordinary energy was possessed with a passion for building. Whenever he could take time off from waging wars, he started some new project, and even today so many of his works remain that whenever there's a question about who erected what, Christian gets the credit. Rosenborg Slot (Rosenborg Castle), the Runde Tårn (the Round Tower) and the Børsen (Stock Exchange) with its exotic dragon spire, were all built by him. He also gave the town an arsenal and a naval dock, and put up the "Nyboder," or rows of small houses which are still inhabited by naval personnel and pensioners.

In 1659, when the Swedish King Carl Gustaf tried to put an end to the continual Dano-Swedish wars by the simple strategy of conquering Denmark outright, Copenhagen found itself in a difficult situation. The town was besieged and everyone, including Frederik III, the then king, took a hand at defending it. After attempting to take the city by storm, the Swedes were routed and driven back to their own shores. This same Frederik thereupon built the Kastellet (Citadel) near Langelinie, which served the reverse of its intended function in 1940 when the Germans initiated their occupation of Denmark by capturing the old fortifications.

Back in 1728 and 1795, fires swept Copenhagen and destroyed vast portions of it. The devastation had scarcely been repaired when a British fleet twice bombarded the city during the Napoleonic Wars in 1801 and 1807. Fortunately the palaces survived—Amalienborg, Christiansborg and Rosenborg—and the vacant sites undoubtedly provided opportunities for rebuilding that might not otherwise have been undertaken. After the Napoleonic Wars, Denmark enjoyed relative peace and Copenhagen expanded far beyond the ramparts and water fortifications. Industries such as brewing, shipbuilding and manufacturing hardware became immensely profitable, and the city grew from a population of 130,000 in 1850 to its present size of well over a million inhabitants, suburbs included.

Strolls About Town

With this partial introduction to the Copenhagen scene, the time has come to sally forth into the bewildering jumble of winding streets, unexpected canals and multitudinous buildings which are the distinguishing features of the Danish capital. The average visitor from abroad, as he steps out of the Central Station into the warm sun of a summer morning, is likely to be a bit baffled at the start. As we've already pointed out, there is a serious scarcity of distinguishing landmarks by which the new arrival can easily chart his course through this intricate city. While it's true that Copenhagen a few years back seemed to be largely a collection of charmingly distinctive spires, there are now so many tall modern buildings that you can no longer see them. And to top it off, about the time you are at last getting yourself oriented, you are so unnerved by the sudden appearance of a platoon of bicyclists bearing down upon you that all idea of where you are or where you intended to go is just as precipitously driven from your head. Watch out too for the special bicycle lanes; the Danes take their cycling seriously and most major roads have bicycle lanes on either side.

Any attempt to plot out some interesting tours for the person bent on discovering the "real" Copenhagen is difficult. Assuming that you master your fear of two-wheeled traffic and have provided yourself with a suitable map, it's more than possible that you'll start off in the wrong direction and be so captivated by what you see that you won't detect your error until you've gone several blocks out of your way. Don't be alarmed, however—before you've had a chance to get the points of the compass properly unscrambled, it's more than likely that a friendly Dane will stop and politely offer to show you the way.

So let's plunge in and start at the Rådhus Pladsen, or Town Hall Square. Dominating the square is the Town Hall itself, an immense and impressive redbrick building surmounted by a tall tower. It was completed in 1905. High above the main entrance is the figure of Bishop Absalon, founder of the city. Inside you see first the World Clock invented and built by Jens

Olsen. They you come to a large hall surrounded by a balcony, which is used for official functions. Here there are marble busts of Hans Christian Andersen, poet, playwright and writer of the famous stories for children, of Bertel Thorvaldsen, the noted sculptor, and of Martin Nyrop, the building's architect.

Above, on the first floor, are the council chamber and the municipal reception room. You can climb up the 105-meter (350-foot) tower, but only on one of the official guided tours. From its top there are fine views of the city and the surrounding countryside.

As you emerge from the Town Hall, a turn to your left would take you up Vesterbrogade, and in a moment you would come to the main entrance of the famous Tivoli Gardens. Just down from here, on Hans Christian Andersens Boulevard, is the city tourist office. Hardly anyone comes to Denmark without first having heard of the Tivoli Gardens. These date back to 1843, when Georg Carstensen, Danish architect and man of letters, persuaded Christian VIII to let him lay out an amusement park on the site of Copenhagen's old fortifications. "If only people are allowed to amuse themselves," he argued, "they will forget to talk politics." Within a few months Tivoli, patterned after London's now long-extinct Vauxhall Gardens, was a reality. In 1951 the wheel turned a full circle when the Festival of Britain organizers used Tivoli as a model for the Festival Gardens in London's Battersea Park. During its short season from May to September, Tivoli welcomes an average of 4 million visitors.

Whatever you happen to be doing in Tivoli, on a Saturday or Sunday you will enjoy the appearance of the Tivoli Guard. This is a group of toy-town soldiers (age limit 17) dressed in the style of the Queen's Guard, who march through the Gardens to the music of their own band.

On certain nights, the Gardens close with a magnificent display of fireworks. As rockets fly to meet the moon and colorful set pieces vie with the electric brilliance of the Chinese Pagoda, the illuminated fountain, and the fairy-like lights among the trees, you will begin to appreciate something of what Tivoli means to the Danes.

At the southern end of the Gardens, again on Hans Christian Andersens Boulevard, is the Glyptotek. It is a rather fanciful neo-Classical building, but contains an excellent collection of French sculpture, with fine pieces by Degas, Gauguin, and other Impressionists. There is also an outstanding collection of Egyptian works, including a famous statue of a hippopotamus, and much Greek and Roman statuary, all well-displayed. A gift to the municipality from Carl Jacobsen, founder of the Carlsberg breweries, the museum is maintained by the Carlsberg Foundation, which has done much to further cultural and scientific activities in Denmark. The winter garden outside contains Kai Nielsen's *Watermother* sculpture, serenely watching the 14 marble babies who tumble over her.

Back again on Vesterbrogade, you'll find the newly opened Scala center, with three floors of shops, cinemas, even a gym and swimming pool. Down the street you'll find the SAS building, one of the city's few skyscrapers. It also contains the Royal Hotel. Opposite is the Central Station, and in the same building, though the entrance is on Bernstorffs Gade, is the Air Terminal. There is an obelisk in front of the station commemorating the freeing of the Danish peasants from the feudal yoke in 1788. Just beyond, in the black Vesterport building, is Den Permanente, The House of Danish Design, where the best of modern Danish arts and crafts are displayed and sold. Ten minutes' walk from here along Vesterbrogade brings you

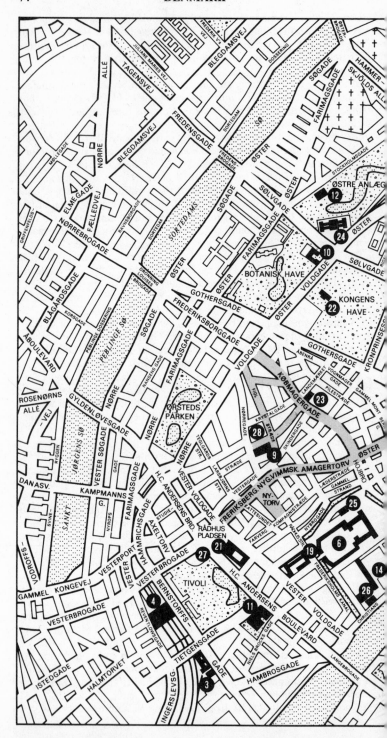

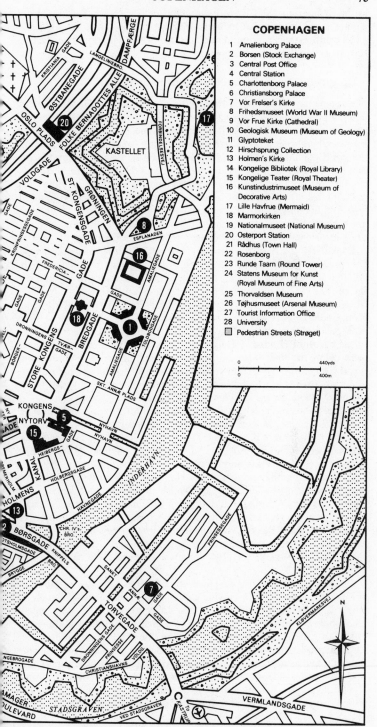

COPENHAGEN

1 Amalienborg Palace
2 Børsen (Stock Exchange)
3 Central Post Office
4 Central Station
5 Charlottenborg Palace
6 Christiansborg Palace
7 Vor Frelser's Kirke
8 Frihedsmuseet (World War II Museum)
9 Vor Frue Kirke (Cathedral)
10 Geologisk Museum (Museum of Geology)
11 Glyptoteket
12 Hirschsprung Collection
13 Holmen's Kirke
14 Kongelige Bibliotek (Royal Library)
15 Kongelige Teater (Royal Theater)
16 Kunstindustrimuseet (Museum of
    Decorative Arts)
17 Lille Havfrue (Mermaid)
18 Marmorkirken
19 Nationalmuseet (National Museum)
20 Østerport Station
21 Rådhus (Town Hall)
22 Rosenborg
23 Runde Taarn (Round Tower)
24 Statens Museum for Kunst
    (Royal Museum of Fine Arts)
25 Thorvaldsen Museum
26 Tøjhusmuseet (Arsenal Museum)
27 Tourist Information Office
28 University
▨ Pedestrian Streets (Strøget)

0   440yds
0   400m

to the Bymuseum, the City Museum. Outside is a model of medieval Copenhagen, while inside are exhibits depicting the city's history. Absalonsgade, a little street running down one side of the Museum, has been returned to its 19th-century appearance.

Up Strøget to Slotsholmen and Christianshavn

The next part of our exploration of the city, again using Rådhus Pladsen as a jumping-off point, takes us to the "Strøget," a series of narrow streets running eastwards from Rådhus Pladsen. The principal street here is Frederiksberggade, a pedestrian-only shopping street that more than any other in Copenhagen is the city's answer to Fifth Avenue or Bond Street. Not far along Frederiksberggade, we come to a double square, the northern half of which is called Gammeltorv and the southern, Nytorv. The most interesting thing about these twin squares is the splendid fountain in the middle of the former. On April 16, the Queen's birthday, children are brought here to see the "golden apples dance." These golden apples are gilded metal balls which "dance" on the jets of water.

Looking to the right from the Nytorv half of this square, you may be able to see a spot of water to the south. A few steps in this direction bring you to Rådhusstraede and then to Frederiksholms Canal, where you'll find the entrance to one of Copenhagen's most fascinating places, the National Museum, built in the 1740s for Crown Prince Frederik, who later became King Frederik V. Inside you can see the world's finest collection of Stone Age tools and runic stones dating from the Viking period. Note particularly the beautiful Hindsgavl Dagger, fashioned and used several thousand years before the birth of Christ. You can also get some idea of Viking camp life, the ships with which they traveled all over the world, and their unusual burial mounds in which it was the custom to put a jug of liquor beside the body of the deceased to assure him happiness in heaven.

One of the featured exhibits in the Historical Music section is a number of Bronze Age *lur,* unusual musical instruments between four and six feet in length, which were popular 3,000 years ago; 36 lurs or fragments have thus far been found in peat bogs all over Denmark. The museum offers for sale interesting silver and bronze replicas of certain of the exhibits.

Directly across the bridge from the National Museum is the Christiansborg Slot, seat of the Folketing, or Danish parliament, and the Supreme Court. It's an imposing building that dominates the little island—Slotsholmen, the very heart of the city—on which it stands. And appropriately, this is where Bishop Absalon built his first fortress in 1167. Its ruins can be visited under the present building, which is the sixth on this site. From 1441 until the fire of 1794 Christiansborg was used as a royal residence.

On the same island with the palace are clustered a number of other important buildings. Set in an idyllic garden is Det Kongelige Bibliotek, the Royal Library, with Denmark's largest collection of books, newspapers, incunabula and manuscripts, including the earliest records of Viking expeditions to America and Greenland. On one side of the library is Tøjhuset, Copenhagen's arms museum, with outstanding displays of uniforms, weapons, and armor, in an arched hall nearly 180 meters (200 yards) long.

On the other side of the library is the low, red-brick Børsen, former Stock Exchange. This fine example of Renaissance architecture is claimed to be the oldest stock exchange in the world still used for its original purpose, though the main part of the business has now been moved to other premises. The Børsen stands in tribute to the skill and originality of Christian IV. Indeed, it is said that he lent a hand in the twisting of the tails of the four dragons that form its spire. The spire, as unusual as it is beautiful, is certainly the most distinctive feature of the Børsen, but the entire structure is one of the city's greatest architectural treasures.

Still on Slotsholmen and on the island side of Christiansborg Slot, we come to the Thorvaldsen Museum. Here the great sculptor is buried, surrounded by the originals or casts of all his works. Beyond and to the north of this museum we recross the canal over Højbro, or High Bridge.

To the left is a delightful row of houses bordering the northern edge of Slotsholmen. The quays in front of them were for long Copenhagen's fish market, and a sadly much-diminished market is still held here regularly. The fishy theme is reflected too by the presence of two excellent and long-established fish restaurants hard by the site of the market.

Let's stand in the middle of Højbro for a moment and look back down the canal to the right. Just across from Børsen is Holmens Kirke, where two of Denmark's greatest naval heroes are entombed. One is Niels Juel, the man who shredded the Swedish fleet at Køge in 1677, and the other is the almost legendary Tordenskjold, who defeated Charles XII of Sweden during the Great Northern War. At the far end of the canal you see Knippelsbro, the big drawbridge leading to the island of Christianshavn. That green and gold spire with the curious spiral staircase winding around it is part of Vor Frelsers Kirke (Our Saviour's Church). After a look inside, you'll find that the excellent view from the tower is well worth the climb.

Christianshavn is one of the oldest quarters of Copenhagen. Though somewhat dilapidated now, and haunt of more than its fair share of low-life types, the area has retained some of its Left Bank charm, not least along the canals that thread through it where old houses lean out over houseboats and yachts. Row boats are available for hire; particularly attractive on a moonlit night. Those nostalgic for the 1960s can get a taste of counter-culture at Christiania, a community founded in 1971 when students occupied army barracks. The giant cartoons and grafitti covering the buildings preach drugs and peace. Up to 1,400 people live here during the summer; the winter population is smaller.

The Runde Tårn and the University

Alternatively, head north from Højbro along Købmagergade. Continue past the equestrian statue of Bishop Absalon and the charming brick Nikolaj Kirke (actually part restaurant and exhibition center today, but still one of the principal landmarks of the city, not least for its towering spire). Cross over the Strøget and continue north. A couple of hundred meters up on the right you'll come to the Runde Tårn, the Round Tower, which Christian IV built as an observatory, not as part of the church to which it is attached, though this, with a handsome interior, is well worth a visit. If you are energetic, you can climb to the top of the Runde Tårn up the internal spiral ramp. Peter the Great of Russia, so the story goes, drove up in a horse-drawn carriage.

Perhaps this is the place for a few more words about Denmark's amazing warrior-architect-scholar-king. Vitally alive to every new idea, Christian IV was much more than a builder. During his busy life he found time to revolutionize farming, reform the administration of his Norwegian kingdom, create seven new chairs of learning at the University and start trading companies to exploit the fabled riches of the East and discover a Northwest Passage. Even when he went for a walk, he would pull a ruler out of his pocket and check the workmanship of local masons and carpenters.

Across the road from the Runde Tårn is the Regensen, since 1628 a residential college for university students. It is worth pushing aside the heavy door and taking a quick look at the courtyard. The old lime tree there celebrates its birthday with a private May lunch, after which the students "shake hands" with a pair of gloves hung up in its branches.

From the Regensen, continue along Krystalgade to the University and, on Nørregade, the Vor Frue Kirke, the Church of Our Lady. The University celebrated its 500th anniversary in 1979, but the bulk of its buildings, including the main university, dates from the period of Copenhagen's great expansion in the 19th century. The growth of the University has lately been such, however, that many departments have had to be moved to more spacious quarters outside the city center.

The Vor Frue Kirke has been Copenhagen's cathedral since 1924. Bishop Absalon is believed to have built a chapel here in the early-13th century. Ravaged by fire in 1728 and hit during Nelson's bombardment in 1807, it was rebuilt in stern neo-Classical style in the early-19th century. The entire structure was extensively restored between 1977 and 1979. Bronze statues of Moses and David flank the entrance, and Thorvaldsen's marble sculptures of Christ and the Apostles can be seen inside. The ruins of the first church (1320) can now be seen in the basement, and a small historical collection has been opened on the first floor. On coming out take a turn to the left down Nørregade and, before you know it, you are back at the twin squares of Gammeltorv and Nytorv, our first stop.

Kongens Nytorv to Langelinie

Thus far we have described a large circle in the older part of town. The trip we are about to start upon will take us pretty much in a straight line. It begins at Kongens Nytorv, which lies at the opposite end of Strøget from Rådhus Pladsen. Strøget, you will recall, is the series of streets with different names that comprise Copenhagen's principal shopping district. The better stores are at the end from which we are about to set out.

In the center of Kongens Nytorv is a mounted statue of Christian V. Near the end of June every year, newly matriculated students arrive here in horse-drawn wagonettes and dance around the silent figure of the king. The southern side of the square is flanked by the Kongelige Theater, featuring ballet and opera as well as classical drama. Next door stands the Theater's annex, popularly called the "Starling Box". The Dutch Baroque building of Charlottenborg, which has housed the Danish Academy of Fine Arts since 1754, is also in Kongens Nytorv.

The stretch of water you see running up to Kongens Nytorv is the Nyhavn Canal. Picturesque 18th-century buildings crowd both sides. Today the area has become fashionable, with one restaurant opening after another. A veritable fleet of old-time sailing ships normally lines the quays along Nyhavn, and on one side the *Fyrskib XVII*, a stout old lightship dating from 1893, permanently moored, is seeing out her days as a floating museum. The far end of Nyhavn is the departure point for the hydrofoil to Malmö in Sweden, while beyond, the passenger ships to Norway and the Baltic dock.

Our path, however, is down Bredgade, a wide street leading north from Kongens Nytorv, to the first turning to the right, Sankt Annae Plads, then the next left into Amaliengade.

Before you stands an imposing colonnade. Although it looks like stone, it is actually made of wood—if you don't believe us, try tapping it. When you've gone through the arches, the square you are in contains the four residences that comprise Amalienborg Palace. The one immediately to the right is used by Queen Margrethe and her family, the following (facing you on the right) is occupied by dowager Queen Ingrid. During the fall and winter, when the Queen lives in Copenhagen, the guards, complete with bearskins and headed by their band, march through the city from the barracks adjoining Rosenborg Slot every day, to relieve the Amalienborg sentries at noon. Colorful, too, is the sight of a royal coach with its scarlet-coated drivers giving the team some brisk trotting exercise through the busy streets.

Turning left out of the palace square we come back to Bredgade. Directly in front of us broods the Marmorkirken, the Marble Church, a somewhat topheavy building with an enormous dome several sizes too large for it. Its ponderous Baroque exterior contrasts a little painfully with the delicate facades of the Amalienborg Palace. Perched around the outside are 16 statues of various religious leaders from Moses to Luther, and below them stand other sculptures of outstanding Danish ministers and bishops. The building was completed in 1894, after having lain in ruins since 1770.

We turn right into Bredgade and continue past the three brilliantly-gilded onion domes of the Russian Church before arriving in front of the Museum of Decorative Arts, the Kunstindustrimuseet, a fine Rococo building that was originally a royal hospital. Today, it contains an excellent collection of artefacts—ceramics, silverware and Flemish tapestries—from the Middle Ages to the present day, as well as a collection of musical instruments.

A few steps more take us up to Esplanaden, where there is a small museum, the Frihedsmuseet, documenting the heroic efforts of the Danish resistance in World War II. Close by, you will see the Gefion Fountain. Powerfully and dramatically this commemorates the legend of the goddess Gefion, who was promised as much of Sweden as she could plough around in one day. Changing her four sons into oxen, she carved out the island of Zealand. Perhaps there may be an element of truth in the story, for if you look at a map of Sweden you'll see that Lake Vänern is much the same size and shape as Zealand itself.

The park in front of us, alongside Esplanaden, is graced by the English Church standing at its entrance. In the center, surrounded by two rings of moats, is the Kastellet, or Citadel. It dates from the late-17th century when it was begun by Frederik III. Much work, renovating and expanding it, was also carried out in the 18th century, by which time it was the principal fortress of the city. The grounds are open to the public. Stretching straight ahead of us is the Langelinie Promenade, where foreign navies moor their ships, and all of Copenhagen meets on Sunday afternoon. About halfway along it, the Little Mermaid of Hans Andersen's famous fairy story perches on a rock by the water's edge and gazes wistfully across the harbor.

Jewels, Flowers and Old Masters

The last of our three excursions begins in Kongens Have, the King's Gardens, where little children play around the statue of Hans Christian Andersen. Our objective is the Renaissance-style Rosenborg Slot, now a museum containing not only a breathtaking display of all the Danish crown jewels but also a fine collection of furniture, together with the personal effects of Danish kings from the time of Christian IV, including that monarch's precious pearl-studded saddle.

Just opposite the palace are some 25 acres of botanical gardens, as well as an observatory and mineralogical museum. Across the street from the north end of these gardens we come to Statens Museum for Kunst, the national art gallery, whose liveried doorkeeper sports buckle shoes and a cocked hat on chilly days. An imposing late neo-Classical facade hides an excellently modernized interior, with a good, though cramped cafeteria. With few exceptions, the collections are generally dull, consisting mainly of second-rate Old Masters and endless rooms of 19th-century Danish pictures. However, the contemporary works should at least provide some light relief. There is also a good collection of works by Matisse. Behind the main building is the Hirschsprung Collection, containing more Danish 19th-century works.

We have now been through most of the better-known parts of the heart of Copenhagen, but it would be an error to forget that the real heart of any city is the living one. The red-coated postmen, the bear-skinned, not over-military-looking Royal Guard, the spirited Tivoli Guard, the cyclists, the little fat man who sells fruit in the street all week and then blossoms out as a racehorse owner on Sundays, Queen Margrethe: all these are the real sights of Copenhagen.

Short Excursions Out of Town

When the sun is shining, whether there is spring in the air or snow on the ground, and the Copenhagener wants a few hours in the country the chances are he will go to Dyrehaven, the Deer Park near Klampenborg. Here nearly 2,000 of these timid, graceful animals wander about at complete ease. A golf course, a summer fun-fair (open mid-April to late August) and several all-year-round restaurants occupy the rest of the 3,500 acres of forest, paths and ponds that make up this lovely park. Near the entrance to the park is the Bellevue bathing beach. Farther along the seaside drive from the capital to Elsinore (Helsingør) are a host of luxurious villas and charming places to stop. Also near Elsinore is Denmark's only casino, the Marienlyst Hotel.

Even closer to Copenhagen than Klampenborg is the fashionable suburb of Charlottenlund. It is a lovely walk from the S-station to Strandvejen where the Akvarium is. Across the road is the beach, popular though less fashionable than the one at Bellevue, and nearby are the picturesque Chalottenlund Fortress and an unofficial, though good, campsite for foreigners only.

Starting from either Lyngby or Holte, you can go for a walk in the woods close by, or else stroll around lakes Lyngbysø and the much larger Furesø. At Lyngby, near Sorgenfri station, you'll find the open-air museum known as Frilandsmuseet. In a park covering 40 acres is a collection of reconstructed old Danish farms, several windmills, and country houses moved here from the other parts of Denmark and southern Sweden.

The Hareskov woods can be reached from Svanemøllen station (train B). From Hareskov you may ramble through the forest to Fiskebaek and have lunch there. Afterwards you might vary your return journey by riding the motorboat to Lyngby or Holte station.

A shorter trip which many enjoy is to Dragør on the island of Amager. This quaint old fishing village, where geese still roam in the crooked streets, has a charm of its very own. The oldest house contains a museum of furniture, costumes, drawings, and model ships. Its chimney is twisted to prevent the Devil finding his way through. The museum in Store Magleby, an old, half-timbered farmhouse, displays Amager furniture, dresses, and needlework.

Another haunt you might enjoy, as much for the trip out as for what you find at your destination, is to Grundtvigs Kirke. Consecrated in 1940 and built in a style based on the typical Danish village church, this building, with its organ-like façade stands in memory of the poet, clergyman and founder of the Folk High School, whose name it bears.

PRACTICAL INFORMATION FOR COPENHAGEN

GETTING TO TOWN FROM THE AIRPORT. There is a frequent bus service from the airport to the Central Station. Airport buses leave every 15 minutes, the journey takes 25 minutes and costs Dkr. 24 (tickets are purchased on the bus). Buses also run to the airport from the station. The bus calls at the Hotel Scandinavia (for information tel. 33–25 24 20). Public buses are half the price and run just as often: routes 32, 32H for Rådhus Pladsen, route 9 for Kongens Nytorv and Østerport, route 38E for Valby Station.

Taxis are expensive, costing around Dkr. 75, but may be practical for groups.

TOURIST INFORMATION. The Tourist Information Office, run by the Danish Tourist Board, is at H.C. Andersens Blvd. 22 (33–11 13 25).

For students and young people "Use it" (*Huset*) at Rådhusstraede 13 (33–15 65 18), has useful information and an accommodations service. Open Mon. to Fri. 10–4 (Tues. and Thurs. 10–6); 15 June to 15 Sept., daily 10–8.

USEFUL ADDRESSES. Embassies. *British Embassy,* Kastelsvej 36–40 (31–26 46 00). *Canadian Embassy,* Kristen Bernikowsgade 1 (33–12 22 99). *U.S. Embassy,* Dag Hammarskiölds Allé 24 (31–42 31 44).

Travel Agents. *American Express,* Dagmarhus, Amagertov 18 (33–12 23 01). *Wagons-Lits/Cooks,* Vesterbrogade 2B (33–14 27 47). *Spies Rejsebureau,* Nyropsgade 41 (31–23 35 00). *Tjåereborg Rejser,* Rådhus Pladsen 75 (33–11 11 00). Charter flights and accommodations in most European destinations can be arranged by the last two companies. *SAS Airlines,* Hammerichsgade 1 (33–13 72 77) for Europe, (33–13 62 66) within Denmark and (33–13 82 88) out of Europe.

Car Hire. *Avis,* Vester Sogade 10 (33–50 42 99); *Hertz,* Ved Vesterport 3 (33–12 77 00). *Inter-Rent,* Jernbanegade 6 (33–11 62 00) offer lowest rates and are highly recommended. *Share-a-Car,* Studiestraede 61 (33–12 06 43), is cheaper and also hires out campers and tents. *Europcar,* Gammel Kongevej 70 (31–24 66 77).

TELEPHONE CODE. The telephone codes for Copenhagen vary according to the area of the city. To call any number in this chapter, including Copenhagen numbers within the city, the prefixes we've included must be used unless otherwise specified.

HOTELS. Hotels in Denmark's capital are numerous and range from the luxurious down to the very plain and modest side-street hotel. During the season (May through Oct.) it is advisable to book your room well in advance, either directly or through your local travel agent. If you happen to come without a reservation, go to the "Room Service" at Kastrup Airport or at the Central Station. Young people may go to "Use it" (*Huset*), Rådhusstraede 13 (33–15 65 18), where there is also a noticeboard indicating room availability outside opening hours.

The accommodations service at the Central Station is at Kiosk P and it is open daily to personal callers from 1 May to 15 Sept. 9 A.M. to midnight (Nov.–Mar. 9–5). There's a Dkr. 13 deposit per person for rooms in private homes, which cost about Dkr. 110 for a single and Dkr. 220 for a double. Telephone inquiries can be made on 33–12 28 80, Mon. to Fri. 9–5. The postal address is *Hotelbooking Copenhagen,* Hovedbanegården, DK-1570 Copenhagen V. There's also a booth at the airport, which is always open.

Many listed hotels do not fall squarely into our price categories (see *Facts at Your Fingertips* for Denmark). In particular, *Moderate* rates for an hotel at the pricier end may overlap into *Expensive,* or at the lower end may stretch into *Inexpensive.* Take special care and always ask. During the off-season (Nov. to Apr.) many hotels, especially the new ones, lower their rates considerably. It is therefore advisable when reserving to have the prices confirmed. Hotels designated (BE) charge for breakfast. The budget hotel area is near the Central Station, around Colbjørnsengade/Helgolandsgade.

Deluxe

D'Angleterre. Kongens Nytorv 34 (33–12 00 95). 189 beds. A classic, ranking first among Copenhagen hotels. It has recently been renovated but retains an Old-World charm. Suites available. Sidewalk terrace café is a popular meeting place all year round. Widely regarded as one of the best hotels in Europe. Bar, restaurant with music, beauty salon, barber shop. (BE). AE, DC, MC, V.

Kong Frederick. Vester Voldgade 23/27 (31–42 59 02). 97 comfortable rooms with private facilities, and good restaurant. English-style "pub." AE, DC, MC, V.

Nyhavn 71. (33–11 85 85). A Romantik Hotel. 113 beds. One of the most charming and atmospheric hotels in Copenhagen, in converted 200-year-old storehouse. Most of the rooms have view of the harbor. Some suites. Excellent restaurant serving Danish Cold Table at lunchtime and *à la carte* in the evenings. AE, DC, MC.

Plaza. Bernstorffsgade 4 (33–14 92 62). Now under the joint banner "Royal Classic Hotels," with the *d'Angleterre* and *Kong Frederik.* 82 rooms. This group offers special weekend winter rates and various off-peak bargains. AE, DC, MC, V.

SAS Royal. Hammerichsgade 1 (33–14 14 12). 447 beds, all rooms with bath. This modern hotel has the best of Danish architecture, art and furniture. Every comfort. Sauna, restaurant, bar. (BE). AE, DC, MC, V.

SAS Scandinavia. Amager Blvd. 70 (33–11 23 24). 1,046 beds. Enormous tower block mid-way between the airport and the city facing the old city moats. Pool, restaurant, bar, coffee shop, sauna. (BE). AE, DC, MC, V.

Sheraton Copenhagen. Vester Søgade 6 (33–14 35 35). 846 beds, 34 suites, all rooms with T.V. Liberal use of blond wood, gray and pink in the decor. Sauna. (BE). AE, DC, MC, V.

Falkoner Hotel. Falkoner Allé 9 (31–19 80 01). 166 beds, and just coming into the lower end of the Deluxe category, so good value. In the Frederiksberg section. Good bus connections and parking facilities. AE, DC, MC, V.

Expensive

Hotel City. Peder Skrams Gade 24 (33–13 06 66). An individually owned tourist hotel, in an old city-center building, newly refurbished to keep traditional atmosphere. Popular with Americans. All rooms have full facilities; telefax and telex services. Breakfast only (included in room price) but many restaurants close by. Good value. AE, DC, MC, V.

Savoy Hotel. Vesterbrogade 324 (31–31 40 73). 67 rooms, all with bath. A surprising oasis of peace in a small garden courtyard off Vesterbrogade. The 1906 building was renovated in 1985. Rooms have all facilities. Breakfast-only restaurant (BE) but affiliated to a first-class restaurant nearby. AE, DC, MC, V.

Sophie Amalie. Sankt. Annae Plads 21 (33–13 34 00). 117 rooms, all with bath, some suites. Completely renovated. Bar. Guests use restaurant of adjoining Copenhagen Admiral. Good value, quiet; some rooms with harbor view. (BE). AE, MC, V.

Hotel Vestersøhus. Vestersøgade 58 (33–11 38 70). 53 large rooms with balconies, all recently redecorated. Recommended is the two-room suite with kitchen and balcony. Also the 15 apartments with bathroom and kitchen are good value for long stays. A family hotel, patronized by the U.S. Embassy, and facing the lakes. Breakfast restaurant. AE, DC, MC, V.

Webers Hotel. Vesterbrogade 118 (31–31 14 32). 80 rooms, all with private facilities. AE, DC, MC, V.

Moderate

Alexandra. H.C. Andersens Blvd. 8 (33–14 22 00). 63 rooms, all private facilities. Close to the Rådhus Pladsen, the center of the capital. Quiet, restaurant. AE, DC, MC.

Ascot Hotel. Studiestraede 57 (33–12 60 00). An attractive old building, with a wrought iron staircase and original features. Centrally located. Popular with Americans, who like facilities such as same-day laundry and dry-cleaning services, and extended room service; all rooms with private facilities. Many have been newly renovated; a few have kitchenettes. Good breakfast buffet in restaurant with bright decor. AE, DC, MC.

Bel Air. Løjtegardsvej 99 (31–51 30 33). 346 rooms, all with bath. Near airport; bus 34 to Copenhagen takes 25 minutes. Restaurant, bar, sauna. DC, MC, V.

Copenhagen Admiral Hotel. Toldbrogade 27/28 (33–11 82 82). A happy surprise to find this interesting conversion of a 1787 granary in the *Moderate* category (overlapping top price end) with a very high standard of facilities. Some two-story suites (Expensive) and restaurant, lobby bar, sidewalk café, shop, sauna. Business and tourist guests from America. MC, V.

Hotel Excelsior. Colbjørnsgade 4 (31–24 50 85). 55 rooms, comfortably furnished in Scandinavian style, 42 with private facilities, in recently renovated building. Bold interior color scheme; the lobby is like a child's post-modern playroom. Pleasant plant-filled atrium for drinks. AE, DC, MC, V.

Hotel Marina. Vedbaek Strandvej 391 (42–89 17 11). At Vedbaek, a residential area 30 minutes north of the city. 100 rooms, all with private facilities, also apartments for 2, 4, and 6, with modern kitchens. Near forest, beach, and yachting harbor. Good restaurant, excellent value. AE, DC, MC, V.

Hotel Neptun. Skt. Annae Plads 18 (33–13 89 00). 66 comfortable rooms, all furnished in mahogany and with private facilities. A classic hotel with 140 years of tradition. Restaurant and café, travel agency. AE, DC, MC, V.

SAS Globetrotter. Envej 171 (31–55 14 33). Near airport. 196 rooms, all with private facilities. Modern, with restaurant, bar and cafeteria, bowling, and sauna. Bus 9 to Børsen takes 15 minutes. AE, DC, MC, V.

Scandic Hotel. Kettevej 4 (31–49 82 22). 210 rooms, all with private facilities. The place to go if you want an indoor pool and sauna. At Hvidovre, western Copenhagen. AE, DC, MC, V.

Triton. Helgolandsgade 7–11 (31–31 32 66). 123 rooms with bath. Streamlined and modern, with large rooms in blond wood and warm tones. Exceptional buffet breakfast. Restaurant, bar. AE, DC, MC, V.

Hotel Østerport. Oslo Plads 5 (33–11 22 66). 73 rooms, 50 with bath. Modern Scandinavian design building, 15-minutes' walk from center, attracting many American summer guests. Meeting room, bar serving light meals. Gourmet restaurant, *Saison,* open for lunch and dinner. AE, DC, MC, V.

Inexpensive

Amager. Amagerbrogade 29 (31–54 40 08). 26 rooms, 16 with private facilities. On the way to the airport but still central. DC, MC.

Missionhotellet Ansgar. Colbjørnsgade 29 (31–21 21 96). 87 rooms, 44 with private facilities. AE, DC, MC, V.

Dragør Faergegård. Drogdensvej 43, Dragør (31–53 05 00). 23 rooms. An idyllic setting in old fishing village, near beach and airport. Buses to Rådhus Pladsen take 40 minutes (BE). DC, MC.

Esplanaden. Bredgade 78 (33–13 212 75). 50 rooms, all with private facilities. Centrally located near Langelinie and Kastellet. Bus and train connections. Good value. DC, MC, V.

Gentofte. Gentoftegarde 29 (31–68 09 11). 71 rooms, all with shower and toilet. Quiet, on the outskirts: bus 24 to Norresport (25 minutes) or train A. AE, DC, MC, V.

Skovshoved. Strandvejen 257, Charlottenlund (31–64 00 28). A charming hotel, about five miles from the center, among old fishing cottages beside the yacht harbor. 20 rooms, all with private facilities, and rooms vary from very large ones overlooking the sea, to smaller rooms overlooking a courtyard. Licensed since 1660, it has retained its Old-World charm, though fully modernized. Gourmet international restaurant (E) attached. (BE costs Dkr. 45). AE, DC, MC, V.

Hotel Viking. Bredgade 65 (33–12 45 50). One hundred-year-old former mansion close to Amalienborg Castle, Nyhaven, and the "Little Mermaid," in an area of palaces and mansions. 90 comfortable and spacious rooms, 19 with private facilities (no TV/radio, which you may find an asset!). Restaurant in same building but not part of Viking. Well managed. Closed to public transportation. AE, DC, MC.

West. Westend 11 (31–24 27 61). 24 rooms. A simple, reasonably priced hotel with few facilities. (BE).

Youth Hostels

Copenhagen Hostel. Sjaellandsbroen 55 (32–52 29 08). 448 beds in 2- and 4-bed rooms. Open all year, 3 miles from center, bus 37 from Holmens Bro near Holmens Kirke.

Vesterbro Ungdomsgård. 8 Absalonsgade (31–31 20 70). Open 5 May–Aug., near Central Station, membership card not required.

Danish Tourist Board list of Youth Hostels available free of charge. Official guide: *Danmarks Vandrehjem,* Vesterbrogade 39, Copenhagen V (32–52 29 08). Dkr. 25 plus postage.

Camping

Absalon Camping. Korsdalsvej 132, Rødovre (31–41 06 00). West of Copenhagen.

Bellahøj Camping, Hvidkildevej (31–10 11 50). In northwest Copenhagen area.

Strandmøllen. DK-2942 Skodsborg (01 80 38 83). North of Copenhagen.

Leaflet with locations, opening times and rating available from Danish Tourist Board free of charge. Complete Guide published by *Campingradet,* Olof Palmes Gade 10, Copenhagen Dk. 2100 (price Dkr. 32 plus Dkr. 20 postage).

HOW TO GET AROUND. By bus and train (S-train). A joint fare system, with optional transfers, covers buses and trains in Copenhagen city and environs. A one-hour ticket for three zones costs Dkr. 8; get it from bus drivers and rail stations. You can save money by buying a packet of 10 basic tickets for 70 Dkr. This system covers an area that stops south of Køge, west of Roskilde, and includes these towns, and Hillerød and Elsinore. Buses and S-trains start as early as 5 A.M. (Sunday 6 A.M.). The last bus and S-train leaves central Copenhagen around half past midnight, but night buses cover certain city routes. Get Zone system details from the 24-hour enquiry service (33–14 17 01).

In and around Copenhagen you can save by buying a *Copenhagen Card,* a ticket valid for one, two, or three days, which costs Dkr. 80, 140, and 180, respectively. It also provides free admission to more than 40 museums and other places of interest, including Tivoli Gardens, and gives a reduction of up to 50% on the ferry crossing to Sweden. You can buy the card at rail stations, tourist offices, travel agents, and some hotels. The card has a 50% discount for children aged 5–11.

By taxi. Taxis are expensive but all are metered. The basic charge is 12 Dkr. plus Dkr. 8–10 per kilometer (including waiting time at traffic lights, etc.). Tipping is optional and rarely expected, although a 4 Dkr. tip is charged for taking baggage to the 2nd floor, or for accompanying less mobile or elderly passengers. Cabs available for hire have the *Fri* sign. They may be hired at taxi stands, en route, or by telephone on 31–35 35 35.

By bicycle. Bicycles may be hired for about Dkr. 30 to 50 per day, deposit Dkr. 100 to 200, from *Danwheel-Rent a Bike,* Colbjørnsensgade 3 (31–21 27 27); *Rent a Bicycle, Jet-Cycles,* Istedgade 71 (31–23 17 60); *Københavns Cyclebørs-Velonia,* Gothersgade 157–159 (33–14 07 17); *Urania Cykler,* Gammel Kongevej 1 (31–21 80 88); *Cykeltanken,* 247 Godthabsvej, near Bellahoj Camping (31–87 14 23). and from Helsingør, Hillerød, Klampenborg and Lyngby rail stations, Apr. through Oct., (33–14 17 01).

By horse-drawn cab. For romantics there are horse-drawn cabs in the famous Deer Park (Dyrehaven), and in the city center. Expensive.

TOURS. From May to October there are various bus tours around the city and beyond. Here we outline the tours of Copenhagen: for further details and tickets contact tourist information offices, travel agents and some hotels. All sightseeing buses depart from Lur Blower Column on Rådhus Pladsden. Although tickets may be purchased from the guide at the point of departure, to be sure of a seat buy them in advance.

The "Grand Tour of Copenhagen" covers all the major sights, with stops at the Gefion Fountain, den Lille Havfrue (the Little Mermaid) and Grundtvigs Kirke. It lasts two and a half hours, and runs twice daily, Apr. through Oct.; in winter, once a weekday, twice on Sat.

The "Royal Tour of Copenhagen" covers Christiansborg Palace with the Royal Reception Rooms, Rosenborg Castle (crown jewels), passes by other royal buildings, and ends at Amalienborg Slot. It takes two and three quarter hours and is available June through Sept. 11, Tues, Thurs., and Sat.

The "City and Harbor Tour" starts by coach and includes a motor boat tour of the charming canals of Christianshavn. Duration is two and a half hours and it takes place from May 1 to Sept. 11 at 9.30 daily.

The "Industrial Art Tour" includes visits to a porcelain factory (either Bing & Grøndahl or Royal Copenhagen Porcelain), the Kunstindustrimuseet (Museum of Decorative and Applied Arts), and Den Permanente, the Danish design center. This tour lasts two and a half hours and runs from May 15 to Sept. 15, every Thurs.

"An Afternoon of History and Romance" includes a visit to an old village in a Copenhagen suburb, a river cruise, the Frilandsmuseet (Open-Air Museum) and the Dyrehaven (Royal Deer Park). Coffee and Danish pastry is included in the price. This tour lasts four hours and runs June 15 to Aug. 31, every Sat.

"Under Sail on the Sound." On the Isefjord, Denmark's oldest schooner. May–Sept. about four hours. Lunch or dinner on board. Departs from Amalienhaven (behind the Copenhagen Admiral Hotel, Toldbodgade 24). For information, tel. 01–15 17 29.

To join a motor boat tour (with or without guide) go to Gammel Strand or Kongens Nytorv. The boats also stop at Den Lille Havfrue and some go to Christianshavn. A fine way to experience Copenhagen.

There are guided walking tours, lasting two hours, with various starting points and routes, July through Aug. Consult the Copenhagen dailies or ask for information at the Tourist Information Office.

Guided tours of the Carlsberg Brewery, Ny Carlsbergvej 140, are on Mon. to Fri. at 9, 11 and 2.30. Meet at Elephant Gate. To make arrangements for groups, tel. 31–21 12 21, ext. 1312. The Tuborg Brewery, Strandvejen 54 (buses 1 and 21) provides tours on weekdays at 10, 12 and 2.30, or by arrangement for groups (tel. 31–29 33 11).

MUSEUMS. Copenhagen is a fine city to stimulate a sense of history and it certainly has its fair share of museums and art galleries. We list here the major museums plus a few smaller ones of special interest, together with opening times. Opening hours and admission fees are subject to change.

Although admission to many museums is free it could pay you to invest in a *Copenhagen Card,* a tourist ticket giving unlimited bus and rail travel in Copenhagen plus free admission to sights including Tivoli. Valid for one, two or three days at Dkr. 80, 140, and 180, respectively, it can be bought from rail stations, the Tourist Information Office, hotels and travel agents.

Davids Samling (C.L. David Collection). Kronprinsessegade 30. Medieval Islamic pottery. European decorative art from 18th cent. Open all year, Sept. 16 through Apr., Tues. to Sun. 11–3; closed Mon.; May through Sept. 15, Tues. to Sun. 10–4, closed Mon. Adm. free.

Frihedsmuseet (Liberty Museum). Churchill parken, Esplanaden. Exhibits detailing the efforts of the Danish Resistance in World War II. Open all year: Tues. to Sat. 10–4, Sun. 10–5; closed Mon. Adm. free.

Fyrskib XVII. Nyhavn 10. Lightship dating from 1895. Open all year, when the gangway is down.

Geologisk Museum (Geological Museum). Øster Voldgade 5–7. Open all year, Tues. to Sun. 1–4. Closed Mon. Adm. free.

Glyptotek. Dantes Plads. Egyptian, Greek, Etruscan and Roman collections, 19th-cent. French and Danish art. Open May through Aug., Tues. to Sun. 10–4; closed Mon. Sept. through Apr., Tues. to Sat. 12–3, Sun. 10–4, closed Mon. Adm. Dkr. 15, children free, Wed. and Sun. free.

Den Hirschsprungske Samling (Hirschsprung Collection). Stockholmsgade 20. 19th-cent. Danish art. Open all year, Wed. to Sun. 1–4; closed Mon. and Tues. Also open Wed. eve. 7–10, Oct. through Apr. Adm. free.

Jagt- og Skovbrugsmuseet (Hunting and Forestry Museum). Hørsholm. Train to Holte then bus to Hørsholm, or bus 84 or faster 75E (weekdays only). Open Feb. to Nov. 10–4 Tues. to Sun., closed Mon. Closed Dec. through Jan. Adm. Dkr. 5.

Kobenhavns Bymuseum (Copenhagen City Museum). Vesterbrogade 59. Guild relics, costumes, paintings and engravings illustrating the history and appearance of the capital through the ages. Also Søren Kierkegaard reliquae. Open May through Sept., Tues. to Sun. 10–4; closed Mon. Oct. through Apr., Tues. to Sun. 1–4. Adm. free.

Kunstindustrimuseet (Museum of Decorative and Applied Arts). Bredgade 68. European and Oriental handicrafts. Open all year, Tues. to Sun. 1–4; closed Mon. Adm. free on weekdays, except July and Aug.; 12 Dkr. on weekends, July and Aug.

Nationalmuseet (National Museum). Frederiksholms Kanal 12. Exhibits illustrate Danish civilization from Stone Age to recent times; also, ethnographical and coin collections. The Prehistoric and Greenland collections are outstanding. Opening times of the different sections are complex (tel. 33–13 44 11), but most sections are open Sun. 10–4, some Tues. to Sun. 10–4, and other 1–4. General admission times are as follows: Sept. 16 through June 15, Tues. to Fri. 11–3, Sat. and Sun. 12–4; June 16 through Sept. 15, Tues. to Sun. 10–4. Closed Mon. Adm. free, except for the special collection *Jugenzeit Interior*—elegant rooms in *fin de siècle* style (1890), adm. Dkr. 10, children Dkr. 3.

Ordrupgårdsamlingen (Ordrupgård Collections). Vilvordevej 110, Charlottenlund. 19th-cent. French paintings, especially Impressionists. Bus 160 from Klampenborg or Lyngby S-stations. Open all year, Tues. to Sun. 1–5; Wed. 7 P.M.–10 P.M.; closed Mon. Adm. Dkr. 5.

Statens Museum for Kunst (National Gallery). Sølvgade Sølvgade 48–50. Danish and European paintings, including Matisse collection. Open all year, Tues. to Sun. 10–5; closed Mon. Adm. free.

Teaterhistorisk Museum (Theater Museum). Christiansborg Ridebane 18. Open June through Sept., Wed., Fri. and Sun. 2–4; Oct. through May, Wed. and Sun. only 2–4. Adm. Dkr. 10, children Dkr. 5.

Thorvaldsens Museum. Porthusgade 2, Slotsholmen. Works by Danish sculptor (1770–1844). Open Tues. to Sun. 10–5. Closed Mon. Adm. free.

Tøjhusmuseet (Royal Arsenal Museum). Tøjhusgade 3. Collection of weapons and uniforms in Royal Arsenal built around 1600. Open May through Sept., Tues. to Sat. 1–4, Sun. 11–4; Oct. through Apr., Tues. to Fri. 1–3, Sat. 1–4, Sun. 11–4. Closed Mon. Adm. free.

Zoologisk Museum (Zoological Museum). Universitetsparken 15. Open Tues. to Sun. 11–5. Closed Mon. Adm. free.

TIVOLI GARDENS. This world-famous amusement park is open daily from Apr. 26 to mid-September, 10 A.M. (amusements all in operation by 2.30 P.M.) to midnight. It covers an area of 850,000 square feet. In May, amusements are cheaper, and on some Wednesdays children get free afternoon tickets for a few amusements. **Concert Hall:** Not only does Tivoli lie in the heart of Copenhagen, but during the summer months it is the city's musical center as well. Symphony concerts are given every evening at 7.30 and 9 (sometimes free). Also free daily "proms".

Pantomime Theater ("Peacock Building" to left of main entrance). Performances every evening except Sun., pantomimes 7.45, ballets 9.45. Pantomime came to Denmark from Italy via France and England about 150 years ago. This is the only place in the world where traditional pantomime is still performed.

Open-air Stage (in middle of gardens). International variety acts every evening at 7 and 10.30, weekends 5, 7, and 10.

Amusements. In the farthest righthand corner of the gardens ("The Fun Corner") and in "The Alley" behind the scenic railway; open from 2 to 4 until midnight.

Variety Theater Glassalen has a varied program with Danish revues during the summer.

Tivoli Boy Guards. Parade every Sat. and Sun., 6.30 and 8.30.

Fireworks. Weds. and Sats. at 11.45 P.M. on lake and open-air stage. Sun., stage fireworks at 11.30 P.M.

Restaurants. Eating places of all categories; open daily 9 A.M.–midnight. *Divan I* and *Divan II* are noteworthy but by no means inexpensive. Of greater gastronomic interest but no cheaper is *Belle Terrasse.* Over beer and sausages at *Ferry Inn* (*Faergekroen*) you can join in the folk singing. Also *Perlen, Balkonen, Grøften* and *Nimb.*

Dancing. Every night from 10–midnight at *Taverna.*

Jazz, Folk. *Slukefter* and *Vise Vers Huset.*

PARKS AND ZOOS. In the **Botanisk Have** (Botanical Gardens), Gothersgade 28 (tel. 33–12 74 60). Gardens open May to Aug. daily 8.30–6. Sept. to April daily 8.30–4. Palmhouse with tropical plants open all year 10–3 daily. Cactus house open all year Sat. and Sun. only 1–3. Adm. free.

Danmarks Akvarium is at Strandvejen, Charlottenlund. Take the S-train and walk, or bus 1 or 27. 90 tanks with about 3,000 fish and other marine animals from all over the world. Open daily Mar. through Nov. 10–6; Dec. through Feb. Mon. to Fri. 10–4, Sat. and Sun. 10–5. Adm. Dkr. 23, children Dkr. 10. The **Zoologisk Have** (Zoo) is at 32 Roskildevej. Founded in 1859, it is the largest and oldest zoo in Scandinavia. Open Apr. through May, Sept. through Oct., daily 9–5; June through Aug., daily 9–6; Nov. through Mar., daily 9–4. Adm. Dkr. 35, children Dkr. 16.

The **Dyrehaven** (Deer Park) is near Klampenborg and can be reached by S-train or bus 27. At Hellerup is the World War II Resistance memorial park, **Mindeparken Ryvangen,** reached by S-train or bus 21, and open 10 A.M. to sunset.

HISTORIC BUILDINGS AND SITES. Devastated over the centuries by war and fire, Copenhagen has been re-built many times. Its surviving genuine Renaissance buildings are therefore especially worthy of attention; however architects of later centuries also put up exceedingly handsome buildings. You may wish to take a trip out of town to see rather more homely historic buildings at Sorgenfri and Dragør. See *Copenhagen This Week* for comprehensive list.

Amalienborg (Amalienborg Palace). Four identical mansions (1740–50) creating a delightful Rococo square. Queen Margrethe sometimes in residence. Changing of the Guard at noon. The equestrian statue in the center is of King Frederik V.

Børsen (Stock Exchange). Slotsholmen. Built by King Christian IV around 1640. Fine Dutch Renaissance building with remarkable dragon-tail spire. Still in use but not open to general public.

Christiansborg Slot (Christiansborg Palace). Slotsholmen. State apartments, knights' hall, palace ruins. Royal Family residence since 1794. Conducted tours in English June to Aug. at 11, 1 and 3, except Mon. Oct. to Apr. at 2 (except Mon. and Sat). Adm. Dkr. 18, children Dkr. 7.

Dragør. Amager. Seaside village settled by Dutch immigrants. Museum open May through Sept., Tues. to Fri., 2–5; Sat. and Sun. 12–6. Closed Mon. Adm. Dkr. 5. Bus 30 or 33 from Rådhus Pladsen.

Folketing (Parliament). Christiansborg Slot. Open June to Sept., Sun. to Fri. 10–4. Closed Sat. Guided tours also Sun. year-round on the hours, 10–4. Adm. free.

Frilandsmuseet (Open-air Museum). Sorgenfri. Original old Scandinavian buildings in natural surroundings. Bus 84, or S-train. Open mid-Apr. through Sept., daily 10–5; closed Mon.; Oct. 1 to 14, 10–3; Oct. 15 to Apr., Sun. only, 10–3. Adm. Dkr. 10.

Grundtvigs Kirke. På Bjerget. Modern cathedral in village-church style. Bus 10, 16, 19, 43. Open Mon. to Sat. 9–4.45; Sun. 12–4, winter 12–1. Except during services (tel. 31–81 54 42). Adm. free.

Holmens Kirke. Holmens Kanal. Royal chapel and naval church, built 1619. Open 15 May to 15 Sept., Mon. to Fri. 9–2; winter Mon. to Sat. 9–12. Closed Sun. Adm. free.

Kastellet (Citadel). At Langelinie: 17th-cent. fortifications. Open year-round daily 6 A.M. to sunset. Adm. free.

Det Kongelige Bibliotek (Royal Library). Christians Brygge 8. Enter from Christiansborg courtyard. National Library of Denmark, topical exhibitions, exquisite gardens. Open all year Mon. to Sat. 9–6. Closed Sun. Adm. free.

Rådhuset (Town Hall). Tel. 33–15 38 00. Open all year. Mon. to Fri. 10–3. History of local city administration. Reception rooms for councillors. 346 ft. tower. Guided tours Mon. to Fri. at 1, Sat. at 10. Tower tours Mon. to Fri. at 11 and 2, Sat. at 11.

Rosenborg Slot (Rosenborg Castle). Øster Voldgade 4a. Built by Christian IV, 1606–17. Crown Jewels. Open May through Sept. 25, daily 10–4; Sept. 26 through mid-Oct., daily 11–3; treasury open Oct. 24 through Apr., Tues. to Sun. 11–3, closed Mon; castle open Oct. 24 through Apr., Tues., Fri., Sun. 11–1. Adm. Dkr. 20, children Dkr. 7.

Runde Tårn (Round Tower). Købmagergade. Christian IV's observatory, built 1642. Open Dec. through Mar., daily 11–4; Apr. through May, Sept. through Oct., daily 10–5; June through Aug., daily 10–8. Adm. 5 Dkr. Observatory open Sept. 15–Apr. 15, Wed. only 7–9.45 P.M. Adm. Dkr. 10, children Dkr. 4.

SPORTS. Copenhagen is a paradise for active sports people. The Tourist Information Office and Copenhagen Idraetsparks Information Office, P. H. Lings Allé 2, DK-2100 (tel. 33–12 68 60), open Mon. to Fri. 8–4, are good sources of information. **Jogging** may be practised in the parks and woods, and there is a fitness-testing course at Brøndbyskoven. For information on **squash** courts and rackets for hire at *Svanemøllehallen* tel. 31–20 77 01. The Copenhagen Squash Club (Vestersøhus, Vester Søgade, tel. 33–11 86 38) charges Dkr. 75 an hour.

Swimming. The nearest sandy beach is at Charlottenlund. More popular is the artificial beach a little further north at Bellevue. Go to Klampenborg by S-train C or bus 27 (from Hellerup). Other good beaches include Amager Strandpark (bus 12) and Dragør Sydstrand (bus, 30, 31). Beaches free. There are several indoor swimming pools around Copenhagen and its suburbs. Details from Tourist Information. Swimming pools, open during the summer are: Frederiksberg Swimming Baths, 29 Helgesvej; Kildesovshallen, 25 Adolphsvej, Gentofte; Vesterbro Swimming Baths, 4 Angelgade; Øbro Hall, Idraetsparken. South of Dragør (bus 30 or 33) are low meadows alongside the beach, with shallow water (the cleanest near Copenhagen): ideal for children. A 5-mile man-made beach is now open to the public at Køge Bugt Strandpark, south of Copenhagen. It is fine, sandy and clean. Bus

121 from Valby Station, or by S-train A to Ishøj or Hundige station and from there by the beach bus (season only) direct to the beach. You can windsurf along most of the coast of North Sealand. Contact local tourist offices for board hire etc.

Sailing is popular in Copenhagen, and the waters are ideally suited to it. Visitors can obtain assistance through the big clubs, especially the *Royal Danish Yacht Club* (33–14 87 87) and the *Copenhagen Amateur Sailing Club,* Klubhuset Svanemølle-havnen (31–20 71 72). Sailing boats and motor boats can be hired from *Maritim Camping* at Jyllinge (31–38 83 58) or *Holiday Charterboat,* Falkonercentret, Copen-hagen (31–19 09 00).

Fishing. Freshwater fishing for rainbow trout, river trout, carp tench, and eel, at Søllerud Naturpark, Langkaerdammen, Attemosevej, Holte. Information on day fishing licenses is available from local tourist offices. You must provide your own equipment. **Sea fishing in the sound** for cod, herring, garfish, mackerel, contact the following: *m/s Kastrup,* Kastrup Industrihavn (31–50 54 38); *m/s Skipper,* Kalk-braenderihavn (42–84 69 53); *m/s Hanne Berit,* Rungsted Havn (42–57 07 24).

Golf. Visiting golfers have a choice of around a dozen nine- or 18-hole golf courses within some 20 miles of the city center. Details from Tourist Information.

Horse riding. This is popular in the Dyrepark at Klampenborg. Experienced rid-ers lead groups and prices (Dkr. 50–95 an hour) vary according to the mount.

Skating from October to the end of March. Copenhagen has five skating rinks. Details from Tourist Information.

Tennis. The following clubs accept guest members for day-time play only: *Boldk-lubben of 1893* (31–38 18 90); *Hellerup Idraetsklub* (31–62 14 28); *Kobenhavns Boldklub* (01–71 41 80); *Kobenhavns Boldklub* (31–30 23 00).

Sports Events. You can find out about sporting events, and have other sports queries answered at Københavns Idraetsparks Information (as above).

Horseracing is accompanied by totalizator betting in Copenhagen. Flat racing takes place between the latter part of Apr. and mid-Dec. at the Klampenborg Race Course. Bus 27 or S-train C to Klampenborg, then bus 160 or bus 176 from station. Trotting events are held year-round, Sun. and Wed., at Charlottenlund Race Course; S-train C or bus 1 to Charlottenlund. **Cycle races** take place on the Ordrup track at Charlottenlund, usually Mon. and Tues. **Soccer** is played at the Idraet-sparken at Østerbro or Valby, Sun. afternoons or evenings, except July.

THE ARTS. For a list of future events in music, theater, film, exhibitions, etc. *Copenhagen This Week* is an excellent source of information. You can also get de-tails on concerts, festivals, etc. from *MIC* (*Dansk Musik Informations Center*), Vim-melskaftet 48, DK-1161 Copenhagen (31–11 20 86), open from 9–4 (personal callers 1–4). The main theater and music season is from September through May, and tick-ets can be obtained either direct from theaters or concert halls, or from ticket agen-cies such as *Wilhelm Hansen* (31–15 54 57) except for Tivoli. Details from Tourist Information.

Concerts and Guest Performances. The Radiohuset Concert Hall has weekly concerts by the Danish Broadcasting Service's three orchestras. The Sealand Sym-phony Orchestra is resident and gives more than 150 concerts every summer, with Danish and foreign soloists. You can hear new music at Ny Carlsberg Glypotek, the Royal Museum of Fine Arts, and the concert hall of the Louisians Museum in North Sealand.

Theater, Opera and Ballet. The Royal Theater is one of the few in the world to have theater, ballet and opera in the same buildings. Performances on the two stages alternate between all three. The *Mermaid Theater* is the only one in Copenha-gen to give its performances in English.

Movies. The Danes rarely dub films; they use subtitles instead. This means that you can often see original British and American films in your language. The same applies to television.

SHOPPING. Copenhagen is something of a shopper's paradise. Prices are high, but then so is the quality. At the same time, many shops offer tax-free shopping— look for the sign; it's always prominently displayed. Note, however, that you can claim back tax only when your total purchases from any one shop exceed Dkr. 1,200 (U.S. residents) or Dkr. 2,300 (U.K./other EEC residents).

The first place to head for on any shopping expedition in Copenhagen are the Strøget, the pedestrians-only streets—all lined with shops—that lace the heart of the old town.

Design. Near the Central Station (10 Frederiksborgade), at *Den Permanente* (The Permanent Exhibition of Danish Arts and Crafts, all exhibits for sale) there is a comprehensive selection of the finest handwork from all over the country.

A store where you'll find a beautiful and large display of Scandinavian design, plus the best of handicrafts from other countries is *Illum,* Østergade 52, the local Harrods. There are over 70 departments, including porcelain, the best names in Danish and Scandinavian furniture, fabrics and Finnish Rya rugs; a tax-free shipping service, two restaurants, a hairdresser, and credit cards are accepted. A shopper's delight.

Illums Bolighus, Amagertorv 10 (not to be confused with the above store), is *the* Center of Modern Scandinavian Design. If you are interested in some of the most attractive and yet practical things that are being marketed today, this is the spot to visit. Many items on sale here are made by famous Scandinavian designers and artists, some of whom have works exhibited in the New York Museum of Modern Art. A wonderful shop for browsing and picking up ideas for decor, entertaining, etc.

Ikea, Mårkaervej 15, Tåstrup (bus 119 from the station), is a huge furniture store with own, often cheaper, designs.

Silver. *Georg Jensen Silver* is at Østergade 40. Here you will find the largest collection of Jensen hollowware in the world. Browse among extensive offerings of gold and silver jewelry and study the permanent exhibit of tables laid with many of the famous patterns in sterling silver and stainless steel. There is also a small museum with original Jensen pieces, exhibits and photographs relating to his life and work. Antique and second-hand items for sale.

Danish design achieves beauty by classic lines and graceful forms, and centuries of sensitive craftsmanship are reflected in every piece of contemporary silver. *Hans Hansen* at Amagertorv 16 features stunning flat ware, cigarette boxes, and such.

Peter Hertz, Købmagergade 34, is one of the oldest silversmiths in town and makes most of his pieces to order. He specializes in marvelous place settings and delicate jewelry.

But moderns must first visit *A. Michelsen,* Bredgade 11—their prize-winning cigarette container and silver pitcher, their graceful tubecluster candelabra and the enameled anniversary and enameled Christmas spoons designed each year, are all collectors' items. The 1984 spoon was designed by Queen Margrethe.

A bit further along Bredgade, at number 36, is *A. Dragsted,* whose jewelry and tableware are favorites with the Royal Court.

Porcelain and Glass. The *Royal Copenhagen Porcelain Manufactory* (actually a shop on the original factory site) at Amagertorv 6. Three floors of beautiful displays from Flora Danica hand-painted dinner services to figurines. Second quality items also available, at reduced prices.

Bing & Grøndahl porcelain is next door and ranks equally high in quality and design. Second quality available from factory at Vesterbrogade 149. *Rosenthal,* Frederiksberggade 21 has a choice of porcelain and glassware primarily by Scandinavian artists such as Bjørn Wiinblad and Tapio Wirkkala. *Match,* Vimmelskaffet 42 (on Strøget) displays of glass and porcelain from Scandinavia, kitchen to table top.

Holmegaard glassware is on display at Østergade 15, offering everything in Danish design from snaps klukflaske to beautiful opalescent vases. A permanent glass exhibition/museum has been opened. Visits can be made to glassworks in Fensmark to see glass being made, also second quality on sale at reduced prices.

Arts and Crafts. At Ny Østergade 11 is the *Bjrn Wiinblad House,* with a sales display of the artist's own products.

For native crafts, see *Håndarbejdets Fremme,* Vimmelskaftet 38, which has embroideries, handprinted fabrics, and trinkets in impeccable taste. Every article is handmade; patterns and materials are also sold.

Clara Waever at Østergade 42 features special embroidery, lace, and linen.

Elling, at Bredgade 24, features materials of fanciful design together with bright printed pieces amusing for a child's room.

In the 1785 Potter's House at Torvegade 38, *P. Brøste* displays modern Danish and foreign arts and crafts.

Form & Farve, Nicolaj Plads 3, offers a host of characteristic Scandinavian designs, from notebooks to clothes.

At Bredgade 47, the captivating wooden toys, bowls, and plates of *Kay Bojesen* are on display.

Department Stores. *Magasin du Nord,* a huge, modern department store at Kongens Nytorv is the biggest of its kind in Denmark, with particularly good buys in silver, ceramics, and furs.

Illum, Østergade 52, see above, under *Design.*

Daells Varehus, Nørregade 12, is a smaller store, but offers good quality at extremely reasonable prices. Cash only sales.

RESTAURANTS. Copenhagen is reputed to have over 2,000 restaurants, and most of the city's hotels have good dining rooms. Prices are high, however, for the most part, so always be sure to check the menu, which by law much be displayed outside, before going in. A number of restaurants, even the more expensive, offer good-value fixed-price menus, usually of three courses. In addition, look out for restaurants displaying the *Dan-Menu* sign, where a two-course meal—either lunch or dinner—will cost Dkr. 75. Lunch is often the Danes' main meal. In many restaurants and cafés, a salad is included in the price of the main dish, and the second cup of coffee is often free, thereby halving the cost of what may seem an expensive cup. Always ask. Most Expensive and Moderate restaurants take credit cards; many Inexpensive only take cash. Service is always included in all bills.

Further budget bets are the many foreign restaurants that have appeared in recent years. You'll also find all the familiar fast food chains here. There are many pizzerias, particularly in the old city, and American-style burgers are sold all over town at **Burger King, McDonalds** and elsewhere. There are cafeterias in the **Magasin, Anva, Daells Varehus** and **Favør** department stores, which close half an hour before the shop. Cheapest of all are sausages and hamburgers from sidewalk vans (*poølsvogn*) which provide excellent, filling fare.

Expensive

L'Alsace. Ny Østergade 9 (33–14 57 43). Braques and Chagalls deck the walls of this elegant restaurant, set in an ancient courtyard; specializes in fish and French cooking. Book ahead; closed Sun. AE, DC, MC, V.

La Brasserie. Hotel d'Angleterre, Kongens Nytorv 34 (33–32 01 22). The place where Copenhagen's see-and-be-seen set goes to eat. French-inspired food in bistro surroundings. AE, DC, MC, V.

Den Sorte Ravn. Nyhvn 14 (33–13 12 33). French/Danish cuisine. 18th-century building on "gentleman's" side of Nyhavn. Specialties include fresh local seafood, sauces. Book ahead. AE, DC, MC, V.

Els. Store Strandstraede 3, off Nyhavn (33–14 13 41). Menu changes daily; gourmet food using fresh produce. Original 1853 decor. Book ahead. AE, DC, MC, V.

Den Glyde Fortun Fiskekaelderen. Ved Stranden 18 (33–12 20 11). Menu includes two meat dishes, otherwise all seafood in delicious sauces. Specialties of the day written on blackboard. Closed Sun. lunch. Book ahead. AE, DC, MC, V.

Gilleleje. Nyhavn 10 (33–12 58 58). Decorated with fascinating antiques from old spice-trading, sailing-ship days. Interesting spicey recipes. Open lunch and dinner except Sun., July. Book ahead. AE, DC, MC, V.

Kong Hans Kaelder. Vingardsstraede 6 (33–11 68 68). Luxury, gourmet food; top prices for highest quality. Closed lunch, Sun. and mid-July to mid-Aug. Book ahead. AE, DC, MC, V.

Langelinie Pavillonen. Langelinie, near Little Mermaid (33–12 12 14). Superb harbor views. Open lunch, tea and dinner; dancing most evenings. International menu. AE, DC, MC, V.

Pakuskaelderen. Nyhavn 71—basement restaurant of hotel (33–11 85 85). Best Cold Table in town, lunch only. International menu and grills in evening. Old restored warehouse in charming area. Book ahead. DC, MC, V.

Le Restaurant. In Hotel d'Angleterre (33–12 00 95). International menu, pleasant atmosphere, lush decor. DC, MC, V.

Skovshoved. Strandvejen 267, Charlottenlund (31–64 00 28). 15 minutes' drive out of town. Gourmet restaurant with idyllic conservatory dining room. Superb food. Book ahead. AE, DC, MC, V.

St. Gertruds Kloster. Hauser Plads 32 (33–14 66 30). Fascinating ancient building with cloisters and antique church artifacts, lit by 1,200 candles. International menu; special children's dishes. Open daily from 4 P.M. Book ahead. AE, DC, MC, V.

Moderate

Bof & Ost. Gråbrødretorv 13 (33–11 99 11). Basement in ancient square. Closed Sun. Informal bistro with Caviar-Vodka Bar. Open 11.30 A.M.–11 P.M.

Café Royal. In SAS Royal Hotel, Hammerichsgade (33–14 14 12). Open 6.30 A.M.–midnight. Light meals and snacks.

Café Victor. Ny Ostergade 8 (33–13 36 13). Open 10 A.M.–11.30 P.M. Very smart, fashionable clientele. International food.

Copenhagen Corner. Rådhus Pladsen (33–91 45 45). Modern, good international food. 11.30 A.M.–midnight.

Havfruen, Nyhavn 39 (33–11 11 39). Copenhagen natives love the maritime-bistro ambience at the "Mermaid", and are drawn by French-inspired fish specialties. Closed Sun.

Hereford Beefstouw. Large restaurant at Vesterbrogade 3 (33–12 74 41) and smaller, more intimate one at Åbrenå 8 (01–11 91 90). Best steaks in town, cooked to your order. Mix-your-own salads with good dressings. Closed for lunch Sat. and Sun. AE, DC, MC, V.

Ida Davidsen. Store Kongensgade 70 (33–91 36 55). Traditional Danish lunch restaurant with very best open sandwiches and specialties. Closed Sat. and Sun.

Mongolian Barbecue. Store Kongensgade 64–66 (33–14 64 66). Also at Stormgade 35 and Strandvejen 26. Hearty all-you-can-eat menus. New and popular.

Peder Oxe. Gråbrødretorv 11 (33–11 00 77). Steaks and salads. Charming area; can be crowded. 11.30 A.M.–10.30 P.M.

Queen's Rib. In Kong Frederik Hotel, Vester Voldgade 23–27 (33–12 59 02). French and Danish cuisine. Open-air eating from May to Sept. Pub for light meals. AE, DC, MC, V.

Stedet. Lavendelstraede 13 (33–15 66 25). Good cooking; relaxed, casual atmosphere. Open 11.30–3, 5–10.30, Sun. 5–10.30. Closed June and July.

Inexpensive

Amagertorv 8. In Royal Copenhagen Porcelain Shop. Open shop hours, closed Sun. Delicious pastries and light meals.

Café Asbaek. Ny Adelgade 8. In modern art gallery. Light meals and specialties. Open 11–3.30. Closed Sun.

Café Nikolaj. In old Nikolaj Church. Good Danish food. Open noon–midnight except Sun. and Mon.

Café Smukke Marie. Knabrostraede 19. Specializes in buckwheat pancakes with various fillings. Open 1 P.M.–midnight Mon. to Fri.; 4 P.M.–midnight Sat. and Sun.

The Cedars. Lavendelstraede 6. Lebanese buffet. Good value. Open 5–12 P.M.

Chico's Cantina. Borgergade 2. Very popular Mexican restaurant. Good atmosphere and excellent value food. Open noon–3 P.M. and 5 P.M.–midnight.

Green's. Grønnegade 12–14. Vegetarian; popular buffet. Classical music plays, chic bohemians chat, and friendly staff serve.

Krasnapolsky. Vestergade 10. Interesting salads, pasta, snacks. Near the university: there's a brooding youth at every table. Lunch only. Open 11.30 A.M.–midnight; 3 P.M.–midnight on Sun.

Mama Rosa. Østergade 59 (Strøget). Italian specialties, pizza and fresh pasta. Open 11 A.M.–midnight.

Mexicali. Åboulevarden 12. Mexican specialties. Open Tues. to Fri. 5 P.M.–midnight; Sat. and Sun. noon–midnight. Closed Mon.

Peppe's Pizza. Gothersgade 101, Rødhus Pladsen 57, Falkoner Allé 17, Frederiksberg and Skt. Pedersvej 1, Hellerup. Open noon–midnight; Fri. and Sat. to 3 A.M. Excellent freshly made pizzas of all types. Good house wine. Take out too.

NIGHTLIFE. Still feeling strong? There's a long way to go before exhausting the city. All-night membership clubs are now things of the past. About 35 restaurants are permitted to stay open until 5 A.M. (ask your hotel porter or see the newspaper). For shows, see the *Ekstrabladet* newspaper advertisements. For the young, many discos have been opened in recent years. Bohemians in general might like to make their way to the district around Nikolaj Kirke, locally known as "The Minefield." Here are dozens of small music and dance spots, and a beer is the price of admission.

The nightspots listed below are moderate to expensive and usually have an admittance fee.

Clubs and Discos

Compass Club. Amager Blvd. 70. In Scandinavia Hotel. Thurs., Fri. and Sat. only, 10 P.M.–5 A.M.

Fellini Nightclub. Hammerichsgade 1. In SAS Royal Hotel. 10 P.M.–4.30 A.M. Closed Sun.

La Fontaine Jazz Club. Kompagnistraede 11. 11 P.M.–6 A.M.

Jazzhus Montmartre. Nørregade 41. Reputed to be one of the best places for modern jazz in Europe. 8 P.M.–1 A.M. (Fri. and Sat. to 5 A.M.).

New Daddy's/Café Rio. Axeltorv 5. Largest disco in town. Mon.–Thurs. 10 P.M.–4 A.M.; Fri. 10 P.M.–7 A.M.; Sat. 10 P.M.–8 A.M.

Penthouse Club. Sheraton Hotel. 10 P.M.–5 A.M.

Privé. Ny Østergade 14. Hot place for the younger crowd. 10 P.M.–5 A.M. Closed Sun.

Slukefter. Tivoli. May to Sept., 8 P.M.–2 A.M.

Three Musketeers. Nikolaj Plads 25. Best place for traditional jazz, dancing. 8 P.M.–2 A.M., Fri. and Sat.–3 A.M. Closed Sun.

U-Matic. Vestergade 10. Mon.–Wed. 9–2, Thurs. 9–3, Fri. and Sat. 9–5.

Bars with Entertainment

After 8. In Hotel Scandinavia. 8.30–4.

Café Royal/Laurits Betjent. Ved Stranden 16. 10 P.M.–5 A.M. Closed Sun.

Kakadu Bar. Colbjørnsensgade 6. 8 P.M.–5 A.M. Popular.

King's Court Piano Bar. In Sheraton Hotel. 5.30 P.M.–2 A.M.

Musikcafé'n. Rådhusstraede 13. Fri. and Sat. 9 P.M.–2 A.M.

Purple Door Music Theater/Club Bluestime. Fiolstraede 28. Thurs. to Sun. only, 8.30 P.M.–1 A.M.

Rådhuskroen. Løongangsstraede 21. 12 P.M.–4 A.M.

Universitetscafeen. Fiolstraede 2. 10 P.M.–5 A.M.; Sun. 5 P.M.–5 A.M.

Vin & Olgod. Skindergade 45. Viking dinners, fanfare on Viking Lures (musical instruments), dancing and singing. 8 P.M.–2 A.M. Closed Sun.

Vinstue. Kongens Nytorv 19. English pub atmosphere. 10 P.M.–1 A.M.

Wonder Bar. Studiestraede 69. Singles bar. 9 P.M.–5 A.M.

ZEALAND AND ITS ISLANDS

Holiday Haunts and History

Next to Copenhagen, Zealand (Danish, Sjaelland) is the part of Denmark that is seen by more visitors than any other. Even so, most visitors see only part of Zealand, a very small part, missing not only the very beautiful island of Møn but also the interesting and lovely Odsherred region. The classic tour—up the coast of the Sound to Helsingør (Elsinore) and Hamlet's castle (Kronborg Slot), down to Hillerød and Frederiksborg Slot and back to Copenhagen—covers no more than a corner of the rolling and often beautiful country which is Zealand.

Helsingør

Helsingør is one of Denmark's oldest towns. Prosperity came to Helsingør when Erik of Pomerania introduced the much-hated Sound Dues in 1429—a fee to be paid to the Danish crown for all ships passing through the Sound to the Baltic. To ensure the collection of the dues, Kronborg Castle (sometimes called Hamlet's Castle) was built. Helsingør has many medieval houses and commercial buildings dating from the days of the Sound Dues, now protected by preservation orders. Whole streets of restored and well-preserved houses retain the atmosphere of this centuries-old provincial town. The Tourist Information Office in the Old Customs House can provide town maps with walks indicated so that visitors can see all the important buildings, streets and squares.

Erected between 1574 and 1582 by Frederik II, the Renaissance Kronborg Slot is a must. Visit the central yard first and then take a walk on the inner and outer ramparts. The visitable parts of the castle include a 60-meter (200-foot) long banqueting hall, a commercial and maritime museum, dungeons and casemates where the sleeping Holger Dansk will awake and fill every Dane with his spirit when Denmark is in danger. The chapel interior is luxurious, and people are still married there. There is a long tradition of performances of *Hamlet* in the courtyard, including many by famous interpreters of the role over the years.

Marienlyst Slot was built in 1587 as a summer house for Kronborg, and was later used by Queen Juliane Marie. It was rebuilt in 1760 and French-style gardens were added. It is now a city museum.

The Carmelite Convent and Sct. Mariae Church were both founded in 1430 and are among the foremost examples of Danish medieval architecture. Although still partly inhabited, both the former chapter hall and refectory can be visited. Skt. Olai was started about 1200 and not completed until 1559. Fragments of the original 13th-century building are still to be seen on the north side.

Danmarks Tekniske Museum contains noteworthy old technical products made in Denmark, for example the 1886 Hammel car. In the Øresundsakvariet are displayed Sound fauna as seen in ten different localities, with emphasis on sea-anemones and crustaceans.

North Zealand

Around Helsingør is a string of quiet seaside resorts with pleasant, sandy beaches inviting you to linger for a day, or longer. On summer Sundays, a veteran railroad goes to Gilleleje instead of the normal "railbus." Vedbaek, Humlebaek and Snekkersten are to the south; Hellebaek and Hornbaek are to the north; and Sweden (Helsingborg) is to the east, with ferries every 20 minutes.

Humlebaek is well worth a visit for the Louisiana Museum, where a world-class modern art collection is housed in a spectacular building. In the elegant, rambling structure, set in a large park at the water's edge, Warhols vie for space with Giacomettis and Picassos. In the summer, Danes bring their children and picnic under the Calder mobile in the sculpture garden, which boasts a great view of the Sound and, on a clear day, of Sweden.

One example of a vacation village is Tisvildeleje. In winter a fishing village, in summer there is an enormous expansion in population. People walk through its only main road with its low, one-story houses, either to the coast and beach behind the dunes, or back to their summer cottages. Or they walk to the funny "railbus" which will take them back to Hillerød and Copenhagen. Other people will throng at the packed parking lot and walk from their cars down to the beach or into the hilly woodland. Some go fishing, others go to the Troldeskoven (Troll Forest), a part of the wood with twisted, mysterious pines. One could instead go inward to Tisvilde or Tibirke and enjoy the village atmosphere.

For the tourist the towns of Hillerød and Fredensborg, only six miles apart, form a unit of the classic tour of north Zealand. South of Hillerød, there's the charming village of Søllerød with its medieval church, terraced yard and thatched-roofed inn. North of Hillerød a belt of fishing-villages are now completely changed into summer bathing resorts. In Hillerød itself is the Nordsjaellandsk Folkemuseum in a 200-year-old smallholding, and there is the fine Renaissance palace, Frederiksborg Castle.

Frederiksborg Castle was built between 1600 and 1621 for Christian IV. A fire destroyed the main building in 1859 but did not reach the chapel. The interiors were redecorated during the following years with large grants made from brewery king J. C. Jacobsen, and the National Historical Museum at Frederiksborg has been part of the Carlsberg Foundation since 1878. The museum illustrates the history of Denmark, with collections of paintings, furniture, and decorative art. Notable are the Audience Chamber, Knight's Hall and the Chapel with its Compenius organ built in 1610. A series of concerts is held in the Chapel during July and August. North of the lake is one of the best Baroque gardens in northern Europe, and to the west a small Renaissance château dating from 1581 called Bad-stuen (Bath House) which has been used as a hunting lodge. In the summer you can take boat trips on the castle lake.

AEbelholt, six km. (four miles) west, is a monastery with ruins dating from 1175.

Fredensborg is known for its palace and its inn. Fredensborg Palace was built in 1721–3. It is still a royal palace, the Queen's residence in spring and fall. With its 420 rooms grouped around the Dome Hall it is an exqui-site setting for royal parties, and also contains some valuable paintings. The park, which runs down to a lake, Esrum Sø, is one of the most beauti-ful in Europe. The Marble Garden is the royal family's private garden. There are Italian Baroque sculptures and a rose garden.

West of Copenhagen

Selsø Herregårdsmuseum, at Skibby between Frederikssund and Roskilde, has been uninhabited since 1829. You will find a 400-year-old Baroque banqueting hall and Louis XVI wallpaper. West of Roskilde is Odsherred with the main towns Holbaek and Nykøbing. The central part of Holbaek grew up around a 14th-century Blackfriars' convent and the museum is in a late 17th-century building. Surroundings include Tuse Kirke with frescos dating from 1450 picturing the childhood of Jesus. Southwest of Holbaek is a miniature Frederiksborg, Løvenborg Slot, erect-ed behind protecting moats in about 1634 (no admission). The architecture of Tveje Merlose is extraordinary, a fine example of an early medieval church. It has a restored ceiling and the western end still contains the gal-lery for the master and mistress.

Nykøbing is the main town in a popular holiday resort area. The west-ern part of this coastal area has a ferry connection with Ebeltoft.

Near the road from Nykøbing to Kalundborg is Dragsholm Manor House, built in the 13th century by the Roskilde bishop as a fortress. After the Reformation, the castle was used as a state prison; one of the "guests" was the Earl of Bothwell, who died here in 1578 and is buried in Fårevejle Church. Now a hotel and restaurant, but house open to visitors mid-June to mid-August, daily 11–5.

To the west in the bottom of a narrow fjord is Kalundborg, basis for ferries to Samsø and Jutland. Until 1658 the city was strongly fortified, but since its castle was destroyed that year, the unusual church is the only unruined part of the fortification. Vor Frue Kirke (Our Lady's Church), circa 1170, has a groundplan shaped like a Grecian cross. With its five towers and Eastern European patterns it serves—together with the radio masts—as a landmark. There are old thatched houses, especially in Pra-estegade and Adelgade, where Lindegården houses the local museum which occupies over 15 rooms, partly Rococo, and has a fine collection of local costumes.

Nearby is Røsnaes, with dolmens, windmill, cliffs and lighthouse. The Rococo Lerchenberg Slot at Asnaes is situated in a marvelous French-style park with rose garden, English-style lawns and summer concerts.

From Lerchenborg, go south to Slagelse; five km. (three miles) west from town you will find Trelleborg, a Viking fortress which is nearly 1,000 years old. Actually there are two forts, one much larger than the other, each with a huge circular rampart and a moat. The remains of some 30 barracks survive, and one has been reconstructed to show the peculiar, slightly curving shape given to the walls of these 30-meter (100-foot) long buildings. The site layout is thought to have been influenced by Byzantine models. Slagelse is on the main road between Korsør and Copenhagen.

Returning to Copenhagen along the main road you will pass the towns of Sorø, Ringsted and Roskilde. Sorø has an old Cistercian abbey dating from the second half of the 12th century. Today it is dominated by the abbey church and its academy serves as a public school. Sorø Kirke is Denmark's largest abbey church, with the tomb of Bishop Absalon, the founder of Copenhagen, behind the altar. Three kings are buried here and so are two well-known Danish poets, Ludvig Holberg and B. S. Ingemann. The latter rests outside the abbey in the churchyard. Sorø Akademi, from 1586 a school, and from 1623 an academy, was destroyed by fire in 1813 and rebuilt 14 years later. Visitors are admitted only during the school's summer holiday.

The Susåen (Suså river) nearby is good for canoeing, and the hilly woodland around the Tystrup-Bavelse-søerne (lakes) are pleasant, as is the walk round Sorø Sø, the lake, from the Academy. At Bjernede, near Sorø, is Zealand's only round church, an early brick-built church dating from about 1170.

Ringsted was an important medieval town, and is today a commercial town of 28,000 inhabitants. The Romanesque Sankt Bendts Kirke (St. Benedict's Church) was originally a Benedictine abbey, and was the first church in Scandinavia to be built of brick. It was built by King Valdemar 1160–70 as a monument over his father, Knud Lavard, who had been murdered in 1131. The Roman Church rewarded him by canonizing Knud Lavard, who is the only Danish saint. During the next 200 years the church served as the royal sepulchral chapel.

Roskilde, with 50,000 inhabitants, is Zealand's second-largest town. It was a royal residence as early as the 10th century. In the Middle Ages the town was the most important spiritual center in northern Europe, with 12 parish churches and eight large convents and charitable institutions apart from the cathedral. The first railroad in Denmark, linking Copenhagen and Roskilde, was opened in 1847. In 1972 Roskilde University was founded.

Roskilde Domkirke (Roskilde Cathedral) was erected by Bishop Absalon about 1170 on the site of a wooden church 200 years older. It is a most important medieval building, where the Romanesque and Gothic styles intermingle. Various porches and chapels have been added or extended from time to time in the prevailing architectural style, so that the result is a longitudinal section of Danish building history. The chapels have been added to serve as royal tombs, today numbering 38, the most recent burial being that of King Frederick IX in 1972. There is also an interesting 500-year-old clock and a pillar on which several royal personages, including Peter the Great and the Duke of Windsor, have marked their heights.

In 1962 five Viking ships were found in Roskilde Fjord and excavated. They had been sunk in the 11th century to form a barrier against enemy ships sailing towards Roskilde. In the Vikingeskibshallen, the museum built near where the ships were discovered, you can see the ships as well as exhibitions and films tracing their history and restoration.

Take a cruise on the Fjord on the veteran ship Skjelskør, visit nearby Ledreborg manor, or the Lejre Forsøgscenter—a working historical-archeological museum and research center at the Iron Age village in Herthadalen Valley.

South through Køge to the Cliffs of Møn

Interesting towns in southern Zealand are Køge, Naestved, and Vordingborg. Køge has more ancient half-timbered houses than any other town in Zealand. The oldest, dated 1527, is at Kirkestraede 20. There are also the smithy at Kirkestraede 13, the mayor's house to Brogade 16, the weaver's house on the square, and, in particular, Vestergadegården (Vestergade 16) which is richly carved and has an overhanging first floor.

Køge Bay was the site of two great naval battles between Danes and Swedes. The Danish national anthem refers to the earlier of these two (1677) in its first line, "King Christian stood by the lofty mast," although some sources claim the King observed the engagement from the tower of Køge's Skt. Nikolai Kirke. This tower was reputed to have been the place where pirates were hung.

In the Køge district are a number of fine castles: Gisselfeld, a stunning two-storied Renaissance edifice moated all round, with a beautiful park; Rococo Bregentved with copper spires and magnificent gardens; Gjorslev, built in 1400 by the Bishop of Roskilde, in the shape of a cross crowned by a tower in the center; Vallø and Vemmetofte, impressive castles, founded as homes for unmarried ladies of rank.

Near Rødvig are the chalk cliffs called Stevns Klint, which are striking, though not as impressive as the ones at Møn, nearly three times higher. The Højerup Kirke on Stevns Klint, however, has rather a pathetic air about it. Built around 1250, the church found its foundation being undermined by the sea and, so the story goes, moved itself an inch inland every Christmas. Unfortunately this retreat was far too cautious, because first the cemetery and then the choir toppled into the sea. In recent years the church has been restored and the cliffs below it bolstered with masonry to prevent further damage.

Naestved also has a number of half-timbered houses. Boderne is a medieval suite of houses, one of them a museum of arts and crafts. Apostelgården in Riddergade dates from about 1500, and is noteworthy for the figures of Christ and the Twelve Apostles carved under its eaves. There are more old houses in Kompagnistraede, as well as the impressive Gothic church of Skt. Peder, which has a fresco depicting King Valdemar Atterdag and Queen Helvig. Also of interest is the 15th-century Helligåndshuset (House of the Holy Ghost) containing a museum with regional collections. A mile outside of town, there's Herlufsholm Manor, once an abbey, with a 13th-century chapel. Holmegårds Glasvaerk (glassworks) makes an interesting visit—and, if you inquire first, you can hear the famous Holmegards glass instrument band—while regional handicrafts can be seen in the museum at Stenboderne.

On a small island just south of Naestved is the beautifully furnished castle of Gavnø, privately-owned but open to visitors. The delightful garden has modern sculptures in wood and stone. There is a flower show here in May.

The best Zealand canoe trip (85 km. or 52 miles up the Suså river) starts in Naestved and takes you through the most beautiful part of this island. There are many resting spaces, and canoes can be hired.

Vordinborg, Zealand's most southerly town, is splendidly situated on the Great Stream or Storstrøm, the strait separating Zealand from Falster. Here are the ruins of King Valdemar Atterdag's castle, the place where he died in 1182. Besides an outer wall nearly one km. (½ mile) long, there is the Gåsetårnet (Goose Tower), 26 meters (115 feet) tall (if you include the Golden Goose on top) from which there is a view over to Falster and Møn. Around the castle are extensive grounds, now a botanical garden.

From Vordingborg a three-km. (two-mile) long bridge runs to the island of Falster, whose rich soil is used to grow most of Denmark's sugar beet. (In 1985 this bridge was supplemented by the impressive Faro Bridges). Nykøbing is the principal town, with excellent hotels and the Czarens Hus, House of the Czar, an 18th-century half-timbered structure where Peter the Great stayed in 1716. Another bridge connects with the island of Lolland. There are good sandy beaches about 10 km. (six miles) away.

Lolland's main attractions are the towns of Maribo and Nysted, the latter known for Ålholm Slot, an old "robbers' castle" dating from the 12th century. Once a royal dwelling, today especially known for the nearby automobile museum with vintage and veteran cars owned by the Ålholm baron. The cars date from 1896 to 1930 and there are about 250 of them. A steam train dating from 1850 crosses the castle park and takes the visitors down to the Baltic. Maribo, in the middle of the island, is dominated by the 15th-century Domkirke (Cathedral), originally a Bridgettine abbey. Ruins of the convent are still to be seen. The open-air museum has a farmhouse representing the original regional dwelling. On summer weekends a veteran railway will take passengers to Bandholm on the northern coast over the lands of Knuthenborg Manor. The Knuthenborg Safari Park contains game, botanical sights, a monkey jungle and other safari animals. There is also a children's zoo. You can drive through the park, but take care to keep the windows closed unless you want to be visited by a baboon.

From Stubbekøbing on Falster, a short ferry crossing takes you to Bogø, with a dam connected with Møn near Fanefjord. Its white 13th-century church has an overwhelming number of frescos.

A few miles east of Stege, the main town, with its 15th-century gate, is the church of Keldby. This 13th-century church contains a lot of frescos, too, painted between 1275 and 1480. Even the royal wedding of King Valdemar and Queen Helvig in 1340 is pictured here. The third frescoed church is at Elmelunde further east. The nave here dates from about 1075.

The east coast of Møn displays 75-million-year-old chalk cliffs, Mons Klint, towering 120 meters (400 feet) above the sea, a great natural sight, seen from the top or the bottom. The charming 18th-century Liselund Slot with its English-style park and pavilions is nearby.

On your way back to Zealand you can make a detour to Nyord, a dammed island with many 250-year-old unspoiled farmhouses. Cars are not allowed in the hamlet, so you should walk there. Via Stege you reach the main road and the bridge to Zealand.

PRACTICAL INFORMATION FOR ZEALAND

TOURIST INFORMATION. The main towns of Zealand and its islands have tourist information offices: **Helsingør,** Havnepladsen 3 (49–21 13 33). **Hillerød,** 52 Slotsgade (42–26 28 52). **Kalundborg,** Volden 12 (53–51 09 15). **Køge,** Vestergade 1 (53–65 58 00). **Maribo,** Torvet 1A (03–88 04 96). **Nykøbing** (Falster), Østergåde 2 (53–85 13 03). **Ringsted,** Sct. Bendtsgade 10 (53–61 34 00). **Roskilde,** Fondens Bro 3 (42–35 27 00). **Sorø,** Rolighed 5C (53–63 02 69). **Stege** (Møn), Storegade 5 (55–81 44 11).

TELEPHONE CODES. We have given telephone codes for all the towns and villages in the hotel and restaurant lists that follow. These codes are necessary both within and from outside the towns or villages concerned.

HOTELS AND RESTAURANTS. The roads running north and south from Copenhagen pass through seaside resorts and small villages, so you can expect accommodations to range in price and comfort accordingly. Remember that the peak season at the seaside places runs from June 15 to August 30, elsewhere from May 1 to September 30. During other months, ask for off-season rates. The local tourist offices will help you with booking. The Danish Tourist Board publish a comprehensive list of hotels, with all details, annually. Available free of charge from their offices.

Albertslund (Tøstrup). *Motel Wittrup* (M) (42–64 95 51). 56 rooms, 48 with private facilities. Near Copenhagen. (BE). DC, MC.

Fredensborg. *Store Kro* (E), (42–28 00 47). 49 rooms, all with bath. Near castle. As comfortable as any hotel in Denmark and food is unrivaled. Many rooms have terrace. DC, MC, V.

Glostrup. *Glostrup Park Hotel* (E), (42–96 00 38). 85 beds; all rooms with bath. Near Copenhagen. AE, DC, MC, V.

Greve. *Strand Motellet* (M), (42–90 11 30). 10 rooms, all with private facilities. Motel between Copenhagen and Køge. (BE). DC, MC, V.

Helsinger. *Marienlyst* (E), (49–21 18 01). 215 rooms, all with bath. Private beach, sauna, roulette, indoor salt pool. Music and dance. There are also 74 apartments, each sleeping 4–6 people, with kitchenette and bath. AE, DC, MC, V. *Hotel Hamlet* (E), (49–21 05 91). 34 rooms, all with private facilities. AE, DC, MC, V.

Holbaek. *Strandparken* (M), (53–43 06 16). 31 rooms, all with bath. In park. DC, MC.

Hornbaek. *Trouville* (E), (02–20 22 00). 49 rooms, all with bath. Near beach; pool, sauna, fishing, sailing, music, garden. DC, MC.

Jyderup. *Bromølle Kro* (I), (53–55 00 90). 6½ km. (4 miles) south off Roskilde-Kalundborg road, Denmark's oldest inn (1198), in beautiful surroundings, opposite children's amusements. A former host supplemented his income by murdering his sleeping guests, but this hobby isn't practised any longer. (BE).

Karrebaeksminde. Restaurant. *De hvide Svaner* (E). Old thatched-roofed buildings, first-class food.

Køge. *Hvide Hus* (E), (53–65 36 90). 119 rooms, all with private facilities. Sauna. AE, DC, MC, V. *Centralhotellet* (M), (03–65 06 96). 14 rooms, all with private facilities. (BE).
Restaurant. *Casino* (M), (53–65 01 75). Good food.

Korsør. *Klarskovgård* (M), (53–57 23 22). 103 rooms, all with shower.

Maribo (Lolland). *Hvide Hus* (M), (53–88 10 11). 69 rooms with private facilities. Modern, with sauna and pool. DC, MC.
Restaurant. *Bang's Have* (E). In lovely surroundings, fine for meals on outings. Music Sat. all year round. DC.

Menstrup. *Menstrup Kro* (M), (53–74 30 03). Near Naestved; 200-year-old inn, part of Romantik group. Open almost round the clock, ideal for travelers arriving by ferry from south of Denmark. 74 rooms.

Mogenstrup. *Mogenstrup Kro* (E), (53–76 11 30). 87 rooms, all with bath. Cozy country inn, renovated. AE, DC, MC.

Mullerup Havn. Between Kalundborg and Slagelse. *Skipperkroen* (E), (53–55 81 95). Accommodations in 10 cottages with 2 beds each, bath and kitchen. Inn has unusual interior. DC, MC.

Naestved. *Vinhuset* (M), (53–72 08 07). 57 rooms, all with private facilities. Very pleasant, nightclub. AE, DC, MC. *Axelhus* (I), (53–72 06 00). 30 beds, no rooms with private bath. Spacious (BE).

Nykøbing (*Falster*). *Falster* (M), (54–85 93 93). 69 rooms, all with private facilities, pleasant. DC, MC, V. *Liselund Motel* (I), (54–85 15 66). 24 rooms, all with private facilities.

Nykøbing (Sjaelland). *Klintekroen* (I), (53–42 11 91). 12 rooms, all with private facilities. DC, MC, V.
Restaurant. *Den gyldene Hane* (I), Sjaellands Odde (53–42 63 86). On road to Ebeltoft ferry. Almost entirely fish dishes. Fresh food. Also hotel (18 beds) (BE). DC, MC.

Ringsted. *Scandic Hotel* (E), (53–61 93 00). 152 rooms, all with private facilities. *Slimminge Kro* (M), (53–67 90 18). 17 rooms, all with private facilities.
Restaurants. *Apotekergården.* Exclusive, good food. DC, MC, V. *Møllekroen.* Good food. DC, MC, V. A good place for a delicious meal is *Beløse Kro* (53–61 54 12) on the outskirts of Ringsted where two famous chefs from Copenhagen reign in the kitchen. DC, MC, V.

Roskilde. *Prindsen* (E), (42–35 80 10). 72 beds. *Osted Kro* (M), (42–39 70 41). 32 rooms with bath. *Roskilde Motor Hotel* (M), (46–72 46 32). 54 rooms, 14 with private facilities; those without are (I). DC, MC, V.
Restaurant. *Prindsen* (M), charming, shrimp a specialty. MC, V.

Slagelse. *Hotel E2* (E), (53–53 03 22). 144 rooms, all with bath. AE, DC, MC, V.
Restaurants. *Centrum; Helene; Postholderen,* for lunch.

Søllerød. Restaurant. *Søllerød Kro* (E), (42–80 25 05). Old thatched inn in idyllic village. One of the best in Denmark. Excellent cuisine. DC, MC, V.

Sorø. *Kongskilde Friluftsgard* (I), (53–64 92 00). 20 rooms, 10 with private facilities. Restaurant and sauna.

Stege (Møn). *Stege Bugt* (M), (53–81 54 54). 22 rooms, all with bath. AE, DC, MC, V.

Tisvildeleje. *Helenkilde Badepension* (I), (48–30 70 01). 36 rooms, 17 with private facilities. Inexpensive summer pension with full board.

Vordingborg. *Kong Valdemar* (E), (47–77 00 95). 65 rooms, 60 with private facilities. Music, dance, garden. AE, DC, MC, V.

Youth Hostels

There are youth hostels in the following towns and villages: Helsingør, Fakse, Frederiksvaerk, Korsør, Maribo, Naestved, Nakskov, Nykøbing Falster, Ringsted, Roskilde, Sakskøbing, Slagelse, Store Heddinge, Vordingborg.

Camping

Camping sites are to be found near all towns, and often on or near beaches. Tourist Information Offices will tell you where they are, or just follow international wigwam signs.

HOW TO GET AROUND. By bus and train. Buses and trains link Copenhagen with all important points in Zealand: to Helsingør in 50 min., Hillerød 40 min., Roskilde 20 min., and Køge 1 hour. Special sightseeing tickets for the DSB (Danish State Railways) comprise day return ticket from Copenhagen Central Station and admission charge. Included in this scheme are the Knuthenborg Safari Park on Lolland, Ålholm Slot og Automobil Museum on Lolland, the Louisiana museum of modern art in Humlebaek, Roskilde with Domkirke and Vikingeskibshallen, Helsingør for a steam train ride, or there is a two-day round trip to Helsingør and Sweden (no admission charges included).

The *Copenhagen Card* can also offer an excellent deal as it gives unlimited travel on buses and trains in Copenhagen and North Zealand—west beyond Roskilde and south as far as Køge, plus admission to many sights. Valid for one, two or three days, at Dkr. 80, 140, and 180 respectively, it can be bought at rail stations, travel agents, tourist information offices and some hotels.

Travel by bus and train without the benefit of a tourist card of some kind can be expensive as there is no discount on round-trip tickets: they cost twice the one-way fare. Bus tickets are usually purchased on the bus, and train tickets at a rail station, or on the train if the station happens to be closed.

By car. For those who are driving, here is a suggested two-day itinerary for Zealand:

First day: Depart Copenhagen–Helsingør–Fredensborg–Hillerød–Frederiksvaerk–Hundested–Rørvig–Nykøbing Sjaelland–Fårevejle–Snertinge/Jyderup–Kalundborg/Ruds Vedby–Slagelse/Trellebord–Skaelskør–Naestved. Distance, 272 km. (170 miles).

Second day: Naestved–Vordingborg–(Møn)–Prasetø–Fakse Ladeplads–Vemmetofte–Rødvig–(Stevns Klint)–Store Heddinge–Køge–Roskilde–return Copenhagen. Distance, 195 km. (122 miles).

By bicycle. Cycling is popular in Denmark and many roads have cycle tracks. Motor traffic uses chiefly motorways, leaving older roads safer for cyclists. Local tourist information offices will either hire bikes out or refer you to a dealer who does. Cycles may also be hired from the following rail stations: Klampenborg, Hillerød, Lyngby, Naestved, Nykøbing Falster, and the hire charge is Dkr. 30 per day, plus a Dkr. 100 deposit.

TOURS. Here we give details of three bus tours of Zealand which start from Copenhagen. The Tourist Information Office and some hotels will be able to supply you with further information. The "Vikingland Tour" takes you to Roskilde with its splendid cathedral, lunch at an inn (not included in fare), a 4,000-year-old passage grave, a typical Danish farm, and the Vikingeskibhallen at Roskilde to see the 1,000-year-old Viking ships. This tour takes six hours and is available Sun. and Wed., May 15 to Sept. 11.

The "Castle Tour of North Zealand—Hamlet Tour" takes you through the beautiful countryside north of Copenhagen to Kronborg Slot at Helsingør, i.e. Hamlet's castle at Elsinore. You will visit the royal residence of Fredensborg Slot as well as Frederiksborg Slot at Hillerød. This tour takes seven hours and is available Sat. and Sun. in April, Wed., Sat. and Sun. May through Oct., and Wed. and Sun. from Nov. to March.

The "Afternoon Castles Tour" is a shorter version of the above. It takes five hours and is available daily, May through Sept.; and Tues., Wed., Thurs. and Fri. in Apr.

PLACES TO VISIT. Zealand offers not only a feast of ancient churches, splendid castles and stately homes set in lovely parks, but also some important museums—for technology, automobiles, archeology, and trading and maritime history. Remember that the Copenhagen Card may be used in North Zealand (see *How to Get Around*). Here we list places to visit described in the chapter on Zealand together with opening times and admission charges.

Fredensborg. Fredensborg Slot (Fredensborg Palace). Queen's summer residence. Garden open July, 1–5. Adm. 10 Dkr.

Helsingør. Danmarks Tekniske Museum (Danish Technical Museum). Nordre Strandvej section open all year, daily 10–5; Old Rømersvej section open all year, Mon. to Fri. 10–4, Sat. and Sun. 10–5. Adm. Dkr. 12.

Karmeliterklosteret og Sct. Mariae Kirke (Carmelite Monastery and St. Mary's Church). Church open all year, 1–4. Guided monastery tours from 15 May through Sept., daily at 11, 2 and 3. 2 P.M. tour is year-round. Adm. Dkr. 5.

Kronborg Slot (Kronborg Castle). Also *Handels- og Søfartsmuseet* (Danish Maritime Museum). Both open May through Sept., daily 10.30–5; Apr. and Oct., Tues. to Sun. 11–4; Nov. through Mar., daily 11–3. Adm. Dkr. 24. Children half price.

Marienlyst Slot (Marienlyst Castle). Open June through Aug., daily 12–5; Sept. 15 to May 14, Wed., Fri., Sat. and Sun. 1–3, gardens all day. Adm. free.

Skt. Olai Kirke (St. Olai's Church). Open Apr. through Sept., daily 10–5; Oct. through Mar., daily 10–3.

Øresundsakvariet (Øresund Aquarium). June 20 to Aug. 10, daily 1–5; rest of year, Sat. and Sun. only, 1–5. Adm. Dkr. 7.

Hillerød. AEbelholt Kloster AEbelholt Monastery). Bus from Hillerod, 5½km. (3½ miles). Open May through Aug., Tues. to Sun. 10–4; Sept., Tues. to Sun. 1–4; closed Mon. Apr. and Oct., Sat. and Sun. 1–4. Adm. Dkr. 10, children Dkr. 3.

Frederiksborg Slot (Frederiksborg Castle). Home of **Nationalhistorisk Museum** (National Historical Museum). Museum and chapel open Apr., daily 10–4; May through Sept., daily 10–5; Oct. daily 10–4; Nov. through March, daily 11–3. Adm. Dkr. 20, children Dkr. 5.

Nordsjaellandsk Folkemuseum (North Zealand Folk Museum). Open June 15 to Sept. 15, Tues. to Sun. 1–4, closed Mon. Adm. Dkr. 3, children Dkr. 1.

Humlebaek.Louisiana. Modern Art Museum in park. Highly recommended for buildings and statues in magnificent setting overlooking the Sound. Major exhibitions and concerts. Open all year, daily 10–5. Adm. Dkr. 35, children free; times and charges for special exhibitions vary.

Køge. Bregentved Slot (Bregentved Castle). Gardens open Wed., Sat., Sun. and public holidays 9–8.

Gisselfeld Slot (Gisselfeld Castle). Free admission to park.

Gjorslev Slot (Gjorslev Castle). Free admission to park.

Vallø Slot (Vallø Castle). Park open daily.

Maribo (Lolland). **Knuthenborg Manor and Safari Park.** At Bandholm. Open May through Sept., 9–6.

Møn. Liselund (Liselund Manor). Open May through Oct. Conducted tours Mon. to Sat. at 10.30, 11, 1.30 and 2; Sun. and public holidays also at 4 and 4.30. Park open all year.

Naestved. Gavnø Slot (Gavnø Castle). Open May through Sept., daily 10–4 or 10–5.

Holmegårds Glasvaerk (Holmegård Glassworks). Open Mon.–Fri. 9–1.30; summer season also Sat. and Sun. 11–3. "Seconds" of famous glassware available at big discount, also glass blowing demonstrations and glass museum.

Herlufsholm (Herlufsholm Manor). Chapel open May through Oct., daily 11–5; winter, daily 11–1.

Nysted (Lolland). **Ålholm Slot og Automobil Museum** (Ålholm Castle and Automobile Museum). Museum open summer, daily 10–6; castle open summer, daily 11–6. Park open all year.

Ringsted. Sankt Bendts Kirke (St. Benedict's Church). Open year round 10–12 and in summer also 1–5. Adm. free. Concerts held June through Aug., on Tues. afternoons and Wed. evenings.

Roskilde. Domkirke (Cathedral). Open Apr. through Sept., Mon. to Fri. 9–5.45, Sat. 11.30–5.45, Sun. 12.30–5.45; Oct. through Mar., Mon. to Fri. 10–3.45, Sat. 11.30–3.45, Sun. 12.30–1.45. Adm. (unless a service is in progress) Dkr. 3.

Ledreborg (Ledreborg Manor). A manor house dating from 1740. Open July, daily 11–5; June and Aug., Sun. 11–5. Adm. Dkr. 20, children Dkr. 5.

Lejre Forsøgscenter (Historical-archeological research center). At Lejre. Train or bus. Open May through Sept. and Oct. 14–22, daily 10–5. Adm. Dkr. 32, children Dkr. 14.

Vikingeskibshallen (Viking Ship Museum). At Havnen. Open Apr. through Oct., daily 9–5; June through Aug., daily 9–6; Nov. through Mar., daily 10–4. Adm. Dkr. 18, children 12 Dkr.

Sorø. Sorø Kirke (Sorø abbey church). Open May 15 to Sept. 15, Mon. to Sat. 11–5, Sun. 1–5.

THE CENTRAL ISLANDS

Funen, the Garden of Denmark

Funen, with its rolling countryside, farms and orchards, has become known as the Garden of Denmark. For tourists it is best known as the birthplace of Hans Christian Andersen.

Its capital is Odense which, despite its inland location, is the nation's fourth-largest port by virtue of a ship canal. Next in importance is beautifully situated Svendborg, a busy seaside town and jumping-off place to the smaller islands in the south. Southern Funen has more lovely old castles and manor houses to the square mile than perhaps anywhere else in Europe.

Exploring the Central Islands

Your first acquaintance with Funen might be Nyborg, the terminal for train ferries from Zealand. Newcastle, as its name is in translation, grew up around the castle, which was built in 1179 as a guard against Wendish pirates; its central position in the Danish kingdom led to its use as the meeting place of the Danehof, an early parliament. The first Danish constitution, the Great Charter, was granted here by Erik Glipping in 1282. Ten years later the town got a charter, too, and today it has about 18,000 inhabitants. Contrasting with the medieval castle, where plays are performed on the ramparts, are the most modern hotels on Funen.

North of Nyborg is Kerteminde, but make a stopover at Ladby. Here, in an air-conditioned underground burial mound, are preserved the remains of the Ladbyskibet, a 1,100-year-old Viking ship, 22 meters (72 feet)

long and 2.7 meters (nine feet) wide. In it was interred a Viking chief together with his arms, his most valuable treasures, four hunting dogs, and
11 horses. Kerteminde itself is Funen's most important fishing town, and
a picturesque summer resort with old half-timbered buildings in Lange-
gade. Nearby are Viby, an unspoiled hamlet, and Munkebo, which underwent a sudden expansion when the Lindø shipyard was started in the
1950s. Today, this small village 16 km. (10 miles) from Odense, has one
of the greatest shipyards in the world.

The two largest towns on the island, Odense and Svendborg, are equally
suited as a center for exploring the Danish "butter hole." Odense, a port
since 987 although 22 km. (14 miles) from the sea, is the third-largest Danish city and above all is known as the birthplace of Hans Christian Andersen, who spent the first 14 years of his life here. The Odense river, where
his mother did her laundrywork, runs through Funen Village to the harbor
at the narrow fjord leading to the sea.

Museums and Sights

Hans Andersen's probable birthplace is today a museum—H.C. Andersens Hus—containing his personal belongings, sketches, works and silhou-
ettes, and letters from Dickens and Jenny Lind.

Hans Andersen's Barndomshjem, childhood home, has been described
by the writer in *The Story of My Life*. From his second to his 14th year
he lived with his parents, the cobbler and the washerwoman in the flat
to the right.

Skt. Knuds Kirke (St. Canute's Cathedral) is Gothic, erected in the 13th
century on the site of St. Alban's Church, where King Canute was killed
and later canonized. Today he is enshrined here. Two royal tombs are
those of King Hans and King Christian II, with their queens. See also
Claus Berg's golden 16th-century altarpiece. The font dates from 1660.

Den fynske Landsby (Funen Village), two miles south, is an open-air
museum of 22 Funen country buildings including a water mill and open-
air theater with Andersen plays for the children in summer. Return to
town along the river (boats, path).

Mønterstraede is a museum street where four houses dating from 1547
to 1646 show the town culture and life of those days. The Stiftsmuseet
has a local prehistoric collection (especially Iron Age) and collection of
Funen art, e.g. Jens Juel. The DSB Jernbanemuseum displays the State
Railway collections: two royal wagons and a Newcastle steam engine from
1869.

Other places of interest are: Skt. Hans Kirke, dating partly from the
13th century; old houses in Overgade; Brandt's Passage, a converted textile factory that is now a chic new exhibition center and a print museum;
the Zoo; Tivoli; town hall and the university (built 1966). There are also
river cruises.

At Nørre Lyndelse, 13 km. (eight miles) south, is the native home of
Carl Nielsen, the best-known Danish composer.

Svendborg and the Southern Isles

To the south is Svendborg and the bordering island of Tåsinge, both
beautifully situated on the sea. Svendborg, second-largest Funen town, got
its town charter in the 13th century. Today it is devoted to industry, com-

merce and navigation and is ideal for stopovers because of good beaches and "unexplored" surrounding isles. The islands of Tåsinge and Langeland are connected by bridges to Svendborg. The other islands are reached by ship only. Among them, visit AEro and if time allows, Hjortø.

While in Svendborg, visit the Skt. Nikolai Kirke, devoted to the sailors' patron, a Romanesque basilica prior to 1200. Restored 1892, it has frescos in the arches. Anne Hvide's Gård is the regional museum in the oldest preserved building, dating from 1560, with medieval material, ship models and local collections. The Zoologisk Museum has a complete collection of Danish mammals, birds and eggs.

Thurø is connected by a dam to Funen at the Christiansminde woods. Thurø is an orchard with 1,600 inhabitants and used to be the home of some Danish painters and poets who were inspired by its doll-like village and sailors.

Tåsinge, south of Svendborg, has 5,000 inhabitants. Here and in Svendborg was the setting of Elvira Madigan's romance, and the movie was made on location here. (The tombs are at Landet churchyard). Visit Bregninge Church which has magnificent views of the Funen archipelago from its tower, and the nearby skipper's home with ship models and mementos of Elvira Madigan. Troense is one of the best preserved Danish villages, with a row of half-timbered houses. The former school is a museum of shipping, which used to be the living of the islanders. Nearby Valdemarsslot dates from around 1640 and is now a naval museum with much sumptuous furnishing.

Langeland, largest in the archipelago, is connected by bridge and dam to Tåsinge. The main town is Rudkøbing, where H. C. Ørsted, the discoverer of electromagnetism, was born. Today it is dominated by merchants' estates. In Brogade and Østergade are many preserved old houses. South of the town are Ristinge and Bagenkop with good beaches, and ferry to Kiel in Germany. North of Rudkøbing are the 13th-century Tranekaer Slot and Egeløkke, a manor which was once the living of Bishop Grundtvig, founder of the Danish Folk High School movement in the 19th century. The northernmost village is Lohals (ferry to Korsør). As a whole Langeland is rich in relics of the past, and you can always find a beach.

AErø has two towns, Marstal and AErøskøbing. Had it not been because of its competitor, Marstal would have been famous. Today its museum houses a collection of model ships, and the church interior and small shipyards tell a story of bygone grandeur one or two centuries ago. The town has ferry connection with Rudkøbing. However, the smaller AErøskøbing has the most to offer the tourist. Even the sparrows sleep in its 17th and 18th-century streets with 36 protected houses. As in Ebeltoft you will find an isolated community, today revived because of tourism. However, you can still see its post office dating from 1749, its wooden pumps and cook house, although the latter serves today's requirements better as a public toilet! Also see the Dukkehuset (Dolls' House) and the unique collection of bottle ships (750 models), plus Gunnar Hammerichs Hus with its old furniture. The attractive church dates from 1756 and has an interesting pulpit with carvings of dubious ladies with fig leaves. The town is still lit by gaslight at night.

When leaving, you can take ferries to Mommark (Als), Fåborg or Svendborg (Funen) or Rudkøbing.

Southern Funen

Along the lanes around Svendborg you find numerous picturesque spots, but one you must visit is Egeskov. The castle here is the best-preserved island castle in Europe. Its name comes from the oak forest which was felled around 1524 to form 30 years later the piles on which was built an impregnable Renaissance castle. It is still impregnable to tourists, but its five gardens and the museum of vintage cars and aircraft can be visited. You are now about halfway between Nyborg and Fåborg, both of which should be seen. On the road to Nyborg is Holckenhavn Manor dating from 1580, where Cortifz Ulfeldt, the most notorious traitor in Danish history, lived with his wife Leonora Christiana, daughter of King Christian IV.

On the road from Egeskov to Fåborg is Brahetrolleborg, a Cistercian abbey dating from 1172. After the Reformation it was crown property, but became a baronial seat in 1668. It was here that Johan Ludvig Reventlow let the peasants burn a wooden horse symbolizing his release of them.

Other interesting châteaux are the somber, moated Broholm; the lovely Renaissance-style Rygård; Hesselagergård, built in 1538 with walls more than six feet thick and encircled by a moat; Glorup, a manor house from 1580, rebuilt in Baroque style in the 18th century; Lykkesholm, Hellerup, Ravnholt, and Ørbaeklunde.

Fåborg was a privileged town in the 13th century but damaged by a fire in 1728, which, however, spared many old houses that can still be seen in Vestergade and Holkegade. Moreover, one of five medieval gates survives, and so does the belfry, all that remains of the Skt. Nikolai Kirke, to which it once belonged. The museum contains the best collection of Funen painters, a private donation, also works by Kai Nielsen, the sculptor who did the controversial Ymerbrønden ("Ymer Well") in the market square. Just east of town is the 600-year-old Kaleko Møllegård, a water mill, now a museum. There are ferry crossings to either Avernakø, which has 120 inhabitants (especially recommended at Shrovetide and Whitsuntide), or to Lyø (200 inhabitants). This will show you idyllic landscapes and Lyø Village. There is another ferry to Gelting near Flensburg, and the main road leads west to the Bøjden ferry for Fynshav, on Als. On the way one passes the round church at Horne, the only one of its kind in Funen. With walls two meters (seven feet) thick it served both as church and fortress, but today only the core of the building remains. North of Fåborg is a former manor house, now the Hotel Stensgård. Between Fåborg and Assens to the northwest lie the Svanninge Bakker, hills known jokingly as the Funen Alps.

The western coast of Funen offers less of interest than the rest of the island. Assens has a church of minor note and a 17th-century house which was the home of Peter Willemoes. At the age of 18, this Danish hero commanded a battery during the bombardment of Copenhagen with such distinction that Lord Nelson complimented him personally. Middelfart claims to have the only suspension bridge in Denmark, built in 1970, and is worth a stop if only for its Folk Museum, housed in Henning Friisers Hus at Brogade 6. Just outside town is Galsklint, a memorial park in honor of British pilots shot down during World War II.

PRACTICAL INFORMATION FOR
THE CENTRAL ISLANDS

TOURIST INFORMATION. The main towns of Funen and the other central islands have tourist information offices: **AErøskøbing,** Torvet (62–52 13 00). **Assens,** Østergade 57 (64–71 20 31). **Fåborg,** Havnegade 2 (62–61 07 07). **Kerteminde,** Strandgade 5A (65–32 11 21). **Middelfart,** Havnegade 10 (64–41 17 88). **Nyborg,** Torvet 9 (65–31 02 80). **Odense,** Rådhuset (Town Hall) (66–12 79 10). **Svendborg,** Møllergade 20 (62–21 09 80).

TELEPHONE CODES. We have given the Central Island telephone code for all the towns and villages in the hotel and restaurant lists that follow. This code should be used at all times whether from inside the Central Islands or from outside.

HOTELS AND RESTAURANTS. Most hotels maintain the same rates throughout the year, but it is worth asking about off-season rates (Oct. through May). Many of the hotels and inns have special weekend rates and you should also inquire about the *Funen Combi Pension,* a flexible package that allows you to stay at one place but lunch and dine en route. Details from any tourist office, or from any inn taking part. "Inn checks" for one night's stay and breakfast at Dkr. 195 per person, are also available in the Central Islands as they are elsewhere in Denmark.

Aerø. *Hotel AErohus,* AErøskøbing (M), (62–52 10 03). Half-timbered family hotel with 30 rooms, some with bath. Also six 2- to 4-bed apartments. Large garden and terrace. Good food and *Danmenu* available. AE. *Hotel Damgarden* (I), (62–52 16 56). 16 rooms, none with bath.

Assens. *Gl. Brydegard* (M), (64–77 14 75). 17 rooms, all with private facilities and three 6-bed apartments. About six miles south of Assens, near Ebberup. Excellent food in what was once a farm. *Stubberup Kro* (M), (62–79 10 15). Five rooms in inn.

Falsled Kro *Falsled* (E), (62–68 11 11). 13 rooms. Near Stensgård, charming country inn, with French food and wines; superb, expensive food; closed Dec. 11 through Mar. and Mon. (BE). DC, MC. *Fåborg Fjord* (E), (62–61 10 10). 132 rooms, 128 with bath. Recent. AE, DC, MC, V. *Steensgaard Herregaardspension* (E), (09–61 94 90). Splendid manor house dating from 1300s; antiques; excellent food, game a specialty. AE, DC, MC, V. *Klinten* (M), (62–61 38 00). 120 apartments with 6 beds, bath and kitchen. Sauna, pools, weekly rentals. (BE). MC, V.

Kerteminde. *Munkebo Kro* (E), (65–97 40 30). 20 rooms, all with private facilities. A genuine, old inn dating from 1816, with an excellent restaurant, famous for fried eel. Closed Dec. 21 to Jan. 5. *Tornøes* (M), (65–32 16 05). 27 rooms, 23 with private facilities. Garden; venison in season. DC, MC, V.

Langeland. *Hotel Faergegårdem* (M), Tranekaer (62–55 14 35). 48 rooms, 40 with private facilities. Sauna. AE, DC, MC, V. *Skandinavien,* Rudkøbing (I), (62–51 14 95). 12 rooms, 9 with private facilities. TV room. (BE).
Restaurant. *Spodsbjerg Kro og Baderhotel,* Rudkøbing (I), (62–50 10 64). Also has rooms.

Middelfart. *Byggecentrums Kursuscenter* (I), Hindsgavl Allé (64–41 14 41). Close to Hindsgavl Manor with lovely park. DC, MC. *Grimmerhus* (I), Kongebrovej 42 (64–41 03 99). 20 beds, doubles with bath. Beatifully situated; closed around Christmas. (BE).

Nyborg. *Hesselet* (E), (65–31 30 29). 46 rooms, all with bath. On beach, close to 18-hole golf course. Sauna and pool. (BE). *Nyborg Strand* (M), (65–31 31 31). 47 rooms, all with private facilities, also some "luxury" rooms (children free). On beach and located close to 18-hole golf course. Indoor pool and sauna. AE, DC, MC, V. *Ullersley Kro* (I), (65–35 10 07). 15 rooms, 14 with private facilities, in a traditional inn. DC.
Restaurant. *Danetopehofkroen* serves good-value tourist menu.

Odense. *Frederik VI* (E), (65–94 13 13). 92 beds, some (M) rooms. Suburban, with garden. MC, V. *Grand* (E), (66–11 71 71). 139 rooms with bath. Ask for new rooms. One of Denmark's best, and with fine cuisine, bar. AE, DC, MC, V. *Hotel H. C. Andersen* (E), (66–14 78 00). Near new concert house. 148 rooms, all with bath. AE, DC, MC, V. *Munkeris* (E), (66–15 90 41). 67 rooms, all with shower. Recent motel. DC, MC, V. *Windsor* (E), (66–12 06 52). 109 beds. Restored, with modern rooms. AE, DC, MC, V. *Brasilia/Blommenslyst Kro* (M), (65–96 70 12). 52 rooms, all with bath. Motel in park 8 km. (five miles) west. DC, MC. *Frederik VI* (M), (65–94 13 13). 74 rooms. Suburban, with garden. DC, MC. *Missionshotel Ansgar* (M), (60–11 96 93). 34 rooms with bath. Modern, clean, near train station. AE, DC, MC, V. *Mørkenborg Kro* (I) (64–83 10 51). 15 rooms, all with private facilities. On beautiful site 11 miles northwest. Has antiques and children's playground. DC.
Restaurants. *Skoven* (E), in Hunderup Forest, excellent. MC, V. *Under Lindetraet* (E), vis-à-vis Andersen's house. Excellent with many awards for food and wine. Closed July. DC, MC, V. *Franck-A* (M). Moderately-priced meals served in differently-styled interiors. MC, V. *Den gamle Kro* (M). Lovely timbered inn with charming atmosphere and long list of specialties. MC, V. *Den grimme AElling* (M), steak house. MC, V. *Hereford Beefstouw* (M), Vestergade 13 (66–12 02 22). Excellent steaks; highly recommended chain. AE, DC, MC, V. *Sortebro Kro* (I), in Funen Village, for simple fare. MC, V. *Cafe Biografen* (I). Chic café with simple fare in Brandt's Passage. *Målet* (I). Sports club decor, soccer memorabilia, good schnitzel.

Svendborg. *Svendborg* (M), (62–21 17 00). 89 rooms, all with bath. Music and dance. AE, DC, MC, V. *Margrethesmind* (I), (62–24 10 44). 10 rooms, some with bath. On main road between Fåborg and Svendborg. Also art gallery. *3 Roser* (I), (62–21 64 26). 70 rooms, all with bath. Also weekly 4–5 bed apartments with kitchen. Modern motel. Free golf and pool. (BE). DC, MC, V. *Stella Maris* (I), (62–21 38 91). 28 beds, 13 rooms with bath. Garden. (BE).
Restaurants. *Valdemars Slot* (E), (62–22 59 00). Elegant food in ancient vaults below castle. MC. *Røde Mølle*, Hvidkilde. In former water mill; venison a specialty. *Svendborg*, hotel restaurant with dancing. *Underground Ice Cream* (I), Kattesundet 10. Fresh sandwiches, home-made bread. Highly recommended chain.

Troense (Tåsinge). *Troense* (M), (62–22 54 12). 33 rooms, all with private facilities, in an old inn. An ideal spot overlooking Svendsborgsund and the yacht harbor. Free golf course nearby. DC, MC, V.

Youth Hostels

There are youth hostels in the following towns and villages: Årup, Assens, FŞborg, Kerteminde (new), Marstal (AErø), Odense, Nyborg, Ringe, Rudkøbing (Langeland), Svendborg.

Camping

Camping sites are dotted along the coast around Funen and its islands, and are also to be found in beautiful locations inland. Tourist Information Offices will tell you where they are, or just follow the international wigwam signs.

HOW TO GET AROUND. Funen is linked to Jutland by the Little Belt bridges (at Middelfart) and ferries (Fynshav-Bøjden); to Zealand by ferry (Nyborg-Korsør and Halsskov-Knudshoved); to the island of Langeland via the Tåsinge bridge; and to AErø by ferry. Its main town of Odense may be reached from Copenhagen in three hours by "L" train, or more quickly by air.

By bus and train. All important towns on the island of Funen are served by local trains and buses. Trains serve the Nyborg-Odense-Middelfart route and Odense-Svendborg route. All other local transport is by bus, as it is on the small islands. Go to the "rutebilstation" (coach station) in towns that are big enough to have one; otherwise consult timetables displayed at bus stops.

Bus tickets are usually purchased on the bus, and train tickets at a rail station, or on the train if the station happens to be closed. There is no discount on return tickets: they cost twice the one-way fare. One-day tourist tickets are available in Odense.

By car. The east-west motorway across Funen is merely functional but the other roads make charming motoring country, with winding but wide roads. A detailed regional map is essential if you plan to explore the smaller byways. To avoid delay book ahead for the car on the ferry between Funen and Zealand. *Dantourist* in Svendborg offers several package tours including Funen in the itinerary: for example, a seven-day "Castle Tour" that includes overnight stay and half board at hotels with private bath.

By bicycle. With short distances everywhere, the central islands are made for cycling. Local tourist offices will be pleased to suggest itineraries through the most characteristic scenery. Cycles are for hire in AErøskøbing, Assens, Fåborg, Kerteminde, Marstal (AErø), Middelfart, Nyborg, Odense, Ringe, and Svendborg.

TOURS. Tours for motorists are mentioned above. Those without their own transport may like to know about two opportunities to visit Odense, the main town, from Copenhagen. Firstly, the "Hans Christian Andersen Tour" takes you by coach from Copenhagen to Odense to see Andersen's birthplace and museum. The tour last 11 hours, and runs every Sun., May 1 to Sept. 11. Further details from tourist information office and some hotels in Copenhagen.

Secondly, Odense, with Andersen's house and two other museums, is included in the DSB (Danish State Railways) special sightseeing ticket scheme. This ticket includes day return by train from Copenhagen Central Station and admission charges.

PLACES TO VISIT. Fåborg. Brahetrolleborg Slot (Brahetrolleborg Castle). Park open daily, 9–5.

Egeskov Slot (Egeskov Castle). N.E. of Fåborg. Vintage car and aircraft museum open Easter to Oct., 10–5; June to Aug., 9–6. Park open all year. Chamber music concerts held in summer.

Nyborg. Glorup (Glorup Manor). Park open Thurs., Sat. and Sun., 9–6.

Holckenhavn (Holckenhavn Manor). Park open daily 9–4. Chapel open by appointment.

Nyborg Slot (Nyborg Castle). Open Mar. through May, Sept. through Nov., Tues. to Sun. 10–3; June through Aug., Tues. to Sun. 9–5; June through Aug. daily 9–6.

Odense. H.C. Andersens Barndomshjem (childhood home), Munkemøllestraede 3. Open daily Apr. through Sept. 10–5; Oct. through Mar. 12–3.

H.C. Andersens Hus (Hans Andersen Museum), Hans Jensensstraede 39–43. Generally open Apr. through May and Sept., daily 10–5; June through Aug., daily 9–6; Oct. through Mar., daily 10–3.

DSB Jernbanemuseum (Danish Railways Museum), Dannebrogsgade. Open May through Sept., daily 10–4; Oct. through Apr., Sun. only, 10–3.

Den fynske Landsby (Funen Village). Open Apr. through May, Sept. through Oct., daily 9–4; June through Aug., daily 9–6.30; Nov. through Mar., Sun. and holidays.

Møntergården, Monterstraede. Open all year, daily 10–4.

Skt. Knuds Kirke (St. Canute's Cathedral). Open May through Aug., Mon. to Sat. 10–5, Sun. 11.30–12.30; Sept. through Apr., Mon. to Sat. 10–4.

Svendborg. Anne Hvide's Gård (regional museum), Fruestraede 3. Open May through Oct., daily 10–4; Dec., daily 12–5.

Skt. Nikolae Kirke (St. Nicholas's Church). Open daily except during services.

Zoologisk Museum (Zoological Museum), Dronningemaen 30. Open Apr. through Sept., daily 9–5; Oct. through Mar., Mon. to Fri. 9–4, Sat. and Sun. 10–4.

JUTLAND

Birds, Beaches and Runic Stones

The peninsula of Jutland (Jylland) is the only part of Denmark that is attached to the continent of Europe. Its southern boundary is the frontier with Germany. A tenth of the peninsula consists of moors and sand dunes, the latter being almost entirely along the west coast. The other nine-tenths are devoted to agriculture and, to a much lesser extent, to forestry. Esbjerg is the main deep-water port on Jutland's west, or North Sea, coast, but in recent years another has developed at Hirtshals, which takes passenger services from Britain and the Faroe Islands as well as cargo and fishing. There is also a fishing harbor at Hvide Sande. Apart from Esbjerg, the main fishing ports are still Skagen and Frederikshavn in the extreme northeast of Jutland. The geography of the eastern side is quite unlike that of the western. Along the shore facing Funen are deep, well-wooded fjords running miles inland.

Exploring Jutland

The region of Jutland bordering Germany is one that has been fought over a number of times. When bricks replaced mud and wood as Denmark's chief building material one of the first uses made of them by the Danes was the construction of the Dannevirke wall across the neck of Jutland to keep the Germans out. Today the people try to invite them into Denmark instead, tempting them with nature, open beaches and signboards with German texts. However, the population is mixed, and the provinces of Schleswig (Slesvig in Danish) and Holstein (Holsten) caused many feuds and wars between Denmark and Germany. A plebiscite in 1920 established the present boundary, when Schleswig-Holstein became part of Germany, and today the inhabitants on either side of the border cooperate or compete in such plans as an extra North Sea dike or in making Danish cultural arrangements south of the border. But still some administrative features indicate that this southernmost area has a history of its own.

Traveling north along the east coast, you first meet the island of Als, with Sønderborg, separated by the Sound. On the way you pass Gråsten Slot, rebuilt after a fire in 1757 and since then much restored. Today it serves as summer residence for the Queen's Mother, Queen Ingrid. Just before Als is Dybbøl Mølle, perhaps the most revered spot in Denmark and today a national symbol that has been re-erected three times. It is the focal point in a memorial park to the wars in 1848 and 1864. Sønderborg Slot is still intact in spite of the wars; parts of it date back to the 12th century, and it is now a museum. If time allows, the rest of Als is also worth a visit. It bears the mark of the Danfoss factories and of "riding at the ring" festivities in Sønderborg (four days, starting the second Saturday in July).

Back on the mainland again, the road is set for Åbenrå, an ancient town that has suffered from fire and bombardment through the ages. Take a walk through Slotsgade and Vaegterpladsen towards the 15th-century Brundlund Slot, a private residence not open to the public, but there is a good view of it from the road. North of Åbenrå you meet Knivsbjerg, the tallest South Jutland hill, which served as a German rallying point and was blown up by the Danes during the German occupation. Haderslev is dominated by the Domkirke (cathedral, dating back to about 1265 and later rebuilt). Christiansfeld was founded on 1 April 1773, by Moravian Brethren, who found here a refuge; their observances were similar to those of the Danish church, but with music and handicrafts playing a leading part. The settlement is still special and was awarded a European medal in 1975 for its intact atmosphere. Also visit their church and churchyard, the Gudsageren (Field of God), with female burials to the right, male burials to the left.

Our next stop is the medium-sized modern town of Kolding, dominated by the Koldinghus ruin, once a 13th-century royal residence surrounded by a moat. The castle and its chapel were burnt down by Spanish troops in 1808. From 1892 onwards the rooms have gradually been restored and house a historical museum in the castle tower. Kolding's other main attraction is Den Geografiske Have (Geographical Garden) where you can see about 2,000 different species of plants from all over the world arranged according to their habitat.

Fredericia is an important railroad junction, trains from Funen and all parts of Jutland meeting here. Before that, it was an important, though not pleasant fortress, the inhabitants being either soldiers or religious fugitives who were granted religious liberty. The ramparts are well preserved and the central part of town has straight, crossing streets, giving unobstructed fields of fire. Take a walk on the ramparts, which are five km. (three miles) long. On 6 July 1849 they withstood the assault of the Slesvig army, and on 5 July every year there is a flower pilgrimage to the soldiers' graves, followed the next day by a trooping parade and procession in the uniforms of 1849.

But don't forget the western coast of this region. From Kolding the road will take you back to the frontier district and the old community of Tønder (founded 1243). This town is known for its exquisite lace. There is a modern art museum (Sønderjyllands Kunstmuseum), but the collections of the old museum, Tønder Museum—lace, Dutch tiles, furniture, silver and faience—might well interest you more. There are many attractive houses and doorways, especially in Østergade, Vestergade and Uldgade. Kristkirken (Christchurch) is richly decorated. Though built in 1591 much of the contents are from an earlier church—a black marble font dates from 1350, the pews and the pulpit from about 1586. Also notice the handcarved epitaphs dating from 1586 to 1695, and the lectern of 1623 with 18 handcarved biblical scenes. The marshes nearby are unique in Denmark in that dikes protect this region against the periodic floods which formerly caused tremendous damage; even so, the town had to be evacuated as recently as 1976 because of the threat of flooding. Now Danish and German authorities have agreed to build an extra dike. Many couples from abroad know Tønder as a continental Las Vegas or Gretna Green because liberal Danish laws have allowed them to marry here.

Five km. (three miles) to the west nestles the lovely, thatch-roofed village of Møgeltønder. Its cobbled main street, bordered by old lime trees and 17th-century Frisian houses, is considered the most beautiful village street in Northern Europe. Here, in a 17-acre park, is the 18th-century Baroque Schackenborg manor house. The 12th-century village church, part of the estate, has 16th-century frescos, a Gothic altar-piece sculpted by Flemish artists, an arch dating back to 1240, and an outstanding 13th-century wooden Madonna and Child. The Baroque organ (1679) is the oldest church organ still in use in Denmark.

Not far away is the remarkable village of Rudbøl. The Danish-German frontier runs right through its center, though the dividing line is no more substantial than a few metal discs set among the Dutch bricks with which the street is paved. Rudbøl's inn has achieved a certain amount of fame. The building stands in Denmark, but the front entrance is in Germany.

Trip to the Past

Ribe is Denmark's oldest town, and the whole medieval town center is preserved by the National Trust. From May to mid-September a "vektor," or nightwatchman, goes around the town, telling of its ancient history and singing traditional songs. Visitors can accompany him, nightly, from the main square at 10 P.M. Ribe Cathedral is built on the site of one of Denmark's earliest wooden churches, built around 860. The present Cathedral was built between 1117 and 1225, but has undergone many alterations. The tower dates from the 14th century, its bell serving as an alarm and storm warning, with its wide view of the surrounding marshland (admission through the church). The "Cat Head Door" is said to be for the exclusive use of the devil.

The market place features the old inn known as Weis' Stue. In the parlor are panels with biblical pictures and a 400-year-old clock. A carved cupboard is dated 1500, and a candelabrum 1599. Hospitality is the rule of the house.

Many half-timbered houses can be seen in Sønderportsgade, Puggårdsgade and Sortebrødregade, many of them dating from the 16th century. Ribe's smallest building huddles at Klostergade 72. Other points of interest are the Sct. Catharinae Kirke and Kloster (Church of St. Catharine and the Black Friars Abbey), both dating from the mid-13th century. The abbey is the best-preserved and most beautiful monastery in Denmark, except for the one at Helsingør. On Slotsbanken you can view all that remains of the huge 12th-century stronghold of Riberhus. Skibbroen is the oldest Danish port. On the quay stands the Floodwave Column, whose marks show the water levels of previous floods—the top level mark is the 1634 flood, which also hit the cathedral. The dikes prevented two new floods in 1976, when the entire coastal region down to Germany was threatened by a sea a mere 12 yards below the dike top.

In days past, every town was free to set its own legislation, and the legend goes that a mother watching her son being hanged in another Jutland town cried out: "Oh, my boy, thank heaven you were not tried at Ribe." However, female criminals were treated with more consideration in Ribe. The town's legal code declared that a thief of the weaker sex should not be hanged—she was to "be buried alive, because she is a woman."

In 1973 traces of the original Ribe were found north of the river, and these excavations have brought to light coins dating from c. 700, proving that the town is the oldest in Denmark.

Esbjerg and the Western Islands

In Esbjerg we have a town that, for a change, is not old. It is, in fact, one of Denmark's youngest and is often the first impression of Denmark for Britons arriving by ship. A hundred years ago only 20 people lived here, now there are over 79,000. Apart from being Denmark's main gateway for imports and exports and an important fishing port, it is West Jutland's cultural and school center with folk high school, conservatory and museum. Being the main deep-water port on the west coast of Jutland, the town is also the home of several hundred fishing cutters, and you might visit the yards where they are built. Also interesting is the trip to the fish auction halls (but be sure to get there early if you are to see anything), and the Sealarium, where you can watch seals swimming both from above and below the surface.

Fanø is the northernmost of the three Danish tidal area islands, reached by a 20-minute ferry crossing from Esbjerg. The islanders were known as sea-faring people, and a shipbuilding industry arose about 1760. The first half of the 19th century was a successful time, and the fleet was the second largest, after Copenhagen. The ferries arrive at Nordby, which has retained its atmosphere of old sea-faring days, its seamen's church and a museum with maritime exhibits and old costumes. At the southern tip of the island, which can be reached by bus which drives along the ten-mile stretch of beach, is the idyllic village of Sønderho. In the tiny winding lanes there are thatched cottages decorated with ship's relics, figureheads and brass lanterns. The inn here is the best in Denmark, with superb decor and delicious food. There are many holiday houses to rent on Fanø and good campsites. The national costume is unchanged and still in use, at least on Sønderhoday (late July).

South of Fanø is the islet of Mandø. To reach it you have to go by the postal van which will carry you along the road at low tide. 125 people live here, they have their own church dating from 1727 and an inn (apply ahead if you want a room). Bird lovers will find this islet a paradise.

Rømø is the largest and southernmost of the islands, access is over a causeway 13 km. (eight miles) long, and the only main road is supplemented at low tide by the five km. (three miles) broad beach which is also used by automobiles. 800 people live here. A few of the farmhouses of the whaling captains from the old sea-faring times remain and one (dated 1744) at Toftum is a museum, the Nationalmuseets Kommandørgård. Nearby is Denmark's smallest school (1784). Rømø church, Sct. Clement Kirke, was a seamen's church. It has wrought-iron hat pegs above each pew and whaling captains are buried in the churchyard beneath interesting gravestones.

Holiday Haunts on the Jutland Coast

Northwest of Esbjerg stretches the promontory known as Blåvandshuk. From here it is possible to drive for miles through wonderful scenery behind the sea and dunes. After Graerup Strand you motor along some 24 km. (15 miles) of sand before reaching Henne Strand. Continuing in your vehicle with the sea on one side and the lagoon on the other, you reach the old fishing village of Hvide Sande, strategically placed between Ringkøbing Fjord and the North Sea, with a canal and locks. At the northern end of the lagoon you arrive at the North Sea resort of Søndervig.

Skipping about 80 km. (50 miles) of dunes and beach, we stop at Bovbjerg, just beyond Lemvig on the western end of the Limfjord. Here, cliffs 42 meters (140 feet) high tower above the ocean. Until breakwaters were built here in 1909 the sea had cut its way nearly 200 meters (700 feet) in less than a century.

If your time is limited and you are not yet tired of sea and sand, you may continue further up north to Thyborøn on the western mouth of the Limfjord and continue on its northern side. However, another longer route inland will offer you more variation and other landscapes and scenery.

From Bovbjerg we continue to the small towns of Lemvig and Struer. Lemvig is terraced in the hilly landscape, and you arrive and depart along hairpin bends. Dominating Struer are the factories of Bang & Olufsen, known the world over for their radio and television products. After Struer and Vinderup is Sahl Kirke with a magnificent golden altarpiece from about 1200. The gold is, in fact, copper. Not far away is the open-air museum at Hjerl Hede, where you'll find several village houses from various regions, one of them dating back to about 1530. At Hjerl Hede is a reconstructed Iron Age house which is occupied in summer. Also visit the magnificent surrounding area around the Flyndersø lake.

Now it is time to go north along the east side of the Limfjord to visit Spøttrup which will give you an impression of a medieval manor, erected about 1500 and now owned by the state and made a museum. Notice the thick walls and the knights' hall and watchmen's gallery. The adjoining gardens have been reconstructed according to old descriptions of medieval spices and medicinal herbs.

Since 1978 a high-level bridge across the Sallingsund has given easier access to the island of Mors in the Limfjord. The bridge runs between the Pain and the Torment (on Mors side), two place-names reminiscent of earlier problems coming to and from the island. The main town is Nykøbing, but the best sights are to be found among the natural sights of Legind Bjerge near the bridge, at Feggeklit, and finally at Hanklit.

We leave Mors across the Vildsund bridge, and via Thisted, where a well-known Danish poet, J. P. Jacobsen, was born. Heading northwest we reach again the North Sea coast at Klitmøller, where the country with its woods and lakes is particularly beautiful. Today it is a favorite summer resort. Off Bulbjerg coast, Denmark lost a major tourist attraction in 1978, when sea undermined the 46-meter (154-foot) high Skarreklit rock. All that now remains is a fast-eroding stump, and only local postcards tell how it once looked. You may make a detour to Frøstrup, where you can find the northernmost European storks in a private garden. Other birds can be studied inland near Bygholm.

Presently we approach a second beach at Blokhus, another popular West Jutland seaside resort, and further up north the somewhat larger Løkken, Lønstrup and Hirtshals (ferries to Norway). North of Tannisby is Råbjerg Mile, a "drifting" dune, now some four km. (2½ miles) inland which, during the past 400–500 years was moved 9 meters (30 feet) east by the west wind every year. This once fruitful area was the setting of some outdoor scenes in Peter Brook's film of *King Lear* and is today a natural dune desert reached on foot only from Kandestederne.

We have now covered so much of Western Jutland that little remains but the very tip of the peninsula where the waters of the North Sea collide with those of the Kattegat at the spit of Skaw. Just south of this point you find Skagen and Old Skagen (Gl. Skagen), popular both among artists and tourists. Many artists and writers have been inspired by the picturesque quality of Skagen and by its wonderful air and light. The local museum has an outstanding collection of paintings of the period 1830–1930 by artists connected with the locality. One of the sights of Skagen is a church tower buried by sand.

Going back south along the east coast we reach Frederikshavn with daily connections to Sweden and Norway. The fishing harbor is one of Denmark's largest. The entire area is popular with holiday-making Danes and is plentifully supplied with summer chalets (some of them for rent) and campsites.

A ferry from Frederikshavn forms the connection to the isle of Laesø, an untouched and unspoiled landscape with rich fauna and 2,600 inhabitants. Byrum's 500 inhabitants live in the biggest town in the middle of the island. If you don't bring your car to Laesø and its beaches, there are bus tours to the various views and the farmhouses with seaweed roofs. On your way you may pass an islander in her national costume richly decorated with forged silver, perhaps the most beautiful in Denmark.

Aalborg

When you reach Aalborg, you have crossed the Limfjord and leave the northern part of Jutland known as Vendsyssel. Aalborg is known for the schnapps produced here, and also the tasty Limfjord oysters which are dredged in the neighborhood. The town is the most important north Jutland town and, together with her twin town north of the fjord, the fourth largest in Denmark. You find charming combinations of new and old, and twisting lanes filled with medieval houses exist side by side with broad modern boulevards. Sights include the magnificent Jens Bangs Stenhus (Jens Bang's stone house), which has a charming wine cellar and restaurant; a 16th-century cathedral, the Budolfi Kirke, dedicated to the English St. Botolph; the early 16th-century Aalborghus and the early 15th-century Helligåndsklosteret (Monastery of the Holy Ghost). Aalborghallen, a colossal modern hall in the middle of town, is a magnificent center for concerts and exhibitions. In 1972 the Nordjyllands Kunstmuseum by the

Finnish architect Alvar Aalto with its open-air theater became the home of Danish paintings and sculptures since 1800 and of modern foreign art. Jomfru Ane Gade is a tiny cobbled street in the center of Aalborg, where there are numerous restaurants, inns, sidewalk cafés; a charming area with a lively, cosmopolitan atmosphere. North of Aalborg at Nørresundby you will find Lindholm Høje, a Viking burial place with 682 graves.

Among the excursions from Aalborg, the one to Himmerland is 160 km. (100 miles). It takes you past the late 16th-century Lindenborg Slot to Lille Vildmose, a 34-square-mile marsh where the rare black stork can still be found. After 43 km. (27 miles) Hadsund is reached and Mariager Fjord crossed. Following the southern bank inland you arrive in rosefilled Mariager, Denmark's smallest market town, and Hobro at the head of the fjord. Near Hobro is Fyrkat, another 1,000-year-old Viking settlement.

Every 4th of July thousands of Danes and Danish-Americans gather at the Rebild National Park near Aalborg to celebrate America's Independence Day. "Old Glory" and "Dannebrog" wave stoutly in the breeze, flanked by the flags of all the 50 states, and important Americans and Danes are invited to take part in speechmaking and other festivities. Since their purchase by Danish-Americans in 1911, these heather-clad hills have been a national park. In it stands the Lincoln Memorial Cabin built of logs from the original 13 states. Also in the neighborhood are the Tingbaek Kalkminer (limestone workings), with the original models of monuments by two well-known Danish sculptors.

1,400-year-old Viborg

The history of Viborg goes back to the 8th century when the town was a trading center and place of pagan sacrifice. The thousand-year-old Haervejen (ancient military road) used to be the most important connection with the outside world. Viborg was once the coronation town for Danish royalty. Legend has it that King Canute set out from here to conquer England. On sale locally are reproductions, made as cuff links, of a silver coin minted on Canute's orders and inscribed, *Knud, Englands Konge:* Canute, King of England.

Dominating Viborg is its Domkirke, at one time the largest granite church in the world. Of the original edifice, built in 1130, only the crypt remains. The cathedral was restored and reopened in 1876 after it had been damaged by fire several times. Its wall-paintings, executed between 1901 and 1913, were the work of a team of artists inspired and supervised by Joakim Skovgaard. Another church worth visiting is Søndre Sogns Kirke, an old monastery with a golden altarpiece (1520) and more than 200 paintings dating from the early 18th century.

About eight km. (five miles) south of Viborg you will find some of the loveliest scenery in Denmark. Hald Sø (Hald Lake) and the rustic heather-clad Dollerup Bakker (Dollerup Hills) together form a district where it is possible to walk for hours on end and still discover new delights. This region is also known as the "fisherman's paradise."

From Viborg Highway 16 continues to Randers. However, you are recommended to use the longer tour via Rødkaersbro and Bjerringbro which will offer you a beautiful ride along the Gudenå, Denmark's longest river.

Randers and Djursland

Randers occupies a niche in Danish history because it was here in 1340 that Niels Ebbesen killed the German oppressor, Count Gert the Bald, commander of a German army which had occupied almost all of Jutland. Ebbesen's statue stands in front of the Rådhus (Town Hall). The 15th-century Skt. Mortens Kirke has been extensively restored. The carved wooden pulpit and screen, the exquisite organ, and the saintly figures have all been re-gilded. One of the most interesting buildings in the narrow streets is the Helligåndshuset (House of the Holy Ghost) on Erik Menveds Plads. In the Middle Ages friars from the nearby monastery nursed the sick here. Today it is occupied by the Tourist Association, and on its roof there is a stork's nest. Storks are well-loved in Randers—try to stay long enough to enquire about the Stork Society, which has strange rules and rituals, and many members from all over the world.

East of Randers lies Djursland, a holiday area which draws people from all over Denmark. Here there are several fine old manor houses, churches, ancient burial places and ruins. Rosenholm Slot, the property of the Rosenkrantz family since its erection in 1560, is an imposing Danish Renaissance structure. Nearer Randers, Gammel Estrup, a grand 17th-century manor house, is now a museum full of rich period furnishings including an alchemist's cellar; and an agricultural museum. About 14 km. (eight miles) southeast of Randers off Highway 10 is the fine Baroque manor of Clausholm, set in a beautiful park with terraces and small cascades. From here, Anna Sophie Reventlow, daughter of the High Chancellor, was abducted by King Frederik IV, who married her morganatically and later made her Queen. To the east of the region is its main town, Grenå, ravaged several times in the 17th century by Swedish troops. Today Swedes still invade the town, but because of the ferry route to Varberg in Sweden. It is also possible to go by ferry to Hundested on Zealand, and there is a ferry to the isle of Anholt 44 km. (27 miles) out in the Kattegat.

A Hidden Gem

Anholt is 22 square kilometers (8½ square miles) of unspoiled nature of a very special kind. You will find here Denmark's only desert, natural beauties, 25 km. (16 miles) of beaches, and three km. (two miles) from the harbor the only town with 160 inhabitants. You can walk here happily for hours, enjoying both the idyllic Anholt Village, the desert consisting of open gravel plains filled with sand, and the viewpoint Sønderbjerg, at 47 meters (157 feet) the highest point on the island. The village has a memorial for Danes who fell against the English in the battle of 1811. To nature-lovers Anholt is a paradise with its many plants and birds. If you cross to the eastern point, Totten, you may be rewarded with the sight of seals.

It is possible to take your car to Anholt, but not necessary since you can drive only to the village. However, since ferry connections are bad, count on an overnight stay in the inn.

Mols and Ebeltoft

Below Djursland stretches the countryside of Mols. The drive to Fuglsø, Agri and Femmøller is magnificent, with rolling hills covered by heather and spruce, sandy roads winding past thatched cottages and peacefully grazing cattle, and dikes everywhere to keep the sea in place. The natives of this region have the reputation of being hillbillies, and an infinite number of stories are told of their simple ways and slow wit.

One place you must be sure to see is Ebeltoft, a miniature town which, like AErøskøbing, belongs to the past. Wandering up and down among the winding, cobbled streets lined with quaint old houses, you will imagine that you have walked out of the present into a fairytale. From Mols or Ebeltoft you are also able to see Århus, situated on a broad bay and surrounded by woods.

Århus, Old and New

Århus is Denmark's second-largest town. Its history goes back more than 1,000 years, but it is also a modern city with a bustling seaport.

The copper roof and red brick walls of the 13th-century Århus Domkirke, Scandinavia's longest church, can be seen for many miles around. Inside is the largest, most highly carved and richly colored reredos in Denmark. The pulpit dates from 1588, and the early 18th-century organ is particularly fine. Just as remarkable is the Rådhuset (Town Hall), built between 1938 and 1942. A Danish showpiece, everything about it is impressive; its unusual architecture, its lavish use of glass, its mural-decorated lobby and its immense carpet depicting a stylized map of Århus. Most people either like it or detest it on sight. Behind the Town Hall, and designed not to conflict with it, is the new Musikhuset (Concert House) inaugurated in 1982.

The best ties with the past are to be found in another church and the open-air museum. The Vor Frue Kirke (Our Lady's Church) and Kloster (monastery) in Vestergade is the oldest building in the city. The friars' court and a number of Gothic arches can still be seen. In the chapter hall are medieval frescos. South of the town, at the Moesgård manor, is the Forhistorisk Museum Moesgård, which houses the 2,000-year-old Grauballe Man, discovered in a peat bog, plus rune stones and an ethnographic collection.

The open-air museum called Den gamle By ("The Old Town") is a collection of town rather than country houses now brought together in the middle of Århus. Here there are 61 homes, each one furnished and equipped according to its period. With their streets and gardens, their shops and markets, the buildings provide an authentic picture of what life was like in the good old days. The houses are populated every year during the Festival Days in the beginning of September, and you are able to taste bread as it was baked in previous times.

The University, started in 1933 and not yet completed, has a spacious 37-acre campus. From the architectural point of view as well as the academic, it has already won an outstanding place for itself in Scandinavia. A corner of the campus grounds houses the new art museum with Danish art since 1770.

Situated on a central spot, Århus is an ideal base for exploring middle Jutland. Some places have already been described but another tour should be made to the Danish lake district.

The Lake District

Silkeborg is a modern town lying on the banks of the river Gudenå west of Århus. It is situated in the middle of some of the loveliest scenery in Denmark. The town has two museums. The Silkeborg Museum houses on its top floor the Tollund Man, dated at 2,200 years old. The new Silkeborg Kunstmuseum gives pride of place to the works of Asger Jorn, who was born here.

Surrounded by the river and lakes, it is quite natural to leave Silkeborg by water. The river winds through an area of hills covered with woods and heather. You can make the tour by rowboat, canoe, punt, or if you are less energetic by a paddle-steamer built in 1861. A *must* for anyone in this region is the ascent of Denmark's second highest hill, the 147-meter (483 foot) high Himmelbjerget (Sky Mountain). The tower on top, another 24 meters (80 feet), was inaugurated on Constitution Day, 1875, in commemoration of King Frederik VII.

Country roads run north and south of the lakes in the direction of Skanderborg. Off the southern banks near Rye are the few remaining stones of Øm. Founded in 1172 by the Cistercian Order, it was once one of the richest monasteries in that part of the world. After the Reformation Frederik II lived here for a while before having it demolished and the stones carried to Skanderborg to be used in the erection of a new castle. The museum there will show you the culture of that time and bones that had been treated surgically by the monks, and there is also a coin collection.

Samsø

Another day trip from Århus could be to the island of Samsø, but the car ferries leave from Hou, northeast of Horsens. Here, on 44 square miles, you can find a cross-section of Danish landscapes. The flora and fauna differs from that which can be found in the rest of Denmark. The Stavns Fjord is a bird sanctuary with many gulls and wading birds. Samsø also has an "English" country house in the shape of Brattingsborg, built in 1870. Other sights include the Ballebjerg viewpoint and the village of Nordby, one of the most beautiful Danish villages. Don't forget to visit the village pond surrounded by the houses of the former day laborers, today now used as summer dwellings.

Around Vejle

South of Silkeborg you find Vejle, another town with a beautiful position among water and forest-clad hills. To the east a lovely tree-lined fjord stretches to the Kattegat. A motorway bridge is being built here. North of Vejle is Grejsdalen, a mysterious valley which you can also see from the train to Jelling. Jelling is the oldest known royal dwelling. King Gorm lived here more than 1,000 years ago with his queen, and two burial mounds have long been known as the King Mound and the Queen Mound. However, the royal tombs are not under them, but, it seems, in the church itself, rather a strange feature, since they were not Christians. However, on the churchyard you will find "Denmark's Certificate of Baptism," the greater of the two runic stones outside the church. It depicts the oldest figure of Christ in Scandinavia, and the text explains that the stone was erected by King Harald over Gorm, his father, and Thyra, hismother, and that Harald christened the Danes. The event took place in about 960. The minor stone was erected by Gorm as a memorial over his queen.

West of Vejle is the little village of Billund, known because of Legoland, founded by the inventor of the famous Lego construction toy. This amusement park is entirely built of his plastic toy bricks and contains miniature copies of the Amalienborg Palace, an English provincial town, the Mount Rushmore presidents and a Wild West saloon. You could spend plenty of time here, and when you are tired of playing, go and see the antique doll collection, dating back to 1580. But the sensation here is "Titania's Palace," originally built by Sir Neville Wilkinson, who started its construction in 1907 as a gift for his daughter. Everything is a correct miniature copy of older models, and includes a bathroom basin, given by Queen Mary, who was herself a dolls house aficionado, which is inscribed "From the Queen of England to the Queen of Fairyland." In 1978 it was sold at Christie's in London to Legoland for £135,000 and was put on display there for the first time in 1979.

The last sight in the neighborhood is at Givskud, further along the Jelling road, where you will find a Lion Park (Løveparken), where 40 lions live in open surroundings. There are other species to be found here, for instance baboons and a "savanna" with elephants and camels. There is a mini-farm with animals for children.

PRACTICAL INFORMATION FOR JUTLAND

TOURIST INFORMATION. All the main towns in Jutland have tourist information offices: **Aalborg**, Østerå 8 (98–12 60 22). **Århus**, Rådhuset (Town Hall) (86–12 60 00). **Ebeltoft**, Torvet 9–11 (86–34 14 00). **Esbjerg**, Skolegade 33 (75–12 55 99). **Fredericia**, Axeltorv (75–92 13 77). **Frederikshavn**, Brotorvet 1 (98–42 32 66). **Herning**, Bredgade 35 (97–12 44 70). **Hjørring**, Akseltorv 5 (98–92 02 32). **Hobro**, Adelgade 26 (98–52 56 66). **Horsens**, Søndergade 26 (75–62 38 22). **Kolding**, Hellingkorsgade 18 (75–53 21 00). **Løkken**, Vrenstedvej 6 (98–99 10 09). **Lønstrup**, Strandvejen 90 (98–96 02 22). **Nykøbing Mors**, Havnen 4 (97–72 04 88). **Randers**, Erik Menveds Plads 1 (86–42 44 77). **Ribe**, Torvet 3–5 (75–42 15 00). **Ringkøbing**, Torvet (97–32 00 31). **Rømø**, Havnebyvej 30, Tvismark (74–75 51 30). **Samsø**, Langgade 32, Tranebjerg (86–59 14 00). **Silkeborg**, Torvet 9 (86–82 19 11). **Skagen**, Sct. Laurentiivej 18 (98–44 13 77). **Skive**, Østerbro 7 (97–52 32 66). **Saeby**, Krystaltorvet 1 (98–46 15 19). **Sønderborg**, Rådhustorvet 7 (74–42 35 55). **Thisted**, Store Torv 6 (97–92 19 00). **Tønder**, Østergade 2A (74–72 12 20). **Vejle**, "Den Smidske Gård," Søndegade 14 (75–82 19 55). **Viborg**, Nytorv 5 (86–62 16 17).

TELEPHONE CODES. We have given telephone codes for all the towns and villages in the hotel and restaurant lists that follow. These codes must be used both for local and long distance calls.

HOTELS AND RESTAURANTS. Inn vouchers are available from the tourist office at Horsens for the majority of Jutland's inns. They cost around Dkr. 195 per night, including breakfast.

Aalborg. *Central* (E), (98–12 69 33). 73 rooms, some with bath, some (M). DC, MC. *Hvide Hus* (E), (98–13 84 00). 199 rooms, all with bath. Sauna, pool, music in winter periods. DC, MC. *Phønix* (E), (98–12 00 11). 180 rooms, all with private facilities. Traditional, good food, music in winter periods. AE, DC, MC. *Scheelsminde* (E), (98–18 32 33). 70 rooms, all with private facilities. Motel with park. *Limfjordshotellet* (E), (98–16 43 33). 165 rooms, all with private facilities. Near harbor and castle. DC, MC. *Hafnia* (M) (98–13 19 00). 46 rooms, 7 with private facilities. *Park* (M), (98–12 31 33). 56 rooms with bath. Restaurant, sauna, rooms with TV. AE, DC, MC.

Restaurants. *Duus Vinkjaelder* (E). Serves wine from centuries-old wine cellars under Jens Bang's house. *Faklen* (E), Jomfru Ane Gade. Waiters wear tartan kilts. International menu. DC, MC, V. *Jomfru Ane* (E), Jomfru Ane Gade. Pleasant. DC. *Stygge Krumpen* (E). AE, DC, MC, V. *Caféen* (M). AE, DC, MC, V. *Fyrtøjet* (M), Jomfru Ane Gade. Open courtyard in summer. DC, MC, V. *Kniv og Gaffel* (M), Maren Turisgade. Specializes in beef, but other dishes available. Open courtyard in summer; in one of Aalborg's oldest houses. *Regensen* (M). Steak house with open grill. AE, DC, MC, V. *Sokrates* (M), Nørregade 29. Greek specialties with appropriate music; sidewalk tables in summer. DC. *Peppe's Pizza* (I), C. W. Obels Plads. Charming courtyard and half-timbered house. Very good value.

Åbenrå. *Hvide Hus* (E), (74–62 47 00). 68 rooms, all with private facilities. Garden, sauna. AE, DC, MC, V. *Missionshotellet* (I), (74–62 36 12). 90 beds. (BE).
Restaurant. *De 3 Makreller.* Quaint cellar restaurant.

Anholt. *Anholt Kro* (I).

Århus. *Atlantic* (E), (74–13 11 11). 90 rooms, all with private facilities. At the harbor; bar, music, dance. AE, DC, MC, V. *Marselis* (E), (74–14 44 11). 102 rooms, all with private facilities. Bar. AE, DC, MC, V. *Royal* (E), (74–12 00 11). Nearly 150 years old but newly restored. Central, with elegant conservatory restaurant, *The Queen's Garden* (serves special tourist dinner). AE, DC, MC, V. *La Tour* (E), (86–16 78 88). 100 beds, all rooms with bath. Motel. (BE). AE, DC, MC, V. *Missionshotellet Ansgar* (M), (74–12 41 22). 169 rooms, 153 with private facilities. At station; garden. DC, MC, V. *Ritz* (M), (74–13 44 44). 70 rooms, all with private facilities. Near station; clean and well-kept. AE, DC, MC, V.

Restaurants. *Café Mahler* (E). Vestergade 39. Excellent food; intimate with few tables. DC, MC, V. *De 4 Årstider* (The 4 Seasons) (E), Åboulevarden. 47. French cuisine, excellent food, one of the finest restaurants in Europe. Closed Sun. and public holidays. AE, DC, MC, V. *Gammel Åbyhøj* (E), Åbyhoj Bakke Allé 1. Excellent French cuisine; dining room in an old villa. AE, DC, MC, V. *Queens Garden* (Royal Hotel) (E), St. Torv 4 (06–12 00 11). Very good food in plant-filled conservatory. Closed Sun. *Restaurant René* (E), (74–12 12 11). Small menu with daily specialties; all fresh food. Closed Sun. and Mon. *Hereford Beefstouw* (M), Skolegade 5 (74–13 53 25). Excellent chain for best quality steaks. *Musikhusets* (M), (74–12 12 33). Modern restaurant, with interesting music and good food. AE, DC, MC.

Near town are *Sjette Frederik's Kro,* Risskov, an old inn situated on cliffs above the bay and among woods. At Marselisborg Wood are *Frederikshøj Kro* with excellent cuisine at moderate prices, and *Skovmøllen,* an old half-timbered water mill.

Billund. (For Legoland). *Hotel Vis-a-Vis* (E), Astvej 10 (75–33 12 44). 108 rooms, all with private facilities; adjacent to Legoland and very near airport and station. AE, DC, MC, V.

Ebeltoft. *Hvide Hus* (E), (74–34 14 66). 110 rooms with private facilities, some with balcony overlooking the bay. Modern; rooftop restaurant, sauna, pool, golf. Also 12 2–6 bed apartments. AE, DC, MC, V. *Molskroen* (M), (74–36 22 00). 22 rooms, 17 with private facilities. Near beach in Fenmøller. DC, MC, V.
Restaurants. *Mellem Jyder,* next to old Town Hall; *Den skaeve Kro.*

Esbjerg. *Scandic Hotel Olympic* (E), (75–18 11 88). 87 rooms, all with private facilities. *Ansgar Missionhotellet* (M), (75–12 82 44). 63 rooms, 53 with private facilities. AE, DC, MC. *Britannia* (M), (75–13 01 11). 79 rooms, all with bath. Music on weekends. AE, DC, MC, V. *Bell-Inn* (I), (75–12 01 22). 32 rooms, all with private facilities. AE, DC, MC, V.

Restaurants. *Art Pavilion* (E). Excellent food with views over harbor. *Sand's* (M), Solegade 60. Good Danish food, large helpings, reasonable prices and pleasant atmosphere. *Hereford Beefstouw* (I), Kongensgade 130 (75–13 04 55). Excellent steaks. DC, MC.

Fanø. *Danland på Fanø* (M), (75–16 32 77). 6-bed apartments with bath and kitchen; weekly rental. Sauna, pool. MC, V. *Kongen af Danmark* (M), (05–16 33 33). 45 rooms, all with private facilities. Also six 2–4 bed apartments, with private facilities, and kitchen. Sauna. *Sønderho Kro* (M), (75–16 40 09). Charming inn in idyllic village. DC. *Golfhotel* (I), (75–16 30 43). 26 beds, private bath. *Kellers Hotel* (I), (75–16 30 88). 15 rooms, 8 with bath.

Fredericia. *Landsoldaten* (M), (75–92 15 55). 49 rooms, most with private facilities. Bar, Music. DC, MC, V.

Frederikshavn. *Jutlandia* (E), (98–42 42 00). 105 rooms, all with bath. Music and dance Fri. and Sat. AE, DC, MC, V. *Hoffmanns* (M), (08–42 21 66). 74 rooms, 37 with bath. Cozy and well-furnished. AE, DC, MC, V. *Lisboa* (M), (98–42 21 33). 42 rooms, all with private facilities. Motel; good service. AE, DC, MC, V.

Grenå. *Du Nord* (M), (86–32 25 00). 100 rooms, all with private facilities, some (E); also apartments with 4 beds, bath and kitchen. Garden, pool, music, dance. AE, DC, MC, V.

Haderslev. *Haderslev* (M), (74–52 60 10). 70 rooms, all with private facilities, some (E). Motel in park; music and dance Sat. in winter. AE, DC, MC, V.

Hanstholm. *Hantsholm* (M), (97–96 10 44). 80 rooms, all with bath. Unusual cliff setting; sauna, pool, golf, garden. AE, DC, MC, V.

Herning. *Birkegården* (E), (97–22 15 22). 55 rooms, all with private facilities. Garden, pool. (BE). AE, DC, MC, V. *Eyde* (E), (97–22 18 00). 96 rooms, all doubles with private facilities. Bar. AE, DC, MC, V. *Hotel Corona* (I), (07–12 54 44). 54 rooms, 17 with private facilities. DC, MC.

Himmelbjerget. *Landsbykroen,* Skanderborg (I), (86–94 37 16). 20 rooms, 14 with private facilities. At Nørre Vissing on Skanderborg-A 15 road. Rural surroundings. Possibilities for angling and boat-hire. DC, MC, *Gl. Rye Kro* (I), (86–89 80 42). 35 rooms, 21 with bath. Modern wing added to old inn. For anglers. (BE). DC, MC, V.

Horsens. *Bygholm Parkhotel* (E), (75–62 23 33). 150 rooms, 130 with bath. 18th-cent. castle in idyllic park. (BE). AE, DC, MC. *Jørgensens* (M), (75–62 16 00). 45 rooms, 20 with bath. In Baroque mansion, modernized. AE, DC, MC, V.

Restaurant. *Steak-House Helene.* Spanish-style, dance. AE, DC, MC, V.

Hovborg. *Hovborg Kro* (M), (75–39 60 33). 58 rooms, 55 with private facilities. Lodgings and food in old inn in rural surroundings. Good for anglers. DC, MC, V.

Hvidsten. Restaurant. *Hvidsten Kro* (I), (06–47 70 22). Historic old country inn with picturesque interior. Also has 12 beds. (BE).

Karup. *Centrum* (M), (97–10 12 80). 14 rooms, 8 with private facilities, some (I). Motel, for anglers. (BE).

Kolding. *Saxildhus* (E), (75–52 12 00). 95 rooms, all with bath and some with balcony. An outstanding hostelry, near castle, bar, music. AE, DC, MC, V. *Tre Roser* (E), (75–53 21 22). 95 rooms with bath; just in (E) category. Motel which also has 4-bed apartments with kitchenette (weekly rentals). Pool, sauna, garden, park. DC, MC, V. *Kolding* (M), (75–52 50 00). 44 rooms, all with bath. Bistro, disco. AE, DC, MC, V.*Saxildhus* (E), 75–52 12 00). 95 rooms, all with bath and some with balcony. An outstanding hostelry, near castle, bar, music. AE, DC, MC, V.

Restaurant. *Krybi-i-Ly* (M), (75–56 25 55). At Taulov on Kolding-Middelfart highway overlooking Kolding Fjord. Also has 76 beds (E). DC, MC, V.

Laesø. *Carlsen's Hotel* (I), Vesterø Havn (98–49 94 15). 20 beds. At ferry berth; restaurant.

Restaurant. *Bakken,* at Byrum.

Nørre Nebel *(Nymindegab).* *Nymindegab Kro* (M), (75–28 82 11). 37 rooms, 23 with private facilities. Magnificent scenery, overlooking Ringkøbing Fjord. Excellent food; sauna, garden, fishing. Also has 5-bed apartments with kitchen (day or weekly rentals). (BE). DC, MC.

Øsløs. *Bygholm Holiday Center* (I), (97–99 31 39). 18 beds. Also motel apartments of 4 or 6 beds and shower. In sanctuary between Thisted and Fjerritsleve on the Limfjorden. Pool, sauna, riding, fishing, own beach, cafeteria; camping.

Randers. *Scandic Hotel Kongens Ege* (E), (86–43 03 00). 88 rooms, all with bath. Nightclub. AE, DC, MC, V. *Randers* (M), (86–42 34 22). 82 rooms, all with bath. One of Denmark's best: attractive decor, personalized service, delicious food. AE, DC, MC, V.

Restaurant. *Grill Room* at Randers Hotel highly recommended.

Ribe. *Dagmar* (E), (75–42 00 33). 50 rooms, all with bath. Atmospheric 16th-cent. building, fine antiques. AE, DC, MC, V. *Weis' Stue* (I), (05–42 07 00). 9 beds, no room with private bath. In a protected 16th-cent. house; interior has the oldest cupboard in Denmark and Dutch tiles (this inn has been copied by an enthusiastic hotel owner in Maine). (BE).

Ringkøbing. *Fjordgården* (M), (97–32 14 00). 60 rooms, all with bath. Music on summer evenings, bar, garden, sauna. AE, DC, MC, V. *Danland i Søndervig* (I), (07–33 92 00). 16 rooms, 5 with bath. Also 90 apartments. MC.

Rold Skov. *Rold Stor-Kro* (M), (98–37 51 00). 27 km. south of Aalborg in Rebild National Park. 73 rooms with bath, 9 without. Rooms in all price categories. Sauna, pool, garden, angling, hunting. DC, MC.

Saeby. *Viking* (I), (98–46 17 00). Modern facilities. DC, MC, V. *Voerså Kro* (I), (98–46 00 06). 12 rooms. 16 km. (10 miles) south, in picturesque surroundings. Inn with folk dancing in summer in garden; music, occasional dancing. Cozy tap room. (BE).

Samsø. *Nordby Kro* (M), (86–59 60 86). 14 rooms, 1 with private facilities. Also eight 2–4 bed apartments with bath and kitchen. *Pension Verona* (I), (06–59 61 20). 13 rooms, 2 with private facilities.

Silkeborg. *Impala* (E), (86–82 03 00). 60 rooms, all with bath. Fine view, color T.V., indoor pool, sauna, garden, music Sat. (BE). AE, DC, MC, V. *Dania* (M), (86–82 01 11). 47 rooms, all with bath. Bar, music. AE, DC, MC, V.

Restaurants. *Dania* has restaurant, bar and lodge.

Skagen. *Skagen* (E), (98–44 22 33). 55 beds, all with private facilities. Pool, garden. *Strandly Skagen* (M), (98–44 11 31). 23 rooms, 9 with private facilities.

Also four 2–4 bed apartments with bathroom and kitchen. *Skagen Sømandshiem* (M), (98–44 21 10). 35 rooms, 17 with private facilities.

Restaurants. *De to Have* (The Two Seas), on the spit of Skaw. Summer restaurant. *Fiskerestauranten,* opposite the fishermen's houses, fish market and boat moorings. All kinds of fish served in traditional atmosphere.

Skanderborg. *Skanderborghus* (E), (86–52 09 55). 47 rooms, 46 with bath. Modern, magnificent lakeside location out of town, with sauna and garden. AE, DC, MC.

Sønderborg. *Interscan Hotel Sønderborg* (E), (04–42 26 00). 102 rooms, all with private facilities. AE, DC, MC, V. *City* (M), (74–42 16 26). 13 rooms, 12 with bath. DC, MC, V. *Ansgar* (I), (74–42 24 72). 44 rooms, 33 with bath. AE, DC, MC, V. *Arnkilhus* (I), (74–42 23 36). 13 rooms, some with bath. *Garni* (I), (74–42 34 33). 17 rooms with bath.

Thisted. *Aalborg* (M), (97–92 35 66). 32 rooms, most with bath. Near swimming pool. (BE). DC, MC, V.

Tønder. *Hostrups* (I), (74–72 21 29). 24 rooms, all with bath. *Hotel Abild* (I), (04–72 22 92). 16 rooms, 9 with private facilities.

Vejle. *Munkebjerg* (E), (75–72 35 00). 148 rooms, all with private facilities. Magnificently located on a fjord 6½ km (4 miles) east. Indoor swimming pool, sauna, tennis and riding. SAS check-in counter and heliport. AE, DC, MC, V. *Scandic Hotel Australia* (E), (75–82 43 11). 85 rooms, all with bath. Bar. AE, DC, MC, V. *Hedegården* (M), (75–82 08 33). 60 rooms, all with bath. Modern motel 3 km. (2 miles) from center. DC, MC, V. *Grejsdalens* (I), (05–85 30 04). 7 rooms without bath. Small with limited facilities, but beautifully situated.

Restaurants. *Flamingo, Grand Bistro, Graddisco* and *Moulin Rouge* have dancing.

Viborg. *Golf Hotel Viborg* (E). 100 rooms, all with private facilities. Sauna and indoor pool. AE, DC, MC, V. *Kongenshus* (I), (97–54 81 25). 10 rooms, none with private facilities. Motel. *Viborg (I), (66–62 27 22).* 20 rooms with bath.

Restaurants. *Salonen,* with concerts and dancing. Closed Mon. MC, V.

Between Viborg and Århus, *Kongensbro Kro* (I), (86–87 01 77), serves simple, typically Danish dishes and has 26 attractive rooms for overnight guests; good fishing and the Gjern automobile museum nearby. AE, DC, MC, V.

Youth Hostels

There are youth hostels at the following places: Åbenrå, Aalborg, Blokhus, Brande, Århus, Bryrup, Ebeltoft, Esbjerg, Farsø, Fredericia, Frederikshavn, Gram, Grenå, Grindsted, Haderslev, Hals, Henne Strand, Herning, Hirstshals, Hjørring, Hobro, Holstebro, Horsens, Hvide Sande, Højer, Juelsminde, Kolding, Kruså, Løgumkloster, Laesø, Nykøbing Mors, Oksbøl, Randers, Ribe, Ringkøbing, Roslev, Ry, Rødding, Rønde, Skagen, Skanderborg, Skørping, Struer, Saeby, Sønderborg, Thisted, Tinglev, Samsø (Tranebjerg), Tønder, Varde, Vejle, Viborg.

Camping

Camp sites are signposted by the international wigwam sign.

HOW TO GET AROUND. By plane. There are direct flights from Copenhagen to Århus, Billund, Aalborg, Karup, Sønderborg, Skrydstrup, Thisted and Esbjerg.

By boat. From Copenhagen a good way to northern Jutland is by comfortable and frequent car and passenger ferries from Kalundborg to Århus or to Juelsminder, Hundested to Grenå, and, shortest, Sjaellands Odde to Ebeltoft. Cars are carried on all these services.

By train. There are "L" and "IC" train services from Copenhagen to the main towns, taking 5–6 hours, and trains connect all important points on the peninsula. The DSB (Danish State Railways) special sightseeing ticket scheme—comprising return fare from Copenhagen Central Station and admission charges—will take you to Legoland in Billund.

By bus. Jutland is covered by a network of buses, most of them run by the DSB (Danish State Railways). As elsewhere in Denmark, bus fares are high, with no reductions on return fares, so it may be worth asking about discount passes ("rabat-kort"). In Århus tickets cost Dkr. 8, but with a discount pass they can cost Dkr. 5.50. Århus also has one-day tourist tickets, valid for a sightseeing tour plus free bus rides in and around the city.

By car. It is advisable to book ahead for ferry crossings, especially in summer. Particularly busy are the Kalundborg–Århus crossing (state run), and Sjaellands Odde–Ebeltoft and Grenå–Hundested (privately run). Consult an FDM office, the car ferry office, or the pamphlet "Car Ferries" on timetables, prices and booking. All you need to do is leave your car's registration number in order to book. Bookings for the state routes can be made at any major rail station 2 months ahead.

Jutland differs from the rest of Denmark in having more open country, and long, lonely stretches of road with little traffic.

By bicycle. Bicycles are available for hire in every sizeable town. Tourist offices either hire out bikes themselves or will refer you to dealers who do so. They will also suggest tours.

PLACES TO VISIT. We give here the opening times of recommended places to visit, details of which you will find in the chapter. For further information consult local tourist information offices. Note that churches and cathedrals are usually open daily except during services.

Aalborg. Aalborghus (Aalborg Castle). Parts (e.g. dungeon) open in summer, Mon. to Fri. 8–4.

Budolfi Kirke (St. Botolph's Cathedral). Open weekdays 9–3, Sat. 9–noon. Carillon plays every hour 9 A.M.–10 P.M. Closed during services.

Helligåndsklosteret (Monastery of the Holy Ghost). Now a residence for senior citizens. Guided tours Mon. to Fri., June 20 to Aug. 19, at 2 P.M. Adm. Dkr. 10. Out of season visits by arrangement with Aalborg Tourist Bureau.

Nordjyllands Kunstmuseum (North Jutland Museum of Art). Open daily 10–5, closed Mon. except in July and Aug. Adm. Dkr. 5. Guided tours by arrangement.

Århus. Forhistorisk Museum Moesgård (Museum of Prehistory at Moesgård Manor). Open Apr. to mid-Sept., daily 10–5; mid-Sept. through Mar., Tues. to Sun. 10–5, closed Mon.

Den gamle By ("The Old Town" open-air museum). Open Apr., daily 10–4; May through Sept., daily 10–5; Oct., Mon. to Sat. 10–4, Sun. 10–Nov. through Mar., daily 11–3.

Billund. Legoland. Open Apr. 29 to Sept. 17, daily 10–8. Adm. Dkr. 40, children half price.

Givskud. Løveparken (Lion Park). Open May to mid-June, daily 10–4.30; mid-June to mid-Aug., daily 10–6; mid-Aug. through Sept., daily 10–4.30.

Hjerl Hede. Hjerl Hede (open-air museum). Open Apr. through Oct., daily 9–5. Demonstrations of old crafts: July, daily 1.30–5. Open weekends in Dec., 10–5 for old-time Christmas preparations.

Hobro. Lincoln Log Cabin (Lincoln Memorial Cabin). In the Rebild Bakker (Rebild Hills). Open mid-May through Aug., daily 10–5.

Thingbaek Kalkminer (Tingbaek Limestone Workings). Opening times as for Lincoln Log Cabin.

Kolding. Den Geografiske Have (Geographical Garden). Open Apr. through May, daily 9–6; June through Aug., daily 9–8; Sept. through Mar., daily 9–6.
Koldinghus. Open Apr. through Sept., Tues. to Sun. 10–5; Oct. through Dec. weekends 12–3.

Randers. Clausholm. Open May 15 through Sept. 15, daily 10–12 and 2–5:30.
Gammel Estrup. Jutland's Manor House Museum in castle, and Danish Agriculture Museum on farm. Open May to Oct. daily 10–5. Nov. to April Castle open Tues. to Sun. 11–3, Farm Sat. and Sun. 11–4.
Rosenholm Slot. Manor, park and gardens open mid-June to Aug. 5, daily 10–5, closed 12–1.

Ribe. Ribe Domkirke (Ribe Cathedral). Open in summer 10–6, Sun. 12.30–6. Oct. through Apr., Mon. to Sat. 10–12 and 2–4, Sun. 2–4. No admittance during services.
Sct. Catharinae Kirke og Kloster (Church of St. Catharine and the Black Friars Abbey). Open all year, 10–12 and 2–4.

Rømø. Nationalmuseets Kommandorgård (island museum), Toftum. Open May through Sept., daily 10–6; Oct. through Dec., 10–3.

Samsø. Brattingsborg. Park open June through Sept., Tues. and Fri. 10–4.

Silkeborg. Silkeborg Kunstmuseum (art museum). Open Apr. through mid-May, daily 10–5; mid-May through Oct., Tues. to Sun. 10–3, closed Mon.; Nov. through mid-Dec., Tues. to Fri. 12–4, Sat. and Sun. 10–4, closed Mon.
Silkeborg Museum. Open Apr., Wed., Sat. and Sun. 12–4; May through Oct., daily 10–5; Nov. through mid-Dec., Wed., Sat. and Sun. 12–4.

Skagen. Skagen Museum. Open Apr., daily 11–3; May, daily 11–5; June through Aug., daily 10–6; Sept., daily 10–5; Oct., daily 11–3; Nov. through Jan. Wed. to Fri. 1–3, Dat. and Sun. 11–3.

Skanderborg. Øm Kloster (Øm Monastery). Open Apr., Tues. to Sun. 9–5, closed Mon.; May through Aug., Tues. to Sun., 9–6, closed Mon.; 1 Sept. to 21 Oct., Tues. to Sun. 9–4, closed Mon.

Sønderborg. Dybbøl Mølle (Dybbøl Mill). Open Apr. through mid-June and mid-Aug. through Sept., 1–4, mid-June through mid-Aug. 10–5.
Gråsten Slot (Gråsten Castle). Except when castle is occupied, chapel is open Apr. through Sept., daily 10–12 and 2–5; and park is open all year from 7 to sunset.
Sønderborg Slot (Sønderborg Castle). Open May through Sept., daily 10–5; Oct. through Mar., 1–4, Apr. and Oct. 10–4.

Spøttrup. Spøttrup. Open Apr., Sun. and bank holidays 11–5, closed Mon. to Sat.; May through Aug., daily 10–6; Sept., daily 10–5.

Tønder. Sønderjyllands Kunstmuseum (South Jutland Museum of Modern Art). Open May through Oct., Tues. to Sun., 10–5; Nov. through Apr., Tues. to Sun. 1–5, closed Mon.
Tønder Museum. Open May through Oct., Tues. to Sun., 10–5; Nov. through Apr., Tues. to Sun., 1–5, closed Mon.

SPORTS. Water sports are understandably popular here. There are over 320 km. (200 miles) of continuous sand beach on the west coast; good bathing can also be had on the eastern side. You can drive on the beach from Løkken to Blokhus as well as the 18-km. (11-mile) stretch of Fanø's coastline. The best known resorts include Skagen, Hirtshals, Løkken, Blokhus, Ålbek, Saeby, Aså, and Hals; Århus and Grenå also have fine beaches.

There's excellent **sailing** on the waters of the East Jutland fjords and the Limfjord, and **fishing** for salmon trout in the West Jutland streams. The river Guden, Denmark's longest, offers wonderful possibilities for a week's **canoeing** or **kayaking** tour from Tørring to Randers.

Aalborg, Århus, Brønderslev, Ebeltoft, Esbjerg, Fanø, Vesterhavsbad, Frederikshavn, Herning, Hobro, Holstebro, Horsens, Kolding, Randers, Silkeborg, Skagen, Skive, Skjern, Vejle and Viborg all have **golf** courses.

There are excellent opportunities for **jogging** in forests and along beaches.

ISLE OF BORNHOLM

The Baltic Hideaway

Far from the rest of Denmark, in the Baltic between Sweden and Poland, is a 225 square mile island. Since 1658, when Jens Kofoed's islanders threw out Swedish troops, the Bornholmers' Danish nationality and feelings have never been doubted. The 150 km. (93 miles) of coastline change from cliffs and rocks to skerries and dunes of the world's finest sand. The flora and fauna is special, too, and here you'll find Almindingen, the third-largest forest in Denmark. Bornholm is the only place in Denmark where towns were built on sloping rocks and the independent farmers never settled in villages. There are many special trades connected with a "Bornholmer," hence the word designates an islander, a grandfather clock—or a smoked herring. Today fortified round churches and ruins still bear witness to times not so idyllic.

Exploring Bornholm

You may wonder how so many natural sights could have been put together as on Bornholm. It seems as if the "splendid isolation" also has concentrated and isolated a lot of nature that was not allowed to spread to the rest of Denmark. So even if you have seen other parts of Denmark you will be surprised here.

Rønne

The main city if Rønne, port for ships to Copenhagen, Sweden and Germany (the latter service is rather erratic). When arriving by ship you will

131

be fascinated by the half-timbered tower which appears before you disembark, but the church is young, from 1915–18, and the real half timber is to be found in the streets behind the church. The majority of those houses were built around 1800, though some go back as far as late 17th century. Notice that nearly all houses have but one story, a fact that has given the city a large extension. The most beautiful of the houses is Erichsen's Farm in Laksegade where Holger Drachmann, the poet, and Dr. Zahrtmann, the Bornholm painter, lived.

An interesting museum, the Forsvarsmuseum, Defense Museum, is at Kastellet in Rønne. On the last Thursday in the month, from April to December, the Rønne Day gives rise to much activity and, among other amenities, free horse-carriage rides are given in the old town.

Jons Kapel and Hammershus

Let us start our island excursions with a visit to the northwest corner. The bicycle is a very popular means of transportation, although many people also travel by car. We pass through Hasle, well suited for discovery walks, and continue to Jons Kapel on the coast. Before reaching it you may make detours to the coast to see tiny Helligpeder and Teglkås.

According to legend, Brother Jon, the monk, lived in a cave on the steep cliff. He gave his sermons from the rock, which since then has borne the name Jons Kapel (Jon's Chapel). He must have had strong legs and lungs, since he lived on a rock 40 meters (130 feet) high and preached from the 22-meter (72-foot) high Pulpit rock.

Jons Kapel is halfway between Hasle and the marvellous ruins of the Hammershus Slot. The castle was built about 1255 as a fortress on a strategic spot. The stronghold was in use until 1743, but before that time its importance had decreased. It was occupied by Swedish troops in 1648, but Jens Kofoed, the Bornholm hero, killed its governor and the castle was given back to Denmark. The remaining ruins were protected in 1822, the biggest in North Europe.

At Borrelyng young children would enjoy a visit to the small zoo where there are animals roaming free in a natural environment.

Fashionable Allinge and Sandvig

The dominating Hammerknude with a good view from the lighthouse stands as the northern protection of Bornholm against the sea and enemy ships of earlier days. It also protects the twin towns of Sandvig and Allinge, together with the fashionable district of Bornholm. Here you find most of the hotels, but also several low half-timbered houses, especially in Allinge. In spite of the modern signs of civilization one of the characteristic Bornholm smokehouse chimneys still dominates the town. Also from these towns you can walk along the coast. Tejn and Sandkås further down the north coast are other popular beach resorts.

A Round Church

But, for a change, go inland to Olsker. Its church will serve as your introduction to the four round churches of Bornholm. They were all erected about 1150, and with their shape and thick walls they served a double purpose as both physical and spiritual protection of the poor souls who were often attacked by pirates or enemy armies. The church was defended from the third story. The church at Olsker is the smallest but tallest of the round churches.

Rø and Its Neighborhood

Our next stop is at Rø between Helligdomsklipperne and Rø Plantage (plantation). If you choose the Helligdomsklipperne on the coast you will meet a famous rock formation towering up to 22 meters (72 feet) above sea level and filled with crevices, caves and rock columns. It is one of the great natural sights of Bornholm, and in summer it is also possible to see it from the sea. You may then realize why it got its name, which may be translated as the Sanctuary or Sacred Thing.

Rø Plantage is a natural sight of quite another kind. Here as you walk in heather, among trees or on stones, you may meet the black woodpecker or deer. Scenery that you won't forget soon surrounds the artificial lake.

Østerlars and Gudhjem

From Rø we go inland once more, now heading for the greatest of the round churches at Østerlars. This church seems to be the most imposing of all because of the strong buttresses. The structure is the same as we saw at Olsker, only this one is better adorned, and better suited for defense purposes. The nave diameter is about 16 meters (18 yards).

You will probably understand why generations of painters have visited Gudhjem, whether you see it from the top of the Bokul Klippeknude (cliff) or from the narrow roads looping down the terraces to the charming little village. The small, well-kept houses have to a great extent been carved out of the rock, and two little harbors and the smokehouses give evidence of the main occupation, at least outside the tourist season.

A Riviera Tour and a Prize Town

Ever been to the Riviera? If so, compare the Bornholm counterpart along the coast road from Gudhjem to Salene on the Svaneke road. Shortly after leaving the coast a path leads from the Hotel Randkløveskår down to the coast. A little inland you find the Randkløveskår, a narrow gorge between tall rock formations, later dividing into two clefts. Now refreshed we continue along the main road to Svaneke.

In 1975 the Council of Europe awarded a gold medal for the "consistent preservation of the historical character of the typical little port" to the easternmost Danish provincial town, Svaneke. So here you will meet mostly 18th- or 19th-century houses. The harbor was cut into the rock, and steep streets and houses on high plinths show the difficulties of constructing this original fishing-hamlet in the Middle Ages. Two different mills are its landmarks. But it seems that conditions were not so harsh as one might believe, because you find here vines, figs and mulberries.

Inland, between Svaneke and Nexø, you find a peculiar landscape known as the Paradisbakkerne (Paradise Hills). A beautiful view will meet you among the valleys full of rocks, woodland and forest lakes. The best "entrance" to this area is from Klinteby west of Nexø. Map and route descriptions for this area have been worked out to secure the best enjoyment from your visit, where you can only move on foot. Marked tours take 1, 2 or 3 hours respectively.

Sand, Dunes and Beaches

The Bornholm coast, from Nexø to Boderne on the south coast, is the area almost entirely devoted to bathing and water sports, although you will also find beaches on other parts of the coast. Some people even bathe from the rocks. The water is shallow and well suited for the children. At Dueodde you find dunes 14 meters (45 feet) high and miles upon miles of beach with the most fine-grained sand in the world. Here is also the 44-meter (145 feet) tall lighthouse with a marvelous view from its top.

Central Bornholm

Let us conclude our visit to the Bornholm landscapes with a glance at the central part. It is dominated by one town, Åkirkeby, and the third-largest Danish forest, the Almindingen. Åkirkeby is the oldest town on the island with a municipal charter from 1346 and in the Middle Ages a spiritual center as well. You can see that when visiting the Å Kirke, Bornholm's largest church, built in the second half of the 13th century. Both walls and tower are well suited for defense purposes, but the church is not round. The church furniture here is worth studying. The altarpiece and pulpit are Dutch Renaissance from about 1600; there is also one of the best examples of a Scandinavian Romanesque font, of the same age as the church. Eleven arcaded panels depict scenes from the life of Christ, and they are explained with more than 500 runic letters also cut into the sandstone. More runes are to be found on stones in the porch.

The Almindingen is one of the most varied Danish forests, with trees, rocks, lakes and ponds. You find here the Rytterknaegten, Bornholm's highest "mountain" (156 meters or 516 feet!) with the Kongeminde tower, even now, it seems, too low to come above the treetops of this vast area. Near the Rytterknaegten you can take a walk in the Echo Valley (Ekkodalen) with walls 22 meters (72 feet) over you.

The forest is only 16 km. (10 miles) from our starting point, Rønne. On your way back you may make detours to the round churches at Nylars (between Åkirkeby and Rønne) and Nyker northeast of Rønne. The one at Nylars is the best preserved and most decorated of the four Bornholm round churches.

Christiansø

Before leaving Bornholm, you should make a point of crossing to the idyllic island of Christiansø (Christian's Island), the largest of the group of islets that includes Frederiksø, Graesholm, and other smaller rock formations. Originally a bastion, only the towers "Storetårn" and "Lilletårn" remain of the fort, which was started in 1684 and dismantled in 1855. The barracks, street and the gardens, for which the earth was transported in boats, have a distinctive atmosphere of their own. Not only was the foundation of the bastion an architectural achievement, but the flora is also something special, with vines and Southern European plants that are watered only by rain water from the basins. There is no ground water on the island.

Although no longer used as a fortification, all the islets come under the Ministry of Defense, and the 118 inhabitants pay no local taxes.

Graesholm is an inaccessible bird sanctuary. It is the only place in Denmark where the razorbill and guillemot breed.

PRACTICAL INFORMATION FOR BORNHOLM

TOURIST INFORMATION. The main tourist information offices are at **Allinge,** Kirkegade 6 (53–98 00 01) and **Rønne,** Havnen (53–95 08 10). There are offices also at: **Åkirkeby, Gudhjem, Hasle, Nexø, Svaneke** and **Tejn.** For activity holidays and all types of bookings: *Bornholms Kongresbureau,* Snellemark 13, DK-300 Rønne (53–95 12 11).

TELEPHONE CODES. We have given the Bornholm telephone code for all the towns and villages in the hotel and restaurant lists that follow. This code must be used for local as well as long distance calls.

HOTELS AND RESTAURANTS. Bornholm has long been a favorite summer holiday resort of Danes and tourists alike. Recent hotel development has provided plenty of modern accommodations, primarily in Rønne and the coastal resorts. As well as the hotels listed, some of which have apartments, Bornholm offers quite a number of small holiday homes for renting, many of which are well built and equipped. The tourist offices at Åkirkeby, Allinge, Nexø, Rønne and Svaneke handle bookings.

There are youth hostels at Gudhjem, Hasle, Neksø (Dueodde), Rønne, Sandvig-Allinge, and Svaneke, and about 20 camping sites are dotted along the coast, with one inland at Åkirkeby.

And, of course—as elsewhere in Denmark—you can eat well practically anywhere.

Åkirkeby. *Kanns* (M), (53–97 40 12). 47 beds, all with bath. Garden. (BE).

Allinge. *Abildgard* (E), at Sandkås (53–98 09 55). 37 rooms with shower. Half-board terms; small apartments with fridge but no cooking facilities. Tennis, garden, sauna, pool, solarium. *Hotel Frieden* (E), at Sandkås (53–98 04 25). 41 rooms with private facilities. Indoor pool and sauna. Also 8 apartments with bath. *AEblehaven* (M), (53–98 12 22). 280 beds in 70 apartments with kitchen (weekly rentals).
Restaurant. *Grotten.* At Sandkås. Dance restaurant, with an underground disco set in the rocks.

Gudhjem. *Ellebaek* (M), (53–98 51 00), some (I); 25 rooms, 16 with private facilities; pension only; garden. *Helligdommen* (M), (53–98 40 20). 21 rooms, 20 with bath. (BE). *Thern's* (I), (53–98 50 99). 45 beds; garden.
Restaurant. *Bokulhus.* On top of Bokul rock; fish specialties.

Hasle. *Herold* (M), (53–98 40 24). 18 rooms, 14 rooms with bath, some (I); harbor view. DC, MC.

Nexø (Neksø). *Bornholm* (E), (53–98 83 83). 27 rooms with private facilities. On Dueodde beach. Garden, heated pool. Also 4–5 bed apartments with kitchen (weekly rentals). *Holms Hotel* (I), (53–99 20 45). 49 rooms, 33 with private facilities. *Linds Pension* (I), (53–98 80 80). 19 rooms, all with private facilities.
Restaurant. *De tre Sostre* (The Three Sisters) (E), (03–99 33 93). An excellent place, with fish specialties (from split cod to lobster) and entertainment. Closed Oct. through Apr. AE, DC, MC, V.

Rønne. *Fredensborg* (E), (53–95 44 44). 72 rooms, all with bath and balcony. Overlooking the sea, beach, sauna. Also 12 apartments. AE, DC, MC, V. *Griffen*

(E), (53–95 51 11). 140 rooms, all with shower. Sauna, tennis, restaurant with local dishes; near airport. DC, MC, V. *Hotel Hoffman* (E), (53–95 03 86). 85 rooms with bath. Sauna, pool. Charming establishment in town center. AE, DC, MC. *Ryttergården* (M), (53–95 19 13). 91 rooms, all with bath. Near beach, pool, riding. Also 30 4–5-bed apartments for weekly rental.

Restaurants. *De fem Stâuerna,* exclusive fish and steak restaurant in Hotel Fredensborg. AE, DC, MC, V. *Rådhuskroen,* old half-timbered house in town center. Excellent smørrebrød, also a few rooms. AE, DC, MC, V.

Sandvig. *Hammerso* (E), (53–98 03 64). 40 rooms, all with bath; pension. Summer hotel, near beach. Garden, pool. *Strandhotellet* (M), (53–98 03 14). 41 rooms, all with shower. Summer hotel, on the beach, with garden; refurnished with modern decor. *Pension Langebierg* (I), (53–98 02 98). 20 rooms, 18 with private facilities. AE.

Restaurant. *Ostersoens Perle,* at Tejn.

Svaneke. *Siemsens Gård* (M), (53–99 61 49). 45 rooms, all with shower. Open Apr. to Nov. Garden, sauna. AE, DC, MC, V.

HOW TO GET AROUND. By bus. There is no railway on Bornholm, but there is a good bus network. A BATkort (discount pass) offers considerable savings on bus fares, and one-day tourist tickets are also available.

By car. There is a car ferry from Ystad in Sweden, but it's more practical to hire a car on Bornholm. Several dealers hire them out. Danish speed limits apply, of course, and good braking will be useful on Bornholm's steep stretches of road. Bornholm's landscape is very unlike the rest of Denmark: rock and cliff dominate every view.

By bicycle. Cycles may be hired in Allinge, Gudhjem, Hasle, Pedersker near Åkirkeby, Rønne and Svaneke. There are splendid cycling routes along the coast, but be sure to check your brakes before setting out.

By boat. The island of Christiansø can be reached by boat year-round from Svaneke, and mid-May to mid-Sept. from Allinge and Gudhjem.

PLACES TO VISIT. Åkirkeby. Å Kirke. One of the island's few churches that *isn't* round. Dates from the 13th century, and retains its original font. The altarpiece and pulpit are Dutch (16th-century). Open May through Sept., Mon. to Sat. 1–5. Key available from verger rest of year.

Allinge-Sandvig. Hammershus. Castle ruins, built originally in about 1250 by archbishop Jakob Erlandsen on high cliff overlooking the sea; the largest ruined castle in northern Europe. Open all year.

Bornholms Dyre- & Naturpark. Zoo, 3 km. south of Allinge. Animals roam free through beautiful grounds. Open May through Sept., daily 10–5.

Nyker. Ny Kirke, 10 km. (6 miles) northeast of Rønne. The smallest round church on the island. Note especially the column with original late-Gothic frescos. Open late-May through late Oct., daily 7–sunset.

Nylars. Nylars Kirke. 10 km. (6 miles) southeast of Rønne. Large round church with attractive 14th-century frescos. Open mid-May through mid-Sept., Mon. to Sat., 9–5.

Olsker. Ols Kirke, 5 km. south of Allinge. The most elevated round church on the island, 113 meters (350 ft.) above sea level; is believed to date from the late-12th century. Also has Renaissance pulpit. Key available from priest.

Østerlars. Østerlars Kirke, 10 km. (6 miles) south of Gudhjem. The largest of the island's many round churches, dating probably from the 12th century. Hollow column in the nave contains the font; another is decorated with frescos that are believed to date from the 14th century. Open Apr. through late Oct., Mon. to Sat. 9–5, closed Sun.

Rønne. Forsvarsmuseum (Defense Museum). In the castle, and charts the military struggles of the island, principally against the Swedes. Open May though Sept., Tues. to Sat. 10–4, closed Sun.

SPORTS. Swimming is excellent—from flat rocks, from the sandy beach that stretches for miles on the south coast, and from sizeable sandy beaches to the west. It is possible to bathe in the sea until late September. There are good swimming pools at Gudhjem, Rønne and Sandvig. Instruction is available in **windsurfing:** short courses at about Dkr. 300; courses leading to a certificate at about Dkr. 800.

Sailing and **fishing** for salmon in the waters offshore attract the deep-sea sportsman, and there's free trout fishing south of Rønne off "Stampen."

Bornholm also has a **golf** course at Rønne.

SHOPPING. Ceramics are manufactured in Rønne and may be bought directly from *Michael Andersen, L. Hjorth, Joghus and Soholm. Gaveboden* at Allinge sells ceramics, glass and trinkets, and there are *Keramikstâuan* shops for ceramics and stoneware at Nexø and Snogebaek. Twenty-three local potters also have workshops around the island where visitors are welcome to watch them work, and buy a souvenir. In Svaneke, three shops are worth noting: *Waldorff* for stoneware, *I Stalden* for textiles and ceramics, and *Staugård* for stoneware, paintings and ceramics. Local folk art may be bought from *Alkemisterne* at Snogebaek, and smoked fish from Espersen, or direct from smokehouses in Svanere harbor at Rønne.

FINLAND

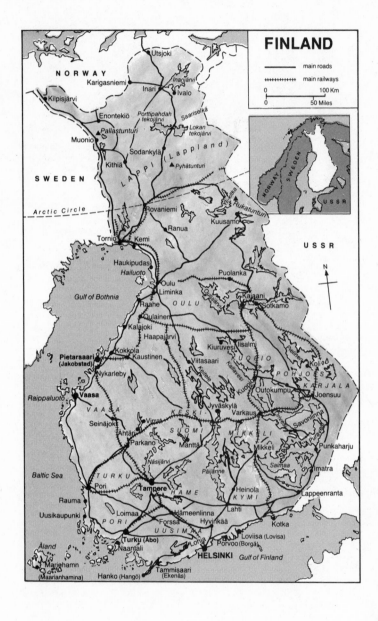

FINLAND

——— main roads

++++++++++ main railways

0   100 Km

0   50 Miles

NORWAY

Utsjoki

Karigasniemi

Inari   *Inarijärvi*

Kilpisjärvi   Ivalo

Enontekiö   *Porttipahdah*
tekojärvi   *Saariselkä*

Pallastunturi   *Lokan*
tekojärvi

Muonio

Sodankylä

Kithiä   *L A P P I*   *(L A P P L A N D)*

SWEDEN   ▲ *Pyhätunturi*

Arctic Circle

Rovaniemi   *Rukatunturi*

Ranua   Kuusamo

Tornio   Kemi

USSR

Haukipudas

Hailuoto

Oulu   Puolanka

Liminka

Gulf of Bothnia   *O U L U*   Kajaani

Raahe   Sotkamo

Oulainen

Kalajoki

Haapajärvi

Kiuruvesi   Iisalmi

Pietarsaari   Kokkola

(Jakobstad)   Kaustinen   Viitasaari

Nykarleby   *K U O P I O*   Koli

P O H J O I S

Raippaluoto   **Vaasa**   Kuopio   *K A R J A L A*

Outokumpu   Joensuu

V A A S A   *K E S K I*

Seinäjoki   Jyväskylä   Varkaus

Virrat   Savonlinna

Ähtäri   *S U O M I*   *M I K K E L I*

Parkano   Punkaharju

Mänttä   Mikkeli

Näsijärvi   *Saimaa*

Päijänne   Imatra

Baltic Sea   *T U R K U*

Pori   **Tampere**   Heinola

H Ä M E   *K Y M I*   Lappeenranta

Rauma   Lahti

Loimaa   Hämeenlinna   Hyvinkää

Uusikaupunki   Forssa   Kotka

P O R I   *U U S I M A A*

Turku (Åbo)   Loviisa (Lovisa)

Åland   Naantali   Lohja   Porvoo (Borgå)

HELSINKI   *Gulf of Finland*

Mariehamn
(Maarianhamina)   Hanko (Hangö)   Tammisaari
(Ekenäs)

NORWAY   SWEDEN   USSR

FINLAND—FACTS AT YOUR FINGERTIPS

NATIONAL TOURIST OFFICE. In the U.S.: *Finnish Tourist Board,* 655 Third Ave., New York, NY 10017 (212–370 5540); 1900 Avenue of the Stars, Suite 1025, Los Angeles, CA 90067 (213–277–5226).

In Canada: *Finnish Tourist Board,* 1200 Bay St., Suite 640, Toronto, Ontario M5R 2A5 (416–964–9159).

In the U.K.: 66–68 Haymarket, London SW1Y 4RF (01–839 4048).

The mailing address for the Finnish Tourist Board's head office in Finland is P.O. Box 53, 00521 Helsinki 52. Its Tourist Information Office, Unioninkatu 26, Helsinki (90–144 511), and most travel agencies in Helsinki can supply personal callers with information on most aspects of travel in Finland. The Finnish Tourist Board also has a Northern office at Maakuntakatu 10, 96101 Rovaniemi (960–17 201). In addition, every town and resort has a tourist office (often identified by the international "i" sign), and usually one or more travel agencies *(matkatoimisto).* We list all the major Finnish tourist offices at the beginning of each *Practical Information* section.

CURRENCY. The unit of Finnish currency is the *markka* (Fmk) divided into 100 *penniä* (singular *penni*). The rate of exchange at press time (mid-1989) was 4.30 Fmk to the U.S. dollar and 7 Fmk to the pound sterling.

You can change money or travelers' checks in banks and exchange bureaux (see *Closing Times*); most hotels will also change money, though the rate is likely to be less favorable.

COSTS IN FINLAND. The standard of living in Finland is high and so are prices, though inflation is reasonably low. You can keep costs down very substantially by following the suggestions given in the following pages, but don't expect to get very far on a shoestring.

Sample costs. Cinema seat, 25–30 Fmk; entrance to museum or castle, 5–15 Fmk; coffee, 4–7 Fmk; medium beer (per bottle), 5.70 Fmk in shops, from 12.60 in restaurants; house wine by the glass in a Moderate restaurant, 13.50 Fmk; by the carafe, from 82 Fmk; Coke, 3 Fmk (shop), 8–9 Fmk (restaurant).

SEASONAL EVENTS. The summer season lasts from mid-May to mid-September, reaching its peak in July, but note that some facilities, such as lake traffic, only operate from June through August. This is also the period of the summer "Finland Festivals," featuring major cultural events. The skiing season begins in January in the southern parts of the country and lasts until the end of April in the north.

A free calendar of events is published every year by the Finnish Tourist Board. The following is a selection of the major ones. Note the solar eclipse in July 1990.

January 1 is the signal for New Year celebrations throughout the country.

March sees the Lahti Games, Finland's premier winter sports event, in early March (can be late Feb.) Major cross-country ski races include the Finlandia Ski Race, Hämeenlinna to Lahti, early March, and the Arctic Circle Ski Race at Rovaniemi, around mid-March. Later in the month the Lady Day Festival is held at Enontekiö in Lapland, a gathering of the Lapps with traditional dress being worn, and reindeer driving and lasso-throwing competitions among the celebrations. The end of March or early April also sees the international Ounasvaara Winter Games at Rovaniemi.

April 30 is Vapunaatto, May Day eve, a nation-wide celebration that combines Labor Day and student festivities into one emphatic welcome to the Spring. Many never see their beds this night.

May 1 is Vappu or May Day itself, essentially a day for family outings. Students and workers also have their own processions. Centered mainly on eastern Finland, the Pradznik Festival, a traditional Orthodox church and folk festival, is held in different areas between May and September.

June has a whole host of activities.

Two events at the beginning of the month are the Vaasa Festival, a puppet theater festival, and the Kuopio Dance and Music Festival, with performances ranging from classical ballet to modern dance. In the second week of June the 10-day Ilmajoki Music Festival begins, with performances of all kinds of music, including open-air Finnish folk opera. The Naantali Music Festival, beginning mid-June, has mainly classical music.

Midsummer Eve, or Juhannusaatto, sees nation-wide celebrations on the weekend closest to the 24th, with festivities around immense bonfires, or, in western Finland, maypoles. At the very end of the month and stretching into July the Jyväskylä Arts Festival is held, with varied cultural events on a different theme every year.

July On July 22, 1990, there will be a total eclipse of the sun, visible from Helsinki along a line northeast to Joensuu—the only part of Western Europe to see it. Further details are given on pg. 188. Otherwise, there's the Savonlinna Opera Festival, four weeks of international performances in the splendid setting of medieval Olavinlinna castle; but there are also many song and orchestral events in various other locations around the country. Earlier in the month, the Aleksis Kivi Festival celebrates Finland's national author in Nurmijärvi, while the Bomba Festival of Karelia folklore takes place in Nurmes throughout the month.

The first half of the month has the Pori Jazz Festival, an international event with open-air concerts and street events. Starting in the middle of the month is the Kuhmo Chamber Music Festival, two weeks of chamber music featuring Finnish and international musicians.

At about the same time begins the one-week Kaustinen Folk Music Festival, when over 1,000 performers participate in dozens of concerts. The most important of the Pradznik festivals (see May) also takes place in mid-July in Ilomantsi. At the very end of the month is Sleepyhead Day in Naantali and Hanko, when the laziest person in town is thrown into the sea; it's a day-long fun event.

August begins with the week-long Lahti Organ Festival, mainly at the beautiful Church of the Cross. Next comes the Turku Music Festival, a week-long celebration of all types of music, and the Tampere Theater Summer. The main venue is the splendid open-air Pyynikki Theater, with its revolving auditorium.

Finally, the Helsinki Festival, two weeks of cultural events of all kinds, begins at the end of the month, lasting into early September.

NATIONAL HOLIDAYS. January 1 (New Year); January 6 (Epiphany); April 13–16 (Easter); April 30–May 1 (Labor Day); May 19 (Ascension); June 2–3 (Pentecost); June 22–23 (midsummer); November 3 (All Saints); December 6 (Independence Day); December 24–26 (Christmas).

LANGUAGE. Finnish and Swedish are both Finland's official languages, but Swedish is the mother tongue of about 6% of the population. Finnish belongs to an entirely different language group (Finno-Ugrian) from Swedish and the other Nordic languages. It's melodic, logical, easy to pronounce but very difficult to learn (it has 14 grammatical cases). Fortunately, English is widely spoken throughout the tourist industry and by many in the young to middle age groups. Older people tend to know German better. It's worth learning some basic phrases in Finnish for the surprised pleasure it will give!

CUSTOMS. Residents of non-European countries may bring duty-free into Finland 400 cigarettes or 500 grams of tobacco products; plus, for persons aged 20 or over, 2 liters of beer, 1 liter of other mild alcoholic drink and 1 liter of spirits, *or* (if aged 18 or over) 2 liters of beer and 2 liters of other mild alcoholic drink; plus non-commercial goods to the value of 1500 Fmk.

For residents of European countries, the same duty-free allowances are valid with the exception that only 200 cigarettes or 250 grams of other tobacco products may be imported.

There is no limit to the amount of foreign currency that may be imported or exported, but no more than 10,000 Fmk may be exported without declaration. Note the restrictions on importing certain foodstuffs.

HOTELS. There is no official grading system for Finnish hotels. Nonetheless, basic standards are very high. Nearly all hotels, except some in the lower price ranges, have baths or showers in all or most rooms. An increasing number offer rooms for non-smokers and those suffering from allergies. Most hotels have restaurants, and in the more expensive there will usually be music or dancing on some or all evenings. A number also offer roulette. Any other special amenities, such as night clubs or sports facilities are indicated in our hotel listings.

For inexpensive accommodations, Finland also boasts a number of summer hotels, most common in larger towns and cities. These usually modern and excellent-value hotels act as student accommodations for the rest of the year, and some are run by students themselves. A new type of Finnish accommodations is the *gasthaus,* usually small and family-run; you can get further information from Finlanida Hotels, Merimiehenkatu 29, 00150 Helsinki. The lowest-priced of all are boarding houses *(matkustajakoti).*

Motorists especially will find the Finn Check scheme useful. The scheme operates from June 1 to August 31 and gives discounts in many hotels throughout the country. You may buy as many of the checks as you want—they operate really as a series of vouchers—and each check costs 150 Fmk per night, per person, inclusive of breakfast. In the most expensive hotels, an additional 75 Fmk will be charged, in less expensive hotels the check also covers the cost of a self-service lunch. Only your first night can be reserved in advance, but reservations for subsequent nights can be made free of charge from any hotel participating in the scheme. Details from travel agents and the Finnish Tourist Board.

Prices. We have divided all the hotels we list into four categories—Deluxe (L), Expensive (E), Moderate (M) and Inexpensive (I). These grades are determined solely by price.

Two people in a double room can expect to pay (prices in Fmk)

	Helsinki	Elsewhere
Deluxe	750 and up	650 and up
Expensive	550–750	450–650
Moderate	350–550	250–450
Inexpensive	under 350	under 250

These prices include breakfast and a 15% service charge. Some hotels also include a free morning sauna and swim. The initials AE, DC, MC, and V stand for American Express, Diner's Club, MasterCard and Visa.

A recently introduced form of bed-and-breakfast accommodations brings costs down to 80–140 Fmk per person (details from Lomarenagas, Museokatu 3, Helsinki). Several major hotel groups, such as Rantasipi, Cumulus, and Scanhotels, offer budget rates in summer.

SELF-CATERING. In summer, most Finnish families disappear to their summer cottages, usually tucked away in the forests by some lake, sea or river shore, or on an island. Visitors can follow suit by renting a summer cottage, either in a holiday village or in a more remote location. In many holiday villages, sports facilities are provided and in most cases a sauna and use of a boat are available free or for a small charge. The range of weekly rentals is from 400–5000 Fmk, average 1000–2500 Fmk, depending on season, size and amenities. Time-share schemes have also been introduced in some holiday villages; the Finnish Tourist Board can advise.

A main booking center for the whole country is *Lomarengas,* Museokatu 3, 00100 Helsinki (90–441 346).

An increasingly popular facility is renting well-equipped apartments in Helsinki and other major towns.

FARM VACATIONS. A free booklet, *Farm Holidays in Finland,* is issued by the Finnish Tourist Board. These increasingly popular accommodations give you an opportunity to participate in rural family life. They are usually available on half- or full-board basis, and include a sauna.

A central booking office for the whole country is *Suomen 4H-liitto,* Uudenmaankatu 24, 00120 Helsinki (90–642 233).

CAMPING. The best way to enjoy Finland's wealth of lake-and-forest scenery is to get out into it. There are camping sites near most cities and throughout the countryside, open to all from May or June to August or September (some open year-round). About 350 camp sites classified into three grades have been established by various organizations in Finland and, as the Finn has an eye for beauty, most of them have choice locations on the shore of lake, river or sea. In about 250 of these, caravans can be linked to the electric current (220 V.). Note that facilities for filling and changing gas bottles is limited to a very few places in western Finland. Outside these sites camping is not generally allowed without the landowner's permission. It is also of the utmost importance in this forest-bound land to take the greatest possible care with regard to fire.

Camping is handled by the *Finnish Travel Association's Camping Department,* Mikonkatu 25, 00100 Helsinki (90–170 868). A system of Finncamping Checks is sold as part of a package arrangement through some travel agencies. Otherwise the charge is usually in the 21–57 Fmk range per family (two adults, two children, a car and tent or caravan). And though services vary, the charge normally includes showers, facilities for cooking, washing, and dish washing. At most sites, those not holding an international camping pass (FICC) must buy a national camping card costing 10 Fmk.

A free list of camp sites is available from the Finnish Tourist Board, and most of them are marked on the excellent *Suomen Tiekartta* (Finnish Road Map) and *Autolijan Tiekartta* (Motorist's Road Map), both available from bookshops or the *Automobile and Touring Club* in Helsinki.

YOUTH AND FAMILY HOSTELS. There are about 160 hostels, graded in four categories, throughout the country. They range from small farms or manor houses to empty schools, many offering "family rooms." There are no age restrictions and all are also open to motorists. Coffee and refreshments are available at most of them, and there are usually cooking facilities. Many have boats or bicycles for hire. Overnight charges range from 26–150 Fmk per night. Sleeping bags may not be used, but sheets can be hired at an additional charge.

Further details from the *Finnish Youth Hostels Association,* Yrjönkatu 38 B, 00100 Helsinki (90–694 0377). A free list of hostels is available from the Finnish Tourist Board.

RESTAURANTS. The choice of eating places in Finland, in main towns and cities at any rate, is varied both in style and price. Away from larger centers, the best restaurants are likely to be in hotels. Considering Finland's high standard of living and consequent reputation for priceyness, meal costs are generally reasonable, especially if you stick to the *table d'hôte,* or suggested menus, served in many hotels and restaurants, though usually only between certain fixed times. This is usually fairly early, especially in more moderately-priced places. You'll find that food is always attractively served.

The Finnish Tourist Board produces a *Lappi à la Carte* leaflet listing gourmet routes in Finnish Lapland, with the emphasis on traditional dishes. There are now also leaflets outlining two gourmet trails respectively in the east and west of the country.

Fast food is readily available in cities, especially Helsinki. Similarly, English-type "pubs," with inexpensive food have become popular.

Prices. We have divided the restaurants in our listings into three categories— Expensive (E), Moderate (M) and Inexpensive (I). These grades are determined solely by price.

Prices, per person, excluding drinks, but including service charge (in Fmk).

	Helsinki	Elsewhere
Expensive	170–220	150–190
Moderate	110–170	90–150
Inexpensive	75–110	60–90

These prices are for à la carte meals. Fixed-price menus, usually covering two courses and coffee, work out at about half the above.

FOOD AND DRINK. The cold table (*voileipäpöytä* in Finnish) is as varied and attractive here as elsewhere in Scandinavia. Other national specialties include *poronkieltä* (reindeer tongue with lemon sauce), *poronkäristys* (reindeer casserole, particularly good in Lapland), *hiilillä paistettua silakkaa* (Baltic herring grilled over charcoal), *kalakukko* (fish and pork baked in a rye flour crust, specialty of Kuopio), *lihapullia* (meat balls with a tasty sauce), and *uunijuustoa* (oven cheese). There is excellent fish, such as burbot, and various members of the salmon family. If you happen to be around from about the end of July to early September, don't miss a crayfish party—when the Finns don bibs and tuck into boiled crayfish, flavored with dill and washed down with fiery *akvavit* far into the white nights. Desserts are good and rich, and to digest them they provide some delicate liqueurs, *Lakka* (cloudberry) and *Mesimarja* (Arctic bramble). These and other fruits of the forest also make popular desserts.

Be warned that imported spirits are very expensive, those bottled in Finland merely expensive! Wines are relatively reasonably priced, especially if bottled in Finland.

Licensing laws are liberal. Beer is served from 9 A.M. onwards and other liquor from noon until the restaurant closes. Beer is now also sold in supermarkets, many cafés and a number of otherwise unlicensed premises. Otherwise ALKO, the Finnish State Alcohol Monopoly, have many shops where you can buy all kinds of alcoholic drinks. But note the strict laws (see *By Car*) governing drinking and driving.

At the other end of the scale, drinking water is safe everywhere, and the excellent coffee is drunk in great quantities, black or with cream. Like other Scandinavians, the Finns drink a lot of milk or *piimä* (skimmed milk).

TIPPING. A general guide line is that you should tip for good service, but that tipping is not otherwise taken for granted. The service charges mentioned under *Hotels* and *Restaurants* (see above) are sufficient, though a few extra coins are usually left. There's an obligatory cloakroom fee to hotel or restaurant doormen—usually 3–4 Fmk. Taxi drivers, theater ushers, washroom attendants, barbers and beauty salon attendants are not normally tipped.

MAIL. Post offices are marked *Posti* and mailing boxes are yellow, normally fixed to a wall. Postage stamps can also be bought in most hotels, many kiosks, tobacconists and some book shops.

Postal rates for airmail letters and postcards to the U.K. are 2.50 Fmk.; to the U.S. 3 Fmk. for letters, 2.50 Fmk. for postcards.

TELEPHONES. Public booths are well distributed. The procedure is to lift the receiver, insert the money and dial; the money is returned if you are not connected. If you're checking a number in the telephone directory, remember that the Finnish letters "å," "ä" and "ö" come at the end of the alphabet.

CLOSING TIMES. Shops are usually open Mon. to Fri., 9–6, Sat. 9–2; they may close an hour earlier in summer. In Helsinki, department stores also stay open until 8 P.M. Mon. to Fri. Additionally, in the subway by Helsinki rail station, shops of all kinds operate until 10 P.M., including Sunday. Shops in Helsinki's Senaatti Center, the Esplanade and the Forum Shopping Center are open Sun. in July and Aug. On national holidays, all shops are closed and on the eve of national holidays they observe Saturday times.

Banks open 9:30–4, Mon. to Fri., Closed Sat. Longer hours apply in international airports, harbors, main rail stations and certain exchange bureaux in main cities.

SPORTS. The Finnish landscapes seem tailor made for a number of outdoor activities, all of which have a very large following among the Finns themselves. The best areas for individual sports are outlined in the regional chapters, but some principal addresses for information are as follows. The Finnish Equestrian Federation, Finnish Golf Union, Finnish Yachting Association, Finnish Motor Boat Association and Finnish Canoe Association are all at Radiokatu 12, 00240 Helsinki. Boat rentals and flotilla sailing are arranged through the Nautic Center, Veneentekijäntie 1, 00210 Helsinki.

GETTING AROUND FINLAND. If you can work out your detailed itinerary in advance, you can buy a tourist ticket, valid one month, combining travel by train, bus and plane, offering savings of about 20%.

By air. Finland has an elaborate service of internal flights operated by *Finnair*. Helsinki is connected with most Finnish towns and there are also cross-country flights linking several of these. Fares are among the lowest in Europe, with special rates for family groups, children, pensioners (over-65s), and young people (12–23). In addition, the *Finnair Holiday Ticket* ($250) and the *Youth Holiday Ticket* ($200) offer unlimited travel on domestic routes for a maximum of 15 days to any non-resident of Finland.

By train. Finland's extensive rail system reaches all main centers of the country. The network stops short a little north of the Arctic Circle. Standards of comfort and cleanliness are high. Most trains have first and second class; a few have second class only. On some long-distance routes, there are special "playroom" cars for children. A *Finnrail Pass* gives unlimited travel for 8, 15 or 22 days; sample cost for 15 days is $135 second class, $203 first class (half fare for children; 20% reduction for groups of at least three persons). Seat tickets (10 Fmk) are recommended and, on special fast trains (15–25 Fmk), are obligatory. Round trip tickets cost slightly less than double one way ones. Reductions apply to groups of a minimum of three persons. Special rates also apply to children, and to over-65s holding a special card available for 50 Fmk. from any rail station in Finland.

A network of car-carrying trains operate from and between Helsinki and several main centers throughout the country.

Finland is also a partner in the following international schemes: *EurailPass* (first class only, unlimited travel); *Eurail Youth Pass* (second class only, unlimited travel for under-26s); *Scanrail Pass* (unlimited travel for 21 days throughout Scandinavia); *Inter Rail Ticket* (for under-26s); *Rail Europ Senior Card* (for men over 65, women over 60). See "Getting Around Scandinavia" in *Planning Your Trip* for further details.

By bus. Bus travel plays a leading role in Finland with an extensive network, linked in many cases to the rail system. In the far north and in parts of the east, it is the only means of public transport. Costs are lower than by rail. There is an additional charge (6 Fmk) for express services. Reductions apply to children, family groups and to over-65s holding a special *65 Card* costing 25 Fmk and available from bus stations in Finland. The new Coach Holiday, valid two weeks, ticket entitles holders to travel 1,000 km. by bus for 230 Fmk.

By car. An extensive road-building programme has resulted in a good network of asphalted main roads throughout much of the country. In the south, four-lane motorways grow a little annually. Other major roads have a surface of oil and sand. Where the old dirt roads still remain, as in many parts of the far north and remoter areas, the gravel is often bound with clay and dustlaying chemicals, thus making the surface even and hard; but when it rains these roads can be somewhat slippery, dirty and smelly. In winter all main roads are kept open for traffic and the going is usually good. During the spring thaw (April–early June, according to latitude), some roads are at times impassable or very difficult to negotiate; look out for the road sign *"kelirikko"* which warns you of bad conditions. Another warning sign, with appropriate drawing, concerns elk (moose) and reindeer; take heed for collision with up to 600 kg. of elk is no joke. They are especially active at dusk.

Speed limits are 60, 80, 100 or 120 km per hour, according to the classification of the road and traffic density, and the limit applicable is indicated by signs. If it is not, the basic speed limit is 50 km.p.h. in built-up areas, 80 km.p.h. in the countryside, or, on motorways, 120 km.p.h.

At intersections, cars coming from the right have priority. The rights of pedestrians on pedestrian crossings must be rigorously observed. The use of seat belts is now compulsory. Outside built-up areas, low-beam headlights must be used at all times of day, regardless of weather conditions. *Important:* the laws regarding drinking and driving are very strict. If you exceed the exact limit of .5 milligrams of alcohol in the blood, the penalty is nearly always imprisonment or a heavy fine.

Gasoline costs around 3.35 Fmk per liter (3.15 Fmk unleaded). There is a good network of service stations and repair garages, but it is wise to keep topped up if you are in less populated regions or taking minor roads in wilderness areas.

The address of the *Automobile and Touring Club of Finland* is Kansakoulukatu 10, 00100 Helsinki (90–694 0022). Should you be involved in an accident, you should contact immediately the Finnish Motor Insurers' Bureau *Liikennevakuutusyhdistys,* Bulevardi 28, 00120 Helsinki (90–19251), which deals with traffic accidents involving foreign vehicles in Finland.

A selection of car hire firms is given under "Useful Addresses" in *Practical Information* sections. A new facility is the rental of motorhomes through Inter-Rent, Hitsaajankatu 7C, 00180 Helsinki, or Touring Cars, Päiväranta, 70420 Kuopio (971–341 800).

By bike. Cycling has become very popular, and planned routes are now arranged in many areas through local tourist offices. Cycles can be hired in most tourist centers.

By boat/cruises. Modern comfortable ferries link Helsinki and Turku with the Åland islands; both cities also have a network of small ferries serving island communities within their orbit.

Lake steamers and motorships, with restaurants on board, ply the inland waterways. Increasingly, trips are organized as cruises, ranging from a few hours or a weekend to several days, but there is still a number of regular schedules (see Regional Chapters) which you can join or leave at will. In addition, boat services operate to the Saimaa Canal from Lappéenranta.

On foot. Almost the whole of Finland is ideal hiking country, and in many areas there are marked trails with refuge huts for overnights. Remember that many of these areas are remote and wild, especially in the north and east, and it is always essential to be properly equipped, to heed local advice, and tell your hotel or friends where you are heading and how long you intend to be away. A free booklet *Hiking Routes* is issued by the Finnish Tourist Board.

PRELUDE TO FINLAND

Scandinavia's Rich Secret

by
ANDREW BROWN

Finland is the toughest of the Scandinavian countries. It is tough in both senses of the word: resilient and difficult. For foreigners it is difficult: Finland is the only European country that had a common border with Russia in 1939 and yet remains independent today. It is also the only country in the world to have fought Communist Russia to a standstill—in the Winter War of 1939–40; and though the Finns lost the "Continuation War" of 1941–44, when they fought alongside the Germans against the Russians, Finland survived even this loss. The Russians annexed a great deal of territory; installed a Proconsul, and extracted very heavy reparations from their defeated foes. But they did not absorb all Finland. The Proconsul went home after three years to die of cirrhosis; the refugees from the ceded territories were settled; the reparations were duly paid. Finland survived and prospers.

But such a history leaves scars: the Finns are nowadays both fiercely patriotic, and quite free of aggressive nationalism. They are not proud of their wars, though they are proud of the way in which they have subsequently learned to live in peace with Russia. They remain resilient, and very difficult for foreigners to understand. The language is part of this difficulty. Finnish is partially comprehensible to Estonians, and related to the

Lapp languages. It is also very distantly related to Hungarian. But it is quite unrelated to the other Scandinavian languages. Nor would the Finns have things otherwise. They think of their language as far more flexible and expressive than either Swedish or English—and most Finns speak both these languages.

Flamboyant Savagery

Language is not the only thing that sets Finland apart from the rest of Scandinavia. Helsinki is probably the least Americanized city in capitalist Europe. The other Scandinavian capitals all have their natures partially concealed by modern buildings. Helsinki remains as it was, and very beautiful. Everything *works* with Scandinavian efficiency, but it all *looks* central European. There is a flamboyant savagery about the Finns quite alien to the rest of Scandinavia: a Finnish writer was once approached by a broke colleague for a loan.

"I can't," he said, "I'm broke myself." And to prove his point, he took from his wallet his last hundred Finnmark bill, tore it into shreds, dumped them in the ashtray—this happened in a pub, of course—and set light to them. This is the sort of behavior one would expect from a Polish or Hungarian nobleman between the wars, not from a phlegmatic Scandinavian. But then, the Finns are anything but phlegmatic. If they seem to accept their appalling history calmly, this is not indifference, but tough-mindedness. They could say with Bishop Burnett that "Things are as they are. They will be as they will be. Why, then, should we wish to be deceived?"

This tough-mindedness sets them apart from practically everyone else in the world; but even if Finland is not like anywhere else—and that is one reason why it is worth visiting—you can at least partly prepare yourself for it by imagining a Central European country that has been shifted 500 miles north into Scandinavia.

The countryside is Scandinavian: smallholdings set among the lakes and forests of the interior, and along the coast the marvellous Baltic archipelagoes. It is a tourist cliché to speak of the lakes and forests of Finland, just as one cannot mention Lapland without talking about the Midnight Sun. But in fact these things do not reward the traveller. They are indeed beautiful, and entirely overwhelming, but once you have seen them that is that; they are not stimulating in themselves. Unless you have business in the forest, or beneath the midnight sun, you will very rapidly get bored. You get nothing for free in Finland, and if you wish to be interested in the wilderness, then you must bring your own interests to it. If you can do that, then you will be repaid handsomely. The fisherman, the hunter, and the botanist will all find their heart's desire in the Finnish wilderness.

Life and Death on the Lakes

The Finnish smallholder must have all these skills and more. It is through this sort of pioneer farming that the Scandinavian element has impressed itself upon Finnish culture. Even well within modern times, times in Finland were very difficult, and the memories of extreme poverty remain potent. A sense of being crushed by unending, almost fruitless toil is perhaps the proper explanation of "Scandinavian gloom." It is an emotion that has little to do with long winter nights—then at least you can

rest—and a great deal to do with constant physical fatigue. Even now there
are stories where the darkness of the forest seems to douse and choke the
clear aseptic brightness of modern life.

Consider the life and death of Lauri Rapala. He was born in 1907, in
great poverty. His father was unknown, so he was given the surname of
Rapala—the name of the village where he was born. After a spell as a lum-
berjack, he set up as a freshwater fisherman, using nets and standing lines
in the lakes of the interior. It was not a profitable life. For 21 years he
lived with his wife—and, eventually, seven children—in a one-room cabin
the size of a modern Finnish living-room, with only one bed. So as not
to waste time while rowing between his nets, he whittled small fish out
of spruce bark, stuck hooks in them, and towed them behind the boat while
he rowed. These "wobblers" caught a great many fish, and Rapala started
to make a little extra money by selling them.

Then the war came. He spent five years on the Russian Front, and survived. He returned to his old way of life: fishing all day, and in the evenings
whittling his "wobblers." He had posted some to Finnish friends in America, where they began to sell. The hobby had become a business, and then
an enormous success. By 1964, Lauri Rapala had set up a factory, and
was selling 800,000 a year. He was rich, though still generous, and he
could move his family to new houses. And then, one night in 1965, his
youngest son drowned in one of the lakes where the original wobblers had
been tested. The circle was closed: the lakes that had first kept the Rapala
family alive, and then made them rich had claimed their price. After the
accident, Lauri Rapala set out to drink himself to death. It took him nine
years: he was a strong man. He is buried beside his drowned son. The business flourishes still.

It is a very Finnish story: one of toughness, and almost unimaginable
resilience; hard work, success, and finally vodka. But anyone who thinks
it shows an unreasonable gloominess, should consider what vast reserves
of courage and cheerfulness Lauri Rapala must have had to get as far as
he got.

Neighbors and Colonizers

In the plain of Western Finland, along the Baltic Coast, another Scandinavian influence is felt. These are the Swedish-speaking regions. The
Swedes and Finns have had a long and complicated relationship, that
somewhat resembles that between England and Ireland. The parallels cannot be drawn too far, but they are nonetheless illuminating. They help one
also to understand the relationship between Finland and Russia. The frontier that Stalin drew in 1940 is almost exactly the same as the frontier that
Peter the Great drew up when Finland was still a Swedish colony in 1721.

In the beginning, the Swedes were military colonizers. The Finnish-
speaking tribesmen of the interior traded in valuable furs, and the Swedes
wished both to control this trade, and to profit from the valuable fishing
in the gulf of Bothnia. These were the days before there were any Russians.
The word "Russian" itself comes from the name that Swedish Vikings for-
aging eastwards gave themselves—"Rus." Then the Swedes settled, like
the Normans in Ireland. They formed the land-owning, aristocratic class-
es, divided by languages from the peasantry that worked for them. And,
just as in Ireland, it was among the these settlers, absorbed in the country
yet still remote from the indigenous population, that nationalism first be-

came an articulate political force. As early as the 14th century, the Swedish ruling class in Finland were championing Finnish interests against central authority.

The differences start in the 16th century, with the Reformation. The Finns did not retain a separate religion to their conquerors, as the Irish did, and this homogeneity of religion helped to preserve the separate languages. When the Swedes and Finns adopted Protestantism, the Bible was translated into Finnish, and this was to prove crucially important. Finnish nationalism in modern times is based on the Finnish language, and without a Finnish Bible, it is questionable whether the language would have survived, any more than Gaelic for example has. Nor have the Finns fought the Swedes as the Irish fought the English. But the two countries have had a long, intimate, and fertile connection, and the Swedish-Finns, like the Anglo-Irish, have made contributions to literature and the arts quite out of proportion to their numbers, which are tiny.

Architecture and the Realities of Life

Culture returns us to the Central European, German influence. This is apparent to the visitor in at least two ways. The first is the astonishing beauty of Finnish buildings. Architecture is an art in Finland, with a power comparable to that of any other art form, and it is taken very seriously. The results do not much resemble anything anywhere else in the world. All one can say about Finnish taste is that it owes nothing to anyone else's ideas of what is beautiful. When it works, it enlarges our ideas of what can be beautiful—and what more can any art achieve? Even when it fails, it both expresses and transmits strong, clear emotions. There is a building in Helsinki that appears to be modelled on the architect's worst hangover: life-sized, or slightly larger, rendered in grey and brown knobbly concrete. No one could call it beautiful, but it is one of the most eloquent buildings you could ever hope to see.

The German influence, too, is apparent in the formality of Finnish manners. Flowers for the hostess at a dinner party; little formal speeches of thanks; a certain reserve symbolized by the use of a formal and an informal pronoun for "you":—socially Finland remains a very old-fashioned place.

A very old-fashioned place, but also a very civilized one. History and geography have forced the Finns to face some of the nastiest aspects of human life. They have faced them with great courage and a certain elegance. Just as their proximity to Russia sharpens their appreciation of the value of their own freedom, so the ghastliness of Finnish history has reinforced their appreciation of the arts of peace. There are a score of theaters and stages for the performing arts in Helsinki, a city of scarcely half-a-million people which also contains the largest and best bookshop in Scandinavia.

Denmark may be more comfortable, and Norway may be more beautiful. Sweden is richer, and easier for the visitor to appreciate. But Finland is the strangest and the most civilized of all the Scandinavian countries, as well as the toughest. It is quite unique; and when you have peeled off all that is Scandinavian, and all that is Central European, there remains a quality that is as rich and secret as the language. You would have to live there for years to discover quite what the secret is—and when you had discovered it, you would probably find it incommunicable.

HELSINKI

Broad Avenues and Bright Prospects

Helsinki (Helsingfors to the Swedish-speaking minority) is very much a city of the sea, sprawling over peninsulas, curving round bays and spilling out across islands that are linked by bridges, causeways or even by boat to the central hub. This hub fills a chunky peninsula where, somehow, without overcrowding, are to be found the single-chamber Parliament, or Eduskuntatalo, the leading technical and educational institutes, art galleries, theaters, museums, business houses, the great Olympic Stadium (scene of the 1952 Olympic Games and 1983 World Athletics Championships), much outstandingly good architecture, the head offices of every big industrial enterprise—in fact all that constitutes the legislative, cultural, scientific, commercial and economic life of the country. And still there is space left for airy parks and broad streets.

Helsinki owes its origin to the chance whims of two monarchs, and its development has largely been the result of a series of accidents. Some 400 years ago King Gustav Vasa of Sweden ordered the citizens of four Finnish towns—Porvoo (Borgå), Tammisaari (Ekenäs), Rauma and Ulvila (Ulfsby)—to leave their homes and proceed to a place on the rapids of the river Vantaa. There they were to build a new town to attract the trade of the Estonian city of Tallinn, thus challenging the power of the Hanseatic League. Like many another city of this period, Helsinki's growth was interrupted by wars, plagues and fires. Not until 1809, when Finland became an autonomous Grand Duchy of Russia, was Helsinki really able to start developing; then three years later, it became the capital of Finland, primarily because the Czar found Turku (Åbo) was too far away from Russia

152

and too close for comfort to Sweden to remain the capital of his newly-acquired territory.

The first of the accidents which stimulated the new capital's growth was the Great Fire in Turku. So much of the latter city was gutted that the University was moved bodily to Helsinki, which at once became the cultural as well as the political center of the country. In 1808, thanks to chance again, another Great Fire played a part in the young city's future. This time it was Helsinki that burned, allowing the German-born architect, Carl Ludvig Engel, an opportunity to plan the rebuilding of the city practically house by house and stone by stone. It is to Engel and to his partner, Ehrenström, that Finland must be grateful for her beautiful capital.

Around the Senate Square which Engel designed stand the Tuomiokirk-ko or Cathedral, the University and the State Council Building—a group built in one of the purest styles European architecture can boast. Perhaps it was Engel's inspiration, but from his day Finland has always had good architects. Two of them, Eliel Saarinen and Alvar Aalto, became world famous. You can hardly walk down any street in Helsinki without seeing splendid examples of the work of modern architects whose fame is already spreading beyond the frontiers of Finland, such as Heikki and Kaija Sirén, Rewell, Ervi, Petäjä, Pietilä, Penttilä.

Under the protective shadows of the island fortress of Suomenlinna (Sveaborg), Helsinki developed rapidly during the 19th century. The lovely park-strewn suburb of Töölö, and the island residential districts of Lauttasaari, and Kulosaari came into being quite recently. Still newer suburbs grew up in the post-World War II period, and the city continues to expand, as indeed it must, for like most capitals, it has not enough accommodations for all who wish to live there.

Exploring Helsinki

From the visitor's point of view, Helsinki has the virtue of compactness. Once you have oriented yourself and found out where you are on the city map, it will be difficult to get lost. The piers where ships from abroad dock, the railway station and, to a lesser extent, the air terminal, are all in the center of the city. So, however you come, you can start wandering around on foot at once.

It's an idea to begin by finding a good viewpoint from which to make your first survey of the city—such as the top of the Olympic Stadium Tower, the hill of Tähtitorninmäki, or comfortably installed in a top floor bar or restaurant as in the Torni, Hesperia, Inter-Continental, Palace or Vaakuna hotels. Probably the first buildings you will notice are the Cathedral and the railway station, both in the center of the town, together with the House of Parliament and the Stadium Tower. The great broad street running from the center of town through the city and out to the main Turku road is Mannerheimintie, or Mannerheimvägen (*tie* in Finnish, and *vägen* in Swedish, mean street or road.) Along this broad avenue, named after Finland's great hero Marshal Mannerheim, you'll be able to pick out the Post Office, the House of Parliament, the National Museum (Suomen Kansallismuseo), the fine new Concert and Congress Center of Finlandia Hall, and the Olympic Stadium.

Another simple introduction to the city is to take the No. 3T or 3B tram which describes a figure of eight through the city, bringing you back to

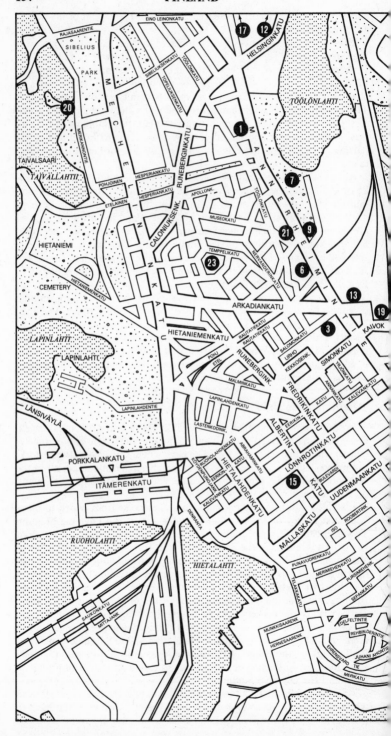

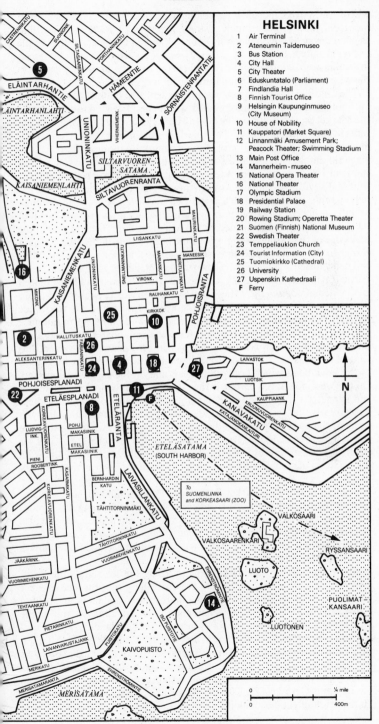

HELSINKI

1 Air Terminal
2 Ateneumin Taidemuseo
3 Bus Station
4 City Hall
5 City Theater
6 Eduskuntatalo (Parliament)
7 Findlandia Hall
8 Finnish Tourist Office
9 Helsingin Kaupunginmuseo
   (City Museum)
10 House of Nobility
11 Kauppatori (Market Square)
12 Linnanmäki Amusement Park;
   Peacock Theater; Swimming Stadium
13 Main Post Office
14 Mannerheim - museo
15 National Opera Theater
16 National Theater
17 Olympic Stadium
18 Presidential Palace
19 Railway Station
20 Rowing Stadium; Operetta Theater
21 Suomen (Finnish) National Museum
22 Swedish Theater
23 Temppeliaukion Church
24 Tourist Information (City)
25 Tuomiokirkko (Cathedral)
26 University
27 Uspenskin Kathedraali
F Ferry

where you started. No. 3T has a commentary in several languages in summer (see "How to get around" in the *Practical Information*). After that, as good a way as any of planning your sightseeing is to start in the middle and work outwards. In point of fact, by far the greatest number of interesting sights are contained in the central part of the city, branching out from the Market Square (or Kauppatori).

The Helsinki Tourist Office has an excellent free booklet "See Helsinki on Foot," detailing six walking tours with maps. Their premises are near the Market Square down by the South Harbor, a few hundred meters from some of the passenger quays. The colorful open-air market flourishes each morning, ending around 1 P.M. and reopening in summer from 3.30–8, when the emphasis is more on arts and crafts. Grouped around the striking statue of Havis Amanda, by Ville Vallgren, are the flower sellers, and the fruit stalls with their mountains of strawberries, raspberries, blueberries, red currants and red whortleberries. You may even be fortunate enough to find the special cloudberry, *suomuurain,* which grows mostly north of the Arctic Circle and is ripened by the Midnight Sun. Fish are sold at the very edge of the harbor, straight from the boats in which they were caught earlier in the morning and so fresh they are still alive and flipping. Meat and dairy produce is sold in the covered market, just beyond the fish stalls.

Havis Amanda, incidentally, the beautiful lady loved by all Helsinkiites, is a center of *vapunaatto* (May Day Eve) revelry. She is crowned again and again on this festive night with the white caps of students who wade through the protective moat surrounding her and climb up to embrace her. Another statue of interest is the stone monument commemorating the time in 1833 when Nicolas I and his consort Feodorovna visited Finland. Known as the Empress Stone, it stands just opposite the quay used by the small boats which head out to the islands of the harbor archipelago. On the west side of the harbor is the Olympia Terminal where passenger and car ferries from Sweden, Poland, and Estonia dock—some of them huge vessels that loom as high as the buildings. Continue south and you come to the pleasant park and district of Kaivopuisto, where most of the embassies are to be found. On the shore, here and elsewhere, you will see small wooden structures from which some Helsinki housewives follow an old tradition of scrubbing their carpets in the sea (or lake, as the case may be).

Leading out of the Market Square are Pohjoisesplanadi and Eteläsplanadi (North and South Esplanades), with gardens running up the middle. Compositely known as Esplanadi, it is a favorite promenade and also features some of the display rooms and shops of Finland's top firms in porcelain, glass, fashion and crafts. Many of them are open on Sundays in July and August.

Along the edge of the Market Square facing the sea stands the President's Palace, with a sentry in field grey patrolling the entrance. Near it you can see the City Hall and various administrative buildings, and behind it towers Helsinki's most famous landmark, the Cathedral. Separating the North and South Harbors, the rocky headland of Katajanokka is dominated by the Orthodox Uspensky Cathedral with its gleaming "onion" domes. This rather neglected area of 19th-century warehouses and naval barracks has been given a new injection of life and is now a developing complex of shops, arts and crafts studios, and restaurants. Passenger ships from Sweden and Germany dock at the Katajanokka terminals on the South Harbor side of the headland.

Senate and Railway Squares: Contrasting Hubs

Only a block away from the South Harbor market is Senate Square, one of the loveliest in northern Europe, with Engel's Cathedral and its domes soaring above it. In the middle of the square is Walter Runeberg's statue of Alexander II of Russia, the enlightened despot who was so well disposed to Finland.

On January 28, 1951, the great Marshal Baron Carl Gustaf Mannerheim, died in Switzerland. He was flown back to his native land and lay in state in the Cathedral for three days before his state funeral. The citizens of Finland were allowed to pay their last respects to him while he lay there in the dim vastness of this lovely church. Young war widows, children, officers and soldiers, who had fought in Finland's wars against Russia under Mannerheim's leadership, filed past in their thousands, and the only sound was one of weeping. Never in Finland's history has there been such an expression of national feeling.

Opposite the Cathedral the lively new Senaatti shopping center adds a new dimension to this gracious but rather quiet district. Most of the streets leading off the Senate Square contain government and administrative offices. Snellmaninkatu is named after J.V. Snellman, whose statue stands in front of the Bank of Finland. Known as the awakener of the Finnish national spirit, he was instrumental in persuading the Russian overlords to accept the idea of a separate Finnish currency and officially recognize the Finnish language. Nearby is the House of the Estates, site of Finland's Parliament during the Russian era, and now occupied by several scientific societies.

But let us leave the Senate Square and the "Whitehall district" of Finland and take a stroll up Aleksanterinkatu, the main shopping center of Helsinki. At its top end, where it runs into Mannerheimintie, is Stockmann's, Finland's largest department store. At this corner is the famous statue of the Three Smiths by Felix Nylund, a common rendezvous for people who have to meet somewhere in town.

Where Mannerheimintie meets Esplanadi stands the Swedish Theater where plays are given in the Swedish language. To reach its Finnish-language rival, the older National Theater, you must turn around and go back down Aleksanterinkatu to the first street on your left, which leads into the huge square in front of the railway station, which is also the hub of the city's impressive new metro network. Here the National Theater is overshadowed by the massive station itself, designed by Eliel Saarinen. Although he became an American citizen during the war, Saarinen's last wish was to be buried in his native country. His ashes were flown to Finland in 1950 and interred in the grounds of the beautiful home he built for himself along the shore of lovely Lake Hvitträsk.

Right opposite the Railway Station is the City Center, a complex of shops, restaurants, cafés, with underground passageway of shops leading to the railway station. Also on the opposite side of the Railway Square and facing the National Theater is the newly renovated Art Museum of the Ateneum (Ateneum in Taidemuseo), which houses specimens of the works of Finland's greatest painters. The paintings of Gallen-Kallela, Hugo Simberg, Albert Edelfelt, Eero Järnefelt, and Magnus Enckell are known far beyond the borders of Finland and are well worth a visit. You'll also find some sculptures by the world-famous Wäinö Aaltonen.

Just behind the railway station stands the Main Post Office. Opposite is Sokos House which contains a large hotel and restaurant, plus numerous business offices and shops. Nearby is one of Helsinki's latest shopping precincts, Kaivopiha, an attractive oasis linked to the railway station, with an entrance from Mannerheimintie.

The Post Office marks one boundary of the "downtown" part of the capital. Across Mannerheimintie from here is the bus station and, in the adjoining block, the glossy new Forum shopping center. A stone's throw north along Mannerheimintie is the House of Parliament, the impressive structure in red granite which seems so striking because of the ample space around it. It looks solid and, if you go inside you will agree that it is solid, built to withstand storms of debate within and criticism from without. It is lavishly and beautifully decorated inside, even to the special caucus room reserved exclusively for the three-score or more of lady representatives. Finland's 200 members of Parliament are elected by proportional representation.

National Museum and Olympic Stadium

A short distance west of Mannerheimintie in Temppeliaukio is the Temppeliaukio church, one of Europe's most unusual modern churches, built into the living rock. Designed by the brothers Timo and Tuomo Suomalainen, it is also used as a concert hall. Returning to Mannerheimintie, just a few hundred meters from the House of Parliament is an odd-looking edifice with a tower which gives it a church-like appearance. This is the National Museum, which houses a large collection of ethnographical exhibits illustrating Finland's history. This area, round the shores of Töölönlahti Bay, is the site of the big new city plan designed by Alvar Aalto. Part of this is Finlandia Hall, the Concert and Congress Center, designed by him, which opened in 1971, close to the shore of the bay and not far from the National Museum. The Intercontinental Hotel is nearby, while the ultramodern City Theater, designed by Timo Pentilä, is across the bay.

About half a mile beyond Finlandia Hall, on the corner of Helsinginkatu, is the site of the glossy new Opera House due to open in 1992. Further along Mannerheimintie, not half an hour's walk from the railway station and but ten minutes by tram, rises the imposing tower of the Olympic Stadium. One of the finest views of Helsinki can be obtained from the top of this tower. Further north still and to the east of Mannerheimintie, less than two miles from the city center, is Helsinki's fine new International Fair Center, which opened in 1975. Exhibition halls, a restaurant, cafeteria and well-planned open spaces make it a showplace of its kind.

The street leading off at right angles from Mannerheimintie, Helsinginkatu, leads to the beautiful Botanical Gardens and the Water Tower, from which there is a fine view. Nearby is Helsinki's Tivoli, or permanent amusement park, called Linnanmäki, offering top-class entertainment of universal family appeal. Continuing along this street we come to the "East End" of Helsinki where there is little to see except proof of the fact that Helsinki has indeed no slums.

If you return to Mannerheimintie and cross the street, you will find yourself in the hospital center of the capital. Actually, it is still Töölö, the biggest residential district, but in this little section are concentrated most of the city's biggest and newest hospitals.

Although it may seem a startling suggestion, you next ought to go and see the Hietaniemi Cemetery. When you get there, you will realize why it is a favorite rendezvous for a promenade, for it is a beautiful place. Marshal Mannerheim is buried in the military section. It is a custom to place candles on each grave on Christmas Eve, a moving sight.

Another place well worth visiting is Arabia. This is one of the largest pottery factories in Europe and can be visited by appointment. Although the Arabia plant is some distance out of town, a tram service runs practically to the gate.

Helsinki's Islands

A number of Helsinki's most interesting sights are on islands, a major one being the fortress of Suomenlinna. In fact, this covers a series of interlinked islands, and the entire Finnish army assisted in its construction, which began in 1748. Under the protection of this fortification, Helsinki first began to develop and flourish. Once called the Gibraltar of the North, it was indeed impregnable, never having been taken by assault. Twice, however, it was surrendered without a fight, first to the Russians in the war of 1808–1809, and then during Finland's war of independence when the German Baltic Division, assisted by the Finnish Civic Guard, captured the city of Helsinki. During the Crimean War a combined British and French fleet bombarded the fortress and the fires caused by the cannonade convinced the army that the fortress could not withstand modern artillery fire.

Yet Suomenlinna is more than an ancient military monument with several museums; its parks and gardens are lovely, especially in the spring. One of the forts near the historic King's Gate has an outstanding restaurant. Bearing the historic name of Walhalla, it has been changed as little as possible. This group of islands has now been developed into an all-purpose center for cultural and leisure activities. It includes the recently completed Nordic Arts Center, partly housed in a restored barracks dating from 1868, and focussing on exhibitions and the promotion and exchange of ideas on Scandinavian art.

Seurasaari, an island linked by bridge to the mainland, is another good spot to visit. It houses a delightful open-air museum which brings together houses, ranging from simple huts with turf roofs to lovely wooden villas furnished with original furniture, transported from various parts of the country.

Yet another island, Korkeasaari, houses Helsinki's zoo, reached by ferry from the South Harbor or by foot bridge from Mustikkamaa. The latter is the home of Helsinki's Summer Theater and is also an island, but accessible by road bridge. Close to Korkeasaari, the islet of Hylkysaari is the setting for the recently opened National Maritime Museum. Still more islands in this sea-girt city feature such amenities as bathing beaches, restaurants, yacht clubs.

Environs

A trip round some of Helsinki's suburbs will give you a fine idea of that special Finnish talent for creating imaginative residential districts in harmony with nature. These provide the theme for some sightseeing tours, but if you want to explore independently, head for Tapiola Garden City, situated in the forests and close to the sea, to the west of town.

PRACTICAL INFORMATION FOR HELSINKI

See pg. 188 for further information on the solar eclipse on July 22, 1990.

GETTING TO TOWN FROM THE AIRPORT. Frequent bus services link Seutula Airport with the air terminal (Hotel Intercontinental, Töölönkatu 21) and Railway Square in the city center. Journey time is 30 minutes. Check-in takes place at the airport.

TOURIST INFORMATION. Free publications such as *Helsinki This Week* and *Helsinki Today* are good sources of information on what's on and where. The City Tourist Office is at Pohjoisesplanadi 19 (169 3757).

Helsinki Card. This entitles you to free entry to about 40 museums and other sights, a guided sightseeing tour and unlimited travel on the city's public transport, and quite a few discounts. The cost is 65 Fmk (one day), 85 Fmk (two days), 105 Fmk (three days); about half-price for children. You can buy it from the City Tourist Office, hotels and some travel agencies.

USEFUL ADDRESSES. Embassies. *Canada,* Pohjoisesplanadi 25B (171 141). *U.K.,* Uudenmaankatu 16–20 (647 922); during 1990 moving to Itäinen Puistotie 19 (90–661 311). *U.S.A.,* I. Puistotie 14A (171 931).

Car Hire. *Avis,* Fredrikinkatu 37 (441 155). *Budget Rent a Car,* Malminkatu 36 (694 5300). *Hertz,* Polarpoint, Hernesaarenranta 11 (622 1100). *Inter-Rent,* Hitsaajankatu 7 (775 6133).

American Express. Katajanokan pohjoisranta 9–13 (661 631).

Main Post Office. Mannerheimintie 11 (1955 117).

Emergency hospital for foreigners. Helsinki University Central Hospital (4711). Information on health care available round the clock on (735 001).

Emergency (police, fire, ambulance) tel. 000.

TELEPHONE CODES. The telephone code for Helsinki is 90. To call any number in this chapter, unless otherwise specified, this prefix must be used. Within the city no prefix is required.

HOTELS. Reservations are highly recommended as the city is busy with conferences and exhibitions when it is not full of tourists. There is a Hotel Booking Service in the railway station for hotel and private accommodations, open mid-May through mid-Sept., Mon. to Fri. 9–9, Sat. 9–7, Sun. 10–6; mid-Sept. through mid-May, Mon. to Fri. 9–6, closed Sat., Sun. Unless otherwise stated, all the hotels listed below are open all the year and have licensed restaurants.

Deluxe

Hesperia. Mannerheimintie 50 (43 101). 385 rooms, pool, night club. A short stroll from center. AE, DC, MC, V.

Inter-Continental. Mannerheimintie 46 (441 331). 555 rooms, pool, nightclub. Perhaps Helsinki's plushest. A short stroll from center. AE, DC, MC, V.

Kalastajatorppa. Kalastajatorpantie 1 (488 011). 235 rooms, pool, tennis, boating, fishing. Glorious seashore situation and linked by underground passage-way with famous *Round Room* restaurant and *Red Room* nightclub. AE, DC, MC, V.

Palace. Eteläranta 10 (171 114). 59 rooms. Stunning view over South Harbor. AE, DC, MC, V.

Ramada Presidentti. E. Rautatiekatu 4 (6911). 500 rooms, several restaurants, pool, nightclub, all-night café. Central. AE, DC, MC, V.

Rivoli Jardin. Kasarmikatu 40 (177 880). 53 rooms; winter garden, no restaurant. New, central, with particularly well-equipped rooms. AE, DC, MC, V.

Strand Inter-Continental. J. Stenberginranta 4 (39 351). Helsinki's latest with all facilities; 200 rooms, waterside location, pool. AE, DC, MC, V.

Expensive

Airport Hotel Rantasipi. Near Seutula Airport (826 822). 300 rooms, pool, nightclub. Excellent for transit stopovers with shuttle service to airport. AE, DC, MC, V.

Dipoli. Otaranta (435 811). 213 rooms, most with sea view, nightclub, disco, sports facilities. In garden suburb of Otaniemi, 9 km. from center. AE, DC, MC, V.

Helsinki. Hallituskatu 12 (171 401). 130 rooms, disco. Very central. AE, DC, MC, V.

Klaus Kurki. Bulevardi 2 (602 322). 130 rooms, central. AE, DC, MC, V.

Korpilampi. (Forest Lake) Lahnus (855 8431). 162 rooms, pool, nightclub, sports facilities, popular for congresses. Lovely forest setting in Espoo, 20 km. northwest of city. Some (M) accommodations. AE, DC, MC, V.

Merihotelli Cumulus. J. Stenberginranta 6 (708 111). 87 rooms, pool. AE, DC, MC, V.

Olympia. L. Brahenkatu 2 (750 801). 100 rooms. AE, DC, MC, V.

Seurahuone. Kaivokatu 12 (170 441). 114 rooms, nightclub, disco, elegant Café Socis. Very central, opposite rail station. AE, DC, MC, V.

Tapiola Garden. Tapiontori (461 711). 82 rooms, pool, nightclub. In the garden suburb of Tapiola. AE, DC, MC, V.

Torni. Yrjönkatu 26 (131 131). 158 rooms, several restaurants with different specialties, in high rise block. Central. AE, DC, MC, V.

Vaakuna. Asema-aukio 2 (171 811). 290 rooms, nightclub, disco. Central location on main railway station square. AE, DC, MC, V.

Moderate

Anna, Annankatu 1 (648 011). 58 rooms, cafeteria only. Nicely renovated small hotel in the center. AE, MC, V.

Aurora. Helsinginkatu 50 (717 400). 75 rooms, pool. AE, DC, MC, V.

Espoo (523 533). 13 km. (8 miles) from city. 94 rooms, rooftop pool. AE, DC, MC, V.

Haaga. Nuijamiestentie 10 (578 311). Not so central, part of the Hotel and Restaurant College, 110 rooms, pool. AE, DC, MC, V.

Helka. P. Rautatienkatu 23 (440 581). 150 rooms, some Expensive. AE, DC, MC, V.

Hospiz. Vuorikatu 17B (170 481). 141 rooms, unlicensed restaurant. AE, DC, MC, V.

Martta. Uudenmaankatu 24 (646 211). 44 rooms, unlicensed restaurant. AE, MC, V.

Ursula. Paasivuorenkatu 1 (750 311). Not so central, 43 rooms, cafeteria. AE, DC, MC, V.

Inexpensive

Academica. Hietaniemenkatu 14 (402 0206). Summer only, 216 rooms, pool, disco, tennis. AE, MC, V.

Dipoli Summer Hotel. Jämeräntaival (460 211). 240 rooms; sports facilities. Summer only. AE, DC, MC, V.

Finn. Kalevankatu 3B (640 904). 28 rooms; no restaurant. MC, V.

Satakuntatalo. Lapinrinne 1 (694 0311). Summer only, 64 rooms. AE, MC, V.

Cheapest accommodations are in boarding houses such as **Kongressikoti,** Snellmaninkatu 15 (174 839). **Clairet,** It. Teatterikuja 3 (669 707). MC, V. **Erottajanpuisto,** Uudenmaankatu 9 (642 169). **Lönnrot,** Lönnrotinkatu 16 (693 2590). **Omapohja,** It. Teatterikuja 3 (666 211). **Pensionat Regina,** Puistokatu 9 (656 937).

Apartment Rentals

Check with Art Travel (753 7018) or Yksitysmajoitus (445 048).

Camping

Rastila. 13 km. (8 miles) east of city center. Open May 15 to Sept. 15.

Youth Hostels

Olympic Stadium Youth and Family Hostel, Pohjoinen Stadionintie 3B (496 071). Open all year.
City Youth and Family Hostel. Porthaninkatu 2 (709 92590). Open May 15 through Aug.

HOW TO GET AROUND. By tram/bus. A ride costs 6.50 Fmk (small reduction for ten-ride tickets), allowing transfers within a one-hour period. A tourist ticket valid for 24 hours for unlimited travel is available from the Helsinki Tourist Office or public transport ticket offices (but not on board the vehicles), but better value is the Helsinki Card (see pg. 160), which gives many benefits including unlimited travel on all public transport within the city. The 3T tram, with commentary in several languages in summer, follows a figure-eight circuit right around the city center.
By metro. The first section of Helsinki's splendid new subway begins one stop beyond the main rail station and goes northeast to Itäkeskus, where it links with bus services to the outer suburbs. Same fare and transfer system as tram/bus above.
By taxi. These bear the sign "taksi." Minimum charge is 10,50 Fmk, with a surcharge added after 6 P.M. and at weekends. The fare increases according to the length of journey, amount of luggage and number of passengers. No tips are necessary or expected.
By boat. Regular ferries link the South Harbor with island communities, in addition to sightseeing boats throughout summer.
On foot. The Helsinki City Tourist Office have worked out some excellent itineraries, with maps. Ask for their free booklet "See Helsinki on Foot."

TOURS. There is a good selection of half- and full-day sightseeing tours of the city, some extending to the suburbs. Sightseeing trips by boat leave from the Market Square (South Harbor) visiting Helsinki's archipelago. Some include a lunch stop ashore.
Further afield is Hvitträsk with its lovely lake and the former studio-home of three leading Finnish architects. Another short excursion is to Ainola, near Järvenpää, the lovely home of Sibelius, now open to the public. The composer is buried in the grounds. Among other trips that can be made in one day, three are especially recommended: Porvoo (Borgå), Hanko and Hämeenlinna combined with Aulanko. You can travel to Porvoo by boat in three hours, returning by bus; or go both ways by boat.
Full details of all these trips are available from the tourist office.

MUSEUMS. The opening times given below are for the summer; check for other seasons. Entrance fees are usually 5–15 Fmk; in a few cases admission is free. Don't forget the Helsinki Card which gives free admission to around 40 museums and other sights.
Ateneumin Taidemuseo (Art Museum of the Ateneum). Railway Square. Reopening in 1990 after extensive renovation. Mainly paintings, sculptures, drawings, etc., by Finnish artists; some foreign and old masters. Open Mon. to Sat. 9–5, Wed. 9–8, Sun. 11–5.
Arabian museo (Museum of Arabia). Hämeentie 135. Table ware and ceramic art by this famous Finnish porcelain factory. Open Mon. 10–8, Tues. to Fri. 10–5, Sta.–Sun. 9–3. By terminal of tram no. 6.

HELSINKI 163

Gallen-Kallelan museo (Gallen-Kallela Museum). Leppävaara, Tarvaspää, reached by no. 4 tram to Munkkiniemi, then pleasant 2 km. walk. The home and works of one of Finland's greatest painters in charming surroundings. Open Tues. to Thurs. 10–8, Fri. to Sun. 10–5.

Helsingin Kaupunginmuseo (Helsinki City Museum). Karamzininkatu 2, beside Finlandia Hall. Art, furniture, archives illustrating history of city. Open Sun. to Fri. 12–4, Thurs. 12–8.

Helsingen kaupungin Taidemuseo (Helsinki City Art Museum). Tamminiementie 6, near Seurasaari. Finnish and French art from 20th century. Open Wed. to Sun. 11–6.30.

Heureka (The Finnish Science Center). Tikkurila in Vantaa, 15 minutes by train from the city center. The surrealist complex of this high-tech wonderland opened in 1989, covering everything from natural phnomena to the latest computer technology, with the whole range of audio-visual displays and working models. You can even conduct your own experiments. In the Center's Verne Theater, you'll get a new dimension on outer space. Open Mon.–Fri., 10–8, Sat.–Sun., 10–6.

Mannerheim-museo (Mannerheim Museum). Kalliolinnantie 14, Kaivopuisto. Home of Marshal Mannerheim, containing his collected trophies. Open Fri. and Sat. 11–3, Sun. 11–4.

Ruiskumestarin talo (Burgher's House). Kristianinkatu 12. Oldest wooden house in Helsinki (1817). Open Sun. to Fri. 12–4, Thurs. 12–8; closed Sat.

Seurasaaren ulkomuseo (Seurasaari Open-air Museum). Seurasaari island. Farm and manor buildings from different parts of the country. Open daily 11.30–5.30, Wed. 11.30–7.

Sinebrychoff Art Museum. Bulevardi 40. Collection of foreign old masters, especially Dutch and Flemish. Open Mon. to Fri. 9–5, Sat., Sun. 11–5.

Sports Museum. Olympic Stadium. Permanent and changing exhibitions, including memorabilia of some of the world's greatest athletes and skiers. There are also "ghosts" from the 1940 Olympics (pre-empted by World War II), such as the winners' podium that was never used. Open Mon.–Fri. 11–5, Thurs. 11–7, Sat.–Sun. 12–4.

Suomen kansallismuseo (National Museum). Mannerheimintie 34. Three sections: prehistoric, historic, ethnographic. Open 11–4 daily, Tues. also 6–9.

Suomen merimuseo (National Maritime Museum). Hylkysaari island, ferry 10 min. from Market Square (South Harbor). Also reached by footbridge from Mustikkamaa via Korkeasaari. Specialized maritime history museum. Open daily 10–3.

Suomen rakennustaiteen museo (Museum of Finnish Architecture). Kasarmikatu 24. Archives of Finnish architecture, past and present. Open 10–4. Closed Mon.

Taideteollisuusmuseo (Museum of Applied Arts), Korkeavuorenkatu 23. Development of design. Open Tues. to Fri. 11–5, Sat. and Sun. 11–4.

Urho Kekkonen Museum. Tamminiemi, Seurasaarentie 15. The late Urho Kekkonen, Finland's longest-serving President, lived here for 30 years. Near Seurasaari. Open daily 11–4.

PARKS AND ZOOS. The *City Conservatories* are in Eläintarha Park, open Mon. to Sat. 12–3, Sun. 11–3. Two central parks are *Tähtitorninmäki* (Observatory Hill) on the west side of the South Harbor and, a little to the south, *Kaivopuisto*—both rather more natural than formal. A beautiful oasis west of the center is the shoreside cemetery of *Hietaniemi;* Marshal Mannerheim is buried here. A little north of this is *Sibelius Park* with its distinctive sculpture by Eila Hiltunen commemorating the great Finnish composer.

Helsinki *zoo* is on the island of Korkeasaari, reached by ferry from the South Harbor, or by foot bridge from Mustikkamaa island which is accessible by road. Open June and July 10–9; shorter hours in other months.

HISTORIC BUILDINGS AND SITES. Eduskuntatalo (Parliament). Mannerheimintie. An imposing granite building, designed by Siren and completed in 1931. For entrance hours, contact the City Tourist Office. Public admitted to gallery during full session.

Stadionin torni (Olympic Stadium Tower). Eteläinen Stadionintie 3. Offers superb views. Open Mon. to Fri. 9–8, Sat. and Sun. 10–5.

Suomenlinna. Frequent ferry service from South Harbor. Fortifications on series of islands, now developed into a multi-purpose center: Nordic Arts center, museums, summer restaurants, summer theater, guided tours. Museums open daily 11–5.

Temppeliaukion kirkko (Temppeliaukio church). Lutherinkatu 3. Beautifully carved out of living rock to the plans of Timo and Tuomo Suomalainen. Open Mon. to Sat. 10–8, Sun. 12–2, 5–8.

Tuomiokirkko (Cathedral). Senaatintori. Fine classical building by Engel dating from the 1830s. Open Mon. to Fri. 9–5, Sat. and Sun. 9–6.

Uspenskin Kathedraali (Uspenski Cathedral). Kanavankatu 1. Completed in 1868, the most important Orthodox church in Finland. Open Mon. to Fri. 10–3.

Vanhakaupunki (Old Town). Original site of city founded in 1550, reached by tram no. 6.

SPORTS. Golf. There is a good 18-hole course at Talin kartano (Tali Manor), some 7 km. (4 miles) from city center. The tourist office can supply details about green fees and playing conditions.

Saunas. Nearly all hotels have them, but also recommended (and inexpensive) are those at swimming halls listed in *Helsinki Tourist Information.*

Swimming. The rocky shores and small beaches in and around the city offer plenty of opportunities. Among them are: Uunisaari, an island opposite the residential and diplomatic district of Kaivopuisto; the sandy beach of Hietaranta; the island of Seurasaari (accessible on foot); Mustikkamaa; farther out on the island of Pihlajasaari; Suomenlinna. Also at the Swimming Stadium or at Kumpula open-air pool.

Tennis. There are indoor courts at: Tennispalatsi, Ruskeasuo, Yrjönkatu 21B, Kulosaari, Meilahti Sports Park, Töölö Sports House, Tali Tennis Center, Myllypuro Tennis Center. Outdoor courts are at: Kaisaniemi, Kalastajatorppa, Kulosaari, Meilahti Sports Park, Taivallahti.

Winter sports. In winter, you can ski in the heart of the city through the parks (as some Helsinkiites do on their way to work!), or anywhere in the surrounding countryside. More specifically, Nuuksionpää, northwest of the city by bus, offers good terrain or, further afield, the ridges of Hyvinkää can be reached by bus or train. There is also ice skating at numerous public rinks in Helsinki.

MUSIC, MOVIES AND THEATERS. Music. The *National Opera Theater* at Bulevardi 23–27 (moving to a brand new complex on Mannerheimintie in 1992) offers performances of international and Finnish operas and ballets. Concerts are often held in the magnificent Aalto-designed *Finlandia Hall* on Mannerheimintie. Musical performances are also held in a number of attractive settings in summer, such as organ recitals on Sunday evenings in the Cathedral, concerts in *Temppeliaukion Church* and the *House of Nobility,* and open-air concerts of various kinds in several parks.

Movies. All films are shown in their original language with Finnish subtitles.

Theaters. The Finns are enthusiastic theatergoers and, though the main theaters will present most visitors with a language problem, it's well worth attending one of the several open-air summer theaters for the atmosphere and setting. The main ones are: *Helsinki Summer Theater* on Mustikkamaa island; *Operetta Theater* at the Rowing Stadium; *Peacock Theater* (variety shows) at Linnanmäki amusement park; *Rhymäteatteri* on Suomenlinna; *Student Theater,* Seurasaari; *Summer Theater,* Central Park, in the grounds of Laakso riding field; *Töölönranta Summer Theater* at Töölölahti Bay.

SHOPPING. Ask for the leaflet with full details of tax-free shopping, giving savings of about 11% on purchases of over 200 Fmk. The shop gives you a check for the appropriate amount which you can cash at most departure points; but you must also produce the items you have bought. Prices may not be low, but quality is high as is the standard of design of most Finnish products. Items to look out for especially are glass, handwoven textiles, fashion wear, furs, stainless steel, metal and semi-precious jewelry, wooden toys. Hand-made candles in brilliant or subtle shades are charming inexpensive buys, while at the other end of the scale, the Finns produce beautifully designed modern furniture!

If you haven't much time to shop around, your best bet is to go to one of the big stores. The most famous is *Stockmann's,* founded in 1862, filling a block between Aleksanterinkatu, Mannerheimintie and Keskuskatu; it has an efficient export service. Nearby is the newly renovated Aleksi 13 department store.

Two big marketing groups with a nationwide network are SOK with their *Sokos* stores and hypermarkets, and E Marketing with their *Centrum* and *EKA-Market* (cut price) department stores.

The main shopping streets are Pohjoisesplanadi and Aleksanterinkatu, and the smaller streets off these. Stroll along Pohjoisesplanadi (North Esplanade) and you'll find the showrooms and shops of many major firms such as *Arabia* (ceramics and porcelain), *Nuutajärvi* (glass), *Marimekko* and *Vuokko* (fashions and fabrics), *Aarikka* (costume jewelry, wooden buttons and other crafts), *Pentik (leather) and Studio Tarja Niskanen* (furs). Most shops on Esplanadikatu are open on Sunday afternoons in summer. *Iso Roobertinkatu* is Helsinki's first pedestrian-only street, popularly known as Roba.

For a selection of small shops, go to the Station Tunnel (linking the rail station with the City Center complex opposite), or *Hakaniemi Market Hall,* where 50 shops above the covered food market in Hämeentie offer interesting variety. Several new and attractive shopping precincts include *Kaivopiha,* off Mannerheimintie and linked to the railway station. Another is the *Senaatti Center* opposite the cathedral.

A "must" is a morning visit to Kauppatori (Market Square) where the lively open-air market flourishes, year-round, by the South Harbor, selling fruit, vegetables, fish and household goods. It reopens in the afternoon in summer when the emphasis is on arts and crafts. Another main market place at Hietalahti includes a flea market from Mon. to Sat. 6.30–2.

Among specialist shops, the following are particularly worth a visit: Jewelry—*Kalevala Koru,* Unioninkatu 25 (especially beautiful traditional Kalevala motifs); *Galerie Björn Weckström,* Unioninkatu 30, or *Lindroos,* Aleksanterinkatu 48 (truly handsome modern jewelry). Furs—*Turkistuottaja* have an auction at Martinkyläntie 40 (in the suburb of Vantaa); *Ali Fur,* Erottaja 1–3; *Fur Shop,* Yrjönkatu 12–14. You can get anything and everything for the sauna from *Sauna-Soppi,* Aleksanterinkatu 28, Senate Square.

Finally Scandinavia's biggest bookshop is *Akateeminen Kirjakauppa* (Academic Bookstore), Keskuskatu 1.

RESTAURANTS. Helsinki's eating houses cater for every taste and pocket, ranging from the gourmet to the budgeteer in a hurry. All establishments listed below are fully licensed unless otherwise stated. Remember that set meals served between certain hours will bring costs down sharply.

Expensive

Alexander Nevski. Pohjoisesplanadi 17 (639 610). Helsinki's latest to capture the style and gastronomy of Imperial Russia. AE, DC, MC, V.

Amadeus. Sofiankatu (626 676). Quiet atmosphere, friendly service, game specialties. AE, DC, MC, V.

Bellevue. Rahapajankatu 3 (179 560). Russian style. AE, DC, MC, V.

Café Adlon. Fabianinkatu 14 (664 611). Smart. DC, MC, V.

Céline. Kasarmikatu 23 (636 921). One of the best. AE, MC, V.

Engel, Tehtaankatu 34 (628 865). One of Helsinki's latest, with ambitious *à la carte* menu. AE, DC, MC, V.

George. Kalevankatu 17 (647 662). Sophisticated gourmet restaurant voted "Restaurant 1987" by a Finnish Gourmet Club. AE, DC, MC, V.

Havis Amanda. Unioninkatu 23 (666 882). By the South Harbor; two sections of which one specializes in fish. AE, DC, MC, V.

Kaivohuone. (177 881). In attractive location in Kaivopuisto Park looking out to the harbor; floorshow. AE, DC, MC, V.

Katajanokka Casino. Laivastokatu 1 (653 401). In fine seashore location. AE, MC, V.

König. Mikonkatu 4 (171 271). Subdued, sophisticated setting, below ground. AE, DC, MC, V.

Kulosaari Casino. Hopeasalmenpolku 1 (688 202). Pleasantly placed on island of the same name, but accessible by road. Dancing. AE, DC, MC, V.

Kultainen Sipuli (Golden Onion). Kanavaranta (179 900). One of Helsiniki's latest and most attractive in restored brick warehouse in the Katajanokka district. AE, DC, V.

Mestaritalli. Toivo Kuulan puisto (440 274). Formerly stables, now an elegant restaurant in a seashore park. Dancing. AE, DC, MC, V.

Piekka Finnish Cuisine. Sibeliuksenkatu 2 (493 591). Finnish specialties prepared in the traditional way in one of Helsinki's newest eating houses. AE, DC, MC, V.

Round House. Kalastajatorpantie 2 (488 011). A famous showpiece, beautifully situated near the seashore, above the Red Room nightclub. Floorshow. Part of the Kalastajatorppa hotel. AE, DC, MC, V.

Savoy. Eteläesplanadi 14 (176 571). A favorite lunch place for Finland's tycoons. Designed by Alvar Aalto. AE, DC, MC, V.

Svenska Klubben. Maurinkatu 6 (628 706). Intimate manorial atmosphere in listed historic house by North Harbor. AE, DC, MC, V.

Walhalla. (668 552). On fortress island of Suomenlinna, reached by short ferry journey from South Harbor. You dine in the authentic 18th-century atmosphere of a fortress never taken by storm, in a setting of ancient ramparts and flowering lilac bushes—one of the memorable sights of Helsinki. Summer only. AE, DC, MC, V.

Moderate

Agora Tea Room. Unioninkatu 30 (607 092). Especially for tea enthusiasts. DC, MC, V.

Amigo. Tehtaankatu 12 (625 311). Good for Spanish food.

Cafe Socis. In Seurahuone hotel, elegant rendezvous, lunch (M), coffee and cakes (E). AE, DC, MC, V.

El' Greco. Eteläesplanadi 22 (607 565). Greek food. AE, MC, V.

Elite. Eteläinen Hesperiankatu (495 542). Recently refurbished but maintaining its appeal to both locals and artists. MC, V.

Happy Days. Pohjoisesplanadi 2 (624 023). Adjoining Swedish Theater, with several restaurants of various price levels and types. MC, V.

Kappeli. (179 242). In the Esplanade near the South Harbor, recently renovated with several sections including open-air summer restaurant. AE, DC, MC, V.

Karelia. Käpylänkuja 1 (799 077). Karelian specialties. AE, DC, MC, V.

Kosmos. Kalevankatu 3 (607 717). Varied home-cooked fare in one of Helsinki's oldest restaurants in the heart of downtown; it's been in the same family since opening in the 1920s—and has kept the original ambience. AE, MC, V.

Omenapuu. Keskuskatu 6 (630 205). Cozy family restaurant in busy shopping center. Can be *Inexpensive.* AE, DC, MC, V.

Ostrobotnia. Museokatu 10 (408 602). Finnish food, good value.

Perho. Mechelininkatu 7 (493 481). Run by the Helsinki Hotel and Restaurant College and recently renovated. Excellent value. AE, DC, MC, V.

Rivoli. Albertinkatu 38 (643 455). French cuisine. AE, DC, MC, V.

Tamminiementien Café. Tamminiementie, near Seurasaari Open Air Museum. Homemade goodies (including Polish specialties) served in the restored faded elegance of the 1740s manor house of Meilahti. Lots of atmosphere, but definitely not for the calorie-conscious. MC, V.

Tervasaaren Aitta. Tervasaari (605 412). Excellent cold table. Summer only. AE, DC, MC, V.

Troikka. Caloniuksenkatu 3 (445 229). One of a chain of three small eating places, specializing in Russian food. AE, DC, MC, V.

Vanha Maestro. Fredrikinkatu 51–53 (644 303). You can dance in the daytime here (Wed. and Sun. are Ladies Invitation Days). AE, MC, V.

Wellamo. Vyökatu 9 (663 139). Small, intimate, rustic atmosphere, good food if you like garlic. AE, MC, V.

Inexpensive

Carrols. Self-service hamburger restaurants in Mannerheimintie 19, in the City Passage, and Keskuskatu 3; disposable plates and cups; good value. Unlicensed.

Chez Marius. Mikonkatu 1 (669 697). French cuisine, beer and wine only.

Eliel. In the railway station (177 900). Genuine *art nouveau* style. Self-service. MC, V.

Kasvisravintola. Korkeavuorenkatu 3 (179 212). Self-service vegetarian restaurant. Unlicensed. DC.

Kellarikrouvi. P. Makasiininkatu 6 (655 198). Cozy wine cellar atmosphere. AE, DC, MC, V.

Kynsilaukka (Garlic). Fredrikinkatu 22 (651 939). Makes good use of garlic in rustic decor. DC, MC, V.

Vanhan Kellari. Mannerheimintie 3 (654 646). In cellar of Old Students' House. MC, V.

Wienerwald, Kaivokatu (663 589) and Lauttasaari (677 400). Part of the Austrian chain. AE, MC, V.

Many modern and attractive cafés (*kahvila* or *baari*), dotted about town, offer refreshments and sometimes hot meals, as well as coffee, cakes, etc. Look out for **Frazer.** AE, MC, V. Several cafés have lovely shoreside locations, such as the **Ursula,** Kaivopuisto.

A selection of English-style pubs includes: **Angleterre** (M), Fredrikinkatu 47 (647 371), AE; **Annan Pub** (M), Annankatu 3 (633 316). MC, V. **Richard's Pub** (M), Rikhardinkatu 4 (667 232); and **St. Urho's Pub** (M), Museokatu 10 (446 940).

NIGHTLIFE. Young people wanting to meet their Finnish counterparts can try one of the following discos: **Alibi,** Hietaniemenkatu 14; **Club Anna and Eric,** Eerikinkatu 3; **Harald's,** Kasarmikatu 40; **Ky-Exit,** Pohj. Rautatiekatu 21; **Tavastia,** Urho Kekkosenkatu 4–6.

For family fun, there's Linnanmäki amusement park (summer only), Helsinki's Tivoli with Peacock Theater, side shows, open-air dancing, Monorail and jungle train.

See under *Hotels* for establishments with nightclubs and under *Restaurants* for those featuring floor shows and dancing.

THE SOUTH COAST AND ISLANDS

The Gateway for Finnish Culture

Anyone with a weakness for islands will find a magic world of them stretching along Finland's coastline. There, in the Gulf of Finland and the Baltic, over 30,000 islands form a magnificent archipelago. Westward from Turku ride the rugged but fascinating Åland Islands group, forming an autonomous province of their own. Turku, the former capital, was also the main gateway through which cultural influences reached Finland over the centuries. The coastal district of Porvoo, east of Helsinki, is another area stuffed with history and cultural associations.

In this section, where two place names are given for a center, the second is the Swedish one and it indicates that there is a substantial Swedish-speaking element in the population. An exception is the Åland archipelago, where the population is entirely Swedish-speaking and therefore preference has been given to Swedish names.

Exploring the South Coast

Fifty km. (31 miles) east of Helsinki and on the coast lies Porvoo (Borgå), one of the oldest towns in Finland. It was only Helsinki's privileged position, plus the usual run of fires and wars, that kept Porvoo from growing into a great port. The major landmark of Porvoo Cathedral dates from the 15th century and it is famous as the setting for the first meeting of the Finnish Diet, called by Czar Alexander I in 1809, at which he proclaimed Finland an autonomous Grand Duchy. Today it is thought of as a town of poets and painters, for it has been the home of many of Finland's most famous names in the realm of arts and letters; the colorful wooden houses and shady alleys of the old district are enchanting. The greatest of Porvoo's sons was J. L. Runeberg, the national poet, whose home, kept as it was when he lived in it, stands at the corner of Runeberginkatu and Aleksanterinkatu in the new part of town. Also worth seeing are the old Town Hall, now a historical museum, and the Ville Vallgren Museum housed in typical 18th-century buildings.

Loviisa comes next, a rather charming summer resort; a special feature is its open-air theater with revolving auditorium, on a smaller scale to the famous one at Tampere.

Farther east are the two islands of Kotka and Hovinsaari, at the mouth of the Kymi river. Kotka was practically unknown until the naval battles of Ruotsinsalmi fought off its shore in 1789 and 1790 revealed its suitability as a harbor. (There is an open-air museum to the battle on Varissaari (Fort Elisabeth) reached by boat.) The Russians also saw the Kotka area as an excellent place to build frontier fortifications against attacks by land or sea from the west. Work on the fortifications was begun in 1791, and at the same time the fortress of Kyminlinna was built on the northern end of Hovinsaari. They were destroyed by a British naval force in 1855, but ten years later a thriving sawmill industry brought the town back to life, and today Kotka is Finland's largest export harbor for timber.

One of the most pleasant spots in the area is the Imperial Fishing Lodge, now a museum, by Langinkoski rapids, built in 1889. An idyllic haven, an hour away by motor boat, is the island of Kaunissaari, with beautiful beaches of fine sand.

West of Helsinki

Hvitträsk, 28 km. (17 miles) west of Helsinki, was the home of famous Finnish architects Eliel Saarinen, Armas Lindgren and Herman Gesellius. Today it is a museum, with an excellent restaurant attached, beautifully situated above Hvitträsk lake. There are Stone Age traces in the vicinity.

Next comes Tammisaari (Ekenäs). Predominantly Swedish-speaking, Tammisaari has little of historical interest, although like most towns along Finland's south coast, it, too, can produce a cannon ball that was fired at it by the British fleet during the time of the Crimean War. But it is a pretty town, with narrow old streets, and the drive to it from the capital is a pleasant one. The forests here are more of the broad-leaved variety, as opposed to the vast majority of Finland's forests, which are of pine and fir. Tammisaari also goes in for the cultivation of what the foresters term exotic plants and trees, and it is interesting to find oak trees here, some of the very few in Finland. An excursion from Tammisaari is to the ruins of medieval Raasepori (Raseborg) Castle, about 16 km. (10 miles) east.

An hour's drive farther to the west is the popular seaside resort of Hanko (Hangö), with its long stretch of sandy beach. This very popular sailing center was once a major launching point for emigrants to the U.S.A., Canada and Australia.

Turku, the Old Capital

Finland's oldest city, founded in the 13th century, and its capital until 1812, Turku is situated on both banks of the Aura river. With a population of 162,000, it is the country's third largest city and is sometimes called "the cradle of Finnish culture". Commercially its great importance lies in the fact that its harbor is the most easily kept open throughout the winter. In fact, the very word, *turku,* means trading post. It is also widely known for its shipyards. It has both Finnish and Swedish Universities, the new buildings of the Finnish one being well worth a visit.

Called Åbo by the Swedish-speaking Finns, Turku is the center of the southwest part of the country, whose land is fertile and winters are milder. With a cathedral over 700 years old, the city is still the seat of the Archbishop of Finland. Although gutted by fire in 1827, the cathedral has been completely restored. In the choir can be seen R. W. Ekman's frescos portraying Bishop Henry (an Englishman) baptizing the heathen Finns, and Mikael Agricola offering the Finnish translation of the New Testament to Gustav Vasa of Sweden.

Where the Aura river flows into the sea stands Turku Castle, the city's second most important historical monument. The oldest part of the fortress was built at the end of the 13th century, whereas the newer part dates back to the 16th century. Once a prison, it has been attractively restored and contains today the Historical Museum, with collections of furniture, portraits, arms and implements covering 400 years.

Like Helsinki, Turku has a lively open-air morning market, which in summer reopens from 4–8 P.M. Among the city's other main sights is the Handicrafts Museum: a street of wooden houses that survived the 1827 fire and now features such craft workshops as the comb-maker, the weaver, and the potter, using equipment and techniques that date back a century and a half. In summer, visitors may also try their hand under expert guidance. Notable, too, is the Resurrection Chapel, one of the outstanding creations of modern Finnish architecture. Also well worth visiting in Turku are the Sibelius Museum and the Wäinö Aaltonen Museum, the latter devoted to the works of Finland's great sculptor and additionally featuring changing exhibitions of contemporary art. Both are on the banks of the River Aura as is the striking modern theater.

Besides several old churches erected during the Middle Ages not far outside the city, there is the Ruissalo National Park, located on an island though accessible by road; it has the largest oak woods in the country. There is also a pleasant sandy beach, modern accommodations and good sports facilities.

But one of the greatest attractions in the vicinity of Turku is the beach at the coastal resort of Naantali (Nådendal), where the President of Finland has his summer residence. Finland's oldest known author, Jöns Budde, was a monk in the 15th-century monastery whose chapel now serves as the church. There are water-bus trips on certain summer evenings from Turku to Naantali. Other good excursions from Turku include the Tour of Seven Churches, covering some of the delightful medieval churches of the area.

Åland Islands

From Turku there are air and sea connections to the Åland (Ahvenan-maa) islands, where rural calm combines with fine coastal scenery. In all, there are over 6,500 islands and skerries, a handful of them inhabited by a total population of 23,000. Virtually all of them are Swedish-speaking and the Ålanders are very proud of their largely autonomous status. Near-ly half the population lives in the pleasant little capital of Mariehamn (Maarianhamina) which straddles a narrow peninsula, its two harbors linked by the shady main avenues of Norra Esplanadgatan and Storagatan. The Maritime Museum near the main harbor is well worth visiting for the islands have a very long seafaring tradition; nearby is the splendid four-masted barque *Pommern*.

Åland is particularly well organized for cycling and fishing packages, motor tours (you can go island-hopping on the network of car or passenger ferries), farmhouse holidays and rental cottages—over 7000 of them scat-tered about the islands, 1200 available for rent. These are marvelous sail-ing waters though, as yet, only a few yachts are available for rent.

There is much of historic interest for the archipelago has been inhabited since prehistoric times. Some of the medieval stone churches on the islands are particularly well preserved, notably those of Jomala, seven km. (four miles) north of Mariehamn; Finström, 25 km. (16 miles) north; Hammar-land, 21 km. (13 miles) northwest; Eckerö, 37 km. (23 miles) northwest; Sund, 25 km. (16 miles) northeast; and Lemland, 13 km. (eight miles) southeast. Also of interest are the scattered ruins of a big naval fortress built by the Russians in the early 19th century and only half completed when it was blasted out of existence by Anglo-French forces during the Crimean War in 1854. These are at Bomarsund, about 35 km. (22 miles) northeast of Mariehamn and, only ten km. (six miles) away, is Kastelholm Castle built by the Swedes in the 14th century, though considerably dam-aged. The castle is currently being completely restored, a process which will take several years though parts of it can be visited. Very close is the excellent open-air museum of Jan Karlsgarden, a collection of farm build-ings from the mid-19th century. In the vicinity is a new golf course.

In prehistoric times, the Åland isles were—relatively speaking—heavily populated, as shown by traces of no less than 10,000 settlements, graves and strongholds from antiquity, though they are mostly difficult to find. One of the largest Viking cemeteries is near the 13th century ruins of Lem-böte chapel in the parish of Lemland.

PRACTICAL INFORMATION FOR
THE SOUTH COAST AND ISLANDS

TOURIST INFORMATION. Hanko. Bulevardi 15 (911–82 239); in summer, In-formation Office at the Eastern Harbor (911–85 617). **Kotka.** (City) Keskuskatu 17 (952–11 736). (Region) Keskuskatu 13 (952–13 284). **Lohja.** Laurinkatu 61 (912–201 217). **Loviisa.** Brandensteinsgatan 13 (915–52 212). **Mariehamn.** Storaga-tan 18 (928–16 575). **Naantali.** Puistotie 24 (921–755 388). **Porvoo.** Rauhankatu 20 (915–170 145); in summer also in the Old Town Hall Square (915–130 747).

Tammisaari. Skillnadsgatan 16 (911–14 600). **Turku.** (City) Käsityöläiskatu 3 (921–336 366). (Region) L. Rantakatu 13 (921–517 333); Information Offices at Aurakatu 4 (921–315 363) and at the harbor (921–303 563).

TELEPHONE CODES. We have given telephone codes for all the towns and villages in the hotel and restaurant lists that follow. These codes need only be used when calling from outside the town or village concerned.

HOTELS AND RESTAURANTS. Unless otherwise stated, all the hotels listed below have all or some rooms with bath or shower, licensed restaurants, and are open all the year.

We have divided the hotels and restaurants in the lists that follow into four categories—Deluxe (L), Expensive (E), Moderate (M) and Inexpensive (I). Where two names are given below for a town or village, the second is the Swedish one (except in the case of Swedish-speaking Mariehamn), and it indicates that there is a substantial Swedish–speaking element in the population.

Hanko (Hangö). Bathing and sailing resort. *Regatta* (E), Merikatu 1 (911–86 491). 32 rooms, near sea. AE, DC, MC, V.
Restaurant. *Casino* (E), Appelgrenintie 10 (911–82 310). Traditional style, summer only. AE, DC, MC, V.
Camping. *Silversand,* late May to late August.
Hanko's Travelers' Home and Hostel. Bulevardi 15 (911–82 239).

Kotka. Major sea port with nearby bathing. *Seurahuone* (E), Kaivokatu 16 (952–11 090). 100 rooms, disco. DC, MC, V. *Kesti–Karhu* (M), Karjalantie 7 (952–63 466). 20 rooms, sports facilities. *Ruotsinsalmi* (M), Kirkkokatu 14 (952–13 440). 24 rooms. DC, MC, V. *Koskisoppi* (I), Keisarinmajantie 4 (952–25 555). 48 rooms, summer only.
Restaurants. *Hamlet* (M), Kymenlaaksonkatu 16 (952–15 240). DC, MC, V. *Meriniemi* (M), Puistola (952–11 945). Summer only. AE, DC, MC, V. *Palski* (M), Satamakatu 9 (952–11 421). AE, DC, MC, V.
Camping. *Santalahti,* Mussalo (952–604 060), open all year.
Youth Hostels. *Municipal youth and family hostel,* Sports Center (952–11 603). *Kärkisaari,* Mussalo (952–604 215).

Lohja. *Gasthaus Laurinportti* (E–M), Laurinkatu 1 (912–11 771). 16 rooms.
Camping. *Haikari* (912–24 735), open June 1 through mid–Aug.

Loviisa (Lovisa). South coast town. *Skandinavia* (M), Karlskronabulevardi 9–11 (915–531 725). 20 rooms, pool. DC, MC, V. *Zilton* (M), Mariankatu 29 (915–52 191). 10 rooms. DC, MC, V.

Mariehamn (Maarianhamina). Cozy capital of the Åland islands. *Arkipelag* (L–E), Strandgatan 31 (928–14 020). 86 rooms, pools, nightclub, tennis, the islands' newest and plushest. AE, DC, MC, V. *Adlon* (E), Hamngatan 7 (928–15 300). 54 rooms, pool. AE, DC, MC, V. *Cikada* (E–M), Hamngatan 1 (928–16 333). 84 rooms, pool, tennis. AE, MC, V. *Park Ålandia* (E–M), Norra Esplanadgatan 3 (928–14 130). 80 rooms, pool. AE, MC, V. *Savoy* (M), Nygatan 12 (928–15 400). 85 rooms, pool. AE, MC, V. *Passat* (M), modern apartments with kitchen, no restaurant, pool, opposite *Pommern* (M), Norragatan 10 (928–15 555). 70 rooms, pool. DC, MC, V.
The islands have many *boarding houses* (M–I) offering half board, and well organized *self-catering accommodations.*
Restaurants. With dancing at several of the hotels and also at the *Sabina* (E), Ålandsvägen 42 (928–11 988). AE, MC, V. *Nautical Club* (E), Hamngatan 2 (928–11 633). AE, MC, V. The *Galleri* disco is near the Arkipelag hotel. DC.
Camping. *Gröna Udden,* near bathing beach, is the nearest to town. *Möckelö,* on peninsula west of town.

Naantali. Attractive small coastal town, near Turku. *Gasthaus Unikeko* (E–M), Luostarinkatu 20 (921–751 881). 50 rooms, unlicensed restaurant, tennis, pool. AE, DC, MC, V. *Naantalin Kylpylä Spa* (E), Kalevanniemi (921–857 711). 92 rooms, pool, near seashore. AE.
Restaurants. *Kaivohuone* (E), Nunnakatu 7 (921–751 291). Summer only. AE, DC, MC, V. *Merenrantaravintola* (M), Mannerheiminkatu 2 (921–751 383). Summer only.
Camping. *Kuparivuori,* (921–751 354), open June 1 through late Aug.

Porvoo (Borgå). Delightful old coastal town, east of Helsinki. *Haikko Manor Hotel and Congress Center* (L), several km. southwest of town in lovely seashore setting (915–123 133). 179 rooms in converted old manor house, superbly furnished, pools, extensive sports facilities, nightclub, health treatment. AE, DC, MC, V. *Seurahovi* (E), Rauhankatu 27 B (915–18 861). 47 rooms. DC, MC, V.
Restaurant. *Wanha Laamanni* (E), Vourikatu 17 (915–130 455). 18th-century décor, excellent food. AE, DC, MC, V.
Camping. Kokonniemi, (915–171 967), 2 km. (just over one mile) from town center, open June to Aug.
Youth and Family Hostel. *Porvoon Retkeilymaja,* Linnankoskenkatu 1–3 (915–130 012).

Tammisaari (Ekenäs). Attractive south coast center. *Marine* (M), Kammantekijänkatu (911–13 833). 24 rooms, unlicensed cafeteria, tennis. AE, DC, MC, V.
Restaurants. *Knipan* (E), Stallörsparken (911–11 169). On the water, summer only. DC, MC, V. *Gnägget* (M), Stallören (911–13 331). Cozy "stable" atmosphere, beer and wine only. DC, MC, V. *Svenska Klubben* (M), Bryggerigatan 9 (911–11 296).
Camping. Ormnäs (911–14 434), open late May through late Aug.
Youth and Family Hostel. *Ekenäs Vandrarhem,* Höijersvagen 10C (911–16 393).

Turku (Åbo). Major sea port and interesting former capital of Finland. *Hamburger Börs* (L), Kauppiaskatu 6 (921–511 211). 160 rooms, recently renovated, pool, nightclub, popular beer garden. AE, DC, MC, V. *Marina Palace* (L–E), Linnankatu 32 (921–336 300). 182 rooms, pool, nightclub, attractive riverside location. AE, DC, MC, V. *Rantasipi Ikituuri* (E), Pispalantie 7 (921–376 111). 150 rooms, nightclub, pool, tennis. AE, DC, MC, V. *Ruissalo Spa* (E), Ruissalo, in lovely park–like setting about 5 km. (three miles) from town (921–605 511). 132 rooms, pool, sports facilities including golf. AE, DC, MC, V. *Seurahuone* (E), Humalistonkatu 2 (921–500 800). 137 rooms, nightclub. AE, DC, MC, V. *Cumulus* (E–M), Eerikinkatu 28 (921–514 111). 208 rooms, pool. AE, DC, MC, V. *Ritz* (E–M), Humalistonkatu 7 (921–337 337). 166 rooms. AE, DC, MC, V. *Ikituuri Summer Hotel* (M), Pispalantie 7 (921–376 111). 144 rooms, pool, nightclub, tennis. AE, DC, MC, V. *Domus Aboensis* (I), Piispankatu 10 (921–329 470). 76 rooms, unlicensed cafeteria, summer only. MC, V. *Turun Karina* (I), Itäinen Pitkäkatu 30B (921–336 666). 27 rooms, unlicensed cafeteria.
Restaurants. *Brahen Kellari* (E), Puolalankatu 1 (921–325 400). AE, DC, MC, V. *Le Pirate* (E–M), Boren puisto (921–511 443). On a boat in the river. AE, DC, MC, V. *Hämeenportti* (M), Hämeenkatu 7 (921–315 054). DC, MC, V. *Martin's* (M), Martinkatu 1 (921–359 829). Spanish décor and food (also Finnish), intimate atmosphere, beer and wine only. DC, MC, V. *Pinella* (M), Porthanin puisto (921–500 074). Traditional style, good atmosphere, open-air section in summer. MC, V. *Pippurimylly* (M), Stalarminkatu 2 (921–359 501). Beer and wine only. MC, V. *Casa Mia Trattoria* (I), It. Pitkäkatu 12–14 (921–321 243). Beer and wine only. DC, MC, V. *Hiivari* (I), Käsityöläiskatu 5 (921–314 008).
Camping. *Saaronniemi,* Ruissalo, (921–589 249), about 10 km. (six miles) from city, open June 1 through Aug. 31.
Youth and Family Hostel. *Turku Youth Hostel,* Linnankatu 39, (921–316 578).

HOW TO GET AROUND. By air. Regular flights serve Mariehamn and Turku.
By train. Apart from the Helsinki–Turku line, train routes in the region are rather devious, so you'd best travel by bus.
By bus. Regular schedules link all parts of the region.
By boat. Regular schedules by modern ferries link Turku with the Åland Islands. There are regular trips by boat from Helsinki to Porvoo in summer, taking three hours one way.
By bike. Planned cycling routes are available on the mainland; details from tourist offices and the Finnish Youth Hostels Association, Yrjönkatu 38B, Helsinki (90–694 0377). Individual packaged cycling tours are organized on the Åland Islands by Ålandsresor, Storagatan 9, Mariehamn, tel. 928–28 040.

TOURS. In summer, sightseeing trips by boat are arranged from Hanko, Kotka, Mariehamn, Porvoo and Turku. Bus tours from Mariehamn take in the principal historic sights of the main island. There are daily city tours of Turku in summer, as well as longer tours into the surrounding countryside, such as the Seven Churches Tour visiting some of the beautiful medieval churches of the area.

PLACES TO VISIT. The heavily indented coastline and thousands of islands and skerries, especially in the southwest, offer a great deal that is scenically beautiful. Much of the country's early history is associated with this region, so this is the area richest in historical monuments. The following is a selection of principal sights. Opening times apply to the peak season.

Kotka. Imperial Czar's Fishing Lodge. By the rapids of Langinkoski, a few km. from town; a favorite spot of Alexander III and Maria Feodorovna. Open daily 10–7.
Karhula Glass Museum and Shop. Open daily 12–5.
Vaarisaari Open-air Museum. Fort Elisabeth, Vaarisaari island; commemorating the naval battle of Ruotsinsalmi, 1790. Motor boat connection.

Mariehamn. Åland Museum. Stadshusparken, Öhbergsvägen 1; official historical museum of the province. Open 10–4, Tues. also 4–8 closed Mon.
Maritime Museum. Devoted to Åland's rich seafaring history. Open daily 9–5 (in July 9–7). to Sat. 9–5, Sun. 10–4.
Pommern. Four-masted barque, now museum ship to the great days when Åland's windjammers carried grain from Australia to England. Open daily 9–7.
Major historic monuments on the main island of the Åland archipelago include the fortifications of **Bomarsund,** the fortress of **Kastelholm,** the farm museum of **Jan Karslgården,** and many medieval churches.

Naantali. Convent Church of St. Birgitta. Founded in 1443. Open daily 11–7.
Kultaranta. Summer residence of the President of Finland; the park is open on Fri. 6–8.

Porvoo. Cathedral. Greystone church from 15th century with old frescoes and statue of Alexander I commemorating historic meeting here in 1809. Open Mon. to Sat. 10–6, Sun. 2–5.
Doll Museum. Open daily 11–3.30.
Edelfelt-Vallgren Art Museum. Commemorating two major Finnish artists. Open daily 11–4.
Historical Museum. In Old Town Hall (1764). Open daily 11–4.
Runeberg's home. Museum to Finland's national poet. Open Mon. to Sat. 9.30–4, Sun. 10.30–5.

Turku. Cathedral. Expanded and restored many times since its founding in the 13th century. Open Mon. to Fri. 9–7, Sat. 9–3, Sun. 2.30–4.30.
Handicrafts Museum. Vartivuorenkatu 4. A surviving street from the great fire of 1827, with original interiors and crafts displays. Open daily 10–6.

Museum Ship Sigyn. Open Tues. to Fri. and Sun. 10–3, Sat. 10–5; closed Mon.

Pharmacy Museum. Läntinen Rantakatu 13, in an 18th century wooden building. Open daily 10–6.

Resurrection Chapel and Holy Cross Chapel. Skanssinmäki, on the city outskirts; fine examples of modern architecture by Erik Bryggman and Pekka Pitkänen. Open by arrangement.

Sibelius Museum. Piispankatu 17, devoted to the great composer. Open Tues. to Sun., 11–3, Wed. also 6–8.

Turku Castle and Provincial Museum. Major historic sight near the mouth of the river Aura. Medieval banquets are regularly held in the Castle in Aug.; group reservations at other times. Open daily 10–6.

Wäinö Aaltonen Museum. Itäinen Rantakatu 38; the works of Finland's great sculptor and others. Open Mon. to Fri. 10–4 and 6–8, Sat. 10–4, Sun. 10–6.

SPORTS. Boating. Row boats are available at all centers. Motor and sailing boats can be rented in Mariehamn, Tammissaari, and Turku.

These island-studded waters offer marvelous opportunities for sailing. The Åland Islands, for example, have nearly 30 marinas.

Cycling. See How to Get Around, above.

Golf. There is an 18-hole course at Turku, a 9-hole course near the fortress of Kastelhom, Åland.

Riding. Available in Hanko, Kotka, Lohja, Mariehamn, Porvoo, Turku.

Swimming. Boundless opportunities, mainly off smooth granite. There are fine sandy beaches on the island of Kaunissaari, reached in an hour by motor boat from Kotka.

Windsurfing. Facilities in Hanko, Mariehamn, Porvoo, Tammissaari, and Turku.

THE CENTRAL PROVINCES

Way of Poets and Pioneers

Romantics sometimes speak of "the land of a thousand lakes," but they don't even come close. A recent re-count puts the figure at 187,888, comprising in all nearly a tenth of the Finnish countryside. Much of the rest of the land is covered with forests. In the midst of all this, the Finns have somehow managed to find space for their cities, homes and farms. Yet though they have built well and solidly, though they have bent the land to their will, Nature is still triumphant. Indeed the magnificent and sometimes wild country Finland possesses is perhaps its most notable attraction. The constant theme of lake and island, forest and ridge may sound potentially monotonous, but the variations are infinite, and the interplay of light and color at different seasons and different times of day provides endless permutations.

Since one of the greatest attractions this nation offers the visitor is the opportunity to come really close to nature, you would be wise to allow a little time to savor the true delight of life outdoors, even if it is just to slip away from your hotel and walk in the forests which will almost certainly be on the doorstep. For the more ambitious, there are plenty of marked trails.

Exploring the Central Provinces

As a first destination we suggest Hämeenlinna, with a couple of stops along the way, just off the main road. The first is Hyvinkää, with its forested ridges and one of Finland's most fascinating museums for railroad buffs, the Railway Museum. Among the exhibits are the two Imperial carriages used by the Russian czars. The second stop is at the outstanding Glass Museum at Riihimäki.

The town of Hämeenlinna, birthplace of Jean Sibelius, boasts a castle, the oldest part of which probably dates from the crusades which Birger Jarl led into Finland in 1249. Ten km. (six miles) away on the road to Tampere is Hattula Church, built of stone about the year 1250. The few remaining old country churches in Finland are well worth visiting because of their unique interior decoration, dominated by paintings covering the walls and ceilings. Artists of those days had a firm belief in all the horrors of hell fire, and spared no pains in depicting their beliefs with the brush. Hattula Church also has some fine wood carvings. Just outside Hämeenlinna is Aulanko National Park, where there is an excellent hotel.

From Hämeenlinna you can travel on to Tampere by one of the sleek water buses of the Finnish Silver Line, a full day's cruise described below under Tampere. If you're motoring, make a point of stopping off at one of Finland's top glass works, Iittala, 20 km. (12 miles) north of Hämeenlinna. Guided factory tours are arranged and there's a museum and shop with irresistible bargains.

Tampere, the Weaving Wonderland

Almost every book, pamphlet, brochure, and guide will inform you that Tampere, the country's second-largest city, is Finland's Pittsburgh. However, the resemblance begins and ends with the concentrated presence here of industry—the settings are quite incomparable.

From about the year 1,000, this part of Finland was a base from which traders and hunters set out on their expeditions to northern Finland and even to Lapland. But it was not until 1779 that a Swedish king actually founded the town of Tampere. Some 41 years later a Scotsman by the name of James Finlayson came to the infant city and established a factory for spinning cotton. This was perhaps the beginning of "big business" in Finland. The firm of Finlayson exists today and is still one of the country's leading industrial enterprises.

Artful location is the secret of Tampere's many factories. An isthmus little more than a kilometer wide at its narrowest point separates the lakes Näsijärvi and Pyhäjärvi, and at one spot the Tammerkoski Rapids provide an outlet for the waters of one to cascade through to the other. Called the "Mother of Tampere", these rapids provide the power on which the town's livelihood depends. Their natural beauty has been preserved in spite of the factories on either bank, and the well-designed public buildings of the city grouped around them enhance their general effect. Also in the heart of town is Hämeensilta bridge with its four statues by the well-known sculptor Wäinö Aaltonen. Just to the south of this is the Tourist Office, close to the glossy high-rise of Hotel Ilves in a newly restored old warehouse area. You'll find some interesting boutiques, art studios and restaurants around here and, close by, the bustling quayside of Laukontori, terminal for the Finnish Silver Line and sightseeing boats.

The high ridge of Pyynikki forms a natural park near the center of town, and on its top is an outlook tower commanding a view of the surrounding countryside. At the foot of this Pyynikki Ridge is the Pynikki Open-air Theater with its revolving auditorium which can be moved even with a full load of spectators to face any one of the sets ready prepared by nature.

On the Särkänniemi peninsula to the north, the even higher, modern observation tower of Näsineula soars above the lake, forest and town, topped by a revolving restaurant. The same building houses the first planetarium in Scandinavia and a well-planned aquarium and, close by, is the Sara Hildén Art Museum set in its own sculpture park on the lake shore. It's a fine modern building with superb changing exhibitions, if you've a taste for the avant-garde.

A number of museums include a pleasantly-situated provincial museum, a good art gallery, the charming Haihara Doll Museum just outside town, and the Lenin Museum (it was in Tampere that Lenin and Stalin first met in 1905). One of the most imaginative museums of all has the unpromising name of The Workers' Museum of Amuri, west of the center. In fact, it's just a block of old timber houses, showing just how the original tenants lived up to 100 years ago—so well done that you expect them to return at any moment.

Tampere Cathedral, a little northeast of the center, is comparatively modern (completed in 1907), but it houses some of the best-known masterpieces of Finnish art, including Magnus Enckell's fresco, *The Resurrection,* and two works by Hugo Simberg, *Wounded Angel* and *Garden of Death.* Further east, beyond the railroad station, is the startling, modern Kaleva Church, designed by Reima and Raili Pietilä. It looks rather like a grain elevator from the outside, but is all soaring light and space within. Outside of town, there are one or two fine 15th-century characteristic small stone churches.

Tampere is a terminal for two major lake routes. To the north, the "Poet's Way" route lies along Näsijärvi, as far as Virrat. It passes through the charming little town of Ruovesi where J.L. Runeberg, Finland's national poet, lived in his student days. At Petoniemi Mansion he collected the material for his famous *Tales of Ensign Stål.* Not far away, artist Akseli Gallen-Kallela built himself a castle-like building in Kalevalan style, alas not open to the public.

North of Virrat is Ähtäri. Here, in a fine forested setting, is Finland's first wildlife park and "Mini Suomi," the latter representing all the regions of Finland and their main features, including many highly sophisticated working models and audio-visual displays. Intended to be educational, it is also fascinating. The extensive Ähtäri complex includes an extraordinary hotel built into the living rock and designed by the Suomalainen brothers, who created the Temppeliaukio rock church in Helsinki.

The second route, that of the Finnish Silver Line, offers two alternative schedules to Aulanko and Hämeenlinna. One features Kangasala, immortalized in Z. Topelius' poem, *A Summer Day at Kangasala.* (The poem has been set to music and is one of the loveliest of many haunting Finnish songs.) Along the way the modern water bus passes by Valkeakoski, a town typical of the many Finnish industrial communities which are set in idyllic surroundings. The other route takes in the home and studio of the sculptor Emil Wikström.

Lahti, Gateway to Central Finland

Let's look now at the center of the country, starting with a short trip to the modern town of Lahti. Located at the southern end of one of Finland's largest lake systems, Vesijärvi-Päijänne, this community is now the sixth-biggest town in the country, with rapidly expanding industries. Its

City Hall was designed by Eliel Saarinen. But there are a number of notable modern buildings, including the Church of the Cross by Alvar Aalto, and a fine theater. The town is also noted for the nearby athletic academy of Vierumäki, possessing an international reputation and an unsurpassed location.

Lahti is better known, however, for winter sports. Good enough, in fact, to have been selected for the 1958 and 1989 World Ski Championships. In general, Finland is comparatively flat, but running across the country is the very prominent Salpausselkä Ridge formed during the Glacial Age. Where this crosses the town boundaries, it has given its name to winter games which attract thousands of Finns and many foreigners every March. In an attractive rural setting only a few miles west of Lahti, the old manor house of Pyhaniemi houses an art gallery, and not far away is the beautiful 15th-century church of Hollola with a separate bell tower designed by Engel. Across the road from this a fine timber building in National Romantic style is now a coffee house offering delicious home-made refreshments.

Twice a week in summer (Sunday and Thursday), a venerable steam train, the *Pikku-Jumpo,* chuffs along the one-hour route from Lahti to Heinola to the northeast. Each journey has a different theme (Wild West, Train Robbery, etc.), complete with appropriate costume, and passengers have the option of returning the same way or by boat. Heinola itself is an extremely pleasant small town on an adjoining lake system and has particularly good facilities for canoeing, with a network of paddling routes that include a 360-km. circuit of great variety through some of the loveliest scenery in unspoilt rural Finland. Right in the heart of town, at Siltasaaren Lohjapaja, you can borrow a rod and hardly fail to make a catch from a pool jam-packed with rainbow trout, which will then be smoked or salted for you to take away or eat on the spot.

At the northern end of Lake Päijänne lies Jyväskylä. Known as a cultural center Jyväskylä was the first to establish a secondary school that used Finnish as the language of instruction and now has its own university by Aalto, who also designed the City Theater. The town has an attractive open-air museum and, on the outskirts, the well-equipped sports center of Laajavuori.

Jyväskylä is also an important woodworking center for it is right in the forested heart of Finland. The whole region and Vitasaari to the north has been developed as a holiday area with delightful holiday villages in log-cabin style scattered about the vast, deeply forested and lake-strewn region. The holiday villages offer sports facilities as well—and also a good opportunity to probe deep into Finland's "off-the-beaten-track." Jyväskylä's annual Arts Festival in summer has become a major event, and the town is also important as a terminal for boat trips to Lahti down Lake Päijänne, the second-largest in Finland. During the early part of the journey the scenery is wildly beautiful, with forest-covered ridges and completely uninhabited rocky shores. The landscape grows milder and more serene as you travel south, and numerous villas are scattered along the banks or built on the many islands that punctuate the lake throughout its 113 km. (70 miles) length. If you're traveling between Lahti and Jyväskylä by car, the eastern route is the more beautiful and takes you through Sysmä, near which is the delightful Suvi-Pinx open-air art exhibition (summer only) in a beautiful forest setting. It has a restaurant and amusements for children.

Saimaa Lake District

Now that we have explored some of the more interesting parts of central Finland, let's move on eastwards to the region known as the Saimaa Lake system. It is in this area that many of the most beautiful places in the country are concentrated, and it is here that some of the most interesting pages of Finnish history have been written. It might be a good idea to adopt Savonlinna as your new headquarters. It is an attractive lakeside resort also noted as a watering place and is a terminus of the Saimaa lake steamers. The healing baths are to be found in the Casino Park. The latter is on one of the many islands, all linked by bridges, which, together with a cape jutting out into the lake, constitute the town of Savonlinna. Besides its location and its baths, Savonlinna's outstanding attraction is the fortress of Olavinlinna, Finland's finest medieval castle and one of the best-preserved historical monuments in Scandinavia. Still surrounded by the water that formed such an essential part of its defensive strength centuries ago, it is in the eastern part of the old section of town.

A Danish-born knight built this fortress with the object of providing a bastion for the eastern frontier of the then kingdom of Sweden-Finland to assist in repulsing attacks and invasions from the east. Apart from the important role it played in the wars of those days, Olavinlinna Castle helped to protect and support the Finnish colonists who began to develop the land for several miles around. During the numerous wars of the 18th century it changed hands repeatedly, but it lost its military significance when Finland became a Grand Duchy of Russia.

In recent years the main courtyard has been the setting for operatic and theatrical performances, and an International Opera Festival is held here throughout July when the town becomes an international musical mecca. There's a marvelous atmosphere at this time, especially in the evenings as the crowds wend their way through the narrow streets to the castle for an opera performance, many dressing up for the occasion, and even more carrying blankets, for it can be chilly on a Finnish summer evening! Arts and crafts are also strongly featured in studios and exhibitions around town in summer.

Not far from the castle, on the headland of Riihisaari, the Provincial Museum gives an excellent picture of the history and development of lake traffic, including the fascinating timber floating trains, which are still a common summer feature of Saimaa today. Near it is the museum ship *Salama,* a steam schooner, built in 1874, shipwrecked in 1898 and raised from the lake in 1971.

Until recently Savonlinna was the central hub of a network of regular lake traffic leaving for and arriving from the four points of the Saimaa compass each morning and evening. Some of these regular schedules have been replaced by sightseeing cruises, but the quaysides of Savonlinna still present a lively scene with the daily to-ing and fro-ing of these venerable vessels. The morning market does brisk business on these same quaysides.

A short distance from Savonlinna is the famous ridge of Punkaharju; eight km. (five miles) long, it rises between the lakes and at some points is no more than eight meters (25 feet) wide though it manages to accommodate both a road and railway. Within recent years, the unique Retretti art center has been created in this area, part of it in a majestic cavern that was literally blasted out of the living rock. In addition to outstanding art exhibitions, the center is also used for classical concerts and evening jazz and pop sessions. Almost next to it is Kesämaa (Summerland), a great funfair place for the children, and next to that is a well-equipped holiday center. Also in the area, Punkaharju's National Hotel, originally built in 1845 as a gamekeeper's lodge by Czar Nicholas I and subsequently enlarged, has been restored as a restful oasis in which to stay or simply enjoy a meal. At Kerimäki, 23 km. (14 miles) east of Savonlinna, is the world's largest wooden church from the 1840s, holding 3,500 people. Both areas offer good water sports facilities, and well equipped camp sites and holiday villages.

You can either continue farther to the north, or start your return, still a leisurely one, towards the capital, and in most directions you can still travel by boat. Southwards the steamer runs through the Saimaa lake system to Lappeenranta. This is a lively resort and town on the southern shores of Saimaa and, from here, trips are available on the Saimaa Canal, re-opened a few years ago. You can continue through the canal to Viiburi (Viborg), now in the Soviet Union, but of course you will need a visa. The old fortress area of Lappeenranta is of particular interest. A half-hour drive from here is Imatra whose magnificent rapids, tamed and diverted to help power the considerable local industry, are released as a tourist attraction on certain Sundays each summer. Other possibilities from Savonlinna are to take a ship in the opposite direction northwest to Kuopio, or train or bus northeast to Joensuu. These routes pick their way through or beside an amazingly long and immensely intricate system of lakes, canals and narrow channels, all part of the Saimaa network, Finland's (and Europe's) largest lake system.

Joensuu and Koli

Joensuu is the only town of any size in the vast area known as North Karelia. Its chief claim to distinction is a town hall which, like the one at Lahti, was designed by Eliel Saarinen. Our objective, however, is Koli on the western shore of Lake Pielinen (Pielisjärvi), nearly 64 km. (40 miles) due north of Joensuu. By boat, twice a week, the journey takes a leisurely six to seven hours, but you can also go by train to Vuonislahti, on the lake's eastern shore, and take a motorboat across to Koli. Alternatively, there is a bus service from Joensuu to Koli.

As we mentioned earlier, Finland is relatively flat; thus, in comparison with the hills found in most parts of the country, Koli is considered a mountain. This is its great appeal. From the rocky summit of Ukko-Koli more than 300 meters (1,000 feet) up, there are some of the most magnificent views to be found anywhere. There is a modern tourist hotel near the hill top and holiday villages on the lake shore. Much has been done for the visitor to Koli in the way of well-marked footpaths and tracks for the hiker and other facilities. On the Pielisjoki river the canoeing is excellent. But it is for winter sports that this region is particularly noted.

The region to the east of Joensuu is little-known to foreign visitors though of special interest as a traditional stronghold of the Orthodox church. The summer calendar features a number of Pradznik festivals, traditional Orthodox church and folk celebrations, the most important being at Ilomantsi in July.

Kuopio

Kuopio is a lively and interesting town and an excellent ski center, with plenty going on throughout the year—notably the Ice Marathon in March, Dance and Music Festival in June, and major sailing and motorcross events. The morning market in the town center is one of the most colorful outside Helsinki, and there are several very good museums, one of the best being the Open-air Museum which re-creates former life styles.

There's an Orthodox as well as a Lutheran Cathedral, and the Orthodox Church Museum, housed in a modern building on the outskirts of town, has collections from Orthodox Karelia that are unique in the western world. Part of the reason for this lies in the removal to this region of the Orthodox convent of Lintula and much larger monastery complex of Valamo, originally sited on the shores of Lake Ladoga which was ceded to the Soviet Union after World War II. Both are in remote and lovely settings and can be visited, either by excursion bus or boat, from Kuopio, which also gives you an opportunity to experience the incredible complexities of these lake- and forest-scapes at close quarters. For a bird's eye view, you need go no further than the slender tower on Puijo hill on Kuopio's outskirts. There is a revolving restaurant near the top and viewing galleries; try to time your visit for sundown when the reflected colors between sky and lake are at their most kaleidoscopic.

Farther north still, you come into the wilderness landscapes of Kainuu, with Kajaani as the main town. It's on the shore of the huge lake of Oulujärvi and was once a major collecting point for the transport of tar by boat to Oulu on the coast. It has 17th-century castle ruins and a town hall designed by Engel; but the region's chief claims for attention are its scenery and amenities for outdoor activities—especially for enthusiasts of fishing or canoeing or, in winter, cross-country skiing. Facilities are particularly well developed in and around the fine Vuokatti Sports Institute, near Sotkamo, about 40 km. (25 miles) east of Kajaani. Farther east still is Kuhmo, which has become an attraction for music lovers with its Chamber Music Festival each July.

PRACTICAL INFORMATION FOR
THE CENTRAL PROVINCES

TOURIST INFORMATION. Hämeenlinna. Palokunnankatu 11 (917–202 388). **Heinola.** Torikatu 8 (910–58 444). **Hyvinkää.** Hämeenkatu 3D (914–2511). **Imatra.** Keskusasema (954–24 666). **Joensuu.** Koskikatu 1 (973–201 362). **Jyväskylä.** (Town) Vapaudenkatu 38 (941–624 903). (Region) Vapaudenkatu 38 (941–610 866). **Kuopio.** (Town) Haapaniemenkatu 17 (971–182 584). (Region) Haapaniemenkatu 17 (971–114 101). **Lahti.** Torikatu 3B (918–182 580). **Lappeenranta.** Bus Station; (953–18 850). **Mikkeli.** (Town) Hallituskatu 3a (955–151 444). (Region) Hallituskatu 2 (955–365 399). **Savonlinna.** Puistokatu 1 (957–13 492); Saimaa Travel, Puistokatu 1 (957–22 508). **Tampere.** (Town) Verkatehtaankatu 2 (931–126 652). (Region) Verkatehtaankatu 2 (931–124 488).

TELEPHONE CODES. We have given telephone codes for all the towns and villages in the hotel and restaurant lists that follow. These codes need only be used when calling from outside the town or village concerned.

HOTELS AND RESTAURANTS. Unless otherwise stated, all the hotels listed below have all or some rooms with bath or shower, licensed restaurants, and are open yearround.

Åhtari. Finland's first wildlife and leisure park. *Mesikämmen* (E) (965–391 111). 103 rooms, disco, pool, sports facilities. Fine building built into the living rock. MC, V.

Hämeenlinna. Sibelius' birthplace and with other cultural associations. *Rantasipi Aulanko* (L), 3 km. (2 miles) from town center (917–29 521). 216 rooms, nightclub, pool, extensive sports facilities. Lovely lake-side location. AE, DC, MC, V. *Cumulus* (E), Raatihuoneenkatu 18 (917–28 811). 101 rooms, pool, newly renovated. AE, DC, MC, V. *Emilia* (E), Raatihuoneenkatu 23 (917–25 928). 41 rooms. AE, DC, MC, V. *Amis Summer Hotel* (I), Lahdensivu (917–25 621). 123 rooms, unlicensed cafeteria.

Restaurants. *Valentinos* (E), Sibeliuksenkatu 3 (917–28 777). AE, MC, V. *Hälläpyörä* (M), Raatihuoneenkatu 3 (917–24 431). MC, V. *Olde William's* (M), Rauhankatu 11 (917–27 380), cozy tavern and restaurant. *Piiparkakkutalo* (M), Kirkkorinne 2 (917–121 606), Finnish fare in renovated old timber building. AE, DC, MC, V.

Camping. *Aulanko,* 3 km. (2 miles) from town (917–28 560), open May 1 through mid-Sept.

Youth and Family Hostel. *Kuusisto,* near camp site at Aulanko (917–28 560).

Heinola. Lakeside town and resort. *Kumpeli* (E–M), Muonamiehenkatu 3 (910–58 214). 77 rooms, pool, sports facilities. Modern, with pleasant riverside location, 1 km. from center. AE, DC, MC, V. *Seurahuone* (E–M), Lampikatu 16 (910–52 061). 25 rooms, old fashioned. AE, DC, MC, V.

Restaurant. *Harjupaviljonki* (M), Harjupuisto (910–52 068). Hill-top location, part of old spa establishment, summer only.

Camping. *Heinäsaari* (910–53 083), open June 1 through Aug. 31.

Youth and Family Hostel. *Retkeilymaja,* Opintie 1 (910–52 425).

Hyvinkää. Small town amidst forested ridges. *Rantasipi Sveitsi* (L), Härkävehmaankatu 4 (914–18 820). 190 rooms, nightclub, pool, sports facilities. Fine location in woods just outside town. AE, DC, MC, V. *Martiina* (M), Hämeenkatu 2–4 (914–12 400). 40 rooms, pool. AE, DC, MC, V.

Restaurants. *Stefan* (E), Hämeenkatu 24–26 (914–11 260). MC, V. *Pieni Huvimaja* (M), Hämeenkatu 13–17 (914–17 093).

Youth and Family Hostel. *Sveitsin Retkeilymaja,* Sveitsi (914–89 444).

Imatra. Industrial center with famous rapids. *Imatran Valtionhotelli* (L–E), Torkkelinkatu 2 (954–63 244). 142 rooms, disco, pool. Located by the rapids (only seen in full flood on selected summer Sundays). AE, DC, MC, V. *Imatran Kylpylä Spa* (E), Vapaa-aikakeskus (954–2051). 95 rooms, pool, sports facilities. AE, DC. *Mansikkala* (I), Rastaankatu 3 (954–22 133). 52 rooms, unlicensed cafeteria, summer only. DC, MC, V.

Camping. *Ukonlinna,* located in the Leisure Center.

Youth and Family Hostels. *Mansikka,* Raastaankatu 3 (954–22 133). *Ukonlinna,* (954–21 270).

Joensuu. Lake resort and industrial town. *Karelia* (E), Kauppakatu 25 (973–24 391). 36 rooms. AE, DC, MC, V. *Kimmel* (E), Itäranta 1 (973–1771). 230 rooms, pool, nightclub. AE, DC, MC, V. *Pohjois-Karjala* (E), Torikatu 20 (973–27 311). 77 rooms. AE, DC, MC, V. *Viehka* (M), Kauppakatu 32 (973–29 531). 40 rooms. AE, DC, MC, V.

184 FINLAND

Restaurants. *Shemeikka* (E), Kauppakatu 29 (973–21 358). MC, V. *Teatteriravintola* (E), Rantakatu 4 (973–29 306). MC, V. *Puikkari* (M), Puronsuunkatu 1 (973–822 136). MC, V.
Camping. Linnunlahti (973–201 364), open June 1 through Aug. 31.
Youth and Family hostels. *Partiotalon retkeilymaja* (Scout Lodge), Vanamokatu 25 (973–23 381.) *Sports Institute,* Kalevankatu 8 (973–201 594).

Jyväskylä. University and industrial town in heart of lakes and forests. *Rantasipi Laajavuori* (L), Laajavuori (941–628 211). 176 rooms, nightclub, pool, extensive sports facilities. Fine location on outskirts of town. AE, DC, MC, V. *Cumulus* (E–M), Väinönkatu 5 (941–215 211). 203 rooms, pool. AE, DC, MC, V. *Jyväshovi* (E), Kauppakatu 35 (941–630 211). 121 rooms, pool. AE, DC, MC, V. *Laajavuori Summer Hotel* (M), Auvilankuja 2 (941–251 323). 78 rooms, beer and wine only. *Milton* (M), Asema-aukio (941–213 411). 35 rooms. AE, DC, MC, V. *Rentukka* (I), Taitoniekantie 9 (941–252 211). 136 rooms, disco, summer only. MC, V.
Restaurants. *Katinhäntä* (E), Asemakatu 7 (941–618 115). Intimate, gracious atmosphere. AE, DC, MC, V. *Ilokivi* (M), Keskushairaalantie 2 (941–619 306). *Kantakrouvi* (M), Hannikaisenkatu 27–29 (941–217 198). MC, V. *Mörssäri* (M), Voionmaankatu 32 (941–618 434). *Priimus* (M), Taulumäentie 45 (941–216 711). Good value in hotel and restaurant school. DC, MC, V.
Camping. *Tuomiojärvi* (941–624 903), open June 1 to Aug. 31.
Youth and Family hostels. *Lajaari,* Laajavuori (941–253 355).

Kajaani. Interesting regional capital of Kainuu district. *Kajaani* (E), Leiripolku 2 (986–38 911). 72 rooms, pool. AE, DC, MC, V. *Kajanus* (E), Koskikatu 3 (986–1641). 156 rooms, pool, sports facilities. AE, DC, MC, V. *Seurahuone* (E), Kauppakatu 11 (986–23 076). 67 rooms. AE, DC, MC, V. *Valjus* (E), Kauppakatu 20 (986–24 191). 32 rooms, pool. AE, DC, MC, V. *Vanha Välskäri* (E), Kauppakatu 21 (986–25 661). 32 rooms. AE, DC, MC, V.
Restaurants. *Martina* (M), Kauppakatu 30 (986–22 808), cozy cellar restaurant, Italian food. *Pikku-Välskäri* (M), Soidinkuja 1 (986–150 562). MC, V. *Sampola* (I), Kalevankatu 2 (986–22 894), beer and wine only.
Camping. *Onnela,* 1 km. (half a mile) from town (986–22 703), open June 1 through Aug. 31.
Youth and Family Hostel. *Kajaani,* Oravantie 3 (986–25 704).

Koli. Small tourist center in beautiful, hilly lake and forest setting. *Koli* (M), Ylä-Koli (973–672 221). 63 rooms, pool, superb views. AE, MC, V. *Kolin Hiisi* (M), Loma-Koli (973–672 241). 36 rooms, sports facilities. MC, V.
Camping. *Loma-Koli* (973–672 241), open early June through mid-Aug.
Kuhmo. In the heart of a wilderness area and famed for tis music festival. *Kainuu* (M), Kainuuntie 84 (986–51 711). 30 rooms, pool. *Kalevala* (M) (986–530 154). 50 rooms, pool, sports facilities.

Kuopio. Lake resort, skiing center and industrial town. *Cumulus* (E–M), Asemakatu 32 (971–123 555). 134 rooms, pool. AE, DC, MC, V. *Rauhalahti* (E–M), Katiskaniementie 8 (971–311 700). 252 rooms plus chalets, pool, disco, extensive sports facilities. 5 km. (3 miles) from center. AE, DC, MC, V. *Rivoli Kuopio* (E), Satamakatu 1 (971–195 111). 141 rooms, pool, sports facilities. Best in town, with lakeside location. AE, DC, MC, V. *Martina* (M), Tullinportinkatu 23 (971–123 522). 37 rooms, disco, newly renovated. *Savonia Summer Hotel* (M), Sammakkolammentie 2 (971–225 333). 50 rooms, pool, summer only. AE, MC, V. *Sport Hotel Puijo* (M), by Puijo Tower (971–114 841). 20 rooms, lovely hilltop location. AE, DC, MC, V. *Tekma* (M), Taivaanpankontie 14 (971–222 925). 60 rooms without bath or shower, beer and wine only, summer only. MC, V.
Restaurants. *Musta Lammas* (E), Satamakatu 4 (971–123 494). Attractively adapted beer cellar. AE, DC, MC, V. *Puijon Torni* (E), (971–114 841). Revolving restaurant on top of tower on outskirts of town. AE, MC, V. *Henry's Pub* (M), Kauppakatu 18 (971–122 002). MC, V. *Kummeli* (M), Puijonkatu 19 (971–127

711). MC, V. *Sampo* (I), Kauppakatu 13 (971–114 677). Fish specialties, unpretentious, but excellent value. MC, V.

Camping. *Rauhalahti,* 6.5 km. (4 miles) from town (971–312 244), open mid-May through end Aug. One of best in Scandinavia.

Youth and Family Hostel. *Jynkkä* (971–312 361). *Tekma* (971–222 925).

Lahti. Lake resort, major skiing center and industrial town. *Ascot* (L–E), Rauhankatu 14 (918–89 711). 144 rooms, pool. AE, DC, MC, V. *Messilä* (E), 8 km. (5 miles) from town (918–86 011). 60 rooms, pool, extensive summer and winter sports facilities, old-time banquets. Centered round old manor house in a charming and peaceful location. AE, MC, V. *Musta Kissa* (E), Rautatienkatu 21 (918–37 851). 71 rooms. DC, MC, V. *Seurahuone* (E), Aleksanterinkatu 14 (918–25 161). 121 rooms, nightclub, pool, long gastronomic tradition. AE, MC, V. *Lahti* (M), Hämeenkatu 4 (918–89 721). 87 rooms. *Mukkulan Kartano* (M), 4 km. (just over 2 miles) from town (918–306 554). 14 rooms, sports facilities. In attractive converted old manor in lovely location. AE, DC, MC, V. *Mukkula Summer Hotel* (M), part of the Mukkula complex above (918–306 251). 80 rooms, sports facilities. AE, DC, MC, V.

Restaurants. *Kommodori* (E), Myllysaari (918–531 272). Summer only. DC, MC, V. *Seurahuone* (E)—see *Hotels* above. The food here is notable. *El Toro* (M), Mariankatu 8 (918–25 388). Spanish style and food (also Finnish). AE, DC, MC, V. *Faarao* (M), Aleksanterinkatu 16 (918–515 535). *Oululaisen kulma* (M), Aleksanterinkatu 10 (918–29 806). *Mandi* (I), Vuorikatu 35 (918–522 553). Finnish food, beer and wine only.

Camping. *Mukkula,* part of the Mukkula tourist complex 4 km. from town (918–306 554), open June 1 through Aug. 31. *Messilä,* near Messilä hotel complex, as above.

Youth and Family Hostel. Kivikatu 1 (918–26 324).

Lappeenranta. Major lake resort with some industry. *Cumulus* (E–M), Valtakatu 31 (953–50 870). 95 rooms, pool. AE, DC, MC, V. *Lappee* (E), Brahenkatu 1 (953–5861), 211 rooms, pool, sports facilities. AE, DC, MC, V. *Lappeenranta Spa* (M), Ainonkatu 17 (953–17 400). 34 rooms, pool. MC, V. *Karelia-Park* (I), Korpraalinkuja 1 (953–552 111). 90 rooms, tennis, summer only. MC, V. *Kesa-Loas* (I), Karankokatu 4 (953–28 111). 100 rooms, unlicensed, cafeteria, summer only. *Rotelli* (I), Huhtiniemi, Kuusimäenkatu 18 (953–15 555). 20 rooms, unlicensed restaurant, pool, tennis.

Restaurants. *Casa Nostra* (E), Kauppakatu 52 (953–18 180). Good Italian food. AE, DC, MC, V. *Kasino* (E), Ainonkatu 10 (953–10 200). Traditional style, near harbor, summer only. AE, MC, V. *Kolme Lyhtyä* (M), Kauppakatu 27 (953–10 100). DC. *Willimies* (M), Kauppakatu 39 (953–15 011). DC, MC, V. *Adriano Bar* (I), Kauppakatu 27 (953–13 454). DC, MC, V. *Pappilan kahvila* (I), attractive coffee house in the fortress area, with Orthodox music and specialties. *The Old Park* (I), Valtakatu 36 (953–12 140).

Camping. *Huhtiniemi* (953–11 888), open May 15 through Aug. 31.

Youth and Family Hostel. *Huhtiniemi Camping,* (953–11 888).

Mikkeli. Lakeside and industrial town. *Cumulus* (E–M), Mikonkatu 9 (955–369 222). 115 rooms, pool. AE, DC, MC, V. *Nuijamies* (E–M), Porrassalmenkatu 21 (955–363 111). 40 rooms, disco. AE, MC, V. *Varsavuori* (E–M), Kirkonvarkaus (955–367 111). 98 rooms, nightclub, pool, sports facilities. Lakeside location 3 km. (2 miles from town). AE, DC, MC, V. *Kaleva* (M), Hallituskatu 5 (955–12 041). 34 rooms. DC, MC, V. *Visulahti Leisure Center* (M), (tel. 955–18 281). Well-equipped chalet accommodations 5 km. (3 miles) from town. *Tekuila* (I), Raviradantie 1 (955–366 542). 96 rooms, unlicensed cafeteria, summer only. DC, MC, V.

Restaurants. *Olorosa* (M), Raatihuoeenkatu 4 (955–13 818). *Päämaja* (M), Raatihuoneenkatu 4 (955–14 616). Pub style. *Teatteri Holvi* (M), Savilahdenkatu 11

(955–10 663). Housed in 19th-century fire station next to the old theater. DC, MC, V.

Camping. *Visulahti Tourist Center* (955–18 281), open all year. *Rauhaniemi* (955–11 416), open June through mid-Aug.

Nurmes. *Bomban Talo* (E), Suojärvenkatu 1 (976–22 260). Charming accommodations in Karelian-style village constructed 2½ km. (1½ miles) from town. 74 rooms, sports facilities. AE, DC, MC, V.

Punkaharju. Ridge and beauty spot near Savonlinna. *Valtionhotelli* (National Hotel) (E–M), (957–311 761). 29 rooms, restaurant, sports facilities. Summer only. In beautifully restored 19th-century building in lovely situation. DC, MC, V.
Camping. *Kultakivi* (957–315 110), open mid-April through mid-Sept. MC, V. *Punkaharju Holiday Center,* (957–311 761), open June 1 through early Sept. DC.

Saarijärvi. Forest and lake center, central Finland. *Rantasipi Summassaari* (E), (944–21 311). A few kilometers to the south in beautiful lakeside location. 240 rooms, disco, pool, sports facilities. AE, DC, MC, V.

Savonlinna. Major lake resort with medieval castle. *Spa Hotel Casino* (E), Kylpylaitoksentie (957–22 864). 79 rooms, pool, sports facilities, health treatment. AE, DC, MC, V. *Seurahuone* (E–M), Kauppatori 4 (957–5731). 84 rooms, disco. AE, DC, MC, V. *Tott* (E), Satamakatu 1 (tel. 957–514 500). 60 rooms, pool, nightclub. An old downtown favorite, completely renovated. AE, DC, MC, V. *Pietari Kylliäinen* (M), Olavinkatu 15 (957–22 901). 46 rooms, use of Casino Hotel's facilities. AE, DC, MC, V. *Malakias* (M), Pihlajavedenkuja 6 (957–23 283). 220 rooms, unlicensed cafeteria, summer only. DC, MC, V. *Vuorilinna* (M), Kasinonsaari (957–24 908). 215 rooms, sports facilities, summer only. AE, DC, MC, V.
Restaurants. *Wanha Kasino* (E), Kylpylaitoksentie (957–22 572). Turn-of-century style, summer only. DC. *Rauhalinna* (E), Lehtiniemi (957–523 119). Charming turn-of-century castle-like villa, 16 km. (10 miles) from town (4 km. (2 miles) by boat). AE, DC, MC, V. *Snellman's* (E, evening, M for lunch), Olavinkatu 31 (957–13 104). Mini-mansion style with classical music. AE, DC, MC, V. *Hopeasalmi* (M), restaurant ship (927–21 701). In the harbor. MC, V. *Kauppaseura* (M), Possenkatu 1 (957–22 415). *Linnaravintola* (M), Olavinlinna (957–23 838), in the castle. DC. *Majakka* (M), Satamakatu 11 (957–21 456). Unpretentious, but good food. AE, DC, MC, V. *San Martin* (M), Olavinkatu 46 (957–13 004). Pizza and steak house. *Musta Pässi* (I), Tulliportinkatu 2 (957–22 228). Beer tavern. AE, DC, MC, V.
Camping. *Vuohimäki,* about 6 km. (4 miles) from town (957–537 353), new, well-equipped. Open June through Aug.
Youth Hostels. *Malakias,* Pihlajavedenkuja 6 (957–23 283). *Mertamalakias* Otavankatu 8 (957–20 685). *Hospits,* Linnankatu 20 (957–22 443).

Sotkamo. In north central district of Kainuu. *Tulikettu* (E), Hiukanharju, near village (986–61 111). 46 rooms, pool, extensive sports facilities. DC, MC, V. *Suvikas* (E), Vuokatti (986–640 401). 16 rooms, sports facilities. Attractive small hotel a few km. from village in fine wilderness setting near major Vuokatti Sports Institute. *Vuokatinhovi* (E–M), Vuokatti (986–640 211). 61 rooms, extensive sports facilities, in same area.

Sysmä. Small, inexpensive lake and forest resort. *Uoti* (M), Keskustie 1 (910–71 351). 8 rooms. DC, MC, V.

Tampere. Finland's second city, major industrial town and lakeside center. *Ilves* (L–E), Hatanpäänvaltatie 1 (931–121 212). 336 rooms, pool, nightclub, top facilities. New in 1986. AE, DC, MC, V. *Rosendahl* (L–M), Pyynikintie 13 (931–112 233). 213 rooms, nightclub, pool, sports facilities. Peaceful lakeside location. AE, DC, MC, V. *Grand Hotel Tammer* (E), Satakunnankatu 13 (931–125 380). 90

rooms, pool. AE, DC, MC, V. *Martina* (E), Hämeenkatu 11 (931–380). 71 rooms. AE, MC, V. *Cumulus* (E–M), Koskikatu 5 (931–35 500). 229 rooms, pool. AE, DC, MC, V. *Motor Hotel Jäähovi* (E–M), Sammonvaltatie 2 (931–559 900). 73 rooms, pool. AE, DC, MC, V. *Pyynikki Residential Hotel* (E–M), Mariankatu 26a (931–134 566). 13 well-equipped rental apartments in the city center. *Victoria* (E–M), Itsenaisyydenkatu 1 (931–30 640). 100 rooms, pool, disco. AE, MC, V. *Tampere* (E–M), Hämeenkatu 1 (931–121 980). 260 rooms, pool. AE, DC, MC, V. *Maisa* (M), Maisansalo (931–789 700). 24 rooms, sports facilities, part of recent tourist center. 36 km. (22 miles) from city. AE, DC, MC, V. *Otavala* (M), Rautatienkatu 22 (931–38 400). 20 rooms, unlicensed cafeteria. MC, V. *Astrum* (I), Viinikankatu 22 (931–35 317). Central, excellent value, unlicensed cafeteria. *Domus* (I), Pellervonkatu 9 (931–550 000). 200 rooms, pool, disco, summer only. MC, V. *Härmälä* (I), Nuolialantie 50 (931–650 400). 117 rooms, summer only.

Restaurants. *Finlayson Palatsi* (E), Kuninkaankatu 11 (931–125 905). Elegant club house atmosphere in former turn-of-the-century home. AE, DC, MC, V. *Hämeensilta* (E), Hämeenkatu 13 (931–27 207). Dancing. AE, DC, MC, V. *Henrik* (E), Satamakatu 7 (931–121 191). Small, unpretentious; good food. DC, MC, V. *Näsinneula* (E), Särkänniemi (931–124 697). Revolving restaurant on top of great tower. AE, DC, MC, V. *Sorsapuiston Grilli* (E), Sorsapuisto 1 (931–556 550). Excellent food including Baltic herring specialties, in pleasant atmosphere. AE, DC, MC, V. *Rustholli* (E–M), Aitolahti (931–620 111). AE, DC, MC, V. On lakeside 8 km. (5 miles) from center, excellent cold table with regional specialties. *Myllarit* (E–M), Åkerlundinkatu 4 (931–149 666). Pleasant old mill decor. *Kaijakka* (M), Laukontori (931–23 494). Afternoon dancing. *Merirosvo* (M), Särkänniemi (931–24 697). Splendid Baltic herring dishes. MC, V. *Ohranjyvä* (M), Näsilinnankatu 15 (931–127 217). Intimate atmosphere. AE, DC, MC, V. *Salud* (M), Otavalankatu 10 (931–35 996). Tasty Spanish specialties. AE, DC, MC, V. *Rapukka* (M–I), Tammelanpuistokatu 34 (931–110 086). Imaginatively presented dishes, including vegetarian. *Silakka* (M–I), Vuolteenkatu 20 (931–149 740). Baltic herring and other fish specialties. Beer and wine only. DC, MC, V.

Camping. *Maisansalo-Camping,* Teisko (931–789 705), open May 10 through mid-Aug. 36 km. (22 miles) from town. *Tampere-Camping,* Härmälä (931–651 250), open June 1 through Aug. 31. *Taulaniemi camping,* Taulaniemi, Teisko (931–785 753), open May 15 through Sept. 30. 35 km. (21 miles) from town.

Youth and Family Hostels. *YWCA's Youth Hostel,* Tuomiokirkonkatu 12A (931–35 900). *Uimahallinmaja.* Pirkankatu 10–12 (931–229 460).

Viitasaari. Forest and lake center, central Finland. *Pihkuri* (M) (946–21 440). 24 rooms, disco, on lakeshore, boating. MC, V. *Ruuppo* (M), Ruuponsaari, (946–21 480). 15 km. (9 miles) from village, in lovely lakeside location. 55 rooms, pool, disco, sports facilities. AE, DC, MC, V.

HOW TO GET AROUND. By air. There are regular flights serving Joensuu, Jyväskylä, Kajaani, Kuopio, Lappeenranta, Mikkeli, Savonlinna, Tampere and Varkaus.

By train. You can reach all main towns and resorts by train, though some routes are inevitably made devious by the lake-strewn nature of the region. There are carcarrying trains on several routes. By fast train, it takes nearly four hours to Jyväskylä, five hours to Kuopio and 5½ hours to Savonlinna.

By bus. Services reach to the remotest corners of the region, with express routes to all main centers.

By boat. The greatest concentration of traffic is on the fabulous labyrinthine waters of Saimaa in the east. The main long distance regular schedules on Saimaa are Kuopio-Savonlinna-Kuopio, taking about 12 hours each way, and Savonlinna-Lappeenranta-Savonlinna, taking 9 hours; but there are any number of shorter local schedules and longer cruises from all the main lake resorts, such as Joensuu, Kuopio, Lappeenranta, Savonlinna, lasting from a few hours to several days. Of special interest are the one-day Monastery cruises from Kuopio to Uusi Valamo and Lintula. Local tourist offices can advise. The longest are six-day cruises operated by Roll-Ships Ltd., Passenger Harbor, Kuopio (971–126 744).

Elsewhere regular schedules include: *Western Lakeland,* the Silverline route Hämeenlinna-Tampere; Poet's Way route Tampere-Virrat; Tampere-Maisansalo. *Central Lakeland* on the Päijänne lake system Lahti-Jyväskylä; Lahti-Heinola. *North Karelia* in the Lake Pielinen region, Joensuu-Nurmes via Koli; Lieksa–Koli.

Most services operate from early or mid-June to mid- or late August. Local cruises are also arranged from most of these centers. On the Päijänne and Saimaa lake systems, evening disco or dance cruises are regularly featured.

By bike. Planned cycling routes are arranged from various centers, such as Imatra, Jyväskylä, Kajaani and Lappeenranta.

TOURS. City tours are organized in summer in Joensuu, Jyväskylä, Kajaani, Kuopio, Lahti, Lappeenranta and Tampere (not always daily); elsewhere by arrangement. Bus tours to places of scenic or historic interest in the surroundings are available from several centers. See also *By boat* above. A wide variety of tours throughout the region are arranged ex-Helsinki by a number of Finnish travel agencies.

SOLAR ECLIPSE. On July 22, 1990 a total eclipse of the sun will be visible along a "lane" about 100 miles long, extending northeast from Helsinki to Joensuu. The following are among the main places from which you should be able to see it: Hämeenlinna, Heinola, Hyvinkää, Imatra, Joensuu, Koli, Lahti, Lappeenranta, Mikkeli and Savonlinna. But you'll need to be up early—the event is scheduled to last about 1½ minutes following sunrise at 4:52 A.M. As the sun will be very low in the northeast horizon, you'll also need to choose your observation spot with care—further advice should be available from finnish tourist Board offices. Statistical surveys on the weather to be expected will also become available in due course. However, hotels in the eclipse area show every sign of being fully booked far ahead, so you may need to take a tent.

PLACES TO VISIT. This is the most watery part of the country, and the permutations on the theme of lake and forest, island and ridge, peninsula and bay, offer endless fascination. Historic sights are concentrated in a few main centers, but there are splendid examples of modern architecture almost anywhere in the region. The following is a selection of principal sights. Opening times apply to the peak season.

Hämeenlinna. Aulanko Tower. View point in Aulanko National Park. Open daily 10–8.

Castle. Dating from medieval times. Open daily 10–6.

Hattula Church. 14th century stone church with splendid interior frescoes from early 16th century. Open daily 10–6.

Sibelius' Home. The composer's childhood home. Open daily 10–4.

Silk House. On grounds of Aulanko Hotel. Exhibition and tax-free shop with silk items from all over the world.

Heinola. Bird Park (and **Bird Hospital**). About 400 tropical and Finnish birds.

Pikku-Jumpo steam train rides; see under Lahti.

Siltisaari Fishing Center. Rainbow trout fishing from specially stocked pool or from lake, near town center.

Hyvinkää. Hyvinkää Church. Designed by A. Ruusuvuori, 1961.

Railway Museum. Hyvinkäänkatu 9; locomotive shed and yard from the 1870s, exhibits include Imperial carriages used by Russian czar—a "must" for railway buffs. Open Tues. to Fri. 11–3, Wed. also 3–7. Sat. 11–4, Sun. 11–5.

Imatra. Church of the Three Crosses. Designed by Alvar Aalto.

Imatrankoski Rapids. A magnificent sight when the harnessed waters are released on Sundays and some holidays in summer.

Karelian Farmhouse. Open-air museum. Open 10–6; closed Mon.

Joensuu. Handicrafts Exhibition. Rantakatu 2.
Karelia House (Karjalan Talo). Ilosaari, including museum of Karelian culture. Open Tues. to Fri. 12–4, Wed. also 4–8, Sat. 10–4, Sun. 10–6.

Jyväskylä. Alvar Aalto Museum. Focusing on this renowned Finnish architect. Open Tues. to Sun. 12–6; closed Mon.
Aviation Museum of Central Finland. 20 km. (12 miles) north of city. Open daily 10–8.
City Theater. Designed by Alvar Aalto.
Handicrafts Museum. Open Tues. to Sun. 12–7; closed Mon.
Museum of Central Finland. With handicraft workers' cottages. Open Tues. to Sun. 12–7; closed Mon.
Muuramme Sauna Village. 15 km. (nine miles) south of city; over 200 years of Finnish sauna tradition.
Savutuvan Apaja. Haapaniemi, 12 km. (7½ miles) from town; a smoke cabin and other old buildings from central Finland. Open on request.
University of Jyväskylä. Designed by Alvar Aalto.

Kajaani. Kajaani Castle. Ruins from 1604.
Kainuu Museum. Asemakatu 4. Open Tues. to Sat. 12–3, Sun. and Wed. 12–6.
Paltaniemi. 8 km. (5 miles) north of town. Pretty village with church from 1726. Czar's stable (relic from visit by Alexander I) in the church yard. Eino Leino Talo (exact copy of Hövelö, birthplace of poet Eino Leino).
Town Hall. Designed by C.L. Engel, 1831.

Kuopio. Cathedral. Completed in 1815. Open daily 10–5.
Kuopio Museum. Kauppakatu 23. Excellent provincial museum, open Mon. to Fri. 9–4, Sat. 10–4, Sun. 11–7.
Market Square. Lively open-air market in center of town.
Open-air Museum. Kirkkokatu. Furnished buildings from 19th century. Open daily 10–5, Wed. also 5–7.
Orthodox Church Museum. Karjalankatu 1, collections from Orthodox Karelia, unique in Western Europe. Open Tues. to Sun. 10–4.
Puijo Tower. Offering superb panorama. Open daily 9 A.M.–1 A.M.

Lahti. Art Museum. Vesijärvenkatu 11, permanent and special exhibitions. Open daily Wed. to Sun. 12–4, Tues. 12–6.
Handicrafts Center. Saimaankatu 23. Exhibitions, demonstrations and sales. Open Mon. to Fri. 10–6, Sat. 10–2.
Hollola Church and Museum. 16 km. (ten miles) from city; dating from the 15th century. Open daily.
Lahti Historical Museum. Lahdenkatu 4. Open Tues. to Sun. 12–4, Tues. also 6–8.
Market Place. Open-air market on weekdays, special market day first Wed. of month.
Pikku-Jumpo. Steam locomotive rides once or twice weekly to Heinola (1 hour), each with a different theme.
Pyhäniemi. Near Hollola. Old manor house with summer art exhibitions.
Ristin Kirkko (Church of Cross). Designed by Alvar Aalto. Open daily 10–3.
Skiing Stadium. Sightseeing platform on top of 90 meter (295 feet) ski jump. Open Mon. to Fri. 11–6, Sat. and Sun. 10–5.

Lappeenranta. Linnoitus (Fortress). The oldest part of town and features many of the principal sights including: **Papilan kahvila** (Vicarage Café) with Orthodox interior and atmosphere, open Tues. to Sun. 12–6; **South Karelian Museum,** open Mon. to Fri. 10–6, Sat. and Sun. 11–5; **Virgin Mary Church,** built 1785, the oldest Orthodox church in Finland, open Tues. to Sun. 10–6.

190 FINLAND

Lappee Church. Central Park, dating from 1794. Open daily 12–5.
Lauritsala Church. Lauritsala, designed by Korhonen and Laapotti, 1969. Open daily 12–5.
Market Place. Open-air market Mon. to Sat. 7–1, summer also Mon. to Fri. 3–7.
Saimaa Canal. Built in 1856, restored in 1968, about 50 km. (31 miles) long, linking Lake Saimaa to Gulf of Finland through Soviet territory. Finnish section visited on sightseeing cruises.
Town Hall. Wooden building from 1829.

Mikkeli. Headquarters Museum. Päämajankuja 1–3. Mannerheim's Headquarters during World War II. Open daily 11–5.
Infantry Museum. Jääkärinkatu 6–8. Open daily 11–6.
Provincial Suur-Savo Museum. Otavankatu. Open Tues. to Sun. 11–3, closed Mon.
Provincial Government House. 1842, by C.L. Engel.
Visulahti Tourist Center. 5 km. (3 miles) from town. Features waxworks, automobile museum, dinosaur park, and Miniland of major Finnish buildings on a scale of 1 to 20. Open 9–9.

Punkaharju. Retretti. Remarkable art center in magnificent lakeside location, partly built underground into rock. A unique setting for exhibitions, concerts and opera performances. Open all year. Nearby **Punkaharju Summerland** (Kesämaa), splendid amusement park for children. Open daily 10–7.

Riihimäki. Finnish Glass Museum in former glass works. Outstanding museum and exhibition dedicated to 300 years of Finland's glass industry. Open daily 10–6.

Savonlinna. (see also *Punkaharju,* 27 km. (17 miles) from town). **Kerimäki Church.** 24 km. (15 miles) to the east. Largest wooden church in the world, built in 1847. Open Mon. to Fri. 9–8, Sat. 9–6, Sun. 11–8.
Olavinlinna. Magnificent medieval castle, best in Finland. Open daily 9–5.
Savonlinna Provincial Museum. Museum ships, including *Salama* (schooner from 1874), and exhibits illustrating history of Saimaa lake traffic. Open 10–8.
Suruton. In restored villa on Kasinosaari, illustrated history of Savonlinna Opera Festival. Open daily 10–6.

Tampere. Ask the Tourist Office about the Tampere Card (1, 2, or 3 days) valid for unlimited travel on local buses and free entrance to many museums. **Aquarium.** See *Särkänniemi.*
Art Museum of Tampere. Puutarhakatu 34, major Finnish collection. Open daily 11–7.
Cathedral (Tuomiokirkko). Designed by Lars Sonck, built 1902–1907; contains works by famous Finnish artists Magnus Enckell and Hugo Simberg. Open daily 10–6.
Children's Zoo. See *Särkänniemi.*
Haihara Doll Museum. Kaukajärvi, about nine km. (six miles) from city center; enchanting collection from different parts of the world. Open daily 12–6.
Häme Museum. Näsilinna, major collection featuring exceptional hand-woven rugs and tapestries and "chimneyless cottage." Open Tues. to Sun. 12–6; closed Mon.
Kaleva Church. Striking modern design by Raili and Reima Pietilä. Open daily 10–6.
Lenin Museum. Hallituskatu 19. Open Tues. to Sat. 11–3, Sun. 11–4; closed Mon.
Messukylä Church. Five km. (three miles) from city center, beautiful 15th-century stone church. Open daily 10–6.

Moomin Valley (Muumilaakso). Hämeenpuisto 20. Moomin house and original sketches of Tove Jansson, author of famous children's Moomin books. Open daily 12–6.

Näsineula Observation Tower and **Planetarium**. See *Särkänniemi*.

Pyynikki Park. With observation tower, open daily 9–6, and Summer Theater with revolving auditorium.

Sara Hildén Art Museum. Särkänniemi. Striking modern building exhibiting foreign and Finnish 20th-century art. Open daily 11–6.

Särkänniemi Tourist Center, Särkänniemi. With Aquarium (10–8), Planetarium, Näsineula Observation Tower (10–8), Children's Zoo (11–7) and Amusement Park (12–8).

Workers' Museum of Amuri. Makasiininkatu 12. Well-arranged museum block of workers' homes illustrating bygone way of life. Open Tues. to Sun. 12–6.

SPORTS. Boating. Rowing boats and canoes are available at all lake resorts; motor boats at many of them, sailing boats at a few. Many canoe tours are organized through the lake systems of the region; check with local tourist offices.

Golf. Imatra and Tampere have 18-hole courses. There are nine-hole courses at Aulanko near Hämeenlinna, Lahti, Lappeenranta and Mikkeli.

Riding. Facilities are available at Hämeenlinna, Hyvinkää, Imatra, Jyväskylä, Kuopio, Lahti, Mikkeli, Savonlinna, Sotkamo and Tampere.

Swimming. Almost anywhere! You'll have no problem in finding a secluded spot, or even an island to yourself. Much of the bathing is off smooth granite, which is also excellent for sunbathing—a favorite Finnish pastime.

Windsurfing. Facilities are available at Hämeenlinna, Heinola, Imatra, Joensuu, Jyväskylä, Kuopio, Lahti, Lappeenranta, Mikkeli, Savonlinna, Sotkamo and Tampere.

Winter sports. You'll find marked trails for cross-country skiing (some illuminated in the evenings) in almost every Finnish community. Centers with the best facilities in this region—usually including one or more ski lifts, ski school and organized ski excursions—are Hyvinkää, Jyväskylä, Koli, Kuopio, Lahti and Sotkamo.

OSTROBOTHNIA

Rural Plains to Forested Ravines

The flatlands of Ostrobothnia are the least visited by tourists, with some reason since they lack that primeval wilderness quality with which so much of the rest of Finland is endowed. Yet there is quite a lot of interest, especially if you want to get to grips with Finnish history and, not least, if you have a taste for huge sandy beaches that you can enjoy with very little interference from other humanity. The coastal towns vary from charming backwaters to busy bustling places, but most of them have played their part in one way or another in shaping Finland's destiny at some time. The land itself, by the way, has noticeably risen over the centuries so that quite a few harbors are now some miles from the modern nucleus of the towns.

Much of the hinterland is agricultural and nearly all of it flat with one notable exception. That is the north-eastern part of the region, close by the Soviet border, where there is as wild and rugged an area as you could wish to meet in the vicinity of Kuusamo.

As many of the coastal towns have a substantially Swedish-speaking population, the Swedish name is also given where appropriate in this section. It is, incidentally, from this province that so many Finns have emigrated to the United States.

Coast and Plains

You may find yourself entering Ostrobothnia either from Turku to the south or from Tampere and the neighboring province of Häme to the southeast. Almost due west of Tampere on the coast is Pori, the biggest industrial town and harbor on the Gulf of Bothnia, and famous for its annual Jazz Festival. This is one of the places where the retreat of the sea is most noticeable. About 19 km. (12 miles) away, the long beach at Yyteri is a favorite summer resort—the sands are really superb and there are all kinds of sports facilities as well as a splendid hotel there. The old fishing communities of Reposaari, an island accessible by road, are other points of interest about 32 km. (20 miles) away. Two charming coastal towns are worth mentioning to the south of Pori, though strictly speaking they are outside Ostrobothnia's boundaries. These are Rauma and Uusikaupunki in both of which some fine old wooden buildings have managed to survive the hazards of fire.

Or you may come into Ostrobothnia further north, taking in on the way Finland's first wild-life park at Ähteri, (see page 176) due north of Tampere and on the boundary of the two provinces. Your first major coastal town then is likely to be Vaasa (Vasa) and, on the way, you will observe how the country begins to flatten out and finally becomes a succession of rolling plains. There is open country in northern Finland too, but nowhere the cultivation that can be seen here. The whole landscape takes on a new aspect, one unlike any in the other regions of Finland: even the houses are different, generally two-storied.

Vaasa is an important port, with regular passenger services across to Swedish ports. After the disastrous fire of 1852 (a few interesting buildings of Old Vaasa can still be seen) the town was moved nearer the sea and given a Russian name. During the 1918 war of independence Vaasa became the capital of "White" Finland, the country's official government having moved there from "Red" Helsinki, and to commemorate the event the city was allowed to include Finland's Cross of Liberty in its coat of arms. In fact, South Ostrobothnia seems to have taken a prominent part in Finnish politics on several occasions. Besides being the site of a Russian defeat in 1808–9, the parish of Lapua is the place where the anti-Communist Lapua Movement originated in 1930. Spreading quickly all over the country, it reached a climax in the so-called Peasants' March, when 12,000 men from all over the country gathered in the capital and forced Parliament to declare Communism illegal.

The plains of Ostrobothnia are strewn with the battlefields of one or another of the numerous wars that the Finns have fought, first against the Swedes, then against the Russians, and for a brief while even among themselves. The coastal scenery is lovely, and there is good sailing in the Gulf of Bothnia. Apart from Vaasa, there are only two other towns of any size in this part of the province: Kokkola (Gamlakarleby) and Pietarsaari (Jakobstad), lying on the coast to the north of Vaasa. Pietarsaari is an attractive place with strong associations with the national poet Runeberg and has an active, modern trade center. Among the smaller coastal towns, Kristiinankaupunki and Uusikaarlepyy are both charming, with a good crop of ancient wooden houses. For beaches, go to Kalajoki where the sands are truly glorious and there are good amenities in the way of accommodations and sports facilities, set amidst the dunes.

Kokkola has one sight of particular interest to English visitors. On the banks of the small stream which runs through town is the English Park, and here in a small building is an English pinnace captured during the Crimean War when a landing was attempted near here in 1854. One British officer and eight seamen fell in the engagement, and they are buried in the Maaria Cemetery just outside the city. A memorial to this small battle stands on Halkokari Point in the old harbor.

Bothnian Gulf to Bear Country

Towards the top of the Gulf of Bothnia is the lively northern university town of Oulu. Originally a fur- and salmon-trading port, it became one of the major tar export harbors of the world in the last century and is today a busy industrial center. You can find out about the historic tar trade at the fascinating Turkansaari outdoor museum and try out regional specialties at the museum's café. Oulu's excellent modern buildings include a fine theater facing ancient warehouses by the harbor, and there are pleasant parks, a colorful market and plenty of cultural activities. Here, in the city's university, a new concept, the Oulu school of architecture, was born in recent years under the inspiration of Reima Pietilä. The emphasis is on making buildings an integral part of their surroundings, using brick and wood as the main materials.

For complete contrasts with the rest of Ostrobothnia, you must turn northeast to the rugged ravines and forested hills that lie just north of Kuusamo, including the fell district of Rukatunturi and Oulanka National Park. It's an area of gorge-like valleys where you have the opportunity to experience the thrills of shooting the rapids. The fishing is particularly good in these parts, and so is the walking, with marked trails to follow such as the 80 km. (50 mile) long Bear's Ring. The rivers also offer excellent waters for canoeing and kayaking. In winter, this is one of the best-equipped areas for all levels of skiing.

PRACTICAL INFORMATION FOR OSTROBOTHNIA

TOURIST INFORMATION. Kalajoki. Bus Station (983–60 591). **Kokkola** (Karleby). Kaarlelankatu 21 (968–311 902). **Kuusamo.** Torangintaival 2 (989–22 131) **Oulu.** (City) Torikatu 10 (981–241 011); (Region) Koulukatu 15 (981–226 744). **Pietarsaari** (Jakobstad). Storgatan 11 (967–31 796). **Pori.** (Town) Antinkatu 5 (939–335 780); (Region) Pohjoiskauppatori 1 C 29 (939–333 708). **Rauma.** Eteläkatu 7 (938–224 555). **Seinäjoki.** Kauppakatu 17 (964–162 184). **Uusikaupunki.** Levysepänkatu 4 A (922–1551); in summer, Alinenkatu 34 (922–21 225). **Vaasa.** (City) Raastuvankatu 30 (961–251 145); (Region) Raastuvankatu 17 A6 (961–114 441).

TELEPHONE CODES. We have given telephone codes for all the towns and villages in the hotel and restaurant lists that follow. These codes need only be used when calling from outside the town or village concerned.

HOTELS AND RESTAURANTS. Unless otherwise stated, all the hotels listed below have all or some rooms with bath or shower, licensed restaurants, and are open all the year. Where two names are given in this section, the second is the Swedish name, and indicates that there is a substantial Swedish-speaking population in the area.

Kalajoki. Small bathing resort with superb sandy beaches. *Rantakalla* (E–M), Hiekkasärkät (983–66 642). 34 rooms, pool, extensive sports facilities. DC, MC, V. *Kalajoki* (M), Hiekkasärkät (983–66 613). 35 rooms, disco. MC, V.
    Camping. *Hiekkasärkät,* near beach (983–60 301), open late May through Aug. 31.

Kaustinen. Small village best known for its annual folk festival. *Marjaana* (M), Teerijärventie 1 (968–611 211). 11 rooms, disco, pool, tennis. DC, MC, V. **Camping.** *Tastula* (968–614 118), open June 1 through Aug. 10.

Kokkola. Town near shores of Gulf of Bothnia. *Chydenius* (E–M), Rautatienkatu 6 (968–14 044). 44 rooms, tennis. AE, DC, MC, V. *Seurahuone* (E), Torikatu 24 (968–12 811). 73 rooms, disco. AE, DC, MC, V. *Vaakuna* (E), Rantakatu 16 (968–15 411). 71 rooms, pool, tennis. AE, DC, MC, V. **Camping.** *Suntinsuu,* two km. (one mile) north of rail station (968–14 006), open June 1 through Aug. 31. **Youth and Family Hostel.** *Tankkari,* Vidnäsinkatu 2 (968–18 274).

Kuusamo. Small town near wild fell and forest country not far from Arctic Circle; summer hiking and winter sports center. *Kuusamo* (E), Kirkkotie 23 (989–2020). 94 rooms, nightclub, disco, pool. AE, DC, MC, V. *Rantasipi Rukahovi* (E), Rukatunturi (989–3131). In splendid fell and forest country about 25 km. (16 miles) north. 108 rooms, pool, excursions into surrounding wilderness landscapes including shooting rapids. AE, DC, MC, V. *Iivaaren Lomakeskus* (M), (989–82 191). 23 rooms, sports facilities. *Martina* (M), Ouluntie 3 (989–22051). 40 rooms. DC, MC, V. **Camping.** More than a dozen camp sites in the area. Open year–round are: *Juuma,* (989–45 112); *Teeriranta* (989–62 141); and *Petäjälampi* (989–2364).

Oulu. Important northern port on Gulf of Bothnia, industrial and university city. *Vaakuna* (E), Hallituskatu 1 (981–224 666). 218 rooms, nightclub, disco, pool, boating. AE, DC, MC, V. *Apollo* (E–M), Asemakatu 31 (981–224 344). 53 rooms. DC, MC, V. *Cumulus* (E–M), Kajaaninkatu 17 (981–220 222). 207 rooms, pool. AE, DC, MC, V. *Lanamäki* (E–M), Rautatienkatu 8 (981–229 555). 36 rooms, beer and wine only. AE, DC, MC, V. *Arina* (M), Pakkahuoneenkatu 16 (981–14 221). 63 rooms. AE, DC, MC, V, *Otokylä* (I), Haapanatie 2 (981–332 672). 196 rooms, disco, summer only. *Välkkylä* (I), Kajaanintie 36 (981–227 707). 74 rooms, disco, pool, summer only. MC, V. **Restaurants.** *Hovinarri* (E), Isokatu 35 (981–222 497). MC, V. *Zivago* (E), Saaristonkatu 12 (981–223 886). DC. *Botnia-pub* (M), Pakkahuoneenkatu 30 (981–228 500). MC, V. *Merikoski* (M), Merikoskenkatu 2 (981–344 376). *Reidar* (M), Välkkylä, Kajaanintie 36 (981–13 321). **Camping.** *Nallikari,* Hietasaari (981–541 541); open early May through Sept. 30. **Youth Hostel.** *Välkkylä,* Kajaanintie 36 (981–227 707).

Pietarsaari (Jakobstad). Attractive small coastal town and birthplace of national poet Runeberg. *Fontell* (E), Kanavapuistikko 13 (967–30 366). 100 rooms, tennis. MC, V. *Pool* (E), Alholmintie (967–13 222). 40 rooms, pool, tennis. DC, MC, V. **Restaurants.** *Ebba* (M), Amerikagatan 2 (967–18 211). *Källären* (M), Rådhusgatan 7 (967–30 355). DC, MC, V. **Camping.** *Joutsen* (967–30 660), open May 15 through Aug. 31. **Youth Hostel.** *Joutsen* (967–30 660).

Pori. Major port on Gulf of Bothnia, industrial center near excellent beaches. *Rantasipi Yyteri* (E), Yyteri (939–343 777). About 20 km. (12 miles) away by the splendid sandy beaches of Yyteri. 113 rooms, nightclub, pool, extensive sports facilities. AE, DC, MC, V. *Satakunta* (E), Gallen-Kallelankatu 7 (939–820 100). 208 rooms, nightclub. AE, DC, MC, V. *Cumulus* (E–M), Itsenäisyydenkatu 37 (939–828 000). 56 rooms, pool. AE, DC, MC, V. *Juhana Herttua* (E–M), Itäpuisto 1 (939–331 841). 58 rooms. AE, DC, MC, V. *Mäntyluodon Hotelli* (I), (939–343 270). 8 rooms without bath or shower. MC, V. **Restaurants.** *Monttu* (E), Antinkatu 15 (939–339 093). MC, V. *Jussikka* (M), Yrjönkatu 10 (939–335 361). MC, V. *Punapaula* (M), Isolinnankatu 19 (939–331 486). *Sarkka* (M), Uusikoivistontie 40 (939–23 874). *Selkämeri* (M), Eteläpuisto 9 (939–332 822).

Camping. *Isomäki,* Isomäki Sports Center (939–410 620), open mid–June through mid–Aug. *Siikaranta,* Reposaari (939–344 120), open May 30 through mid–Aug. *Yyteri,* by Yyteri beach 20 km. (12 miles) from town (939–343 778); open May 30 through Aug. 25.
Youth and Family Hostel. *Retkeilymaja,* Korventie 52 (939–28 125).

Rauma. Coastal town with attractive old districts. *Cumulus* (E–M), Aittakarinkatu 9 (938–221 122). 104 rooms, pool. AE, DC, MC, V. *Raumanlinna* (E), Valtakatu 5 (938–221 111). 74 rooms, pool. AE, DC, MC, V.
Camping. *Poroholma,* open May 15 through Aug. 31, by the sea 1½ km. (1 mile) from town. *Reksaari,* on island with daily waterbus connections.
Youth and Family Hostel. *Poroholma* (938–224 666).

Rukatunturi. See *Kuusamo.*

Seinäjoki. Inland town, east of Vaasa. *Kantakievari* (E), Kalevankatu 2 (964–142 111). 49 rooms. AE, MC, V. *Rantasipi Sorsanpesä* (E), Törnäväntie 27 (964–120 100). 90 rooms, disco, pool. AE, DC, MC, V. *Cumulus Seinäjoki* (E–M), Kauppakatu 10 (964–141 620). 71 rooms, disco, pool. AE, DC, MC, V. *Seurahuone* (M), Keskuskatu 12 (964–131 944). 12 rooms, disco.
Camping. *Törnävä,* three km. (two miles) from center (964–120 784), open June 1 through Aug. 31.
Youth and Family Hostels. Bothnia Center Sahalankatu 11 (964–142 662). *Kortteri Youth and Family Hostel,* Puskantie 38 (964–144 800).

Uusikaupunki. Attractive small coastal town. *Lännentie* (E), Levysepänkatu 1 (922–12 636). 35 rooms, pool. AE, MC, V.
Camping. *Santtionranta* (922–23 862), open June 1 through mid-Aug.

Vaasa. Major west coast port and historic town. *Wasa* (L–E), Hoviokeudenpuistikko 18 (961–123 353). 150 rooms, pool. AE, DC, MC, V. *Central* (E), Hoviokeudenpuistikko 21 (961–111 211). 145 rooms, pool. AE, DC, MC, V. *Coronet* (E), Ylätori (961–121 044). 53 rooms. AE, DC, MC, V. *Waskia* (E), Lemmenpolku 3 (961–121 444). 184 rooms, nightclub, pool, sports facilities. AE, DC, MC, V. *Villitys* (I), Pitkäkatu 21 (961–122 581). 64 rooms, unlicensed cafeteria, summer only. AE, MC, V.
Restaurants. *Caribbean People,* (E–M), Vaasanpuistikko 22 (961–115 245). *Fondis* Källäre (E), Hovioikeudenpuistikko 15 (961–111 018). AE, MC, V. *Sekstantti* (M), Kauppapuistikko 40 (961–112 429). *Koti* (I), Raastuvankatu 15 (961–113 039), beer and wine only.
Camping. *Vaskiluoto* (961–113 852), 2 km. (1 mile) from town, open June 1 through Aug. 31.
Youth and Family Hostel. *Tekla,* Palosaarentie 58 (961–117 850).

HOW TO GET AROUND. By air. Regular flights serve Kokkola/Pietarsaari, Kuusamo, Oulu, Pori and Vaasa. **By train.** Main train routes are to Pori, Vaasa and to Oulu (via Kokkola), including car-carrying trains Helsinki–Oulu. Journey time Helsinki–Oulu by fast train is under seven hours. There are no train routes along the coast.

By bus. Services reach to every corner of the region, with express routes to main centers. This is the principal means of transport linking coastal communities.

By bike. Planned cycling routes are organized from Kokkola and Kuusamo.

TOURS. During the summer, sightseeing tours are arranged in Pietarsaari, Seinäjoki and Vaasa. There are also archipelago cruises which are available from Rauma, Uusikaupunki and Vaasa.

PLACES TO VISIT. The main scenic features of the region are its sandy beaches (the best in Finland), small island groups that lie just off the coast and, in the northeast, the magnificently wild fell and forest landscapes just south of the Arctic Circle. Some of the coastal communities have a very long trading tradition, and some have played a major part in Finland's more recent history. Opening times below apply to the peak season.

Kokkola. English Boathouse. Containing a landing craft captured from the British in the Crimean War.

Kaarlela Church. Two km. (one mile) from town, built in 1460.

Renlund Art Gallery. Pitkänsillankatu 39.

Oulu. Botanical Gardens. In attractive Hupisaaret park area at mouth of Oulujoki river.

Cathedral (Tuomiokirkko). Renovated after a fire according to a design by C.L. Engel in early-19th century. Open daily 10–7.

Market Place. With lively open-air market, near ancient salt storehouses on waterfront.

Museum of North Ostrobothnia. Ainola Park. Open Mon. to Thurs. 11–6, Wed. also 6–8, Sat. 11–3, Sun. 12–6.

Turkansaari. Church and open-air museum on island in Oulujoki river 13 km. (eight miles) east of town. Open daily 11–9.

Pietarsaari (Jakobstad). **Pedersöre.** Kyrkostrand, on southern outskirts of town; founded in 13th century. Open by appointment.

Runeberg's Cottage. Home of national poet J.L. Runeberg. Open Tues. to Sun. 10–3.

Runeberg's Fishing Hut. Four km. (two miles) north of town, near camp site Joutsen. Open daily 9–9.

Strengberg Tobacco Museum. Strengbergsgatan 1. Open by appointment.

Viexpo. Strengbergsgatan, permanent exhibition of export goods. Open Mon. to Fri. 8–4, Sat. and Sun. 11–2.

Pori. Central Pori Church. Between bridges over Kokemäenjoki river. Neo-Gothic, built in 1863, with altarpiece by Ekman and stained glass windows by Magnus Enckell.

Juselius Mausoleum. In Käppärä cemetery; erected by a businessman in memory of his young daughter with paintings by Pekka Halonen and frescoes by Gallen-Kallela. Open 12–3, Sat. 10–12; closed Mon.

Pori Art Museum, Eteläranta. Notable changing exhibitions of international modern art. Open Tues. to Sun. 11–6.

Reposaari. Flourishing old island community, accessible by road, 30 km. (19 miles) from town.

Town Hall. Formerly Junnelius Palace, Hallituskatu 12; built in Venetian style in 1895. Open by arrangement.

Rauma. Kirsti. Craftsman's home from the 18th century.

Marela Museum. A ship owner's house from the 19th century.

Pyhän Kolminaisuuden Kirkko (Church of the Holy Trinity). Ruins from the 14th century.

Pyhän Ristin Kirkko (Church of the Holy Cross). Founded in the 15th century, with Renaissance ceiling paintings and wooden sculptures.

Vanhakaupunki (Old Town). Old district south of the canal, with wooden houses based on city plan from 16th century.

Seinäjoki. Cultural and Administrative Center. By Alvar Aalto.

Museum of Southern Ostrobothnia. Including Gunpowder, Agricultural, Pharmacy and Open-air Museums. Open Tues. to Sun. 11–7.

Uusikaupunki. Cultural Museum. Including maritime section with exhibits from the era of sail. Open Thurs. and Fri. 10–5, Sat. and Sun. 12–3.

Lokalahti Church. Wooden church from 1763. 15 km. (9 miles) from town.
Old Church. From 1629. Open Mon.–Sat. 11–3, Sun. 12–4.
Myllymäki Park. With four old windmills. Open 10–8.
Pyhämaan Uhrikirkko (Sacrificial Church of Pyhämaa). Wooden church from the early 17th century 20 km. (12 miles) from town.

Vaasa. Art Hall (Taidehalli). Changing Finnish and foreign exhibitions.
Brage Open-air Museum. Hietalahti; seal hunting and folk museum. Open Mon. to Fri. 4–7, Sat. and Sun. 1–4.
Mustasaari Church. Old Vaasa. Open daily 9–4.
Orthodox Church. Kasarmintori; includes items from Valamo Monastery. Open Tues. to Sat. 10–3.
Ostrobothnian Museum. Museokatu 3; gentry and folk museum; also fine art section. Open Mon. to Fri. 12–8, Sat. and Sun. 1–6.
St. Mary's Church. Ruins in Old Vaasa. Dates from 14th century.
Stundars Handicraft Village. Solf. Open daily 12–6. 17 km. (11 miles) from town.
Vaasa Church. From 19th century with altar–piece by A. Edelfelt. Open Tues. to Fri. 10–3 and 6–8, Sat. 10–2.
Vaasa Court of Appeal. With fine portrait collection.
Wasastjerna–House Museum. Special section of Ostrobothnian Museum in Old Vaasa. Open daily 12–6; closed Mon.

SPORTS. Boating. Rowing boats are available at Kokkola, Oulu, Pietarsaari, Rauma, Uusikaupunki, Vaasa. There is excellent and varied canoeing and kayaking in the Kuusamo area.
Golf. There are 9-hole courses at Kokkola, Oulu, Pori, and Vaasa.
Riding. Facilities at Kalajoki, Kokkola, Oulu, Pietarsaari, Rauma, Seinäjoki, Uusikaupunki and Vaasa.
Swimming. Finland's finest sandy beaches are to be found on the west coast, some stretching for miles. Kalajoki and Yyteri, near Pori, have excellent tourist facilities.
Windsurfing. Facilities at Kalajoki, Oulu, Pietarsaari, Pori, Rauma, Seinäjoki, Uusikaupunki, and Vaasa.
Winter sports. Top center of the region is Rukatunturi, near Kuusamo, with ski trails, ski lifts, ski school and all kinds of excursions organized. Winter fishing through the ice and snow safaris are also arranged.

FINNISH LAPLAND

Arctic Contrasts

Lapland is a twofold miracle, a product of man and nature working in close harmony. Nature fashioned a wilderness of endless forests, fells, and great silences. So often the human footstep has obliterated all that came before, but here man has walked gently and left the virgin solitude of this country almost unspoiled. Now easily accessible by plane, train or bus, this Arctic outpost offers comfortable hotels and modern amenities, yet you won't have to go very far to find yourself in an almost primordial solitude.

Exploring Finnish Lapland

The oldest traces of human habitation in Finland have been found in Lapland, and hoards of Danish, English and even Arabian coins indicate trade activities many centuries ago. The origins of the Lapps themselves are lost in the mists of history. There are only some 2,500 pure Lapps still living here; the remainder of the provinces' population of some 220,000 are Finns. Until the 1930s, Lapland was still largely unexploited, still a region where any trip was an expedition of exploration. Then the Canadian-owned Petsamo Nickel Company (now in Soviet hands) completed the great road which connects Rovaniemi with the Arctic Sea. Building activities increased along this route (later to be known as the Arctic Road), the land was turned and sown, and a few hotels were built to cater to the increasing numbers of visitors.

Next came World War II with the Soviet Union still the enemy. In September, 1944, in conformity with the terms of the Armistice Treaty with their foe, the Finns started to drive out the considerable number of German troops then stationed in Lapland. Methodical to the last, they retreated destroying all they could. The capital Rovaniemi was levelled; almost every farmhouse, cottage and cattle-shed was burned down or blown up.

Barely giving the ruins time to cease smoking, the Finns started back again in a few weeks to create modern communities out of the desolation. Certain areas of Lapland had to be ceded to the Soviet Union (the Arctic coastline, Petsamo, and part of the Salla district on the east frontier), but their inhabitants were settled within the new boundaries. They included some 250 Skolt Lapps, a unique Lapp tribe, who were settled at Sevettijärvi on the northern shores of Lake Inari.

Along the Arctic Road

To get down to rather more practical details for the intending visitor, let us find a base in Lapland itself from which we can explore the country. The southernmost town of the province, Kemi, is somewhat south of the Arctic Circle on the coast of the Gulf of Bothnia. But practically on the Arctic Circle is the "Gateway to Lapland," Rovaniemi, the administrative hub and communications center of the province where the Ounas and Kemi rivers meet.

In the process of post-World War II rebuilding, Rovaniemi's population shot up from 8,000 to its present 33,000, so don't expect to arrive in a backwoods shanty town. This modern city on the edge of the wilderness comes as a surprise to most people with its excellent architecture and amenities—quite a lot of it, including the layout of the town, the work of Alvar Aalto. Note especially Lappia Hall, the concert and congress center which also houses the Lapland Provincial Museum, the world's northernmost professional theater, and the Library, both beautifully designed by Aalto. Also based on Aalto's plans is the new City Hall next door.

Quite a lot of light industry has come to Rovaniemi, too, and with all the varied amenities it has to offer, it attracts visitors from all over the province on business or pleasure, for health or further education, or simply because it has the best selection of shops of anywhere on or north of the Arctic Circle. Among other places to visit here are the modern church with its impressive mural, and various museum collections devoted to the region and its different features. Local sightseeing also includes summer trips on the Kemi river.

But interesting though it is, Rovaniemi is by no means typical of Lapland and to explore the province you have several alternatives. If you're in search of adventure, a number of small firms in Rovaniemi arrange safaris of up to one week with themes ranging from summer hiking or canoeing to winter reindeer or snowmobile trips into the wilderness. There are also a number of packages from Helsinki or from Rovaniemi that take in some of the Lapland highlights, albeit at greater speed than is ideal. There are even one-night trips by Concorde ex-London to see the midnight sun at midsummer or meet Santa Claus at Christmas. From Rovaniemi, independent travelers have various options. One is to fly or take the Arctic Road from Rovaniemi to Ivalo, the main artery of central and northern Lapland and, like other roads in the region, an important post-bus route. Ten kms. (six miles) from Rovaniemi, on the Arctic Circle, is a restaurant and—no less—Santa Claus' village and workshops where gifts can be bought in midsummer for mailing any day you like, with Santa Claus Land stamp. Santa Claus himself is in daily attendance year round. In the same Arctic Circle complex are the Hundred Elves' House illustrating Christmas celebrations in different countries, a glassworks, and a reindeer farm. A lot farther north at Sodankylä (where there is also a Northern Lights Observatory) is an ancient wooden church under which mysterious mummies were discovered. The nearby fells have been developed into a holiday area; and at Vuotso, further north still, you can even try your hand at goldwashing for an hour, a day or several days under expert guidance at Tankavaara, about ½ km. (¼ mile) east of the Artic Road there is now an extremely well arranged Gold Museum here, with a restaurant and self-catering accommodation.

Goldwashing is also practised on remoter parts of the Ivalojoki river to the northwest where a goldwashing station, built as long ago as 1870 at Kultala, still stands. Most of the Ivalojoki passes through remote landscapes, but from just south of Ivalo township it flows alongside the Arctic Highway for a while. It's an excellent canoeing river and there are now arrangements for renting canoes to paddle down to lake Inari, returning by bus to holiday centers such as Saariselkä.

The latter lies a little north of Tankavaara and is an expanding complex in a fine setting, with a varied range of accommodations from which to embark on lone or guided trips into the true wilderness. Over 2,500 square km. (965 square miles) of this magnificent area has recently been named the Urho Kekkonen National Park after Finland's former president. Further north, the sprawling small township of Ivalo is a main center for northern Lapland with a top class hotel and all the amenities of a modern community.

The huge island-studded expanses of Lake Inari, north of Ivalo, offer endless possibilities for wilderness exploration, and the village of Inari on its southwest shore is a good center from which to radiate in almost any direction. It has a charming modern church and sightseeing cruises on the lake are arranged in summer. West of it lies the Lemmenjoki (River of Love) where there is a small holiday village from which wilderness treks or boat trips are organized, including into a remote goldwashing district where a few hardy souls are still trying their luck.

In recent years, a growing number of small holiday villages have blossomed on or near the Arctic Road near Inari and to the north of it, usually with a small restaurant and shop attached. Amenities are simple, but the situations are often magnificent and bring you very close to the true pulse of Lapland. Usually there will be a boat at your disposal, fishing possibilities and the experience of preparing your own sauna. From Kaamanen, north of Inari, a side road leads to Sevettijärvi, home of the Skolt Lapps, and eventually into Norway.

Further north still is Utsjoki, a most straggling village on the Norwegian border. This is the country's northernmost parish in which you can travel by boat on the Teno river—famed for its salmon waters and called Finland's most beautiful river. Should you wish to take a trip into Norway, you can drive over the border at Nuorgam northeast of Utsjoki, or from Karigasniemi over the Norwegian Arctic Highway, eventually returning into Finland at Kilpisjärvi in the far northwest, though this is a very long detour. However, Utsjoki and Karigasniemi are now also linked by a minor road following the Teno river, a road which continues further south

still along the border with Norway to Angell from which you can return
east to Inari, so that there are now several round-trip possibilities of various lengths.

To the Three Countries Boundary

Another alternative from Rovaniemi is to head via Pello and the Tornio
valley or Kittilä into western Lapland, reaching right up to the meeting
point with Norway and Sweden near Kilpisjärvi. Along minor roads about
60 km. (37 miles) to the west of Kittilä, the rural community of Äkäslompolo has blossomed into one of the best-equipped summer and winter resorts resorts in Lapland. It is located by a small lake at the foot of the
fell of Yllästunturi, at the hub of a network of walking trails. You'll pass
another well-equipped tourist complex 20 km. (12 miles) north of Kittilä,
at the foot of Levitunturi near Sirkka. It's of a particularly attractive design and caters especially to health fanatics.

The fells are higher and the scenery more impressive on this side of Lapland, and the fell group of Pallastunturi and the villages of Enontekiö and
Kilpisjärvi are particularly recommended. A superb wilderness trail,
about 96 km. (60 miles) long, links Pallastunturi and Enontekiö across
the fells, with unattended huts along the way in which to overnight. To
the east of the fells, a relatively recent minor road passes through Raatta-
ma and a number of hamlets whose remoteness at that time protected them
from war devastation so that a number of farm buildings survive from
quite ancient times. Enontekiö straggles along a lake shore and from it
a road leads to Kautokeino in Norway, eventually linking up with the rest
of the Norwegian road network. The road from Muonio to Kilpisjärvi,
paralleling the Swedish border, is known as the Way of the Four Winds
(after the four points of the male Lapp headgear). Along this route, Karesuvanto is well placed for excursions into the wilderness and trips over
into Sweden. From Kilpisjärvi itself, a popular excursion is to the simple
granite Stone of the Three Countries, marking the boundary of Sweden,
Norway and Finland. There are marvelous views for those with energy
to climb Saana fell, looming over Kilpisjärvi and, to the northeast, rise
more fells including the highest in Finland, Haltia at over 1,220 meters
(4,000 feet).

The Wild and Not-So-Wild

But what are those special features that draw some people back to Lapland again and again? It is difficult to put your finger on them for they
are made up of many factors as intangible as the Northern Lights that
send their flickering veils of color weaving across the winter sky. If you
can take the intense but dry cold, winter is a fascinating time in Lapland,
not only for the Northern Lights, but for experiences such as the unique
reindeer round-ups.

Depending how far north of the Arctic Circle you go, the sun doesn't
rise for anything up to several weeks around mid–winter. Don't imagine
it is pitch dark, though. There is reflected light from the invisible sun below
the horizon during the middle hours of the day, and a luminosity drawn
from the ever–present snow.

From December to March, reindeer owners round up their herds all
over the Lapland map, and collect them in their thousands into huge cor-

rals. Sometimes dressed in their colorful costumes, the Lapps and also many Finns lasso the reindeer in true Wild West fashion, recognizing their own animals by brand marks on the ear. Once sorted into individual herds, they are counted, some selected for slaughter and the rest go free again. The round-ups are also attended by many buyers, for reindeer meat is considered quite a delicacy not only for eating locally, but for "export" to the south and even abroad.

To get to some of the remoter round-ups you may have to travel by taxi plane, though other corrals are near the road, especially around Ivalo, Inari and Enontekiö. Most Lapps and northern Finns get there on skis or by one of those motorized sledges which rather sadly have replaced the much more attractive (and silent) reindeer-drawn *pulkka* (a kind of boat-shaped sleigh on one runner). In southern Lapland especially, an increasing number of round-ups occur in the fall. Finding out exactly when and where a round-up is taking place is not easy, for much depends on the whims of the weather and the reindeer, so you must check locally. The information offices in Rovaniemi, however, will be able to give some guidance.

A few words should be said about the Lapps—a proud, sensitive and intelligent people some of whom, with justification, resent the attitude of those visitors who regard them as a tourist attraction put there for their benefit. The word for Lapp in their language is *Same* (pronounced Saa-me) and this is how they prefer to be known. Remember this is their country and they have an ancient culture, language and customs of their own. Modern influences (and intermarriage) have rather regrettably changed many aspects of their traditional way of life; for example, the attractive costumes are less frequently seen, except on festive occasions. The young especially have been affected by the changes and many of them are far more interested in becoming teachers, lawyers or engineers than breeding reindeer or hunting from their remote homesteads. Yet others have found profit from selling souvenirs to the tourists. But most prefer to go about their daily life minding their own business. The Lady Day Church Festival in Enontekiö in March and Easter Church Festival in Inari are particularly colorful events, attended by many Lapps in their most brilliant costumes, and usually featuring reindeer racing or lassoing competitions.

Of other winter attractions such as skiing, reindeer safaris and dog sledge tours, more has been said under *Winter Sports* at the end of this section. Summer has the blessing of daylight up to 24 hours long, and often beautiful weather to go with it, but beware of the mosquitoes. In the fall—usually early September—the colors are so fabulous that the Finns have a special word for it—*ruska*.

So the new and the old intermingle in this remote northern corner of Europe. The new Lapland is a place of modern techniques in which careful management is gradually driving back the wilderness and creating cornfields beyond the Arctic Circle. The forests are being exploited and managed with expert care, and light industry and hydro-electric projects have added their mark to the Lapland map. Yet goldwashers still wash the gravel of the Lemmenjoki river, cut off from the world except for occasional visitors and the aircraft that swoop down with their mail and provisions, and the rhythm of the seasons still governs the life of all those connected with reindeer. And the experienced traveler who would like to roam through the wilds for days on end without meeting a fellow human being can still do so without any problem at all. Be warned, however, that climatic conditions change rapidly and often unpredictably, especially on those lonely Arctic fells. Always seek and heed local advice, and tell your hotel or friends where you are heading and how long you intend to be away. An attractive alternative is provided by organized canoeing or hiking trips with nights in huts or tents in the wilderness.

PRACTICAL INFORMATION FOR
FINNISH LAPLAND

TOURIST INFORMATION. Ivalo. Bus Station. Piiskuntie 5 (9697–12 521). **Kemi.** Torikatu 4 (9698–299 450). **Rovaniemi.** (Town) Aallonkatu 2 (960–16 270); in summer also at the railroad station (960–22 218); (Region) Lapland Travel (Lapin Matkailu), Maakuntakatu 10 (960–16 052). **Tornio.** Lukiokatu 10 (9698–40 048).

Details of the many facilities and types of holiday in the region are given in the annually revised brochure *Finnish Lapland* produced by Lapland Travel in Rovaniemi and available from Finnish Tourist Board offices. There is also a separate brochure covering amenities along the Arctic Road.

TELEPHONE CODES. We have given telephone codes for all the towns and villages in the hotel and restaurant lists that follow. These codes need only be used when calling from outside the town or village concerned.

HOTELS AND RESTAURANTS. Unless otherwise stated, all the hotels listed below have all or some rooms with bath or shower, licensed restaurants, and are open all year.

Äkäslompolo. Well-equipped summer and winter resort. *Akas-Hotelli* (E–M), (9695–69 171). 84 rooms, pool, disco, summer and winter sports facilities. AE, MC, V.

Enontekiö. Lakeside village in western fell district. *Hetta* (E–M), (9696–51 361). 39 rooms, pool, boating, lovely location overlooking lake. AE, MC, V. *Jussan Tupa* (M) (9696–51 101). 34 rooms, pool, boating. *Hetan Matkailumaja* (I), (9696–51 361). 18 rooms, no restaurant.

Camping. *Hetta* (9696–51 008), open year round. *Kotakieva* (9696–51 063), open June 1 through Sept. 30. *Galdotieva* (9696–58 064), near Palojärvi on the road to Kautokeino (Norway), best facilities, open year round.

Youth Hostel. *Hetan Retkeilymaja* (9696–51 016).

Inari. Pleasant village by huge lake of same name in northern Lapland. *Inarin Kultahovi* (M), (9697–51 221). 29 rooms, fine riverside location. AE, MC, V. The area to the north offers several small, simple holiday villages including: *Kaamasen Kievari,* simple huts, restaurant serving excellent local specialties; *Muotkan Ruoktu,* cafeteria; *Neljän tuulentupa,* accommodations in 3- or 4-bed rooms in main buildings, pleasant café and restaurant; *Kiellatupa,* modern, 3- or 4-bed rooms in main buildings. West of Inari is *Lemmenjoen Lomamajat* in a fine riverside wilderness setting up the Lemmenjoki river, cafeteria, shop, fishing.

Camping. There are about ten camp sites in the area, including at or near all the holiday villages mentioned above. *Lomakylä Inari* (9697–51 108), has the best facilities, open March 1 through late Sept. *Hostel Retkeilymaja Kukkula* (9697–51 244).

Ivalo. Main village and communication center in northern Lapland. *Ivalo* (E), Ivalontie 34 (9697–21 911). 62 rooms, pool, boating, on banks of river. AE, DC, MC, V.

Camping. *Näverniemi* (9697–21 621), open year round.

Karesuvanto. Village near Swedish border, northwest Lapland. *Ratkin* (M) (9696–42 101). 26 rooms, attractive local style. MC, V.

Kemi. Port and industrial center on far north of Gulf of Bothnia. *Cumulus* (E–M), Hahtisaarenkatu 3 (980–20 931). 119 rooms, pool. AE, DC, MC, V. *Merihovi* (E–M), Keskuspuistokatu 6–8 (9698–23 431). 70 rooms, DC, MC, V. *Relletti Summer Hotel* (I), Miilukatu 1 (9698–20 941). 34 rooms without bath or shower, no restaurant.

Restaurants. *Kaleva* (M), Valtakatu 3 (9698–15 624). *Martina Café* (M), Keskuspuistokatu 15 (9698–23 502). MC, V. *Roma* (I), Valtakatu 12 (9698–16 812), beer and wine only. MC, V.

Kilpisjärvi. Beautiful situation by lake and beneath fells in far northwest. *Kilpisjärvi Tourist Hotel* (E–M), (9696–77 761). 49 rooms, beautiful setting. AE, DC, MC, V. *Saananmaja* (M) (9696–77 746). 15 rooms, unlicensed restaurant.

Camping. *Kilpisjärvi* (9696–77 771), open mid-June through mid-Sept.

Youth Hostel. *Retkeilykeskus* (9696–77 771), good facilities. MC, V.

Kittilä. Main village at road junction in west central Lapland. *Kittilä* (E–M), Valtatie 47 (9694–13 201). 37 rooms, pool. MC, V. *Levitunturi* (E) (9694–81 301). 82 rooms, pool, well-equipped winter and summer resort in nearby fells. AE, MC, V.

Camping. *Kittilä* (9694–13 221), open June 1 through Aug. 31.

Youth Hostel. *Retkeilymaja* (9694–13 221).

Muonio. Main village near western fell districts on Swedish border. *Olostunturi* (E–M) (9696–2001). 85 rooms, pool, a little outside village at foot of fell. DC.

Camping. *Harriniva* (9696–2491), open year round. *Olostunturi* (9696–1200), open June 15 through Aug. 15.

Pallastunturi. Splendid group of western fells, near Muonio, 50 km. (31 miles). *Pallastunturi Tourist Hotel* (E–M), (9696–2441). 69 rooms, in lonely splendor. AE, MC, V.

Pyhätunturi. Fine group of southern fells north of Kemijärvi. *Kultakero* (E–M) (9692–12 081). 48 rooms, pool. AE, MC, V.

Camping. *Pyhätunturi Kotakylä* (9692–52 120), open mid-June to mid-Sept.

Rovaniemi. Modern capital of Lapland province; winter sports center. *Rantasipi Pohjanhovi* (L), Pohjanpuistikko 2 (960–313 731). 214 rooms, disco, pool. AE, DC, MC, V. *Ounasvaara* (E), (960–23 371). 52 rooms, tennis, lovely hilltop position on outskirts of town. AE, DC, MC, V. *Polar* (E), Valtakatu 23 (960–23 751). 64 rooms, pool. AE, DC, MC, V. *Aakenus* (M–I), Koskikatu 47 (960–22 051). 45 rooms, unlicensed restaurant. *Gasthof* (M–I), Koskikatu 41 (960–23 222). 42 rooms, pool. AE, DC, MC. *Lapinportti* (M), Pohlojankatu 19 (960–22 555). 46 rooms, pool. DC, MC, V. *Oppipoika* (M), Korkalonkatu 33 (960–20 321). 40 rooms, pool. AE, DC, MC, V. *Rovaniemen Ammattikoulun Kesähotelli* (I), Kairatie 75 (960–392 651). 36 rooms, cafeteria only, summer only.

Restaurants. *Bel-Giovanni* (M–I), Valtakatu 34 (960–16 406). Lively bistro atmosphere, beer and wine only. AE, MC, V. *Lapinpoika* (M), Ruokasenkatu 2 (960–16 890), excellent cold table, intimate atmosphere. MC, V. *Pinja* (M), Valtakatu 19 (960–14 272). Quiet, intimate—and non-smoking; beer and wine only. DC, MC. *Sampo* (M), Korkalonkatu 32 (960–312 574). Lapland specialties, popular with the young. DC, MC, V.

Camping. *Ounaskoski,* Jäämerentie 1 (960–15 304), open June 1 through Aug. 31, by the river. *Ounasvaara,* at the skiing stadium (960–60 606).

Youth and Family Hostel. *Kaupungin Retkeilymaja,* Hallituskatu 16 (960–14 644).

Saariselkä. Expanding tourist and walking center with modern facilities near virgin wilderness area east of the Arctic Highway; guided hiking trips and gold-panning excursions to old gold workings in the area. *Riekonlinna* (L–E) (9697–81 601). 66 rooms, extensive sports facilities. AE, DC, MC, V. *Riekonkieppi* (E), Raitopolku 2 (9697–81 711). 103 rooms, sports facilities. AE, DC, MC, V. *Saariselkä Recreation Center* (E), Saariseläntie 25 (9697–81 826). 133 rooms, disco. *Kelohovi* (E–M) (9697–81 891). 10 rooms, sports facilities. *Laanihovi* (E–M), (9697–81 816). 36 rooms. MC, V. Several well-equipped holiday villages in the area include *Kelohovi* and *Kakslauttanen.*

Youth Hostel. *Kiilopään Eräkeskus* (9697–87 101).

Sodankylä. Main village on major route north. *Kantakievari Luosto* (E–M) (9693–13 681). 50 rooms, in nearby Luostotunturi fell district, disco, sports facilities. AE, DC, MC, V. Also well-equipped self-catering cottages.

Camping. *Nilimella* (9693–12 181), open mid-June through late Aug. *Orakoski* (9693–11 965), open late May through mid-Sept.

Youth Hostel. *Retkeilymaja,* Lapinpisto (9693–11 960).

Suomutunturi. Fell district on the Arctic Circle, 40 km. (25 miles) southeast of Kemijärvi. *Suommu* (E–M) (9692–12 951). 61 rooms, disco, pool, boating. AE, DC, MC, V.

Tankavaara. Goldwashing center near Arctic Highway. Simple self-catering accommodations, attractive restaurant (9693–461 58). DC.

Tornio. On Swedish border at northern tip of Gulf of Bothnia. *Kaupunginhotelli* (E), Itäranta 4 (9698–43 311), 100 rooms, disco, pool. AE, DC, MC, V. *Tornio* (M), Keskikatu 1 (9698–42 401). 14 rooms, boating. AE, DC, MC, V.

Restaurant. *Dar Menga,* Kauppakatu 12–14 (9698–42 353). Beer and wine only. MC, V.

Camping. *Aittaniemi* (9698–40 917), open June 15 through Aug. 31. *Kalliopudas* (9698–445 945), open June 1 through Aug. 31.

Youth and Family Hostels. *Kivirannan Retkeilymaja* (9698–40 146). *Suensaari,* Kirkkotie 1 (9698–41 682).

Utsjoki. Village in northernmost fell district by Norwegian border. *Utsjoki Tourist Hotel* (M) (9697–71 121). 32 rooms, boating. AE, MC, V.

Camping. *Ailigas* (9697–71 229), open June 15 through Aug. 30. *Kenestupa* (9697–72 531), open mid-June through mid-Aug., some distance south of village. *Kevon Lomakeskus* (9697–72 506), open mid-June through mid-Aug., some distance south of village. *Nuorgam* (9697–74 312), open year round, some distance northeast of village by road to Nuorgam.

HOW TO GET AROUND. By air. Regular flights serve Ivalo, Kittilä and Rovaniemi. **By train.** There are excellent services to Rovaniemi from the south, and car-carrying trains to both Rovaniemi and Kolari. Rail routes end at Kemijärvi or Kolari, both north of the Arctic Circle. **By bus.** This is the main form of surface transport throughout the province and extending into northern Norway. **By boat.** Sightseeing excursions are arranged on Lake Inari from Inari, and on the Kemi river from Rovaniemi.

TOURS. City sightseeing tours are arranged in summer in Rovaniemi; also available are river excursions. A variety of special interest tours to various parts of Finnish Lapland are marketed by Lapland Travel, **Maakuntakatu 10,** Rovaniemi. These feature fishing, canoeing, sailing, trekking, jeep safaris, and gold panning in summer; skiing, snowmobile tours and reindeer safaries in winter. Lapland tours, some extending into northern Norway, are also available ex-Helsinki or ex-Rovaniemi through a number of Finnish travel agencies.

PLACES TO VISIT. The magnificent wilderness scenery of the province is its top attraction at any season. Major winter features are the magical Northern Lights and the thrilling spectacle offered by reindeer roundups. Fall colors (usually September) are of outstanding beauty. Historic monuments are few and far between, but there is some splendid modern architecture and fascinating museums devoted to this unique region, including the culture of the Same (Lapp) people. Opening times below apply to the peak season.

Inari. Lapp Museum. Open-air museum displaying Lapp dwellings and traditional way of life. Open daily 8 A.M.–10 P.M.

Pielppäjärvi Church. About 7 km. (four miles) east of village; some 200 years old, wood-built.

Kemi. Gemstone Gallery, Kauppakatu 29. New and unusual collection of gold and jewellery, including handmade replicas of many crown jewels and other art treasures. Open daily 10–8.

Rovaniemi. Forestry Museum. Salmijärvi. Open Tues. to Sun. 12–6.

Lapland Provincial Museum. Lappia House (Lapland Collection) and Poromiehentie 1A (birds and minerals). Open Tues. to Sun. 10–6.

Lappia House. Hallituskatu 11; modern theater, concert and congress center designed by Alvar Aalto. Open 8–4. Guided tours Mon. to Fri. 10, 1 and 4.

Library. Hallituskatu 9, designed by Alvar Aalto, features art exhibition.

Lutheran Church. Kirkkotie 1, with important altar fresco *Source of Life* by Lennart Segerstråle. Open daily 9–8.

Pöykkölä Museum. On the outskirts of town. Local farm buildings from the 18th century. Open 12–4.

Santa Claus's Workshop. On the Arctic Circle 10 km. (6 miles) from town. Open daily 9–8.

Sodankylä. Church. Wood-built, nearly 300 years old.

Tankavaara. Gold Museum. Illustrating history of goldwashing since 19th century, including open-air section. Open daily 9–6.

Tornio. Church. Dating from 1686. Open Mon. to Fri. 9–5.

Kukkolankoski Rapids. 16 km. (ten miles) north of town. The biggest unharnessed rapids in Finland.

Tornio Valley Museum. Keskikatu 22. Open Tues. to Fri. 12–7, Sat. and Sun. 12–5.

SPORTS. (See also Tours above.) **Boating.** Rowing boats or canoes are available in Inari, Kemi, Kemijärvi, Rovaniemi, Sodankylä, Tornio and from many small tourist centers. There are some particularly good canoeing rivers, such as the Ounasjoki (from Enontekiö to Rovaniemi) and the Tornionjoki. The latter and its tributaries form the boundary between Finland and Sweden and annually provide the scene of the 537–km. long International Canoe Race. Canoeing tours are arranged from a number of centers.

Riding. Facilities exist in Kemi, Kemijärvi, Rovaniemi, Sodankylä and Tornio.

Swimming. Secluded spots are legion and settings almost invariably superb, but don't expect the temperature of the water to be anything much above chilly!

Windsurfing. There are facilities in Inari, Kemi, Kemijärvi, Rovaniemi, Sodankylä.

Winter sports. The long treeless slopes of the Lapland fells offer excellent terrain, though in many cases you will have to climb to the top of them first in order to ski down. However, there is now a good selection of centers provided with a ski lift or two, a ski school and the possibility of hiring equipment. From any of them, you can also practice cross-country skiing (it doesn't have to be far!), which is the best way of all of experiencing these far northern landscapes. All offer marked trails of varying lengths, usually with one or more illuminated to compensate for the shorter winter days, though by March there are already 12 hours of daylight and, by April, 16. The following is a selection of the best-equipped centers, all of them—with the exception of Rovaniemi—consisting either of a lone hotel or a small scattered group of establishments, invariably in a glorious setting: Äkäslompolo, Levin-tunturi (near Kittilä), Luostotunturi (near Sodankylä), Pallastunturi, Pyhätunturi, Rovaniemi, Saariselkä, and Suomutunturi. In addition, the villages of Enontekiö, Inari and Kilpisjärvi are excellent centers for cross-country skiing with good accommodations.

Other winter activities include the possibility to test your skill at the world's only reindeer-driving school, near Rovaniemi. In quite a few centers, rides by reindeer-drawn sleigh are arranged and in a few places, notably Rovaniemi, skidoos can be rented. Reindeer safaris provide an unforgettable experience but are expensive. Ice fishing (through a hole in the ice of a frozen lake) is another popular feature. Wind-surfing on ice and snow is the latest sport which looks set to win a big following.

ICELAND

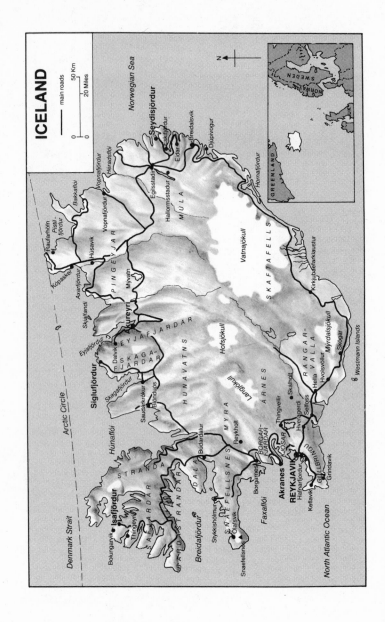

ICELAND

main roads

0 ____ 50 Km
0 ____ 20 Miles

ICELAND—FACTS AT YOUR FINGERTIPS

NATIONAL TOURIST OFFICE. The Iceland Tourist Bureau publish a number of pamphlets on all aspects of tourism within the country, and they will be able to supply information on a wide range of travel topics.

Their addresses are:

In North America: *Iceland Tourist Board,* 655 Third Ave., New York, NY 10017 (212–949–2333).

In the U.K.: 3rd Floor, Tottenham Court Rd., London W1P 9LG (01–388 5599).

Within Iceland are several tourist bureaus. The majority are in Reykjavik. All have free pamphlets and are most helpful. The National Tourist Offices are at: Reyjkanesbraut 6 (25855), and the Tourist Information Center, Ingolfsstraeti 5 (623045).

CURRENCY. In 1981 Iceland adjusted its currency to New Krona (Nkr.), where 1 new krona equals 100 old kronur; new bank notes and coins were also introduced. 1 krona has 100 aurar. The coins in use are 5, 10 and 50 aurar, 1 krona, 5 kronur, 10 kronur and 50 kronur, with notes of 10, 50, 100, 500, 1000 and 5000 kronur. The 10 kronur note is being withdrawn but is still valid. All banks have foreign exchange departments which handle both hard currency and travelers cheques. The latter can also be cashed at hotels, major travel bureaus, and many restaurants. Note that many goods are priced in dollars and can be bought with that currency or with most credit cards. We give most prices in this chapter in U.S. dollars. At the time of writing the exchange rate was 52 Ikr. to the U.S. dollar, 90 Ikr. to the pound sterling.

COSTS IN ICELAND. There is no such thing as a cheap trip to Iceland at the present time, as very high rates of inflation and the necessity to import most consumer items have brought the cost of living to a very high level. Your bill at restaurants and hotels will include a hefty 24% state tax and service charge; keep this in mind when planning your budget. Certain items are relatively inexpensive however, those being cinema tickets, public transport, petrol, tobacco, and coffee.

Sample costs. A cinema seat, 250 Ikr.; theater seat, 800 Ikr.; a coffee in snack bar, 40 Ikr.; a beer 90 Ikr. in snack bar or 140 Ikr. in Moderate restaurant; bottle of wine in Moderate restauarnt, 450 Ikr.

SEASONAL EVENTS. Icelanders celebrate as many holidays as they possibly can! Christmas Eve marks the start of the main midwinter celebrations, which last until *Threttándi* (The Thirteenth—January 6). December 24th is the family celebration, the 25th the religious one, and December 31st and January 6th are the main evenings for social events. In April they greet the First Day of Summer. May 1st and Whitmonday (May 15) are other days when tourists might find some offices are closed.

Iceland has a small population, and large-scale festivals are only rarely undertaken. However, every second year in Reykjavik there is a major international Arts Festival, in early June (due in 1990). The Westman Islanders also celebrate a festival of their own, and this is treated as a sports and social carnival which is held each year on the first weekend in August.

NATIONAL HOLIDAYS. Jan. 1 (New Year's Day); Mar. 12 (Maundy Thursday); Mar. 14, 15, 16 (Easter); Apr. 20 (First Day of Summer); May 1 (Labor Day); May 25 (Ascension Day); June 4–5 (Whitsun); Jun. 17 (National Day); Aug. 7 (Bank Holiday); Dec. 25 and 26 (Christmas); Dec. 31 (New Year's Eve).

LANGUAGE. Icelandic is a Germanic tongue first brought to the island by settlers from Norway. The modern language has changed so little from the Old Norse of ancient times that Icelandic children can understand the Sagas fairly well, though these works date from the 12th to the 14th centuries!

However, it is a difficult language to master thanks to an extremely difficult set of pronunciation rules, and many tourists (most, in fact) will find it nigh on impossible, what with words and constructions like this: "haestaréttarmálaflutnigsmanns-skrifstofustúlkuútidyralykill," meaning "a latch key belonging to a girl working in a lawyer's office." Fear not though, as most Icelanders you meet will almost certainly speak fairly good English, some Danish or German, and possibly French as well.

CUSTOMS. Visitors to Iceland are allowed to import the following items duty-free: 200 cigarettes or 250 grams of tobacco products; plus 1 liter of alcoholic beverage, and 1 liter wine less than 21% alcoholic content, or 12 bottles of beer (note that only those over 20 years of age can import alcohol, over 16 for tobacco products). Prescription drugs for personal use are also permitted. No limit is put on the amount of foreign currency which may be imported or exported, but no more than Ikr. 2,100 may be exported.

HOTELS. The best hotels are in the capital and the other main town, Akureyri. The chain of Edda hotels, found all over the country, are clean and simple and moderately priced. Don't forget that a state and service tax is 24% is included in your bill (this is contained in the prices quoted below). Breakfast is extra, usual price $10 per person. Somewhat less expensive accommodations are available in private homes within Reykjavik, which usually run about $37 a night for a single room, $55 for a double. Check with the Iceland Tourist Bureau for lists of homes participating in this scheme.

Prices. We have divided the hotels we list into three categories: Expensive (E), Moderate (M), and Inexpensive (I). These gradings are determined solely by price. The prices behind these gradings vary between hotels within Reykjavik and those elsewhere in the country.

Two people in a double room can expect to pay (in U.S. dollars):

	Reykjavik	Elsewhere
Expensive	$120–$150	$90–$140
Moderate	$100–$120	$55–$90
Inexpensive	$50–$100	$30–$55

These prices include service charges and tax. The abbreviations AE, DC, MC, and V in the listings stand for American Express, Diner's Club, MasterCard (incorporating Access and EuroCard), and Visa.

Icelandic villages are very small, so for the most part hotels there do not have any addresses as such—you simply enter the village and the hotel will probably be the first thing you see. All of the "Edda" hotels we list are boarding schools throughout the winter, and it's only during the summer tourist season that they are turned into hotels. These are often built out in the middle of nowhere, the location being usually by a hot spring, which explains the numerous swimming pools and saunas that Edda hotels offer.

FARM VACATIONS. Besides being one of the least expensive means of accommodation, farm holidays are an excellent way of meeting the natives to gain an insight into their way of life, and are ideal for those who would happily spend a week or two berry-picking, fishing, rambling, hiking and ponytrekking. *Samvinn-Travel,* Austurstraeti 12, Reykjavik (27077), is just one of the many agents which book farm holidays; contact the Tourist Bureau for more information.

CAMPING. Over a score of camp sites have been created in Iceland, and a list of these, with their amenities, can be obtained from the Tourist Bureau. Most of them are fairly basic, but usually provide camp toilets and running water, in a few cases hot water and electrical outlets. The site at Reykjavik is well placed next to the swimming pool and sports stadium; in Akureyri, it is adjacent to an open-air swimming pool near the town center. Charges are about $6 per night or less.

The best equipped camping grounds are found in Reykjavik, Húsafell, Ísafjördur, Varmahlid, Akureyri, Mývatn, Egilsstadir, Laugavatn, Thingvellir, Jökulsárgljúfur and Skaftafell. Where there is no site, tents may be pitched in any suitable spot, though campers should request permission (which is usually granted) of the local farmer to camp on any cultivated ground or fenced-in areas.

Where camping is prohibited, such as in parts of a national park, signs are displayed reading *Tjaldstaedi bönnud.* In other places areas have been marked out for camping, frequently marked *Tjaldstaedi,* and no special permission is then necessary. In some areas international signs are posted.

As no firewood or other fuel is to be found in Iceland, and it is forbidden by law to use the scant scrub found in some areas, campers should bring along paraffin or gas stoves for cooking and heating. Supplies of paraffin are available at gas stations and a few stores in Reykjavik, and at gas stations in Keflavik, Hafnarfjördur, Akureyri and Húsavik. Propane gas is sold at Shell gas stations in Reykjavik and at the larger Shell gas stations throughout the country. Butane gas and Camping Gaz are available in Reykjavik (at Sölvhólsgata 1), and at most co-operative stores throughout the country.

Camping equipment can be rented only in Reykjavik and advance reservations are advisable. For rates see the Reykjavik *Camping* section below.

YOUTH HOSTELS. There are hostels located countrywide, though the Y.H.A. headquarters are at Laufásveg 41, Reykjavik (24950); they will supply all details. In Akureyri, the Youth Hostel is at Stórholt 1 (96–23657).

Ferdafélag Íslands (Touring Club of Iceland), Öldugata 3, Reykjavik (19533 and 11798), oversee a number of huts in somewhat less inhabited areas where travelers can stay overnight, provided they bring their own sleeping bags and food. Groups which are traveling with the Club have priority over others.

For those which are traveling independently by car, we suggest you buy the *Iceland Road Guide,* an excellent book which marks hostels, sleeping bag cabins, and Edda hotels throughout the country.

RESTAURANTS. Icelandic restaurants have improved a great deal over the past 10 years. There are many good eating places suitable for all budgets to be found in Reykjavik and Akureyri, as well as in many of the suburban areas. Down-market, the snack bars usually found adjacent to gas stations are good and reasonably priced, and you can re-fill your coffee cup free! Budgeteers should note that while restaurant prices will most likely be comparable with what you're used to paying, wine is fiendishly expensive as it is imported, so keep this in mind as you order your magnum! We particularly recommend the fish dishes, since Icelandic fish is always fresh and tasty.

Some of the more expensive Reykjavik and Akureyri restaurants have dancing, particularly at weekends, with singing and modest cabaret shows.

Prices. We have divided the restaurants in our listings into three categories—Expensive (E), Moderate (M), and Inexpensive (I). These gradings are determined solely by price and usually include both tax and service charges, though do check.

Prices, per person, excluding drinks, in U.S. dollars:

	Reykjavik and elsewhere
Expensive	over $45
Moderate	$25–$45
Inexpensive	less than $25

FOOD AND DRINK. Iceland has to import most of her goods, so prices are quite high. Supermarkets are stocked with a good variety of food, but tinned food is especially expensive. Best to go for local foods which are fresher and cheaper. Milk is excellent, and *skyr,* which is made from milk and tastes a little like yogurt, is delicious with fresh blueberries, served in late summer. Another specialty is *hardfiskur* (dried fish), best in small bits spread with butter. The fish, usually haddock, is dressed, cleaned, and washed, then hung up in airy sheds where it dries until becoming hard and brittle. It is almost as common a sight in Iceland to see row upon row of drying fish as it is in Greece to see the grapes picked and laid out to dry.

An unusual Icelandic dish is cured shark meat, known locally as *hákarl.* Fresh shark meat is not edible and has to be cured before being eaten. The shark is cut into strips which are placed on a clean gravel bed and covered with stones. After several weeks, it is removed, washed, and hung up to dry. The curing process is difficult and only those with experience can turn out a first-class product. Shark meat has a rather pungent odour; it has been said that when eating it, the most ticklish operation is to get it past your nose! To obtain maximum gastronomical enjoyment, it should be washed down liberally with ice-cold Icelandic *brennivin.*

Of the meat dishes, lamb is especially recommended. Smoked lamb, called *hangikjöt,* is used on festive occasions and as a traditional main course for Christmas dinner.

Icelandic cuisine has improved immensely over the past two decades, and fish, in particular, is fresh and delicious. The following dishes are recommended: *Íslenzkur kaviar* (Icelandic caviar), *sherry síld* (marinated herring in sherry), *smokkfiskur Lisbon* (cuttlefish Lisbon), *graflax* (raw pickled salmon, a national dish), *marineradar gellur* (marinated codgills), and *lambalundir* (tenderloin of lamb). For dessert, try *Íslenzkar pönnukökur* (Icelandic pancakes).

As mentioned before, wine is expensive since it, too, must be imported. The local beers are good, and much more widely available since the laws restricting its sale were overturned in 1989.

TIPPING. Hotels and restaurants usually include in the bill both a service charge and sales tax of 24%. Extra tipping is not expected, and may in some cases even be resented. Taxi drivers, hairdressers, and washroom attendants are not tipped. There is a small charge for leaving coats in cloakrooms, though no more than 60¢ A cover charge is added to the bill in some licensed restaurants.

MAIL. At presstime: airmail letters to the U.S., 34 Ikr., to the U.K., 24 Ikr.; postcards to the U.S., 24 Ikr., to the U.K., 18 Ikr. Mail boxes are red. The main post office in Reykjavik is on the corner of Austurstraeti and Pósthússtraeti; open weekdays 9–5, Saturday 9–12.

TELEPHONES. An efficient telephone and telegraph service is available throughout the country, both for inter-Iceland and overseas calls; the latter can be booked day and night. You can dial direct almost anywhere in Europe, otherwise telephone "09" for assistance on overseas calls, "02" for local calls. The operator will speak English and will connect you with the required number.

CLOSING TIMES. Shops are open on weekdays from 9–6; some remain open on Fri. till 8 or 9 P.M. Candy stores and flower shops do not shut until 11 P.M. Sat., shops are open from 9–12 during the summer, 9–4 in winter. Banks are open for business Mon. to Fri. 9.15–4. On Thur., most banks remain open until 5 or 6 P.M.; note that banks are closed Sat. Offices are open 9–5 weekdays, and close on weekends.

SPORTS. Hiking through the extensive uninhabited interior and **mountaineering** are two of the favorite pastimes. A leaflet *Climbing and Skiing in Iceland,* obtainable from the Iceland Tourist Board, gives excellent guidance on some of the best areas and advice on equipment and guides. There are ramblers' clubs in main towns which organize both day and weekend outings; for more details, contact *Ferdafélag Íslands,* Öldugata 3, Reykjavik (19533) or Utivist, Grófin 1, Reykjavik (14606).

Iceland offers some of the best salmon and trout fishing in all Europe, while sea angling for cod, habbock, etc., at Grindavik, and halibut fishing in Breidafjördur is also good. Reindeer **hunting** (low quota) in Aug. and Sept., and some wild goose shooting from Aug. 20–Nov. 20.

Icelandic ponies can be hired in most places for those who want to get in a spot of **riding**. These sturdy steeds are direct descendants of those brought over by the Vikings and are ideally suited to the rough terrain. Riding possibilities range from a few hours to much longer treks with a guide, staying at hotels, hostels or camping. There is a Horse Hire Service at Laugarvatn (50 miles from Reykjavik). Check the Tourist Bureau's pamphlet entitled The *Viking Horse* for more details.

Swimming is considered the national sport, and excellent facilities are available countrywide.

There is enough snow most winters for **skiing**, and most of the population gets out into it. There are a few skiing centers, notably near Akureyri in the north and, in summer, in the Kerlingarfjöll mountains in remote south central Iceland, about 125 miles from Reykjavik. The latter are best explored from the little valley of Askard where weekly courses are arranged (hostel and camping facilities). In the summer you can ski in shorts. During the winter skiing is available 20 miles from Reykjavik; there is a frequent service from the Bus Terminal.

GETTING AROUND ICELAND. By air. *Icelandair* (Flugleidir) flies the domestic routes which link about a dozen of the country's main towns and villages, as well as the Westmann Islands. *Arnarflug* (Eagle Air) also has services across the country; contact their head office at Lágmúla 7, 105 Reykjavik, for further information.

By bus. There is no train service in Iceland, but the country has a comprehensive network of bus services reaching to all but the most isolated communities. Though the road may often seem rough, the routes take you through some incredible and quite unforgettable scenery. There are a number of special runabout tickets available, such as the *Full Circle Passport*, which is good for travel on the main ring route around Iceland. There is no time limit and you can stop-over along the route as often as you like; cost at presstime was $145. The *Omnibus Passport* gives unlimited travel on all scheduled bus routes, main and secondary roads; cost at presstime was $170 for 1 week, rising to $310 for four weeks. Children's discounts are available. *Air-Bus Rover* tickets—fly one way, bus the other—are also very popular and economical, as well as being conveniently time-saving. *Icelandair Air Rover Ticket,* valid for 30 days, fly or travel by bus, starting at any point of the circle: Reykjavik–Ísafjördur–Akureyri–Egilsstadir–Höfn–Reykjavik. The airline has also introduced "Fly As You Please" tickets, valid May through Sept., that allow you four flights.

By car. Apart from the asphalt roads through and around the towns, the highway between Keflavik and Reykjavik and a fairly good road to Selfoss, motoring can be a hazardous exercise, often along lava track or dirt and gravel surfaces. The ring route around Iceland can hardly be called a highway. One motors—and arrives—eventually, and seldom without some minor excitement en route, such as the disappearance of a road under a small river, which wasn't there the day before—but it is a fascinating exercise. On the whole, you must be prepared to handle small repairs and maintenance yourself though there are a few small garages. Fuel service stations are few and far between; at presstime, 1 liter of petrol *(bensín)* was about 85¢. You drive on the right. An international driving license is necessary.

See the *Useful Addresses* section, page 231, for the names of some car hire firms within Reykjavik.

By boat. There is a boat service from Reykjavik to almost all of Iceland's harbour towns; contact *Ríkisskip, Skipaútgerd Ríkisins,* Hafnarhúsi v/Tryggvabraut 101, Reykjavik (28822), for detailed information on fares and schedules.

By bike. On the whole, Icelandic country roads are not suitable for bicycling, though many visitors find it enjoyable to explore some of the cities and towns by bike. Details of rental fees and bike hire establishments are available from both tourist offices and youth hostels.

On foot. As mentioned in the *Sports* section earlier, hiking is very popular and a marvelous opportunity to experience Iceland's rugged landscape. However, we stress that no expedition should be undertaken lightly, certainly never without advising local people where you are going, and in many cases you should consider taking a guide.

PRELUDE TO ICELAND

Land of Ice and Fire

When the Vikings landed in Iceland, they thought they had discovered the entrance to the Netherworld. Centuries later, the cone-shaped Snaefellsjökull glacier was made famous by Jules Verne in his *Journey to the Center of the Earth*. In Iceland you are on the edge of the world—and it feels that way too. This is a land of eerie icescapes and petrified lava fields, steaming thermal springs and spectacular glaciers. It is estimated that over the last 500 years a third of the volcanic lava to have reached the surface of the earth emerged in Iceland. Such is the pressure beneath the surface that the Giant Geysir, which gave its name to geysers all over the world, spouted boiling water and steam over 150 feet in the air. By contrast, the largest glacier here, Vatna-jökull, occupies an area equal to all the other glaciers in Europe put together.

Iceland has always been different—and in many different ways. The country is barren, with hardly a tree to be seen, but, with stark multicolored mountains, magnificent waterfalls, lakes and green valleys, is nonetheless strikingly beautiful. There are no frogs, snakes or reptiles. When the Vikings arrived, foxes were the only indigenous mammals. Since then, man has imported a wide range of animal inhabitants, including inadvertently-introduced mice and rats. Reindeer were first brought from Norway in the 18th century, and small herds can be found in the eastern counties.

Modern Comforts the Natural Way

Despite all this, Iceland is a modern Scandinavian country—though it is 500 miles from the nearest European landfall (Scotland) and nearly 1,000 miles from Copenhagen, which used to be its administrative capital. Nowadays the population is around 245,000—the same as the city of Derby in Britain, or just over half the size of Omaha, Nebraska. Half the Icelanders live in the capital Reykjavik, while over 80% of the rest of the island's 40,000 square miles remains uninhabited.

As its name suggests, Iceland is a chilly country. Though the Gulf Stream may keep its winters slightly warmer than those of New York, in summer a temperature of 70°F has them all swooning. But the summers here have one great advantage—it practically never becomes dark. And even in spring and fall there are long, long twilit evenings. But despite the tempting blue sea washing the weird black volcanic sand of the beaches, the sea is always too cold for swimming.

By contrast, Iceland has a flourishing horticultural industry, producing vegetables to meet the domestic demand, flowers for export, fruit—even bananas! This is all achieved by harnessing the abundant geothermal energy, which is put to a wide variety of use. For instance, most of the houses in Reykjavik are heated by naturally-produced near-boiling water. This is carried by two ten-mile-long, heavily insulated pipelines from the nearby hot spring. The heat lost while the water is running from the underground streams to the kitchen tap is less than 2°F, enabling the Icelanders to keep their houses at around 70°–75°F both winter and summer. However, you may sometimes notice a rather odd sulfur smell in the bathrooms.

If you happen to visit in winter, you'll find that it's dark for all but a few hours, partially explaining why the Icelanders are such good chess players. The real wizards come from the island of Grimsey, 30 miles off the northern shore on the Arctic Circle, where in mid-winter they only have a few hours of twilight every day. These long nights also explain why, per capita, more books are written, printed, bought and read in Iceland than anywhere else in the world.

However, before you set out for Iceland, there's one vital point you should know. Iceland is an expensive country. In 1987 record fish catches brought the country's balance of payments out of the red for the first time since 1978, and inflation is now at a manageable 11–12%. The falling value of the krona means your dollars and pounds go that much further. The main cause of inflation is that despite its small population, the island is anything but self-sufficient. Only just over 1% of the land is under permanent cultivation (hardly surprising when you realise that Reykjavik is on the same latitude as Archangel in Russia, and the Yukon in Canada). This lack of land development means that a high proportion of foodstuff has to be imported—and at a considerable expense owing to the distances involved. Indeed, Iceland's whole economy is based upon its sole major industry—fishing.

Despite these drawbacks, Iceland is host to a wide range of visitors, including many biologists, geologists, bird-watchers and photographers: all attracted by the unique colorfulness of the landscape—with its black lava, red sulfur, blue hotsprings, grey and white rivers with spectacular waterfalls creating high arching rainbows, and green, green valleys (unlike Greenland, which, paradoxically, is covered in ice). However, as you trek the wilderness you must be prepared for temperamental weather. Here you can have all four seasons in one day. Even so, when you step inside off the tundra, you enter Scandinavian-style living quarters: this is a land where primeval landscapes and modern comforts exist side by side.

Iceland may not be to everyone's taste—but there's no denying that it's different.

History and Development

The first people to arrive in Iceland were Irish monks. However, their time here was neither long or happy and they were either enslaved, or driven out, by the first recorded settlers, the Norsemen, who arrived in the year 874. The Norsemen were led by Ingólfur Arnarson, who was fleeing from the tyranny of Harold Fairhair in Norway. When Ingólfur first saw Iceland rising out of the sea before his longboat, he threw overboard a pair of high seat pillars carved with images of the heathen gods. He swore that he would make his home wherever the wooden pillars landed. Some time later they were found washed up in a mysterious smoke-shrouded bay. The smoke was caused by the steam from the nearby hot springs. The Icelandic word for smoke is "reykur," and for bay is "vík"—and that is how the capital of Iceland, Reykjavik, got its name.

To begin with the new colony prospered, attracting many Norsemen who had already settled in parts of Ireland, Scotland and the Faroe Islands. These new settlers brought with them their wives and slaves, which accounts for the preponderance of Celtic blood in the Icelandic population. Even to this day many of the natives have the appearance and temperament of Irish people.

In 930 the settlers established their first parliament—the Althing. Thus they created the first republic north of the Alps. The Althing still operates today, and is now the world's oldest surviving national legislature.

With prosperity, the forests melted before the axe, the sod was turned with primitive ploughs, imported sheep grazed the uplands, fish thronged the rivers, lakes and bays, and the skalds sang eulogies to the pagan gods. But with prosperity came rivalry and power-struggles. The Icelandic chieftain Eric the Red was forced to flee from his enemies (and in so doing discovered Greenland, founding an Icelandic settlement there). When Eric's son Leif fled, he discovered a land called Vinland—now widely believed to have been the northern shores of America. It was this era which gave birth to the famous Icelandic sagas. These sagas describe the life of the early powerful Viking settlers, their heroic deeds at home and overseas, their vicious blood-feuds, and their great love stories.

Meanwhile, the country continued to be rent by quarrels, feuds and power-struggles. By the beginning of the 13th century there was general civil war. Fratricidal strife continued for more than 50 years, periodically stirred up by the Norwegian kings who hoped to claim Iceland as their own. Their hopes were realized in 1264, when the Norwegian king stepped in as "arbiter" and sovereign. However, in 1380, both Iceland and Norway came under the Danish crown. The islanders then had to cope with the encroachment of Danish officials as well as natural calamities caused by volcanic eruptions. Their problems were further increased in the mid-16th century when the Reformation was imposed by the Danish king, and the last Catholic bishop, Jon Arason, was beheaded without trial. The king confiscated the property of the monasteries and churches, consolidating still more his grip on the country. At the same time, Spanish, Moorish and English pirates also raided the country. Then came famine, smallpox, leprosy, the Black Death, and worst of all, the imposition by the Danish king of a trade monopoly.

Iceland's unhappy story continued until the early 19th century when Icelandic nationalism began slowly to emerge in opposition to the oppressive Danish trade monopolies. But the movement thereafter gained popular momentum rapidly. Partial Home Rule came in 1904, and full sovereignty under the Danish King in 1918. When Denmark was invaded by Germany in 1940, Britain occupied undefended Iceland to keep it from falling into the hands of the Axis. A year later American forces replaced the British (and built Keflavík Airport); and on June 17th 1944, Iceland severed its remaining ties with Copenhagen to become a republic once more. The Icelanders then elected their first president. And in 1980, the Icelanders elected Vigdís Finnbogadóttir as president—the first woman to be elected a president in Europe.

Sagas, Song and Seafaring—Iceland Today

Alone among the world's myriad tongues, modern Icelandic has changed so little since early pagan times that reading the ancient sagas presents no more of a problem to the present-day Icelander than do Shakespeare's works to the average educated Englishman or American. Swedish, Danish and Norwegian all developed from the same stem, of course, but Icelandic bears about the same relationship to them as Anglo-Saxon does to English, and it's an exceptional Scandinavian who can make his way through Icelandic literature without the aid of dictionary and grammar. Even at this late date, Icelandic retains two peculiar letters of the alphabet which long ago disappeared from the other northern languages. One letter looks like a *b* combined with a *p,* and is pronounced like the *th* in *thin;* the other, pronounced like *th* in *leather* resembles a lazy *d* with a horizontal line drawn through the stem. Both look formidable on first acquaintance but yield to a little persistent lisping and buzzing.

In addition to its literary achievements, Icelandic has had a novel effect on matrimony and the position of women. In Iceland the custom persists of giving children the *first* instead of the *last* name of their father. Thus Magnus, the son of Svein, becomes Magnus Sveinsson, while Gudrún, the daughter of Einar, is known as Gudrún Einarsdóttir. What's more, Gudrún keeps her maiden name even after she marries, though her children will bear her husband's name.

Another custom is preserved amongst the older women. Many still wear the graceful national costume, which consists of a long, full black skirt and a black bodice, embroidered in gold and laced with gold cord over a colored blouse. An apron, worn as an ornamental panel, is usually of the same material as the blouse. Their hair is done up in two long braids which are looped up behind, and on their heads they wear small black velvet caps, with long black tassels, which are bound by two- or three-inch rings of gold or silver. Many of the younger women treasure the beautiful embroidered costumes worn by their mothers or grandmothers, though they do not wear them except on gala occasions.

Besides chess and books, singing has long been a favourite pastime to while away the long winter evenings. Even today the influence of medieval church music is revealed by the use of harmonies long ago superseded elsewhere. Choral groups are numerous and active—again there are more per capita than in any other country—and Iceland produces international opera singers. Singing developed naturally from ballad and saga recitals, and the tradition persists.

But fishing is really what Iceland is all about. The fishing industry and its by-products dominate the national economy. The main commodity available for export is fish, and about 75% of Iceland's trade is based in fish products. Per fisherman, the annual catch amounts to a staggering 290 tons, another world record.

Several years ago, over-fishing began to have a serious effect on Iceland's traditional fishing grounds. In consequence, Iceland extended her territorial limit to 200 miles, in a desperate effort to preserve stocks. More than this, it was also designed to protect the jobs of the more than one-in-seven of Iceland's workforce who are employed in the fishing industry. This action by Iceland led to a dispute with Britain—the so-called "Cod War"—which is now, fortunately, a thing of the past. A compromise was reached, and the rich harvest of the Arctic seas remains protected.

EXPLORING ICELAND

Volcanos, Hot Springs and Glaciers

Iceland is the second-largest island in Europe (only Great Britain is larger). It has approximately the same land area as England, or Kentucky, and for many years its strategic position in the north Atlantic made it an important staging post on trans-Atlantic flights. Nowadays, practically all flights go direct between Europe and America—though advantageous rates apply for those willing to make a short stop-over at Keflavik, Iceland's international airport, which is just 29 miles from Reykjavik.

Iceland's Capital

At the turn of the century, Reykjavik was a sleepy fishing village of just 6,000 people. Though it's now 20 times this size, its expansion has been carefully planned. The new apartment blocks are earthquake-proof, and the city is completely smokeless as all its heating is provided by the nearby hot springs. The city's resourcefulness was tested to the full in the fall of 1986 when, with all of one week's notice, President Reagan and Mikhail Gorbachev, plus attendant aides, advisors and sundry other camp followers—not to mention several thousand journalists—descended on it for an unexpected round of Disarmament talks. The talks may have failed, but they put Reykjavik firmly on the international map.

Set in its fjord, overlooked by snow-capped mountains, Reykjavik presents a colorful sight—with its concrete houses painted in light colors, and their striking red, blue and green roofs. Among the more important buildings are the Parliament or Althing, the Lutheran cathedral, the National

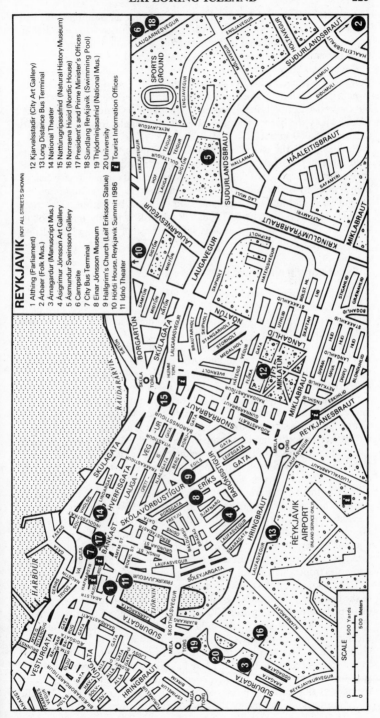

Theater, the University and the National Museum on Sudurgata beyond Mela Torg. Hallgrim's Church, with its famous statue of Leif Eiriksson, dominates a rocky plateau and a cluster of small wooden houses dating from the end of the last century.

Reykjavik's streets are ideal for window-shopping, but you'll find everything very expensive though some bargains can be found in street markets. Even so, an Icelandic sweater is a must. You'll find them all over town, but the best selection is in the Icelandic Handicrafts Center at Hafnarstraeti 3, down by the harbor near the City Bus Terminal. Good sweaters start at around 2,000 krona.

Besides being the island's center of government, Reykjavik is also its cultural center. Largely owing to those long dark winter evenings, the arts thrive here. Despite its comparatively small population, the city has its own symphony orchestra, two professional theaters, several museums and art galleries, and numerous cinemas and excellent bookstores. The more popular arts also exist here. Though Reykjavik is hardly known for its night life, there are some good discos. But a word of warning here: drinks in such places cost the earth.

Excursions from Reykjavik

Reykjavik makes a good base for exploring other parts of the country. About 56 km. (35 miles) east of the capital stretches the broad lava plain of Thingvellir, site of the first parliament and now a national park. A placid lake, Thingvallavatn, the biggest in Iceland, lends a deceptively idyllic air, for it was on this plain that chieftains and citizens from every village and farm met each summer to make the law. Here the decision was taken around the year A.D. 1000 to lay aside pagan ways and adopt the tenets of Christianity. The speaker's rock and the hollowed-out seats reserved for the most important men can still be seen, together with the ancient fairgrounds where wrestling matches took place, weddings were contracted and old scores settled. Nowadays Thingvellir is a favorite place for holiday-makers, and the modern campers' tents in the summer do, in a sense, carry on the tradition of the great meeting place, but in a much more gentle form. Do not miss a stroll along the Almannagja chasm, and the magnificent view from its upper rim.

A little further out from Reykjavik, the Great Geysir, which gave its name to hot springs around the world, bubbles away oblivious of the expectant crowds which gather there daily in hopes of some excitement. Geysir is getting old these days and cannot be relied upon to perform, but a junior geyser, Strokkur, seldom fails, throwing up boiling water to considerable heights at five-minute intervals. In the same area there are small boreholes from which steam arises, as well as beautiful pools of blue water.

Twenty km. (12 miles) away there is more thunder, this time in the form of the deafening Gullfoss waterfall. The river Hvitá plunges down a series of steps before throwing itself 30 meters (95 ft.) into a narrow canyon. The noise—and the spray—are on a heroic scale, and towards afternoon the sun illuminates the moist air, making it in fact, as well as name, the Golden Falls. Twenty nine km. (18 miles) from Geysir is Skálholt, a hallowed spot in Icelandic history. There has been a Christian church on this spot for nine centuries, and the present exquisitely simple building with its modern altar piece is the eleventh in its line. Jón Arason, last Catholic bishop in Iceland, and martyr to the Reformation, was beheaded without trial at Skálholt in 1550. A plaque marks the spot. A variety of one-day tours from Rekjavik are available for approximately $50.

To ascend 1,615 meter (5,000 ft.) volcanic Mount Hekla requires two full days, although by road it's only 120 km. (75 miles) from the capital. Getting up and down the mountain is a ten hour undertaking in itself, but the view into the crater, as well as out from the crater's edge, fully justifies the strenuous climb to the top. Hekla has erupted several times in recent years, and the new lava fields stretch for some miles around the crater. For those who dislike trudging, a four-hour plane trip combines a good look at Hekla with a glimpse of the glacier Vatnajökull, and a flight north to the Arctic Circle.

West Iceland

It's a long, sometimes monotonous drive to the Snaefellsnes peninsula. But you call always break it on the way by calling in at the whaling station at the head of Hvalfjördur. If you arrive at the same time as a whale, be prepared for a pungent and bloody experience. It is possible to shorten the journey by taking the ferry from Reykjavik to Akranes. Further north, turn inland to visit Reykholt, where you can see the small hot pool which belonged to Snorri Sturluson, Iceland's famous poet, who recorded the sagas. Touring westwards you reach Snaefellsnes peninsula with its glacier, Snaefellsjökull. This is the glacier where Jules Verne set the starting point for the *Journey to the Center of the Earth.* It is a wild beautiful place, where the main attractions are the hosts of seabirds nesting along the basalt cliffs, and the seals who pop up to gaze curiously at intruders.

On the other side of the peninsula there are weirdly shaped rock castles which are reached by crossing a grey lavafield. Continue along the northern side of the peninsula and you come to Stykkishólmur. The town is popular with many sea-sports fishermen who come for the halibut in Breidafjördur. It is a pleasant little place with a modern hospital run by Belgian nuns. Behind the town is a hill known as Helgafell. According to local superstition, anyone who climbs Helgafell for the first time will be granted three wishes—provided he doesn't look back or talk on the way up.

There are several islands in the large bay of Breidafjördur. A few are inhabited, and all have large colonies of birds and seals. A local ferry passing close to some of these islands takes you across the bay to Brjánslaekur Farm, on the remote Vestfirdir, the isolated region of the Western Fjords.

East Iceland

Not until 1974, when the final bridge was completed across the treacherous glacier waters pouring from the tongues of Vatnajökull glacier, was this area accessible by car from Reykjavik. It is still a long journey, but you can watch the miniature icebergs sliding towards the sea while the great skuas swoop overhead and across the black sands.

Following the southern road, you come to Skógar, a tiny settlement beside the impressive Skógafoss. Here you can lunch at the Edda hotel by prior arrangement, then visit the small museum consisting of turf houses brought from elsewhere in the district and re-erected. The locals used to fish this treacherous coast in small boats, and the last of these boats rests in the little museum together with many other interesting mementos from a tough and primitive way of life which persisted until comparatively recent times.

Press on eastward and you come to the Skaftafell reserve. This contains the famous Svartifoss waterfall, dropping thinly over a cliff whose sides resemble the pipes of a great organ. It's possible to walk on the glacier tongues here, but this should not be attempted without expert guidance and correct equipment. Höfn on the east coast is developing as a popular center from which to explore the extraordinary landscapes created by the outlying glaciers of Vatnajökull and the wild coastline. From here excursions are arranged to these, as well as to Skaftafell National Park.

On the very eastern tip of Iceland, you come to Borgarfjördur Eystri (a village and fjord with the same name). This is renowned as one of the most beautiful spots in the country. It takes its name from Álfaborg, a hillock just outside the village, reputed to be the legendary home of elves. Iceland's famous painter, Kjarval, lived here for a time. The village has a small hotel and restaurant.

South Iceland, Westmann Islands and Surtsey

The remote Westmann Islands are off the southwest coast of Iceland, and amongst them only Heimaey is inhabited. In 1973, after lying dormant for nearly 5,000 years the Helgafell (Holy Mountain) on Heimaey erupted, and the entire population of 5,000 was immediately evacuated by local fishing boats to the mainland. This was a disaster for the islanders. Their main industry was fishing, and they were dependent on the safe harbor at Heimaey as well as upon the fish processing plants there. However, with the grit and determination of people long used to living with the forces of nature, the inhabitants started to dig themselves out long before the eruption had ceased, removing tons of black lava dust from their buried houses and streets. Now the streets are cleared, the houses rebuilt and re-painted, and fishing and processing working normally, though some of the plants were seriously damaged. However, the island now has 600 meters (1,900 ft.) of lava on the approaches to the harbor, and many of the houses which were closest to the eruption were buried for ever. The lava, still hot, is used for thermal heat by the islanders. Cold waterpipes are run through it, giving boiling water straight from the tap.

The islands are rich in sea birds, especially puffins, which are used in large quantities for food. The puffins were not too greatly affected by the eruption, but a considerable number of sea birds were lost and this has affected the task of egg-pickers, who estimate that it will take several more years before the colonies fully establish themselves again. Egg-picking is hazardous work. Dangling from ropes, the men swing from ledge to ledge down sheer volcanic cliffs to collect eggs from the nests, often attacked fiercely by the birds. Primitive winches haul the men back up with their fragile loads. Throughout the years there have been 18 fatal accidents, and legend has it that when the 19th man falls to his death the volcano Katla on the mainland opposite will erupt. (Its next eruption is in fact long over-due.)

A highlight of the Icelandic calendar is the festival held on the first weekend in August on Heimaey. It is well worth taking time to visit the Westmann Islands, despite the fact that the round-trip flight might be canceled by bad weather and you'll face a 10-hour sea journey instead. But if you really cannot spare more than a few hours, you can always take a shorter sightseeing tour from Reykjavik. A few miles west of the West-mann Islands is the new volcanic island of Surtsey, which was thrown up out of the sea by a submarine volcanic eruption in 1963. Already it is several hundred feet high. Scientists work there recording the progress of nature, but lesser folk are not allowed ashore. Sightseeing trips usually include a sail around the island and also to the multi-colored sea cave Kafhellir, on the island of Haena nearby.

Akureyri and the North

The north of Iceland was created by the interplay of fire and ice. The largest lava fields on earth are to be found here, for instance Odádahraun, some with plants and mosses, others barren and bare. The country is not all forbidding, and the valleys sheltered by the mountains are lush with vegetation and rich in color. There are also many rivers with good salmon and trout fishing, magnificent waterfalls and strange formations of basalt rock columns.

Iceland's second-largest town, Akureyri, is an hour from Reykjavik by plane. Ranged up and down a series of irregular hills on the western side of Eyjafjördur, the town is dominated by a simple ultra-modern Lutheran church whose twin spires accent the barren and treeless landscape. Some of the surrounding mountains reach a height of 1,400 meters (4,500 ft.) and offer fine climbs and ski runs.

Beside the Edda summer hotel there is an interesting statue. In bygone times, if a man transgressed the laws of the community, he was often banished, along with his family, to the lava fields. This was virtually a death sentence, for nothing could sustain life in those regions. This poignant statue, called the *Outlaw,* is by Einar Jonsson and depicts a man carrying his wife and child and accompanied by his dog, walking into outlawry.

From Akureyri you can get a boat to Grimsey, a particularly interesting spot for sea bird enthusiasts. This island is over 32 km. (20 miles) from the mainland and actually straddles the Arctic Circle. From Akureyri you can also take a long jolting bus ride over the weird volcanic plateaux to the magnificent waterfall of Godafoss, where the local chieftain threw his pagan household gods into its foaming depths when he was converted to Christianity in A.D. 1000. In the adjoining district is Glerárdalur, a valley where petrified wood is found. The bus continues to Lake Mývatn, a birdwatchers' paradise, where vast numbers of waterfowl make their homes. One can get a guide to some of the more remote nesting areas.

Mývatn also has an especially tasty breed of trout, which feeds on the midges that give the lake its name. Here there are all kinds of exotic phenomena, including Dimmuborgir (the black castles) where the fantastic landscape is said to resemble the lunar surface more closely than anywhere else on earth; Stóragjá and Grjótagjá, two pools of natural hot water in underground caves, where one can enjoy wonderful bathing; and Námaskard, where the purple sulfur boils like a witches' cauldron in the strange red and yellow valleys.

When the volcano Askja erupted here two centuries ago, the lava ran directly towards the lake and the small settlement which lay beside it. But in the path of the lava stood the settlement's tiny church; while the congregation prayed inside, the molten mass came to a halt within inches of its walls. There is a new church now, but the remains of the old one can still be seen, surrounded on three sides by solidified lava. Farther afield are Dettifoss, Europe's largest waterfall, and the fascinating lush national park of Ásbyrgi with the curious echoing rocks of Hljódaklettar. From here you can continue to Húsavik, an attractive port on the north coast, and thence back to Akureyri.

Central Iceland

The interior of Iceland is virtually uninhabited apart from the occasional isolated meteorological or scientific station. Though the Icelanders may get rather tired of having it likened to the Moon, the landscape really is strangely reminiscent of some science fiction vision—with its great stony deserts, extravagantly contorted lava fields, and towering glaciers from which crystal clear streams and green rivers drain across the land. The colors are superb, and there is a feeling of timelessness that few other places in the world can match.

This is *not* an area where you go exploring on your own. But there are excellent overland tours escorted by experienced guides. You don't have to be young and hearty or tremendously energetic to enjoy these, but you do need to be an outdoor enthusiast and prepared to camp. Transport is in specially constructed buses, and tents and all necessary equipment are provided; you are usually expected to be in charge of your tent during the trip, but meals are provided for you. Since this kind of tour tends to attract those who are interested in birds or flowers or geology, it's usually a fine meeting ground for like-minded souls of all ages and many nationalities. Over-night stops may be made near a small community or in the heart of a rugged uninhabited wilderness, perhaps on the edge of a lava field or at the foot of some craggy white glacier. There are opportunities to bathe in clear, naturally hot spring-water under the open sky, peer into volcanic craters, walk among wild lansdcapes, and experience a stillness that has barely been disturbed by human presence since time began.

These, then, are the distinctive features of Iceland, a land which beguiles all who have once stood on its grey shores, and felt the rock tremble beneath them with the subterranean forces of an unseen world.

PRACTICAL INFORMATION FOR REYKJAVIK

GETTING TO TOWN FROM THE AIRPORT. For arrivals at Keflavík International Airport, a bus service is stationed outside the terminal entrance which will provide transportation into Reykjavik. Fare at time of writing is $7, but sometimes your ticket includes the fare. Taxis are also available, though as driving time to Reykjavik is approximately 45 minutes, cost will be quite high.

From the town terminal there are bus connections and taxis on hand, night and day, to other parts of the city.

TOURIST INFORMATION. There are five main centers for tourist information in Reykjavik: The Information Center, Ingólfsstraeti 5 (623045); the nearby *Gimli*, Laekjargata 3 (28025); *Útsýn*, Austurstraeti 17 (26611); and the Iceland Tourist Bureaus at Reykjanesbraut (27488) and in Hotel Loftleidir at Reykjavik Airport (22322); also at Skógarhlid 6, (25855). There is also a branch office at Keflavík Airport Terminal. All these bureaus will be able to supply information on the city as well as for the rest of Iceland. Information can also be had concerning local and not-so-local accommodations, as well as special discount fares on city and country-wide bus services.

EXPLORING ICELAND

USEFUL ADDRESSES. Travel Agents. *Gudmundur Jónasson Tours,* Borgartúni 34 (83222). *Samvinn-Travel,* Austurstraeti 12 (27077). *Úlfar Jacobsen Tourist Bureau,* Austurstraeti 9 (13499). *BSI Travel,* Hringbraut (22300).

Embassies. *U.S. Embassy,* 21 Laufásvegur (29100). *Canadian Consulate,* Laufásvegur 77, (13721). *British Embassy,* 49 Laufásvegur (15883).

Car Hire. *ALP Car Rental,* Hladbrekka 2 Kopavogi (42837). *Geysir,* Borgartún 24 (11015). *Icelandair Car Rental* (22322).

Police. Headquarters at Hverfisgata 113, and at Hlemmtorg, tel. 11166.

Medical Services. Emergency telephone no. is 81200. From 8 A.M.–9 P.M., *Landspitalinn,* tel. 21230 and 29000. *Drugstore* (Apótek), tel. 18888.

TELEPHONE CODES. The telephone code for Reykjavik is 91 when calling from outside the capital. When calling Iceland from overseas the 9 is dropped and 1 becomes the code for Reykjavik. Within the city, however, no prefix is required. For all establishments outside Reykjavik, we have listed the necessary prefix immediately before the telephone number.

HOTELS. Apart from the top hotels in Reykjavik, Iceland's hotels are modest and simple. Breakfast is not included in the hotel price. However, all prices include 24% state tax and service charge. Somewhat less expensive accommodations are available in private homes; check with the Tourist Bureau for a list of homes participating. Students and other adventurous travelers who want to tour the countryside can usually obtain a night's lodging from $15, provided they supply their own sleeping bags. The summer hotels known as "Edda" hotels (university and school hostels used for tourists during the summer vacation) are moderately priced, but demand for rooms is high so book in advance if possible.

Expensive

Holiday Inn. Sigtún 38 (689000). 100 rooms. New, with restaurant and coffee shop. Fairly central. AE, DC, MC, V.

Hotel Esja. Sudurlandsbraut 2 (82200). 134 rooms. Conveniently located and with an exceptionally good view. AE, DC, MC, V.

Hotel Holt. Bergstadastraeti 37 (25700). 50 rooms. Central location. Decor features original works by leading Icelandic painters. AE, DC, MC, V.

Hotel Lind. Raudarárstíg 18 (623350). 44 rooms. A new hotel near to the city's main bus terminal. AE, DC, MC, V.

Hotel Loftleidir. Reykjavik Airport (22322). 227 rooms with bath or shower. All amenities, including theater, sauna, and solarium. AE, DC, MC, V.

Hotel Saga. Hagatorg (29900). 219 rooms, all above 4th floor. Recommended rooftop restaurant. All amenities. AE, DC, MC, V.

Moderate

Hotel Borg. Pósthússtraeti 11 (11440). 46 rooms. A traditional hotel; very central, beside the Cathedral. AE, DC, MC, V.

Hotel City. Ránargata 4a (18650). 31 rooms. Central.

Gardur. Hringbraut (15656). 44 rooms. Open summer only.

Ødinsvé. Odinstorg (25224). 20 rooms. 2 restaurants.

Stadur. Skipholt 27 (26210). 23 rooms. Open June 1 to Sept. 30.

Inexpensive

Guesthouse. Brautarholt 22 (20986). 24 rooms. Open summer only.

Guesthouse. Flókagata 5 (19828). 11 rooms. Central.

Guesthouse. Snorrabraut 52 (16522). 18 rooms. Comfortable.

Hotel Jörd. Skólavördustíg 13a (621739). 8 rooms. Central.

Royal Inn. Laugavegur 11 (24513). 11 rooms, in heart of town.

Salvation Army Guesthouse. Kirkjustraeti 2 (13203). 24 rooms.

Viking Guesthouse. Ránargata 12 (19367). 11 rooms.

Youth Hostel, Laufásvegur 41. Short walk from the center.

230 ICELAND

Camping

Reykjavik has only one campsite, and a pleasant one at that, conveniently located on Sundlaugarvegur, next to the largest swimming pool and near the sports stadium. Note that fires are not allowed, and all garbage must be collected and disposed of properly. All details from the Iceland Tourist Bureau.

Tjaldaleigan Rent-a-Tent, at Hringbraut v/Umferdarmidstodina 101 (13072), rents out all sorts of camping equipment, from cars with tent-trailers to camping kits including tent, sleeping bag, mattress, gas stove, and even a set of pots and pans. Prices run about $40 per person per week for the kit.

Youth Hostels

There are several hostels in Reykjavik; full details are available from the Youth Hostels Association (Farfugladeild Reykjavikur), Laufásveg 41 (24950). These hostels are well-equipped and very popular during the holiday season, so it's best to book beforehand. The Y.H.A. will also be able to give addresses of other inexpensive sleeping accommodations for those who have their own sleeping bags; cost usually as little as $15.

HOW TO GET AROUND. By bus. The major form of city transport is by buses which bear the letters S.V.R.—Straetisvaganar Reykjavikur (Reykjavik Buses). The two main stopping points are at Hlemmtorg in the eastern part of town, and the terminal at Laekjartog in the city center. These buses run fairly frequently, while most services start at 7 A.M. and finish at midnight. At weekends, the last buses finish at 1 A.M.

There are usually no ticket conductors on Icelandic buses. Tickets are bought directly from the driver (either individually or in sheets, which is cheaper), and then placed in a receptacle close to the driver's seat. Smoking is not allowed. If you want to get off, just press one of the buttons placed intermittently throughout the bus.

By taxi. Taxis are expensive, though you aren't expected to tip the driver anything over the metered amount. There are taxi stands in many parts of the city, and they also pick up en route. The sign *Laus* means that the cab is available for hire.

TOURS. An excellent way of getting acquainted with Reykjavik is to take one of the city's guided bus tours. Usually lasting around 2½ hours, these tours introduce the capital's past and present, and include a visit to the Museum and Art Gallery. Departures daily at 10 A.M. and 2 P.M. May through Sept.; cost approximately $21–$32.

A varied itinerary of day excursions is also available to and around the surrounding countryside. These day-tours include pony trekking on the Icelandic hills; the starkly dramatic lava arena of Thingvellir, where the ancient Viking parliament met for centuries; the famous Great Geysir, a seething area of erupting hot springs, mud pools, and geysirs, of which Strokkur, the world's most active geysir, is likely to spurt several times up to a height of 100 ft.; Reykholt, home of the famous Saga historian, Snorri Sturluson; and even an aerial tour for an eagle's-eye view of the rugged lavafields, volcanoes, and glaciers of southern Iceland.

All cost and departure details from the Icelandic Tourist Board; day excursion information can also be had from *Reykjavik Excursions* at Hotel Loftleidir at the airport (22322), or from *Gimli,* Laekjargata 3 (28025).

MUSEUMS. Being a small nation, Iceland cannot offer museums on the scale of the Louvre, the Prado, or the Metropolitan Museum of Art. She has, however, produced some very fine artists, many of whom have bequeathed their houses to the nation upon their death and whose works are displayed therein. These museums are normally open from 1.30–4 P.M., closed Mon. Admission is generally free, but occasionally there is a nominal charge.

Árbaer (Folk Museum). On the city outskirts. An interesting collection of old buildings, depicting rural life in the past.

Árnagardur (Árni Magnússon Manuscript Museum). Interesting collection of ancient manuscripts.

Ásgrímur Jónsson Art Gallery. Bergstadastraeti 74. An excellent collection of watercolors and oils by this well-beloved Icelandic painter.

Ásmundur Sveinsson Gallery. Kirkjumyrarbletti 10, Sigtún. An unusual dome-like house built by the artist himself, where you can see his creations throughout both house and garden. Open Sun.

Einar Jónsson Museum. Beside Eiríksgata, in the older part of the city. Most of the sculptures are displayed in the garden.

Gallerí Borg. Austurvöllur. Close to Hotel Borg. A modern gallery which sometimes has an art auction.

Hladvarpinn. The Women's Center; theater and exhibition hall. Vesturgata 3. Hours vary.

Kjarvalsstadir (City Art Gallery). Miklatún. Dedicated to the memory of the great Icelandic painter Johannes S. Kjarval, many of whose works are displayed here, along with those of other Icelandic and foreign artists.

Museum of Natural History, Hverfisgata. Open Sun., Tues., Thurs. and Sat.

National Art Museum. Sudurgata. A comprehensive collection of Icelandic art. Open Sun.

Norraena Húsid (Nordic House). Close to the University. A cultural center rather than just a museum, with exhibitions, lectures, and concerts.

Thjódminjasafnid (National Museum). On Hringbraut, close to the University. Viking artifacts, plus national costumes and silver work. Also displays of weaving and woodcarving, an ancient craft which has revived in recent years, and some unusual whalebone carvings.

PARKS AND GARDENS. Great efforts are being made to beautify Iceland's cities and towns by planting trees, flowers, and shrubs in parks and gardens, though the persistent wind prevents them blooming until June or even July. Tjarnargardar (Lakeside Gardens) are spread around Lake Tjörnin within Reykjavik's city center. The small but pretty garden behind the Parliament building is called Althingishússgardur. Overlooking the harbour and close to the National Theater is Arnarhóll, a grassy hill crowned by a statue of Ingólfur Arnarson, the first settler. Near the sports stadium and main swimming pool blooms Laugardalur, a lovely botanical garden.

SPORTS. Swimming. Every Icelandic primary school registers swimming as a compulsory subject, and it has become the national sport, somewhat like football to the Americans and cricket to the British. Most travelers will enjoy the marvelous swimming pools, and Reykjavik has many which are open year-round. It is particularly invigorating in winter months to dive from a snow-laden poolside into the warm waters of an open-air pool. All bathers are required to take a shower both before and after swimming.

Following are some Reykjavik pools and their addresses: *Sundlaugar Reykjavikur,* Laugardal (34039); *Sundlaug Vesturbaejar,* Hofsvallagata (15004); *Sundlaug Kópavogs,* Borgarholtsbraut (41299); *Sundlaug Breidagerdisskóla,* Breidagerdi (85860); *Sunóll Reykjavikur,* Barónsstig (14059); and *Sundhöll Hafnarfjardar,* Herjólfsgata 10 (50088).

Golf. The city has a number of golf clubs, though most boast only nine holes, except for the main club, *Golfklúbbur Reykjavikur,* (84735), which is about 8 km. (5 miles) east of the city center and has 18 holes. Another smaller golf club is at *Seltjarnarnes,* in the western part of the city. Clubs are open daily from May to Nov., and play continues as long as the daylight lasts (it's scarcely necessary to stop at all during June!).

Gliding. Gliding enthusiasts should contact *Flugmálafélag Íslands* (the Icelandic Gliding Club), on (24354).

Fishing. Many foreign anglers return year after year for the excellent fishing opportunities that Iceland offers, Prince Charles among them. Trout and salmon are especially good, and sea angling is also possible. Check with the Tourist Office for more details. Remember that not only is a permit necessary, but the angler must usually limit his catch to a quota.

Hiking. For information on day and weekend outings, contact *Ferdafélag Íslands,* Oldugata 3 (19533).

Winter Sports. Skating is popular; Lake Tjörnin in particular, in the heart of the capital, is a bustling spot for skaters.

Skiing is practised on the slopes between Reykjavik and Selfoss. Regular bus service from Hlemmtorg and Lackjartorg during the winter. Summer skiing at Kerlingarfjöll.

The Sports Stadium in Laugardal (83377), next to the large swimming pool, has excellent facilities, both indoor and outdoor, including **badminton** and **tennis.**

Details of all sports and facilities from the Tourist Office.

MUSIC, MOVIES, AND THEATERS. Music. Reykjavik has an active symphony orchestra, with several well-known Icelandic and foreign guest conductors. An opera, operetta, or musical is staged at least once a year at the National Theater. The Icelandic Opera has been operating for some years with a great response by the public, and some Icelandic opera singers are internationally known. As in other Scandinavian countries, there are several male-voice choirs and some mixed ones. Brass bands are very popular.

Movies. There are several cinemas in Reykjavik and its suburbs. Most films shown are British or American with Icelandic subtitles. Now, however, some new Icelandic films are coming onto the circuit which usually portray life from the Saga Times. Icelandic nature and volcano films are shown daily in the *Osvaldur Knudsen Film Studio,* near the Hotel Holt. The *Volcano Show,* Hellusundi 6a (13230), consists of two hours of Icelandic volcano and nature films.

Theaters. Reykjavik's *National Theater,* opened in 1950, is a splendid building at Hverfisgata (11200), close to the city center. The Theater performs both classical and modern works, but be warned that these are in Icelandic and will therefore be somewhat impenetrable to most (though the spectacle itself is still enjoyable). Ballet is also performed here, and though not as advanced as drama productions, some good programs can be seen, usually during the winter months. Another smaller theater is the *L.R.* (Reykjavik Theater) in Vonarstraeti by the lake (16620), which is planning to move its productions in the near future to the new City Theater in the New Center of Kringlumyri. The National Theater, Reykjavik Theater, and the Icelandic Opera are all closed during Aug.

The Icelandic Marionette Show at Jón Gudmundsson, Kaplaskjólsveg 61 (16167) gives performances to both large and small groups. *Light Nights* is a multi-media show in English, depicting Icelandic culture through the ages; it appears regularly during the summer tourist season at Tjarnarbió, near the lake. Performances start at 9 P.M., Thurs. through Sun.

SHOPPING. Iceland does not exactly qualify as a shopper's paradise, but locally-made sweaters and scarves of undyed Icelandic wool are beautiful and extremely soft and warm. Also worth considering are the sheepskins, lava ceramics, and silver items. Beware of the duty-free shop at Keflavík Airport. Some items are more expensive than in shops in town. The following shops are also recommended: *Álafoss Store,* Vesturgata 2, *Framtidin,* Laugavegur 45, *Gallerí Langbrók,* Amtmannstigur 1, *The Handknitting Association of Iceland,* Skólavördustig 19, *Hilda,* Borgartún 22, *The Icelandic Handicrafts' Center,* Hafnarstraeti 3, *Kúnst,* Laugavegur 40, *Parisartízkan,* Laugavegi, and *Rammagerdin,* Hafnarstraeti 19.

In food stores you can buy specially packed samples of Icelandic food to take home yourself or to mail to your friends. The smoked salmon, herring, and shrimps are all excellent.

RESTAURANTS. Reykjavik and the surrounding suburbs have seen some welcome additions recently as far as restaurants go, and there is now an attractive selection of eating places catering for all pocketbooks. Note that all of the expensive hotels mentioned earlier in this chapter have reasonable restaurants. Reservations are necessary from Thurs. to Mon. during the summer.

Expensive

Alex. Laugavegur 126 (24631). A popular all-rounder. AE, DC, MC, V.

Arnarhóll. Hverfisgata 8–10 (18833). Very exclusive and formal. Central location. AE, DC, MC, V.

Hotel Holt. Bergstadastraeti 37 (25700). The best hotel-restaurant in town. Exclusive and business-like ambience.

Vid Sjavarsduna. Tryggvagat (15520). Good French cuisine; lamb and seafood specialties. Close to the harbor—you can watch the boats sailing in and out. AE, DC, MC, V.

Vid Tjörnina. Templarasund 3 (18666). Highly recommended. This unique restaurant is located just behind the Parliament building and the Cathedral; and has a typical late 19th-century Scandinavian decor. The chef is a pioneer of modern Icelandic seafood cuisine; try the marinated codgills. AE, DC, MC, V.

Thrir Frakkar. Baldursgata 14 (23929). French cuisine. AE, DC, MC, V.

Moderate

Hard Rock Café. Kringlan (689888).

Hornid Restaurant. Hafnarstraeti 15 (20366). Attractive atmosphere, and very central. Icelandic lamb among specialties. AE, MC, V.

Krákan. Laugavegur 22 (13628). Very popular. AE, MC, V.

Potturinn og pannan. Brautarholt 22 (11690). Excellent food in a pleasant setting. American salads. Unlicensed. AE, MC, V.

Náttúran. Laugavegur 20b (28410). Vegetarian. Reasonably priced.

Torfan. Amtmannsstígur 1 (13303). Icelandic specialties in charming 19th-century atmosphere. AE, MC, V.

Inexpensive

Café Hressó. Austurstraeti 20 (14353). Popular meeting place. AE, MC, V.

El Sombrero. Laugavegur 73 (23866). Spanish food and pizzas. AE, MC, V.

Múlakaffi. Hallarmúli (37737). Typical Icelandic meals.

Pítuhornid. Bergthórugata 21 (12400). Pita, soups, and salads. Value for money.

Saelkerinn. Austurstraeti 22 (11633). Central. Italian dishes. AE, MC, V.

NIGHTLIFE. As your grandmother probably used to say, a word to the wise is sufficient: Iceland doesn't have what you would call a red-hot after-hours scene, and some tourists might find it unbearably tame or quaint. But following is a list of the more popular Reykjavik discos, one of which may take your fancy: *Broadway,* Álfabakka 8, Breidholti (77500); *Europa Discotek,* Borgatun 32 (35355); *Hotel Isleand,* Armuli 9 (687111); *Glaesibaer,* Álfheimar 74 (86220); *Hollywood,* Ármúli 5 (83715); *Klúbburinn,* Borgartún 32 (35355); *Kreml,* Austurvelli (11322) and *Odal,* Austurvöllur (11322, 11630).

Bars

All the major hotels in Reykjavik listed earlier in this chapter have licensed bars. It's important to note that the term "bar" to the Icelander refers to snack bars selling fast foods and soft drinks, so don't get confused. Icelandic law prohibits the sale of strong beers, but low alcohol beers are readily available. Wine bars in restaurants are new.

PRACTICAL INFORMATION FOR
THE REST OF ICELAND

TOURIST INFORMATION. Akureyri. Ferdaskrifstofan Akureyri, Rádhústorg 3 (96–25000). **Westmann Islands.** Ferdaskrifstofan Utsýn, Hólgata 6 (98–1515).

TELEPHONE CODES. We have given telephone codes for all the towns and villages in the hotel and restaurant lists that follow. These codes need only be used when calling from outside the town or village concerned.

HOTELS AND RESTAURANTS. It's important to note that although Iceland is a large island, the total population is only around 240,000, so it's not overflowing with huge, sprawling urban areas by any means. Given which, we haven't been able to provide many addresses for hotels and restaurants outside of those in Reykajavik and Akuyeri.

In the following sections, we have divided Iceland into four areas—North, South, East, and West—and list all hotels and restaurants under the appropriate town or village name. In most of the smaller places, there are no other restaurants except for those in the hotels, but these are usually quite adequate.

The hotels and restaurants listed below fall into three categories: Expensive (E), Moderate (M), and Inexpensive (I). We give approximate prices for these gradings in the *Facts at Your Fingertips* section.

NORTH ICELAND

Akureyri. *Hotel K.E.A.* (E), Hafnarstraeti 89 (96–22200). 28 rooms, all with bath or shower. First-class hotel with a friendly atmosphere; several bars, a restaurant and cafeteria. AE, MC, V. *Hotel Akureyri* (M), Hafnarstraeti 98 (96–22525). Comfortable hotel in the town center. V. *Hotel Vardborg* (M), Geislagata 7 (96–22600). 24 rooms. Very close to the center, with personal service and a good restaurant. AE, MC. *Skídahotel Hlídarfjall* (M), 96–22930. A ski-hotel in the hills about 2 miles above the town; open Jan. through May. Four chair-lifts, and floodlit ski-trails. *Dalakofinn* (I), Lyngholt 20 (96–23035). Very small (4 guest maximum), with bath, private entrance, and breakfast available on request. Good cooking facilities. *Edda* (I), (96–24055). 68 rooms without bath. Summer only. V. *Guesthouse Árgerdi* (I), Túngusída 2 (96–24849). Bed and breakfast for one to four persons. Swimming pool and sauna. Buses nos. 3, 4, and 5 all days from central square.

Restaurants. *Sjallinn* (M), Geislagata 12 (96–22770). Popular restaurant serving all sorts of seafood. Disco and band from Thurs. to Sun. V. *Smidjan* (M), adjacent to Bautinn (96–21818). Try the spiced lamb chop. MC, V. *Bautinn* (I), Hafnarstraeti 92 (96–21818). First-class restaurant near the town center. MC, V. *H. 100* (I), Hafnarstraeti 100 (96–25500). Combination restaurant and disco.

Camping. The camping site is at Thórunnarstraeti, just south of the swimming pool (96–23379). Toilet facilities, and hot and cold water available.

Youth Hostel. Stórholt 1 (96–23657).

Blönduós. *Edda* (M), (95–4126). 30 rooms, all with bath or shower. V.

Dalvík. *Hotel Vikurröst* (M), (96–61354). 20 rooms. Swimming pool and restaurant. Also allows sleeping bag stays. MC.

Hrútafjördur. *Edda Reykir* (M), (95–1003). 28 rooms. Swimming pool and steam bath. Summer only. V. *Stadarskáli* (M), (95–1150). Motel with good restaurant. MC.

Húnavellir. *Edda Svínavatn* (M), (95–4370). 23 rooms. Very comfortable hotel in a picturesque setting near Lake Svínavatn. Swimming pool and sauna. V.

Húsavik. *Hotel Húsavik* (E), Ketilsbraut (96–41220). 34 rooms with bath or shower. AE, V.

Kópasker. *Guesthouse* (I), (96–52121). 3 rooms.

Laugar. *Hotel Laugar S. Thingeyjarsýsla* (M), (96–43120). 70 rooms; summer only.

Mývath. *Reykjahlíd* (M), (96–441412). 12 rooms without bath; summer only. *Reynihlíd* (M), (96–44170). 44 rooms, swimming pool. U.S. astronauts were trained in the lunar-like atmosphere of the surrounding area. AE, MC, V.

Raufarhöfn. *Hotel Nordurljós* (M), (96–51223). 30 rooms; summer only.

Saudárkrókur. *Hotel Maelifell* (I), Adalgata 7 (95–5265). 7 rooms. MC.

Siglufjördur. *Hotel Höfn* (M), Laekjargata 10 (96–71514). 14 rooms, none with private bath. MC, V.

Skagafjördur. *Hotel Varmahlíd* (M), (95–6170). 17 rooms, none with private bath.

Stórutjarnir. Alongside Lake Ljósavatn. *Edda* (M), 96–43221. Comfortable, with 24 rooms. On route from Akureyri to Húsavik. Not far from the magnificent waterfall of Godafoss. Summer only.

SOUTH ICELAND

Flúdir. *Summerhotel Flúdir* (M), (99–6630). 27 rooms; summer only. *Motel Skjólborg* (I), (99–6624). 8 rooms.

Grindavik. *Guesthouse Bláa Lónid Svartsengi* (M), (92–8650). 10 rooms. Hot sea baths for sufferers from rheumatism and psoriasis. Good restaurant. Transport from airport.

Hella. *Guesthouse Mosfell* (I), (99–5828). 20 rooms without private bath.

Hveragerdi. *Hotel Ork* (E), (99–4700). 59 rooms with showers. Brand new, modern hotel. MC. *Hotel Hveragerdi* (M), Breidamörk 25 (99–4231). 12 rooms; summer only. MC. *Hotel Ljósbrá* (M), (4588). 10 rooms. MC.

Hvolsvöllur. *Hotel Hvolsvöllur* (M), (99–8187). 20 rooms, some with bath.

Keflavík. *Hotel Keflavík* (M), (92–4377). 27 rooms with showers. MC.

Kirkjubaejarklaustur. *Hotel Edda* (M), (99–7626). 32 rooms, some with bath or shower. Open all year. V.

Laugarvatn. *Hotel New Edda* (M), (99–6154). 27 rooms; summer only. *Edda Hotel* (I), (99–6118). 88 rooms, all with bath or shower. Swimming pool and steam baths; situated close by a lake. V.

Njardvík. *Hotel Kristina* (M), (92–4444). 10 rooms with showers. MC.

Selfoss. *Thóristún* (M), (99–1633). 17 rooms.

Skálholt. *Guesthouse Skálholt* (M), (99–6870). 10 rooms with bath; summer only.

Skógar. *Hotel Edda* (I), (99–8870). 34 rooms without bath; summer only. V.

Thingvellir. *Valhöll* (M), Lyngas 4 (99–4080). 37 rooms; summer only. AE, DC, MC.

Vík Mýrdal. *Hotel K.S.* (I), (99–7193). 10 rooms.

Westmann Islands. *Hotel Gestgjafinn* (M), (98–2577). 14 rooms, all with bath or shower. V. *Guesthouse Heimir* (I), (98–1515). 22 rooms, none with bath.

EAST ICELAND

Breidalsvík. *Hotel Bláfell* (M), (97–5770). 8 rooms, none with private bath. *Hotel Edda Stadarborg* (M), (96–5683). 9 rooms; summer only.

Djúpivogur. *Hotel Framtid* (I), (97–8887). 9 rooms.

Egilsstadir. *Hotel Valaskjálf* (M), (97–1500). 24 rooms, all with bath. V. *Hotel Egilstadir* (I), (97–1114). 15 rooms with bath; summer only.

Eidar. *Hotel Edda* (I), (97–3803). 60 rooms, none with bath. Summer only. V.

Eskifjördur. *Hotel Askja* (I), (97–6261). 7 rooms.

Hallormsstadir. *Hotel Edda* (I), (97–1683). 22 rooms, none with private bath. Summer only. V.

Hornafjördur. *Hotel Höfn* (E), (97–8240). 40 rooms, all with bath or shower. DC, V. *Hotel Edda Nesjaskóli* (I), (97–8470). 30 rooms, none with bath. Summer only. V.

Raufarhöfn. *Nordurljós* (I), (96–51233). 8 rooms.

Reydarfjördur. *Guesthouse K.B.H.* (I), (97–4200). 3 rooms without bath.

Seydisfjördur. *Snaefell* (M), (97–21460). 9 rooms. Restaurant.

Vopnafjördur. *Guesthouse Tangi* (M), (97–3224). 12 rooms without bath.

WEST ICELAND

Akranes. *Hotel Akranes Bárugata* (M), (97–2020). 11 rooms, none with bath.

Borgarfjördur. *Hotel Bifröst* (M), (93–5000). 31 rooms; summer only.

Borgarnes. *Hotel Borgarnes* (M), Egilsgötu (93–7119). 35 rooms, all with bath or shower. MC, V.

Búdardalur. *Hotel Bjarg* (I), (93–4161). 7 rooms.

Isafjördur. *Hotel Isafjördur* (E), (94–4111). 31 rooms, all with bath or shower. V. *Hotel Hamrabaer* (M), (94–3777). 8 rooms. *Guesthouse Isafjördur* (I), (94–3043). 17 rooms.

Króksfjördur. *Hotel Edda Bjarkalundur* (M), (94–4762). 12 rooms; summer only.

Ólafsvik. *Hotel Nes* (M), (93–6300). 38 rooms, none with bath.

Reykholt. *Hotel Edda* (M), (93–5260). Summer only. V.

Saelinsdalur. *Hotel Laugar* (M), (93–4111). 27 rooms, none with bath. Summer only.

Snaefellsnes. *Hotel Búdir* (M), (93–8111). 20 rooms, none with bath. Summer only.

Stykkishólmur. *Hotel Stykkishólmur* (E), (93–8330). 26 rooms, all with bath or shower. MC, V.

Thingeyri. *Guesthouse Höfn* (I), (94–8151). 3 rooms.

Vatnsfjördur. *Hotel Edda Flókalundur* (M), (94–2011). 14 rooms, all with bath or shower. Summer only. V.

NORWAY

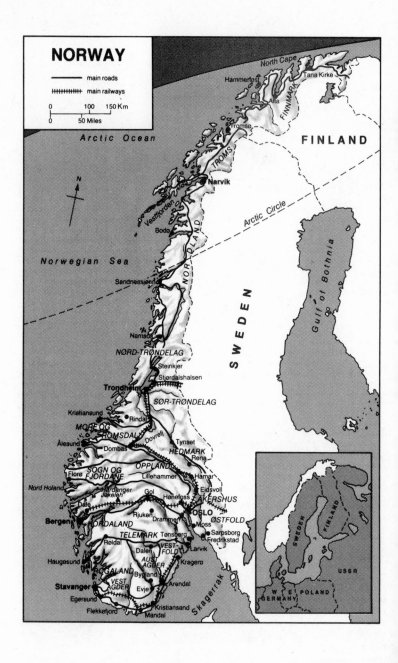

NORWAY

main roads

HHHHHHHH main railways

0 ——— 100 ——— 150 Km

0 — 50 Miles

Arctic Ocean

North Cape

Hammerfest   Tana Kirke

Alta   FINNMARK

Tromsø

FINLAND

TROMS

Narvik

Arctic Circle

Vestfjorden

Bodø

NORDLAND

Norwegian Sea

Gulf of Bothnia

Sandnessjøen

SWEDEN

Namsos

NORD-TRØNDELAG

Steinkjer

Stjørdalshalsen

Trondheim

SØR-TRØNDELAG

Kristiansund   •Rindal

MØRE OG

ROMSDAL   Dovrell

Ålesund   Tynset

Dombås   *HEDMARK*

Rena

SOGN OG   *OPPLAND*

Florø   *FJORDANE*   Lillehammer

Hamar

Nord Holand   Hardanger   Gol   Eidsvoll

Jøkelen   Hønefoss   *AKERSHUS*

Dale   **OSLO**

Bergen   Rjuken   Drammen   *ØSTFOLD*

HORDALAND   Moss

TELEMARK   Tønsberg   Sarpsborg

Røldal   Fredrikstad

Dalen   *VEST-*   Larvik

Haugesund   *FOLD*

AUST-   Kragerø

ROGALAND   *AGDER*

Bygland   Arendal

VEST-

Stavanger   *AGDER*   Evje

Egersund   *Skagerrak*

Flekkefjord   Kristiansand

Mandal

SWEDEN

FINLAND

USSR

W E

S

POLAND

W.

GERMANY

NORWAY—FACTS AT YOUR FINGERTIPS

NATIONAL TOURIST OFFICE. In North America: *Norwegian Tourist Office,* 655 Third Ave., New York, NY 10017 (212–949–2333).
In the U.K.: 20 Pall Mall, London S.W.1 (01–839 6255).

Within Norway, there are numerous local tourist offices, all identified by the international "i" sign. Many are only open during the summer, but all the major offices are open year round. As well as providing information on their own regions, they will also help in finding accommodations and making reservations for trains, boats, buses and ferries. We list all the major tourist offices at the beginning of each *Practical Information* section.

CURRENCY. The unit of currency in Norway is the *krone,* written as NOK and divided into 100 *ore.* The rate of exchange at the time of writing (mid-1989) was NOK 6.06 to the U.S. dollar and NOK 11.50 to the pound sterling. These rates will certainly change before and during 1990, so check them carefully both when planning your trip and during it.

COSTS IN NORWAY. As a result of both its North Sea oil boom and the natural industriousness of its hard-working people, Norway has an extremely high standard of living. Costs, for the most part, are therefore naturally very high. In fact certain items, in particular food but above all alcohol, are extremely expensive and above average even by Scandinavian standards.

The Norwegians are conscious of their high-price-tag reputation, however, and have made significant efforts to keep down costs for visitors. We give details of the many hotel, restaurant and travel bargains to be had in the relevant sections below. But at the same time, you should be prepared for some fairly high costs.

Sample costs. A cinema seat for one, NOK 35; visit to a museum, NOK 5 to 12; beer (per bottle), NOK 35; house wine—by the glass in a café, NOK 25, by the bottle in a restaurant, NOK 160; a Coke, NOK 15; a moderate taxi ride in Oslo, NOK 70; an average bus ride in Oslo, NOK 12.

SEASONAL EVENTS. Like all the Scandinavian countries, the majority of Norway's special and seasonal events take place in the summer, especially in June. However, as is only appropriate in the country that claims to be the home of winter sports, there are also a large number of winter sports events.

The Norwegian Tourist Board publishes an annual list of all Norway's major festivals, but among the more important are:

January begins the year with various New Year competitions, including men's speed skating in Oslo. The Monolith Cross Country Ski Race, for both men and women, is held in Oslo's Frogner Park at the beginning of the month, while a week or so later Lillehammer holds its ski festival.

February sees the Norwegian Ski Jumping championships—an event long dominated by the Scandinavians—also at Lillehammer.

March is similarly full of winter sports competitions, of which the most important by far is the Holmenkollen Ski Festival in Oslo. But there's also the Mjøsløpene marathon ski race—114 miles, in fact—on Lake Mjøsa outside Lillehammer at the start of the month, while mid-March sees a whole host of other gruelling cross-country ski races, including the Norway–Sweden race at Engerdal. The most historical race is the Birkebeiner Ski Race from Lillehammer to Rena—30 miles. At the end of the month, there is a Winter Festival up beyond the Arctic Circle at Narvik, with skating and skiing competitions and much other wintery celebrating. But maybe the most unusual event is the Ridderrennet Knights Race, a competition for the disabled at Beitostølen.

April sees a winter festival with a difference, also up beyond the Arctic Circle: reindeer races at Karasjok and Kautokeino. April also sees the last major cross-country ski race of the year, at Skarverennet, 37 km. (23 miles), Finse to Ustaoset.

May gets under way with another gruelling sporting event, the Ancient Marathon at Fredrikstad, a 38-km. (24-mile) hike along a route containing numerous historical and archeological landmarks. May also has two major celebrations: May Day itself, on the 1st, and May 17, Constitution Day, celebrated with processions of schoolchildren led by their own brass bands. They march through the streets of Oslo and up to the Royal Palace where the King and royal family greet them from the balcony. Two cultural festivals held now are the International Church Festival at Kristiansand, and the Bergen International Festival, with music, theater and ballet.

June has a host of special events. There's the Grieg Festival in Lofthus, commemorating the birth of Norway's most celebrated composer; the Stor Mart'n, a traditional Fair at Nidaroshallen, Trondheim; the North Norway Festival at Harstad, when exhibitions, folklore and an historical play at the open-air theater near the ancient Trondenes church are presented; and the Kongsberg International Jazz Festival. June is also packed with sporting events, of which perhaps the most unusual is the Midnight Cup golf tournament at Trondheim, when play continues throughout the night. But there's also the North Sea Fishing Festival, for both individuals and teams, at Haugesund. Finally, June is probably most famous for the myriad celebrations that take place on Midsummer Night: bonfires, fireworks and revelry go on all night long throughout the country.

July. International athletics are represented at the Bislett Games, held in Oslo during June and July. American Independence Day is celebrated in Frogner Park, Oslo, at the statue of Abraham Lincoln. Molde hosts an international Jazz Festival, while at the end of the month there is an historical open-air play at Stiklestad, the Olsokspelet.

August. The Tananger International Sea Fishing Festival at Stavanger, for both individuals and teams, starts off the month. On a more cultural note, Elverum hosts a Music Festival, also at the beginning of the month, while in the church ruins at Maridalen in Oslo, the Maridalspillet, an historical drama, is presented. Last week of the month sees "Oslo Days," Oslo's culture festival, which ends with a marathon street race.

September sees the last of the summer's festivities, the Dølajazz festival in Lillehammer.

December is most notable for the presentation of the Nobel Peace Prize on the 10th in the Aula at Oslo's university. Christmas is celebrated with gusto throughout Norway and is really a week's holiday, until Jan. 2.

NATIONAL HOLIDAYS. January 1 (New Year's Day); April 12–16 (Easter); May 1 (Labor Day); May 17 (Constitution Day); May 24 (Ascension Day); June 4 (Whit Monday) December 25 and 26 (Christmas).

LANGUAGE. Many Norwegians, especially younger people and those in cities and larger centers, speak English, generally to a very high standard. Certainly in tourist offices, hotels, restaurants, bars, museums and so forth, you will have no difficulties. In rural areas, you will still find English-speakers in most places, but you might have difficulty in understanding any Norwegian words you may have picked up because dialects vary tremendously.

CUSTOMS. Residents of non-European countries may import duty-free into Norway: 400 cigarettes or 50 grams of cigars or tobacco and 200 leaves of cigarette papers (except those under 15); plus, 2 liters of spirits or 2 liters of wine and 2 liters of beer; plus, 50 grams of perfume and ½ liter of eau de Cologne; plus, other goods to the value of NOK 3,500.

Residents of European countries may import duty-free into Norway: 200 cigarettes or 250 grams of cigars or tobacco and 200 leaves of cigarette papers (except those under 15); plus, 1 liter of spirits and 1 liter of fortified wine or two liters of table wine or 2 liters of wine and 2 liters of beer (except those under 20); plus, a small quantity of perfume and/or eau de Cologne (in opened bottles); plus, other goods to the value of NOK 700.

Note that alcoholic beverages over 60° (120° proof) may not be imported.

You may also bring in any amount of foreign and Norwegian currency but must declare it on arrival. You may export no more than the equivalent of NOK 10,000 in foreign currency. No more than NOK 5,000 may be exported.

So far, Norway is rabies free. No animals may be imported without a permit from the Ministry of Agriculture. Fines for smuggling are very high and the animal(s) will almost certainly be destroyed, or sent home immediately at the owner's expense.

HOTELS. The Norwegians are strict about hotels, as indeed they are about many things, and any establishment calling itself a hotel must match up to certain minimum legal standards. As a result, you can be sure that any Norwegian "hotel" will be spotlessly clean, comfortable and very well run. In addition, many outside larger cities are still family-owned and run and offer a degree of personal service and hospitality only rarely found elsewhere. With the exception only of the likes of Oslo and Stavanger, the majority of Norwegian hotels are neither especially expensive or particularly cheap, tending instead to be moderately-priced—by Norwegian standards anyway—and perhaps a little unspectacular and staid. But anyone in search of quiet and good service is likely to be satisfied.

We give basic prices below, but note that almost all hotels, especially in resort areas, will charge "en pension" rates for stays longer than five, or sometimes three, days; that is, charges will be reduced for anyone staying longer than these minimum periods. In addition, many resort hotels also have special summer and weekend rates with reductions of as much as 30 to 40%. Note also that resort hotels offering superior accommodations are called "tourist" hotels. You might also discover a breed of hotel known as a "mountain" or *Høyfjellshotel;* to qualify, they must be located at least 2,500 ft. above sea level.

The Scandinavia Bonus Pass, costing approximately $20 and valid also in Denmark, Finland and Sweden, gives average discounts of 15–40% in selected Norwegian hotels from June 1 to September 1. In addition, children under 16 stay in their parents' room at no extra charge. This scheme is particularly useful for anyone planning to tour more than one Scandinavian country by car. For full details, write *Inter Nor Hotels,* Kronprinsensgt. 5, Oslo 2, Norway. *Nordturist* (or Scanrail) gives you discounts at 100 first class hotels from June 13–Aug. 17.

The Fjord Pass works on a similar basis. It costs approximately NOK 50 for two adults and their children under 15 and is valid at 200 Norwegian hotels. Large discounts are given between May 15 and September 15; children under 3 stay free in their parents' room (without an extra bed), while 50% of the adult tariff is charged for 3–14 year olds.

Summer Hotels consist of student accommodations that are opened to the public during the summer at low rates. Though housed in modern and cheerful buildings, they lack finesse, but are more than adequate. Young people and budget travelers will find them appealing.

Prices. We have divided all the hotels we list into four categories—Deluxe (L), Expensive (E), Moderate (M) and Inexpensive (I). These grades are determined solely by price.

Two people in a double room in **Oslo** can expect to pay (prices in NOK):

Deluxe	950 and up
Expensive	650–950
Moderate	500–600
Inexpensive	350–400

These prices include breakfast and taxes. Outside Oslo, you can expect to pay considerably less, especially in rural districts. In the listings, the abbreviations AE,

DC, MC, and V stand for American Express, Diner's Club, MasterCard (including Access and EuroCard), and Visa.

SELF-CATERING. A vacation where you stay in a cabin and cook for yourself is a Norwegian way of life, an escape from the daily routine, a chance to live in close contact with nature. Bear in mind that facilities vary considerably, from well-equipped chalets with electric cooking, heating and frigidaire to cabins with no running water and outdoor sanitation only. Prices vary accordingly. Full details are available from *Den Norske Hytteformidlingen,* Kierschowsgt. 7, 0405 Oslo 4 (02–356710), the Norwegian Tourist Board, at the Rådhus (City Hall) or Postbox 499 Sentrum, 0105 Oslo 1 (02–427044), and many travel agents. Norwegian tourist offices in the U.K. and North America also carry brochures with full information on this class of accommodations.

The most inexpensive self-catering vacation is to be had by renting a *rorbu,* a fisherman's dwelling. These are available to visitors during the summer and are located in the Lofoten isles in North Norway, and on the South Coast.

Farm vacations are available in several regions, but the most popular area is the Gudbrandsdal valley along the Dovre railroad. These holidays are offered by working farms, and either self-catering or full board with the farmer's family is available. Best contact Lillehammer Tourist Office, Storgaten 56, Lillehammer, or the Norwegian Tourist Board or a good travel agent.

CAMPING. There are over 1,400 authorized campsites in Norway. The Norwegians are great believers in camping, one reason for the high standards encountered almost everywhere.

Several campsites provide log cabins or wooden huts at reasonable rates. Bogstad Camping in Oslo—Norway's largest campsite with space for over 1,200 tents—also offers 20 furnished and well-equipped log cabins, each with four to five beds. The *Kongelig Norsk Automobilklub* or *KNA* (Royal Norwegian Automobile Club) owns a number of tourist huts, which are available to members of AAA and AA at bargain rates. The KNA is at Parkveien 68, Oslo 2 (02–562690). *NAF,* the *Norges Automobil Forbund* (Norwegian Automobile Association), produces a guide called *Camping Norway,* available from tourist offices or Storgaten 2–6, Oslo 1 (02–337080).

A useful folder on campsites and youth hostels in Norway is available from the Norwegian Tourist Board. Campsites are listed with 1, 2 or 3 stars according to their facilities. The cost per night for car and tent is around NOK 80. Camping huts—where available—can be rented at NOK 70 to 220 per night. Reservations are facilitated by the purchase of a *Campingkort* (camping card) for NOK 10.

YOUTH HOSTELS. There are some 100 youth hostels spread all over Norway. Some are built especially for the purpose and are among the best in Europe. Sleeping bags are obligatory, so bring your own or hire one at the hostel. If you are not a member of YHA in your country, you can buy an international membership card at most youth hostels. There is no age limit. The charge for a bed is generally NOK 100 per night in the best hostels, or NOK 65 to 82 in more modest hostels. A useful list is available from the *Norwegian Youth Hostels Association,* Dronningensgate 26, Oslo 1.

RESTAURANTS. Eating out in Norway is expensive, especially if you have even a glass of wine, let alone a bottle, with your meal. Over the last few years Norwegian cuisine has improved considerably, mainly due to the competition from the many international restaurants in the main cities. You'll also find that away from towns and cities nearly all restaurants are in hotels.

A great many of them offer fixed-price menus or *table d'hôte* menus, suggested menus that is, both of which are good value, even if they do not offer a great deal in the way of choice. Keep an eye open too for the *ferie meny,* or vacation menu, where a main course with coffee costs around NOK 50 to 60.

Most larger centers also have good-value pizza and Chinese restaurants, and even occasionally the odd Greek spot. Similarly fast food chains are commonplace.

Prices. We have divided the restaurants in our listings into three categories—Expensive (E), Moderate (M) and Inexpensive (I). These grades are determined solely by price.

Prices, per person, with service charges but excluding drinks (in NOK)

Expensive	200 and up
Moderate	100–200
Inexpensive	60–100

Outside Oslo, prices are often considerably lower.

FOOD AND DRINK. Breakfasts are often enormous with a variety of fish, meats and cheese, and fine bread served from the cold buffet along with coffee and boiled or fried eggs. Many city hotels also offer a smaller Continental breakfast. A national institution is the *koldtbord* (cold table) which will often be in evidence at lunch time, featuring smoked salmon, fresh lobster, shrimp and other products of the sea, also assorted meats, salads, cheese, desserts and hot dishes. The sandwiches are a meal in their own right, single-decker meat, cheese, fish or salad concoctions as open and friendly as the Norwegians themselves. They are called *smørbrød*. Equally appreciated by Norwegians and their visitors are the roast venison, ptarmigan in cream sauce, wild cranberries and cloudberries *(multer)* with a flavor all its own. If you have a strong palate and really want to go Norwegian, try *lutefisk,* a highly flavored codfish that tastes as though it had been preserved in a potash lye. After that even the fiery Norwegian schnaps, *aquavit,* seems cool by comparison

As well as the very high taxes on alcohol, Norway has strict laws governing its sale. Spirits may not be served on Sundays, national holidays and after midnight. Similarly barmen may not serve you more than one drink at a time, to prevent people from stocking up drinks at midnight. After midnight you can still drink beer and wine in some places. Outside restaurants and bars, alcohol can otherwise only be bought at the state-run Vinmonopol liquor stores, open regular shopping hours during the week and until 1 P.M. on Saturdays. Note that these are not open on Sundays. Finally, avoid imported spirits—a bottle of scotch will cost upwards of $30.

TIPPING. The Norwegians do not generally expect tips. Taxes and service are always added to your bill in hotels and restaurants, so only exceptional service should warrant a tip. If you do feel your waiter deserves a tip, round up the bill to the nearest 10 krone; this is generally considered adequate. Similarly, taxi drivers do not expect tips, but on guided tours it is usual to tip if satisfied.

MAIL. Postal rates for airmail letters to the U.S. are NOK 4.50 and postcards to the U.S. are NOK 4.00 and to the U.K. NOK 3.50 for up to 20 grams. Rate of letters and postcards within Scandinavia, NOK 2.70.

CLOSING TIMES. Shops open 9–5 (4 in summer). On Sat. they may close as early as 1 P.M., especially in summer. Banking hours are 8.30–3.30, Mon. to Fri., but closed on Sat. Many banks close at 3 P.M. during summer. Museums are usually open until 6 during the summer season, but consult the local guide for details.

SPORTS. Although spectator sports exist, they do not satisfy the Norwegian individualist. He must have his own skis, his own skates, and his own boat, and these he uses whenever he can and whatever his age or walk of life. The Norwegians are, to put it mildly, *very* fond of the outdoor life, but they are most famous for their skiing, both alpine and cross-country. Come winter, there's nowhere in Norway where you can't ski, including Oslo. Local tourist boards will direct you to the nearest slopes and trails, or simply follow the Norwegians. (*See* Winter Sports below.)

The south coast and the region around Oslo have several seaside spots where the weather is reliable and the facilities for swimming and other water sports are plentiful. Mandal, on the southwest coast, has fine sandy beaches. Sailing is enjoyed in Norway all around the coast from Trondheim to Oslo. The capital itself, situated at the head of the picturesque island-studded Oslo Fjord, is the most important yachting center.

Norway's mountain districts are easily reached from all parts of the country. In a few hours' walk from road or railway you can reach beautiful country off the beaten track. The great mountain ranges are ideal for hiking and offer excellent holiday facilities. Although most—but not all—have been climbed, there is still scope for further exploratory mountaineering. All the popular rock climbs are well marked, making these ideal for parties of some experience wishing to learn guideless climbing.

Over 200 rivers provide salmon and sea-trout fishing. The season extends from June to September. It is no exaggeration to say that some of the best salmon fishing in the world can be had in these Norwegian rivers. A fishing permit must be obtained first—details from the Norwegian Tourist Board, or the Directorate for Wildlife and Freshwater Fish, 7000 Trondheim. (Tourist boards and post offices usually dispense permits; they cost NOK 10 for a week, NOK 40 for a year.) In addition, Norway is honeycombed with several thousand lakes. There are trout in practically every lake and river, even high up among the mountain ranges.

The Norwegian Tourist Board's inexpensive guide book *Mountain Touring in Norway* is indispensable for hikers, and anglers should get their invaluable guide *Angling in Norway*.

Salmon fishing is offered by *Fly-spesialisten,* Kronprinsesse Marthas plass 1, Oslo 1, while hunting trips are organised by *Trønderreiser,* Kongensgate 30, N-7000 Trondheim.

WINTER SPORTS. Norway, the home of skiing, has terrains to fit the abilities of expert and novice, the tastes of ski tourer and downhill runner. Ski lifts are available at all the major centers, and skis may be hired for a small fee. Prices and fares are reduced in January, when the snow also is at its best. However, there is ample snow from Christmas until the end of April, with plenty of warm sunshine and dry, inland air. Cross-country ski package tours from the U.S. and Canada are very popular to such centers as Lillehammer, Voss, Geilo and Hemsedal. Check with a travel agent or the Norwegian Tourist Board.

Norway is so mountainous that you can ski almost anywhere, but the Norwegians have their favorite places. Oslo—with the wooded hills of Nordmarka—is the biggest winter sports center of east Norway. Oslo-Marka's varying terrain covers a vast area of unspoiled, hilly forest and lakeland rising to altitudes of 2,100 ft. There are 1,500 miles of well-prepared trails, 60 miles of which are floodlit at night. Other resorts within easy reach of the capital are Kongsberg and Norefjell.

Woodland settings characterize the Telemark resorts of Bolkesjø, Morgedal, Vrådal and Vråliosen, whereas more mountainous country is found at Rjukan, Rauland and Tuddal. West Norway has developed skiing resorts at Kvamskog and Seljestad. Along the Bergen railway are such well-known resorts as Voss, Mjølfjell, and Vatnahalsen in alpine terrain; Finse—the highest resort on the Bergen-Oslo railway—where skiing continues until June; while Ustaoset and Geilo (the biggest and, for alpine skiing, the most popular resort), Ål, Gol, and Nesbyen, are set in more rolling country.

The top winter sports center on the Dovre railway in the Gudbrandsdal country is Lillehammer—host of the 1994 Winter Olympics. Similar undulating terrain is found at Tretten, Espedal, Harpefoss, Vinstra, and Dombås. Oppdal offers more rugged country, Hamar is set in typical wooded terrain. The hotels in the Jotunheimen mountains—Bygdin, Tyin and Spiterstulen—are all situated in alpine terrain. Valdres offers a great variety of skiing country: typical woodland skiing down in the valleys, and mountainous terrain at Beitostølen, Grindaheim, Nystova, Nøsen and Maristova, with excellent alpine skiing at the new Aurdal alpine center.

Although skiing is the big sport, there is curling and tobogganing as well, and many resorts have excellent skating rinks. You may even indulge in a week or two of dogsled touring on skis—not for novices, but you needn't be an expert skier either.

GETTING AROUND NORWAY. By air. Norway has an excellent internal air network. *SAS,* Braathens *SAFE* and *Wideroe's* are the principal carriers. Fares are on the high side, but discounts for weekend travel, families, the disabled, senior citizens, and youth travel—details from the Norwegian Tourist Board and travel agents—help keep costs manageable. Inquire about "Visit Norway" passes, relatively cheap packages of domestic flight coupons (usually only good for summer travel) at SAS, SAS Building, Ruseløkkveien 6, Oslo 2 (02–429970); Braathens SAFE AS, Ruseløkkveien 26, Oslo 2 (02–411020); Widerøes Flyveselskap AS, Mustadsveien 1, Oslo 2 (02–555960).

By train. Most long-distance trains leave from *Sentralstasjon* or Oslo-S (Central Station), while suburban trains usually leave from *Vestbanestasjon* or Oslo-V (West Station). Norwegian trains offer punctuality, comfort—and scenery. Most routes fan out from Oslo though, and leave the coasts (except in the south, where service is much more comprehensive) to buses and ferries. Not all trains travel quickly, but otherwise train travel in Norway is to be recommended. A number of express trains have special viewing coaches, and all principal trains carry both first- and second-class carriages and have either dining or buffet cars. Sleeping cars are available on overnight services, for which a supplement is payable; there are no couchettes, however. Reservations are required on all Express *(Ekspresstog)* and some Fast *(Hurtigtog)* services.

Generally speaking, the longer your journey, the less expensive proportionately it becomes. However, a number of good-value discounts for family groups, young people, senior citizens, and mid-week travel are also on offer. Details from travel agents, the Norwegian Tourist Board and local tourist offices. The Norwegian State Railway (NSR) office is at Stortingate 28, Oslo 1 (02–429460). They are open Monday to Friday 8.30–3.30 and serve as a travel bureau as well as a train information service.

In addition to these exclusively Norwegian discounts, the *Nordturist* (or Scanrail Card), the *Inter-Rail* card, the *Eurailpass* and *Eurail Youthpass,* and the *Rail Europ Senior Card* are all valid within Norway. See "Getting Around Scandinavia by Rail" in *Planning Your Trip* for further details.

By car. Motoring in Norway is very different from most other European countries. The scenery is constantly changing in all its breath-taking beauty. Many roads are outstanding tourist attractions on their own merit—particularly in the Fjord Country—with hair-pin bends and mountain passes, smiling lakes and thundering waterfalls. There are good hotels along every major tourist route. Roads are often narrow, so you should plan to cover no more than 250 km. (155 miles) per day. As filling stations may be far apart, particularly in the north and on the mountain roads, stock up. Gas costs about NOK 5.30 a liter. Remember that from September 1 until April 30 low-beam headlights are mandatory at all times. (Drivers of British automobiles must adjust beams so that they sweep right.) NAF can assist you: Storgaten 2–6, Oslo 1 (02–337080). Also remember that at intersections cars approaching from the right have right of way.

The ideal starting point for any motoring vacation in Scandinavia is Bergen on the west coast, reached by direct flights from New York or London. Visitors should first explore the Fjord Country, then drive across the mountain ranges to Oslo and onwards to Stockholm and Copenhagen.

Starting from Bergen, there is a choice of four major routes to Oslo, each of such great scenic beauty that it is difficult to choose among them. All take in the fantastic Tokagjel canyon east of Bergen and the giant Hardanger fjord with stunning vistas of the huge Folgefonn glacier, but here they part. One route goes through the Telemark region to Oslo (538 km. or 334 miles), and another across the Hardanger mountain plateau via Geilo to Oslo (489 km. or 303 miles).

Two other routes from Bergen continue via Voss and the stupendous zig-zag road through Stalheim canyon to Gudvangen on the narrow Naerøy fjord—a branch of the Sogne fjord, longest and deepest in Norway. One route goes by ferry to Revsnes and then via the Tyin mountain road to Oslo (565 km. or 350 miles), whereas the other route goes by ferry to Kaupanger and then along Sogne fjord and across Sognefjell mountain pass—highest in Norway at 1,440 meters or 4,690 ft.—down to Otta and Oslo (735 km. or 456 miles).

Any of these four routes could be covered in two days, but there is great scope for excursions en route, so you could easily spend three or four days on the trip. The Telemark route is open throughout the year, because two mountain passes are now bypassed by tunnels. The other routes are blocked by snow from November to May. See the *Fjord Country* chapter for many other tours of the western fjords. Any combination of two eastern valleys with one or more western fjords invariably makes a perfect itinerary. The fifth alternative is to go by car and ferry south to Stavanger, then continue by car to Kristiansand and along the picturesque south coast to Oslo (550 km., 350 miles).

Ambitious motoring buffs may like to drive all the way from Oslo to North Cape—a distance of 2,233 km. or 1,383 miles, including three ferry crossings and several mountain passes. You drive through Trondheim, Bodø, Narvik and Tromsø, but in between every town you will see fjords, rivers, waterfalls, mountains, glaciers and even Lapps, or Samis as they are now called, with their reindeer herds.

By boat/cruises. Norway's immense, fjord-indented coast has an intricate network of ferries and larger passenger ships serving it, in many places providing an essential means of transport. A wide choice of services is available, from simple hops across fjords (saving many miles of driving) and delightful one-day excursions among the thousands of islands to luxury cruises. Every local tourist office can supply full details of services and excursions in their region. We also give general information on sailings in the *Practical Information* sections at the end of every chapter.

In addition, Norway also boasts the world-famous coastal express service, *Hurtigrute,* from Bergen in the southwest to Kirkenes in the far north, beyond the North Cape. There's one sailing daily from Bergen throughout the summer, and the round-trip takes 11 days calling in at 35 harbors—where side trips are easily arranged—en route. The boats sail along one of the most dramatic coastlines in the world, guaranteeing spectacular views almost the whole way. It is, however, extremely popular, and you should book at least six months in advance. All the *Hurtigrutes* take some cars, but the newer ships take far more and cars can be driven on rather than winched on. Any travel agent can supply details, as can the Norwegian Tourist Board who also produce an excellent book, *2,500 Miles on the Coastal Express.* A Coastal Pass is available for young people between the ages of 16 and 26, costing NOK 1,300 and valid for unlimited travel for 21 days. Available from Norwegian travel agents.

By bus. The country is well covered by bus services. Several of the long-distances buses are of great interest to the tourist. For example the North Norway bus service starting at Fauske (on the railway to Bodø) goes right up to Kirkenes on the Russian-Norwegian border covering some 1,000 km. (625 miles) in four days. There are also long-distance international buses linking the Nordic countries, for example from Trondheim (Norway) to Stockholm (Sweden), Mo i Rana (Norway) to Umeå (Sweden), Bodø (Norway) to Skellefteå (Sweden) and Tromsø to Rovaniemi (Finland). Detailed planning information for Bus/Rail Ferry services is available in the *Tourist Timetable for Norway,* available from the Norwegian Tourist Board and published annually in April.

PRELUDE TO NORWAY

Something New Under the Midnight Sun

by
ANDREW BROWN

Every Norwegian, so the joke goes, can speak four languages, and three of these are Norwegian. There is a reasonable explanation for this: the country consists of different pockets of civilization, cut off from each other by mountains and vast distances, but rejoined today by television. The name of the country confirms this: Denmark, Sweden, and Finland all derive their names from their inhabitants. "Norway" meant originally "The Way Northwards": instead of giving their name to a place, the Norwegians took their name from the route on which they lived.

It is a very long route: if you set out from Oslo in the south to Alta or Kirkenes in the far north, you are attempting a journey as long as from Oslo to Sicily. To get from Oslo to Sicily, you would pass through some of the most densely-inhabited areas of Europe, but there are only four-and-a-half million people in the whole of Norway, so it is not surprising that their towns and villages have preserved a great deal of the individuality that other parts of Europe have lost.

A Constantly Changing Delight

This diversity makes Norway difficult to describe. Wherever you go, you can hope to find something peculiar, different, and diverting in the next valley. The scaly wooden stave churches in the south of the country—a number dating from late-Viking times—are the best-known examples of this. None of them looks like a church nearly so much as they look like frozen dinosaurs or trolls. Similarly, it is easy enough to drive from A to B in Sweden and Finland, even if they are 500 miles apart (if you drive even 200 miles in any direction in Denmark, you will end up either in Germany or in the sea). It is easy to drive long distances through these other Scandinavian countries. The countryside looks like A for 200 miles, then it looks like B for another 200, then you have arrived. Norway, most famous for the spectacular, inhuman beauty of the fjords, is a marvelous country to drive through, a constantly changing delight to see. The only snag is Norwegian roads.

Winter retreats through Scandinavia like a Russian army, devastating the country that it must leave behind. It is March, April, and, further north, May, that are intolerable to live through, not the proper winter. The seemingly unending sequence of thaws and refreezings, sleet and rain, ice and slush, when dirty brown snow lies like scabs on the dead grey earth, makes it seem that nothing will ever live anywhere again. These times, not the sparkling winter, explain the Scandinavian longing for the sun.

There are probably more potholes than cars in Norway. The main roads, though narrow, are promptly repaired each spring. But any road too small to be marked on a map of the whole country is likely to be rougher than you would have thought possible. There is nothing to be done about this except to relax (bounce) enjoy the view (bone-jarring crunch) and plan your (bump) itinerary accordingly. The most beautiful view I ever saw from a car in Norway I saw from behind a herd of cows.

This may give the impression that Norway is a primitive country. It is not. Even before the discovery of oil in the North Sea, Norway was one of the most prosperous countries in the world. Now it is one of the very richest (and most expensive) but there is so much of the country, and there are so few people in it, that it is impossible to keep all the roads in order.

Sweden and Finland are mostly forest; Denmark is all meadow and parkland; Norway looks as if people live there. The valleys are astonishingly fertile, almost as rich, in fact, as the sea. Even the Alta valley at the foot of the North Cape, which looks as desolate as any place on earth, supports nearly 1,000 fishermen and small farmers.

Dambusters and Dynamite

Alta is a good town from which to consider the rest of Norway. It lies at the mouth of the Alta river, which runs north across the bleak plateaux of Finnmark, 200 miles above the Arctic Circle. The river is—or was—one of the best salmon rivers in the world. Norway is famous for its salmon rivers, but the Alta was extraordinary even by Norwegian standards. The average weight of the fish there was 25 pounds, and in good years 20 tons of fish would be caught by rods alone, and far more than that netted in the fjord outside.

The government in Oslo proposed to dam the river. Finnmark needed the electricity. In some ways, this dam is a symbol of everything admirable about modern Norway. It is an astonishing feat to build anything in Finnmark in winter, when the temperature can drop to 50 below in a cold snap, and the sun sets for a fortnight around Christmas. And winter lasts a long time up there. (There are firms that will fly you out for fishing through the ice of lakes still frozen at midsummer).

Yet the dam was not welcomed by the inhabitants of Alta, and it was hated by the Lapps, or Samis as they now prefer to be called, who live in the bleak hills around the headwaters of the river. One Lapp lost an arm in an accident with explosives when he was attempting to sabotage a bridge necessary to the construction of it. Others went on hunger strikes outside the Parliament building in Oslo. When Parliament decided for the third time that work on the dam must start in 1981, the passive resistance of demonstrators who had come from all over the country demanded enormous resources to overcome. Every traffic policeman in the country was taken from his duties and quartered on a converted passenger ferry moored in Alta harbor.

Helicopters, snow-scooters, snow-cats: every resource of modern technology was deployed against the demonstrators; but just when everyone was expecting a tremendous dust-up, resistance was broken by the imposition of very heavy fines on any unauthorized people found within 10 miles of the construction site. Now the affair is almost forgotten in southern Norway; yet the story is an illuminating one. It contains all the essential elements of modern Norway: vast distances; great wealth and impressive technology; the slightly giddying profusion of riches from the sea; and the whole thing administered by a stubborn people never afraid to pick a good fight for their rights.

Illusion or Idyll?

This last is not obvious about the Norwegians: they tend to strike the visitor as remote and placid beings, like the Eloi in H.G.Wells's novel *The Time Machine.* The hero of this book mounts a Victorian time machine, the first in literature, that resembles nothing so much as a brass-bound bicycle and pedals away from suburbia into the future. After 30,000 years he reaches a country that seems like paradise. The inhabitants, known as the Eloi, are pale and delicate. They live like children, and appear to know nothing of sin. The only things to frighten them are the mysterious towers that stud the parkland where they live. Eventually the hero descends through one of these towers to an underworld where gnarled and dark creatures—the Morlocks—work unremittingly to sustain the Eloi in their carefree existence up above. The hero finally precipitates a revolution and then pedals back home again.

There are no Morlocks beneath Norway. They represent a nightmare of industrialism, and the Norwegians, like all the Scandinavians, were able, when they had their industrial revolution, to benefit from the experience of the countries that had gone through it before. The Scandinavians are among the richest people in Europe now partly because they were among the poorest 100 years ago. The lessons of the 19th century reached Scandinavia at the same time as the technology, whereas the rest of us got the technology first and the lessons second, the hard way. And it is the Norwegians who most closely approximate to the 19th-century idea of the future as expressed by the lives of the Eloi.

This is not simply a matter of material wealth. The Norwegians have a gloss of health about them. Their cheeks are ruddy; everyone seems to ski or skate or walk in the mountains whenever they get the chance.

In fact the Norwegians can easily seem too good to be true; an impression that Norwegian writers and artists have done their best to dispel. The very best of these—Ibsen, Knut Hamsun, Edvard Munch—have been as good as any in the world, but for that very reason they are not particularly illuminating about specifically Norwegian traits, any more than Shakespeare provides a reliable guide to the English character. Two lesser figures, though, are very illuminating. Aksel Sandemose was a writer who promulgated the ten commandments of village life in the 1930s. The most memorable of these laws were: You must not think that you are worth anything; you must not think yourself better than anyone else; you must not think yourself capable of anything worthwhile; and you must not think that you are in any way exceptional.

The life of small communities is not always that claustrophobic, but Sandemose certainly touched a nerve. His commandments, known as the *Janteloven,* have passed into Scandinavian folklore, and when the book came out, he received letters from all over to thank him for saying so clearly what so many had felt and suffered from.

The most impressive illustration of the Norwegian psyche is the sculpture park in Oslo. Here a sculptor named Gustav Vigeland spent 20 years in seclusion, protected by a fence, and supported by the city's municipal authorities. He produced an enormous amount of statuary. The centerpiece, known as the Monolith, is a tangled Joycean nightmare—a sort of *Finnegans Wake* done in stone—representing a struggle for air and for life. When asked what his religion was, Vigeland replied, "Look at the Monolith." It is an extraordinary monument, representing nothing but itself, and is well worth a visit, along with the rest of the 80-acre park, which many consider to be Oslo's highlight.

Oslo is a pleasant town, but it is the least pretentious capital in the world, and country Norwegians aren't unduly impressed by it. This is not because it is small, which it is, or shabby, which it isn't; but because the idea that one city or one central ruling body should lead the nation seems alien to the Norwegian character. Oslo is dominated architecturally by the City Hall, which stands above the Royal Palace and the Parliament building like a hippopotamus watching a pair of chihuahuas. This disproportion seems to say that only local politics are real and worth bothering about. The rest is just a stage set, to be used on high days and holy days, but not to be worried about otherwise.

While the Swedes are entranced by the idea of themselves as a nation, Norwegians tend to think of themselves as inhabitants of a particular town or valley. When a foreigner is someone who lives up the next fjord and speaks a different dialect, who needs to worry about the rest of the world? But this attitude has changed over the past decade as more and more Norwegians travel abroad.

Of Fish and Fjords

But the rest of the world can profit greatly from Norway. This is most obviously true of fishermen. Alaska, like Norway, combines enormous numbers of fish with very small numbers of fishermen. Even the most famous rivers like the upper Glomma are not at all crowded by American standards; anyone prepared to walk a little can find a private paradise with very little trouble.

And then there is the sea, where the fishing is easy and a boat-ride up the Norwegian coast is marvelous. The fjords are as wonderful as their reputation. No amount of anticipation—and no photographs—can ever prepare the traveler for the real thing.

The Norwegian landscape, at its most spectacular, can make you feel that you have been unwrapped: the cling-film memories and expectations that keep us from really seeing anything new and wholly unexpected are here peeled away. There is something new under the midnight sun for everyone.

OSLO

The Countryside Capital

The bright, breezy and outdoorsy capital of Norway is an hospitable city of some 450,000 people located at the head of the long, low Oslo fjord. Here is a world capital with nature at its very doorstep, a perfect place to adjust from the frenetic, over-civilized existence of some Western countries to the simpler, more wholesome values of Norwegian life.

Oslo is not a city of great architecture, sweeping boulevards and imposing buildings, yet in the somewhat haphazard arrangement of the streets there is a certain charm. And if you really go looking, you will certainly find buildings both old and modern of distinction. But, as every Oslonian says, "The surroundings!" Yes, they are magnificent, and the view of the town from any of the easily-reached heights that surround it is superb. But do not jump to the conclusion that the first thing to do is to rush out of town. That's only part of the program—there is plenty to do in Oslo before you head for the hills.

But hills, forests, fjords and farms, mountains and meadows there are aplenty, all encompassed within the nominal city limits of Oslo. The city is in fact the tenth-largest in the world in total area, but this statistic is really no more than a bureaucratic convenience. The built-up area of Oslo is small and in no way compares even with Stockholm and Copenhagen, let alone the likes of London, Paris or Rome. Thus the presence of a fairly rumbustious Nature close at hand is more than any other the most distinctive feature of this little capital.

So be warned. Anyone coming to Oslo in pursuit of sophisticated urban high-living is liable to be somewhat disappointed. Indeed, it should also

be added that the rather puritanical Norwegians actively frown on anything that might be considered high living, principally by imposing sting-
ing taxes and strict regulations on the sale of alcohol. However, those in
search of gentle relaxation, with the accent on the great outdoors, though
perhaps with just a dash of sophistication to spice up the mixture, will
find the Norwegian capital very much to their liking.

By Way of Background

Oslo is an ancient city, founded in 1050 by King Harald Hardraarda
(or Hard Counsel), yet in contrast to most European capitals, very little
remains that is more than a couple of hundred years old at most. The reasons for this apparently paradoxical state of affairs are not so hard to find,
however.

Despite its antiquity and despite having been capital of Norway since
the middle ages, for much of its history Oslo has really been no more than
a bit-part player on the European stage, and an unfortunate one at that.
With Norway falling under the influence and rule of first Denmark and
then Sweden, Oslo was little more than a pawn, intermittently besieged,
conquered, traded-off and reconquered. The city, or more exactly the
Akershus Fortress that was its strategic heart, was attacked first by Duke
Erik of Sweden in 1310—no more than 10 years after it had been completed by Haakon V. It was subsequently besieged (successfully) by Christian
II of Denmark in 1531–2 and by the Swedes again in 1537 and 1716, who
on both occasions were attempting to wrest it from the Danes. As if this
was not enough, the old wooden city was also periodically ravaged by fire,
culminating in the disastrous fire of 1624 when practically the whole town
was burned to the ground. Thus in contrast to Stockholm, for example,
which has rarely been seriously attacked, Oslo's tempestuous past has seen
the repeated destruction of much of the city, explaining the relative scarcity of older buildings today.

1624 in fact marks the beginning of the development of the modern city.
Following this second fire, Christian IV, Danish ruler of Norway, decided
to rebuild the town about a mile to the west of its original location so as
to bring it closer to the protecting walls of the Akershus Fortress. He also
decreed the houses be built of stone or brick and that the streets be a certain width. As a final flourish, he then renamed the city Christiania.

For the next two hundred years or so the little capital enjoyed a reasonable degree of prosperity, though it also suffered further severe fires in 1686
and 1708. But its growth was never more than steady and was in any case
punctuated by regular political and economic setbacks, chiefly the result
of Norway's continued domination by Denmark. During the Napoleonic
Wars, for example, Norway was forced by the Danes to commit herself
to the French cause, despite the close ties that by that point existed between Norway and Great Britain. The inevitable result was a British
blockade of Norwegian ports with grave consequences for Norwegian
trade.

On May 17, 1814, a Norwegian constitution was formulated at Eidsvoll
(just north of Oslo at the southern end of Lake Mjøsa), and later a Norwegian king was proclaimed. It was only after 1814 that Norway finally
achieved her independence from the Danes (though at the cost of renewed
domination by Sweden) and the little city began to grow significantly. And
it is from the middle years of the 19th century that the majority of Oslo's

principal buildings date: The Royal Palace, the Stortinget (or Parliament) and the University were all constructed between about 1820 and 1860, while Karl Johans Gate, still the principal thoroughfare, was laid out between 1818 and 1848. The 19th century also witnessed a considerable increase in both trade and population (in 1855 Oslo's population was still less than 40,000, by 1900 it was 150,000; similarly, by the same date Oslo had overtaken Bergen as Norway's principal port). The growth of the city also gave rise to a considerable housing shortage, with the result that many small wooden houses were built, outside the then city limits, by workers flooding into Oslo from elsewhere in Norway. A number of these little buildings can still be seen in areas such as Valerengen, Kampen and Rodeløkka, many of them now modernized, expensive, and much sought-after private homes.

Following Norway's emergence into total independence in 1905, when King Haakon VII was crowned as the first king of Norway since the Middle Ages, the city continued to grow (and, on January 1 1925, reverted to its original medieval name of Oslo), but it was the immediate post-war period that witnessed the greatest period of expansion. The striking and monumental City Hall, completed in 1950, is the most obvious symbol of this growth and the spurt of building that accompanied it. Similarly, much of suburban Oslo dates from this period. Today, though still something of a toy town, Oslo is an harmonious, stable and civilized capital, that has put its troubled history behind it.

Exploring Oslo

The heart of Oslo is Karl Johans Gate, a spacious street (much of it now for pedestrians only) about a mile long that runs east to west from the Sentralstasjon or Oslo-S (Central Station) to the Slottet (Royal Palace). About half-way along is a little park, Studenterlunden, which for the sake of argument we'll use as the starting point for our exploration of Oslo. The most obvious feature here is the late-19th-century Nationalteatret (National Theater), an attractive classical building at one end of the little park. It's one of the focal points of the capital's cultural life and, appropriately, twin statues of Henrik Ibsen and Bjørnstjerne Bjørnson, Norway's most distinguished men of letters, flank the entrance. The theater has been newly renovated after a backstage fire in 1982 closed its main stage and auditorium. Its intimate amphitheater carried on as usual. No performances, however, are given in the summer. (On either side of the theater, by the way, are the city's principal bus stops and the entrance to the electric tram that runs up to Holmenkollen).

Immediately to the north of the National Theater is the handsome neo-Classical facade of the University of Oslo, built from 1811. In fact, most of the University's departments have long since been moved to more spacious quarters at Blindern, to the north of the city. But the building remains the administrative center of the University and examinations are still conducted here in the *Aula,* or Central Hall, which is famous also for the murals of Edvard Munch that cover its walls. The Aula is also the venue for the presentation of the Nobel Peace Prize.

The forecourt of the University is the scene every fall of the inmatriculation of new students to the University every year. But it's also an excellent vantage point from which to watch the procession on May 17, Constitution Day, of thousands of schoolchildren, marching behind brass bands

banners, as they wend their way along Karl Johans Gate before climbing
the hill to the Palace to greet the royal family.

From the University, in fact, it's no more than a few hundred yards
up to the Palace, standing in its fine park (which unfortunately is very
much less salubrious at night). The Palace is not open to the public, but
you can watch the changing of the guard every day at 1.30. The band plays
when the King is in residence (all year round except mid-May to October
when he moves out to his country home at Bygdøy). The statue on the
parade in front of the Palace is of King Karl Johan, a Swedish king of
Norway after whom the city's main street is named. To the west is another
statue, this time of Queen Maud, daughter of Edward VII, King of England, and mother of the present king, Olav. Across the road is a third statue. This is Haakon VII, who was Norway's king from 1905 to 1957 and
presided over his country's independence in 1905. He is still regarded with
great affection by the Norwegians, not least for keeping alive the hopes
of his beleaguered people during World War II when Norway labored
under the Nazi occupation. His son Olav today enjoys the same deep hold
on the affection of his people.

Again using the park by the National Theater as a base, this time head
east away from the Palace and towards the Stortinget, Norway's Parliament. It's quite a striking building, heavy and sturdy, in parts more like
a cathedral than a Government building. Inside, it has been richly decorated by modern Norwegian artists. It can be visited during the summer re-
cess. (July and August, Monday to Saturday 12–2; admission free). Leave
the Storting to the right and continue up Karl Johans Gate, here paved
over and a bustling shopping center, towards the Domkirken, the Cathedral. Just before you reach the Cathedral, you pass through Stortorget,
a busy flower market in the spring and summer. Though small, the Cathedral is an attractive church, if a little dour from the exterior. It was consecrated in 1697 and contains a fine carved wooden pulpit dating from 1699.
However, it has since been substantially remodeled, notably in 1849–50
and just after the last war, when the striking ceiling frescos, by Hugo Lous
Mohr, illustrating the perpetual battle between the forces of light and
darkness, and the stained glass windows, designed by Emanuel Vigeland,
brother of the more famous Gustav, were executed.

In the arcades behind the Cathedral, where there has been a market
since the middle ages, you will today find the Arts and Crafts Center. It's
a good place to potter around for an unusual souvenir. In front of the Cathedral there's another statue, this one of Christian IV, King of Norway
and Denmark, who moved the site of Oslo nearer to the Akershus Fortress
after the disastrous fire of 1624.

The National Gallery

The third and final exploration of the center of Oslo is to the cluster
of museums behind and to the north of the University. Here you will find
the Nasjongalleriet (National Gallery), the Historisk Museum (Historical
Museum) and the Kunstindustrimuseet (Museum of Applied Art).

The National Gallery, established originally in 1836, is Norway's foremost art collection, containing some 3,000 paintings by Norwegian artists
and about 1,000 by other artists. In addition, there are large collections
of engravings, drawings, prints and water colors, the whole amounting to
a very creditable 40,000 catalogued works. Though the emphasis is

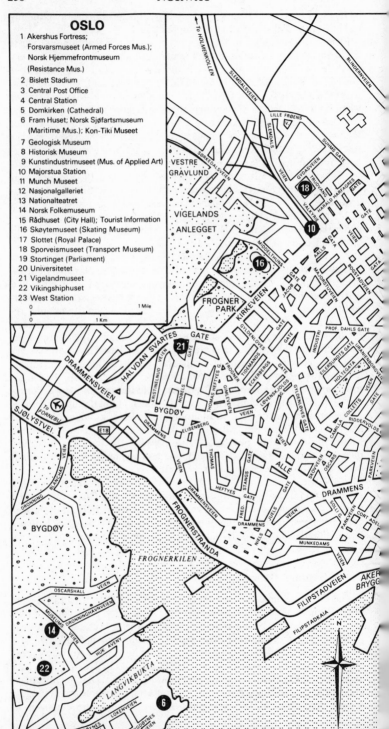

OSLO

1 Akershus Fortress;
Forsvarsmuseet (Armed Forces Mus.);
Norsk Hjemmefrontmuseum
(Resistance Mus.)
2 Bislett Stadium
3 Central Post Office
4 Central Station
5 Domkirken (Cathedral)
6 Fram Huset; Norsk Sjøfartsmuseum
(Maritime Mus.); Kon-Tiki Museet
7 Geologisk Museum
8 Historisk Museum
9 Kunstindustrimuseet (Mus. of Applied Art)
10 Majorstua Station
11 Munch Museet
12 Nasjonalgalleriet
13 Nationalteatret
14 Norsk Folkemuseum
15 Rådhuset (City Hall); Tourist Information
16 Skøytemuseet (Skating Museum)
17 Slottet (Royal Palace)
18 Sporveismuseet (Transport Museum)
19 Stortinget (Parliament)
20 Universitetet
21 Vigelandmuseet
22 Vikingshiphuset
23 West Station

0 _____ 1 Mile
0 _____ 1 Km

perhaps not surprisingly on Norwegian works from 1800 onwards, there are also many works dating from the Renaissance to the 19th century by both Norwegian and foreign artists. However, perhaps the highlight of the collection are the paintings by Edvard Munch, by some way Norway's most famous and influential painter. In spite of its all round excellence, however, the National Gallery, in common with many leading museums around the world, is severely handicapped by a lack of display space. The modern collections in particular have long been crammed into inadequate galleries. But the gallery's modern works were moved to a new home in the adjacent Bank of Norway's old building at the end of 1987, which by a happy coincidence was also the gallery's 150th anniversary. The building is now an independent Museum of Modern Art.

Back to back with the National Gallery is the Historical Museum, containing the University's collection of antiquities. Of particular interest is the fine display of Viking artefacts, especially jewelry. And a visit here is a useful supplement to one to the Viking ships at Bygdøy (of which more later) on the other side of the harbor.

Finally, continue up St. Olavs Gate, which runs diagonally away from the entrance to the Historical Museum, to the fascinating Museum of Applied Art, or Kunstindustrimuseum. Here you'll find furniture, silver, china, clothes—in short all the bric a brac and clutter that help bring the past alive—from the middle ages to the present, displayed against an imaginative background of music from each period. The emphasis is on Norwegian artefacts, but there are also sizeable collections from other lands, including the Far East.

Toward the Harbor

Having by now explored much of the center of the city, head down toward the harbor and the Akershus Fortress, Oslo's most ancient and historic building. The long, low bulk of the Fortress was built by King Haakon V in the early-14th century and has seen much violent military activity during its troubled life. It's an impressive building, by turns gloomy and romantic, with many spires and unexpected jutting roofs. As befits its military status, the Nazis used it as their headquarters during their occupation of Oslo in the war, and appropriately the Fortress today houses the excellent Hjemmefrontmuseum (Resistance Museum) which graphically and imaginatively charts the progress of the occupation from 1940–45, and the heroic efforts of Norway's Resistance. The fortress also contains a stone monument honoring the memory of those Norwegians who were executed by the Nazis.

Visit the State Apartments here—tours, in English, by guides dressed in period costume—or take in one of the Sunday lunch-time concerts in the chapel. Alternatively, you may just like to wander around the attractive grounds and along the ramparts, from where there is a magnificent view over the harbor and the city. Just outside, and to the east of the Fortress is the Forsvarsmuseet (Armed Forces Museum), latest addition to Oslo's museums. It too is well worth a visit for those with a military turn of mind.

From Akershus, it is no more than a few minutes' walk, past the martial figure pointing out to sea (an impressive statue of one Peter Wessel Tordenskiold, Admiral of the Danish/Norwegian fleet from 1715–20) to the red-brick Rådhuset (City Hall), its twin blunt towers looming over Rådhusplass. Outside, on the harbor side, you'll find another statue, F.D.R. in fact, holding a copy of the Atlantic Charter. The statue was unveiled by his wife Eleanor in 1950.

The main entrance to the City Hall is on the opposite side of the building, away from the harbor. But there's a second entrance on this, the harbor side which leads to the Tourist Information office. (Similarly, city sightseeing buses leave from this side, as do the sightseeing boats from the quays just across the road). But walk around to the principal entrance on the city side. It's well worth having a look inside at the massive central hall and the other rooms—the council chamber, the anterooms and the Munch room—open to the public. The whole of the interior is commandingly impressive, but by far and away the most eye-catching features are the murals, some 2,000 square feet in all, illustrating aspects of life in and around the city. They were produced during the '30s and '40s, but the building wasn't finished until 1950—work on the City Hall actually began in 1930 but had to be suspended during the war—and not surprisingly many of them, notably that on the left hand wall of the central hall, also deal with the Nazi occupation. Some may find them gaudy and rather wooden, as well as being perhaps a little dated, but they are undeniably impressive for all that. For those who wish, there are guides on hand to show you around.

The latest attraction is Aker Brygge, only a few minutes away from the City Hall, by the harbor. In this new shopping and leisure center are a myriad of small cafés and ethnic restaurants, both indoor and outdoor, as well as several theaters and restaurants.

The Environs of Oslo

To some extent, one can fairly claim that the principal attractions outside Oslo proper are, quite simply, the hills, forests and fjords that encroach so closely on the city and are so distinct a feature of life here. But there are also five specific places of interest outside the city, none of which should be missed by anyone intent on doing justice to a visit here. These are: the Frogner Park, northwest of the city; Bygdøy, just across the fjord from the harbor; Holmenkollen, north of the city; and two museums, the Henie-Onstad Art Center, overlooking the Oslo fjord at Høvikodden, and the Munch Museum to the northeast.

Frogner, or Vigeland, Park (easily reached by tram no. 2, or bus nos. 72 and 73 from the National Theater) contains perhaps the most startling sight in Oslo. This is the 60-foot high monolith, carved from a single block of stone weighing in at 200 tons, by the sculptor Gustav Vigeland (1869–1943). But as well as the monolith, the park, which was also designed by Vigeland, contains a further 650 statues by the sculptor which took him a total of 40 years to complete and which combine to illustrate and illuminate Vigeland's central theme: the cycle of life. Thus the entire park and its accompanying statues chart man's birth, growth and inevitable decay, the whole climaxed by the giant monolith. As you walk around the park, starting at the imposing bronze gates, you follow the progress of man's life, beginning naturally with birth and progressing through childhood, adolescence, maturity, old age and death. In addition, there is a massive fountain supported by six monumental figures symbolizing man's burden. Further evidence of Vigeland's prolific output is provided by the adjoining Vigeland Museum. (There is a good open-air restaurant here to revive those whose spirits may have flagged after confronting Vigeland's work in the raw). The museum contains 1,650 sculptures, 12,000 sketches and 3,700 woodcuts, all the work of this indefatigable artist.

Opinions have long been divided as to the artistic merit of Vigeland's work. Certainly, it is hard to see Vigeland's output as part of any wider European movements or schools. Nonetheless the park as a whole can have an overwhelmingly powerful impact and many visitors have commented that it provided the high point of their stay here. See it for yourself and make up your own mind. A large outdoor swimming pool is just one of its many attractions.

The museums at Bygdøy, however, present no such problems. They're easily reached by ferry from in front of the City Hall in summer, or by half-hourly bus (no. 30 or 30X) from the side of the National Theater. The most conspicuous of the buildings at Bygdøy is not actually a museum at all; rather, it's a huge tent-like structure (the traditional shape of a Viking boathouse)—known as the Framhuset —housing the sturdy little polar ship *Fram.* Actually, "little" is possibly a misleading term—the *Fram* is by no means a large vessel, even by the standards of her day (she was built in 1892), but housed in her permanent enclosed dry dock she appears positively massive. She was built for Fritjof Nansen, earliest of the many remarkable Norwegian polar explorers of the late-19th and early-20th centuries, for his three-year drift across the permanently frozen waters surrounding the North Pole. She was subsequently used by Otto Sverdrup on his journey to map the west coast of Greenland, and then to take Roald Amundsen on the first leg of his successful journey to the South Pole in 1911. She has been beautifully preserved and the visitor can clamber all over this most famous of polar vessels. Outside, you will find another famous Norwegian polar ship, even smaller than the *Fram.* This is the *Gjoa,* built originally as a fishing boat, and subsequently used by Amundsen on his discovery of the Northwest Passage (1903–6). Like the *Fram,* the *Gjoa* spent over three years gripped in the ice of the Arctic making her slow way across the roof of the world, eloquent proof of the skills of Norwegian shipwrights. Visitors are not, unfortunately, allowed on board.

A harpoon's throw from the *Fram* building is Oslo's Sjøfartsmuseum, or Maritime Museum. It's excellently laid out and graphically charts Norway's illustrious seafaring traditions and triumphs from the Vikings to the present day. The museum contains a veritable treasure chest of models, pictures, nautical bric-a-brac, even the interior of a passenger ship from the early years of this century. An interesting annex contains a number of actual vessels, from early fishing boats to a beautifully built and finished Olympic sailing dinghy. There's a good restaurant and cafeteria in the museum (in summer the cafeteria moves outside).

Opposite the Maritime Museum is the third in this trio of nautical haunts, the Kon-Tiki Museum, home of Thor Heyerdahl's famous balsa wood raft of the same name in which he caught the imagination of the world by sailing over 5,000 miles from Peru to Polynesia in 1947. The raft, never presumably too sturdy at the best of times, is showing its age somewhat these days, but is still an impressive sight. Underneath it there's an interesting and convincing mock up of the many different types of fish that congregated under its frail balsa wood timbers during the crossing, including a splendid whale shark, almost as long as the raft itself. The museum also houses *Ra II,* the papyrus boat in which Heyerdahl sailed from Morocco to Barbados in 1970, again in an attempt to prove that ancient man undertook long ocean crossings.

A little inland from the three museums is an equally impressive museum celebrating Norway's maritime exploits, though of a very much earlier period—the Vikingshiphuset or Viking Ship Museum. The museum is some 15 minutes' walk from the Maritime Museum, but well signposted and easy to find. (Coming from the city, the no. 30 or 30X bus stops right outside). Opened in 1936, it houses three remarkable and very beautiful Viking ships dating from A.D. 800–900, all discovered at the turn of the century. Almost as interesting as the vessels themselves are the various artefacts which were found on board, for these were burial ships, buried with Viking chieftains and intended to serve them in the next world as they had in this. Thus the ships were piled high with the goods and chattels of the chieftains, all of which have helped to build our remarkably complete picture of Viking life.

Finally, visit the immense Norsk Folkemuseum, the Norwegian Folk Museum, located just up the road from the Viking ships. Principally an outdoor museum (though no more than a couple of miles from the city center, the museum is practically in the country), it contains some 150 original wooden farmhouses and other buildings from all over Norway, many dating from the middle ages, that have been reassembled here. The chief treasure is one of Norway's unique stave churches, its roofs piled high like a pagoda, dating from the 13th century.

The museum was founded originally in 1894 and moved to Bygdøy in 1902 under the patronage of King Oscar II when the king's collection, which included the stave church, was added. Over the years, collections from other museums have also been transferred here. As well as the buildings themselves, the museum has an extensive collection of interiors, notably Ibsen's study, preserved exactly as it was when he lived in Oslo. There are goings-on galore at the museum in summer, especially on Sundays when there are displays of folk dancing, puppet shows, movies, handicraft demonstrations and lectures.

Up to Holmenkollen

The next excursion out of Oslo will take you in a completely different direction, northwest out of the city in fact and up into the hills to Holmenkollen and the Tryvannshøgda observation tower. Board any Frognerseter/Holmenkollen suburban train (T-bane) from the Nationaltheateret station and disembark at Holmenkollen. (If you want to stop at the observation tower first, get off at Frognerseter and walk up—it takes about 15 minutes. Holmenkollen will be visible, and from the tower at Tryvannshøgda, it is a 20-minute downhill walk.)

Norway is generally regarded as the home of modern skiing and no single place played a more significant role in its development than Holmenkollen. Indeed, to many Norwegians, Holmenkollen possesses a near-mystic significance and is regarded almost as a symbol of Norway. This reverence reaches a peak during the annual Holmenkollen championships, normally held in March. They have been held every year since the beginning of the century—except during World War II—and grip the attention of the entire nation. The King—no mean ski jumper himself in his youth—is one of the staunchest supporters. For the visitor, however, the principal attraction of Holmenkollen is the ski jump itself, a towering ramp stretching skywards down which the intrepid jumpers (once you've seen the jump, you may not think "intrepid" quite strong enough an adjective) hurtle before hurling themselves into space. If you've got a head for heights, take the elevator to the top of the tower—the view is predictably sensational.

Blasted into the rock by the side of the jump is the little ski museum—there's a statue of Nansen outside—which illustrates the development of skiing in Norway. Highlights of the museum are a ski over 2,500 years old and a display of polar equipment used by Nansen and Amundsen on their journeys to the North and South Poles respectively (including a phlegmatic stuffed dog taken—before it was stuffed—to the South Pole).

Finally, walk down the hill again from the jump to the Holmenkollen Park Hotel, a matter of 200 yards or so, to have a look at this marvelous late 19th-century building. It's been substantially renovated and a brand new annex added, but the original wooden building, with its multitude of projecting balconies, gables and overlapping roofs, has been lovingly preserved. The hotel has a variety of cafés and restaurants, though all are pricey. Less expensive refreshments are available at the Holmenkollen restaurant a little further down the hill, where you can sit on the terrace and enjoy the view in rather more comfort than from the top of the ski jump. The tram station for the ride back into town is located just below the restaurant.

Our final two excursions—to the Munch Museum and the Henie-Onstad Senteret, the Henie-Onstad Art Center—will not take you far from the city center, but are nonetheless well outside the downtown area.

The Munch Museum lies to the northeast of the city and can be reached by subway from Jernbanetorget in front of the Sentralstasjon to Tøyen (any train) or by bus (no. 29) from the City Hall, again to Tøyen. Edvard Munch (1863–1944) is the only Norwegian painter who can be claimed to have exercised a decisive influence on the wider European stage, and his work—tormented and expressionist—remains hugely popular today. The museum, opened in 1963, the centenary of the artist's birth, is thus a fitting memorial to Norway's most famous painter. It includes all those works—some 22,000 in all—in the artist's possession at the time of his death, all of which he left to the city. Needless to say, it is not possible to display anything more than a small fraction of this vast collection at any one time, so the exhibits are changed regularly, making repeated visits here a pleasure (though the most important works are generally on view at all times). But as well as Munch's work, the museum also holds regular exhibitions of works by other artists and presents lectures, concerts and films. Guided tours in English are available. The museum has undergone a lot of alterations in order to display a larger collection of Munch's paintings.

Across the street from the Museum are the Natural History museums and the Botanical Gardens, the latter an oasis on a hot summer's day. There is also a large open-air swimming pool close by.

Finally, visit the Henie-Onstad Art Center, 20 minutes west from the National Theater by bus no. 32 or buses 151, 161, 162, 252 or 261 from Universitetplassen, overlooking the fjord at Høvikodden. It's a modern art center in the widest sense. At the heart of the complex is the collection of 20th-century paintings donated by ice skater Sonja Henie and Niels Onstad, her husband. But the center also puts on concerts, film shows, the-

ater, ballet, lectures and the like. A good cafeteria and restaurant complete
the picture.

PRACTICAL INFORMATION FOR OSLO

GETTING TO TOWN FROM THE AIRPORT. There is a regular bus service
(every 15 minutes) from Oslo airport (Fornebu) stopping at the Scandinavia Hotel
(opposite the Royal Palace) and at the Central Station; cost is NOK 20 and journey
time is around 15 minutes; to/from Gardemoen airport, NOK 50, journey time
50 mins. There are also city buses from the airport which cost around NOK 15.
A taxi from the airport to the city center will run about NOK 80 to NOK 100.

TOURIST INFORMATION. The city tourist office is located in the City Hall
on Rådhusplassen (harbor side), Oslo 1 (414863). They can supply information on
all aspects of the city from sightseeing trips to renting bicycles. In addition, they
publish annually the *Oslo Guide,* which gives details of hotels, museums, restaurants
etc., in the city, and the monthly *Oslo This Week,* which lists all current activities
in the city. The excellent-value *Oslo Card* is also available from the tourist office.
Valid for one, two or three days and costing 75, 110 and 140 NOK, respectively,
the card gives unlimited free travel on all public transport within the city and free
entry to all museums, as well as discounts on many sightseeing buses and boats
and car hire, and special rates in some restaurants. It also entitles you to free parking on any city-owned parking lot. (The Oslo Card is also available from hotels,
travel agents, larger stores and branches of the ABC Bank in the city center.)
The City Hall tourist office is open May 15 through Sept. 15, Mon. to Sat.
8.30–7, Sun. 9–5; Sept. 16 through May 14, Mon. to Fri. 8.30–4, Sat. 8.30–
2.30; closed Sun. There is a second tourist office in the Sentralstasjon (at
the eastern end of Karl Johans Gate), tel. 02–416221. It is open daily 8
A.M.–11 P.M. This office also helps tourists find accommodations. The *Lands-
laget for Reiselivet: Norge* (Norwegian Travel Association), Langkai 1,
Oslo 1 (02–427044), is a good place for long-distance travel inquiries. All
these offices close on national holidays.

USEFUL ADDRESSES. Travel Agents. *Winge Reisebureau* (agent for American Express), Karl Johansgt. 33/35 (412030). *Bennett Reisebureau,* Karl Johansgt,
3 (209090). *Mytravel International,* Karl Johansgt, 35 (412030). *Berg-Nansen Reisebureau,* Arbiensgt 3 (591901).
Embassies. *U.S. Embassy,* Drammensveien 18 (448550). *Canadian Embassy,*
Oscarsgate 20 (466955). *British Embassy,* Ths Heftyesgate 8 (552400).
Car Hire. *Avis,* Munkedamsveien 27 (410060). *Europcar,* Fredensborgveien 33
(202150). *Hertz,* Wergelandsvn 1 (205212).
All the leading car hire companies also have desks at Fornebu airport.

TELEPHONE CODES. The telephone code for Oslo is 02. To call any number
in this chapter, unless otherwise specified, this prefix must be used. Within the city,
no prefix is required.

HOTELS. Oslo is well supplied with hotels in all price ranges, many offering
excellent-value special deals at all times of year. For example, from the end of June
to early August, 23 Oslo hotels give substantial discounts and this offer is also valid
at weekends all year round. Similarly, two children under 15 can stay in their parents' room at no extra charge. Full details of all Oslo hotels are given in the tourist
office's *Oslo Guide.*
The tourist office also runs an accommodations office at the Central Station for
hotels, pensions and rooms in private houses. You must, however, apply in person

at the office and no advance bookings will be taken. There is a fee of 10 NOK, NOK 5 for will be refunded when you check in. This office is open daily, 8 A.M.–11 P.M. Closed national holidays.

Deluxe

Ambassadeur. Camilla Collettsvei 15 (441835). 50 beds. Near Royal Palace, with indoor pool and sauna. AE, DC, MC, V.

Bristol. Kristian IV's Gate (415840). 220 beds, all rooms with bath. Quietly located on a side street, the Bristol has an excellent restaurant, the *Bristol Grill,* while *El Toro* is a Spanish restaurant with dancing and floor shows. There is also the *Leopard Grill,* plus a nightclub and disco on the second floor. The *Trafalgar* bar, the *Library* bar and the *Winter Garden* complete the picture. AE, MC, V.

Continental. Stortinsgate 24/26 (419060). 304 beds, all rooms with bath. Opposite the National Theater and with view of the Royal Palace. Its *Annen Étage* restaurant is one of the most elegant in Oslo, and produces excellent food. The *Loftet* is a beer and wine restaurant with billiards and disco. There is also the *Tivoli* grill, a modern and inexpensive restaurant, and the *Continental* bar near the lobby. However, of outstanding interest is the *Theatercaféen* on the ground floor, an elegant and hardly changed late-19th-century meeting place much frequented by Oslo high society and media folk. AE, DC, MC, V.

Gabelshus Hotel. Gabelsgt 16 (55 22 60). 85 rooms, all with bath. Only 5 mins. from city center in quiet street, this hotel is more like a large country house. Good restaurant, spacious bedrooms.

Grand. Karl Johansgate 31 (429390). 525 rooms, all with bath or shower and all with color T.V. On Oslo's main street and opposite Parliament and city park. Indoor pool, sauna and solarium. The *Speilen* restaurant is Oslo's most exclusive and has dancing; but the hotel's other restaurants include the *Étoile,* for French cuisine, the *Palmen,* a sandwich buffet, and the *Fritzner* grill, a top-grade spot. The *Grand Café* is a famous Oslo rendezvous, where Ibsen had his permanent chair, and with murals depicting life in late-19th-century Oslo; the *Bonanza* is a restaurant and nightclub with a Western theme. AE, DC, MC, V.

SAS Park Royal Hotel. Fornebuparken, 1324 Lysaker (120220). 500 beds, 10 suites, all with bath. Located near the airport; ten minutes from center. Restaurant seating 230, bar, sauna, fitness room, tennis, direct check-in to airport, executive office for hire; ample parking spaces. AE, DC, MC, V.

Expensive

Europa. St. Olavsgate 31 (209990). 285 beds, all rooms with bath and color T.V. Centrally located and modern. Special reductions for children. DC, MC, V.

Fønix. Dronningensgate 19 (425957). 98 beds, most rooms with bath or shower. Restaurant and bar—wine and beer only. Located near Central Station. AE, MC, V.

Gyldenløve. Bogstadveien 20 (601090). 30 beds. Bed and breakfast only, no alcohol. AE, MC, V.

Holmen Fjord. Slemmestadvn. 64, 1360 Nesbru (847280). 108 beds. 20 minutes west of Oslo on E18. Right on waterside with marina, sailboats, motor boats and windsurfboards for hire. Trim room, sports facilities, restaurant, nightclub.

Holmenkollen Park. Kongeveien 26 (146090). 278 rooms., all with bath and most with balconies. Magnificent old Norse-style building overlooking the city and located by the Holmenkollen ski jump. Luxurious annex added in 1981, but the original log-cabin part of the building remains the chief attraction. Facilities include gourmet restaurant, coffee shop, bar and nightclub, indoor pool, whirlpool, sauna, gym, squash court, curling rink and parking for 90 cars. AE, DC, MC, V.

KNA Park Avenue Hotel. Parkveien 68 (446970). 289 beds, all rooms with bath or shower. Run by the Royal Norwegian Automobile Club. Intimate restaurant and bar, and good bistro. AE, DC, MC, V.

Nobel. Karl Johansgate 33 (427 80). 148 beds., most rooms with bath or shower. On Oslo's main street, with bistro and bar. Special summer rates. Good restaurant. AE, DC, MC, V.

Rica Oslofjord. PO Box 160, 1330 Sandvika (545700). 486 beds, all rooms with bath, T.V., etc. 7 km. (4 miles) from Fornebu airport, 15 km. (9 miles) from center of Oslo. Shuttle bus. Restaurants, nightclub, bar. All rooms around marble atrium. Local bus and train services to center. AE, DC, MC, V.

Ritz. Fr. Stangsgate 3 (443960). 90 beds. Hotel and pension; with restaurant. Attractive place in quiet side street. 7-minute tram ride from center. AE, DC, MC, V.

Sara. Gunnerusgate 11–13 (429410). 464 beds, 100 rooms with bath. Opposite Central Station. *Crystal Garden* restaurant has both Scandinavian and international menus. *Glamrik* pub has Viking-style decor; coffee shop. DC, MC, V.

Savoy. Universitetsgate 11 (202655). 105 beds. Near the National Gallery; with restaurant. AE, DC, MC, V.

Scandic. Drammensveien, 1322 Høvik (121740). 230 beds, all rooms with bath or shower. At Høvik, 6 km. (4 miles) west of city on E18. Restaurant, cafeteria, sauna, parking. AE, MC, V.

Standard. Pilestredet 27 (203555). 72 beds. With restaurant. MC, V.

Stefanhotellet. Rosenkranzgate 1 (429250). 200 beds, all rooms with bath or shower. Centrally located, with popular 8th-floor restaurant—no alcohol but a superb lunch buffet, including traditional sour cream porridge eaten with smoked meats. AE, MC, V.

Triangel Hotel. Holbergs plass (208855). 192 beds, 103 rooms with bath or shower. Fully renovated in 1984. À la carte and buffet restaurant. Garage. No alcohol. AE, V.

West. Skovveien 15 (554030). 76 beds, all rooms with bath or shower. Renovations completed in 1987. Ideally located in West End near the Palace. Good restaurant; fully licensed. DC, MC, V.

Moderate

Anker Stiftelsens Yrkesskolens Hybelhus. Storgata 55 (114005). 500 beds, many rooms with 4 beds. Centrally located, with cooking facilities, supermarket, cafeteria, and restaurant. Open May to Aug. only. AE, DC, MC, V.

Bondeheimen. Rosenkrantzgate 8 (429530). 135 beds, all rooms with bath or shower. Located in a side street off Karl Johansgate in city center. Some family rooms. Cafeteria, no alcohol. Disabled access. AE, DC, MC, V.

Majorstuen. Bogstadun 64 (693495). 80 beds, all rooms with bath or shower. Friendly restaurant and pub—wine and beer only. Located in the busy shopping area of Oslo west. Reached by metro from the National Theater to Majorstuen. AE, DC, MC, V.

Munch. Munchsgate 5 (424275). 225 beds, all rooms with bath or shower. Restaurant with wine and beer. Located in pleasant surroundings near the Munch Museum in Oslo east. Disabled access. AE, DC, MC, V.

Norrøna. Grensen 19 (426400). 61 beds. With cafeteria, but no alcohol. AE, DC, MC, V.

Norum. Bygdøy Alle 53 (447990). 90 beds, all rooms with bath. In residential area west of the city center; bistro with good food. AE, DC, MC, V.

Inexpensive

Bella Vista. Årrundundveien 11B (654588). 18 beds, all rooms with bath or shower. Self-catering.

Blindern Studenthjem. Blindernveien 41 (461281). 300 beds, all rooms with bath or shower. Cafeteria. Located to the northwest of city center. Students' residence in winter.

Youth Hostel

Haraldsheim Youth Hostel, Haraldsheimvn 4 (155043). 4 km. (2½ miles) from city center, with 300 beds, family rooms, restaurant, lounge, T.V. Great views across Oslofjord. Take tram 1 from National Theater to Sinsen. Closed Christmas week.

Camping

Bogstad Camp and Tourist Center, Ankerveien 117, (507680). Open all year. Take bus 41 to Bogstad. Situated by large lake in scenic surroundings. Windsurfing, swimming a few mins. from Holmenkollen.

Ekeberg Camping, (198568). 3 km. (just under 2 miles) from city center. Open June 20 to Aug. 20. Bus 24 from Jernbanetorget or 74 from Parliament.

Stubljan Camping, (612706). Bus 75 to Ingierstrand from Oslo S.

HOW TO GET AROUND. By bus and tram. The bus and tram network is generally good. The heart of the network is by the National Theater in the city center. All stops here give details of schedules, but details are also available from the tourist office. There is a flat fare of NOK 12 for all journeys, but there is an "inner circle" ticket, NOK 6, for a limited area in the center. A number of good-value discount tickets are available. Best of all is the *Oslo Card* (available from the tourist office) which gives unlimited free travel on all public transport for one, two or three days at a cost of NOK 75, 110, and 140 respectively (children half price). The *Oslo Card* also entitles you to free admission to museums, discounts on car rentals and in certain restaurants, and on sightseeing tours. Alternatively, there is a *Tourist Ticket,* again available from the tourist office, which gives 24 hours' unlimited travel on all public transport for 30 NOK. (children half price). There are also two multi-journey tickets called *maxikort* and *minikort.* The first, costing NOK 120, gives you 14 coupons, each entitling you to one hour's travel with unlimited transfers. The second, costing NOK 40, contains four coupons. Both are half price for children.

By metro. The Oslo metro, currently divided into eastern and western sectors— the western sector radiating from the National Theater and the eastern sector from Stortinget—was linked in 1986. A single ticket, valid for one hour and no transfers costs NOK 12. But the Oslo Card is also good for metro travel. The most important line for most visitors is that from the National Theater to the Frognerseter station on the Holmenkollen line high above the city. But the metro services, some supplemented by electric trains, also extend into the suburbs.

By taxi. Cabs are expensive but numerous. They can be hailed in the street if the light on the roof is on, as long as they are more than 100 yards from the rank, but there are also cab stands at the Central and West rail stations. Otherwise, call 388090 (or 388080 for an advance booking, at least 1 hour in advance). There is an additional charge for more than two passengers and at night. Tip around 10% of the fare.

By bicycle. The tourist office can supply lists of all places where bikes can be rented. Deposit NOK 200. Oslo, not least because of its small scale, is a delightful city to cycle around, though hilly in parts, and rides out into the country are easy to make.

On foot. The city is easily explored on foot and the tourist office can supply lists of suggested walks.

TOURS. *H.M. Kristiansen* provides three tours, all lasting three hours, and all starting from the City Hall harbor side. Tickets are available on the bus or from the Oslo Tourist Information Office. The "Oslo Highlights" morning tour goes to the Vigeland Sculpture Park, Holmenkollen, the Viking Ship Museum, and the *Kon-Tiki.* May through Sept., daily at 10 A.M. NOK 100 adults, NOK 50 children. The "Morning Sightseeing" tour visits Akerhus Castle, Vigeland Sculpture Park, the Munch Museum, and Holmenkollen. Apr. through Oct., daily at 10 A.M. NOK 100 adults, NOK 50 children. The "Afternoon Tour" goes to the Norwegian Folk Museum, Viking Ships, *Kon-Tiki,* and the Polar Ship *Fram.* Apr. through Oct., daily at 2.30 P.M. NOK 120.

The *Oslo Guide* brochure (free from the tourist office) has several walking tours on its map. Some go farther afield and link up with public transportation. Taxis also give sightseeing tours in English for a fee of NOK 200 per hour. Cal 02–388090 or 02–388000 to reserve a personal tour.

If you're allergic to crowds, you'll get a more authentic picture of life in Oslo's seaside suburbs by taking one of the regular passenger ferries that ply between the city and Nesodden. Travel by return boat, or get off at Nesodden to explore, and return by a later boat. Ferries start from Aker Brygge.

Or you can take the bus (starts from Grønlandstorg, but best entered outside the University), to Sundvollen, final destination Hønefoss. For the next hour you will see some of the most magnificent scenery to be found in the Oslo region as you wind and climb your way around the precipitous edges of the crystal blue Tyri Fjord. At Sundvollen you can walk up Dronningveien, or go by car, to the top of Krokkleiva with famous views from Kongens Utsikt (the King's View), one of the most beautiful in Norway. The walk is quite stiff (takes about 3 hours altogether). Alternatively, take the 36 bus to Jevnaker, where you can visit the Hadeland Glass Works, the largest of its kind in Scandinavia. Founded in 1762, the work is still performed by craftsmen and visitors may see glassblowing, cutting and etching of crystal.

Blaafarvevaerket, a former cobalt works, at Åmot, is also worth a visit, and is best reached by car or sightseeing bus. Open late May through late Sept., Mon. to Sat. 10–8.

English language guides are available from tourist office. All guides are licensed.

MUSEUMS. Most cities in the world have museums of the traditional kind, and Oslo has its share—but in addition, Oslo has a series of unique museums, particularly its "one man" and "one ship" museums.

Barnekunst Museet (International Children's Art Museum). Lille Frogner Alle 4. Children's art—drawings, paintings, ceramics, tapestries and handicrafts collected from more than 100 countries. Children's workshop. Open all year; closed Mon. and Thurs. Admission NOK 20, reduced rates for groups, families, children.

Forsvarsmuseet (The Norwegian Armed Forces Museum). Situated in the old arsenal building in the lower grounds of Akershus fortress. A new construction, when completed, will cover the history of Norwegian defence from the late Middle Ages to contemporary times. Open May through Sept., Mon., Wed., and Fri. 10–3, Tues. and Thurs. 10–8, Sat. 10–4; Oct. through Apr., Mon. to Fri. 10–3, Sat. 10–4, Sun. 11–4. Admission free.

Framhuset (The Polar Exploration Ship). *Fram* was built by the well-known designer Colin Archer for Nansen's Polar expedition 1893–96. It was also used by Otto Sverdrup 1889–1902, and later by Roald Amundsen on his expedition to the South Pole 1910–12. Open Mon. to Sat. 10–6, Sun. 11–6; closed in winter. Admission NOK 7.

Henie-Onstad Kunstsenter (The Sonja Henie-Niels Onstad Art Center). At Høvikodden, 11 km. (7 miles) from Oslo. The Center was opened in 1968 and contains a permanent collection of 20th-century art, donated by Sonja Henie and her husband Niels Onstad. Displays are changed regularly to reflect current trends and ideas in literature, film, dance, music, architecture and applied arts: other events like concerts are also staged here. Buses 32, 34, 36 and 37 leave regularly from the city center. Open all year Mon. to Fri. 9 A.M.–9.30 P.M., Sat. and Sun. 11–9.30. Admission NOK 20 adults, NOK 10 students, children, servicemen and senior citizens; NOK 40 family ticket.

Historisk Museum (The Historical Museum). Frederiksgate 2. Contains the University's Ethnographical Museum, Numismatic Collection and its Collection of Antiquities, Viking artefacts and jewelry. The collection from the Middle Ages is Oslo's richest art collection from that period. Open mid-Sept. through mid-May, Tues. to Sun. 12–3. Admission free.

Kon-Tiki Museet (The Kon-Tiki Museum). At Bygdøynes, the museum contains the raft on which Thor Heyerdahl and five companions drifted over 8,000 km. (5,000 miles) across the Pacific from Peru to Polynesia. It also houses the 14-meter (46-foot) reed boat *Ra II* and items belonging to it from Heyerdahl's 1970 expedition across the Atlantic Ocean. Open mid-May through Aug., daily 10–6; Sept. and

Oct., daily 10.30–5; Nov. through mid-May, daily 10.30–4. Admission NOK 10 adults, NOK 4 children, NOK 6 students, servicemen and senior citizens.

Kunstindustrimuseet (The Museum of Applied Art). St. Olavsgate 1. Collections of both Norwegian and foreign applied arts from the Middle Ages through to the 20th century. Displayed are furniture, silver, glass, ceramics and textiles. Of note is the Baldishol tapestry, woven in Hedmark in the 1180s, one of the five tapestries which have been preserved from the Romanesque era. Open all year Tues. to Fri. 11–3, Sat. and Sun. 12–4; late opening Tues. 7 P.M.–9 P.M. Admission NOK 10 adults, NOK 5 students, servicemen and senior citizens, children free. Free admission in mid-winter.

Kunstnerforbundet (Artists Association). Kjeld Stubsgate 3. Contemporary Norwegian art, also handicrafts. Open July through Aug., Mon. to Fri. 10–4, Sat. 10–2; Sept. through June, Mon. to Fri. 10–5, Sat. 10–3, Sun. 12–4.

Kunstnernes Hus (Artists' Center). Wergelandsveien 17. Changing exhibitions of contemporary Norwegian and foreign paintings, sculpture and prints. Open Tues. to Fri. 10–6, Sat. and Sun. 12–4; closed Mon. Admission NOK 10 adults, NOK 5 children.

Munch-Museet (The Munch Museum). Tøyengaten 53. In 1940 Edvard Munch bequeathed the City of Oslo many of his works; paintings, drawings, water colours, prints and sculptures, books, letters and private papers. The collection has been increased by gifts from individuals. Lectures and concerts. Guided tours available. Open Tues. to Sat. 10–8, Sun. 12–8; closed Mon. Admission free during low season (mid-Sept. to mid-May); mid-May to mid-Sept. admission NOK 10.

Nasjonalgalleriet (The National Gallery). Universitetsgaten 13. Norway's largest public collection, with emphasis on Norwegian painting, sculpture and lithographs. Also has a collection of French and modern European paintings. Open Mon. to Fri. 10–4, Sat. 10–3, Sun. 12–3; late opening Wed. and Thurs. 6 P.M.–8 P.M. Admission free.

De Naturhistoriske Museet (Natural History Museum). Sarsgata 1. Botanical garden and conservatories, mineralogical and geological museum, paleontological museum with fossil plants and animals, and zoological museum. Botanical gardens open May through Aug., Mon. to Fri. 7 A.M.–8 P.M., Sat. and Sun. 10–8; Oct. through Dec., Mon. to Fri. 7–7, Sat. and Sun. 10–7; Jan. through Mar., Mon. to Fri. 7–5, Sat. and Sun. 10–5; Apr., Mon. to Fri. 7–6, Sat. and Sun. 10–6. All other museums open all year, Tues. to Sun. 12–3, except the Botanical Museum which is open Wed. to Sat. 12–3.

Norsk Arkitektmuseum (Norwegian Architecture Museum). Josefinesgt. 32. Alternating exhibitions. Library. Open Mon. to Fri. 9–3; closed Sat. and Sun. Admission free.

Norsk Folkemuseum (The Norwegian Folk Museum). Museumsveien 10 Bygdøy. Outdoor collection of 170 buildings, including 13th-century stave church. Indoor collection designed to illustrate Norway's urban and rural culture. Henrik Ibsen's study, a Lapp (Sami) collection and a pharmacy museum are also to be seen here. In summer: restaurant, folk dancing, concerts. Open mid-May through Aug., Mon. to Sat. 10–6, Sun. 11–6; Sept., Mon. to Sat. 11–4, Sun. 12–5; Oct. through mid-May, Mon. to Sat. 11–4, Sun. 12–3. Admission NOK 20 adults (NOK 10 in winter), NOK 10 children (NOK 4 in winter).

Norsk Hjemmefrontmuseum (Norway's Resistance Museum). Situated in an old building in the grounds of Akershus Fortress, close to the monument to patriots who gave their lives in World War II. Attempts to give a true picture of major events in Norway during the German occupation. Lecture hall, library, war publication archives. Open May through Sept., Mon. to Sat. 10–4, Sun. 11–4; Oct. through Apr., Mon. to Sat. 10–3, Sun. 11–4. Admission NOK 10.

Norsk Sjøfartsmuseum (The Norwegian Maritime Museum). Bygdøynes. Contains a collection of boats used along the Norwegian coast, models of sailing ships and a model shipyard. Ocean navigation is presented through models, paintings and objects. Slide projectors, radar instruments, library, restaurants, cafeteria. Open May through Sept., daily 10–8; Oct. through Dec., Mon., Wed., Fri. and Sat. 10.30–4, Tues., Thurs. and Sun. 10.30–5; Mar. and Apr., Mon., Wed., Fri. and Sat. 10.30–

4, Tues. and Thurs. 10.30–8, Sun. 10.30–5. Admission NOK 10 adults, NOK 4 children.

Norsk Teknisk Museum (Norwegian Museum of Science & Industry). Kjelsåsvn. 143, (adjoining Frysja park). Vast exhibition halls displaying industrial and technical development in Norway right up to the space age. Telecommunications exhibition with models. Open Tues. to Sun. 10–7; closed Mon. Admission NOK 10. Cafeteria, picnic area, swimming in Frysja park. Open mid-May through mid-Sept., Tues. to Sun. 10–7; mid-Sept. through mid-May, Tues. 10–7, Wed. to Sun. 10–4. Admission NOK 10 adults, NOK 5 children.

Oslo Bymuseum (The City Museum). Frognerveien 67. Situated in Frogner Hovedgård (Frogner Manor), built around 1790. Contains maps, portrait gallery, views of Oslo, rooms furnished as in former days. New display showing development of Oslo from Viking times to present day with models. Open May through Aug., Mon. to Fri. 10–6, Sat. and Sun. 11–5; Sept. through mid-Dec. and Jan. through Apr., Mon. to Fri. 10–4, Sat. and Sun. 11–4. Admission NOK 10 adults, NOK 5 children.

Oslo Kunstforening (Oslo Art Association). Rådhusgate 19. Situated in residence dating from 1626; exhibitions of paintings, sculpture, prints and etchings. Open Tues. to Fri. 11–5, Sat. 11–4, Sun. 12–4.

Postmuseet (Postal Museum). Dronningensgt. 15. Contains displays of stamps, postal accessories, and the development of communications over three centuries. Open Mon. to Fri. 10–3, Sat. 10–1; closed Sun. Admission free.

Skimuseet (The Ski Museum). Collections of skis, including the 2,500 year old Øvrebø ski and part of Nansen's and Amundsen's polar equipment. Shows history of skiing and ski jumping. A lift gives access to the 55–meter (180–foot) tower, which has a magnificent view. Open Apr., daily 10–3; May, daily 10–5; June, daily 10–7; July through mid-Aug., daily 9 A.M.–10 P.M.; mid- to late Aug., daily 10–7; Sept., daily 10–5; Oct. through Dec., daily 10–3. Admission NOK 12 adults, inclusive ticket (museum, ski jump and observation tower) NOK 23, NOK 6 children, students and servicemen for museum only.

Skøytemuseet (Skating Museum). Frogner Stadium, entrance Middelthungsgt. Focus on Norwegian speed-skating champions. Open Wed. 6–8 P.M. and Sat. 12 noon–2 P.M., or by appointment (tel. 500993). Admission free.

Sporveismuseet (Transport Museum). Vognhall 5, Slemdalsvn. 1–3. Norway's only collection of veteran trams and buses. Pictures and artifacts connected with public transport. Open Sun. all year, 12–3; Apr. through Sept., Sat. also, 12–3. Admission NOK 10 adults, NOK 5 children.

Teatermuseet (Theater Museum). Nedre Slottsgt. 1. On second floor above Gamle Rådhus restaurant. Traces the development of Oslo's theater from the beginning of the 19th century up to 1950. It is situated in one of the oldest buildings in Oslo, built around 1600. Open Wed. 11–3, Sun. 12–4. Admission NOK. 5.

Vigelandmuseet (The Vigeland Museum). Nobelsgate 32. Formerly Gustav Vigeland's studio and residence. It contains 1,650 sculptures, 3,700 woodcuts, 423 plates for woodcuts and around 11,000 sketches. Concerts in summer. Guided tours. Open May through Oct., Tues. to Sat. 12–7; Nov. through Apr., Tues. to Sat. 1–7.

Vikingskiphuset (The Viking Ships and Archeological Finds). Huk Aveny 35, Bygdøy. Remarkable relics of the Viking Age, all found near the Oslo fjord. Open May through Sept. daily 10–6; Oct., daily 11–5; Nov. and Dec., daily 11–4; mid-Jan. through Mar., daily 11–3. Admission NOK 10 adults, NOK 5 children and students.

PARKS, ZOOS AND GARDENS. Botanisk Hage (Botanical Garden and Museum). Trondheimsveien 23. Hot houses, geological and zoological collections. Open Tues. to Sun. 12–3; closed Mon. Admission free.

Dyreparken Tusenfryd (Zoo). Located in the suburb of Ås. Opened in June 1988. Animals, funfair, minigolf, cafeteria. Open daily throughout the summer. Admission NOK 90 (children 70).

Frognerparken (The Vigeland Sculptures in Frogner Park). Gustav Vigeland's gigantic work—a world of people carved in granite, iron and bronze. Open-air swimming pool, cafeteria, sports arena, tennis courts, restaurants. Open 24 hours a day all year. Admission free.

Gamlebyen Ruiner in park with archeological excavations, part of the center of ecclesiastical affairs in medieval Oslo. Open summer only. Admission free.

Sørenga Ruiner. Ruins of the earliest buildings in Oslo: The Royal Palace and the Maria Church from approx. 1050. This was the king's center of power. Open summer only. Admission free.

HISTORIC BUILDINGS AND SITES. Akershus Slott og Festning (Akershus Castle). One of Oslo's most formidable buildings, first built by Haakon V around 1300. It was then rebuilt by Christian IV around 1620 and has subsequently been restored and redecorated. It contains the royal mausoleums, state apartments (16th cent.) and World War II Resistance Museum and the Armed Forces Museum. Open Mon. to Sat. 10–4, Sun. 12.30–4. Admission NOK 10.

Bogstad Gård (Bogstad Manor). Sørkedalen. Patrician manor built around 1760, once owned by prime minister Peder Anker. Landscaped garden and art treasures. Open mid-May through mid-Sept., Wed. 6–7, Sun. 12–5. Admission NOK 20 adults, NOK 5 children.

Damstredet. Picturesque wooden houses from early 19th century; many are today the homes of artists.

Domkirken (Oslo Cathedral). At Stortorvet. Built between 1694 and 1699, the exterior was restored in 1849–50. The interior was restored in 1949–50. Altar piece and pulpit from 1699. Concerts. Open Mon. to Fri. 10–3, Sat. 10–1; closed Sun. except divine service 11 and 7.30. Admission free.

Gamle Aker Kirke (Old Aker Church). Akersbakken 26. Built around 1100, this is the oldest stone church in Scandinavia still in use as parish church. Tues. and Thurs. 12–2, Sun. service 11. Admission free.

Hovedøya Klosterruiner (Monastery Ruins). Constructed by Cistercian Monks, who arrived from Kirkstead in England in 1147. Ferry from Vippetangen to open-air site. Admission free.

Konserthuset (Concert Hall). Johan Svendsens plass. Inaugurated 1977, designed by Gøsta Åbergh. Facade covered with polished light Tolga granite. Concert hall and chamber music hall. Concerts of all kinds. Open for touring by appointment. See daily press and *Oslo This Week*.

Ladegården (Oslo Ladegård). Oslogate 13. Medieval Bishop's residence. The ecclesiastic center of ancient Oslo, together with the St. Hallvard Church. Later the Mayor's residence then pleasure residence. The present Baroque building dates from the 17th century, with vaults from the Middle Ages. Restored by the City of Oslo 1957–68. Open May through Sept., Wed. 6–7, Sun. 1–2. Admission free.

Oscarshall. Bygdøy. Pleasure palace built in 1847–52 by King Oscar I of Norway and Sweden. Open June through Sept., Sun. 11–4. Admission NOK 5 adults, NOK 1 children.

Rådhuset (Oslo City Hall). Foundation stone laid in 1931, inaugurated in 1950 for the celebration of Oslo's 900th anniversary. Lavishly decorated by Norway's leading painters and sculptors during the 1930s and 40s. Guided tours available. Open Apr. through Sept., Mon. to Sat. 10–3, Sun. 12–3; Jan. through Mar., Mon. to Sat. 11–2, Sun. 12–3. Admission free.

Slottet (Royal Palace). Drammensveien 1. Constructed 1825–48. Residence of King Olav V, King of Norway. Public admitted to the park only. Changing of the guard takes places at 1.30 P.M. When the King is in residence the band of the Royal Guard plays Mon. to Fri.

Stortinget (Parliament). Karl Johansgt. Built 1861–66. Richly decorated by contemporary Norwegian artists. Open July through Aug., Mon. to Sat. 11–3. Guided tours July through mid-Sept. at 11, 12 and 1. Admission free.

Tryvannstårnet (Tryvann Observation Tower). The largest observation tower in the north, with an optical horizon covering about 30,044 sq. km. (11,600 sq. miles). It is situated on the Tryvann hill on the outskirts of Oslo. Lift, binoculars, refreshments, souvenirs. Reached by Holmenkollen Railway from the National Theater to Frognerseteren, then a 25-minute walk. Open Mar. through Apr., Tues. to Sun. 10–6; May, daily 10–8; June and July, daily 9.30 A.M.–10 P.M.; Aug., daily 10–8; Sept., daily 10–6; Oct., Tues. to Sun. 10–4; Nov. through Feb., Sat. and Sun. 10–4. Admission NOK 11. adults, NOK 6 children.

Universitetet (Oslo University). Karl Johansgt. 47. The *Aula* (Hall) of the University with murals by Edvard Munch. Open July, Mon. to Fri. 12–2, otherwise on request by calling 02–330070 ext. 756.

SPORTS. Swimming. There are excellent bathing beaches on both sides of the fjord, all easily reached by bus from the City Hall. Out at Bygdøy, there is a popular beach at Huk, plus one reserved for nudists. On the east side you'll find: Ingierstrand, Katten, Hvervenbukta, Ljanskollen and Bestemorstrand, all reached by bus 75. On the west side, Hvalstrand, Asker, reached by bus nos. 261, 252, half-an-hour from the center. Also good are the two adjoining islands of Langøyene, owned by the city and with good sandy beaches; take the ferry from pier 4. Water temperatures in July and August average about 68° F (20° C). There are a number of very popular swimming pools dotted around the city, of which the most popular are by the Vigeland sculpture park and at Tøyen by the Munch Museum.

Tennis. Courts are available at Frogner Stadium near Vigeland Park.

Fishing. Good trout fishing can be had in many places around the city. Permits are necessary but may be bought at the many sports shops in Oslo and in the fishing chalets of Kobberhaughytta, Kikutstua and Løvliseter, where fishermen can also stay overnight.

Golf. The Bogstad golf course is 10 km. (6 miles) from the city center, enjoys unrivalled surroundings, and offers excellent golf from May to October.

Winter Sports. The season runs from Christmas to the end of March. There is fine skiing country in the hills around the city. Although the emphasis is naturally on cross country rather than downhill skiing, there are many fine slalom hills in Oslo and environs. All the trails and runs around the city can easily be reached from the center of town, and many are also floodlit. Ski schools and ski rental companies are plentiful. In addition, there are a number of skating and curling rinks and tobogganing trails. Details of all from the tourist office.

MUSIC, MOVIES AND THEATERS. Music. The musical life of the Norwegian capital is impressive, to say the least. The Oslo Philharmonic is the city's principal orchestra and has achieved much renown under its conductor Mariss Jansons for its recordings of Tchaikovsky's symphonies. It has frequent visits from soloists and conductors of international fame. Concerts are normally held in the *Konserthuset,* the Oslo Concert Hall, at Ruseløkkveien, a modern and lavish building completed in 1977. As well as the main auditorium there is also a smaller hall for chamber music and folk dance performances in summer on Mon. and Thurs. at 9 P.M.

In addition to the orchestra, the city has a thriving opera and ballet company, whose season generally lasts from September to June. Performances are most usually given at the *Den Norske Opera,* Storgaten 21. But there are also some performances at the *Henie-Onstad Art Center* at Høvikodden. For details of performances, see *Oslo This Week.*

Movies. There are numerous movie theaters around town. See the daily press or ask at the tourist office to see what's playing and when. A wide range of American and British movies are shown. Films are always screened in their original language with Norwegian subtitles. Smoking is not permitted in Norwegian cinemas.

Theaters. Oslo's principal theater is the *Nationalteatret* at Stortingsgaten 15 in the heart of the city. The main stage has now been renovated after a backstage fire. Note, however, that it is not open during the summer. Performances are in Norwegian, naturally enough, making their appeal somewhat limited as far as foreign visitors are concerned. But if you know, say, an Ibsen play well, it may be worth the experience. In the same building is the little *Amfiscenen,* used for both classical drama and more experimental work.

Among Oslo's other leading theaters are the *ABC Teatret,* St. Olavs plass 1; *Det Norske Teatret,* Kristian IV's gt. 8, Norway's most modern theater, opened in 1985, which presents works in *Nynorsk* or "new" Norwegian; the *Oslo Nye Teater,* Rosenkrantzgt. 10, which presents predominantly comedies and musicals, though again principally in Norwegian; the *Dukketeatret* in the City Museum, the Bymuseet, at Frognerveien 67, a puppet theater and an excellent place for families and children; the *Centralteateret,* Akersgaten 38, presents plays for children and young people. At Aker Brygge you will find smaller theater companies performing. For details of all performances, check *Oslo This Week.*

Finally, there are performances of folk dancing throughout the summer. The best and most colorful are held on Sundays at the *Folk Museum* at Bygdøy, and at the *Oslo Concert Hall* during July & Aug., but there are also displays, which you can join in if the spirit so moves you, at *Bygdelagssamskipnaden,* Nordahl Brunsgate 22, in the winter.

SHOPPING. In Norway, as in the other Scandinavian countries, you will find evidence of the peasant heritage in handicrafts—ceramics and textile weaving, wood carving and decorative painting. As prices are controlled, you may as well shop in Oslo where you will have the greatest choice. About 20% is charged (included in the price) in Value Added Tax (VAT), which will be refunded to any visitor who spends more than NOK 300 in any one shop. Ask for a special tax-free cheque and show your passport. All articles purchased must be presented together with the required tax-free cheque at the tax-free service counter at ports, airports, and border posts. The VAT will then be refunded minus 4½% service charge.

Glasmagasinet, at Stortorget 10, and *Steen & Strøm,* at Koagensgate 23, are Oslo's foremost department stores. The quayside *Aker Brygge* stores stay open late, until 8 P.M. (7 P.M. on Thursdays).

Arts and Crafts. *Basarhalene (Bazaar Arcade),* behind Oslo Cathedral, is a center for applied art, open all year. Artists present their own work. *Forum,* Rosenkrantzgate 7 (opposite the Bristol Hotel), has permanent exhibitions of contemporary Norwegian arts and crafts. Each item on display must first be accepted by a jury.

A similar establishment is *Norway Designs,* Stortingsgate 28 (entrance from Roald Amundsengate), the capital's largest center for the exhibition and sale of top quality Norwegian applied art, with special facilities for export.

For the most indigenous Norwegian handicraft try *Husfliden* (Norwegian Association for Home Arts and Crafts), Møllergate 4, near the cathedral and just behind the *Glasmagasin* department store. A non-profit organization for preserving and continuing the traditions of Norwegian handicrafts and rustic culture, it offers a wide range of home industry products including the well-known knitted sweaters, woven tapestries, dolls in national costumes, woodcarvings, ceramics etc.

Pewter, Ceramics and Crystal. A great Norwegian specialty is its pewterware: sugar bowls and creamers, all sizes of trays and bowls, candlesticks and pitchers. With a light-finish technique, Gunnar Havstad has created the best contemporary works, whereas the Groseth pewter bears the marks of the heavy sandstone presses that formed them after the old English manner.

Tinnboden, Tordenskioldsgate 7, has a good selection, as well as a splendid array of dolls in colorful regional dresses. *Glasmagasin* Department Store has a good selection of all three.

These ceramics are perhaps more primitive than those you have found in Denmark and Sweden—the plates and bowls often thicker and embellished with peasant figures and symbols of the life they know. Norway's best-known porcelain factory is Porsgrund. Also outstanding are the pottery works at Egersund and Stavanger, and the Hadeland Glass Works. Their products, however, should be available in Oslo pottery and ceramics stores and in larger department stores. Since their production, though of top quality, cannot incorporate all the vigorous ideas of young creative innovators, the works of individual craftsmen are equally numerous. Originality and taste are the rule in even the most common art glass, ceramics, and porcelain.

For the very best in crystal and glass etching be sure to go to *Christiania Glasmagasin,* Stortorget 10. In the glass department here you will find distinguished modern glassware, amusing cocktail glasses, and exquisite art glass in a range of delectable colors.

Knitwear. All department stores have good stocks of traditional Norwegian sweaters, but certain specialist shops also have particularly fine designs. Among them are:

Heimen, Rosenkrantzgt. 8, with handknitted sweaters and mittens. They can also make up authentic Norwegian costumes—each valley has its own—to order.

The *Oslo Sweater Shop* is in the arcade under the Hotel Scandinavia; *Maurtua,* Fridjof Nansensplass, opposite the City Hall, has a wide range of knitwear and textiles; *Trønderstna,* Vikaterrace, also has textiles and knitwear and a good selection of wool and patterns. If you can't find what you're looking for in these shops, try *Steen and Strøm,* the largest department store in Oslo.

Sports Shops. In Oslo the sports lover comes into his own. *Gresvig Sports Shop,* Storgata 20, also *Christiania Glasmagasin* at Stortorget 10, are probably the best in town and, in this sportsman's paradise, that means a lot. Norwegian packs, flies for your fishing rod—or the rod itself—skis, any kind of sports equipment for use during your trek through the countryside or for shipment home (which *Gresvig's* will happily and efficiently handle for you) are featured here.

Norway's famous ski jumper, *Sigmund Ruud,* has a shop at Kirkeveien 57.

RESTAURANTS. Oslo is singularly blessed with great numbers of excellent restaurants, particularly at the top end of the scale. Similarly, many of the more expensive hotels also have first-class restaurants, details of which are given in the Hotel listings above. But bear in mind that expensive restaurants here are very expensive, even by Scandinavian standards, while even a quick bite at one of the fast food spots, of which there are many, will also cost significantly more than in the U.S. Alcohol, especially wine, is also extremely pricey in all restaurants, with a humble bottle of table wine costing upwards of $35. Be careful!

For fast food, try the city center, which has any number of pizza and hamburger joints and small trendy cafés much favored by the young. Likewise, both the *Steen & Strøm* and *Glasmagasin* department stores have several restaurants featuring lunch buffets, ranging from the inexpensive to something a little more elaborate. A fair number of restaurants are closed on Sundays.

Expensive

Aker Brygge. Oslo's quayside pleasure park has restaurants in all price ranges and all nationalities.

Annen Etage. Hotel Continental, Stortingsgt 24/26 (419060). One of the very few Norwegian restaurants that has been internationally recognized. Excellent atmosphere and cuisine. Open daily except Sat.; piano music on Sun. from 3–7. AE, DC, MC, V.

Bagatelle. Bygdøy Alle 3 (446397). Sophisticated and elegant French spot to the west of the Royal Palace with excellent food. AE, DC, MC, V.

Blom. Karl Johansgate 41 (427300). Traditional artists' restaurant for nearly a century. Norwegian and international cuisine. Lunch buffet, "Fru Blom", lively café with outdoor terrace in more moderate price range; pâté, cheese, snacks and vintage wine by the glass. MC, V.

Caravelle. Fornebu Airport (122929). International restaurant overlooking the runways with excellent salad bar. Also has less expensive *Caravelle Cabin* (M), for pizzas, steaks and sandwiches, and *Caravelle Cafeteria* (M). AE, DC, MC, V.

De Fem Stuer. Holmenkollen Park Hotel, Kongevn. 26 (146090). Gourmet restaurant in traditional 19th-century timber building furnished in period style. Expensive, but good value; and interiors alone justify a visit. AE, DC, MC, V.

Frognerseteren. Holmenkollveien 200 (143736). By the Holmenkollen ski jump with spectacular views over the city. Old timber building in traditional Norse style with open hearth and Norwegian specialties. A must. MC, DC, V.

Grotten. Wergelandsveien 5 (209604). Located near the Royal Palace. Small, intimate restaurant with extensive à la carte menu. Closed on Sun. AE, MC.

Holmenkollen. Holmenkollveien 119 (146226). Also up on the hill by the ski jump and with the same wonderful views. AE, DC, MC, V. Cafeteria (M) in same building.

La Brochette. Dr. Maudsgt 1/3 (416733). Select your own steak in this fine French spot; distinctive milieu and personal attention. AE, MC, V.

Ludvik. Torggt. 16 (42 88 80) (also at Aker Brygge). Specializes in fish. Situated in old city baths building. Good and unusual menu. AE, DC, MC, V.

Mølla. Sagvn 21 (375450). Charmingly-renovated spinning mill on the Aker river. Unique 19th-century atmosphere. Live music, cabaret and dancing in candlelit vaults; fish and game a specialty. AE, DC, MC, V.

La P'tite Cuisine. Solligaten 2 (444575). Grill restaurant with French atmosphere and cuisine in the west of the city. Fine wines. AE, DC, MC, V.

Tre Kokker. Drammensveien 30 (442650). Norwegian-style charcoal grill with excellent international cuisine near the Royal Palace; run by Norway's top gourmet. Dancing in bar. AE, DC, MC, V.

Moderate

Bella Napoli. Storgt. 26 (410052). Italian dishes and pizza. Friendly, informal atmosphere. Popular with young people. AE, MC, V.

Carl Johan Bistro. Karl Johansgt. 37 (417790). Good lunch buffet, special "dish of the day." Right in center of main street. AE, DC, MC, V.

Charly's. SAS Hotel Scandinavia (entrance from street only), St. Olavsgt. (113000). Salad bar, light meals, wine and beer; busy, noisy atmosphere. AE, DC, MC, V.

Engebret Café. Bankplassen 1 (360783). Newly renovated. Famous for its fish; cozy interior; piano music. Closed on Sun. AE, DC, MC, V.

Gamle Raadhus (old Town Hall), Nedre Slottsgt. 1 (420107). Oslo's oldest restaurant in building from 1640. Specializes in fish; noted for mussels and fresh shrimp. Closed Sun. AE, DC, MC, V.

Mamma Rosa. Øvre Slottsgt. 12 (420130). Informal Italian atmosphere, guitar music in evening; pasta and pizza as well as international menu. AE, MC, V.

La Mer. Pilestredet 31 (203445/203469). Fish and shellfish specialties. Closed Sun. AE, DC, V.

L'Océan. M/S Pibervigen, Rådhusbrygge 6, (419996/419997). Good fish restaurant on ship moored in front of the City Hall. In summer tours down the fjord during the day. Closed Sun.

Peking House. St. Olavsgt. 23 (114878). Good Chinese food. Pleasant interior, quick service. Near SAS hotel. One of three of the same name.

Stortorvets (Estasje) Gjestiveri. Grensen 1 (428863). Traditional restaurant in building from 1700. Outdoor courtyard service in summer. A genuine Christiania inn. AE, DC, MC, V.

Storyville, Chez Bendriss. Universitetsgt. 26 (429635). French and creole cuisine—barbecued spare ribs a specialty, and so is the Dixieland jazz. In same building, *Humla* (424420), with live music, cabaret, dancing in young atmosphere. Closed Sun. AE, DC, MC, V.

Theatercaféen. Stortingsgt. 24/26. Oslo's most visited restaurant; in the Hotel Continental. Good food, but best known for its lively, sophisticated atmosphere. AE, DC, MC, V.

Tostrupkjelleren. Karl Johansgt. 25 (421470). International restaurant, popular with those in the media; piano music. Closed on Sun. AE, DC, MC, V.

Inexpensive

Albin Upp (Gallery and Art Café). Briskebyv. 42 (557192). A real find for lovers of something different. Intimate wine and snack bar in renovated farmer's cottage right in the center of town. Contemporary Norwegian art on display includes graphics, jewelry, ceramics, watercolors. Open all year, but from June to Aug. on weekdays only 12–5. Tram no. 1 (Briskeby) from National Theater stops outside; get off at Uranienborg school stop. Good parking.

Café Frølich. Drammensvn. 20 (443737). Oslo's only music café in old Viennese style. Several instruments including grand piano used by music students or any guest competent enough to play them—anything from classical to jazz and rock. Varied menu of small dishes, plus ice cream specials.

Café Sjakk Matt. Haakon VII's gt. 5 (423227). Popular with younger set. Snacks, salads, sandwiches, hot and cold meals.

Den Lille Fondue. President Harbitzgate 18 (441960). Oslo's only fondue restaurant; small and intimate; music. AE, DC, MC, V.

Herregårdsbroen. Frognerparken (552089). Features an open-air restaurant with à la carte menu. Open in summer.

Kaffistova, Grillstova, Torgstova. Recommended chain of coffee shops and cafeterias with generous helpings; check the *Oslo Guide* for locations.

Pinocchio Rica. Bogstadvn 53 (607786). Just by Colosseum cinema. Cheap and good. Closed Sun. AE, DC, MC, V.

Vega Vertshus Friskpartrestaurant. Munkedamsvn. 36 (428557). Vegetarian, salads, hot and cold meals; near National Theater station. AE, DC, MC, V.

NIGHTLIFE. A combination of high prices and puritanism have long conspired to render Norwegian nightlife a somewhat low key, not to say dormant affair. However, despite still strict licensing laws—no spirits can be served after midnight and not at all on Sundays and national holidays, and a bottle of scotch in a nightclub will certainly cost in excess of $50—the oil boom and its attendant influx of big-spending oil men, coupled with Norway's high standard of living, have resulted in a gradual hotting up of the nighttime tempo over the last few years. Over 90 restaurants, cafés and nightclubs are open after 1 A.M. Among the most popular spots are: *Sardines, Stravinsky* (very expensive), *Barock,* and *Cruise* (Aker Brygge).

A number of the larger and more expensive hotels have cabarets and dancing—either discos or to bands. Similarly, some, though by no means all, restaurants have entertainment of one sort or another. See our *Hotel* and *Restaurant* listings for details. In addition there are also a growing number of regular night spots, though their ranks are still thin. Most, not least as a result of their scarcity, tend to get very crowded, especially at weekends. The city also boasts a thriving jazz scene, not perhaps to be compared to Copenhagen's but lively enough nonetheless.

Among the recommended spots are:

Amalienborg Jazzhouse, Arbeidergate 2 (423024). Unpretentious with some frequently excellent jazz.

Ben Joseph (La Petite Cuisine). Solligate 2 (444575). Grill restaurant and nightclub in one.

Grand Café (Grand Hotel). Karl Johansgt. 31 (429390). Sunday Brunch, lunch with jazz concert.

Guldfisken. Rådhusgate 2 (411489). Good spot for trad. jazz.

Hot House. Pilestredet 15B (203989). Definitely for swingers; lots of jazz.

Jazz Alive. Observatoriegate 2B (440745). Live bands every night; one of the top jazz spots.

Stortorvets Gjaestiveri. Grensen 1 (428863). Beside the cathedral. Lunchtime jazz sessions on Saturdays in 18th-century building kept in period style. International menu, sandwich buffet, service in courtyard in summer. Attractive place even without the jazz.

THE OSLO FJORD DISTRICT

Vikings, Whalers and Twisting Valleys

Østfold is that section of Norway lying between the Oslo region, its major towns of Moss, Fredrikstad, Sarpsborg, and Halden are all points on the main rail line to the capital. At the same time Østfold also belongs economically to the forest and lumber district of eastern Norway and to the great valley of Østerdal, whose river Glomma flows through Sarpsborg to empty into the fjord just beyond Fredrikstad. It is a small section of the country, rich in history and modern industry. On the west side of the Oslo Fjord is located another small district, the opposite number of Østfold, quite logically called Vestfold.

Exploring the Oslo Fjord District

By leaving Oslo's Central Station some morning on a southbound express you will reach Moss in about an hour (if the wind's right, you'll know it by the smell!). Formerly known for its tremendous distillery, the town has now both paper and pulp and other types of industries. It is also the eastern terminus of the cross-fjord Horten-Moss ferry which links Østfold and Vestfold. Unless you intend to cross on this ferry, stay aboard the train another half-hour, then descend at Fredrikstad. Here is a thriving industrial town which converts animal and vegetable oil into many useful products, cans first-class anchovies, exports lumber, etc., yet is at the same time filled with historical monuments. Across the Glomma river in the New Town there is a super-cafeteria, part of Scandinavia's biggest food center—"Stabburet."

The fortified Old Town, with its earthen and stone ramparts, built in the 17th century as a protection against the Swedes, is fully worth wandering about. Particularly fascinating is the great stone fortress of Kongsten standing alone beyond the ramparts as an outpost to meet the first waves of attackers.

In Old Town, is the arts and crafts center—"PLUS." Many of its workshops are open for demonstrations and sales. You will find PLUS represented in many of the leading stores and centers for good Norwegian design.

East of Fredrikstad, route 110 runs in the direction of Halden. This road—also known as the Antiquity Road—is only 16 km. (ten miles) long but takes visitors back 3,000 years. Along it can be seen some of Norway's finest prehistoric finds, notably rock carvings and grave mounds, not all very clearly marked—you may want to get detailed directions from the local tourist office. The road also passes "Tomta," Roald Amundsen's birthplace at Borge.

Home of the internationally-known Borregaard Paper Mills, Sarpsborg has had a long and checkered history since its founding in 1016 by St. Olav. Like Fredrikstad, it was burned down many times during the conflicts with Sweden, but with the expansion of its paper industry in recent decades Sarpsborg is now a thriving and stable industrial town. Sarpsborg's only real attraction for visitors is the waterfall which the Glomma River forms in the middle of the town. This 20-meter (64-foot) waterfall is always impressive and simply marvellous at flood periods. Visitors interested in history might browse around the grounds of the Borgarsyssel Museum, where the ruins of St. Nikolas Church are found, or if it happens to be a Sunday, visit the charming Hafslund Manor.

Stay overnight at Halden and devote the next morning to visiting the Fredriksten Fortress, constructed on a steep hill in the town. The views over the border country and the tales told by the guide about sieges and sorties during the 17th and 18th centuries will amply reward one for the effort expended. The theater here is the only surviving Baroque theater in the country.

Vestfold, Home of the Vikings

Even smaller than its eastern twin, Vestfold has many links with the Oslo region as well as a thriving industrial life of its own which included until 1968 that unique occupation, Antarctic whaling. Historically Vestfold, like southern Norway, has had more contacts with Denmark than with Sweden, but what will stir the imagination most of all are the traces of Viking kings and seafarers to be found there. This district has no clear-cut boundary such as the Swedish border provides for Østfold, but merges into the mountain district of Telemark.

The first half hour of the journey takes one as far as Drammen on the same main line that leads to Kristiansand and Stavanger.

The scenery is interesting but not spectacular; and it demonstrates, moreover, how quickly one gets from Oslo to the land of farms, forests and bare rock. And if you are wondering why more Norwegian railroads haven't been laid down in duplicate, the answer is easily seen on this 48-km. (30-mile) stretch to Drammen which has just been made doubletrack at staggering costs. Here you can see some of the difficulties that Norwegian railroad engineers encounter all over the country: steep up and down

grades, cuts through solid rocks and tunnels. In fact the Norwegian State
Railways on the Oslo–Drammen run has blasted Norway's longest tunnel
(11 km./seven miles) through the mountains to open the double track.
The Sisyphean job was completed in 1973. After the tunnel is passed there
is a view over the valley and across Drammensfjord to the lumber, paper
and shipping town of Drammen, sixth-largest city in Norway. Located
at the mouth of the large timber-floating river, Drammen has the same
strategic location as Fredrikstad on the other side of the Oslo Fjord, albeit
without any walled town or fortress. The "Corkscrew Road" tunneled
through the mountain to the top of the Bragernes Hill is a unique attraction.

The Vestfold express branches off here and inside an hour we pass
through long, narrow Holmestrand, squeezed in between fjord and hillside, and Skoppum, from where the bus runs to the former naval base (also
car-ferry) town of Horten. It is well worth making a detour to the coastal
village of Åsgårdstrand, where Edvard Munch painted many of his well
known works. His small, whiteframe house is open to the public from May
to September. This unspoilt village is now a popular holiday resort. A
short ride beyond brings Tønsberg which the inhabitants proudly claim
as Norway's oldest town, founded in the year 870. The hill rising steeply
beside the railway station demands a visit even though all that is left of
the extensive fortress, castle and abbey which once crowned it are some
ruined foundations. The outlook tower on top is of modern construction,
erected in 1870 to commemorate the 1,000th anniversary of Tønsberg's
founding, and it offers a panorama comparable in sweep to that from
Frognerseteren in Oslo.

Because of the passages both to the Oslo Fjord eastwards and to the
open sea southwards you can see at once why Tønsberg was a strategic
place, not only for the old Viking raiders but also for shipping. From the
sailing ships of the 18th and 19th centuries there has been a steady peaceful
development to today's fleet of cargo liners and oil tankers which has won
Tønsberg fourth place among shipping ports in Norway.

Looking back north along the railway from the Millenium Tower, one
can almost locate Borre, site of many ancient Viking burial mounds; while
much nearer Tønsberg is another famous site: Oseberg, where one of the
Viking ships now at Bygdøy was found. You should really have a guide
or Norwegian friend along to point out other historic spots, such as Ram-
nes, where rival pretenders to the throne fought decisive battles in the 12th
century, and the old manor house at Jarlsberg, the seat of Norway's last
family of nobility and still occupied by the family today. Hereditary titles
were abolished by parliament early in the 19th century, but Count Wedel
Jarlsberg was permitted to keep his distinction until he died in 1893.

Sandefjord and the World's Largest Mammal

Next stop is the picturesque town of Sandefjord, which was once the
main base for the Norwegian whaling fleet. Sven Foyn, a native of Tønsberg, invented the explosive harpoon, but it was the skippers from Sandefjord who developed the business of Antarctic whaling to its recent level.
The sight of the huge floating factories—up to 25,000 tonnes—and of their
dozens of attending whale-catchers, tiny 200-tonners, used to be a fascinating and instructive sight. The great era of Antarctic whaling, nevertheless,
has come to an end. With Japanese and Russian whalers joining the Nor-

wegians after the last war, the whales are becoming fewer and fewer, and Sandefjord has withdrawn from the great hunt. However, in compensation, Sandefjord has acquired Norway's fifth-largest merchant fleet. By all means visit the Whaling Museum given to the town by the local "whale king", Consul Lars Christensen.

An interesting side-trip by taxi from Sandefjord is to Gokstad Mound where another of the Viking ships at Bygdøy was found in 1880. Only a grass-covered mound can be seen there now, but it will give some idea of the magnitude and pomp of medieval Viking burials.

Larvik is another of Vestfold's busy ports but it combines this with important lumbering activities, lying as it does at the mouth of another great timber-floating river; the Lågen from Numedal Valley.

Continue a few miles south from Larvik along road 301 to the coastal town of Stavern, famous for its many well-preserved 18th-century wooden houses. The Citadel here, once used by naval hero Tordenskjiold, is now an artists' colony. Stavern has good bathing spots, particularly at the nearby fishing village of Nevlunghavn and a salmon fishing river.

PRACTICAL INFORMATION FOR
THE OSLO FJORD DISTRICT

TOURIST INFORMATION. Tourist Information Offices are located in the following places: **Fredrikstad** (09–320330). **Halden,** Kongens Brygge (09–182487). **Larvik,** Stogaten 20 (034–82 623). **Horten,** Torggt. 2 (033–43 390). **Moss,** Christiesgt 3 (09–255451). **Sandefjord,** in the Town Hall (034–68 100). **Sarpsborg,** St. Mariegt 96 (09–153629). **Tønsberg,** Storgt 55 (033–14 819/10211).

TELEPHONE CODES. We have given telephone codes for all the towns and villages in the hotel and restaurant lists that follow. These codes need only be used when calling from outside the town or village concerned.

HOTELS AND RESTAURANTS. The region has a number of new hotels and modest family establishments. But in this district, as in other places, it is perfectly feasible to stay in modern town hotels and enjoy swimming on the neighboring beaches. The town hotels are mostly unpretentious, but the *Grand* at Larvik, the *Klubben* at Tønsberg, and the *Park* at Sandefjord are among the best in Norway. Some of the seaside resort hotels offer reduced terms before and after the peak season.

Drammen (Buskerud). *Rica Park* (L), Gamle Kirkeplass 3 (03–838280). 190 beds, all rooms with facilities, restaurant. MC, V. *Müllerhotel Drammen* (E), Strømsø Torg 7 (03–831590). 350 beds. All rooms with facilities.
Restaurant. *Skansen Restaurant.* At the top of the Spiral, a tunnel hewn out of the rock, running in six convolutions to a superb viewpoint at Skansen.
Youth Hostel. *Drammen Youth Hostel* (I), Korsvegen 62. 150 beds.

Fredrikstad (Østfold). *City* (E), Nygaardsgt 44–46 (09–317750). 250 beds. 50 rooms with bath, restaurant. AE, DC, MC, V. *Britannia* (I), Gunnar Nilsensgt 4 (09–311131). 23 beds, no rooms with bath or shower. Restaurant with à la carte menu. *Victoria* (M), Turngt 3 (09–311165). 82 beds, most rooms with facilities. AE, DC, MC, V. *Fredrikstad Motel og Camping* (I), Torsnesveien 16 (09–320315). 52 beds. Swimming.

Restaurants. *Hawk Club A/S,* Storgt 20 (09–311035). *Løwendals Galei,* Storgt 4 (09–316944). *Peppe's Pizza,* Torvgt 57 (09–322202). *Tamburen,* Faergeportgt 78 (09–320313). *Tordenskiol Danserest,* Storgt 4 (09–316944).

Halden (Østfold). *Park* (E), Marcus Thranesgt 30 (09–184044). 90 beds, restaurant. MC, V. *Grand* (M), Jernbanetorget 1 (09–187200). 60 beds, all rooms with facilities. Fully-licensed restaurant. MC, V.
Restaurants. *Friluften,* Storgt 18 (09–181340). *Dickens,* Storgt 9 (09–183503). *Fredriksten Kro,* Fredricksten Festning (09–185425).
Youth Hostel. *Stangeløkka Youth Hostel* (I), 031–83 046. 40 beds.

Hankø (Østfold). Famous yachting center, summer only. *Hankø Fjordhotel* (L), 1620 Gresvik (09–332105). 140 beds, most rooms with facilities. Restaurant.

Holmestrand (Vestfold). *Holmestrand* (M), Langgt. 1 (033–53 100). 96 beds, 48 rooms with all facilities. Family rooms, many with panoramic views over fjord. Right on the waterfront. Restaurant, bar, and own pier for visiting boats.

Horten (Vestfold). *Grand* (M), Jernbanegt 1 (033–41 722). 48 beds, most rooms with facilities, all with TV, fridge, telephone; restaurant, bar, hire of sailboats and instruction.

Larvik (Vestfold). *Grand* (M), Storgaten 38–40 (034–83 800). 200 beds, most rooms with facilities. Overlooking fjord. Restaurants. AE, MC, V. *Holms Motel* (I), Amundrød E–18 (034–11 482). 126 beds. Cafeteria. AE, DC, MC. *Seierstad Gjestagård* (I), (034–11 092). 26 beds, no rooms with bath or shower. Self-catering,. Boats for hire.
Restaurants. *Hansemann,* Kongensgt 33 (034–86 148). *Blomsterhaven* (Grand Hotel), Storgt 38 (034–87 800). *Carina,* Jegersborggt. 4 (034–81360). AE, MC, V. *Otto Mat and Vinhus,* Torget 6 (034–81 811). *Hvalen Kro, Ø.* Halsen (034–26 099).

Moss (Østfold). *Refsnes Gods* (L), Godset 5 (09–270411). On Jeløy island. 90 beds, 30 rooms with bath. Charming. AE, MC. *Moss Hotel* (M), Dronningensgt. 21 (09–255080). 84 beds. Outstanding restaurant. MC, V.
Restaurant. *Ebas A/S,* Dronningens 1 (09–253898).
Youth Hostel. *Vansjøheimen Youth Hostel* (I), (032–55 334). 64 beds.

Sandefjord (Vestfold). *Park* (E). Strandpromenaden 9 (034–65 550). 270 beds, all rooms with facilities: Overlooking harbor, one of Norway's best hotels. Restaurant, bar, swimming, saunas. AE, DC, MC, V. *Atlantic* (M), Jernbanealléen 31 (034–63 104). 70 beds, some rooms with bath. AE, DC, V. *Granerød* (M), (034–77077). 250 beds, all rooms with all facilities. 12 rooms specially designed for handicapped guests. Conference center. *Kong Carl* (M), Torggt. 9 (034–63 117). 49 beds, all rooms with facilities.

Sarpsborg (Østfold). Industrial town with spectacular waterfall. *Grand* (M), Oskarsgt. 67 (09–154400). 53 beds, most rooms with bath or shower. Fully-licensed restaurant. AE, DC, MC, V. *Saga* (M), Sannessundvn 1 (09–154044). 120 beds, all rooms with facilities. AE, DC, MC, V. *St. Olav* (E), St. Olav's Plass, Glengsgt 21 (09–152055). 132 beds, 25 rooms with bath. AE, DC, MC, V.
Restaurant. *Dickens A/S,* St. Mariegt 109 (09–152892).
Youth Hostel. *Tuneheimen Youth Hostel* (I), (031–45 001). 70 beds.

Stavern (Vestfold). *Hotel Wassilioff* (E), Havngt. 1–3 (034–98 311). 88 beds, most rooms with facilities. At harbor's edge; outdoor terrace, pub, disco, new gourmet restaurant.
Restaurants. *Selma and Tatjanas Kjeller,* Hotel Wassilioff.

Tjøme (Vestfold). *Rica Havna* (E), (033–90 802), on coast in park. Chalets, hire of boats, wind surfers, cycles, tennis and squash courts, swimming pool, solarium. *Tjøme* (M), (033–90 232). 35 beds. Restaurant, café.

Restaurant. *Verdens Ende* (033–90 517). Overlooking rocks and sea.

Tønsberg (Vestfold). *Klubben* (E), Nedre Langgt 49 (033–15 111). 175 beds, all rooms with facilities, restaurant. AE, DC, MC. *Grand* (E), Øvre Langgt 65 (033–12 203). 160 beds, all rooms with facilities. *Maritim* (M), Storgt. 17 (033–17 100). 50 beds, all rooms with facilities.

Restaurants. *Bamboo Gardens,* Ø Langgt 49 (033–12 325). Good Chinese cuisine in intimate atmosphere. *Baronen & Baronessen,* Rådhusgt 2 (033–15 837). *Bonanza,* Ø. Langgt 65 inng. Møllegt (033–12 606). *Fregatten,* Storgt 17 (033–14 776). *Håndverkeren,* Kammegt 6 (033–12 388). *Kong Sverre,* Tollbugt. 14 (033–12 903). Pizza, grills. *Le-Ni Swing In Steak House,* Storgt 32 (033–11 892). *Pizzanini,* Munkegt 10 (033–11 915). *Vaegteren,* Storgt. 29 (033–13 909). *Vertshuset Greven,* Grev Wedelsgt. 3 (033–13 113).

Youth Hostel. *Tønsberg Youth Hostel* (I), (033–12 848). 47 beds.

Camping

There are good campsites near most towns by the Oslo Fjord, particularly along the main road in Østfold from Sweden to Oslo. *Kajerstranden* (Stavern) and *Oddane Sand* (Nevlunghavn) are 3-star camping sites. *Havna Skjaegardspark,* Tjøme. *Fjaerholmen Caravan/Camping,* close by Tønsberg Sailing Club on Nøtteroy Island.

HOW TO GET AROUND. There are good train services from Oslo down both sides of the Oslofjord—on the west side to Drammen, Tønsberg, Sandefjord and Larvik, and on the east side to Moss, Fredrikstad, Sarpsborg and Halden. It is possible to do a one-day round trip to either of these areas, allowing an hour or two in any one of the towns. There is a 40-minute car and passenger ferry crossing between Moss and Horten. Torp airport, between Tønsberg and Sandefjord, has regular connections with Stavanger, Bergen and Copenhagen. There are passenger ferries between Sandefjord and Strømstad (Sweden), Tønsberg and Strømstad, and Larvik and Fredrickshavn.

TOURS. For information on suggested touring routes, guided tours, boat trips and car ferries, visit the local Tourist Information Offices, listed at the beginning of this *Practical Information* section.

PLACES TO VISIT. The Oslo Fjord District has many churches and cathedrals of historical interest. The area also has its share of galleries and museums for the tourist to enjoy. Some of these places are listed below.

Drammen. Drammen Museum. Outdoor museum, with Marienlyst Manor from the 1770s. At Bragernesåsen.

Rock carvings. On Skogerveien road, these carvings are 6,000 years old.

Fredrikstad. Fredrikstad Domkirke. The cathedral is richly decorated by Norwegian artists. One of the largest and best organs in Norway.

Fredrikstad Museum. At the Gamle Slaveri. Open daily 10–4.

Gamelbyen (The Old Town). Scandinavia's oldest preserved fortress town, dating back to 1663.

Glemmen Church. Built in stone around 1100, with a Roman font. Crucifix and apostle sculpture from Lubeck, around 1450.

Kongsten Fort. Dates back to 1685. Now the property of the Town of Fredrikstad.

Oldtidsveien (Highway of the Ancients). The most concentrated collection of archaeological monuments in the country is to be found along Highway No. 110, between Fredrikstad and Skjeberg.

Halden. Fredristen Festning. Mountain Fortress from the end of 1600s, empire style buildings. War and cultural history museum in the old prisons.

Larvik. Larvik Bymuseum. A manor house from 1673; the town museum. **Larvik Maritime Museum.** In the old customs house (1714).

Sarpsborg. Borgarsyssel Museum. County museum for Østfold with cultural history collections and old buildings.

Stavern. Fredriksvern. Naval station dating from 1750, now training school for air force. Open July through Sept. 9–8 daily. Many well-preserved 18th-century buildings.
Citadel. Artists colony in summer. 18th-century building; open to public.
Stavern Church. Baroque/Roccoco building dating from 1751.

Tønsberg. The oldest town in the north—once capital of Norway. **Haugar.** In the center of town, with old burial mounds. Site of local assembly in olden times.
Memorial Park. With sculptures by Gustav Vigeland and glass mosaics by Per Vigeland.
Oseberg Mound (where Oseberg ship, now in Viking Ship Museum in Oslo, was found). Borre National Park has several Viking burial mounds.
Slottsfjelle. Once the largest castle in Norway. Contains one of the largest collections of medieval ruins in Northern Europe.
St. Olav's Church. The largest circular church in the North. There has been a monastery in Tönsberg since the 1190s.
Tönsberg Cathedral. Erected in 1858 on the site of the old Lavran Church.
Vestfold County Museum. Includes outdoor museum, whaling and shipping sections. Viking ship from 800. Archeological section. Café serving waffles and traditional sour cream porridge *(rømmegrøt).*

SPORTS. Swimming everywhere outside the Drøbak Narrows is pleasant in crystal-clear and surprisingly warm water (averaging 68°F. throughout the season). The bathing beaches at Ula and Lille Skagen at Hvasser are particularly good.
Sailing and boating are in evidence everywhere; the waters of the outer Oslo Fjord, with the mixture of open stretches and sheltered channels, are ideal for this activity. A sailing school with first-class instructors is run by the Hankø Hotel.
Faerder Lighthouse outside Hvasser marks entrance to the inner Oslofjord and is the scene of one of the first annual regattas marking the start of the sailing season: down the fjord from Oslo, round Faerder and back up the fjord again to Oslo. Boat trips round the lighthouse also possible from Hvasser. **Fishing** from a boat—or with a spinning-rod from the rocks—is a popular sport, best early (May) and late (September) in the season.

TELEMARK AND THE SOUTH COAST

A Land Fit for Heroes

The Telemark district, whose name has become a part of the skier's lore, is among Norway's most beautiful and most interesting. Winding valleys, precipitous gorges, silvery lakes, snow-covered mountains, pastoral farmlands with their ancient stave churches—all present an unforgettable picture of contrasts and surprises. Dotting the islands and inlets of the South Coast are delightful resorts forming a holiday paradise, ideal for exploring or just basking in the sun. Telemark is well served by public transport—as described below—but the best way of seeing this remarkable area is to go by car.

Exploring Telemark and the South Coast

The Vestfold express train takes you from Oslo via Larvik to the end of the line at Skien. Besides serving as terminus, Skien is also the beginning of another rail line to Oslo via Kongsberg and Drammen if you want to return to the capital by another route. Even more important, however, is Skien's position as a main gateway to Telemark, for no eager tourist should leave Norway without at least a glimpse of that ruggedly charming mountain district.

First, though, look at the city from Brekke Park on the high ridge back of Høyer's Hotel, where not only a fine outdoor Folk Museum is located but also an excellent collection of Ibseniana. For Henrik Ibsen was born in Skien in 1828 and grew up on Venstøp farm (now an Ibsen memorial), five km. (three miles) from the town center, and in Snipetorget 27. Today Ibsen House is a modern cultural center with art gallery, theater and library.

The classic approach to Telemark from Skien is the Bandak Canal. The charming old ship *Victoria* makes the journey from Skien to Dalen in one day, by lock and lake through the province of Telemark.

Leaving Skien at 8:30 sharp you have got a glorious 108 km. (65 miles) in front of you, out of which 100 (60) stay quiet, the rest are streams, canals and locks. *Victoria* is in no particular hurry to get you to Dalen. There is too much to show: the park-like lower Telemark, manor houses and timber industry at Ulefoss, winding streams, locks and narrows between Lake Norsjø and Lake Kviteseidvatn and wild Lake Bandak with precipitous mountain sides. While the boat is negotiating the locks you may stroll along the canal path, visit the local shop, chat with the locals—in fact imbibe the peaceful charm which is the very essence of this water excursion.

If this does not appeal, you may board a morning bus from Skien and skirt Lake Norsjø, passing through Ulefoss, with its manor houses on the hills and timber industry along the river en route to Bø, one of the famous districts of Telemark. You might well make the Lifjell Hotel, in the hills above the station, your first stay, for the view from there is probably Telemark's most panoramic, which is saying quite a lot. Bø is the traffic hub of central Telemark. Travelers direct from Oslo alight from the express trains at this junction and board the buses of the efficient West Telemark Bus Company for a ride along the silvery bank of Lake Seljord to the village of Seljord, with its medieval church and wealth of local tradition, thereafter continuing to Brunkeberg crossroads. The main bus line continues straight west from Brunkeberg, heading for the Hardanger Fjord. En route it passes through the steep valley of Morgedal, famous as the cradle of modern skiing. The Bjåland Museum in Morgedal contains an interesting collection of Antarctic items, as well as old skis.

But our aim is to ramble about a bit in Telemark, in the general direction of Dalen. Thus we catch an afternoon bus from Brunkeberg (a study of timetables is important when traveling within criss-cross Telemark), and wind down a "vistaful" road to Kviteseid and across the hills to Vrådal. This resort is located at an altitude of about 300 meters (1,000 feet), and anyone wanting a quiet stay, with fishing and rowing, on a beautiful mountain-fringed lake, should stop here for a few days.

You can proceed southward by bus from Vrådal along Lake Nisser to Nelaug, and reach Arendal on the South Coast by train from there. But that's another trip. Our route takes us along another beautiful lake, the Vråvatn, to Vråliosen and across the mountains, but if traveling by car make a short detour to Skafså to visit Anne Grimsdalen's sculpture museum, before hairpinning down to Dalen, with a breathtaking view of Lake Bandak. Dalen, formerly the tourist pivot of Telemark, is today the center of the gigantic Tokke hydro-electric scheme which involves great areas of Telemark; the power station of Dalen (Tokke I) yields 400,000 kilowatts, and has few competitors in Europe.

If you decide to explore Dalen more closely, you should take a taxi up the north wall of Lake Bankad the eight km. (five miles) to Eidsborg for a most impressive hairpin climb from the water's edge up to the mountains. Here is a small but ancient stave church. Visit the old building close to it, which has been turned into a local museum and boasts the oldest washing-machine in the world, invented a couple of centuries ago by an imaginative Telemark farmer. From Dalen you can also go by taxi to another of the wonders of Telemark, the Ravnejuvet ravine, dropping some 300 meters (1,000 feet) into the valley of Tokke and having peculiar air currents that bring papers—and even such heavier objects as bushes—thrown down into it back over the brink. Throw in your banknotes and they should return to you.

From Dalen we travel along the Tokke Valley to Åmot, where the beautiful Hyllandsfoss Falls disappeared into the Tokke project, and head for the village of Rauland.

Culture and Sabotage

Located 1,000 meters (3,300 feet) above sea level, the Rauland Hotel is your best base of operations to combine fishing, hunting, or hiking with a study of the genuine rural culture of Telemark. From the hilltop near the hotel one can see far across Lake Mösvatn into the wild Hardanger plateau and, in the opposite direction, many of the mountain summits of Telemark. Southeast lies Lake Totak and Rauland village—15 minutes by car—with a concentration of more *stabburs,* (storehouses on stilts) farm buildings, etc., than can be found anywhere except in the Oslo Folk Museum. But here they have the added charm of completely natural surroundings and are still in use. Beyond Lake Totak the horizon is formed by a long row of peaks running north-south: the mountains guarding the approach to Setesdal valley.

Rauland was the home of the late Dyre Vaa, the sculptor who designed the Swans Fountain in the courtyard of the Oslo Rådhus. A collection of his work is open during the summer season. (Some of his later efforts in modern painting are displayed on the walls of the hotel salons.) One of the most famous country fiddlers in Norway, Myllargutten (The Miller Boy), lived at the west end of Totak, and either the hotel manager or local guides can tell you any number of stories and legends about him and the "old days" in Rauland.

Whatever the complications in choosing your route to Rauland, there is one best way out: the bus trip along the edge of Lake Møsvatn and down to Rjukan. As you cut across this southeast corner of the Hardanger plateau you are again on historic ground. In a solitary hut not far from the mountain hotel, the Norwegian leader of the famous Linge Company of saboteurs, Major Leif Tronstad, was killed in early 1945. And during the winter of 1943 this whole area was the scene of dramatic actions by the Norwegian underground against the Vemork Plant of Norsk Hydro where "heavy water" was produced by the Nazis for their atomic bomb experiments in Germany. Thus, when the bus halts at the Skinnerbu stop on Lake Møsvatn near the big dam, you may have time to buy postcards at the mountain chalet run by one of the saboteurs.

Beyond the dam the road enters a canyon which grows steadily deeper and with more precipitous walls until, in a hairpin swing, it brings you right opposite Vemork, scene of the daring coup now so widely known through the film reconstruction, *Heroes of Telemark.* In spite of the thousands of Nazi soldiers guarding the entire valley, Norwegian saboteurs climbed down into this steep-sided, snow-filled gulch on a bright moonlit night to set off dynamite charges that destroyed the heavy-water plant.

Still further down the canyon is the electric power and industrial town of Rjukan, squeezed in between the river and cliffs, while overhead towers the great peak of Mount Gausta, almost 1,850 meters (6,000 feet) high. Small wonder that the sun does not shine at the bottom for five months of the year. However, the inhabitants of Rjukan can quickly get up into the sunshine on the northern rim of the canyon by means of a cable car that rises over 500 meters (1,600 feet) in a trajectory of 1,000 meters (3,000 feet).

From Rjukan you have two glorious ways of leaving Telemark, each with its particular attractions. One is by bus around the head of Lake Tinnsjø and across more mountains with farms and *stabburs* to Bolkesjø and then to Kongsberg. An important junction on the main Oslo-Stavanger railway, Kongsberg, an old silver mining town and still the seat of the Royal Norwegian Mint, is today famous for its remarkable 18th-century church, its Mining Museum and the miniature train taking visitors down into the old mines, 350 meters (1,140 feet) below the surface.

The other way out is by bus from Rjukan to Mel, and by train-ferry down nearly the entire length of Lake Tinnsjø: a wild, roadless district much like Bandak. At Tinnoset the train takes to dry land once again, pauses briefly at the industrial town of Notodden and then joins the main railway at Hjuksebø Junction below Kongsberg. For an appropriate leave-taking of Telemark, stop over at Notodden long enough to take a bus or taxi the few miles to Heddal and see that largest of Norwegian stave churches.

Exploring the South Coast

The south coast railroad from Oslo to Kristiansand and onwards to Stavanger, forces its way through crevasses and along lakes and rivers as far as Kristiansand; then there is no alternative but to go right through the mountains, bridging the rivers in vast spans of concrete and steel. Thus you will become acquainted with some of Europe's largest rail tunnels and loftiest bridges, and a wild and desolate interior, but the south coast itself will still escape you—unless you take the sidetracks to Kragerø, Arendal and Flekkefjord. During the summer a boat leaves Oslo daily for Arendal, with stopovers at Kragerø, Jomfruland, Risør—all popular holiday resorts. You can return to Oslo on the same day. Refreshments are served on board. Tickets and details from Tourist Information Office in Oslo.

Therefore our suggestion is that you should go by bus, (or car), starting in Porsgrunn (which we presume you have reached via Oslo). The famous 100-year-old Porsgrunn Porcelain Factory is open to visitors and worth a visit. Much of the work is still done by hand. However, by bus it is a question of detours if you wish to imbibe the atmosphere of Kragerø and Risør, resuming travel by a later bus. Anybody might be tempted to stay over in Kragerø until the next day, for here is a picturesqueness that has inspired generations of painters to haunt the little town and its many islands. In any case, reserve a few hours to wander through the narrow and winding streets in the old part of Kragerø. The Berg-Kragerø Museum is housed in a period building of great beauty, and contains collections illustrating the life and history of the coastal population.

Risør is even more romantic than Kragerø, with its stately patrician houses from the early 19th century lining the harbor. Don't worry about missing the winding streets of little Tvedestrand, your bus will take you right into them. We suggest you "jump ship" in Tvedestrand, leave the through-service bus to find its own way to Arendal, and enter the coastal bus which will take you to Arendal via Flosta.

Once known as "Little Venice," Arendal's canals have been turned into wide streets, but it still retains its beautiful harbor. The town is a center for holiday-makers and offers interesting boat trips among the skerries and on the delta of the River Nid.

Despite nature's charm on the south coast and despite the bustle of modern industry and communications there is a slight atmosphere of sadness about Sørlandet (the "south land"), a hint of bygone and better days. For all of these small towns and hamlets had their heyday when sailing ships were the masters of the sea. These were the times that brought the small white cottages and the large white mansion houses into being—the times described in Jonas Lie's novels, when skippers and pilots were the heroes and their wives the heroines.

You can recapture a bit of this spirit, if you stay in Arendal, by taking a trip to the large island of Tromøy and visiting the old church of the same name; and by crossing over to little Merdøy Island, where a typical skipper's home has been taken over unchanged, forming a part of the Aust-Agder Museum, and kept exactly as it was in its owner's day.

Between Arendal and Grimstad you may be tempted to step off the bus in Fevik and entrust yourself to the Strand Hotel there, facing the Skagerak from a bathing beach position. Grimstad brings back the history of both sailing ships and Ibsen, for it was here that the great dramatist served as a druggist's apprentice and began writing his first works.

Lillesand, further on, will delight your eye not only by its fine mansion houses, but also by its location behind a complicated maze of channels and skerries. This is where you should finally abandon your bus—if the weather is fine—and lodge at the intimate Hotel Norge, because we suggest you investigate those skerries which are the essence of the south coast.

Kristiansand, Capital of Sørlandet

You can take the south coast railway for a dramatic but comfortable and quick ride to Stavanger, or continue to rough it along the highroad. One bus service links up with the other, and there is no doubt about it, you will reach Stavanger in the end, especially if you have been provident enough to supply yourself with the latest Norwegian timetable (Rutebok for Norge). Moreover, you will have had a marvellous time, if you are the type of adventurer and Norway-lover that we suspect. You will probably fall in love with Mandal's narrow streets which are lined with 18th- and 19th-century houses. You will be thrilled by the view of Kvinesdal and the Fedafjord, almost scared by the wildness of Jøssingfjord, and amazed at the number of fishing vessels in the harbor of Egersund. Your last surprise on the journey will probably be that mountainous Norway contains a stretch of flat farming land the size of Jaeren, south of Stavanger.

But now let's assume that, having decided to make the journey to Stavanger another time, you have stayed overnight in Kristiansand. Formerly the arch-enemy of the other southern towns, because of its founding by the Danish king in 1641 and special royal privileges, Kristiansand is now a major Norwegian port.

Kristiansand is the capital of Sørlandet, and offers good shopping facilities. Take a stroll through the old–world Kvadratur area, the checker–

board plan of streets between the harbor on two sides and the Otra River on the third, the old fortress of Christiansholm, (where exhibitions are often held in summer), and the cathedral. An exceedingly visible but non-cultural landmark is the tall chimney of the nickel-refining plant on the east side of the harbor approach, claimed to be the highest stack in Europe. Despite the regularity of the old part of the city, there are many delightful houses of typical southern Norway style and neatness, but most of them are jammed so tightly against each other that there is no place for the little garden in front. Apparently Kristiansand has always been crowded, for Gabriel Scott quotes a visitor in 1799 as having said that if a man absent-mindedly smoked his pipe by his own open window, he might easily happen to spit into a neighbor's parlor. At Kristiansand you also find Norway's largest animal and amusement park, covering more than 40 hectares (100 acres), and the Ravnedalen Nature Park.

The Otra River, which flows into the sea at Kristiansand, provides the clue for our next move: namely, to follow it upstream about 160 km. (100 miles) through Setesdal to its source. The charming narrow-gauged Setesdal Railway runs no more, except as a hobby train along a five-km. (three-mile) track on summer weekends. Therefore, we enter a morning bus at Kristiansand in the direction of Setesdalen. The first two hours are un-eventful. Whereas the old railway criss-crossed the foaming Otra, the Setesdal highway, to begin with, roams about the provinces miles away from the lively river. At Haegeland, river contact is once more established and we advise you to discontinue your morning nap. At Evje a wide flat area suddenly appears and, sure enough, here is Evje-*moen,* or the military training ground, for there are not too many places in upland Norway where naturally level drilling grounds are available.

Byglandsfjord, former terminus of the Setesdal Line, is reached in 2½ hours. The Otra is called Byglandsfjord at this point, for it's now a lake two km. (one mile) wide in places and at least 40 km. (25 miles) in rambling length. We are now entering the real Setesdal, that formerly most isolated and inaccessible of all Norwegian valleys, and the one which still bears many traces of its erstwhile quaint manners and culture.

Cliffs and Cutthroats of Setesdal

In olden days its inhabitants were not the most peaceful and lawabiding of citizens—witness the "Robbers' Hole" (Tjuvehola) in the mountain side just beyond the hamlet of Byglandsfjord, where thieves used to waylay farmers returning from town and relieve them of their purchases and left-over cash. And not far beyond there, we have dramatic evidence of how natural barriers for ages cut off Setesdal, not only from the outside world, but from itself. Just above the water's edge the road runs through a 550-meter (600-yard) tunnel blasted out of a cliff which, before the highway engineers came along, rose perpendicularly from the lake without offering even enough foothold for a mountain climber.

Byglandsfjord is the undisputed central point in lower Setesdal, as well as a convenient stopping place for tourists. However, another couple of hours will bring you to Valle which, in our opinion, is the most rewarding part of all Setesdal. Spend a day or two in Valle, trying trout fishing in the river (permission must be obtained), and go walking among the remarkable old farms that line the lower, moderately sloping hillsides. This will enable you to see more closely the unusual outfit that a few older men still wear while working in the fields. It consists of a white shirt and black trousers that give a remarkably dressed up appearance to men pitching hay; an appearance partly comprised, however, by the very battered and narrowrimmed black felt hat which completes the costume. Some elderly women may also be seen in the fields raking hay and hanging it up to dry on racks in their distinctive attire: black woolen stockings, white woolen skirt with black edgings, white blouse, black bolero or red jacket; while the older ones also wear a curious scarf-like headgear which shades their eyes like a bonnet in front and hangs down at back like a pigtail.

Yet these working clothes in Setesdal are nothing compared to the Sunday and festive costumes. The women put on black skirts and blouses over the white ones for church-going, while for weddings they add a bright red skirt, also over the previous foundation. The men change to black trousers with a heavy piece of leather reinforcing the seat and with gaily colored cuffs, and wear a heavy pullover with decorations in front and at the wrists to match the trouser cuffs. But again all this pales in contrast to what the bride and groom must don for their wedding! To the basic festive outfit are added embroideries, silver, ornaments and a bridal crown, said to be worth at least a thousand dollars. However, everyone can afford it in this valley, for helpful neighbors each lend a certain item, or else the young couple can rent a complete set of finery from the local "Housewives Association" just as one hires a dress suit in a city.

Hikes and Hideouts

The history of Setesdal is as interesting as its costumes, yet one would need to be something of a hiker to appreciate it at first hand. At Valle begins the old "Skin Trail", so called because it took the peasants westward over the mountains to the nearest tax-collector's office where they paid in skins, a 2-day journey that was extremely unpopular with the inhabitants. East from Valle the energetic tourist can take a 2-hour hike along the road leading to the *seters* (mountain farms) where the cattle graze in summer and where *seter*-maidens make cheese. Or he can follow the "Bishop's Trail" into Telemark, along which church officials made their way in olden times on their not too frequent visits to the "stubborn devils" in Setesdal.

Indeed, the valley's parishioners were so averse to change in the early days of the Reformation that they killed or drove out more than one of the new Lutheran priests. Tax-collectors and sheriffs were equally disliked, and some natives carried on feuds with the royal officials which remind one of the encounters between American hillbillies and revenue officers.

Such a famous local character was "Bad Aasmund", and you should not miss a visit to his hideout four km. (six miles) up the valley from Valle. He tangled with the law four centuries ago, fled to Holland, returned after many years but just in time—according to the legends—to abduct his former fiancée as she was about to be married to a persistent farmer she didn't like. Again outlawed, "Bad Aasmund" lived with his bride in the farm at Rygnestad, taking refuge in a stoutly fortified *stabbur* or *loft* whenever the sheriff was so rash as to put in a decidedly apprehensive appearance.

However, the gentleman apparently didn't call very often, for Aasmund was as handy with a bow and arrow as Robin Hood, and the massive logs of his *loft* still stand there today as impregnable as ever. But strangely enough, after all the glamorous days of adventure and rebellion, the bad man settled down, and in later life became a sheriff and tax-collector himself.

The bus ride north from Valle to Bykle and Hovden is perhaps the most exciting part of the trip. The road climbs steeply, now running close to the rushing torrent Otra, now hugging the valley walls. Like all other mountain highways in Norway, this one has its share of curves with the customary steep slope or even precipice on the outside edge. Low cement parapets or large stones are set up along this edge as guard-rails and there is usually room for two vehicles to pass. Nevertheless, the tourist driving his own car should exercise particular caution at such points and make his presence known by sounding the horn before entering a blind curve.

Near Bykle you will see another dramatic reminder of former hardships in communication: the Byklestigen or Bykle-ladder. This is a narrow path cut across the face of a cliff, which used to be the only way people could get from the lower valley to Bykle. Supplies had to be carried on their own backs, for not even pack-horses were able to negotiate Byklestigen. A full-width roadway has been carved out at the bottom of the rock wall along the river, so the distance which formerly took hours of toil is now made in a few minutes.

An hour later you are at Hovden, where there is easy access to both mountain lakes and rivers, in case you are a fisherman. (By the way, the source of the Otra River lies up in one of these lakes.) Hovden is also the end of the Setesdal bus line and here we change to another bus whose ultimate destination is Odda on the Sør Fjord.

You may think that you've seen everything in the way of wild scenery by this time but there is still much more in store along our *northbound* route. The great advantage of traveling upstream through Setesdal rather than down is that one can thus enjoy the natural crescendo of change from miniature Sørlandet up through the ever-higher, ever-shifting Setesdal to something even more magnificent but as yet unknown, which you sense lies right ahead.

And sure enough, just beyond Hovden comes another climax. There's a long straight piece of road ahead bordered on either side by a forest of dwarf birches which grow smaller and sparser for each kilometer. Beyond and above them on all sides rises a vast mountain plateau with snow patches here and there on the heights. This is the great central massif of the Hardangervidda: thousands of square kilometers of heath, lakes and mountain peaks.

The bus follows this road for many minutes but then, just as you think you are reaching these highlands, a deep, broad valley appears 300 meters (1,000 feet) below with the familiar pattern of cultivated fields and green meadows with golden hay drying on the racks. This is Haukeligrend village, an important road junction. If the purpose has been only to discover Telemark and the South Coast, this is where we turn east and take a bus that will bring us through the winding valleys of Telemark to Bø, and from there by train to Oslo. If you wish to wander farther afield, the direction to follow is westward across the mountain passes to Hardanger. Magnificent scenery and stupendous hairpin curves await you along this route— the high mountains around Haukeliseter, the steep and winding ascent into Røldal with its pilgrim stave church, the unsurpassed view of Lake Røldal from the mountain road to Seljestad, the Seljestad Gorge and the view of the Folgefonn Glacier. Without a doubt, this can be an immensely impressive journey.

PRACTICAL INFORMATION FOR
TELEMARK AND THE SOUTH COAST

TELEPHONE CODES. We have given telephone codes for all the towns and villages in the hotel and restaurant lists that follow. These codes need only be used when calling from outside the town or village concerned.

HOTELS AND RESTAURANTS. The majority of Telemark hostelries are in the moderate price category. Since they are for the most part "tourist" or "mountain" hotels, you can rest assured that they will automatically reach the high standards of equipment, service and food required by law.

Arendal (Aust Agder). *Central* (E), Vestregt 11 (041–22 020). 71 beds, restaurant. DC, MC, V. *Müllerhotel Phonix* (M), Friergangen (041–25 160). 155 beds, restaurant, dancing, bar, disco. DC, MC, V.

Restaurants. *Breidablikk Vertshus,* Faervik, Tromøy (041–85 127). *El Paso Western Saloon,* Havnegt 8 (041–21 805). *Grand Restaurant,* Langbryggen 19 (041–25 160). *Teje Vigen Café,* Langbryggen 3 (041–21 972).

Bø (Telemark). *Lifjell Turisthotell* (E), (03–950011). Situated below Mt Lifjell, 150 beds. AE, MC, V. *Bø Hotel* (M), (03–95 011). 100 beds. AE, MC. *Lifjellstua* (M), (03–953380. 50 beds.

Restaurant. *Vertshuset Bø* (036–61 099).

Bolkesjø (Telemark). *Bolkesjø* (E), (036–18 600). Built in 1881, rebuilt and enlarged, old interiors preserved, fine views of Telemark, 335 beds, all rooms with bath or shower, restaurant. Indoor swimming pool, sauna. MC, V. *Gran* (E), 3670 Notodden (036–18 640). 160 beds. MC, V. The hotels are 300 yards from each other, under same family ownership.

Byglandsfjord (Aust Agder). *Revsnes* (M), (043–34 105). 84 beds, most rooms with facilities. DC.

Farsund (Vest–Agder). *Farsund Fjordhotel* (E), Floridaodden (043–91 022). 126 beds, all rooms with bath/shower. AE, DC, MC. *Farsund Pensjonat* (I), Kjørestadveien 52 (043–91 573). None of the rooms have bath/shower. DC, V.

Restaurants. *Henrich og Pernille,* Nytorvet 1 (043–91 443). *Kaperstuen,* Listerv. 6 (043–91 502). *La Mer Restaurant,* Vanse (043–93 622).

Fevik (Aust Agder). *Strand* (E), 4870 Fevik (041–47 322). 80 beds, most rooms with bath, restaurant, sea view, sandy beach. AE, DC, MC, V.

Flekkefjord (Vest–Agder). *Grand* (M), Anders Beersgt. 9 (043–22 355). 40 beds, most with bath/shower. *Maritim* (M), Sundegt (043–23 333). 99 beds, all rooms with bath/shower. AE, DC, MC, V. *Bondeheimen* (I), Elvegt. 9 (043–22 171). 17 beds.

Grimstad (Aust Agder). *Helmershus* (M), Vesterled 23 (041–41 022). 76 beds, all rooms with bath or shower. DC, MC, V.

Restaurants. *Furuly Cafeteria,* Øvre Fevik (041–47 109). *La Pepita Pizza,* Juskerstr. 4 (041–41 641). *Spisekrogen,* Juskerstr. 2 (041–40 300). *Villa Ernst,* Arendalsvn 19 (041–40 300).

Youth Hostel. *Grimstad Youth Hostel* (I), (041–41 410). 21 beds.

Hovden (Aust Agder). *Hovden Høyfjellshotell* (E), (043–39 600). 180 beds, all rooms with bath or shower. AE, DC, MC, V. *Hovdestøylen Hotell og Hyttetun* (E), (043–39 552). 143 beds, some in cabins. AE, DC, MC, V. *Hovden Apartmentshotell* (M), (043–39 606). Weekly rental, 300 beds. DC, MC, V.

Kongsberg (Buskerud). *Grand* (E), Kristian Augustgt 2 (03–732029), 160 beds, 64 rooms with bath. DC, MC, V. *Gyldenløve* (E), Herm. Fossgate 1 (03–731744). 110 beds, 12 rooms with bath. AE, DC, MC, V.

Restaurants. *Cafena,* Storgt 12 (03–732758). *Ernst's Kafeteria,* Drammensvn 87 (03–733 530).

Youth Hostel. *Kongsberg Youth Hostel* (I), (03–732024). 90 beds.

Kragerø (Telemark). *Victoria* (M), (03–981066). 55 beds, 6 rooms with bath. DC, MC, V.

Restaurants. *Bucholmen Café,* Hovedbyen 13 (036–80 123). *El Paso Western Saloon,* Hovedbyen 12 (036–81 532).

Youth Hostel. *Kragerø Youth Hostel* (I), (03–732024). 90 beds.

Kristiansand (Vest–Agder). *Caledonien* (E), Vestre Strandgt 7 (042–29 100). 400 beds, all rooms with facilities, restaurants. AE, DC, MC, V. *Christian Quart* (E), Markensgate 39 (042–22 210). 220 beds, all rooms with facilities, restaurant. AE, DC, MC, V. *Ernst Park Hotel* (E), Rådhusgate 2 (042–21 400). 191 beds, many rooms with bath, restaurant. AE, DC, MC, V. *Savoy* (E), Kristian IV's gate 1 (042–24 175). 48 beds, most rooms with facilities. Restaurant. AE, DC, MC, V.

Bondeheimen (M), Kirkegate 15 (042–24 440). 64 beds.

Restaurants. *Kafé Jens,* Vestre Strandgt. 7 and *Veteranen,* both (043–29 100). *Bowlers Steakhouse,* Kirkegt. (042–29 009). *Bølgen Grill,* Elvegt. 1 (042–25 838). *Captain's Table* and *Down Town Key Club,* Dronningens gt. 66, (042–21 500). *Peppe's Pizza,* Gyldenløvesgt 7 (042–25 715). *Ravnedalens Friluftscafe* (042–21 344). *Restaurant Sjøhuset, Østre Strandgt. 12a (042–26 260). Skipperstua,* Skippergt 21 (042–29 075).

Youth Hostel. *Roligheden Youth Hostel* (I), Marviksvn 98 (042–94 947). 135 beds.

Kvinesdal (Vest–Agder). *Rafoss* (M), (043–50 388). 34 beds, all rooms with facilities. Restaurant. Boat rental. DC, V. *Utsikten* (M), (043–50 444). 49 beds, all rooms with bath/shower. MC, V.

Mandal (Vest–Agder). Adjoining popular Sjøsanden sandy beach. *Mandalitten* (E), (043–61 422). 70 beds, some with shower. *Solborg* (E), Neseveien 1 (043–61 311). 120 beds, 40 rooms with facilities, restaurant, swimming, sauna, sightseeing boat. AE, DC, MC, V.

Restaurants. *Café Amaldus,* S-varehus (043–64 860). *Café Clubben Store,* Elvegt 59 (043–62 660). *Lodsen,* Store Elvegt. 43 (043–63 376). *Puben,* Store Elvegt. 9. *Sjøstjerne Kro,* øsandvn 2 (043–63 005).

Youth Hostel. *Mandal Youth Hostel* (I), (043–61 501). 48 beds.

Morgedal. (Telemark). *Morgedal Turisthotell* (E), (036–54 144). 130 beds in 70 rooms, all with bath/shower. AE, DC, MC, V.

Rauland (Telemark). 1,000 meters (3,300 feet). *Rauland Høgsfjellshotell* (M), (036–73 222). 27 beds, 23 rooms with bath. AE, DC, MC, V. *Austbøo Hostel Rauland* (I), (036–73 425). 75 beds. DC, MC.

Rjukan (Telemark). The Gaustablikk holiday center is situated 15 km. (nine miles) southwest of Rjukan, access by road throughout the year, 970 meters (3180 feet), views of Mt. Gausta. *Gaustablikk Høgsfjellshotell* (E), (036–91 422). 91 beds,

all rooms with shower or toilet. DC, MC, V. *Kvitåvatn Fjellstoge* (I), (036–91 174). 139 beds in family rooms.
Restaurant. *Kinokaféen,* Storstulsgt 1 (036–91 265).
Youth Hostel. *Rjukan Youth Hostel* (I), (036–90 527). 90 beds.

Skien (Telemark). *Rica Ibsen Hotel* (E), Kongensgt 33 (03–524990). 236 beds, all rooms with bath/shower, restaurants, swimming. AE, DC, MC, V. *Høyes* (M), Kongensgt 6 (03–520540) 120 beds, 35 rooms with bath. DC, MC, V.
Restaurants. *Brekke Parkkafe,* Brekkeparken (035–23 873). *Café Henrik Ibsen-huset* (035–23 670). *El Bravo Western Saloon,* Torggt 18 (035–21 222). *Gregorious Restaurant,* Torggt 10 (035–27 398).

Valle (Aust Agder). *Bergtun* (M), (043–37 270). 20 beds.
Restaurants. *Noreheim Kafé* (043–36 629). *Setesdalsstoga Kro* (043–36 832).

Vrådal (Telemark). *Straand* (E), (036–56 100). 235 beds, most rooms with facilities, dining room, cafeteria, swimming, sauna. DC, MC, V. *Vrådal Hotell og Hytte-park* (E), (036–56 127). 58 rooms, 30 with bath. MC, V.

HOW TO GET AROUND. From Oslo, Sørlandsbanen railroads run through Kongsberg, Kristiansand and Egersund to Stavanger, with branches to Arendal and Flekkefjord. In addition, connecting bus services go from the main line to other towns and villages, both on the coast and inland, generally connecting with the trains. Fastest trains to Kristiansand take between 4½ and 5 hours. Several services daily to Kristiansand with the majority running through to Stavanger or with good connections.

TOURS. There are many excursions offered by boat and ferry, throughout Telemark and the South Coast. One of particular interest is at Skien, where the passenger vessel *Victoria* cruises Telemark's Inland Waterway. The Waterway is a system of canals and locks linking lakes and rivers, and it stretches from the Skagerak to Dalen, 130 km. (80 miles) inland. Information on these cruises from the Tourist Information Center (Turisttrafikk) in Skien (03–528227).

PLACES TO VISIT. The highlights of Telemark include the lakes of Bandak, Fyresvatn, and Tinnsjø; the views from Lifjell, Nutheim (across Flatdal), Brunkeberg, and Bolkesjø; the majestic Mount Gausta and the stupendous Vestifjord valley at Rjukan; the old farms at Rauland and the stave churches of Heddal and Eidsborg.

No such inventory can be made up for the South Coast, where the charm is every where—in the white-painted towns and fishing villages, and the tang of sea.

As well as the natural beauties of the area, there are also museums, preserved houses, and churches and other buildings of historical interest. Some of these are listed below.

Arendal. Aust–Agder Museum. At Langsae Manor.
City Hall and Old Town on Tyholmen. The City Hall, in Empire style from 1813, is one of the largest wooden buildings in Norway.
Merdøgård Museum. A sailing-ship captain's home from 1700s, beaches, boat from Langbryggen pier in town.

Farsund. Farsund Museum. Laid out as a South Coast skipper's house.

Grimstad. Burial grounds. From the Iron Age with mounds, monoliths and stone circles.
Town Museum. In the old pharmacy where Henrik Ibsen was an assistant.

Kongsberg. Kongsberg Church (1761). With Baroque interiors.
Lågdals Open-air Museum. With many fine lofthouses and cottages.
Mining Museum. In the old melting hut, history of the silver works.

Kragerø. Berg-Kragerø Museum. Four km. (two miles) from the town center, in a summer residence dating from around 1800. Open May through Sept. 12–7; Tues., Thurs., Sat. 5–7.

Kristiansand. Arne Vigeland Collections. 130 works of art, primarily sculptures cast in gypsum and bronze.

Christiansholm Fortress. Built 1674 by Fredrik III.

Gimle Estate Museum. From 1820; furniture and paintings from 17th and 18th centuries.

Oddernes Church. Built 1040. Baroque pulpit from 1704. Runic stone.

The Setesdal Railway. Grovane-Vennesla. Steam train from 1901. Reopened as veteran railway on a 5 km.-long narrow track.

Vest-Agder County Museum. 28 old buildings originally from Setesdal and Kristiansand. Church furnishings/urban and rural furniture textiles etc.

Zoo and Amusement Park. 1,000 animals, fun center, sports, activities, café, restaurant.

Boat sightseeing with M/S Maarten. Daily except Sun. from mid-June to mid-Aug.

Ravnedalen Nature Park. Marked trails, café.

Mandal. Mandal Church. Norway's largest wooden church in empire style. Built 1821.

Morgedal. Olav Bjåland's Museum. Shows the development of skis. Open July 1 through Aug. 20.

Sondre Norheimstogo. The cotter's farm where the ski pioneer S. Norheim (1825–97) was born.

Skien. Ibsen House. Skien's community center, opened in 1973. Library, art-exhibitions, concerts, theater performances and cinema.

Ibsen's Venstop. The farm where Henrik Ibsen spent his childhood, now a museum north of the town center.

Gjerpen Church. Is built around a Romanesque stone church erected before 1200. Rebuilt and restored several times.

Kapitelberget. Is the ruin of a medieval crypt church believed to have been built during the 1100s.

Maehlum Church. Timber-constructed from 1728. Altarpiece from 1618. Restored in 1968.

Rock Carvings. At Norde Maele, Fossum and Loberhaugen.

SPORTS. In summer there is quite good **fishing** in the mountains of western Telemark, very good on the Hardanger Plateau. **Hiking** from chalet to chalet on the Hardanger Plateau is another attraction. The South Coast offers **swimming** from the cliffs or lovely beaches (best are Sjøsanden near Mandal, Hamresanden near Kristiansand, and the beach at Fevik), **boating** among the skerries, and **fishing** in the sounds. The mountain lakes of Setesdal hold plenty of sleek trout.

Telemark, the birthplace of alpine **skiing**, is today one of Norway's most popular winter sports areas. The principal resorts are Bø/Lifjell, Bolkesjø, Morgedal, Rauland, Rjukan, Vrådal and Gautefall. The season extends from Christmas until after Easter. Most hotels have ski lifts of various types, employ their own ski instructors, and have ski equipment for hire.

THE FJORD COUNTRY

Wonders and Waterfalls

Norway's Fjord Country provides one of the world's unique travel experiences. The fjords tell different things to different people, with their awesome power and majesty, their changing moods. More likely than not, however, the visitor will recall something more, something of the atmosphere of quiet beauty. Whether it might be on the banks of one of the fjord's famous salmon or trout streams, or rowing in the shadow of a 300-meter (1,000-foot) rock face, or relaxing with a pot of good coffee and pleasant company on some fjord farm, there will always be that element of tranquil calm unique to this part of the world.

Exploring the Fjord Country

Conspicuously located in downtown Stavanger, only a stone's throw from the busy wharves with their hundreds of larger and smaller craft, is a monument to Alexander L. Kielland, the city's literary light and chronicler. With a good view from his pedestal, he stands there somewhat critically appraising the scene before him. Today it's certainly not the same town which he so vividly described some 80 or 90 years ago. But neither has it acquired the impersonal self-absorbed air which one might expect in the former fish canning capital of the world, now one of the headquarters of Norway's North Sea oil fleet.

Today, a new Stavanger has emerged, in keeping with the city's new role as headquarters of the Norwegian oil industry. The town has a distinctly cosmopolitan flavor in fact, legacy of the substantial overseas population attracted by the oil boom. It's an interesting spot in which to spend some time. With a population of over 92,000, Stavanger is the fourth-largest city in Norway. It was founded in 1100, and boasts a stately Anglo-Norman cathedral well over 800 years old.

Every visitor to Stavanger should walk around the older quarters with their picturesque alleyways, old style wooden structures and cobblestone streets. The venerable Kongsgaard school, as well as Ledaal—the old Kielland estate which is now public property—and the royal residence in Stavanger, should also be seen. Like so many Norwegian cities, Stavanger appears to be in a period of transition when the old must adjust itself to the demands of the times, while the new, in turn, must temper its urge to tear down and modernize. Stavanger has often been called the city with the many churches and has long enjoyed an active highly individualist spiritual life. One of its streets, Berglandsgate, is lined practically solid on both sides with a spectrum of churches, chapels and missions representing a large number of dissenting faiths and groups.

The Ryfylke fjords north and east of Stavanger form the southernmost part of the Fjord Country. Stavanger is well suited for its part as port of entry to this district, because the "White Fleet", consisting of low-slung, speedy craft known as "sea buses", provides swift and comfortable transport for both passengers and cars to the surrounding fjords. You may stay in Stavanger's fine hotels and make daily excursions on the ships of the "White Fleet" even to the most distant fjords of Ryfylke and return to your base in the afternoon. Stavanger is also the western terminus for the South Norway Railway.

The visitor should also make it a point to visit the Lyse Fjord. This trip should be made if for no other reason than to see the fjord's "cliff-dweller" communities, where farms cling to narrow ledges hundreds of meters above the sea, and the Pulpit Rock, some 610 meters (2,000 ft.) high. There is also a new road from Lysebotn to Sirdal, with 27 hairpin bends, climbing up the mountainside.

Though Stavanger has been primarily oriented towards the sea, it has more recently recognized its role as the gate to what has become one of Norway's leading agricultural counties. Stretching southward along the coast is a huge glacial moraine known as Jaeren. Flat and stony, it is probably the largest expanse of level ground to be found in all of Norway. But it is practically without harbors, nor is there much fishing. The inhabitants were therefore forced to turn to farming at an early date, and the district's hundreds of kilometers of stone fences stand today as monuments to centuries of back-breaking labor.

Once freed from stones, however, the soil was capable of growing crops of all kinds. There is little if any snow here, the climate is mild and the growing season long. Today, Jaeren is the country's leading producer of eggs and wool.

The "Discovery Route"

The "Discovery Route" is the classic route through the Ryfylke fjords to Hardanger and Bergen, with traditions dating back to the days of the pony cart. Thanks to the "White Fleet" and modern buses, this time-honored route has become popular lately.

The fjord boat leaves Stavanger early in the morning for Jelsa at the entrance to the Sand Fjord, where your bus is waiting. It takes you via

Sand, along the famous Suldalslågen salmon river to Solheimsvik, and around Lake Suldal to Nesflaten along the impressive new road. The journey then leads through the narrow and rugged Bratlandsdal Valley, where the road is hewn from the steep mountainside. At Breifonn you join the main Telemark road from Oslo to Bergen. Years ago it was blocked by snow every winter, but by means of huge tunnels, the road now goes straight through the impeding mountains.

At Breifonn you change to another bus, to Odda, which takes the zigzag road to the Seljestad mountain pass (now bypassed in tunnel) with fine views of Lake Røldal and the Breifonn Glacier. Descending on the Seljestad side, the bus will make a short stop at the Låtefoss waterfall, tumbling down the mountainside in a double avalanche and gently spraying the road. The Discovery Route terminates in Odda, the industrial center at the very head of the Sør Fjord—a branch of the mighty Hardanger Fjord.

Of all the popular spots in Hardanger, Sør Fjord is perhaps the most memorable. This fjord arm extends from Utne, almost due south to Odda, its east shore a continuous sweep of orchards—in springtime an undulating sea of white and pink blossoms. This setting, with its old farms, orchards, green plots and eternal mountains, has provided inspiration for great works of art, literature and music during the resurgence of national romanticism in the last century. Paintings of Adolf Tidemand and Hans Gude, songs like Ole Bull's *Seter Maiden's Sunday,* and many of Grieg's melodies had their origin in this part of the Hardanger Fjord. Visitors to Sør Fjord should not fail to see the old farm community at Aga on the west shore. The old buildings preserved here in their natural setting have retained an air of antiquity which no outdoor museum can match. A rather narrow road on the left of Sør Fjord leads through Aga to the charming resort of Utne. Utne can be reached by ferry from Kinsarvik on the other side of the fjord.

Out of the Sør Fjord and continuing almost due east, the Eid Fjord comprises the eastern extremity of the Hardanger Fjord, pushing inland almost to the very base of the Hardangerjøklen, a high-lying glacier. Eidfjord village, at the head of this fjord arm, has for centuries been a junction point between eastern and western Norway. From the earliest times, travelers on foot, horseback or on skis have followed this natural declivity down from the Hardanger plateau. Today, one of the main east-west highways follows this route through the magnificent Måbødal valley, passing by the well-known waterfall, the Vøringfoss, 182 meters (600 ft.) high. The nearby Sima power plant, the largest in Europe, is situated deep inside the mountain. Guided tours can be arranged by the local tourist office.

It is time now to look around for some of those renowned Hardanger beauty spots in which to relax. We have already passed the peaceful villages of Røldal and Seljestad, and on the eastern shore of the Sør Fjord there is the district of Ullensvang, with more fruit trees than any other Norwegian community, with a medieval church on a romantic point in the fjord, waterfalls draping the cliffs, the Folgefonn glacier capping the mountains across the fjord, and Edvard Grieg's studio hut. Exuding the same charm is lovely Utne on the point between the main fjord and Sør Fjord, Ulvik nestling at the head of its own little fjord and with terraced farms climbing the steep hills. Granvin is also an attractive resort.

Continuing from Odda along Sør Fjord, we ferry across the Hardanger Fjord from Bruravik to Brimnes and via the new Vallavik tunnel (opened

1985) to Granvin, and ride along the northern shores of the mighty main fjord. The high road takes us across the Fyksesund bridge, spanning the 230-meter (755-foot) gap of that imposing offshoot of the Hardanger Fjord, and along it we ride into the charming villages of Øystese and Norheimsund, both famous Hardanger resorts.

From Norheimsund we have the choice of two roads to Bergen. The main route takes us through another of those wild canyons—the Tokagjel Gorge—and across the mountain moors of Kvamskogen to the "Capital of the Fjords". The other route, narrower but no less interesting, continues along the Hardanger Fjord to Strandebarm, another flourishing Hardanger resort, and via Mundheim westwards to Bergen. Alternatively, you can take the E-68 road to Voss, the principal town in Hardanger and an international ski center. There are good road and rail connections to Bergen from here.

Waterways to Haugesund

Catamaran boats have been introduced between Stavanger and Bergen making the trip to Haugesund in 75 minutes and Bergen in four hours. However, the more leisurely way of going by ferry to the delightful old harbor town of Skudeneshavn and bus to Haugesund fits in better with most itineraries. Haugesund, built, it is said, on a foundation of herring bones, is a major shipping center.

Just north of the city is King Harald's Column, a monument raised on the burial mound where the Viking King Harald the Fairhaired is believed to lie. The column was dedicated in 1872, presumably 1,000 years after the battle of Hafrs Fjord, when Norway was united into a single kingdom. This historic battleground is located a short distance southwest of Stavanger.

Across the channel from Haugesund is the level, treeless island of Karmøy, the site of one of King Harald's favorite estates. A wealth of finds have verified the island's importance during Viking times.

Northward by boat or northeast from Haugesund via Highway E76 the destination is the same. By highway, one enters the back door, by boat the wide-open front door of Hardanger, loveliest of the fjords. Going by road a dilemma arises. By following Highway E76 all the way we travel along one of the finest fjordside roads hewn into the vertical wall of the Åkrafjord. By branching left at Håland, however, we include such gems as the villages of Skånevik and Rosendal, with modern hotels. Rosendal estate, which became a barony in 1678, has a history going right back to the days of the ancient Norse king, Håkon Håkonsson. The main building dates from the 1650s and is one of the most beautiful in all Norway, while the Rosendal Gardens are a sight long to be remembered. Estate and gardens were deeded to the University of Oslo in 1927 and the property is now being operated as an experimental farm.

While Hardanger is a tourist's paradise from early spring to late fall, one is in the habit of thinking of this fjord in terms of blossomtime. For Hardanger is the richest orchard district in Norway, with fruit trees often forming a seemingly endless border between fjord edge and the snow-capped mountains.

Northward to Sogne Fjord

Sailing northward from Bergen, we keep pretty well within the island fringe that provides a good sheltered waterway along much of the Norwegian coast. Inland the mountains rise range upon range, but along the coast the land is scraped and bare—nothing but smooth rounded stones with an occasional farm wherever a handful of soil made it possible. These weathered, rocky islands were evidently former mountain tops, and even farther inland the mountains seem rounded and worn. In fact only a few peaks in these parts protruded above the vast ice field that covered this whole fjord district in the Ice Age. When this huge blanket began to slip from east to west, it ground off the mountain tops and chiseled a series of deep valleys extending westward to the sea.

Then followed a period of upheaval while the coastline rose and fell, finally sinking until the tops of former peaks had been turned into islands, and long fingers of sea water had been sent probing into the innermost recesses of the valleys—in the case of the Sogne Fjord, a good 200 km. (125 miles). In the latter, the present sea level is halfway up the former valley wall, and the water is 1,128 meters (3,700 feet) deep at one point. Here in the fjord country people are now living five or six hundred meters above what was the valley floor some millions of years ago. Hence the fjords, and so much for a second-hand geography lesson.

Bypassing a little spot called Eivindvik, about three quarters of the way up the coast between Bergen and the mouth of the Sogne Fjord, you may notice two old stone crosses on the shore. It seems that these fjord districts were popular spots with the chieftains and clan leaders, most of whom preferred the rough, bald coastal tracts to the more protected and fertile inner fjords, a preference based on tactical rather than personal considerations. By establishing himself at a strategic point on the island-protected waterway which extends along a good length of the Norwegian coast, a chief who used foresight could secure himself a little Norwegian Gibraltar. Back in those early days, the landed peasants, clansmen and chieftains from the fjord districts used to meet somewhere in this section for their Gula Parliament, the laws of which have served as a model for the parliament of Iceland. Its location, as well as the stone crosses, suggest that Eivindvik was the site of this ancient legislative body.

Rounding the corner and swinging eastward into the Sogne Fjord, some interesting changes take place. As you push deeper into the fjord, the strip of land between the water's edge and the mountain wall becomes broader and greener. There are more farms, and the bald, naked rocks of the outer coast disappear. By the time Lavik is passed, you can begin to get an insight into the true fjord country.

Lavik sits just inside the outer Sogne Fjord, where the main highway leading northward to Sunn Fjord and Nord Fjord connects with a side road leading to the aluminum center of Høyanger. Thanks to quantities of cheap hydro-electric power, bauxite can be shipped in and processed into aluminum more cheaply here than in any other part of the world. The same is being done at Ardal, all the way at the end of the fjord. Høyanger itself is one of the best planned industrial towns on the globe. High, and near the top of one of the two peaks between which the town nestles, fumes pour out of a hole in the mountain top through a tunnel which functions as a gigantic smokestack. Here mountain breezes carry it away so that none of it ever reaches the town.

About halfway up the fjord at Balestrand begins the true fjord country. For generations this has been the most famous tourist region in Sogne. Here the harsh and bare landscape of the coast and outer fjord has gradually been building up to something surprising and exciting. By the time you push as far inland as Balestrand the world is new, and the inner Sogne lies before you. Here it's the magnitude that impresses. Towering snow-capped mountains drop 1,200 meters (4,000 feet) into the fjord often no wider than a city block. Against a background like this, a tourist steamer can look as insignificant as a water bug. In many places there's no shore at all; the perpendicular mountain faces continue right down beneath the water for hundreds, thousands of meters, and even the largest boats can slip along these rock walls at hand-shaking distance without worrying about where the bottom is.

From Balestrand, the long, narrow Fjaerlands Fjord probes northward towards Jostedalsbreen, Norway's mighty glacier. Fjaerland, at the fjord's head, has formerly only been accessible by boat, but this picturesque village can now be reached by road from Balestrand and other places along the fjord thanks to a new tunnel under the glacier opened in May 1986. A short distance inland are the Suphelle and Bøyum glaciers. Resembling a massive waterfall, the slow forward movement of the glacier pushes ice over the precipice and adds to the glittering blue-white wall along one side of the valley.

Second only to the magnitude of Norway's longest and mightiest fjord, it is the color and the ordered neatness of man's contribution to the scene that makes inner Sogne an event of discovery. There are green, well-kept fields, separated by fences of a million stones plucked from the land, and orchards of fruit trees turning a whole fjord rim into a single great orchard. It is easy to see why farming is the major source of livelihood here.

Like many of the innermost fjord communities on the Norwegian coast, this district enjoys an inland climate even though it is located on salt water. Fjord-ends and narrow valleys between these huge bastions of sheer rock are natural greenhouses. Rock walls absorb the heat from the sun during the daylight hours and radiate it after sundown. Crops are heavy, the fruit is the finest in Norway and even tobacco may be grown.

Four Fingers of the Sogne Fjord

About two-thirds of the way along its length, Sogne Fjord branches off in four different directions. The southernmost finger worms due south past Aurland and finally lodges fast between two mountain peaks at Flåm. From that point an electric spur line carries visitors up 1,000 meters (3,000 feet) in 45 minutes to Myrdal on the Oslo-Bergen railway. The next, and shortest, of these fingers comes to rest at Laerdal, near which is the famed Borgund Stave Church. This is one of the most interesting and best preserved of these early medieval edifices. Constructed of hewn timber and roofed and sided with long round-tipped shingles, the church dates from the middle 12th century and presents an amazing insight into the period when Norway was newly Christianized. Crosses vie with dragons, reflecting a charming indecision on the part of the builders as to just what would do proper justice to their new-found faith. Standing there on the earth floor of that gloomy interior, with the scent of century-old wood smoke and tar in his nostrils, the visitor can't help but imagine gruff and probably faltering voices intoning the strange new chants to the Church of Rome.

Notice the worn round hole in one wall; this was the lepers' hole, through which the afflicted who stood outside could hear the priest.

Continuing northward, the third of these four fjord fingers was once probably longer than it is now. Millenniums ago a huge glacial dump was deposited about midway up this fjord valley, forming what is now a large fresh-water lake. Here at Årdal is one of Norway's largest aluminum factories based on hydro-electric power from Tyin Lake, some 1,000 meters (3,000 feet) above the plant, and the Jotunheim Mountains. The water drops that full distance through underground conduits to a turbine-generator room blasted out of solid rock deep in the mountain. From outside, there is little in the diminutive tunnel entrance to suggest that you are looking at one of Norway's mightiest power plants.

The fourth and longest of these fingers of the Sogne Fjord, known as the Luster Fjord, extends almost due north, terminating between the Jotunheim range to the east and the Jostedal Glacier to the west. What this scenery may lack in wild gradeur it makes up for in pastoral beauty and neatness, but if you sidetrack to Nigard glacier (a "tongue" of the massive Jostedal) you'll find all the spectacle you could wish for. Guides wait at the ice tip which is reached by boat across the glacier lake, twice a day in summer. Remember to wear sensible clothing. The Urnes Stave Church, dating from 1070 and probably the oldest of its kind in Norway, is an easier excursion from Sogndal via Solvorn, across Luster Fjord. From Fortun, at the end of this fjord, a highway climbs over Jotunheimen to Lom in Ottadal.

Going to the Sogne Fjord by boat is only one of the methods—though certainly one of the best—to probe its wonders. Another way of approach from Bergen is by railway to Myrdal and down the stupendous Flåm Line, one of the most remarkable pieces of railway engineering in the world. From Flåm a tourist steamer plies daily to Balestrand and Fjaerland on the northern shores.

Another superb route is the one from Voss by bus via Stalheim—a true eyrie overlooking the Naerøydal valley with rainbow-dancing waterfalls and sugarloaf mountains—and out to the finest piece of fjord scenery belonging to Sogne, the Naerøyfjord, often not more than 500 meters (1,650 feet) across, with mountains towering to 1,000 meters (3,000 feet) and more on both sides, and sprinkled with waterfalls. By an ingenious system of connections (boarding one boat from another in mid-fjord) not only Laerdal but Balestrand and other important places on the northern shore are reached.

The straightest approach to the Sogne Fjord is a variation of this latter route, branching off at Vinje from the main road, and crossing the mountain plateau before gently unwinding itself down to the village of Vik, with its characteristic stave church. From Vangsnes, where Emperor Wilhelm II of Germany saw fit to erect a Viking monument of gigantic dimensions, there is a ferry across the fjord to Balestrand, the central point.

The Nord Fjord and the Geiranger Fjord

Exploring the Nord Fjord can again be done by fjord steamer from Bergen or by choosing one of the scenic overland routes from the Sogne Fjord area, such as the one from Lavik via beautiful Lake Jølster, which at Moskog is joined by the route across the Gaularfjell Mountains from Balestrand. The most impressive of these routes, however, is the Sognefjell

road, which climbs in magnificent curves from the head of the Luster
Fjord to the high mountains of Jotunheimen and Norway's highest mountain pass 1,430 meters (4,690 feet) to descend into the romantic Bøverdal
valley. At the village of Lom you turn westward again, climbing to the
mountain plateau at Grotli. Here there is a choice of two routes, the one
heading northwest to Geiranger, and the other one southwest to Nord
Fjord. By choosing the second, you will more or less complete a circuit
around the mightiest glacier of the European continent, Jostedalsbreen.

By steamer, you continue on from Sogne Fjord to Måløy and Nordfjordeid. As at Årdal, a glacial moraine has filled in the natural fjord valley, separating Nordfjordeid from Hornindal Lake by a barrier of land
about two km. (one mile) wide. Much of this is cultivated, but these lush
fields represent generations of work.

At Loen you may follow the Loen valley up to a long, narrow lake where
blue-white glaciers overhang the valley walls. It is here that subterranean
rumblings have twice preceded natural catastrophes when a part of the
mountain has crashed down into the lake. From the road, you will notice
Loen Lake practically filled in at one point; whole communities have simply disappeared here in the course of minutes. At the extreme end of the
valley the road peters out amid a moraine at the foot of cliffs whose walls
are laced with glacial brooks.

There are many who regard Nord Fjord as the most beautiful of Norway's fjords. It is more gentle, but at the same time just a little more forbidding than the other districts we explored. There seems to linger something
of the old days of trolls and giants and a strain of that mystery which in
Grieg's music belittles the man who believes only what he sees.

In Geiranger the mountains tower upward for thousands of meters
straight out of a channel so narrow that the boat seems barely to squeeze
through. Yet here, high on what appears to be a notch on the mountain
face, people actually lived and farmed a generation ago on the few hundred
square meters of soil that Nature has scattered in this niche.

The road to Geiranger from Nordfjord worms its way upward via a series of switchbacks to a height of over 1,000 meters (3,000 feet). After some
20 bends there is a stop at Videseter to enjoy the view of one of the world's
wildest valleys—the Hjelledal. As you progress upward, you enter a
strange, new world—the roof of Norway, a vastness of snowcapped peaks,
lakes, stone and more stone. From Djupvasshytta a private toll road leads
upwards another 450 meters (1,500 feet) to the top of Mount Dalsnibba,
from whose peak it is possible to see for more than 150 km. (93 miles).

The spectacular "Eagle Road" with its unforgettable view of the Seven
Sisters waterfalls, zigzags from Geiranger to Eidsdal. Stop at the "Eagle's
Turn" to take in one of the outstanding views of the fjord country. It is
also possible to take a sightseeing tour on the Geirangerfjord and look at
these spectacular waterfalls from sea level. From the village of Eidsdal
there is a ferry across the fjord to Linge, where the road leads on to Valldal. Here you may notice the zig-zag stripe in the mountain wall—this
was the sea monster that Norway's holy king, St. Olav, smashed against
that cliff when it tried to oppose his landing in Valldal some 900 years
ago. The "Trolls' Path" (Trollstigveien), between Valldal and Åndalsnes,
is a giant among Norway's serpentine roads, coming down the vertical
cliff-face in 11 unbelievably audacious bends, among majestic mountains—the "King", the "Queen", and the "Bishop" (all of which challenge

the rock climber)—with the 150-km. (500-foot) Stigfoss fall and fantastic views.

Another wonderful route runs north from Geiranger. You go by ferry on the Geiranger Fjord past the Seven Sisters waterfalls to Hellesylt, where you take a bus for a breathtaking ride high above the Sunnylvs Fjord, via Stranda and Sykkylven to Ålesund.

"Top of the Fjord Country"

Thus we have arrived at the "Top of the Fjord Country", a title aptly applied to the northernmost fjords of Vestlandet as it indicates both their geographical position and their striking character. It comprises such fjords as the Geiranger Fjord—the very quintessence of fjords—the Hjørund Fjord, magnificent nave of a Gothic Cathedral, the Romsdal Fjord surrounded by alpine peaks, and the Sunndalsfjord, a water-filled canyon among towering cliffs. There are valleys of almost supernatural grandeur and beauty—the Innerdal, Eikesdal, and Norangsdal; waterfalls among the world's highest, such as the Mardalsfoss of Eikesdal, with an uninterrupted fall of 297 meters (975 feet), followed by one of 220 meters (722 feet), the total measuring 656 meters (2,150 feet) and appearing from the valley in spring as one unbroken whole; mountains like the wild formations of Trollheimen, the vertical cliffs of Sunndal, the unruly sea of alpine peaks in Sunmøre, and the "troll" pinnacles of Romsdal. Åndalsnes and Geiranger are the main resorts, second come Ørsta, Hellesylt, Stranda and Øye.

The three towns of the "Top of the Fjord Country" are tourist attractions in their own right. The *klipp*-fish town of Kristiansund, built out on islands facing the sea, connected by bridges and ferry boats, and almost totally rebuilt in colorful architecture after World War II, is extremely pleasing to the modern eye. In the ocean outside lies the island of Grip, Norway's smallest community, until it was incorporated into Kristiansund, clustering round an old stave church. The sea has taken its toll of the Grip people; after the catastrophes of 1640 and 1802 only the church remained. No wonder that the surrounding skerries have such names as "Devils", "Man Killer", and "Hard Skull". As late as 1897, Grip was without franchise or taxation.

The residential town of Molde is known for its panorama that takes in the 87 snow-crowned peaks of the Romsdal mountains. This is a typical resort town, offering a host of interesting excursions, fishing in sea and lake, mountaineering and other activities and an annual and highly popular jazz festival. Molde is called the "town of roses" and if you visit in summer you'll soon see why.

The biggest town of Møre and Romsdal, Ålesund, has its own "Acropolis" with no temple but with a restaurant and a stadium on top and a view of ocean, fjords, and mountains that rivals the view from Fløyen, Bergen. The fjord flights starting from Oslo offered by the Braathen SAFE Airline are something very much out of the ordinary walks of life and travel. Just south of Ålesund is the island of Runde, Norway's southernmost bird sanctuary, with 700,000 inhabitants, including some very rare species, sea-grottos and needle-shaped cliffs. About five km. (three miles) to the east of Ålesund, at Borgund, is the open-air Sunmøre Museum comprising 30 old timber dwellings, a medieval church and the excavated sites of a Viking town.

PRACTICAL INFORMATION FOR
THE FJORD COUNTRY

TELEPHONE CODES. We have given telephone codes for all the towns and villages in the hotel and restaurant lists that follow. These codes need only be used when calling from outside the town or village concerned.

HOTELS AND RESTAURANTS. The Fjord Country has been popular for nearly a century so it has an impressive array of small attractive resorts and a high assortment of hotels. Most of those listed below are licensed but the smaller pensions *(gjestgiveri)* and farm-pensions sometimes are not; if it's important to you, check first. Many hotels offer reduced rates before June 15 and after August 25, *the* season to see the fjords. For easier reference, localities are listed under the districts in which they are situated.

Rogaland District

Bryne (Rogaland). *Rica Jaeren* (L), Arne Garborgsvei (04–482488). 110 beds, 51 rooms with facilities, restaurant, swimming, sauna. AE, DC, MC, V.
Restaurants. *Guddy's,* Meierigt 28 (04–482472).

Haugesund (Rogaland). *Rica Park Hotel* (E), Ystadvn 1 (04–712000). 201 beds. AE. *Rica Saga Hotel* (E), Skippergt, 11 (04–711100). 150 beds. AE, DC, MC, V. *Haugaland* (M), Flotmyr (04–713466). 54 beds. MC, V. *IMI* (M), Strandgt 192 (04–723699). 40 beds, mission hotel, unlicenced. *Rica Maritim* (M), Åsbygt 3 (04–711100). 430 beds. AE, DC, MC, V.
Restaurants. *Captains Cabin,* Skjoldavn 1 (04–721440). *Den Lille Café,* Haraldsgt 139 (04–714767). *The Shakespeare,* Haraldsgt 169 (04–723414). *Tante Louise,* Haradlsgt 133 (04–725069). *Williams Grill,* Haraldsgt 70 (04–724108).
Youth Hostel. *Skeisvang Youth Hostel* (I), (04–712146). 52 beds.

Sandnes (Rogaland). *Kronen Guard* (E), Vatne (04–621400). 50 beds, all rooms with bath. Located 30 minutes by car from Stavanger. Offers something more than an ordinary hotel with excellent service. Very good restaurant, particularly recommended on Sundays. AE, DC, MC, V. *Sandnes Motorhotell* (M), R. Amundsensgt 115 (04–663088). 100 beds, all rooms with bath/shower. AE, DC, MC, V. *Sverre* (M), Storgt 45 (04–66 1086). 125 beds. *Holiday Motel* (I), Granddal Rte. 44 (04–674811). 97 beds, 25 rooms with bath/shower. MC, V.
Restaurants. *Den Lille Café Huset Vårt,* Solavn 3 (04–665 910). *Kalles Kafteria,* Industrigt 1 (04–662 829). *Nille Café,* Gjesdalv. 29 (04–661 111). *Sandnes Kafeteria,* Vågsgt 34 (04–661 502).

Sauda (Rogaland). *Kløver* (E), (04–782633). 38 beds, all rooms with bath/shower. *Grand* (M), (04–782148). 50 beds. DC. *Sauda Fjord Hotel* (M), at Saudasjøen (04–781211). 78 beds, good restaurant. DC, MC, V.
Restaurants. *Kroa,* Brugaten 19 (04–782057).

Stavanger (Rogaland). *KNA Hotellet* (E), Lagårdsvei 61 (04–528500). 332 beds, 120 rooms with bath/shower, restaurant, grill, bar. AE, DC, MC, V. *SAS Royal* (E), Løkkevn. 26, (04–567000). 290 rooms with all facilities, bar, health club with swimming pool and sauna, business service center, airline check-in, garage. *Scandic* (E), Eiganesvei 181, Madla (04–526500). 270 beds, all rooms with facilities, restaurant, grill, bar. DC, MC, V. *Alstor Hotel* (M), Tjensvollvn 31 (04–

527020). 128 beds, all with facilities. AE, DC, MC, V. *Sola Strand* (M), Axel Lund-sv. 27 (04–650222). Near airport on beach. 150 beds, most rooms with facilities. *Victoria* (M), Skansegaten 1 (04–520526). On quay, 204 beds, 97 rooms with bath/shower, restaurant, bar. AE, DC, MC, V.

Pensions. *Bergeland* Gjestegiveri (M), Vikedalsgate la (04–534110). 100 beds. *City Gjestehuset* (M), Madlaveien 18–20 (04–520437). 45 beds. *Commandor* (M), Valbergsgate 9 (04–528000). 52 beds, 48 rooms with bath. AE, DC, MC, V. *Havly* (I), Valberggt. 1 (04–533114). 46 beds. *Rogalandsheimen* (I), Musegate 18 (04–520188). 25 beds.

Restaurants. *Angus House,* Østervåg 25 (04–531636). Chinese. *Jan's Mat og Vin-hus,* Breitorget (04–524502). *La Gondola,* Nytorget 8 (04–534235). *Pernille,* Kirkegt 36 (04–521287). *Viking Restaurant,* Jernbanen (04–528747). *Moon House* (Chinese), Sølvberggt. 9 (04–534343). *De Røde Sjønhus,* N. Holmegt. 14–20 (04–520194). *Straen,* N. Strandgt. 15 (04–526100). Fish specialties.

Youth Hostel. *Mosvangen Youth Hostel* (I), Ibsensgt 21 (04–527560). 80 beds. 3 kms. (2 miles) from station.

Bergen District and Hardanger Fjord

Godøysund (Hordaland). A cluster of small islands, famous yachting center. *Godøysund Fjord Hotel* (E), (054–31 404). 90 beds, 45 rooms with facilities, restaurant. DC, MC, V.

Kinsarvik (Hardanger fjord). Busy ferry point in Hardanger, fine views of fjord and glacier. *Kinsarvik Fjord Hotel* (M), (054–63 100). 135 beds, all rooms with bath/shower. Restaurant Fjord-Kroa. AE, MC, V.

Restaurants. *Harding Hage–Kro* (054–63 182). *Kinsarvik Kafé* (054–63390).

Kvamskogen. (Hordaland). Skiing center, 370 meters (1,200 feet). *Ungdomshei-men* (I), (05–558947). Kvernavollen, popular youth center, 101 beds, cafeteria. **Restaurant.** *Veikroa* (05–558960).

Leirvik (Hordaland). Village on Stord island, bathing, boating, fishing, riding. *Stord Hotel* (E), (054–10 544). 160 beds, all rooms with bath/shower. Restaurant. *Grand* (M), (054–10 233). 76 beds, 50 rooms with facilities. Restaurant.

Youth Hostel. *Lillebø Youth Hostel* (I), (054–14 310). 45 beds.

Lofthus (Hardanger fjord). Famous resort in fruit growing district, facing Sør fjord and Folgefonn glacier. *Ullensvang* (L), (054–61 100). Outstanding, 250 beds, all rooms with facilities, Edvard Grieg's composing cabin in garden. Restaurant. AE, DC, MC, V.

Norheimsund (Hardanger fjord). Resort. *Norheimsund Fjord Hotel* (E), (05–551522). Facing fjord, 76 beds, all rooms with bath/shower. AE, DC, MC, V. *Sand-ven* (M), (05–551911). Facing fjord, 70 beds, 23 rooms with bath/shower, large restaurant used in many package tours. AE, MC, V.

Restaurants. *Fossatun Kafé* (05–551677). *Grillkroa* (05–552340). *Sjøbotn Ka-feteria* (05–551215).

Odda (Hardanger fjord). At head of Sør fjord, industrial center with outstanding surroundings. *Hardanger* (M), Eitrheimsv 13 (054–42 133). 128 beds, 32 rooms with bath. Restaurant. DC, MC, V. *Sørfjordheimen Hotell* (M), Bustetungt 2 (054–41 411). 63 beds, 10 rooms with bath.

Restaurants. *Hjørna Kro og Kafé* (054–41 356). *Iris Kafé* (054–41 105). *Sportskaféen* (054–42 278). *Vasstun Café* (054–41 505).

Youth Hostel. *Odda Youth Hostel* (I), Eidsbratet 1 (054–42 005). 110 beds.

Os (Hordaland). *Solstrand* (E), (05–300099). Facing fjord, one of finest hotels on west coast, 260 beds, all rooms with facilities, restaurant, swimming, sauna. AE, DC, MC, V.

Øystese (Hardanger fjord). *Hardangerfjord* (M), (05–555333). 170 beds, most rooms with facilities. Cafeteria/restaurant. AE, DC, MC.
Restaurants. Øystese Kafé (05–555305). *Sjøbua and Nøring Spisested* (05–555523).

Rosendal (Hordaland). Ancient manor, medieval stone church. *Rosendal Fjord Hotel* (E), (054–81 511). 120 beds, all rooms with facilities. AE, DC, MC, V.

Seljestad (Hordaland). 300 meters (980 feet), fine views of Folgefonn glacier, ski center with lifts and instructors. *Seljestad* (M), 5763 Skarde (054–45 155). 121 beds, 43 rooms with facilities. Cafeteria. DC, MC, V. *Solfonn* (M), (054–45 122). 155 beds, 64 rooms with facilities.

Strandebarm (Hardanger fjord). *Strandebarm Fjord Hotel* (M), (05–559150). 50 beds, vegetarian food. MC.

Ulvik (Hardanger fjord). Fashionable resort at head of narrow Ulvik fjord. *Brakanes* (E), (05–526105). Outstanding, 200 beds, all rooms with facilities, restaurant, boats, private beach, windsurfing, dancing bar, sauna, putting green, tennis. AE, DC, MC, V. *Strand* (E), (05–526305). 120 beds, 30 rooms with bath. AE, MC, V. *Ulvik Tourist Hotel* (E), (05–526200). 120 beds, all rooms with bath. Cafeteria. AE, DC, MC, V.

Utne (Hardanger fjord). Idyllic village, orchards, views of Folgefonn glacier. *Utne* (M), (054–66 983). Lovely old house built in 1722, on the shore of the fjord. Five generations of the same family have run the hotel, which is full of beautiful furniture. 45 beds, all rooms with bath or shower. Restaurant. AE, DC, MC.

Sogne Fjord

Balestrand. One of Norway's oldest tourist centers. *Dragsvik* (M), (056–91 293). 80 beds, most rooms with facilities. AE, DC, V. *Kvikne* (M), (056–91 101). 210 beds, 95 rooms with facilities. AE, DC, MC, V. *Bøyum Pensjonat* (I), (056–91 114). 24 beds, most rooms with facilities. DC, V. *Kringsjå* (I), (056–91 303). 75 beds, 17 rooms with bath, private ketch for fjord trips.
Youth Hostel. *Balestrand Youth Hostel* (I), (056–91303). 90 beds.

Fjaerland (Balestrand). Fjord village, formerly only accessible by boat, now reached by new road and tunnel under glacier. Excursions to glaciers. *Mundal* (E), (056–93 101). Good family hotel, 60 beds, 30 rooms with bath. AE. *Fjaerland Fjord hotell* (M), (056–93 161). 40 beds, 21 rooms with bath.

Flåm (Aurland). Terminal of railroad, descending 866 meters (2,840 feet) from Myrdal through a string of tunnels. *Fretheim* (E), (056–32 200). 140 beds, all rooms with facilities, salmon and sea trout fishing, boats. *Heimly Lodge* (M), (056–32 241). 68 beds.

Hermansverk (Leikanger). *Sognefjord Turisthotell* (E), (056–53 444). 87 beds, all rooms with facilities. AE, DC, MC, V.
Restaurants. *Elvegard Café* (056–53 224). *K–senteret Kafé* (056–53 422).

Laerdal. Fjord village on famous Laerdal salmon river. *Fjordstuen* (E), (056–66 507). 180 beds, all rooms with facilities. Restaurant. Swimming pool, boat rental. AE, DC, MC, V. *Lindstrøm* (E), (056–66 202). 160 beds, all rooms with bath/shower. *Offerdal Hotel and Youth Hostel* (I), (056–66 101). 90 beds.

Leikanger. Leikanger Fjordhotell (E), (056–53 622). 85 beds, 33 rooms with bath. MC.

Skjolden. Fjord village in fruit-growing district. *Skjolden* (I), (056–86 606). 100 beds, 40 rooms with bath.
Youth Hostel. *Skjolden Youth Hostel* (I), (056–86 615). 30 beds.

Sogndal. Village with orchards, salmon fishing. *Hofslund* (M), (056–71 (022). 90 beds, all rooms with bath.
Youth Hostel. *Sogndal Youth Hostel* (I), (056–71 061). 90 beds.

Solvorn. Fjord village opposite Urnes stave church. *Walaker Hotell and Motel* (M), (056–84 207). Originally old posting inn, family owned since 1690. Situated on the banks of Lusterfjord, an arm of the larger Sognefjord. 40 beds, all with bath. Delicious homemade fare—bread, preserves, Fish is one of the specialties. Self-catering apartments available.

Turtagrø. 990 meters (3,250 feet), ideal starting point for walks into Jotunheimen mountain ranges. *Turtagrø* (M), (056–86 116). 65 beds, 5 rooms with bath.

Vik I Sogn. Old churches. *Hopstock* (M), (056–95 102). 58 beds, all rooms with bath/shower. DC, MC, V.
Restaurant. *Viking Cafeteria* (056–95334).

Sunn Fjord and Nord Fjord

Florø (Sunn fjord). Norway's most westerly town, sheltered by numerous islands. *Victoria* (L), Markegt 43 (057–41 033). 170 beds, 55 rooms with bath. AE, DC, MC, V.

Førde (Sunn fjord). At head of Førde fjord. *Sunnfjord* (E), (057–21 622). 330 beds, all rooms with facilities, salmon and trout fishing, angling school. AE, DC, MC, V. *Nye Førde* (M), Hafstadvegen 26 (057–21 411). 64 beds, 50 rooms with bath. AE, DC, MC, V.
Restaurants. *Firdatun Kafé,* Storehagen (057–21 832).

Loen (Styrn—Nord fjord). A fine resort, excursions to Jostedal glacier. *Alexandra* (E), (057–77 660). Outstanding family hotel, 386 beds, all rooms with facilities, folk dancing. AE, DC, MC, V. *Richards* (M), (057–77 657). 45 beds, all rooms with facilities. AE, DC, MC, *Loen Pensjonat* (I), (057–77 624). 48 beds. MC, V.

Måløy (Nord fjord). On island connected with mainland by 1,224–meter (4,016 feet) long bridge. *Kaptein Linge* (E), (057–51 800). 100 beds, 30 rooms with facilities. MC.
Restaurant. *Kannestein Kro* (057–51 699).

Nordfjordeid (Eid—Nord fjord. *Hoddeviks* (M), (057–60 622). 75 beds, most rooms with facilities. Restaurant. Suitable for the disabled. *Nordfjord* (M), (057–60 433). 110 beds, all rooms with facilities. DC, MC, V.
Restaurants. *Eid Cafeteria* (057–60 464). *Sjøsanden Kro* (057–60 060).

Olden (Stryn—Nord fjord). Excursions to Jostedal glacier. *Olden Fjordhotell* (E), (057–73 400). 80 beds, 36 rooms with bath. AE, DC, MC. *Yris* (E), (057–73 240). 78 beds, 59 rooms with bath. DC, MC. *Olden Krotell* (I), (057–73 296). 33 beds, all rooms with bath/shower. AE, MC.
Restaurant. *Briksdalsbre Fjellstove* (057–73 811).

Sandane (Gloppen—Nord fjord). Folk museum, church. *Sivertsen* (E), (057–65 333). 60 beds, 26 rooms with bath/shower. *Vertshuset A/S* (M), (057–66 177). 38 beds, 17 rooms with showers

Stryn (Nord fjord). Traffic junction for regional bus services. *Hjelle Hotel* (M), Hjelledalen (057–75 250). 42 beds. *Karistova* (I), (057–76513). 48 beds. Several inexpensive pensions.
Youth Hostel. *Stryn Youth Hostel* (I), (057–71 106). 88 beds.

Møre and Romsdal

Åesund (Sunnmøre). *Baronen* (E), Vikasenteret (071–47 000). 36 beds, all rooms with bath/shower. Restaurant. DC, MC, V. *Rica Parken* (E), Storgaten 16 (071–25 050). 248 beds, all with facilities., large restaurant, bar, grill, sauna, whirl pool. DC, MC, V. *Rica Skansen* (M), Kongensgate 27 (071–22 938). 179 beds, 44 rooms with bath. AE, DC, MC, V. *Scandinavie* (M), Løvendolgate 8 (071–23 131). 120 beds in 63 rooms, all with facilities, restaurants. AE, DC, MC, V. *Havly Hotel* (I), Rønnebergsgate 4 (071–24 960). 85 beds, 10 rooms with facilities. DC, MC.
Restaurants. *Fregatten Mat og Vinhus,* Keiser Wilhelmsgt 25 (071–27 014). *Skateflua Kafeteria,* Skaregt 1 (071–24253).

Åndalsnes (Rauma—Romsdal). *Grand Hotell Bellevue* (E), (072–21 011). 90 beds, 35 rooms with bath. MC, V. *Rauma Pension* (M), (072–21 233). 19 beds.
Restaurants. *Go'bitn Kafé,* Måndalen (072–23 580). *N-Kafé,* Jernbanegt 1. *Vengetind Kafé,* Vollan 5 (072–21 437).

Geiranger. (Stranda—Sunnmøre). Fjord boat trips. *Geiranger Hotel* (E), (071–63 005). 125 beds, 60 rooms with bath, swimming. AE, DC, MC, V. *Meroks Fjord Hotel* (E), (071–63 002). 105 beds, 33 rooms with bath. AE, DC, MC, V. *Union* (E), (071–63 000). 250 beds, 68 rooms with bath, swimming, sauna. AE, DC, MC, V.

Kristiansund (Nordmøre). *Fosna Hotell Atlantic* (E), Hauggt 16 (073–74 011). 75 beds, all rooms with bath. AE, DC, MC, V. *Grand* (M), Bernstorffstredet 1 (073–73 011). 226 beds, all rooms with bath. AE, DC, MC, V. *Kristiansund* (M), Storgt. 17 (073–73–211). 55 beds, all rooms with bath/shower. Restaurant, fully licensed. *Rica Hotel Kristiansund* (M), Storgt 41–43 (073–76 411). 204 beds, all rooms with bath/shower. Restaurant. Fully licensed.
Restaurants. *Maritim Café,* Storgt 34 (073–72 002). *Nordmørskafeen,* Fosnagt 3 (073–74 547). *Utsyn,* Kongens plass 4 (073–72 414).
Youth Hostel. *Kristiansund Youth Hostel* (I), (073–71 104). 31 beds.

Molde (Romsdal). *Alexandra* (E), Storgt 1–7 (072–51 133). Magnificent views of fjord and mountains, 250 beds, most rooms with facilities, swimming, sauna, sun terrace. AE, DC, MC, V. *Novel* (E), Amtm Kroghsgt 5 (072–51 555). 76 beds, all rooms with bath. AE, DC, MC, V. *Romsdal* (M), Storgt 19 (072–51 711). 49 beds, all rooms with bath. MC, V.
Restaurants. *Gimle,* Hammegt 35 (072–54 122). *Kaffistova,* Storgt 19 (072–51 711). *Najaden Mat og Vinhus,* Romsdalsgt 20 (072–56 965). *Naust-Gryta,* Hamnegt 47 (072–51 030).
Youth Hostel. *Rimo Hostel* (I), Fabrikvn 4–8 (072–54 330). 266 beds, summer.

Ørsta (Sunnmøre). *Viking Fjord Hotel* (M), (070–66 800). 86 beds, 44 rooms with bath, salmon fishing, deer shooting. MC.

Sunndalsøra (Nordmøre). At head of Sunndal fjord. *Müllerhotell Sunndalen* (M), (073–91 655). 103 beds, all rooms with bath. MC, V.
Youth Hostel. *Sunndalsøra Youth Hostel* (I), (073–91 301). 30 beds.

Surnadal (Nordmøre). *Surnadal Hotel* (M), (073–61 544). 175 beds, 17 rooms with bath. DC, MC.

Volda (Sunnmøre). *Svendsen* (M), (071–76 034). 48 beds, 3 rooms with bath. *Volda Turisthotell* (M), (071–77 050). 48 beds, some rooms with bath. AE, DC, MC, V.

Restaurants. *Porse,* Skjervav (070–77 050).

HOW TO GET AROUND. If coming from Oslo you can travel by train to Stavanger (about 8 hours), to Bergen (6–8 hours) and to Åndalsnes (7–8 hours) with both day and overnight services. These places are connected by air with the capital either directly, or via nearby airports with onward bus connections. And the internal air services go to a number of other small towns in the region.

Getting about in this large area is a matter of judicious combination of ferries, buses and trains, allowing you to reach even the smallest community. There are express coastal boat services from Bergen to the Sognefjord as well as the daily "trunk route" ship service to the Far North. Coastal ferries to the south link Bergen with Haugesund and Stavanger (plus other places en route) with both express and local services. Both hydrofoils and catamarans are used on some of these. As the whole system is somewhat complicated, you should enquire locally about those routes of particular interest. Apart from one of two summer "specials," they all operate through the year.

By car. The coastal road from Oslo to Stavanger and many mountain roads (among which the Haukeli, Valdres-Fillefjell, Romsdal, and Sunndal roads are open all year) run into the Fjord Country. Bergen is an excellent starting point for a circuit north to Kristiansund (via Voss-Gudvangen-Balestrand, lake Jølster and the Geirangerfjord, returning by Nordfjord and the Vadheim-Bergen ferry: about 1,220 km., 757 miles) or south to Stavanger along the "Discovery Route" (via Røldal and Sand, returning via Haugesund). Motoring in the fjord country is by nature a leisurely affair, interrupted by spectacular trips across blue fjords. Along these winding roads and in such scenic surroundings there is little sense in covering more than 150–200 km. (100–125 miles) a day.

TOURS. As is appropriate to the Fjord Country, there are many, many boat excursions available throughout the area. There are fjord cruises, trips out to the islands, fishing trips and visits to local beauty spots. There are also plenty of road tours, walking routes and even seaplane and helicopter excursions. The local Tourist Information Offices will have details of guided tours, and suggestions for those who prefer to explore on their own.

PLACES TO VISIT. Glaciers and waterfalls are a particular feature of this beautiful region, and every district has its share of natural wonders that shouldn't be missed. The local Tourist Information Offices will have maps and suggestions as to which ones you should see. There are also a number of museums, and farm and church buildings of interest. Some of these places, both natural and man-made, are listed below.

Rogaland District

Haugesund. The City Hall with Haugesund Museum.

The Five Foolish Virgins. Monoliths from around A.D. 300, by Karmsund bridge.

Haraldshaugen. Where Norway's first king, Harald Hårfagre, is buried. The stone cross on Krosshaugen nearby is from the very early Christian era.

St. Olav's Church. Avaldsnes. Stone church built in 1250 by King Håkon Håkonsson.

Stavanger. Old Stavanger is not a museum, but a living part of the town between Øvre and Nedre Strandgate, with some 130 lived-in white wooden houses from 1800s.

Stavanger Domkirke (Stavanger Cathedral). Norway's best-preserved medieval church. Anglo-Norman style, construction probably started around 1125.

Stavanger Museum. Musegt 16. Archeological, cultural and natural history collections. New trade and maritime museum.

Ullandhaug Farm. A reconstructed farm from the migration period on an archeological site with burial mounds from the Bronze and Iron ages.

Utstein Cloister. Augustinian cloister from the second half of the 13th century. Restored 1965; the only preserved cloister in Norway.

Bergen District and Hardanger Fjord

Kinsarvik. Bu Museum. The Bu Museum is a branch of the Hardanger Folk Museum. It occupies an open site to the left of Highway 7 from Kinsarvik to Eidfjord, 15 km. (nine miles) from Kinsarvik. There are three old houses containing furniture and domestic and craft equipment and the basement of a farmhouse stocked with an immense variety of relics from the stone age to modern times.

Skredhaugen Museum. About 6 km. (four miles) from Kinsarvik on highway 47 to Odda a minor road forks left and provides an alternative route to Lofthus. A few hundred meters from the fork is the Skredhaugen branch of the Hardanger Folk Museum, a collection of seven timber houses gathered from the area and furnished and equipped in the period.

Lofthus. Edvard Grieg's cabin. Where he composed some of his famous works, in the hotel garden.

Rosendal. Kvinnherad Church from mid–1200.

Rosendal Barony. A Renaissance castle from the 1600s, surrounded by a garden and park.

Sogne Fjord

Flåm. Flåm Church from 1600 with stone age graves nearby.

Laerdal. Borgund stave church from 1150.

Leikanger Church. Erected in 1250. Restored to its form of the 17th century. Altar and pulpit from 1606.

Sogndal. Kaupanger Stave Church. Largest in the area, from 1200. Alterations made in 1862. Today restored to its original form and decor.

Sogn Museum "The Heiberg Collection". The most comprehensive museum in Western Norway particularly strong on Norwegian agricultural history.

Stedje Church (1867). The third church on the same site. The first was built when King Olav christened Norway.

Vik. Hopperstad Stave Church from 1130, a fine example of medieval building style.

Hove Stone Church. The oldest stone building in Sogn, from medieval times.

Sunn Fjord and Nord Fjord

Florø. Kinn Church. Romanesque stone church from 1100 on the island of Kinn, one hour by boat from Florø.

Møre and Romsdal

Ålesund. Ålesund Aquarium. With coastal, North Sea and Norwegian Sea species.

Ålesund Museum. Including fishery section with old boats.

Molde. The Fishery Museum. Built as a small fishing village, on Hjertøya island (boat from Torgkaien).
Romsdalsmuseet. The Romsdall Museum with 27 old houses in farmyards.

Ørsta. Ørsta Church (1864). With a Flemish altarpiece from 1520.
Iron Age area. With burial mounds, cairns and stone circles at Løken.
Sunndal Open-air Museum. On Leikvin farm which in the 1860s belonged to Lady Arbuthnott, an English lady known as Sunndal's uncrowned queen.

SPORTS. Angling is a time-honored sport in the fjord country. For generations fine salmon rivers, such as the Sand, Laerdal, Årøy, Flåm, Rauma, and Sunndal have attracted sportsmen from all over the world. Oslo travel agencies *Mytravel,* N. Vollgate 19, and *Flyspesialisten,* Kronprinsesse Märthasplass 1, offer first rate salmon fishing in the fjord country. Deep sea fishing jaunts, run on the principle "no catch—no cash" on board the *Sea Queen* are a Stavanger must. **Mountaineering** is another specialty of this land of fjords and mountains. Expert **rock climbing** can be done from such centers as Turtagrø in Sogne; Øye, Åndalsnes, Sunndalsøra, and Innerdalen in Møre and Romsdal; and ordinary "Sunday climbing" almost everywhere. The fells of Ryfylke, the Hardangervidda mountain plateau, the Finse-Aurland-Fillefjell district, the Jotunheimen-Jostedal area, the mountains south and north of the Rauma Railway, and the Trollheimen mountains all have well-marked paths with pleasant and fully staffed chalets among them. Thus it is perfectly feasible to walk carrying a light rucksack through the Fjord Country or parts of it. **Swimming** in the fjords at the height of summer is extensively done; **waterskiing** is practised at Ulvik and Balestrand; fine beaches and bathing resorts are found near Stavanger. The honeymoon island of Godøysund, south of Bergen, is ideal for **boating** (hotel has boats). A number of centers have sprung up in the Hardanger area, and in the superb **skiing** country along the Bergen Railway. At its highest station, Finse, you can ski until well into June—later still on the glacier. Finse in summer is also a geologist's and botanist's delight. As at other Norwegian winter sports resorts, skiing and skating equipment may be hired for a small fee. It is well to remember, too, that winter sports equipment is not very different in price from other countries, but the quality is very high. There are well-stocked sports shops in such Bergen Railway area resorts as Ål, Geilo, and Voss.

CENTRAL MOUNTAINS, EASTERN VALLEYS

Cradle of Liberty—Home of Giants

The area which this chapter describes contains some scenery which can compete with the northern parts of Norway for breathtaking things to see. In the eastern valleys holidaymakers will find a wealth of beautiful countryside, dappled with lakes, swift-flowing streams, and silent forests, while the Jotunheimen—"Home of the Giants"—mountain range is a paradise for nature lovers and hikers.

Exploring the Central Mountains and Eastern Valleys

First we shall follow the great valley of Østerdal, which runs southward parallel to the Swedish border for about 320 km. (200 miles). From Trondheim we follow the bends of the Gauldal until, at 600 meters (2,000 feet) above sea level, we reach Røros, once the center of Norway's coppermining region.

With its heaps of slag and its many unpainted timber houses, Røros looks like a mining town, and it has had such a character since its founding three centuries ago. A dominating landmark is the town's main building in stone, the late 18th-century church, one of Norway's best examples of Baroque architecture. The countryside around is nearly bare of trees; for most of the forests were cut down years ago when charcoal was the chief fuel for the smelting ovens.

Don't be frightened away by the drab side, however; Røros has many attractions. And there is the great plateau, Rørosvidda, stretching north and east to the Swedish border and inhabited by Lapps with herds of reindeer. The Röros plateau is crisscrossed by marked trails and dotted with tourist-huts, mountain farm *(seter)* quarters, etc., so it is quite possible—given good feet and some ambition—to walk from Lake Aursunden near Røros all the way to the Trondheim-Sweden railway, about 95 km. (60 miles) north. Røros also had its great writer, Johan Falkberget, who died in 1967. His novels about past and present life in this mining district have become literary classics.

Norway's longest river, the 595-km. (370-mile) Glomma, rises just north of Røros and meanders the entire length of the vast eastern forests to empty into the outer Oslo Fjord beyond Fredrikstad. The train from Trondheim parallels the Glomma for about half the distance, or for six hours. This river's chief task is to float logs downstream to the sawmills and paper factories, and the traveler also might as well follow the current. In this way you can watch the Glomma start as a mountain stream in the copper mining district, and finally develop into the mighty timber conveyor that sweeps through Elverum and Kongsvinger.

Elverum serves as junction point for the railway west to Hamar and for a main road leading east to Sweden. It is famous for the final meeting of the Norwegian Parliament in April, 1940, just before the town was destroyed by bombing. It gave King Håkon power to carry on the war outside Norway.

You are now in the region of the great forests which some writers have described as the "ocean of east Norway". Vast, undulating expanses of pine trees whose sounds and whose silence have shaped the lives of people just as the sea has on the west coast, or the long winter nights and long summer days have in Finnmark. Here are persistent influences, reflected not only in literature but in the folk customs, superstitions and tales of trolls, *huldra* (witch-like figures) and other supernatural forest creatures which have been handed down for untold generations.

Gudbrandsdal

If in possession of a good walking outfit, you start out from Oslo's Central Station for the central mountains by way of Lake Mjøsa and that greatest of Norwegian valleys, Gudbrandsdal, which is 200 km. (124 miles) long. The area is rich in traditional Norwegian arts, and folk music and dancing are both popular. Wood carving and painting are also held in high esteem.

Eidsvoll, on the south end of Mjøsa, is perhaps the most resounding name in Norwegian history, for it was here that the Norwegian Constitution was framed and adopted in mid-May of the year 1814. This event marked Norway's emancipation from Danish rule and gave her that now-famous Independence Day, the 17th of May, as widely and enthusiastically celebrated as the American 4th of July. However, the main feature of the celebration—as you will discover if you are in any town in May—is not shooting off fire-crackers but the huge and colorful parades of school children.

While the Eidsvoll "Cradle of Liberty" is well worth a visit for its own sake and for the excellent collection of contemporary furniture, engravings, etc., you will not be able to combine it on the same day with the abso-

lute *must* for travelers in this area: the boat trip on Lake Mjøsa. The Eidsvoll Building lies about three km. from the station, and since the early
morning train from Oslo which connects with the steamer gives you only
ten minutes' leeway, you'll have to board her right away.

By Steamer to Lillehammer

This steamer, the old side-wheeler *Skibladner,* will probably remind you
of Mark Twain and the old days on the Mississippi, for in 1976 she celebrated 120 years of service. She takes almost six hours to reach Lillehammer at the head of Mjøsa, but dinner is served on board, and on a warm
day it's a fine trip. You stop briefly at Hamar on the eastern shore, and
have, both when approaching and leaving, excellent views of its hinterland
of fertile farms. Hamar has the ruins of what was once an impressive stone
cathedral.

From Hamar you cross the widest part of the lake, passing near Helgøy
or Saints' Island, where many leading Norwegian churchmen were in-
terned during the war because of anti-Nazi activities, and call at Gjøvik
on the west side. Gjøvik is an active industrial town, the terminus of a
railway that connects with the Valdres-bane train at Eina. Side-wheeling
northwards from Gjøvik, you see that both shores are more rugged and
forest-covered and come closer together until, just above Lillehammer,
Lake Mjøsa narrows into a non-navigable river, the Lågen. Here is the
entrance to Gudbrandsdal.

Lillehammer is well aware of being a tourist center, and has won its
bid to host the 1994 Winter Olympics. Many of the new facilities are already set up for sports-minded visitors to take advantage of, like new
jumps and a year-round roller-skating rink. Lillehammer is also a cultural
center, thanks to the famous Sandvig Collection at Maihaugen, an open-
air museum much like the Folk Museum in Oslo, but specializing in farm
buildings, *stabburs,* waterwheels, etc., of Gudbrandsdal. There is also an
interesting art gallery and the museum of Norwegian historical vehicles
in Lillehammer, which features vintage cars, the country's largest miniature railway, bicycles and motorcycles.

The town is also famous as having been the residence for many years
of the well-known author and Nobel prize winner Sigrid Undset; while
the Nansen School, Norway's only "academy of humanism", was founded
here in 1939. And at Aulestad, a few miles northwest of Lillehammer, in
Østre Gausdal Valley, stands the former home of the great 19th-century
poet, Bjørnstjerne Bjørnson, author of the Norwegian national anthem.
Hunderfossen "Playland" offers various activities for children and adults.

Throughout most of this stretch the valley of Gudbrandsdal has nearly
the same topographical pattern: fertile fields on the level ground on either
side of the river, patches of cleared farmlands on the wide sloping hillsides,
sometimes way up to the first shoulders, but intermingled with wooded
patches. Beyond the forests on top begin those *seter* highlands and mountains so prized by skiers in winter and hikers in summer. The district of
Vinstra is associated with Henrik Ibsen's famous drama "Peer Gynt".

Across Dovrefjell and from Otta to Vågå and Lom

If you are making the journey between Trondheim and Oslo by car, you
will be certain to travel over the impressive Dovrefjell plateau and, sooner

or later, arrive at Dovregubbens Hall, a delightful place at which to stop and have coffee. Take a look at the shapes formed by the trees. Legend has it that every stone, every tree in Norway has its own troll or fairy and who are we to argue?

Just beyond Otta, you skirt the Rondane Mountains and adjacent hiking areas that extend clear to Østerdalen. At Dombås, the railway divides in two lines: the Rauma line to Åndalsnes, and the Dovre line which crosses over the Dovre Mountains to Trondheim. In between the forking rail lines and beyond are the trails and huts of three other upland Norwegian playgrounds: the Romsdal Alps, Trollheimen, and Dovre.

For our purposes, however, it's best to leave the train at Otta, an hour and a half above Lillehammer, and change to a westbound bus. This vehicle will soon bring you to Lake Vågå and the village of Vågå in the midst of a district as historically interesting as Telemark and with an abundance of grass-roofed timber houses, *stabburs,* and legends of ominous monsters who lived in the surrounding mountains.

A tale is told, for example, about Johannes Blessom, a native of Vågå, who had to spend considerable time in Copenhagen because of a lawsuit, but who kept pining away for his native hills. He was walking the streets in the Danish capital on Christmas Eve when a stranger driving a horse and sleigh accosted him and asked if he wanted to go home. Blessom said yes, and in an instant he was whirled through the air and shortly afterwards deposited on the ground just outside his own farm in Norway. The stranger then drove full speed into a mountainside which opened in a blaze of light to let him enter, for he was, of course, the Jutul or Vågå-giant.

There is an interesting stave church at Vågå, and another at Lom, half an hour further west, at both of which you can take a quick look while the bus has a rest-stop. At Lom two possibilities open up: to continue westwards to Grotli and the notorious zig-zag descent to Geiranger (or the new year-round road to Stryn), or to branch off southwest on the Sognefjell highway which crosses part of Jotunheimen. This time suppose you take the latter road up Bøverdal Valley as far as Elvesaeter.

Aerial Vistas over the Jotunheimen

Next morning step aboard the bus that makes the daily ascent from Bøverdal to a tourist hut called Juvass-hytta. The rough ride up a very rocky trail will certainly lead you to suspect that altitude is being gained—but you will be thoroughly amazed to learn that Juvass-hytta is over 1,675 meters (5,500 feet) above the sea. Stay overnight to get acclimatized and then join the forenoon promenade of roped-together guests and guide across Styggebreen Glacier and up to the summit of Galdhøpiggen, Norway's highest rock peak at 2,495 meters (8,181 feet).

Once on top, and with good visibility, you will agree that this is the place to look at Jotunheimen. On every hand there stretches an overwhelming ocean of cliffs and deep valleys, peaks and glaciers: a sight as spectacular as anything to be seen in Norway.

From Galdhøpiggen you can make the same sort of survey of this part of the world as you did of the Oslo region from Kolsås. Your compass and the detailed maps of Jotunheimen will show you, for example, the location of Mount Glittertind, whose thick snowcovering on top gives it a 12-meter (40-foot) margin over your vantage point; or of the many other peaks on all sides. When you tire of mountain identification, turn to the generally available maps of trails and huts to help you plan what to do next.

You could, for example, try out the summer ski center on Galdhöpiggen that opened in 1986. Alternatively, there's the three-hour descent to Spiterstulen in the valley between the two rival peaks and from there a long walk to Gjendebu on Lake Gjende; seven hours by land or eight if you choose the route over Memuru Glacier. Or you can do it the really hard way by toiling from Spiterstulen up over Glittertind and down to the hut at Glitterheim (seven hours) and then—preferably another day—cross the eastern edge of Memuru Glacier to reach Memurubu (nine hours). Either way you arrive in one of the most famous parts of Giant-Land.

This is the Gjende country, haunt of both historical and legendary characters. For instance, Jo Gjende himself, the mighty reindeer hunter and mountain philosopher who served as guide to many visiting sportsmen and alpinists during the last century, and whose exploits are part of the modern saga of Jotunheimen. Then, of course, there is the Peer Gynt of folklore and the one in Ibsen's great drama, both of whom were well acquainted with these hills.

By all means take the hike from Memurubu to Gjendesheim, a five-hour jaunt, via the famous Besseggen or Edge of Bess. This brings you along that scenic but narrow pinnacle path where you can look down on one side to Lake Bess and 610 meters (2,000 feet) on the other to Lake Gjende. But there's plenty of room for your feet, and if dizzy, just think of Peer Gynt, who claimed to have ridden this path one night at top speed on the back of a reindeer.

Safely down at Gjendesheim, you will find many alternatives lying in wait. The trail east to Sikkilsdalseter (four hours) and the bus down to Vinstra in Gudbrandsdal; or the trail or bus southwards to Bygdin and Beitostølen Tourist Center, whence you can continue all the way by bus to Fagernes. From there the Valdres Railway can take you either to its junction with the Bergens-bane at Roa, or all the way to Oslo.

If this Besseggen excursion sounds too strenuous, a boat plies from Memurubu to both Gjendesheim and Gjendebu at opposite ends of the lake. From the latter hut you can elect the two-day trip to Leirvassbu and Skogadalsbøen, which in turn provides possibilities too numerous to describe here. Suffice it to say that from Skogadalsbøen you can proceed to the Sogne Fjord either west via Turtagrø and by bus on the cross-mountain highway from Lom, or south all the way by foot through Vetti (275-meter (900-foot) Vettisfoss waterfall) to Upper Årdal. Inveterate alpinists, who naturally snort at such tame hiking, may seek their thrills by climbing about in the Hurrungene Range, that chaos of pinnacles and precipices which lies between the Vetti trail and the road to Sogne Fjord. Upper Årdal is the site of one of Norway's newest aluminum processing plants.

But in planning your route through the Home of the Giants, keep two points in mind. First, that at least 20 per cent must be added to the times given in the trail maps for the various journeys from hut to hut; and even more if you intend to proceed at a leisurely pace, take photographs, etc. Second, that ropes and guides are necessary when crossing glaciers as on many of the longer routes. That boaster, Peer Gynt, may have performed reckless deeds in his imagination, but real mountaineers like Jo Gjende never took foolhardy chances.

Valdres and Hallingdal

Let's say that after criss-crossing Jotunheimen we have decided to end up in Årdal, ferry to Revsnes (Laerdal), and wind our way back to Oslo via Valdres. The first part of our bus ride is as wild as they come, up through the canyon-like Laerdal valley to the village of Borgund, where the best-preserved of Norway's stave churches is in perfect keeping with the stern surroundings; and across the high fells of Fillefjell, where the hostels (now modern resorts) date back to medieval times.

The first part of Valdres, Lake Vangsmjøsi, is surrounded by fierce mountains, making it reminiscent of the West Country we have just left. But hardly is the lake left before the farm-dotted Valdres landscape— lakes, silvery rivers, ancient farms on sloping hillsides—opens out, then continues all the way down to the railhead at Fagernes. The Valdres Express—as it proudly used to call itself in posters all over Norway during the late '20s—is not exactly flying along. It is more of a "Berg und Thalbahn", which climbs painstakingly to the top of a pass to rattle triumphantly down into the following valley, repeating this process on diminishing scales time and again before reaching Oslo. But all the charm of Norway's railways is here to feel and enjoy for those who are not speed maniacs; the open hospitality and friendliness of the conductors, the somewhat inexplicable halts; the breathtaking scenery, the peace that follows from gentle travel through generous landscapes in good company.

From Fagernes, instead of returning by the Valdres Railway, we could take a bus to an even more scenic line—the Bergen Railway—at Gol in the Hallingdal. The most spectacular part of that railway lies west of Gol—that part which leads across the high mountains to the fjord country. If one includes the Flåm Railway into the bargain, it is indeed doubtful whether there is anything in the way of railroads to match it in Europe. East of Gol the railway follows impulsive Hallingdal valley, where abrupt changes of scenery and the funniest mountains crop up at every swerve and squiggle of the snake-like train. Now put these east and west parts of the Bergen Railway together, and the whole magnificent Oslo-Bergen run is complete, giving a cross-section of Norway that is hard to beat.

PRACTICAL INFORMATION FOR CENTRAL
MOUNTAINS AND EASTERN VALLEYS

HOTELS. This area, particularly in the mountains lining the Gudbrandsdal valley, boasts the finest group of resort hotels in Norway. Resorts are so numerous that we list only the best known. Some open only for the summer and winter seasons, others all the year.

Beitostølen (Oppland). 905 meters (2,970 feet), ski touring area, ski lifts, ski school. *Beito Høyfjellshotell* (L), (061–41 050). 278 beds, all rooms with facilities. AE, DC, MC, V. *Beitostølen Høyfjellshotell* (M), (061–41 300). 290 beds, 80 rooms, all with shower and toilet. AE, DC, MC, V. *Bitihorn Fjellstue* (M), (061–41 043). 126 beds. *Bergo Hotell* (M), (061–41 045). 70 beds.

Bøverdalen (Oppland). Romantic entrance to Jotunheimen. *Spiterstulen Lodge* (E), (062–11 480). 1,100 meters (3,610 feet), situated between the two highest peaks in Norway, Galdhøpiggen and Glittertind, 160 beds, some rooms with bath. *Jotunheimen Mountain Lodge* (M), at 1,000 meters (3200 ft.), (062–14 700). Open all year. *Elvester* (I), (062–12 000). 698 meters (2,290 feet), 200 beds, 47 rooms with bath/shower. Open only in summer season. *Leirvassbu Fjellstue* (I), (062–12 932). 1,491 meters (4,890 feet), across by jeep from Elveseter, 190 beds, many rooms with shower.
Youth Hostel. *Bøverdalen Youth Hostel* (I), (062–12 064). 38 beds.

Dombås (Oppland). 659 meters (2,160 feet), good ski touring; ski lift, ski school. *Dombås* (E), (062–41 001). 149 beds, many rooms with bath. AE, MC, V. *Dovrefjell* (E), (062–41 005). 160 beds, most rooms with bath or shower. MC, V.
Youth Hostel. *Dombås Youth Hostel* (I), (062–41 045). 85 beds.

Elverum (Hedmark). *Elgstua Pension* (M), (064–10 122). 43 beds. *Glommen Pensjonat* (I), (064–11 267). 34 beds, some rooms with facilities. Restaurant, fully licensed. Also, self-catering chalets.

Espedalen (Oppland). 300 to 930 meters (985 to 3,050 feet). popular for ski touring. *Dalseter Høyfjellshotell* (M), (062–99 910). 150 beds, most rooms with facilities. *Espedalen Fjellstue* (M), (062–99 912). 60 beds.

Fagerness (Oppland). 360 meters (1,180 feet), ski touring. *Fagernes* (M), Jernbanevn (063–61 100). 110 beds, all rooms with facilities, swimming. AE, DC, MC, V. *Fagerlund Hotel* (M), (063–60 600). 30 beds. AE, DC, MC, V.

Gjøvik (Oppland). Facing lake Mjøsa. *Gjovik* (M), Kirkegt 4 (061–78 600). Opened 1985. 102 beds, with all facilities. Grill restaurant, bar, sauna, hairdresser. *Rica* (M), Strandgate 15 (061–72 120). 150 beds, most rooms with facilities, swimming, sauna. AE, DC, MC, V.
Youth Hostel. *Hovdetun Youth Hostel* (I), (061–71 011). 156 beds.

Grindaheim (Oppland). *Grindaheim* (M), (061–67 005). 110 beds, 38 rooms with bath/shower. AE, MC, V. *Mjøsvang Pensjon og Motell* (M), (061–67 077). 70 beds.

Hamar (Hedmark). *Victoria* (E), Strandgaten 21 (065–30 500). 230 beds, all rooms with facilities, sauna. AE, MC, V. *Astoria* (M), Torggt 23 (065–21 690). 120 beds, all rooms with facilities. DC, MC, V. *Rica Olrud* (I), (065–50 100). 350 beds, all rooms with bath/shower. DC, MC, V.
Youth Hostel. *Hamar Youth Hostel* (I), (065–23 641). 98 beds.

Harpefoss (Oppland). 222 to 930 meters (730 to 3,050 feet), popular skiing area; ski lifts at Golå and Wadahl. *Golå Høifjellshotell* (E), (062–98 109). 200 beds, all rooms with facilities, sauna. *Wadahl Hogfjellshotell* (E), (062–98 300). 170 beds, 90 rooms with facilities, swimming, sauna. AE, MC, V.

Høvringen (Oppland). 952 meters (3,120 feet), ideal terrain for ski touring. *Haukliseter Fjellstue* (I), (062–33 717). 54 beds. AE. *Høvringen Høgfjellshotell* (I), (062–33 722). 100 beds, 31 rooms with bath. DC. *Øigardseter Fjellstue* (I), (062–33 713). 96 beds, all rooms with facilities.

Lillehammer (Oppland). 180 meters (590 feet), probably Norway's largest tourist resort, on hillside overlooking lake Mjøsa, grand terrain for ski touring, many ski lifts, ski school, marked trails, skating rink. *Lillehammer* (E), Turisthotellvn 27B (062–54 800). 350 beds, most rooms with facilities, swimming, sauna. AE, MC. *Oppland* (E), Hamarvn 2 (062–58 500). 140 beds, many rooms with bath, swimming, sauna. AE, DC, MC, V. *Rica Victoria* (E), Storgt 84B (062–50 049). 159 beds,

93 rooms with facilities. AE, DC, MC, V. *Dolaheimen* (M), Jernbanegt 3 (062–58 866). 49 beds, all rooms with shower. *Breiseth* (I) (062–50 060). 80 beds, some rooms with bath. *Smestad Summer Hotel* (I), (062–50 987). 345 beds, all rooms with shower, summer only (June to Aug.). MC.

Youth Hostel. *Birkebeiner'n Youth Hostel* (I), (062–51 994). 88 beds.

Lom (Oppland). 381 meters (1,250 feet). *Fossheim* (M), (062–11 105). Traditional Norse style, 120 beds, 54 rooms with bath/shower. AE, DC, MC, V.

Norefjell (Buskerud). 836 meters (2,740 feet), Oslo's nearest mountain resort, wonderful view of lake Krøderen. *Fjellhvil* (I), (067–46 174). 98 beds, many rooms with bath, sauna.

Otta (Oppland). 290 meters (950 feet). *Müllerhotell* (E), (062–30 033). 200 beds, all rooms with facilities, swimming, sauna. AE, DC, MC, V. *Rondane* (E), (062–33 910). 230 beds, 35 rooms with bath/shower, swimming, sauna. AE, DC. *Rapham* (M), (062–30 266). 115 beds.

Tretten (Oppland). Fine skiing terrain, 805 meters (2,640 feet); ski lifts. *Gausdal* (E), (062–28 500). 240 beds, 55 rooms with bath, swimming, sauna. *Skeikampen* (M), (062–28 505). 142 beds, 45 rooms with bath, swimming, sauna.

Vinstra (Oppland). Fine views. *Amundsen Guest House* (M), (062–90 045). 42 beds. *Fefor* (E), (062–90 099). 930 meters (3,050 feet). 220 beds, 45 rooms with bath; sauna, ski lift. AE, DC, MC, V. *Sødorp* (I), (062–91 000). 78 beds. AE, DC, MC.

Vågåmo (Oppland). Mountain village, stave church, old farms. *Villa* (E), (062–37 071). 110 beds, all rooms with facilities; sauna, swimming pool. AE, DC, MC, V.

HOW TO GET AROUND. By train. Getting about is fairly simple as the main valleys are served efficiently by railways. The Røros Railway runs through the entire length of forestclad Østerdal; the Dovre Railway covers the Gudbrandsdal both with express and express special trains and night trains; the same services are effected by the Bergen Railway through the Hallingdal; the Valdres Railway charmingly deals with that province, and even the Numedal has its little railway running between Kongsberg and Rødberg. If you want to get from one valley across to the next one, have a look at the map, pick out the connecting roads, and at those junctions of roads and railways you will find buses waiting to perform exactly the service you desire.

MOTORING. By car. The combination of beautiful scenery, excellent accommodations, and varied excursion possibilities, makes touring this area by car especially rewarding. Note that some of the smaller roads are fairly bumpy.

SPORTS. Sports play an important part in the holiday life of this region. **Fishing** comes first. The lakes and rivers are too many to be mentioned. The best fishing in lakes and rivers above 1,500 feet is available after June 15, and above 2,500 feet after July 15. Mountain **hiking** comes second. The Jotunheimen mountain ranges are the finest in northern Europe, with more than 200 peaks above 6,500 feet, glaciers, wild valleys, and mountains lakes of great beauty. There's **skiing** here summer and winter. The other famous mountain area is the Rondane mountains. Both Jotunheimen and Rondane are perfectly organized from the hiker's point of view, with cairned routes between the staffed chalets. The chalets open at the end of June. (Remember to get a copy of the Norway Travel Association guide book, "Mountain Touring in Norway".) The best period for walking would be in July and August. The many first class resort hotels of the Eastern Valleys offer good **tennis, boating** and **bathing** in pools or nearby lakes. Some offer **riding** also.

WINTER SPORTS. This is excellent **skiing** country, with plenty of snow and terrain to suit every degree of skill—nursery slopes for beginners, downhill and slalom runs for experts, and ski touring. Skis can be hired at most of the resorts. Many resorts have their own skating rinks which are floodlit at night, and **sleigh** rides by the light of pitchpine torches are an added feature.

BERGEN
CAPITAL OF WEST LAND

City of Quays and Grieg

Walking along the quay of Olav Kyrre's old town at night, you will see the thousands of lights that mark the houses, streets and highways as they follow the valleys and shores, now concentrated in narrow belts, now spreading out widely. Meanwhile, out in the fjords, heading north and south and west, are other lights. Those are the fishing boats, cargo liners, and passenger ships to which Bergen mainly owes its position as Norway's second city and capital of Vestlandet.

Bergensers do not suffer from any inferiority complex and particularly not as far as the capital of Norway is concerned. They point out that Bergen was an important commercial and military center when Oslo was still a village, and further, that until as late as the 1830s their town had the larger population. (Today Oslo has just over twice as many people as Bergen.) But they are especially proud of their cultural achievements and point to the great playwright Ludvig Holberg, the National Theater founded in 1859 (which they claim to be the first in Norway), their symphony orchestra, organized way back in 1765, and their annual International Festival of Music and the Arts in May.

Exploring Bergen

The steepest 300-meter mountain in the world is surely Bergen's own Fløyen. A visitor once made this remark about the most renowned of the seven hills among which Bergen has grown up. But he must have been inspired by a native, for the words reflect perfectly the pride, independence and not-too-carefully-hidden superiority complex which mark the true Bergenser. In any case, jump on the funicular which leaves the head of Vetrlids-almenning every 30 minutes, ride up those lofty 300 meters (1,000 feet), and have a bird's-eye view of this westernmost city in Norway.

Fløyen is a perfect place from which to plan sightseeing, since the whole city is spread out below like a relief-map. (But bring a conventional map along for reference.) See how Bergen stretches out in an elongated form running roughly from north to south, bounded for the most part by the fjord on one side and steep mountain slopes on the other. Sandviken, with its old warehouses at the seashore and contrasting new villa sections, is the most northern part, Paradis and Fjøsanger the most southern; while farthest to the west are the industrial sections of Laksevåg and others along the Pudde Fjord. The central part in between is of most interest to us, and we shall descend for a look. Almost underfoot, and near the octagonal but somewhat lopsided lake called Lille Lungegårdsvann, lies the railway station.

Continuing our round-up from the air, we turn to the right bank of the central harbor, where the original town was founded by Olav Kyrre in 1070. There is the age-old fish market and, farther inland, Maria Church, which dates from about 1100, easily recognizable by its square twin steeples. Near the waterfront are the old warehouses of Hanseatic times, while beyond medieval Håkon's Hall, a long pier juts out into the fjord. That is Skoltegrunds-quay, where the Newcastle steamers dock. Directly opposite, on the southwest side of Vågen as the inner harbor is called, we see the park on Nordnes Point and back towards town, more of that complex pattern of wharves, warehouses, cottages, office buildings, narrow lanes and wide fire-prevention avenues or *almenninger,* which is the unmistakable trademark of Bergen.

Now the funicular lowers us swiftly down the inclined railway, which is so steep that one involuntarily shivers a bit. There's no reason for alarm, since every existing safety device is installed on the car, and the trackgripping brakes work automatically in case of emergency. We reach the bottom in a few minutes and walk down the Vetrlids-almenning into the midst of history.

First, a pause at the well-known fish market—Torget—at the inner end of Vågen, to observe or photograph the thousand-year-old scene of thrifty housewives negotiating for their daily supply of fish with the men who caught them a few hours ago. Then we pass by two short blocks of modern buildings and arrive at that world-famous monument to medieval life and trade, the old warehouses of the Hanseatic period in the 14th and 15th centuries.

Bryggen

"Yes, it used to be called Tyskebryggen, or the German Quay," admits the guide, "but by unanimous vote at the first meeting of the city council after the liberation, we decided to call it Bryggen, or The Quay." And, as if by way of further explanation, he looks down the waterfront towards the restored Bergenhus Fortress and Håkon's Hall, Bergen's most prized examples of 13th-century architecture.

The old wooden warehouses, long and narrow, jammed so closely against each other that air and daylight can enter only through tiny slits, are both the acme of picturesqueness and a working model of life in bygone times. They are still used for storage and for offices, and wares are still hauled up by hand pulleys from the narrow planked alleyways to the lofts above. The Hanseatic Museum and the old Schøtstuene, in nearby Engelsgaarden, complete the medieval picture with their collections of ancient documents, coins, furniture, etc.

Nevertheless, this quarter is not equally reverenced by all Bergensers. A good-sized fraction of the public, including a few town-planners, look on it more as a rat-ridden firetrap than as a sacred memorial. Others say that these buildings are unpleasant reminders of a previous period of national downfall and of occupation by an enemy, so why preserve them? And they frankly bemoan the fact that a north gale was blowing that night in January, 1916, when the central town was burned down; an east wind would perhaps have taken care of Tyskebryggen as well. This school of thought had no regrets when, in July of 1955, part of the Quay was devastated by fire.

Fire has been the greatest enemy of Bergen and has harried it far longer than the Hansa ever did. As in old Oslo, fate seemed to decree that some careless person would let his house catch fire every 50 or 100 years, with the result that whole areas would be destroyed. But whereas Oslo was simply abandoned after the fire of 1624 and rebuilt on a new site, the citizens of Bergen had to rebuild on the old foundations. As they learned from each catastrophe, the town planning became more safety-conscious, until after 1916 the present series of broad streets was developed in addition to the crosstown *almenninger* (old streets) at regular intervals. Today, it is said that in the main business section streets occupy almost as much area as the buildings.

Ferry and Fortress

We take the little ferry which plies from near the Rosenkrantz Tower across to the middle of Nordnes, and walk out to the point. Here there is much of interest: another old fortress called Frederiksberg, a beautiful park, the Nordnes bathing establishment, and a fascinating Aquarium. From the south side of the point is a good view down Pudde Fjord to Laksevåg and the other modern industrial suburbs which have spread out along the narrow stretch between shore and steep mountainside. Just north of Laksevåg the Naval Academy is located at Gravdal.

On top of Sydnes Hill is the former Bergens Museum, where Fridtjof Nansen worked as an assistant before making his astounding trip across Greenland on skis, and where the meteorologist Vilhelm Bjerknes first worked out his now internationally known methods of weatherforecasting. The museum is at present part of the new University of Bergen, which was created in 1948. The Graduate School of Business Administration is very appropriately located in Bergen, for this is the city with the longest and strongest traditions in commerce and trade, yet also one of the most progressive business centers in Norway. It has its new and monumental headquarters at Helleveien in the northern outskirts of Bergen.

Famous Sons

If you bring up the subject of Vigeland and the sculpture-park in Oslo, the guide from Bergen admits that there is nothing like it here, "not even in the Fish Market!" But he says it with such a glint in his eye that it's hard to know whether he's bragging or complaining. At least until he starts to point out how many well-placed statues there are in Bergen. In the City Park is Edvard Grieg, for example; and on the steps of the National Theater, Bjørnstjerne Bjørnson, who was its director for a time. This statue, by the way, is the work of Vigeland. But our guide's favorite is obviously sculptor Stephen Sinding's highly original likeness in bronze of Ole Bull. For here is the giant violinist standing on some rocks beside a waterfall, right in the heart of Norwegian nature, yet transplanted to the center of Bergen.

Many famous men have come from Bergen, like the painter I. C. Dahl, and the statesman Christian Michelsen, who was Prime Minister in 1905 when Norway finally succeeded in breaking out of the union with Sweden. But unquestionably the greatest is that trio: Ludvig Holberg, Ole Bull and Edvard Grieg. And while Holberg lived his adult life in Copenhagen, both the violinist and the composer not only claimed Bergen as home but actually lived there even after they had achieved fame. Consequently, we can visit their homes, Ole Bull's at Lysøya, and Grieg's Troldhaugen, which has now become a museum. Situated in a beautiful natural part of Hop, five miles from Bergen, Troldhaugen (whose name means "hill of trolls") has become a Norwegian national shrine. Grieg's studio, his piano, his notes, are all to be seen.

No mention of famous sons can omit those who in every generation have taken the initiative in maintaining or improving Bergen's economy. Such pillars of society range from the untold numbers of fishermen and skippers, like those in Revold's murals in the Stock Exchange, to scores of organizers of great shipping, canning and manufacturing concerns. It was they who created Bergen when the town was almost entirely dependent on sea communications with the rest of Norway; that is until the railway to Oslo was cut through the barricade of mountains and opened for traffic in 1909. And today the sea is still the only connection with many parts of Vestlandet, though since the Flesland airport, 19 km. (12 miles) away, was opened Bergen has been on both domestic and international air routes communicating with places as widely diverse as Bangkok and Vancouver. It is this mixture of remoteness and integration into the modern world which gives Norway its peculiar fascination.

PRACTICAL INFORMATION FOR BERGEN

GETTING TO TOWN FROM THE AIRPORT. There is a frequent bus service running between the airport and the Bergen Bus Station. For departure times, inquire at the airlines, or at the Tourist Information Center.

TOURIST INFORMATION. Bergen Tourist Board run a special Tourist Information Center, Torvalmenningen (05–321480). They publish information of various kinds and also provide assistance in obtaining accommodations and in changing currency after banking hours. The Center sells tickets for city sightseeing by bus or boat and tickets for fjord tours of one or more days. They can also give advice and information on events taking place in Bergen and on tours that are available.

The Tourist Center is open May, Mon. to Sat. 8.30 A.M. –8 P.M., Sun. 9.30–8; June through Mid-Sept., Mon. to Sat. 8.30 A.M. –10 P.M., Sun. 9.30 A.M. –10 P.M.; mid-Sept.

through mid-Oct., Mon. to Sat. 8.30A.M. –8 P.M., Sun. 9.30–8; mid-Sept. through Apr., Mon. to Sat. 10–3.

USEFUL ADDRESSES. Travel Agents. *Bennett Reisebureau A/S,* Ole Bulls plass 9–11 (323010). *Berg-Hansen Travel Bureau,* Olav Kyrresgt. 7 (318140). *Norwegian State Railways,* Bergen Railway Station (319615). *Winge Travel Bureau Ltd.,* Michelsensgt. 1–3 (321080).
Car Hire. *Avis,* Lars Hillesgt. 15 (320130) and at airport (227618). *Hertz,* Lars Hillesgt. 18 (327920). *Europcar,* Markeveien 8–10 (327048). *Budget,* Bilutlei 57 C. Sundtsgt (311413) and at airport (2275527).

TELEPHONE CODES. The telephone code for Bergen is 05. To call any number in this chapter, unless otherwise specified, this prefix must be used. Within the city, no prefix is required. In the final section *Hotels Along the Bergen Railroad,* we have given telephone codes for each town or village. These codes need only be used when calling from outside the town or village concerned.

HOTELS. The overcrowding that has plagued the Bergen hotel scene has eased, and there is space for visitors all year round. However, it is always wise to make reservations ahead, especially at festival times (May).

Deluxe

Admiral. C. Sundtsgt. 9 (324730). 190 beds, all rooms with bath. Superbly located in city center, close to the fish market, aquarium, and shopping district. Restaurant *Emily,* with a fantastic view, is renowned for its seafood delicacies. AE, DC, MC, V.
Grand Hotel Terminus. Kong Oscarsgt. 71 (311655). 220 beds, 130 rooms with all facilities. Located near the bus and rail stations. Restaurants, garage. AE, DC, MC, V.
Norge. Ole Bulls plass 4 (210100). 680 beds, with all facilities. 12 suites, eight restaurants, bars. Garden room with nightly dancing June/Aug. AE, DC, MC, V.
Rosenkrantz. Rosenkrantzgate 7 (315000). 210 beds, 118 rooms with bath; restaurant. AE, DC, MC, V.
SAS Royal. Bryggen (318000). Opened in Feb. 1982 on side of old warehouses ravaged by fire nine times since 1170. The houses were rebuilt each time in the same style and SAS has incorporated this ancient architecture in the hotel, which makes it one of the most interesting in Europe. 500 beds in 265 rooms, all with facilities incl. piped music/radio, swimming, exhibition of Hanseatic artifacts unearthed during construction. AE, DC, MC, V.

Expensive

Bergen Hotell, Håkonsgate 2 (233962). Two km. from station; 135 beds, all rooms with facilities; breakfast included. MC.
Gjestehuset Rica. Vestre Torggate 20a (319666). Central location, 40 beds. MC, V.
Hordaheimen. C. Sundtsgt. 18 (232320). 120 beds, rooms with or without facilities. Centrally located. Restaurant, unlicensed. AE, DC, MC, V.
Neptun. Walckendorffsgate 8 (326000). 214 beds, all rooms with facilities. AE, DC, MC, V.

Moderate

Hotel Hanseaten. Sandbrogate 3 (316155). One km. from station; 44 beds, 21 rooms with bath/shower, restaurant, grill. No credit cards.
Scandic Hotel. Kokstad (227150). Near Fleshland Airport, new in 1982; 411 beds, all rooms with facilities, restaurant, tavern, indoor pool, sauna, ample parking. DC, MC, V.
Strand. Strandkaien 2120 (310815). Facing harbor; 50 beds, 15 rooms with bath, dining room. AE, DC, MC, V.

Toms. C Sundtsgate 52 (232335). Near the station; 78 beds, all rooms with facilities inc. refrigerator; dining room. AE, DC, MC, V.

Victoria. Kong Oscarsgt. 29 (315030). 83 beds; bed and breakfast only. Restaurant *Valente* (Italian) in same building.

Inexpensive

Park Pension. Harold Håfresgt. 35 (320960). 56 beds, rooms with or without facilities. Bed and breakfast. AE, DC, MC, V.

Camping

Bergenshallens Camping. Wilh. Bjerknesvei 24 (282840). Ten minutes from city center, bus no. 3. Open late June to early Aug. All facilities.

Bratland Camping. Haukeland, on road E68 (101338), (16 km., 10 miles from Bergen). Open June through August only.

Grimen Camping. Helldal (100615). On road E68. Camping huts open from May to end Oct. Rooms with access to kitchen and bath open all year.

Lone Camping. (240820). Main camping site for the Bergen area, 19 km. (12 miles) from town on main road E68. All modern conveniences. Service shop and hostel with 128 beds. TV room. Lakeside position. Open all year. Resident watchman.

Midttun Camping. (136036, 101269, 101095). On the main road E68, 11 km. (seven miles) south of Bergen; 12 camping huts, 23 rooms, 127 beds. Most rooms with toilet, shower and mini-kitchen. All modern conveniences. Sauna, laundry. Open all year.

Tennisparadis Caravan-Camping. On E68, 6 km. (4 miles) from city center. All facilities, including cafeteria. Located next to Bergen's big indoor sports center. Open mid-June through mid-Aug.

Youth Hostels

Montana Youth Hostel. Johan Blydtsv. 30 (292900). Wonderful view of the town and surroundings. 250 beds in five-bedded rooms, all with H&C water. Family rooms. Showers in corridors. Ample parking. Inexpensive. Apply to IYHA information office at Strandgaten 4 (326880). Open from mid-May to early October.

HOW TO GET AROUND. By bus. The central bus station is at 8 Strømgaten (326780). It is the terminal for all buses serving the environs of Bergen and the Hardanger area. There are luggage deposits, shops, a cafeteria and a restaurant there.

All buses are marked with destination and route number. Special tourist tickets for unlimited travel in the city of Bergen, within 48 hours, from May 1 to Sept. 15, are available from the Tourist Information Office and at Bergens Sporveis Office. The cost is NOK 25.

By Air. Several planes a day from/to Oslo. Special rates during summer season. Flight takes about 45 mins.

By train. There are day and night trains to and from Oslo and en route stations. The railway station (319640). has luggage deposits and a cafeteria.

By taxi. To order a taxi, phone (990990).

By ferry. Across the harbor, Mon. to Fri. 6.30 A.M.–5 P.M., Sat. 10 A.M.–2 P.M., no ferries Sun. Fare NOK 5, children NOK 3.

From Nøstekaien there are frequent ferries to the island Askøy (20 mins.).

On foot. The mountains surrounding Bergen offer a wide range of walks in mountainous and wooded country. Information about walking routes, and maps for walkers are available at Bergen Turlag, 3C Sundtsgate (322230). Maps are also available from booksellers.

By fjord and coastal steamer. Coastal steamers (*Hurtigrute*) for North Norway leave daily from Ookkeskjaers Kaien. There are hydrofoil boats to Stavanger and Haugesund. Steamers for Hardanger fjord and Sunnhordland leave from Holberg-kaien. Steamers for Sognefjord, Nordfjord and Sunnfjord leave from Nykirkekaien, with express steamers from Strandkaien. Local steamers serving the islands and fjords immediately north and south of Bergen, dock at the inner harbor on the west side of the fish market.

TOURS. The Tourist Information Center, Torgalmenning (321480), can give advice and information on tours that are available. They also sell maps, including maps for walkers.

MUSEUMS. Bergen Billedgalleri (Municipal Art Museum). (311130). Notable collection of Norwegian paintings covering the last 150 years. Also fine examples of European art. Open mid–May through Mid–Sept., Mon. to Sat. 11–4, Sun. 12–3; mid-Sept. through mid-May, Tues. to Sun. 12–3; closed Mon. Admission NOK 5.

Bryggen Museum. (316710). Erling Dekke Naess Institute for Medieval Archaeology. A cultural history museum based on extensive excavations of Bryggen. Displays of artefacts illustrate commerce, shipping, handicrafts, daily life and cultural activities in the Middle Ages. Open May to Aug. 31, Mon., Wed., Fri. 10–4, Tues. and Thurs. 10–8, Sat. and Sun. 11–3; Sept. through Apr., Mon. to Fri. 11–3, Sat. and Sun. 12–4. Admission NOK 10, children free.

Buekorps Museum. A collection of pictures and other items showing the activities over 125 years of the Buekorps, a kind of boys' brigade found only in Bergen and best known for their drill, usually with crossbows. Information on opening hours from the Tourist Office. Admission free.

Fishery Museum (Permanenten). (321249). A cross-section of Norwegian fisheries and their natural foundation. Has served as a model for similar collections abroad. Open mid-May through Aug. Mon. to Sat. 10–3, Sun. 12–3; off season, Wed. and Sun. 12–3. Admission NOK 4, children NOK 2. Closed in 1989 for renovations. Phone ahead to check re-opening date in 1990.

Hanseatic Museum. Bryggen (314189). One of the oldest and best-preserved wooden buildings in Bergen, furnished in 16th-century style. Open June through Aug., daily 10–4; May and Sept., daily 11–2; Oct. through Apr., Sun., Mon., Wed., Fri. 11–2. Admission NOK 10, children NOK 5.

Historical Museum. Sydneshaugen (213116). Fine collections showing West Norwegian culture from prehistoric and medieval times to about 1850, as well as good ethnographical collections. Open Sat. to Thurs. 11–2; closed Fri. Admission free.

Hilmar Rekstens Art Collection. Stamerbakken 7, Fjøsanger (135010). Permanent exhibition of pictorial art, oriental carpets and old English silver. During May—the Festival period—guided tours daily at noon. Admission NOK 35. The rest of the year, open by appointment.

Hordamuseet. Stend (915130). Folk museum for agriculture and fishing. Open Tues. to Fri. and Sun. 12–3. Admission NOK 10, children NOK 5.

Kunstforeningen (Bergen Fine Arts Society). Rasmus Meyers Alle 5 (321460). Alternating exhibitions of contemporary art. Open Tues. to Fri. 12–4, Thurs. also 6–8, Sat. and Sun. 12–3; closed Mon. Admission NOK 10, students NOK 5, artists, art students and children free.

Langegaarden–Fjøsanger Hovedgård. Manor farm, with art gallery and handicraft center, surrounded by beautiful woodlands. Six km. (four miles) from city center.

Leprosy Museum—St. George's Hospital. Kong Oscarsgate 59. The Bergen Collections of the History of Medicine. In the Middle Ages a hospital for lepers. The present buildings date back to the beginning of the 18th century. Open mid–May through late Aug., daily 11–3. Audiovisual programmes in English, French, German and Spanish. Admission NOK 12, children NOK 2.

Maritime Museum. Sydneshaugen (327980). A modern museum of great interest to those who wish to follow the development of shipping from the Old Norse period up to the present day. Open Sun. to Fri. 11–2. Admission NOK 5, children free.

Museum of Natural History. Muséplass 3 (213050). Displays of botany, geology and zoology. Open Fri. to Wed. 11–2; closed Thurs. Admission free.

Old Bergen. Elsesro, Sandviken (256307). An open-air museum with more than 35 wooden houses and stores representative of Bergen architecture in the 18th and 19th century; interiors from the 18th, 19th and 20th centuries. Guided tours every hour. Restaurant with hot and cold meals (256307). Open mid-May through mid-June, daily 12–6; mid-June through mid-Aug., daily 11–7; mid-Aug. through mid-Sept., daily 12–6. Admission NOK 15, children, students, pensioners NOK 10. Family tickets NOK 30.

Rasmus Meyer's Collection. (311130). Fine collection of Norwegian paintings, including many works by Edvard Munch. Open mid-May through mid-Sept. Mon. to Sat. 11–4, Sun. 12–3. Off season, Wed. to Mon. 12–3; closed Tues. Admission NOK 5.

Schøtstuene. Øvregaten 50 (316020). Old assembly rooms, which vividly illustrate social life among the Hanseatic merchants in Bergen. Open June through Aug. daily 10–4; May and Sept., daily 11–2; off season, Sun., Tues., Thurs. and Sat. 11–2. Admission NOK 10, children NOK 5.

Seter Museum (Hill Farm Museum). (915130). Recently erected on Fanafjell near Bergen, showing features of early Norwegian farming.

Stenersen's Collection. (311130). 250 works by well-known modern artists (Munch, Picasso, Klee). Open mid-May through mid-Sept. Mon. to Sat. 11–4, Sun. 12–3; mid-Sept. through mid-May Tues. to Sun. 12–3; closed Mon. Admission NOK 5.

Theta Museum (Resistance Museum). Enhjørningsgården Bryggen. Open mid-May to mid-Sept. mid-May through Aug., Tues., Sat. and Sun. 2–3 P.M. Admission NOK 10, children free.

Vestlandske Kunstindustrimuseum (West Norway Museum of Applied Art). (325108). Collections of European arts and crafts, antique Bergen silver, contemporary Norwegian and foreign ceramics, glass, furnitures, metalwork and Chinese art. Open May 15 through Aug. 31, Mon. to Sat. 10–3, Sun. 12–3; Sept. 1 through May 14, Tues. to Sun. 12–3; closed Mon. Admission NOK 5, children NOK 2.50. Closed in 1989 for renovations. Phone ahead to check re-opening date in 1990.

PARKS, ZOOS AND GARDENS. Milde Arboretum (The Norwegian Arboretum). (991612). The arboretum was founded in 1971 and only a few of its 50 hectares have been planted. In spite of this, a lot of trees and shrubs from different parts of the world may be found. The area is very attractive with hills, rocky gorges, a small lake and a shoreline of several kilometers length. Bus from Bergen Bus Station to Mildevågen, then a 15 minute walk. Open daily. Admission free.

HISTORIC BUILDINGS AND SITES. Alvøen Main Building. (325108). The discontinued Alvøen paper–factory is located 18 km. (11 miles) west of Bergen city. It opened as a museum in 1983. The main building, dating from 1797, contains a collection of old furniture, silver, East–Indian porcelain and pictures. Open May 10 to Aug. 31. Admission free.

Bryggen. Wooden buildings with characteristic pointed gables facing the harbor. A unique example of Norwegian medieval architecture. Today it is a growing center for arts and crafts, where painters, weavers and craftsmen have their workshops, some of them open to the public.

Fana Folklore. An evening spent in true Norwegian tradition with old farm customs, traditional Norwegian food, lively dances and folk music. For details phone Fana Folklore (117240).

Fantoft Stave Church. (280710/135888). A fine example of a Norwegian stave church. Built in the early-12th century in the Sognefjord area, it was later moved to its present site. Open May 15 through Sept. 15, daily 10.30–1.30, 2.30–5.30. Admission NOK 5, children free.

Gamlehaugen. Fjøsanger (133620). Residence of the King when visiting Bergen. Open June through Sept., Mon. to Fri. 10–1. Garden open at all times. Admission NOK 5, children NOK 2.

Håkonshallen. (316067). King Håkon's hall was built in the mid–13th century. It was badly damaged by an explosion and fire in 1944 and restored 1957–61. Open mid-May through mid-Sept., daily 10–4; mid-Sept. through mid-May, Fri. to Wed. 12–3, Thurs. 3–6. Closed during the Festival and Christmas and Easter. Admission NOK 4, children NOK 2.

The Island Lysøen, and Ole Bull's villa. (309077). This distinctive villa and concert hall were built in 1872 by the world-famous violin virtuoso Ole Bull, as a summer residence and meeting place for his many friends. The villa is largely unchanged since Bull's death there in 1880. Ole Bull built a network of walking paths all over the island, with a total length of some 13 km. (eight miles). These paths provide pleasant rural walking for the visitor.

For information on access and guided tours call 309077.

Rosenkrantz Tower. (314380). Erected by the feudal lord of Bergenhus in the 1560s as a fortified official residence, the tower was badly damaged by an explosion in 1944. It was restored 1945–65. Open mid-May through mid-Sept., daily 10–4; mid-Sept. through mid-May, Sun. 12–3. Admission NOK 4, children NOK 2.

Troldhaugen. Hop (135438). Edvard Grieg's home for 22 years, situated beside the Nordås lake. Grieg composed many of his best–known works here, and he and his wife are buried here. Open May through Sept., daily 10.30–1.30, 2.30–5.30. Open only in the afternoon during the Festival period. Admission NOK 10, children NOK 5. New chamber music concert hall built in the grounds, opened 1985. Recitals also given in the house.

Wall Gate. Built in 1562 by the feudal lord of Bergenhus. On the ground floor, trade has been carried out in much the same way for 400 years.

SPORTS. Swimming. The *Nordnes sjøbad,* an outdoor heated swimming pool, is situated near the Aquarium and Helleneset. South of Bergen there are swimming places at *Gronevika* near the Arboretum at Milde; *Austrevågen,* Krokeide; *Mjølkevika,* Stend; and *Os.* North of Bergen there are swimming areas at *Tømmervågen; Våganeset,* and *Vollane,* Eidsvåg.

MUSIC, MOVIES AND THEATERS. The most important event of the Bergen cultural year is the *Bergen International Festival,* which takes place over 12 days in late-May and early-June, with a splendid programme of music, drama, ballet, folklore, arts and entertainment. Details of the great variety of events are published in a separate festival brochure. Tickets are available from the Festival Office, Grieg Hall (tel. 310954 or 320400).

Music. The music of Edvard Grieg is often featured in Bergen. From June 1 to Sept. 10 there are daily recitals of his work at the *Rasmus Meyer Art Collection,* Rasmus Meyer's Alle 7. These recitals are for one hour, beginning at 4 P.M. Tickets at the entrance. There are also recitals of Grieg's music at *Troldhaugen,* his home, every Wednesday during the summer, and daily during the festival period.

A special feature is the *Grieg Hall,* Bergen's new concert hall, with its unusual architecture.

The city Brass Band plays in the *City Park* many evenings in summer, and sometimes at lunchtime if the weather is good. They also play at the entrance to King Haakon's Hall on Thursdays from 12–1, during summer.

Movies. All movies shown in the cinemas of Bergen are in the original language with subtitles in Norwegian. Performances from 11 A.M.–11 P.M.

Theaters. A permanent theater was founded in 1838, the oldest in the country— *Den Nationale Scene.* Note that it is closed in July and August. They perform Norwegian plays alternating with musicals and light entertainment.

SHOPPING. Bergen is as good a place for shopping as Oslo, if smaller.

For department stores, try *Sundt,* at Torgalmenningen 14, which is in the heart of Bergen near *Galleriet,* a major new mall also on Torgalmenningen.

Fur. *Motepels* may be the best place to find furs and it caters to overseas visitors— refunds on VAT are 16⅔%. You will find it at Kong Oscarsgate 14.

Handcrafts. *Husfliden* on Vagsalmenning and Østre Skostredet has a range of authentic crafts.

Pewter and Textiles. These popular Norwegian purchases can be found at *Prydkunst Hjertholm,* Torgalmenningen 8.

Silver. The artist himself attends at *Theodor Olsen,* offering handwrought silver.

RESTAURANTS. Bergen's "vista-vision" restaurant, *Bellevue,* provides magnificent views of the city and fjord beyond. In town are a number of fashionable restaurants, particularly in the two luxury hotels (*Norge* and *SAS Royal*). The following restaurants can also be recommended.

Expensive

Bellevue. Bellevuebakken 9 (310240). On hillside overlooking city and fjord, in charming 17th century manor, silver, crystal, good food and personalized service. AE, DC, MC, V.

Moderate

Bryggen Tracteursted. Bryggen (314046). In Hanseatic surroundings. You may buy live fish from the fish market and ask the chef to prepare it any way you want it! DC.

Bryggestuen Restaurant. Bryggen 6 (310630). Popular for morning coffee and light lunch. AE, DC, MC, V.

Chinatown. Torvgaten 1 (327735). AE, DC, MC, V.

Dickens. Ole Bulls plass 8–10 (328482). Fine old building located right opposite Torgalmenningen. Pleasant restaurant, open from lunchtime to late evening.

Grand Café. Olav Kyrresgate 11 (317732). Opposite Norge Hotel, specialty Chinese food and—in season—boiled cod; pavement café in summer.

Holbergstuen. Torvalmenning 6 (318015). Will serve fish any way you want it, popular meeting place.

Holms Discosteak House. Kong Oscarsgate 45 (315930). Grill, dancing daily, DC.

Michelangelo. Neumannsgaten 25 (319760). Italian restaurant with authentic atmosphere. DC, MC, V.

Villa Amorini. Rasmus Meyer's Allà 5 City Park (310039). New, good food. AE, DC, MC, V.

Wesselstuen. Engen 14 (322900). Pot luck and fish, much frequented any time of day, favorite haunt of the Bergensers.

NIGHTLIFE. There are not many nightclubs in Bergen, but several of the restaurants provide some sort of entertainment, often with music and dancing until the small hours of the morning. The two big hotels (*Norge* and *SAS Royal*) both have night spots, with dancing until 3 A.M. every night. There is also *Christian,* in Chr. Michelsensgate (320 262), which remains popular.

Hotels Along the Bergen Railroad

Ål (Buskerud). 436 to 1,100 meters (1,430 to 3,610 feet). *Bergsjøstolen* (E), (067–84 618). 25 km. (15 miles) by bus from station, 70 beds, most rooms with facilities, swimming, sauna, solarium, trout fishing, ptarmigan shooting (Sept.), fine skiing terrain, ski lift, ski school. MC, V.

Finse (Hordaland). Magnificent high mountain touring area winter and summer. 4 hrs. by train from Oslo, 2½ hrs. from Bergen. Skiing season from Christmas to May but you can climb the glacier on skis in midsummer. 60 kms. of marked trails. Courses arranged in glacier touring. In summer, cycle and canoe hire. From 1986 slalom hill. *Finse* (E), (05–526711). 150 beds, all rooms with bath, with 2 to 6 beds, no singles; partly self-service; cafeteria; center for touring. The Norwegian Tourist Association (Den Norske Turistforeningen) has one of its largest lodges at Finse; reductions for members, but all are welcome.

Geilo (Buskerud). 800 meters (2,625 feet), renowned tourist center and ski resort of high international standing. World Cup alpine events. *Bardøla* (E), (067–85 400). 200 beds, 95 rooms with facilities, swimming, sauna, resident orchestra. AE, DC, MC, V. *Dr. Holms* (E), (067–85 622). One of the most famous resort hotels in Norway, 275 beds, all rooms with facilities. AE, DC, MC, V. *Geilo Apartment Hotel* (M), (067–86 200). 230 beds, 56 apartments, each for 4 persons. *Geilo Hotel* (M), (067–85 511). 145 beds, all rooms with bath/shower. DC, MC, V. *Highland* (M), (067–85 600). 230 beds, most rooms with facilities. AE, DC, MC, V. *Ustedalen* (M), (067–85 111). 170 beds, all rooms with facilities. DC, MC, V. *Vestlia* (M), (067–85 611). 314 beds, all rooms with facilities, swimming. AE, DC, MC, V.

Youth Hostel. *Geilo Youth Hostel* (I), (067–85 300). 140 beds, comfortable.

Gol (Buskerud). 207 meters (680 feet), ski center, lift, marked trails. *Eidsgaard* (M), (067–74 955). 60 rooms. AE, DC, MC, V. *Pers* (M), (067–74 500). 500 beds, all rooms with facilities, swimming. AE, MC, V. *Gol Campingsenter/Apartment* (I), (067–74 144). 160 beds.

Hemsedal. Scandinavia's best alpine center. 24 km. (15 miles) of downhill runs, the longest, 4 km. 14 pistes of varying grades. Accommodations in all price ranges. *Hemsedal Alpin Apartments* (M), (067–79 100). 300 beds. Next to ski lifts. *Hemsedal* (I), (067–79 102). 140 beds, and new family section. 5 mins. from center; 3 mins. from hills. *Skogstad* (E), (067–78 333). Completely refurbished. 149 beds in 85 rooms.

Mjølfjell (Hordaland). 714 meters (2,340 feet), grand area for ski touring.
Youth Hostel. *Mjølfjell Youth Hostel* (I), (05–518111). Six km. (four miles) from station, 140 beds, sauna, all meals, popular.

Oppheim (Hordaland). 26 km. (16 miles) by bus from Voss, 332 meters (1,090 feet), good skiing country, chairlift. *Oppheim* (E), (05–522500). 102 beds, some rooms with bath. AE, DC, MC, V.

Stalheim (Hordaland). 35 km. (22 miles) by bus from Voss, overlooking the Nerøy valley. Zig-zag road now bypassed by giant tunnel, opened 1980, but hairpin bends still there in summer for venturesome motorists. *Stalheim* (E), (05–520122). Outstanding, 212 beds, all rooms with facilities, souvenir shop with local arts and crafts, museum. MC, V.

Ustaoset (Geilo—Buskerud). 991 meters (3,250 feet), views of Mt. Hallingskarvet, good ski touring. *Ustaoset Høyfjellshotell* (M), (067–87 161). 147 beds, all rooms with facilities. AE, DC, MC, V. *Ustaoset Fjellstue and Motell* (I), (067–87 123). 50 beds.

Voss (Hordaland). 55 meters (180 feet). Principal town in Hardanger, situated on the lake and surrounded by mountains. Tourist center summer and winter. St. Olav stone cross from 1023. Finneloftet, built around 1250, Norway's oldest nonecclesiastical timber building. Voss Folk Museum, ancient farmhouses at Mølster and Nesheim. Voss church, completed 1277 with two–meter (seven–foot) thick walls. Cablecar to mountain top with panoramic restaurant. *Park* (L), (05–511322). 106 beds, all rooms with facilities. AE, DC, MC, V. *Jarl* (E), (05–511933). 150 beds, 35 rooms with facilities, sauna. AE, DC, MC, V. *Vossevangen* (E), (05–512144). 140 beds, all with bath/shower. DC. *Fleischer's Hotel and Motel* (M), Evangervn. 13 (05–511155). 120 beds, all rooms with facilities, swimming, sauna. AE, DC, MC, V. *Kringsjå Pensjonat* (M), (05–511627). 32 beds, all rooms with facilities. MC, V. *Noring Pensjonat* (I), (05–511211). 45 beds. *Rondo Pension* (I), (05–511980). 45 beds, 10 rooms with bath. MC.
Youth Hostel. *Voss Youth Hostel* (I), (05–512017). Facing lake Vang, special facilities for handicapped, 160 beds, cafeteria.

ANCIENT TRONDHEIM AND DISTRICT

Stronghold of Crown and Church

A glance at the map will show you that Trondheim is situated more or less where Norway's long tadpole-like tail joins the rounded body of southern Norway, and it is not surprising that the Viking kings should have chosen this site for their first capital. From the sheltered waters of Trondheim Fjord their longboats would sail out on raids that carried them west to the coast of America and east to the shores of the Byzantine Empire.

Norwegian towns have a disconcerting habit of reverting to their former names, but you may rest assured that Trondheim has now made up its mind as to what it wants to be called. This city was once the capital of Norway under the name of Nidaros, and when the Norwegian people were seized 60 years ago with a burning desire to toss aside newfangled names of a mere 300 years' standing, the authorities in Oslo (then Christiania) decided to change Trondheim back to Nidaros. However, they were reckoning without the proverbial obstinacy of the locals, and Trondheim it remains to this day.

Exploring Trondheim and District

Trondheim is a delightful city, possibly the only one in Norway with a genuine air of the medieval about it. King Olav Tryggvason founded the town in the 10th century on the southern shores of the fjord of the same name, where the Nid River runs into the sea. Just before the river pours its waters into the fjord, it makes an abrupt loop, so that the triangle of land on which Trondheim stands is surrounded on two sides by the river and on one side by the sea, and is thus a sort of peninsula connected to the mainland by a narrow strip. A number of bridges cross the Nid River to modern suburbs, but the essential Trondheim is to be found north and west of the Nid.

The cathedral occupies an imposing position to the south. From it a broad avenue runs straight through the central part of the old town to the statue of King Olav in the marketplace.

You may imagine that a visit to Trondheim would resemble one of Amundsen's polar explorations, but the climate is essentially continental, with surprisingly warm summers. Furthermore, Trondheim is not only a cultural and industrial center, but the hub of a large agricultural district which in some years actually exports hay to the British Isles. Trondheim is also an excellent winter sports center, and local skiers and skaters have created almost a monopoly of championships in Norwegian winter sports.

Cathedral, Capital and Court

In the Middle Ages Trondheim enjoyed a European reputation when the great Nidaros Cathedral, begun in 1150, was raised as a shrine to Saint Olav, King of Norway and one of the greatest figures from the Saga Age. King Olav's shrine was visited by pilgrims from every Christian land in the world, and a chain of inns or hostels was built all the way from Oslo in the south, through the broad-bosomed Gudbrandsdal, over the mighty back of Mount Dovre and down to the Gothic cathedral by the banks of the Nid River. This cathedral, now almost completely restored, still stands in all its pristine glory, and it is not only the pride of the citizens, but Trondheim's chief claim to fame. The architecture bears clear marks of the influence of the English Gothic style. It is Scandinavia's largest medieval building.

When the cathedral was built, Trondheim was the undisputed capital of Norway: here the king had his court and here the ecclesiastical dignitaries had their seat. On the little island of Munkholmen, which lies like a cruiser at anchor in the bay, you can still see the ruins of an old monastery, bringing to mind Longfellow's own description of the island in his poem *The Saga of King Olav,* where he says, "At Nidarholm the priests are all singing."

King Haakon VII of Norway was crowned here in 1906, but formal coronations are no longer a part of the ceremonies of state in Norway. Still, it is interesting to know that it was here that all Norway's kings—including Canute, King of Denmark, Norway and England—were elected by the old Norse *tings,* the 10th-century forerunners of the modern Norwegian Storting, or Parliament.

Like most Norwegian towns, Trondheim has from time to time suffered devastating fires, but in one respect Trondheim was more fortunate than either Oslo or Bergen. In the 17th century, after most of the residential quarters had been razed to the ground, a town planning scheme was carried out by Johan Cicignon, a Norwegian of French extraction, who replaced many of the narrow twisting streets with broad avenues. To this canny "foreigner" the people of Trondheim owe the spacious layout of their town. Some people may consider it a little too spread out for its size, though the narrow streets which survived the first contrast charmingly with the well-planned, orderly alleys and streets of Cicignon.

Other Notable Buildings

The Stiftsgården, or royal residence, used by the King whenever he visits Trondheim, is a magnificent structure in late baroque style dating from 1775. Incidentally, this is the second largest wooden building in Scandinavia, and doubtless provides the local firemen with an oversize headache. The largest, Singsaker Studenthjem, also belongs to Trondheim. The Bishop's Palace, only a stone's throw from the cathedral, is another interesting relic of the medieval days when Trondheim had some 16 churches and two monasteries. From the nearby market place the statue of King Olav Tryggvason, Carlyle's "wildly beautifullest" king, surveys the town he founded in the year 997.

In the Folk Museum you will find an excellent collection of buildings and implements illustrating the life in Trondheim and surrounding districts in medieval times. The Kunstforeningen Art Gallery, with a fine collection of paintings by representative Norwegian artists, and the Fortress of Kristianstein, which in the old heroic days guarded Trondheim from the landward side, are also both worth a visit. The latter is situated on a rocky eminence to the east of the city, where it commands a magnificent view of the fjord and of Munkholmen.

On another rise overlooking Trondheim Fjord is Ringve. The estate dates from the 1600s but was given to the city, as a music center, by the will of the last owner, who was responsible for acquiring many of the fine and rare instruments including a magnificent harpsichord once housed at Versailles.

Trondheim, in common with Bergen, has older cultural traditions than Oslo, which both cities regard as somewhat of an interloper, or at best an upstart. While Bergen glories in a Philharmonic Orchestra which is the third oldest in the world, antedating its counterpart in Vienna by a good 70 years, Trondheim has a number of cultural societies which make their opposite numbers in Oslo mere striplings by comparison. Chief among these is the Videnskapsselskapet, or Academy of Sciences, which has been running ever since the 18th century.

Trondheim is also the site of Norway's Tekniske Høgskole, where Norway's architects and engineers receive their training. This institute is now part of the university, and in the course of time a student milieu has grown up in the town unlike that of any other Norwegian city. The University of Bergen, founded in 1948, is as yet only an infant in arms, while the students at the University of Oslo tend to be swallowed up in the capital and have little chance of giving it the stamp of a university town. Not so Trondheim, where the students have their own special societies, clubs and restaurants, and put on a musical revue every other year that is not only traditional, but a box-office success as well.

The Trøndelag Provinces

Few parts of Norway are so varied in their scenery as the twin counties of North Trøndelag and South Trøndelag, of which Trondheim is the capital. Apart from the agricultural districts, there are vast forests, rivers and waterfalls, fjords and mountains.

These provinces are also unusually rich in historical mementos, including such sights as the old *ting*-place at Frosta, where representatives from eight counties met regularly to pass laws and mete out justice from A.D. 940 right up to the 16th century. No place in Norwegian history is better known than the battlefield of Stiklestad, where St. Olav met his death in A.D. 1030, and where the church was built, on the very spot he was slain, a hundred years after the battle. On July 29, the anniversary of the battle, there is an annual performance of the St. Olav play at the open-air theater, the largest and most beautiful in the Nordic countries. The Reformation proved a stirring time for Trøndelag, the citadel of Roman Catholicism in the north. Olav Engelbriktsson, last archbishop of Norway, held out in his fortified castle of Steinvikholm (interesting ruins) before fleeing the country. Austråt Castle, at the mouth of the Trondheim Fjord, has been described as the most original building of the Norwegian Renaissance, and in the 17th century the copper-mining town of Røros was founded. Røros is a favorite excursion from Trondheim by rail or road, as this remarkable little town, immortalized in the great novels of Johan Falkberget, has retained its original appearance right down to the present. The old mines were closed in 1978, but have now been re-opened as a unique museum. There are guided tours throughout the year to the Olav mine.

The other great resort of Trøndelag is the mountain village of Oppdal on the Dovre railway. At Oppdal, some of Norway's longest lifts whisk the visitor up to the Troll Eye Restaurant, 1,037 meters (3,400 feet) above sea level.

If you have a sense of the macabre, you might go to Hell—quite literally. Hell in this case is a charming little railway station not more than half an hour by train from Trondheim. You will have the satisfaction of being able to buy a round-trip ticket, and you should not miss the opportunity of mailing a letter or two and taking advantage of the unique postmark.

PRACTICAL INFORMATION FOR
TRONDHEIM AND DISTRICT

TOURIST INFORMATION. *Trondheim Travel Association,* Torget, Kongensgate 7, 7000 Trondheim (07–511466). Accommodations service, guides, sightseeing, brochures, etc. Open Mon. to Sat. 9–8, Sun. 10–6.

USEFUL ADDRESSES. Travel Agents. *Bennett Reisebureau A/S,* Dronningensgt 12 (07–520620). *Unit Reisebyrå,* NTH Gløshaugen (07–593277) and Avd. Dragvoll (07–596759). *Winge Reisebureau A/S,* O. Tryggvasonsgt. 30 (07–533000).
Consulates. *Great Britain,* Sluppenvn. 10 (07–968211).

TELEPHONE CODES. We have given telephone codes for all the towns and villages in the hotel and restaurant lists that follow. These codes need only be used when calling from outside the town or village concerned. The telephone code for Trondheim is 07.

HOTELS AND RESTAURANTS. Trondheim is well provided with both hotels and restaurants in most price ranges, and is considered *the* restaurant city in Norway.

Levanger (Nord–Trøndelag). Area rich in archeological finds. *Backlund* (E), Kirkegt 41 (076–81 600). 130 beds, most rooms with bath. DC, MC.
Youth Hostel. *Levanger Youth Hostel* (I), (076–81 638). 48 beds.

Meråker (Nord–Trøndelag). Folk museum, old copper mines, skiing, chairlift. *Teveltunet* (I), (07–813611). 96 beds in cabins and main building, most rooms with shower/toilet. Fishing, riding.

Namsos (Nord–Trøndelag). Small mountain in center of town, Namdal folk museum. *Namsen Motor Hotel* (M), Nararvn 2 (077–76 100). 107 beds, all rooms with bath/shower. *Central Hotel Namsos* (I), Kirbegt 7–9 (077–71 000). 90 beds, all rooms with facilities. DC, V.

Oppdal (Sør–Trøndelag). 537 meters (1,790 feet), popular ski resort with all facilities, curling, skating. *Nor Alpin* (E), (074–21 611). 195 beds, all rooms shower/toilet. Dancing, bar, restaurant. DC, V. *Hotell Oppdal* (E), O. Skasliens vei (074–21 111). 160 beds, many rooms with shower/toilet. Swimming, sauna, dancing, bar, good restaurant. DC, MC, V. *Hovdin Hotell* (M), Gamle Kongvei (074–21 911). 114 beds, all rooms with facilities, swimming, sauna. AE, DC, MC, V.
Youth Hostel. *Turistheimen* (I), (074–21 330). 49 beds, cafeteria.

Orkanger (Sør–Trøndelag). *Bårdshaug Herregård* (E), (074–81 055). Converted manor, 120 beds, many rooms with bath, swimming, sauna. MC, V.

Røros (Sør–Trøndelag). *Bergstadens Turisthotel* (E), Osloveien 2 (074–11111). 130 beds, all rooms with facilities, swimming, sauna. AE, DC, MC. *Røros Hotel* (M), An Magritsvei (074–11 011). 226 beds, all rooms with facilities, swimming, sauna. MC.
Youth Hostel. *Røros Youth Hostel* (I), Idrettsheimen, Øravn (074–11 089). 110 beds.

Steinkjer (Nord–Trøndelag). Folk museum, burial mounds, salmon fishing. *Tingvold Park Hotell* (E), Gamle Kongvei 47 (077–61 100). 62 beds. *Grand* (M), Kongensgt 37 (077–64 700). 220 beds, most rooms with facilities, sauna, restaurant. DC, MC, V. *Kaffistova* (M), Kongensgt 36 (077–65 099). 40 beds.

Trondheim. *Britannia* (E), Dronningensgate 5 (07–530040). 280 beds, all rooms with facilities, excellent Palm Garden restaurant, breakfast/lunch restaurant, bar. AE, DC, MC, V. *Larssens* (E), Ths Angellsgate 10B (07–528851). 42 beds, most rooms with facilities, restaurant. AE, MC, V. *Neptun* (E), Ths Angellsgate 12b (07–512133). 80 beds with facilities, bistro, AE, MC, V. *Royal Garden Hotel* (E), Kjøpmannsgt. 73 (07–521100). 600 beds ,top standard, three restaurants, indoor pool, gymnasium, solarium, sauna. MC, V.
Ambassadeur (M), Elvegate 18 (07–527050). 85 beds, all rooms with facilities, roof terrace. AE, DC, MC, V. *Augustin* (M), Kongensgate 26 (07–528348). 110 beds, all rooms with facilities. Restaurant, fully licensed. *Gildevangen* (M), Søndregate, 22b (07–528340). 130 beds, some rooms with bath/shower, dining rooms and cafeteria, unlicensed. AE, DC, MC, V. *Norrøna Misjonshospits* (M), Ths Angellsgate 20 (07–532020). Mission hotel, 31 beds, cafeteria, unlicensed. *Prinsen* (M), Kongensgate 30 (07–530650). 140 beds, 70 rooms with facilities, excellent Coq d'Or restaurant, bistro, cafeteria, grill, wine lodge, beer garden. AE, DC, MC, V. *Residence Hotel* (M), Torvet (07–528380). 117 beds, most rooms with facilities, bar, restaurant, open-air restaurant in summer. DC, MC, V. *Scandic Hotel* (M), Brøsetveien 186 (07–939500). 250 beds, all rooms with facilities, sauna, restaurant, bar. AE, DC, MC, V. *Sentrum Nye* (M), Lilletorget (07–520524). 78 beds, most rooms with facilities, restaurant and cafeteria. DC, MC, V. *Singsaker Sommerhotell* (M), Rogersgate 1 (07–520092). Summer only (June 15 through Aug. 15), 200 beds, some rooms with bath/shower, sauna, restaurant. AE, MC, V. *Trondheim* (M), Kongensgate 15 (07–527030). 147 beds, some rooms with bath/shower, dining room, cafeteria. AE, MC.

Restaurants. The most elegant restaurants in Trondheim are found in the leading hotels, such as *Britannia, Prinsen* and *Royal Garden,* described above, but in addition the following restaurants can be recommended. *Bryggen* (E), Ø Bakklandet 66 (07–534055). Beside Old Town Bridge. French cuisine; closed Sun. *Bajazzo Rica* (M), Søndregate 15 (07–516746). Grill, dancing, disco, billiards, nightclub. AE, DC, MC, V. *Benito's Mat og Vinhus* (M), Vår Fruegate 4 (07–511030). Italian food, wine lodge. AE, V. *Braseriet* (M), Nordregate 11, Pizzeria, disco, open-air café in summer. *Cavalero* (M), Kongensgate 3 (07–524730). Restaurant, grill, bar. MC. *China House* (M), Søndregate 220 (07–525220). Chinese food, closed Mon. MC, V. *Daniel* (M), Tinghusplass 1 (07–525160). Steakhouse and grill. *Erichsen* (M), Nordregt 8 (07–520281). Lunch and dinner, bar. AE, MC. *Grenaderen* (M), Kongs-gården (07–522006). Music, open-air restaurant in summer. AE, DC, MC, V. *Munken Kro, Pizzeria* (M), Frati Munkegt 25 (07–525733). Italian food and pizza. *Peppe's Pizza Pub* (M), Kjøpmannsgate 25 (07–532920). American pizza parlor in old warehouse. *Zia Teresa, Pizzeria* (M), Vår Frue Strete (07–526422)

Youth Hostel. *Rosenborg Youth Hostel (Ungdomsherberget)* (I), Weidenmanns-vei 41 (07–530490). 200 beds, in 2-, 3- and 6-bedded rooms, cafeteria.

Camping. *Flak Camping.* Flak ferry harbor, highway 715, 11 km. (seven miles) west. (07–835800). 2 cabins, 60 caravans. *Sandmoen Camping.* Heimdal, 11 km. (seven miles) south. (07–886135). 27 cabins, 14 rooms, minigolf. *Storsand Gård, Motell and Camping.* Malvik (07–976360). 40 cabins, tents and caravans, minigolf, open-air bathing.

HOW TO GET AROUND. By bus. The bus station in Trondheim is situated at Sverresgt. 3 (07–527322). The staff can be contacted for information on itineraries and prices for services throughout the district. The bus station also has a separate office dealing with longer trips. Motor coaches can be booked through the Tourist Information Office.

By steamship. The coastal express steamer Bergen—Kirkenes northbound and southbound calls daily at Trondheim. For reservations and timetables inquire at any travel agent. There are also express steamer services from Trondheim to Vanvi-kan (190 passengers, frequent departures daily) and from Trondheim, via Brekstad, Hitra, and Frøya to Sula (140 passengers, at least two departures daily).

By car ferry. The most important are: Flakk (Trondheim)—Rørvik (Fosen); Val-set (Agdenes)—Brekstad (Ørland); Sunde (Snillfjord)—Sandstad (Hitra); and Kjer-ringvåg (Hitra)—Flatval (Frøya). All have frequent departures all year round, and the crossings take 20–25 minutes. Tickets can be bought at travel agents or *Fosen Trafikklag,* Fosenkaia, Post Box 512, N–7001 Trondheim (07–525540). Advance bookings cannot be accepted.

By train. The Nordland Railway goes through the entire length of North Trön-delag, and the Dovre and Röros Railways go through South Trödelag. There is also the Meråker–Sweden Railway, which goes through to Stockholm once daily. For information call 526469.

By taxi. In Trondheim, to call a taxi day or night, phone (07–527600). There are taxi stands at Torget (Market Place), Søndregt., Nordregt., Studentersamfun-net, the train station, the Royal Garden Hotel, and Ilevoilen.

TOURS. There are many interesting tours of one to four days, that can be made around the Trondheim district, either by car or by bus. The Trondheim Travel As-sociation, at Torget, Kongensgate 7 (07–511466), should be contacted for details and further suggestions. Some examples are: the Atlantic tour to Hitra and Frøya, a three–day round trip from Trondheim, through Orkanger, Sunde and on to Sand-stad (Hitra); a fishing trip to Åfjord, for which a stay of at least two days is recommended, for deep sea fishing, salmon fishing in rivers, and brown trout fishing in lakes and streams; and a trip around the Trollheimen (a "see–Norway–in–a–nutshell" tour) going Trondheim—Oppdal—Sunndalsøra—Orkanger—Trondheim. From Oppdal (E6 from Trondheim) take the state road 16—called the "Adventure Road"—to Sunndalsøra and Kristiansund. A more spectacular route for scenery would be hard to find.

There are also short tours around Trondheim itself, by bus, tram or even on foot. Ask the Travel Association for details.

PLACES TO VISIT. The principal sights of the district include: *Røros,* with its old copper mines; *Oppdal,* a big alpine winter sports center, but still attractive in summer; *Austrât Castle* at the mouth of the Trondheim Fjord; the battlefield and church at *Stiklestad;* the Frosta *ting*-place; the village of *Hell;* and the rock drawings at *Hegra.* Trondheim itself has quite a number of museums, art galleries and places of historic interest. The Tourist Office will have further details; however, among the more interesting places are: the *Folkemuseet* (Folk Museum) at Sverresborg, which is Trøndelag's museum of urban and rural culture. Buildings have been brought to the site from all over the country and reassembled to provide an authentic cross–section of life and architecture of the past; the island of *Munkholmen,* which in pagan times was a place of execution. In early Christian times an abbey was built there, probably the first in Norway. After the Reformation it was converted into a fortress. Today the island is a public bathing resort; the *Nidaros Cathedral,* Scandinavia's largest medieval building, erected on the shrine of St. Olav. The cathedral (built around 1150) is the center of the annual festivals that commemorate the traditions that surround the name and person of St. Olav; and the *Ringve Gods* (Ringve Museum of Musical History), which is at Ringve Manor, Lade. Visits are based exclusively on conducted tours run by the museum's own guides. Each tour (in Norwegian, English or German) lasts about 80 minutes and includes demonstrations of musical instruments.

PARKS. At the Ringve Music Museum is the Ringve Botanical Garden, at the University of Trondheim, Lade Alle (07–922411). The garden is open all year and admission is free. Conducted tours of the open-air exhibitions are available by appointment.

MUSEUMS AND SITES. The Maritime Museum. This is the result of careful private collecting over a period of 50 years, and skilfully shows the different maritime stages of development in the Trøndelag area from the middle of the 16th century up to the present day. Located in the Old Slavery building, once a prison, in the port area of Trondheim. Open from mid-June through Aug., Mon. to Sat. from 10–3; open year-round on Sun. 12–3. Admission NOK 10, children NOK 5.

Archeological Excavations. The remains of a medieval church, St. Olav's can be found in the courtyard behind the public library, Kongensgate 2. Admission free.

SPORTS. Outdoor life is the chief attraction. **Swimming** in the Trondheim Fjord may be chilly, but is popular with the locals themselves. Excellent trout and salmon **fishing** is within reach; in the Nidelven (River Nid), Namsen, Gaula, Nea, Orkla, and Stjørdal rivers. Salmon fishing in the Verdal river and Lake Leksdalsvatn. The mountains of Snasa and Namdal in the north, and Sylene in the south, also provide good angling. Elk **hunting** in the Snåsa forests is the best in Norway, and the coastal islands, especially Hitra, are the haunt of red deer. Ptarmigan, a game bird similar to grouse, can be shot during September and October.

Mountaineering and **hiking** in the Trollheimen and Sylene districts, where there are trails and attractive chalets.

Trondheim is one of the few towns to boast a **golf course** (9 holes), which is situated at an elevation of 215 meters (700 feet), overlooking the cathedral city and the fjord. Famous for its annual Midnight Sun Golf Tournament. On the outskirts of town, Trondheim, much the same as Oslo, has its own private stretch of **skiing** country, Bymarka. Easily reached from the center of town by bus or train (20 minutes), it is a sportsman's paradise. **Skistua,** opposite the Gråkallen ski jump, is the center. Ski lift and ski trails in all directions.

Other centers include Meråker, Oppdal and Røros, as described above.

WAY TO THE NORTH

Folklore, Finnmark and the Midnight Sun

Norway's main problem was how to care for tourists, not how to attract them. This is still true of northern Norway. From Steinkjer at latitude 64° on up towards the Arctic Ocean, it's just one feast of scenic beauty after another, and the whole, incredible northern outdoors is lit up by both the noonday and the midnight sun. From the moment you pull away from the quay and head out of the Trondheim Fjord, you know that a new kind of adventure has begun.

Exploring North Norway

The great charm of the express steamer trip is seeing the sights when they appear, no matter how awkward the hour. The 240-meter (800-foot) stone mountain, Torghatten, for example, is passed about 1 A.M., and in summer there's enough light to observe the famous hole clear through the rock about halfway up and a good 150 meters (500 feet) long. Geologists talk about the action of waves washing out this tunnel when the shoreline was much higher, but local folklore has a far more colorful explanation which we'll come to shortly. At 4 A.M. you pass the Seven Sisters—seven snow-covered peaks, each more jagged than the last.

If you're breakfasting around eight, you'll have to stop and run out on deck when the approach to Hestmannen or The Horseman is announced. Not just because the silhouette of this rocky island, from a certain point, looks remarkably like a horse and rider, but because he is the clue to

Torghatten. It seems that Hestmannen, quite some time ago, was enam-
ored of the Leka-Maiden near Rørvik, but she paid no attention to him.
Whereupon the enraged Horseman shot a long-distance arrow at her, only
to have it intercepted by Torg who threw his hat in the way; hence the
great hole. To top things off, when the sun rose, everyone involved in the
affair was turned into stone, including the Seven Sisters, who fled with
the Leka-Maiden.

At the north end of the petrified Hestmannen you encounter something
far more stimulating to the imagination than folklore, though quite invisible. This is the imaginary parallel of 66° 32' North of the Arctic Circle,
and once it is crossed, you are in that much-advertised, much-described
Land of the Midnight Sun. The coastal express boat calls at the little village of Ørnes, and overland excursions are arranged by bus via the
Saltstraumen *maelstrom* (or whirlpool) to Bodø.

After a forenoon among the ever-present islands you dock at Bodø
where you stay for a couple of hours.

By engaging a cab, you may even have time to combine looking across
the Salt Fjord south of Bodø towards the spot where the notorious Sal-
straumen churns and eddies during each change of tide, with a quick trip
to the Rønvik Restaurant three km. (two miles) north of town. From here
there's a panorama of rock masses, islands, valleys and fjords that will
open the eyes of the most scenery-satiated traveler.

There would also be a fine view of the Midnight Sun from Rønvik if
you stayed there long enough, but by midnight the *Hurtigrute* is steaming
through Raft Sound in the Lofoten Islands. In fact, by supper time you
are close upon the "Lofot-Wall", as the Norwegians so aptly describe the
jagged series of mountain peaks of this island-chain.

Catch as Catch Can

First it's Stamsund at 7 P.M., one of the largest of the many fishing ports
and shipping centers in the Lofotens, where the scenery consists of boats,
warehouses, rocky shores covered with wooden racks for drying codfish,
and steep snow-covered mountains in the not-distant background. About
two hours later it's Svolvaer, largest town of the islands and with the same
sights, only more of them.

Svolvaer is also the fishing capital of the north during the cod season
each winter in February and March. Furthermore, it is already something
of a tourist center at that time, since many hardy travelers each winter
take advantage of special excursions by boat to witness this fantastic spectacle. Thousands of craft of all kinds engage in fishing with all kinds of
gear. But there's plenty of fish for everyone, no matter what his apparatus,
and, in a good season, all return loaded to the gunwales. On shore the
activity is equally hectic, for all these tons of cod must be cleaned and
processed; fillets are sent away for deep-freezing, livers for stewing, roe
for canning and the split cod is hung up to dry into *tørr-fisk*.

"But some places they don't bother with such drying contrivances,"
says the friendly captain. "Near Kristiansund, for example, the cod are
just spread out on the bare rocks along the shore. That's why around there,
they're called *klipp-fisk*, for *klipp* means cliff."

"Where's that Midnight Sun?" you'll sooner or later ask. The answer
will be disappointing. Throughout June and most of July there is plenty
of twilight, or rather a combined sunset and sunrise effect, but there are

too many islands and mountain walls for you to see the sun when it approaches the horizon at midnight. So, after looking at the wildest parts of the Lofot Wall—Digermulen Mountain and the narrow Raft Sound which you sail through after leaving Svolvaer—you may as well turn in for some much-needed sleep. Of course, if you are troubled with insomnia you'll find plenty to look at all night while the steamer winds among the Vesteralen Islands, which in contrast to the Lofotens, are amazingly flat.

Before breakfast the second full day from Trondheim, you can go ashore in Harstad for an hour and a half. Not only is this an important fish-canning and shipping town, but it can show, a couple of miles north, the curious fortified church of Trondenes. Built in the 13th century, this edifice has stone walls two and a half meters thick and is one of the very few church-fortresses in Norway. Harstad is one of the few ports where the coastal steamers call simultaneously on their daily sailings southwards and northwards. Harstad, with some 22,000 inhabitants, is today a modern center of the region comprising southern parts of Troms county and northern parts of Nordland county.

Senja island, between Harstad and Tromsø, is the second-largest island in Norway, with interesting small fishing and farming communities; there is a link with the mainland via Finnsnes. Fjords and mountains there are aplenty—visit Tranøy, Berg and Torsken.

Approaching Tromsø you pass the Rystraumen whirlpool, which can move dramatically fast. On the Rya island, in the middle of Rystraumen, a small colony of musk oxen live and thrive.

At Tromsø, the capital of Troms Province and the largest city above the Arctic Circle, the Midnight Sun is still elusive because of mountains to the north, but you can take the cable car to the top of the mountain where the view of the sun is quite fantastic. Other sights include the longest bridge in Northern Europe spanning the Tromsø Sound, the gondola lift to Storsteinen, the Tromsdalen Church, the Observatory for Northern Lights—which devotes the long Arctic night to studying the Aurora Borealis—and another well-known scientific institution, the Tromsø Arctic Museum.

If you don't want to go on an expedition for your polar bear, you can meet one in the street in Tromsø itself, but stuffed into immobility. You'll find others, the alive kind, at the zoo, together with seals and otters. But don't wander too far if you want to continue on the 6 P.M. *Hurtigrute*. This night will be your first real chance for a look at the sun, weather permitting, for here's an open space northward between the two islands of Vannøy and Arnøy which the steamer should cross around midnight.

At about 4.30 A.M., the steamer reaches Hammerfest. Again there's an hour for sightseeing, and this time you are in the northernmost city in the world. (By the way, Hammerfest was also the first town in Norway to install electric lights, in 1891). Climb the 100-meter hill just behind the town for a good look at this plucky little community and its not-too-friendly natural environment. Not only was it completely razed in late 1944 by the retreating Nazis, who applied scorched earth destruction to almost all of Finnmark county, but it has also been damaged repeatedly by avalanches. Yet in spite of all handicaps the town was rebuilt, and one of its most impressive sights is the church with its tall tower shaped like an elongated Lapp tent or *kåta*.

Fish export is the main industry of Hammerfest, together with tourist trade in normal times, and here you will see another of the deep-freezing plants which have revolutionized the processing of fish in these parts. Fresh frozen fillets are rapidly replacing the age-old dried *klipp-fisk* and *stokk-fisk* as export items, and are bringing a correspondingly new year-round prosperity to communities which formerly suffered much from seasonal unemployment.

The North Cape

On leaving Hammerfest, you have only 24 hours left of the four-day cruise from Trondheim, but most of them will be spent on the very top of Norway. The steamer crosses several stretches of water that open directly north of the Arctic Ocean, and on approaching the big island of Mager-øy, it may be that you'll head into the "Ice-Sea" as the natives call it.

There's not much to see except a cliff of blackish granite, rising almost vertically from the sea, but if your life ambition has been to follow the example of King Oscar II of Norway and Sweden, who climbed this northernmost piece of Europe in 1873, you can do so. An even earlier tourist was Louis Philippe d'Orleans, later King of France, who visited the North Cape in 1795! The ships call at Honningsvåg, from where buses are run to North Cape to save a really steep 300-meter (1,000-foot) climb. Perhaps the best idea is to step off the ship at Honningsvåg and take an evening bus for the 34 km. (21 miles) to the North Cape across arctic Mageröy (literally Meager Island). The North Cape Hall affords a panoramic view and, in season, a long look at the Midnight Sun hanging above the Arctic Ocean.

The road itself was opened by King Olav (then Crown Prince) in 1956. It offers magnificent views of the Cape itself. Honningsvåg is connected by an auto-ferry with Kåfjord, the nearest point on the mainland.

The steamer now crosses the mouths of three vast fjords—Porsanger, Lakse, and Tana—all of which cut far south into the mainland, and call at some fishing villages. But the main sight after the North Cape is the enormous bird-rock of Svaerholtklubben on the tip of the peninsula between Porsanger Fjord and Lakse Fjord. Midnight will again find you with an unobstructed view to the north so, weather permitting, you'll have another chance to watch the sun toy with the horizon as it passes without interruption from setting to rising.

There'll be an opportunity to walk around the historic fortress of Vard-øhus at Vardø, the easternmost town in Norway. The most ancient part of the stronghold, now long disappeared, was constructed in the early 1300s, while the present ramparts, shaped like an eight-pointed star, date from the 1730s.

Depending on which day of the week it is, the express steamer may or may not call at Vadsø, the administrative capital of Finnmark. This town is located on the upper edge of the wide Varanger Fjord which, unlike the previous three, cuts westward instead of south. In any case, early in the morning next day, you will reach the end station of the North Norway *Hurtigrute:* the important mining town of Kirkenes.

Between Allied bombing raids and Nazi earth-scorching, both Kirkenes and the Syd-Varanger iron mines were almost totally wrecked at the end of World War II. Today, the huge plant in Kirkenes produces by magnetic separation about 1 million tonnes of iron-ore concentrate annually.

Many interesting side-trips can be made from Kirkenes. First of all, a visit to the iron mines a few kilometers from town which, being open-pit affairs, can be seen just by looking at them from the road. Then there's the road south along the Pasvik River which forms most of the boundary between Norway and Soviet Russia. The 64-km. (40-mile) drive to Skogfoss, for example, will provide a good view of the friendly scenery—birch trees, green fields and rolling hills—which is astonishingly different from the stern rockiness of the North Cape country. And you can also have a glimpse of the land on the other shore, behind the Iron Curtain. Incidentally, it's forbidden to carry cameras into this area near the Soviet border, a regulation strictly enforced by Norwegian guards.

From Kirkenes you have two new ways of returning to Trondheim: swiftly and spectacularly by plane with landings at Tromsø, Evenes, Alta, Bardufoss and Bodø; or slowly and fascinatingly by bus or car, "slowly" meaning in this case exactly three days to either Tromsø or Narvik, with two overnight stops; or via the returning *Hurtigrute*. While the plane trip presents a wonderful bird's-eye view of the top of Norway, the slower route overland is more rewarding.

Finnmark by Bus

You leave Kirkenes after early breakfast and drive along the lower side of Varanger Fjord to Tana bridge. Then the new road runs alongside the River Tana into Lapp country. The Tana is a long and interesting river, famous for heavy salmon. It also forms the border between Norway and Finland over a long distance. The road leaves Tana river at Karasjok, one of the largest Lapp villages on the Finnmark mountain plateau, and the day's journey ends at Lakselv on the Porsanger Fjord.

Of the many things which impress you on this tour, probably the most remarkable is the tremendous difference between the rocky bareness of the Arctic coast, and the mildness and fertility of inland Finnmark. Here are farms with pastures as green as any you saw in western Norway, with healthy-looking cows, goats and sheep. True enough, little grain will ripen in this far north, even with 24 hours of sunshine during part of the summer, but potatoes and other root crops give a good yield.

Another striking characteristic is that everything up here is new: houses, barns, boats, piers, even the telegraph poles. All is new for the simple reason that the Nazis burned nearly everything in 1944; hence any manmade structure dates from 1946 or later. But in between the villages, one can drive for scores of kilometers without seeing habitation and sometimes without even meeting another vehicle.

Next morning you leave Lakselv for another day of scenic beauty. At Skaidi, you may make a detour to Hammerfest, but the main road continues southwards along Repparfjord salmon river to Alta on the Alta Fjord. The Alta River is one of the world's best salmon waters, and millionaires have been competing throughout the last century for fishing rights.

From Alta a highway runs about 129 km. (80 miles) south to Kautokeino, a village chiefly inhabited by Lapps. This is a side-trip which can be made the year round and will let you see the semi-nomads in their own setting rather than as a tourist attraction on the side of the road. There are a number of souvenir shops in the village, as well as the atelier of Regine and Frank Juhls whose design jewelry has become famous outside Norway too. There are designs based on traditional Lappish jewelry as well as modern ones. Even if you don't intend buying any jewelry go and visit Juhls' atelier.

The Arctic Highway continues along several fjords, also across the Kvenangen peninsula, on the Sørkjosen in Troms county, where you spend the night.

Troms by Bus

The third day you have a pleasant change in routine by riding the ferry straight across Lyngen Fjord instead of following around its shores, or you may go by the new road along the eastern side of the fjord.

Soon you are speeding nearly south along the west shore of Lyngen Fjord to Nordkjosbotn, at the south end of still another fjord, Bals Fjord, which stretches more or less north for 64 km. (40 miles) to Tromsø.

Olsborg is a hamlet consisting of a small inn, a service station and a few houses, in the picturesque district bordering the Målselv River. This part of Troms Province was colonized 150 years ago by pioneers from the eastern valleys in lower Norway, and today is a thriving agricultural district with solid houses and barns, and, in good years, a harvest of grain beyond the needs of the inhabitants.

In the afternoon the bus passes the sprawling Bardufoss Airport and climbs over a 425-meter (1,400-foot) pass. Here there is a good view out to sea, or rather towards the Vågs Fjord through which you sailed after leaving Harstad. Then it's down to sea level again at Bjerkvik in the midst of both spectacular and historic country, for here are many scenes of battle from World War II. Within an hour you will have crossed the magnificent new bridge across Rombaken Fjord and entered Narvik in Nordland county.

Nordland by Bus and Train

Narvik is a name that awakes a response in most travelers, whether from the Continent or from English-speaking lands. For here occurred the great naval engagement in the Ofot Fjord in April, 1940, when the Germans seized Narvik, and the ensuing campaign in which Norwegian troops, aided by British, French and Polish detachments, inflicted the first defeat of World War II upon the Nazi military machine by recapturing the town. General Fleischer of Norway was thus the first field commander to defeat Hitler in battle. Narvik was, of course, a much sought-after prize because of its importance as the shipping port for the valuable iron ore from the Swedish mines located a short way over the border at Kiruna. The town has been rebuilt and is a pleasant place. While you are there, take a look at the small museum which commemorates the action with a model reconstruction.

Besides the economic importance of Narvik, it can well stand on its own feet as a tourist center in competition with any part of Norway for its panorama of fjords with rows of snow-topped peaks in the background. During the Midnight Sun season, the combination sunset-sunrises enhance the scene with incredible color and light effects. However, for a really breathtaking view of all this the cable railway (Fjellheisen) will carry you from the town to the Fagerness mountain plateau.

Ore-Train Route

The best way to combine economic studies with sightseeing is to ride the ore-carrying railway up to the mines and back, or at least as far as

Bjørnefjell on the Norwegian-Swedish border. You can ride the regular passenger trains up and back, about one hour each way, returning in time to have dinner in Narvik and spend the evening looking around the town. As at Kirkenes there is great activity in Narvik. Ore trains run day and night, unloading their valuable contents at the tremendous quay installations where several freighters are always tied up having their holds filled, while out in the fjord are others waiting their turn. Along the streets at night and in the cafés you'll see and hear the sailors of a dozen nationalities; all of which adds to the impression of a busy cosmopolitan port.

The fourth and final day of the bus journey provides even more scenic variation and grandeur than before. Now begins a really amphibious part of the journey which we'll summarize as follows: first, a mixed run of 80 km. (50 miles) on dry land and a 40-minute cruise across a genuine fjord, Tys Fjord. Again there's a pleasant 32-km. (20-mile) dry run to Innhavet. Here you can look out over the Sag Fjord towards Svolvaer and the Lofoten Islands. But your day has only begun; moreover, you find that the stages are now getting longer. Thus it's 71 km. (44 miles) over rising and falling land to Bonåsjøen, a 15-minute sail across Leirfjord, and then a mere 48 km. (30 miles) to Fauske. From late-fall 1986, the ferry route Sommarset–Bonåsjøen will be replaced by a new road around the Leir Fjord. At this far-inland port town you must make up your mind whether to return to Bodø—due west of here on the Skjerstad Fjord—for a closer look at the Saltstraumen *maelstrom* or to continue southward.

Fauske is your junction for the Nordlandsbane (train) to Trondheim or Bodø. Hardy travelers may want to take the night express that same evening to Trondheim. But a better plan is to take this train to Lønsdal only, spend a night or a couple of days there in magnificent mountain scenery, with a Lapp encampment, excellent trout fishing, and the wildly luxurious Junkerdal valley close at hand, and continue by day train. About a half-hour from Lønsdal there will be a long blast on the locomotive's whistle. Nothing to cause alarm—it merely marks the crossing of the Arctic Circle.

Mo-i-Rana is only a brief stop for the summer expresses, but it's a fascinating place for anyone wishing to combine hiking, glacier-exploration, etc., with the study of the Norwegian kind of industrialization based on abundant hydro-electric power. The largest electric-process steel mill in Scandinavia was built by the Norwegian Government, partly financed by American contributions to the European Recovery Program which released Norwegian capital for this project.

The afternoon brings you down the long narrow handle of Norway, with stops every half-hour or so at the most important places. There's Grong, junction for the side-line to Namsos, and Steinkjer, scene of crushing air attacks upon the British Expeditionary Force which, in 1940, was trying to make its way south from Namsos.

You are now in sight of the upper end of the Trondheim Fjord, and back in North Trøndelag province. The express next stops at Verdal, where it's possible to alight and make the brief side-trip by bus or taxi to Stiklestad, catching a local train afterwards to Trondheim.

Spitsbergen

Although it's highly unlikely you'll spend any time on the inhospitable archipelago which comprises Spitsbergen, a number of cruise ships do call in at Longyearbyen, its administrative center. Since the treaty of 1920, Spitsbergen has been recognized as Norwegian territory but Russia still mines coal there and there is a sizeable Russian community at Barentsberg. For the visitor, however, it's the sheer magnificence of the icy wastes which provide the attraction, especially in good weather. The icefloes provide a glimpse of a world far removed from everyday surroundings. Walking trips of 4 or 11 days were introduced in 1982. Programs are available from the Norwegian Tourist Board.

PRACTICAL INFORMATION FOR THE NORTH

TOURIST INFORMATION. Tourist information offices are located in the following places: **Alta,** (084–35 041). **Bodø,** Sjøgt 21 (081–21 240). **Fauske,** Busstorvet (081–43 303). **Hammerfest,** Rådhusplassen 2 (084–12 185). **Harstad,** Torvet 7 (082–63 235). **Honningsvåg,** Holmen (084–72 894). **Karasjok** (084–66 902). **Kautokeino** (084–56 500). **Kirkenes,** Parkveien (085–92 544). **Mo I Rana** (087–50 421). **Lakselv** (084–61 022). **Narvik,** Kongensgt. 66 (082–43 309). **Tromsø** (083–84 776). **Vadsø,** (085–53 055).

TELEPHONE CODES. We have given telephone codes for all the towns and villages in the hotel and restaurant lists that follow. These codes need only be used when calling from outside the town or village concerned.

HOTELS AND RESTAURANTS. It is advisable to plan any trip north of Trondheim well in advance in view of the limited accommodations. Generally speaking, the best hotels in North Norway are found in the towns, which are in themselves sufficiently small and picturesque to provide a resort atmosphere. In Finnmark there are several inns along the Arctic Highway, which cater to the in-transit tourist. The best known of these inns are located in Alta, Karasjok, Levajok, Skaidi, Lakselv, Vadsø, Kirkenes, Båtsfjord, Berlevåg, Havøysund, Hasvik and Kantokeino. The best inns and hotels along the Arctic Highway in Troms are found in Kvaenangsfjell, Sørkjosen, Olderdalen, Nordkjosbotn, Skibotn, Setermoen and Øse. Fine inns along the Arctic Highway in Nordland at Innhavet, Rognan and Majavatn.

Alta (Finnmark). Salmon fishing in river Alta. *Alta Sommerhotell* (M), (084–35 000). 210 beds, all rooms with bath/shower. AE, DC, MC, V.*Alta Gjestestue* (I), (084–35 336).
Restaurants. *Alta Gjestestue* (I), Bekkefaret 2 (084–35 336).
Youth Hostel. *Alta Youth Hostel* (I), Frikirkens Elevhjem, Midtbakkvn 52 (084–34 409). 55 beds.

Bakkehaug (Troms). *Rundhaug* (M), (089–37 311). 52 beds, some rooms with facilities. *Målselvfossen Turistsenter* (I), (089–35 213). 120 beds, some rooms with facilities; also apartments.

Bardu (Troms). *Bardu Motor Hotel* (E), Setermoen (089–81 022). 78 beds, all with bath.
Restaurants. *og Feriesenter,* Idrettsv .2 *Setermoen Camping and Holiday Center* (I), (089–81 558).

Bodø (Nordland). Excursion to Saltstraumen maelstrom, 33 km. (30 miles) from town. *Diplomat* (E), Sjøgaten 23 (081–27 000). 170 beds, all rooms with facilities. Restaurant. AE, DC, MC, V. *Norton Grand* (E), Storgaten 3 (081–20 000). 91 rooms, many with bath/shower. AE, MC, V. *SAS Royal* (E), Storgaten 2 (081–24

100). 360 beds, all rooms with facilities. AE, DC, MC, V. *Central Hotel* (M), Prof. Schytesgt. 7 (081–23 585). 74 beds, all rooms with facilities. *Norrøna* (I), Storgaten 4 (081–25 550). 170 beds, most rooms with facilities. AE, DC.

Restaurants. *Løold Kafeteria* (I), Tollbugt 9 (081–24 080). Cafeteria in the center of Bodø overlooking the harbor.

Youth Hostel. *Flatvold Youth Hostel* (I), Ronvik Erysset (081–25 666). 160 beds.

Båtsfjord (Finnmark). Characteristic fishing village. *Båtsfjord Royal* (E), (085–83 100). 44 beds all with facilities.

Fauske (Nordland). *Fauske* (E), Storgt. 82 (081–43 833). 200 beds. DC, MC, V.

Restaurants. *Tom's Gatekjøkken,* Storgt 92 (081–44 442). *Tuva Leirsted* (I), (081–42 927).

Youth Hostel. *Fauske Youth Hostel* (I), Nyvn 6 (081–44 706). 124 beds.

Hammerfest (Finnmark). *Brassica* (M), Storgaten 9–11 (084–11 822). 37 beds. DC, V. *Hammerfest Hotel* (E), Strandgt 2–4 (084–11 622). 56 beds, all facilities. *Rica Hotel* (M), Sørøygt 15 (084–11 333). 115 beds, many rooms with bath/shower. AE, DC, MC. *Hammerfest Motel og Camping* (I), (084–11 126). 180 beds, in apartments for 2 or 4 persons.

Harstad (Troms). *Grand Nordic* (E), Strandgate 2 (082–62 170). 125 beds, most rooms with facilities. DC, MC, V. *Viking Nordic* (M), Fjordgate 2 (082–64 080). 170 beds, all rooms with facilities, swimming, sauna. AE, DC, MC, V.

Youth Hostel. *Stangnes Youth Hostel* (I), Plassenvn 27 (082–73 820). 80 beds.

Hasvik. *Hasvik Gjestiveri* (M), Storgt 18 (084–21 207). 18 beds.

Havøysund. *Havøysund* (E), (084–23 103). 30 beds.

Honningsvåg (Finnmark). Small town on Magerøy island, situated 2,110 km. (1,308 miles) from North Pole. *SAS Nordkapp Hotell* (E), Nordkappgt 4 (084–72 333). Special sightseeing trips by fishing vessel to bird sanctuaries at Svaerholtklubben. 266 beds, all rooms with facilities, restaurant, cafeteria. DC, MC, V. *Rogers Inn* (I), Nordkappvn 79 (084–72 465). 16 beds.

Restaurants. *Lagunen Restaurant and Cabins* (M), (084–72 702). *Café Corner* (I), (084–72 701). *Café Ritz* (I), (084–72 711).

Youth Hostel. *Lagunen Nordkapp Youth Hostel* (I), (084–75 113). At North Cape, 34 km. (21 miles) from town, 58 beds.

Karasjok (Finnmark). Lapp village, 30,000 reindeer, Lapp museum, Karasjok library has world's greatest collection of literature on Lapps. *Karasjok SAS Turisthotell* (E), (084–66 203). 140 beds. AE, DC, MC, V. *Karakroa* (I), Kautokeinov 9 (084–66 446). 60 beds, sauna, camping huts and youth hostel.

Kautokeino (Finnmark). Lapp village on Finnmark mountain plateau, famous Easter race by Lapps and reindeer on ice-bound river. *Kautokeino Tourist Hotel* (E), (084–56 205). 114 beds, all rooms with facilities, sauna. AE, DC, MC, V.

Youth Hostel. *Kautokeino Youth Hostel* (I), (084–56 118). 35 beds, modern.

Kirkenes (Finnmark). 50 km. (31 miles) from Soviet frontier, large iron ore mines at Bjørnevatn, 11 km. (seven miles) from Kirkenes. *Rica Kirkenes* (E), Pasvikvn 63 (085–91 491). 160 beds, all rooms with facilities, sauna. AE, DC, MC, V.

Restaurants. *Grillstua,* Dr. Wesselsgt 18 (085–91 287).

Lakselv (Finnmark). *Lakselv* (E), Karasjokvn (084–61 066). 86 beds. *Porsangerfjord* (E), (084–61 377). 88 beds.

Lønsdal (Nordland). 509 méters (1,670 feet), situated near "Arctic Circle" on Saltfjell mountain plateau, good ski touring. *Polarsirkelen Høyfjellshotell* (E), (081–94 122). 87 beds, most rooms with facilities, sauna. DC, MC, V.

Mo I Rana (Nordland). *Holmen* (E), Th. von Westensgt 2 (087–51 444). 80 beds, all rooms with bath/shower, grill, cafeteria, swimming. AE, DC, MC, V. *Meyergården* (M), (087–50 555). 320 beds, most rooms with facilities. AE, DC, MC, V.
Youth Hostel. *Fageråsen Youth Hostel* (I), (087–50 963). 64 beds.

Mosjøen (Nordland). Salmon fishing in river Vefsna, folk museum. *Fru Haugans* (E), (087–70 477). 120 beds, 38 rooms with bath/shower. MC, V. *Lyngengården* (E), (087–74 800). 103 beds, 17 rooms with bath/shower. MC.
Youth Hostel. *Mosjøen Youth Hostel* (I), (087–87 843). In Sandvik folk high school, 140 beds, swimming, sauna.

Narvik (Nordland). Major export harbor for iron ore from Sweden, chairlift to top of Fagernesfjell at 600 meters (1,970 feet), grand skiing terrain. *Grand Royal Hotel* (E), Kongensgate 64 (082–41 500). 220 beds, 118 rooms with bath/shower and radio, restaurant, bars. AE, DC, MC, V. *Nordstjernen Pension* (M), Kongensgate 26 (082–44 120). 50 beds, some rooms with bath/shower.
Youth Hostel. *Nordkalotten Youth Hostel* (I), Havnegate 3 (082–42 598). 110 beds, modern and popular.

Nordkjosbotn (Troms). Road E6/E78. *Vollan Gjestestue* (M), (089–28 103). 33 beds.

Skaidi (Finnmark). Salmon fishing in Repparfjord and Skaidi rivers. *Skaidi Arctic Hotel* (E), (084–16 120). 60 beds. *Repparfjord Ungdomssenter* (Youth Center), (I), Kvalsund (084–16 165). 39 beds.

Sortland (Nordland). On Langøy island in the Lofotens. *Sortland Nordic* (E), Vesterålsgaten 59 (088–21 833). 134 beds, most rooms with facilities. AE, DC, MC, V.

Stamsund (Nordland). On Vestågøy island in the Lofotens. *Stamsund Lofoten* (M), (088–89 228). 60 beds, most rooms with facilities, swimming, sauna. AE, DC, MC.
Youth Hostel. *Justad Rorbu Youth Hostel* (I), (088–89 166). In fishermen's dwelling, 50 beds, primitive.

Svolvaer (Nordland). On Austvågøy island in the Lofotens, the most important tourist center in Lofoten islands, and a mecca for artists. Main Port for annual cod fishinig in Feb./March. *Svolvaer Hotel Lofoten* (E), Austnesfjordgt 24 (088–71 999). 50 beds, all rooms with facilities. Restaurant. Fully licensed. AE, DC, MC, V. *Norton Hotell Lofoten* (E), (088–71 200). 90 beds, all rooms with facilities. AE, DC, MC, V.
Youth Hostel. *Svolvaer Youth Hostel* (I), (088–70 777). 88 beds.

Tromsø (Troms). On island in a narrow sound, hemmed in by mountains, connected with mainland by 1,036 meter (3,398 feet) long bridge. Arctic museum, aquarium, Northern Lights observatory, whaling station at Skjelnan, chairlift to top of Storsteinen. *SAS Royal* (L), Sjøgate 87 (083–56 000). 350 beds, all rooms with facilities. AE, DC, MC, V. *Grand Nordic* (E), Storgate 44 (083–85 500). 171 beds, all rooms with facilities. AE, DC, MC, V. *Saga* (M), Rich Withs Plass 2 (083–81 180). 100 beds, all rooms with facilities. AE, DC, MC, V. *Tromsdalen* (M), (083–35 944). 50 beds, most rooms with facilities. *Tromsø Hotel* (M), Grønnegt. 50 (083–87 520). 70 beds, all rooms with facilities. Breakfast only.
Youth Hostel. *Elverhøy* (I), (083–85 319). 74 beds.

Vadsø (Finnmark). On Varanger fjord, town museum, Esbensen manor is only remaining patrician building left in Finnmark, airship tower used by Amundsen's "Norge" in 1926 and Nobile's "Italia" in 1928. *SAS Vadsø* (E), Oscarsgt 4 (085–53 335). 110 beds, most rooms with facilities. AE, DC, MC, V. *Lailas Gjestehus* (I), Brugt 2 (085–51 681). 54 beds, some rooms with facilities.

Vardø (Finnmark). On an island; connected with the mainland by a 2,800 m (9,240 ft) tunnel. Vardøhus octagonal fortress built in 1737, Vardø museum, Rein-øya island with large bird sanctuaries. *Norton Hotell Barents* (M), (085–87 761). 86 beds, all rooms with facilities, sauna. MC, V. *Lailas Gjestehus* (I), Strandgt. 72 (085–87 529). 11 beds. Breakfast only.

HOW TO GET AROUND. The enormous distances of North Norway demand time. Chief means of transport is the daily year-round service maintained by the fine **coastal express steamers,** sailing from Bergen to Kirkenes and back in 11 days and calling at important coastal places en route. In Finnmark there are 13 airports, several car hire companies and a bus and ferry company with routes right across the country.

From Trondheim, the **North Norway Railway** (Nordlandsbanen) will take you to Fauske and Bodø north of the Arctic Circle in a day. On top of that comes a one day bus ride to Narvik, two days to Tromsø, and four days to reach Kirkenes on this longest **bus** line in Europe, called Nord-Norge-Bussen.

Narvik can be reached **by train** from Stockholm (25 hours), and Narvik is an excellent place to enter the North Cape Bus for a ride to Kirkenes. Return by coastal steamer or plane, as time and purse allow.

By air. One can go from Oslo to Bodø (1½ hrs), Evenes (1½ hrs), Tromsø (1¼ hrs) and Bardufoss (3 hrs), Alta (3 hrs), Lakselv (4 hrs), and Kirkenes (4 hrs). Special inland rates during the summer.

By car. Norway's Number One highway—E6—will take you from Oslo and right across the Arctic Circle to Kirkenes near the Soviet Russian frontier. It is also the gateway to North Cape, but since the road distance from Oslo to North Cape is 2,233 km. or 1,383 miles, there are few people who can afford the time to do it. Many prefer to travel by air to one of the northernmost towns and rent a car there. The distance from North Cape to Tromsø is 484 km. (299 miles), Narvik 750 (464) and Bodø 925 (572). The return trip can be made via Finland or Sweden or by coastal steamer—but in the latter case it is essential to have reservations long in advance.

TOURS. There are tours available throughout the region, with the emphasis on the water. There are many boating excursions—river boats, steamers, catamarans and ferries. Most areas also offer fishing trips, on river, sea or lake.

In some areas there are helicopter or plane tours, and at Narvik and Tromsø there are cable cars going up into the mountains.

For those who prefer to keep their feet on solid ground, there are plenty of conventional road tours to places of great natural beauty, and interest. For example there are trips from Karasjok to a gold diggers' camp; from both Karasjok and Kautokeino to visit reindeer herds; from Kirkenes to the Soviet border; and from Tromsø to see the rock carvings at Kvaløy. Tours go from Tromsø to Spitsbergen in summer.

Details of all tours are available from the local Tourist Information offices, the addresses of which are listed under "Tourist Information" at the beginning of this *Practical Information* section.

PLACES TO VISIT. The North abounds with places of scenic beauty, but there are also many museums, and buildings of historic and architectural interest, for the tourist to visit. Some of these places, both natural and man-made, are listed below.

Alta. Alta Church. One of only two buildings left after the last war, the other being Kåfjord Church.

Alta Museum. Komsa School. Open all year Wed. 6–8. Additional opening times published locally.

Kåfjord Church. Typical English "village church," constructed in 1837. Gift from the English owners of the coppermine in Kåfjord; quite an extraordinary little church.

Bardu. Bardu Church at Setermoen, octagonal all-timber structure, built in 1829 and a perfect replica of the Tynset Church.

Bardustua, at Eggen Farm near Bardujord. This building was erected by settlers newly arrived in the valley. Exhibition of tools, implements etc. owned and used by these immigrants.

Bodø. Bodin Church, a medieval stone church built about 1200; has an alter panel of rich Baroque design from 1670.

Bodø Cathedral. Modern three-nave basilica with separate clock-tower.

Nordland County Museum, has a particularly interesting fisheries section.

Saltstraumen. 34 km. (21 miles) from Bodø, the world's strongest whirlpool.

Fauske. Røsvik Manor. A trading center from 1760. Picturesque collection of houses around a courtyard. Main building (built 1832) is in Bergen style.

Sulitjelma Mining Center. 30 km. (19 miles) east of the Fauske center. Mining Museum.

Hammerfest. Meridianstøtten. The Meredian Stone was erected to commemorate the first international measurement of the world's size—1816—1852.

Polar Bear Club. Hammerfest City Hall. The Royal and Ancient Polar Bear Society where membership can be obtained by personal application. Open all summer 8–6. For special arrangements contact the local tourist office.

Harstad. Grytøy Bygdetun. At Lundenes. An ancient building, parts of which date back to 1770. Some 2,000 items on show, also an old boathouse with a number of boats, including a Nordland boat fully equipped for sailing.

Trondenes Church. Built in 1250, the world's northernmost medieval stone church. Open daily.

Honningsvåg. The North Cape Museum, Havnegata. In addition to the local collections, the museum has specialized in fishing–and coast–culture.

Karasjok. Karasjok Churches. One built in 1807, the oldest in Finnmark; the other consecrated in 1974.

Karasjok Smithy and **Isak Strømeng's Knife Workshop** at Badenjarg.

The Samic Collections. Norway's only specialist museum of Samic culture.

Kautokeino. Lapp Traditional Crafts. Silversmiths, with Lapp collections.

Kirkenes. King Oscar II's Chapel. At Jacobselv border, 61 km. (38 miles) from Kirkenes, this is a stone building with the U.S.S.R. and the Arctic Ocean as its nearest neighbours. It was erected as a spiritual watchtower in 1869.

Øvre Pasvik National Park. The Pasvik valley on Soviet border southwest from Kirkenes is known for its abundance of flora and fauna. Good fishing in Pasvik river.

Sør-Varanger Museum. Main building at Strand. In addition, two farms, Bjørklund (085–91 601) and Noatun (085–95 525). Admission fee.

St. George's Chapel. Neiden. Only Greek Orthodox chapel in Norway—built 1560. Annual memorial service. Belongs to Sør-Varanger Museum. For guided tour contact Neiden Camping (085–96 131). Admission fee.

Målselv. Fossmustua Regional Museum. Near Bardufoss.

Konglistua Bygdetun. Farmstead and buildings from 1840, situated near lake Rostavatn.

Mo I Rana. Grønligrotten. Stalactite cave with underground waterfall.
Stenneset. Open-air museum at the restored parsonage.

Mosjøen. Dolstad Church. Norway's oldest octagonal church; dates from 1732.
Vefsn Museum. Local open-air museum. Ancient farm buildings. Most comprehensive of its kind.

Narvik. Rock Carvings. In the Brennholtet Park.
The War Museum. Near Torghallene; uniforms and weapons from World War II.

Svolvaer. Lofoten Aquarium and Fishery Museum. At Kabelvåg, Svolaer, Lofoten Islands.
Vågan Church. The Lofoten Cathedral built in 1898 is the largest timber church north of Trondheim.

Tromsø. The Arctic Ocean Cathedral. Tromsdal church, a modern masterpiece in glass and concrete. Large stained glass painting.
Polar Museum. Opened in 1978.
Tromsø Cathedral. One of the largest wooden churches in Norway.
Tromsø Museum. Established in 1872, the largest in North Norway; central research institute and interesting range of collections.

Vadsø. Museum. Airship mast used to moor airships *Norge* and *Italia* (used by Roald Amundsen and Umberto Nobile respectively).

Varangerbotn. Sami (Lapp) museum.

Vardø. Norway's easternmost town, near the Soviet border and connected to the mainland by submarine tunnel 2½ km. (1½ miles) long.
Fortress. The world's northernmost fortress; built 1738. Open to the public.

SPORTS. Fishing is *the* pastime in North Norway. The salmon rivers are famous, particularly those in Finnmark, where you may fish for a trifling fee: star attractions are the world famous Alta River in Finnmark and the Malangsfoss in Troms, where salmon is a certainty. The trout fishing on the Finnmark mountain plateau is fabulous, but includes a bit of walking.

The mountains of Lyngen, Lofoten, and the Narvik district lend themselves to strenuous **rock climbing**. Here there is still scope for exploring new routes. **Hiking** in the mountains of North Norway is only for the experienced, as the trails are seldom marked and staffed huts are few and far between. But from Kåfjord, approximately 100 yards from the church, there is a path to Haldde (about 3,000 ft. above sea level), a four-hour walk. Ruins of the world's first Northern Light Observatory. Also dog-team excursions with guide—contact Sven Engholm, Muotkenjarg, N-9730 Karasjok (084–68 163), for group excursions on foot or skis.

Boats can be rented for trips on the Reisa, Karasjokka, Kautokeino, and Tana rivers; there's a good selection of boat tours with guide. There's excellent **skiing** in March, preferably around Narvik (Narvik and Gratangen 300 meters), and Lønsdal (500 meters), south of Bodø.

Lofoten Islands Shanty Hire. Fishermen's shanties (*rorbu*), built on the waterside, can be rented from about NOK 80–400 per night (2–4 bunks). In many of them accommodations were originally basic and meant for the adventurous who seek the world's best sea-fishing off Europe's wildest coastal scenery. Today, standards have been raised considerably and you can rent a *rorbu* varying from simple shanties to those equipped with all mod. cons. *Rorbuer* are listed under categories A, B and C and priced accordingly. Details from tourist information offices. There's always a general store nearby and a road right to the door.

SWEDEN

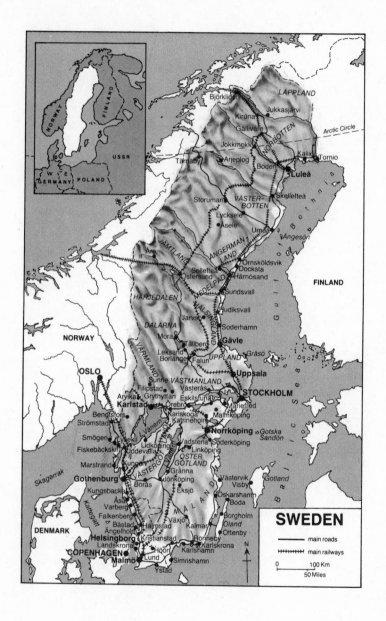

SWEDEN

— main roads

++++++ main railways

0   100 Km
—————————————
    50 Miles

SWEDEN—FACTS AT YOUR FINGERTIPS

NATIONAL TOURIST OFFICE. In North America: *Swedish Tourist Board,* 655 Third Ave., New York, NY 10017 (212–949–2333).

In the U.K.: *Swedish National Tourist Office,* 3 Cork St., London W.1 (01–437 5816).

Within Sweden, there are around 380 local tourist offices, about 180 of which are open all year round. Lists are available from the Swedish Tourist Board, but we also give addresses and telephone numbers of all the major tourist offices at the beginning of each *Practical Information* section. Local tourist offices are usually located in the center of towns and can be identified by a green "i" symbol.

CURRENCY. The unit of currency in Sweden is the *krona* (plural, *kronor*), or crown. It is divided into 100 *öre* and written as SEK. There are coins (all silver) of 10 and 50 öre and of 1 and 5 SEK; notes come in denominations of 10, 50, 100, 500, 1,000, and 10,000 SEK. The rate of exchange at the time of writing (mid-1989) was 6.38 SEK to the U.S. dollar and 10.80 SEK to the pound sterling. However, these rates will certainly change both before and during 1990, so check them carefully when planning your trip and on it.

You can change money or traveler's checks in banks, exchange offices and many post offices. Some hotels will also change money for you, but their rate is likely to be much less favorable.

COSTS IN SWEDEN. Sweden is a country with a high standard of living and many costs are correspondingly high. Some items—liquor especially, particularly the imported variety—are very expensive, while most are perhaps no more than 10–15% more expensive than their equivalents in the U.S.

Inflation has been creeping up in recent years and is now around the 6–7% mark, but the Swedes are only too conscious of their high-price-tag reputation and most visitors should be able to keep expenses within reasonable bounds with a bit of planning. Many hotels, for example, have special low rates throughout the summer and also cut costs during weekends in winter. Many restaurants offer, throughout the year, a low-cost menu at an all-in price for a special dish of the day, salad, light beer or milk, bread and butter and coffee. There are likewise many discounts available for train, plane and bus travel, and most larger cities also have inexpensive tourist cards giving free travel on public transport and free entry into many museums. We give details of all these schemes in the sections that follow. The Swedish Tourist Board also has full details; alternatively, ask your travel agent.

Sample costs. A cinema seat for one, SEK 45; visit to a museum, SEK 15; coffee, SEK 10–15; glass of beer, SEK 15–40 depending on strength bottle of wine, SEK 80–120; Coke, SEK 10–12; moderate taxi ride, SEK 50; an average bus or subway ride, SEK 8. Check on local discount cards, which often give free local transportation as well as free or discounted admission to museums and other attractions.

SEASONAL EVENTS. Summer sees the bulk of Sweden's seasonal events and the Swedish Tourist Board and local tourist offices will be able to advise what's happening where. But the following are some of the major events.

February has the Great Lapp Winter Fair in Jokkmokk in the far north of Sweden.

March sees a major winter event, the 55-mile cross-country Vasaloppet ski race from Sälen to Mora; over 10,000 people take part.

April sees a major horse show at the Scandinavium, Gothenburg.

April 30 is Walpurgis Night, when the end of the winter is celebrated; fires are lit throughout the country.

June 6 is Swedish National Day, with celebrations the length and breadth of the country. Stockholm's Skansen Park is the site of the most dramatic festivities. Midsummer Day is celebrated with equal gusto over the period June 23–25, especially in the provinces of Dalarna and Hälsingland.

July sees the Visby Festival, held in the ruins of the medieval cathedral there. The Swedish Derby is also held now, at Jägersro in Malmö.

August has a series of Swedish-American days, notably at Skansen Park in Stockholm and at Växjö in southern Sweden.

September—the International Consumer Goods Fair at Gothenburg, incorporating the "Household of Today" exhibition.

December has many events celebrating the imminent arrival of Christmas, notably St. Lucia's Day on the 13th, celebrated throughout Sweden (you'll also find a picture of St. Lucia in every hotel). The Nobel Prize awards take place in December in Stockholm (by invitation only).

NATIONAL HOLIDAYS. Jan. 1 (New Year's Day); April 13 (Good Friday); April 16 (Easter Monday); May 1 (Labor Day); May 24 (Ascension Day); June 4 (Pentecost); December 25 (Christmas Day); December 26 (St. Stephen's Day).

LANGUAGE. The Swedes are great linguists. Most speak excellent English, and a good number also manage more than just a smattering of French and German. Most films and many TV programs are also in English with Swedish subtitles.

CUSTOMS. Residents of non-European countries may bring duty-free into Sweden 400 cigarettes or 200 cigarillos or 100 cigars or 500 grams of tobacco; plus, for visitors aged 20 or over, 1 liter of spirits, 1 liter of wine (or 2 liters if no spirits taken in) and 2 liters of beer; plus a reasonable amount of perfume; plus, goods to the value of SEK 600.

Residents of European countries may bring duty-free into Sweden, if they are 15 or over, 200 cigarettes or 100 cigarillos or 50 cigars or 250 grams of tobacco; the allowances for alcohol and other goods are the same as those which apply to non-European visitors.

Alcoholic beverages over 60% (120 proof) may not be imported.

There is no limit to the amount of foreign currency that may be imported or exported, but no more than SEK 6,000 may be imported or exported.

HOTELS. Hotel standards in Sweden are generally very high, even in the lowest price categories. As well as the larger and more expensive establishments—in almost every town you will find a "Grand Hotel," "Stadshotellet," or "Stora Hotellet"—the country is well provided with inexpensive guesthouses and pensions. In addition, all cities and most towns have a centrally-located hotel booking office *(Hotellcentral* or *Rumsförmedling),* usually operated by the local tourist office. Nonetheless, advance reservations, particularly in larger towns, are recommended during the high season (May 15 to Sept. 30).

Prices can be high, but many hotels offer discounted rates all week during the summer and at weekends during the winter, while some chains offer special deals which can be booked through travel agencies in advance. The SARA group, for example, has a Scandinavian Bonus Pass, which costs $24 and entitles the holder to discounts ranging between 15% and 40% at some 100 first-class hotels, not only in Sweden but also in Denmark, Norway, Finland and Iceland. The pass is valid for an unlimited number of overnight stays from June 1 through August 31.

The Scandic Hotel group, which has hotels in 70 locations throughout Scandinavia, has a hotel check scheme which enables you to pay for your accommodations in advance. Weekend Checks are valid every weekend in all Scandic hotels from January through mid-May and from mid-September to the year-end, while Summer Checks are valid every day between mid-May and mid-September. The 1989 price was about $28 per person per night, including breakfast, for Weekend Checks and $33 for Summer Checks, but supplements are payable at some city-center hotels.

The Sweden Hotels group of privately owned hotels has a Hotel Pass program which offers 50% discounts on normal room rates at more than 100 hotels throughout Sweden between mid-June and early September. The Pass costs SEK 100 and is valid for an unlimited number of nights.

Prices. We have divided all the hotels we list into four categories—Deluxe (L), Expensive (E), Moderate (M) and Inexpensive (I). These grades are determined solely by price.

Two people in a double room can expect to pay (prices in SEK)

Deluxe	1,000 and over
Expensive	800–1,000
Moderate	600–800
Inexpensive	under 600

These prices include breakfast and a 15% service charge. The abbreviations AE, DC, MC, and V stand for American Express, Diner's Club, Mastercard (including Access and EuroCard), and Visa (Barclaycard).

CAMPING. Sweden boasts about 750 campsites, about 200 of which are open all year round. Most, however, are open only from late May to early September. All sites are inspected and classified—from one to three stars—by the Swedish Tourist Board and all authorized sites display a green sign with a white "C" against a black tent. Most sites are located by the sea or on a lake and facilities such as mini-golf, windsurfing, riding and tennis are common.

Charges average about SEK 50 per tent. An international camping carnet is required for all sites; alternatively, buy a Swedish Camping Card at any site. The Swedish Tourist Board publishes an abbreviated list of camping sites in English.

For those who fancy the simple life but draw the line at being under canvas, some 300 sites also have "camping cottages" for hire. These have between two and four beds. Top prices are around SEK 250 per night. Sheets and blankets can be rented at camp sites; alternatively, bring your own.

YOUTH HOSTELS. There are almost 300 youth hostels in Sweden, all operated by the Swedish Touring Club (STF). Hostels range from simple, student-type accommodations to restored manor houses and, in the case of the *af Chapman* in Stockholm, a 100-year-old restored sailing ship. Some can provide lunch and dinner, as well as breakfast, and a number also have hot and cold running water in every room. Linen may be rented in all hostels.

Prices range from SEK 40 to SEK 55 per night for members of STF or national youth hostel organizations affiliated to the International Youth Hostel Federation. For nonmembers there is an extra charge ranging between SEK 20 and 35 per night. It is advisable to make reservations in advance. For further details, contact the Swedish Tourist Board or the *Swedish Touring Club,* PO Box 25, S-101 20 Stockholm (08–790 31 00).

RESTAURANTS. Swedish restaurants, especially in more cosmopolitan centers, are varied both in style and price. At the top end of the spectrum, especially in Stockholm, you will find restaurants the equal of those anywhere in the world, while lower down the scale restaurants are generally of a high standard if somewhat more expensive than in the U.S.

Fast food of every variety is now available everywhere. Similarly, Chinese and Greek restaurants—all generally inexpensive—abound. Alternatively, anywhere calling itself a Bar will also provide self-service food but not, confusingly, alcohol.

Away from larger centers, the majority of restaurants are in hotels, though you will still find the occasional regular spot. Many restaurants also provide "office menus," or *dagens rätt* (dish of the day); these normally cost about SEK 40 and include a main dish, salad, beer or milk, bread and butter, coffee and service. Alcohol is generally very expensive in all restaurants.

Prices. We have divided the restaurants in our listings into three categories—Expensive (E), Moderate (M) and Inexpensive (I). These grades are determined solely by price.

Prices, per person, excluding drinks (in SEK)

Expensive	200 and up
Moderate	100–200
Inexpensive	100 or less

All prices are inclusive of service.

FOOD AND DRINK. The Swedish *smörgåsbord,* someone once said, is often abused in spelling, pronunciation and preparation. *Smörgåsbordet* is a large table usually placed in the middle of the dining room and easily accessible to all guests. It is piled high with a large number of delicacies to which you help yourself as often as you like. To appreciate it properly, however, the various dishes should be eaten in proper succession and not helter-skelter. Traditionally, the order goes something like this: pickled herring (possibly more than one kind) with a boiled potato; a couple more fish courses, probably cold smoked salmon, fried Baltic Sea herring, and sardines in oil; the meats, liver paste, boiled ham, sliced beef, not uncommonly smoked reindeer; a salad, fruit and/or vegetable; and finally the cheeses. Bread and butter is served throughout.

Many of the items that appear in the *smörgåsbord* may be familiar to you. Some of the appetizers which you may not have tasted, and which are recommended, are herring on ice with chives and sour cream sauce, fried Baltic Sea herring, smoked eel (delicious, really), smoked reindeer (likewise), and the Swedish Chantilly-type cheese, milder and firmer than its French cousin.

And finally you end up with a dessert such as fruit salad or pastry. A main dish after the *smörgåsbord* is optional (you are unlikely to need one!) and costs extra. Sadly, however, *smörgåsbord* is not so common as it once was, but the tradition is still well maintained in many country inns in the southern province of Skåne.

Other national dishes are crayfish, in season from August to September and the occasion for a rash of informal parties, preferably outdoors; pea soup and pork, followed by pancakes, traditional Thursday supper from autumn through spring; and in November, particularly in southern Sweden, goose.

Generally, the Swedes do better with fish than they do with meat. If you like good, tender beef, stick to the *à la carte* menu.

Practically everything in the way of wines and liquors is regularly available at the better restaurants and bars, even the latest cocktail, although any kind of mixed drink seems somehow out of place in this land where liquor is traditionally drunk straight (neat) with no nonsense, thank you.

Quite another matter is the question of drinking hours. Before noon (1 P.M. on Sundays) you're doomed to soft drinks (not even wine or beer), unless you buy your own bottle at one of the state-owned liquor shops, known as Systembolag. These, however, are closed on Saturdays and Sundays and are by no means thick on the ground. At midnight everything is put away again except at those nightspots with licenses to stay open to 2 or 3 A.M.

Anyhow, if you're going to eat Swedish, order snaps and beer or table water with the *smörgåsbord. Snaps* is the collective name for *aquavit* or *brännvin,* Swedish liquor made under a variety of brand names and with flavors varying from practically tasteless to sweetly spiced. Recommended brands: Skåne, Herrgårds, and O.P. Andersson. Swedish beers are good—made in a variety of light and dark qualities and strengths.

But do remember that almost all alcohol is expensive in Sweden—even a beer can cost upwards of $2.

TIPPING. Tipping in hotels, restaurants and bars is not generally necessary in Sweden as the service charge is always included in your check. However, exceptional service may warrant a tip. Similarly, many round up restaurant bills to the nearest 5 or 10 kronor. There are only a few exceptions to the no-tipping rule. Taxi drivers—who pay tax on tips whether they get them or not—should always be given between 10% and 15%. Hairdressers should be tipped about 10%, and coat check attendants in restaurants should be given about SEK 7 per coat. Otherwise, tipping is the exception rather than the rule.

MAIL. Post offices are open from 9 to 6 Monday to Friday and 10 to 1 on Saturdays. During the summer, some do not open on Saturdays. Aside from post offices, you can also buy stamps from the machines outside post offices, in department stores and hotels. These take 1 and 5 krona coins. Similarly, some shops selling postcards also sell stamps. Mail boxes are painted a distinctive yellow.

Airmail letters to the U.S.A. and Canada weighing less than 20 grams cost SEK 3.60; airmail postcards, SEK 3.10. Postcards and letters within Europe cost SEK 2.50 and 3.10 respectively.

CLOSING TIMES. Shops are generally open 9–6, Mon. to Fri. On Sat. and the day before a holiday, closing time varies between 1 and 4. Department stores and many other shops in the larger cities stay open until 8 or 10 one evening in the week (usually Mon. or Fri.), but not in June or July, and some of the larger stores open on Sun. Banks are open 9.30–3 Mon. to Fri.; many also open in the evening between 4.30 and 6. In many larger cities the banks are open for business from 9.30–5.30. The bank at Stockholm's Arlanda International Airport is open daily from 7 A.M. to 10 P.M. There is also a bank at Gothenburg's Landvetter Airport, open daily from 8 A.M. to 8 P.M.

TAX-FREE SHOPPING. About 19,000 Swedish shops—more than 1,000 in Stockholm alone—participate in a tax-free shopping scheme for visitors enabling you to save around 15% on all buys exported within one week of purchase. Take your passport with you to shops and ask for the special tax-free check. All airports and ports have repayment offices which will refund in cash—deducting a 5% service charge—the tax paid. In some cases the refunds are made on board the ferries. Some stores will offer the tax-free shopping service only on transactions of SEK 200 or more.

GETTING AROUND SWEDEN. By Air. Sweden has a good internal air network, with *SAS* and *Linjeflyg* the main carriers. To give a rough idea of flying times, Stockholm to Kiruna, north of the Arctic Circle, takes around 90 minutes, while Stockholm to Gothenburg, on the west coast, takes around 55 minutes.

Outside peak times, there are many fare bargains to be had. All off-peak fares are some 30% below peak rates for one-way trips. Similarly, senior citizens pay only SEK 200 on all one-way fares in offpeak periods.

Anyone planning to stay away for more than two nights or over a Saturday or Sunday night is entitled to a "mini-fare," valid only for round trips using specified flights. This gives a 50% discount, and in addition your wife or husband and young people between 12 and 25 traveling with you pay only SEK 300 each (plus an extra SEK 100 if a change of flights in Stockholm is necessary), while the fare for children between 2 and 11 is SEK 100. In 1989 SAS and Linjeflyg introduced new "microfares" for Swedish domestic routes priced at 65% below normal fares. They are available on selected flights on all routes but have to be booked at least 14 days in advance. SAS also offer "Visit Scandinavia" fares in July and August for passengers using its intercontinental services on a round-trip basis and starting their journey at a U.S. or Asian gateway. For 250, passengers receive five flight coupons for trips within Scandinavia (excluding Greenland and the Faroe Islands). The "Visit Scandinavia" fares are not available for purchases within Scandinavia and have to be bought at the same time as the intercontinental trip.

By train. Swedish trains are comfortable, clean and reliable with efficient express services linking all main cities. First and second class carriages and dining or self-service cars are carried on most trains. Sleeping cars—costing from about SEK 100 in addition to the normal fare—and couchettes—costing approximately SEK 70—are also available on all overnight runs. No smoking signs must be strictly observed. Note also that the Letter "R" in timetables means that seat reservations—SEK 15—are required.

The Swedish railfare structure was radically changed during 1989. Normal full fares now apply throughout the week, instead of only on Friday and Sunday as previously. However, on certain trains now listed as "Low price" or "Red" departures, fares are reduced by 50%. Passengers traveling on these low fares cannot make any stopovers and the tickets are valid for only 36 hours. There is a flat-rate maximum fare for all journeys of 560 miles (900 kilometers) or more. Passengers holding the European senior citizens' railcard qualify for a 50% reduction on Swedish rail fares.

In addition to these exclusively Swedish discounts, the *Nordturist* (or Scandrail card), the *Inter-Rail* card, the *Eurailpass* and *Eurail Youthpass,* and the *Rail Europ Senior Card* are all valid within Sweden. See "Getting Around Scandinavia by Rail" in *Planning Your Trip* for further details.

By car. Given its vast size and the excellence of the air and rail network, car travel in Sweden may seem a less than ideal means of getting around, especially as only main roads, particularly in the north of the country, are paved, all others being gravel. Having said this, however, roads are very well engineered, and the small population also means that there is generally very little traffic. Similarly, there are no toll roads anywhere.

There are strict speed limits, however, even outside built-up areas. These are 110, 90 or 70 km.p.h. (68, 56 or 43 m.p.h.). In built up areas the speed limit is always 50 km.p.h. (31 m.p.h.), and 30 km.p.h. (19 m.p.h.) outside schools. Speed limits are always well sign-posted. Towing a trailer with brakes, the limit is 70 km.p.h. (43 m.p.h.); without brakes, it is 40 km.p.h. (25 m.p.h.).

Note also that seat belts are compulsory for drivers and all passengers and that you must *always* use dipped headlights, both at night and during the day. U.S. drivers' licenses are valid in Sweden.

Parking restrictions are strictly observed. You should always park only in designated areas. Parking meters accept one krona coins. Wrongly-parked cars will be towed away.

The best people to contact in the event of a breakdown are the police or "Larmtjänst," a 24-hour service run by the Swedish insurance companies, with branches all over the country; its phone numbers are listed in local telephone directories. The toll-free number 90 000 should be used only in an emergency. English is always spoken.

Finally, it is very important to observe the extremely strict (and equally strictly-enforced) drink/drive regulations. Anything in excess of two bottles of beer will be enough for a conviction, and tests are made frequently. Fines are very heavy and imprisonment by no means rare. On the whole, the smart thing is simply not to drink if you're driving.

By bus. Swedish buses are run by the national rail network and a small number of private companies. Prices are very low, but services relatively slow. In more remote parts of the country, however, a reasonable Post Bus service knits the scattered communities together.

By bicycle. Bikes can be rented throughout Sweden. For a complete list of rental companies, write *Cykelfrämjandet,* P.O. Box 3070, S-103 61, Stockholm, which also publishes a useful guide in English to cycling vacations in Sweden. The *Swedish Touring Club,* P.O. Box 25, S-101 20 Stockholm, can also provide details of organized bike tours in practically every province. Prices are very reasonable.

Many buses and trains will also carry bikes free of charge; inquire at tourist offices or write *Svenska Cykelsällskapet,* P.O. Box 6006, S-164 06 Kista, for details.

PRELUDE TO SWEDEN

Dolls' Houses in the Wilderness

by
ANDREW BROWN

Because Sweden is the largest and the richest of the Scandinavian countries, it is also the most typical: any idea of what is "Scandinavian" is informed by Sweden. If the other countries differ from the Swedish model, this tends to suggest that they are not truly "Scandinavian."

The word suggests a combination of gloom and cleanliness; efficiency combined with joyless affluence, conjuring up a vision of somewhere very impressive, but not really suited to human life. Moose and mosquitoes thrive; other lifeforms do not.

It is easy enough to find parts of Sweden that correspond to this stereotype—and they are almost certainly the first parts that the tourist will see. But the tension and the interest of Swedish life comes from the fact that the Swedes themselves could no more stand to live as they seem to do than anybody else could. If the foreigner recoils from certain aspects of Swedish life, so do the Swedes themselves. The result can be extremely confusing, but it is both more interesting and a great deal more pleasant than the rather inhuman front presented to the world would suggest. The moral, for anyone who wants to enjoy Sweden—and there is much here to enjoy— is 'Get off the Main Street'.

The Minor Arts of Peace

A perfect example of this is provided by Uddevalla, a town on the west coast that looks from the main road like every other town in Sweden. Admittedly, there is nowhere in Europe but Sweden where you will find towns that look good from a four-lane highway, but the drabness of Uddevalla is remarked upon even by guidebooks.

Between the main road and the sea is a low-lying area that floods after westerly gales every year. Every fall the octagonal tourist office in Uddevalla is surrounded by water and accessible only to those tourists who had the foresight to pack canoes or waders. It makes an annual splash on the TV news.

On the other side of the road, the town itself is concealed by a line of modern developments: car lots and demolition sites, and large grey concrete buildings that look like overgrown Lego models without either the color or the imagination of the originals.

Seeing all this, the average traveler gets away down the highway as quickly as possible. He may admire the engineering that has made the highway possible, but if he thinks anything at all about the town, it is only that Uddevalla is one of those places that Nature meant to be bypassed. But the wise man turns off the main road into the town, and gets lost in the one-way system. The belt of nastiness is only one block deep. The buildings behind are not particularly beautiful, but they are not inhuman. One conceals a rocky garden, where you can sit on terraces drinking beer all through the summer twilight, moving occasionally to keep within the shade of trees. The streets are crowded with people, not with cars. There is an open-air market. A little more exploration discovers a comfortable cafe, and a shop that sells foreign newspapers. An indoor market sells fish so fresh their eyes and flanks still gleam. Much more surprisingly, it sells kippers, which you can only otherwise buy in Great Britain. These are the minor arts of peace. They may not be spectacular, but they're important; and very well done throughout Scandinavia, but to find them in Sweden you must go behind the facade of grey modernity.

In a Meadow by a Lake

The town of Uddevalla, however, is still public Sweden. Even after you have learned to find and enjoy the shops and cafés, the houses on the hills around remain closed and mysterious. The less privacy people have, the more closely they guard it. To discover what makes Swedes tick, you must go still further from the main road, perhaps to a house that stands some miles south of Uddevalla. It's not a tourist attraction: in fact it is a private house, though people are encouraged to visit the lakes and the woods around it. And those with a taste for the outdoor life can spend a night in the cabin across the meadow.

The house is not far from the main road, but you must travel for some time to get there. The branch road starts at a modern gas station on a highway, leads past a couple of supermarkets and then a much older general store. When it climbs into the hills there is no metalled surface. In the space of a mile you have traveled back 30 years. Five miles of gravel road lead to a track through the forest that only a tractor could get down.

The woods around are typical of Southern Sweden. They seem untamed—moose hairs lie in clumps along the tracks—but they are not oppressive. The lack of undergrowth makes the forest seem extraordinarily spacious, and though the trees are almost all conifers, they're not monotonous. No one who has not seen a Scandinavian forest in early summer can imagine how many shades of green there are in the world, each one distinct and bright and clear. The elements of the view are limited, but they are never quite the same; which keeps the forest beautiful however far you walk, but makes it very easy to get lost in. So be a little careful.

The house stands at the end of this track, in a meadow by a lake. It was built 50 years ago by two Finnish lumberjacks, who lived what must have been a life of monotony remarkable even by the standards of immigrant Finnish lumberjacks. In winter they worked in the forests; in summer they netted pike out of the lake and sold what they could not eat. Eventually they moved away. The house fell into disrepair. This is an old pattern. You *can* live off the land in Sweden, but few would choose to do so. (In the 19th century, Sweden was so poor that a quarter of all the descendants of Swedes living then are now Americans). Walking through the woods in the south of the country you will often come across the remains of cabins from this time, their stone foundations worn down like old teeth.

Even the lake where the lumberjacks had netted their pike died, poisoned by acid rain. The prevailing winds from England and Germany are loaded with sulphur dioxide from factories and car exhausts. This turns to weak sulphuric acid and falls on Sweden, where the peat and granite cannot buffer it as English soil can. The snow that looks so pure in winter is actually weak sulphuric acid, frozen, fluffy, and deadly. When it melts each spring, four months' worth of acid runs into the lakes and rivers in a week, killing fish fry and eggs, most forms of algae, and most insects too. The lakes are neatly sterilized. Of the thousand or so lakes in Bohuslän, only a handful can now support any lifeform higher than the waterlouse.

So far this story has dealt with the effects of the country on the people who live there. The point, however, is how they have changed the country. In the early 70s the house and the lake were taken over by a group of local fishermen. They filled the lakes with trout—each one of which had to be carried down the track in rucksacks full of water—and arranged to have lime spread on the ice each spring to counteract the acid rain. All this is paid for by selling fishing permits for the lakes, but by this time catching fish had become a secondary consideration for the fishermen. Their treasure was the house.

It has been lovingly restored, with stripped and polished pine floors, prints and ornamental driftwood on the walls. It seems that the attraction is that they can get away from all respectable life here. They can drink all night and not worry about driving in the morning; they can chop wood and cover themselves with paint; they chew tobacco and spit into an open fire. It is a small boys' paradise, and irresistible to anyone over the age of 15.

But these small boys in their 30s and 40s turn into old maids in the morning. They tiptoe around in their socks, brushing and sweeping; they agonize over the exact placement of a hat-stand; they would, if they could, reintroduce the death penalty for littering. The wilderness camp is turned into a dolls' house.

It is this clearing up that is the point of the whole thing. This is Sweden in microcosm. The fishermen do not go into the woods to get away from it all, but to extend it all: to build a perfect, private society together in the middle of nowhere. All Swedish life is best understood as conducted in dolls' houses in the wilderness, and it demands of its participants the same passion and concentration as a children's game.

Just as heroism is the Polish vice, sincerity is the curse of the Swedes. They can believe anything—and they do—but this belief is almost always a communal activity. Swedes in discussion are like a shoal of fish. They all point in the same direction, and if they change direction, all do so at once. Sometimes they split into competing shoals, but within each group the discipline remains. What's rare in Sweden, and always seems slightly ridiculous, are self-sufficient individuals, or, if you like, lone fish.

How to Move a Mountain

These attitudes are easily misunderstood. Because belief—sincerity—comes so naturally to the Swedes, they may seem to outsiders insincere, just as the girl who can't say "No" seems incapable of loving because she falls in love so easily. But this is unfair. If the sceptical British, for example, strike ridiculous attitudes, they are being hypocritical. If the Swedish do the same, this is not hypocrisy, but wholly sincere self-deception. And they could easily justify this quirk of character if they ever felt the need to justify something that is to them so self-evident. Faith *has* moved mountains in Sweden, most obviously in the iron-mining town of Kiruna, above the Arctic Circle.

But there is no need to go as far as Kiruna to see this, even though it is one of the most remarkable towns in the world. Stockholm itself is best enjoyed as the most beautiful dolls' house in the world. The most famous sights of the city all have this quality of toys: there is the restored 17th-century warship, the *Wasa;* the royal palace, for show rather than for living in; the open-air museum at Skansen, where houses, churches, and workshops from all over Sweden have been re-erected on the slopes around a zoo. In the workshops there are real craftsmen playing at being real craftsmen; in the zoo there are wolverines and seals playing in beautifully landscaped enclosures.

The modern center of the city is extremely ugly, but this, too, is the result of a communal fantasy. This was the dream of the American '50s (and the Swedish '60s) that with enough money and enough cars, everyone would be happy if there were no buildings in sight more than five years old to remind them of what they had lost. The tourist office in Sweden House marks the furthest outpost of this dream. Beyond it lies a park—the Kungsträdgården—and when the city council proposed to ruin that, too, for the sake of a new subway station, mass demonstrations stopped the plan. Respectable Swedes, who would tell you even then that they were the most buttoned-up and formal people in the world, climbed the trees that were to be cut down, and clung to the branches with the workmen poised below, axes at the ready, until the city council gave way, as they were forced to do. Opposition broke the spell; when communal belief was no longer possible, the ideas that had laid waste the city center lost all their power.

This is not to say that all modern Swedish architecture is ugly; bits of it are extremely beautiful, though nowhere as lovely as in Finland. But again, this beauty is to be found in hidden places, not in public ones. The beautiful public buildings of Stockholm are all old, and almost all of them are built at the edge of islands which greatly increase their beauty.

Angst and Taboos

Of course, one of the things the visitor to Stockholm expects to see is porn. This is most odd for anyone who lives in Sweden—we cannot imagine how the legend of "Swedish Sin" arose. There was admittedly a period in the late '60s when the Swedes decided that since pornography is unavoidable, it must be good for you. That decision later came to seem foolish. Now they are just confused, but not very worried. The guilt, fear, and anguish that Anglo-Saxons lavish on sex are devoted by the Swedes to alcohol.

The Swedish attitude to drink is one of the things that most intensely irritates the foreigner. Drink is not so much difficult as inconvenient to obtain; in those few restaurants that serve it, it is extremely expensive. An elaborate network of law and taboo has almost eliminated drunken driving, except for those drivers too drunk to remember the consequences. This may have kept death off the roads (moose cause more car crashes every year in Sweden than ever humans do) but it has also eliminated social drinking, except in large towns. No amount of pleasure is worth the risk of losing your license in a country where cars are as common and as vital as they are in Sweden. In the countryside there is no-one who can afford to drink with strangers except the town drunk, and who would want to drink with him?

It sometimes seems that the Swedes cannot enjoy a drink unless they are convinced that it is harming them. The windows of the state liquor stores are lined with anti-alcohol posters displayed behind ramparts of a purplish fluid called *Schloss Boosenburg,* an "alcohol-free wine." But things are loosening up nowadays, largely as a result of the introduction of real wine, which women can drink and enjoy with men. The old Swedish taboos on drink had a partially sexual underpinning: men drank; women picked up the pieces, and resented having to do so. This was clearly unsatisfactory, though it did produce one marvelous recipe: Put a small silver coin in the bottom of a cup; add sweetened black coffee till you can no longer see the coin; then pour in vodka until the coin becomes visible again. This is not a drink for those who wish to remain gentlemen in their cups.

It's worth dwelling on this subject because the taboos of a country are more informative even than the local newspapers. The superstitious horror with which the Swedes regarded drink is really a result of the fact that drunks quarrel. They forget the rules of the communal game, and stumble through the dolls' house, breaking things and shouting, interrupting everybody else. No wonder their fellows turn on them with the ferocity of children. For a children's game has power only when all the players believe in it. Otherwise the dolls have no life, and will quickly be broken.

This need not worry the visitor. The Swedes treat foreigners with great courtesy and kindness. Almost all of them speak English, and all are delighted to show you their splendid game. They will perhaps complain that theirs is the most regulated and tightly controlled society in the Western world; and in a sense they are right. For the last 12 years, the Swedish parliament has been passing laws and regulations at a rate of one every eight hours of the day and night, or more than 1,000 a year. But for the most part the citizens treat this activity as lightly as do the parliamentarians themselves. The system has reached such a pitch of complication that no-one takes very much notice of it any more. The Swedes obey such rules as they feel are sensible, and ignore the others. They feel entitled to do so because it is, after all, their game. This sense of belonging makes them a very restful people to be among; nor can anyone who has known a Swedish summer feel that there is anywhere in the world that is more beautiful in the months of May and June.

STOCKHOLM

Open Nature and City Planning

Stockholm, Sweden's capital, has been called the most beautiful city in the world. This is open to debate, but few will deny that it is a handsome and civilized capital with a natural setting that would be hard to beat anywhere. When it was founded as a fortress on a little stone island where Lake Mälaren reaches the Baltic, nobody cared much about natural beauty. It was protection the founders were after, military defense. But around the year 1250, the fortress became a town, and the town, spreading to nearby islands and finally to the mainland, became a city. And, though Nature remained the same, men's opinion of it changed, and Stockholm delights the tourist today with its openness, its space, its vistas over a great expanse of water. Of course it's been called the "Venice of the North," but that happens sooner or later to any northern city with more water than can be supplied by a fire hydrant.

Stockholm's beauty has been jealously guarded by the city fathers. The town is full of parks, tree-lined squares and boulevards, playgrounds, wading pools and other amenities of urban life, and the building codes are extremely strict. Nature and city planning have thus combined to create a pleasing metropolis, and it is hard to realize as you gaze out over the water from a table on the Strömparterren terrace that you are in the heart of a bustling metropolis, a town that has grown from less than 100,000 inhabitants to over a million in the space of a century.

Nowhere is the striking modernity of much of Stockholm more obvious than in the brand new streets and squares around Sergels Torg, a startling glass and steel tower in the heart of the new city, and the rail station, where multi-lane highways, skyscrapers and underground shopping malls have all sprung up in the space of a few years. Yet no more than five minutes' walk will bring you to the medieval heart of the city on the islands of Gamla Stan (Old Town), where narrow twisting streets huddle around the bulk of the imposing Royal Palace, the Cathedral and the Riksdag, the Parliament.

June, July and August are the best months to visit this capital. Then you have the best weather and the greatest variety of sight-seeing facilities. Bring a reasonably warm coat along. What most people would call a mild summer day is apt to be announced in the Stockholm papers as a heat wave. In May or October the weather is brisker, but so is the normal life of Stockholm.

History and Growth

The earliest origins of Stockholm are largely unknown. Perhaps the first somewhat reliable report is a Viking saga, which, as all Viking sagas should, ends in violence. It seems that Agne, a warrior king of the Ynglinga dynasty, had been off on a visit to Finland. There, among other treasures, he had acquired a chieftain's daughter named Skjalf, by the effective if crude device of cutting down her father. Coming home, he stopped on the shore of an island which is now a part of Stockholm, to drink the health of his new bride and a proper toast to his late father-in-law. The mead flowed freely, Agne slept, Skjalf freed her fellow Finnish prisoners, and they hanged Agne. Then the Finns safely sailed home. The place was subsequently called Agnefit, or Agne Strand.

The first written mention of Stockholm in preserved chronicles gives the date 1252. Tradition—and some historical evidence—has it that a powerful regent named Birger Jarl here founded a fortified castle and city, locking off the entrance to Lake Mälaren and the region around it. At all events, it is known that a castle of substance was built in the 13th century, and during the same period the Great Church was begun (dedicated to St. Nicholas, patron saint of shipping) and the first monasteries.

From these dim beginnings the history of the city can be divided into four fairly distinct epochs: the erratic, confused first centuries; the arrival of King Gustav Vasa, who made Stockholm a capital beginning in 1523; King Gustavus Adolphus, who made it the heart of an empire a century later; and the modern era.

After the time of Birger Jarl the Swedish nation, still unorganized, groped its way forward. Up to this time Stockholm had not been the capital; the latest city to enjoy the favor had been Sigtuna. The real physical heart of Sweden remained uncertain. Nevertheless, Magnus Eriksson, a king of some importance, was crowned here in 1336. Toward the end of the century Sweden, Norway, and Denmark were united under one ruler. A period of confusion and revolt followed. Stockholm continued to be a commercial center, with monopoly trading rights for much of the territory around.

On Midsummer's Eve, 1523, when King Gustav Vasa returned from his victorious uprising for Swedish independence from the union (and from a Danish king), the real history of Stockholm began. Vasa was a powerful figure, sometimes called the George Washington of Sweden, and, although he moved from castle to castle throughout the country, his treasure chamber was in the old Stockholm Royal Palace. Succeeding kings tended in the same direction, making Stockholm more and more important.

Under Gustavus Adolphus, a great organizer as well as a military leader, who reigned from 1611 to 1632, the city became a capital in fact as well as name. Sweden had already begun to engage in political machinations and wars on the Continent and in Russia. It was partly his need to keep his military forces at top efficiency, his need for tax money, for supplies and for men that led Gustavus to concentrate the administration of the country in Stockholm. When he died on the battlefield of Lützen in 1632, Protestantism had been saved, Sweden had become an empire and Stockholm was its capital.

Prosperity and population grew accordingly. Gustavus himself, in a farewell address of 1630, had told the citizens of Sweden's cities that he hoped "your small cottages may become large stone houses". Many of them did. From a population of perhaps 3,000 when Gustav Vasa came home victorious, the number of inhabitants had grown to some 9,000 by the time Gustavus Adolphus fell, and rose to perhaps 35,000 by 1660. Meanwhile, the wars continued. Fortunately for Stockholm, they were fought on foreign soil. This did not, however, diminish the importance of the city, for it functioned as the capital even during the long absence of hero King Charles XII, who spent almost his entire reign in the field—losing much of what Gustavus Adolphus had won.

Rulers came and went, political battles were fought, won, and lost. But the building of Stockholm went on, sometimes in the hands of eminent architects like Nicodemus Tessin and his son, who are responsible for both the Royal Palace and Drottningholm Palace, as well as many other buildings which still stand. In the 18th century, Stockholm began to attract scientists and scholars, to share the spotlight with Lund and Uppsala as a center of learning. Gustav III (assassinated in 1792), a dilettante who could put on steel gauntlets when required, did much to make Stockholm a cultural, musical, and dramatic capital.

In 1850 Stockholm was still a quiet town. It had many of the stately buildings which even now give it its characteristic profile, but it numbered less than 100,000 people—a peaceful administrative center, perhaps dreaming of past glories. The first municipal cleaning department was established in 1859, the first waterworks in 1861, and gaslights had arrived but a few years earlier. As late as 1860, Drottninggatan, the most prominent commercial street, had no sidewalks. But the same year the first train arrived from Södertälje, 25 miles away. Modern communications had been born. The new era had begun.

Modern Development

The last 100 years of Stockholm's history are the story of a peaceful revolution, of industrialization, and of the remaking of a government from a monarchy with four estates in the parliament—nobles, clergy, farmers, as well as burghers—into a full parliamentary democracy with a king at its head. As the country has progressed and grown, Stockholm has progressed and grown with it. You will see the physical evidence wherever you go—the squat Parliament House on the site of one-time royal stables; the City Hall, a splendidly quirky and lavish brick creation overlooking the waters of Lake Mälaren; the extensive and striking developments in the center of the city; and two huge satellite suburbs to the west and east of the city.

Exploring Stockholm

If Stockholm's island geography poses communication problems, it has the advantage of dividing the city neatly into sections and of making it possible to know easily where you are.

Gamla Stan. The Old Town, site of the Royal Palace and center of the city and nation, and the adjoining islands, Riddarholmen (The Isle of Knights), and Helgeandsholmen (Island of the Holy Spirit).

Södermalm. As the name implies, this is the southern section, across the bridge leading from the Old Town.

Norrmalm. North of the Old Town, the financial and business heart of the city. The new building construction from Hötorget to Klarabergsgatan, which forms the new commercial center of Stockholm, constitutes the most important part of the redevelopment of Nedre Norrmalm (Lower Norrmalm).

Kungsholmen. A large island west of Norrmalm, site of the Town Hall, and most of the offices of the city government.

Östermalm. East of Norrmalm, largely residential, many embassies and consulates.

Djurgården. The huge island which is mostly park, projecting east toward the Baltic Sea in the channels between Östermalm and Södermalm. Here are concentrated museums, including Skansen, the open-air museum, amusement parks, and restaurants.

Regardless of how long you intend to stay and how thoroughly you expect to see the city, begin by one or more boat excursions. Nothing else can give you a quick idea of the unique nature of Stockholm.

Let's take as a starting point the south of the large downtown park known as the Royal Gardens (Kungsträdgården), just across the rushing channel from the Royal Palace. It's an ummistakable point, easy to find. Immediately beside you is the striking profile of the statue of King Charles XII, arm raised and pointing east; behind him stretches the long park; to his right the unmistakable solid stone of the Royal Opera House, a block or so to his left the familiar façade of the Grand Hotel; and across the water the dominating walls of the palace. Furthermore, just at the water's edge at both sides of the bridge there are kiosks that serve as starting points for some of the boat and bus excursions which show you the city.

The best way to see the city is by boat—there is practically no major place of interest in and around Stockholm that isn't within easy reach of the many little boats that ply around the busy harbor. But you'll find it equally easy to explore the city on foot. Most of the principal sights are concentrated in the center of Stockholm and are relatively close to one another. If you feel like venturing further afield, use the excellent subway system, the T-banan; many of the stations are carved from solid rock, creating an eerie, grotto-like atmosphere.

Gamla Stan

The best place to begin your exploration of the city is the Old Town, Gamla Stan, situated on three little islands. From the statue of Charles XII at the foot of the Kungsträdgården, there are two bridges leading to the Old Town, both no more than a couple of minutes' walk away. The more interesting, however, is the second, the Norrbro, leading directly to the imposing bulk of the Royal Palace. As you cross the bridge, you'll also see the Parliament building, a ponderous stone structure dating from the turn of the century, on your right. And just behind and to one side of the Parliament building is the one-time building of the Bank of Sweden, the oldest existing bank in the world, founded in 1656.

The Royal Palace is not old, as palaces go, but the site is. It was here that Stockholm was born. The original palace, the Three Crowns, burned down one night in 1697, with the exception of the northern wing of today's palace. A new palace on the old site was ordered immediately. Three generations of Sweden's most famous architectural dynasty had an important part in its creation—Nicodemus Tessin the Elder planned the exterior and began the interior decoration, which was continued by his son, Tessin the Younger, and grandson, Carl Gustav Tessin. The whole project took more than 60 years, and was not completed until 1760. The building consists basically of a perfect square—enclosing a large court—with two wings sticking out on the east side and another on the west.

A number of interiors are open to the public. You may be interested in the Hall of State, which contains the king's silver throne. The Chapel Royal in the same wing has, among other impressive historical and artistic treasures, pews saved from the old palace. If you have time, look in on the Apartments of State, the Apartments of King Oscar II and Queen Sophie, and the Guest Apartments, notable for the furnishings and extremely fine Gobelin tapestries. There's also a palace museum, with bits of the previous palace, other historical finds, and the collection of classical sculpture brought from Italy by King Gustav III in the 1780s. The Royal Treasury, in the old vaults, can now be visited.

Diagonally across the street from the south side of the palace, and intimately associated with it, is the Great Church, the Stockholm cathedral and, in a sense, the national church. You would hardly guess from the well-kept exterior that it is believed to be the oldest building in the city, dating from about 1250. Many Swedish kings have been crowned here (until Gustav V gave up the custom when he ascended the throne in 1907), and it is still used for solemn celebrations attended by the king. There are a number of art treasures, of which perhaps the oldest, best known, and most distinguished is the statue carved in wood of St. George and the Dragon by Bernt Notke of Lübeck, which was presented to the church in 1489 to commemorate a Swedish victory over the Danes some 18 years earlier. A sound and light show is performed here for a few weeks during summer.

You are in the heart of the Old Town now and there are several ways of continuing your look about. Here are two good suggestions immediately at hand. The first is to walk downhill on the lane called Storkyrkobrinken, to the right of the main entrance of the Great Church as you come out. This lane, like practically all those of the Old Town, follows the same route it did in the Middle Ages. Everywhere around you are buildings centuries old, living history. At the base of the hill you step out in a little square called Riddarhustorget. The two dominating buildings, across the square from where you enter, both date from the 17th century. One is Riddarhuset, House of the Nobility, in which you will find the crests of Swedish noble families. The white palace to its right was once a private possession, became the city courthouse in the 18th century, and is now occupied by the Supreme Court.

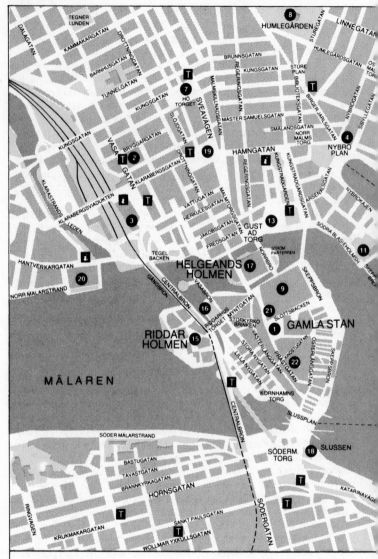

Points of Interest

1 Börsen (Stock Exchange)
2 Centralpostkontoret
  (Central Post Office)
3 Central Rail Station
4 Dramatiska Teatern
  (Royal Dramatic Theater)
5 Historiska Museet (Museum of
  National Antiquities)

6 Kaknästornet (Kaknäs Tower)
7 Konserthuset (Concert Hall)
8 Kungliga Biblioteket
  (Royal Library)
9 Kungliga Slottet (Royal Palace);
  Livrustkammaren (Royal Armory)
10 Moderna Museet (Museum of
   Modern Art)
11 Nationalmuseet
   (National Museum)

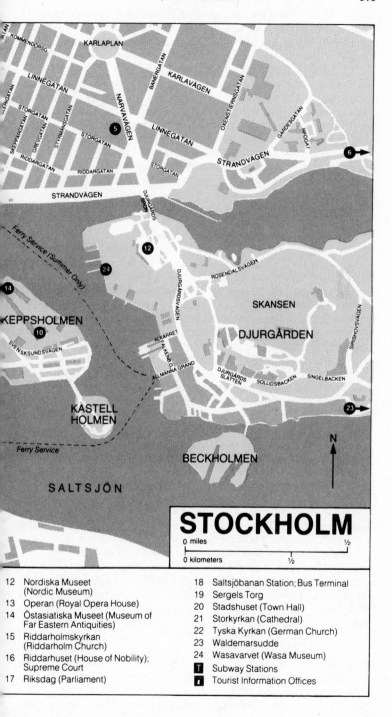

STOCKHOLM

0 miles   ½

0 kilometers   ½

12	Nordiska Museet (Nordic Museum)
13	Operan (Royal Opera House)
14	Östasiatiska Museet (Museum of Far Eastern Antiquities)
15	Riddarholmskyrkan (Riddarholm Church)
16	Riddarhuset (House of Nobility); Supreme Court
17	Riksdag (Parliament)
18	Saltsjöbanan Station; Bus Terminal
19	Sergels Torg
20	Stadshuset (Town Hall)
21	Storkyrkan (Cathedral)
22	Tyska Kyrkan (German Church)
23	Waldemarsudde
24	Wasavarvet (Wasa Museum)
T	Subway Stations
i	Tourist Information Offices

From here you will see the weathered red brick and openwork spire of Riddarholm Church. This is the Swedish Pantheon, burial place of Swedish kings for about four centuries. The most famous figures buried here are King Gustavus Adolphus, hero of the Thirty Years' War, and Charles XII (in Swedish, Karl XII), who is renowned for his signal victories over the Russian and Continental armies, with inferior forces, until the tide turned against him and he fell in Norway in 1718. Two medieval kings, Magnus Ladulås, who died in 1290, and Karl Knutson Bonde, some 180 years later, are also buried here. The latest king to be put to rest was Gustav V, on November 9, 1950. Except for the funeral of a king, the church has not been used for services for a long time. The sarcophagi of the various rulers, usually embellished with their monograms, are clearly visible in the small chapels given over to the various dynasties. The church building itself is interesting as the second oldest structure in Stockholm. It is a former monastery church completed about 1290, with many additions since.

Take five minutes to continue past the church down to the quay on Lake Mälaren. It's well worth it. You get a fine view of the lake, the magnificent arches of the West Bridge in the distance, the southern heights, and above all the imposing profile of the Town Hall, which appears to be almost floating on the water. At the quay you may see one of the Göta Canal ships.

The second alternative to continuing your stroll from the Great Church is to turn left as you come out of the main entrance and walk up Trångsund to a little square called Stortorget, the oldest square in Stockholm. The dominating building, on the north side, is the Stock Exchange. This is also the headquarters of the Swedish Academy, which awards the Nobel Prize in literature. The other buildings are also old; note the tall, narrow, red merchant house and its sculptured portal from the 17th century.

The Old Town is the perfect kind of place to wander around without any decided aim, looking at the old portals, poking about in crowded antique shops, savoring the Bohemian atmosphere and the sense of age, peeking into doll-sized courtyards, making your way through curving, narrow lanes. There is little auto traffic, and the passages are too narrow to provide both streets and sidewalks. Go along Skomakaregatan to the German Church (Tyska Kyrkan), turn right for a few meters, then left again on Prästgatan. Keep your eyes open as you near the end of Prästgatan, on the right you will see one of the narrowest thoroughfares in the world. It is called Mårten Trotzigs Gränd (*gränd* means lane), and leads down to Västerlånggatan. It is scarcely a meter wide, half of it is a stairway, yet it is a public thoroughfare maintained and lighted by the city.

It's only a couple of short blocks from here to the south end of the Old Town. You should really stroll on to that point. Above you are the southern heights, connected with the Old Town by an intricate cloverleaf of bridges and streets at about four levels, called Slussen. Katarina elevator—you see it poking up all by itself on the other side of the channel—takes you up to a platform with a fine view of Stockholm.

Though the Old Town is, of course, the most ancient and historic part of the city, you will have noticed by now that it is by no means lacking in modern chic. In fact it is very definitely the trendiest area of the city, both for shopping and eating, with a veritable surfeit of expensive and glamorous restaurants and shops: there are some 300 restaurants alone.

Skansen

After the sophistication and history of the Old Town, the open-air amusement park of Skansen, founded in 1891, provides a striking contrast. It is situated on the large island of Djurgården, located to the east of the city. The park contains a museum, a zoo, numerous restaurants and cafés, a circus, an aquarium, a theater, a concert hall and much else besides, all combining to make it one of the enduring highlights of the city. One of its principal delights are the buildings—farm houses, windmills, barns, whole estates almost—that have been brought here from all parts of the country, giving even the most casual visitor a taste of traditional rural Sweden. There is even an 18th-century church that is still used for divine services and weddings. But many of the other buildings are in use too. Geese cackle near the entrance to the farm houses from southern Sweden; glass blowers blow glass—you can help blow it if you want to—in the old-time glass blower's hut.

Here also are moose, wolves, foxes and other Nordic animals; Sweden's largest aquarium with Cuban crocodiles; and nocturnal bush-babies, pygmy kangaroos and other strange animals in the Moonlight Hall. Many activities designed especially for children include a children's zoo.

You can walk to Skansen from the statue of Charles XII in about 30 minutes. It is a long walk, but it will take you through much of Stockholm's most gracious and substantial waterfront areas, past elegant apartment blocks and smart shops, with yachts and ferry boats ever-present, particularly on the broad expanse of Strandvägen.

Djurgården is also home to three outstanding museums: the Nordiska Museum, the Waldemarsudde and the *Wasa*. The *Wasa* is a 17th-century warship, once the pride of the Swedish navy, built at vast expense and the most powerful fighting ship of her day in the Baltic. Launched amid great pomp, she set out on her maiden voyage on August 10, 1628 in full view of the population of Stockholm, including of course the King himself. She had sailed less than a mile when a gust caught her, and she heeled over and unceremoniously sank—the *Titanic* of her day. Her precious guns were immediately salvaged, but with the passage of time the *Wasa* faded from memory.

However, in 1956 her position was rediscovered and it was found that, remarkably, the briny waters of the harbor had all but preserved her intact. A complex and difficult salvage operation was begun and in May 1961 the *Wasa* was raised to the surface. Painstaking restoration has returned the ship almost to her original condition, providing the visitor with an unparalleled experience of life afloat in a great warship of the past. The site where she had been displayed for many years was closed in 1988 and a new museum a few hundred meters away is scheduled to open in June 1990.

The Nordiska Museum (the Nordic Museum), housed in a splendid late-Victorian pile, is located just by the Djurgårdsbron, the bridge leading to Djurgården. It contains a vast collection of exhibits that chart Sweden's progress from 1500. Of particular interest are some magnificent fabrics, costumes and rugs, a lovely collection of bridal gowns and the charming gold and silver coronets traditionally worn by Swedish brides.

Finally, visit Prince Eugen's "Waldemarsudde," the former home of "the Painter Prince," brother of the late King Gustav V, which was bequeathed to the people on the prince's death. The many paintings, some by Eugen himself, constitute a fine collection of Swedish art, and the mansion, art gallery, and beautiful grounds are well worth seeing.

Treasures of the City Hall

The Stockholm City Hall, one of the great architectural works of the 20th century, is another appropriate excursion that you can manage in a couple of hours—more if you like. Starting at the statue of Charles XII, turn to the right and merely follow the waterfront until you arrive at its massive portal. The distance is less than a couple of kilometers.

Superlatives have not been lacking in describing the structure. It has sometimes been called "the most beautiful building of this century in Europe." This opinion is not unanimous, of course; some people have reacted violently against it, but even this sharp reaction is a measure of the strength of the total impression. The building was completed and dedicated in 1923, and has become a symbol of the city. It is the seat of the city council and central administration.

The building is certainly unusual—a massive square tower rising from the corner of a graceful central block, the whole built of dark and delicately worked brick and topped by pale-green roofs with spires, domes and minarets abounding. It successfully synthesizes elements of traditional Swedish architecture, notably in the tower, which is derived from the massive castles of 16th-century Sweden, with classical elements, the resulting mixture spiced by Oriental and Byzantine windows and spires. It is difficult to decide finally whether the end-product is beautiful or kitsch—it is undoubtedly impressive.

You can go inside and look around. Among the highlights are the Golden Hall, whose walls are decorated lavishly with mosaics; the Blue Hall, confusingly named perhaps, as the only blue visible is the sky glimpsed through the windows ranged around the top of the walls; and the Prince's Gallery, with large murals by Prince Eugene. You can also go up the 106-meter (348-foot) tower (don't worry, there's an elevator) for a predictably spectacular view. At noon and 6 P.M. the carillon plays the medieval war song of the Swedes that helped gird their loins at the Battle of Brunkeberg in 1471. The adjoining Maiden Tower is surmounted by a bronze St. George and the Dragon. Finally, visit the Terrace, a formal garden on the banks of Lake Mälaren with wonderful views of the Old Town and the southern heights rising beyond it.

Other Sights

Depending on the amount of time you have available and your special interests, there are many other places and institutions well worth a visit. Among the dozens of museums, these are particularly recommended: The National Museum, just a few doors down the quay from the Grand Hotel, which is home to the largest collection of paintings and sculptures, by both Swedish and foreign artists, in the country.

A few minutes' walk from here on the island of Skeppsholmen are the Museum of Modern Art and the Museum of Far Eastern Antiquities, both with fine collections, the latter a pleasing spot to explore or simply from which to admire the view of the Old Town.

The National Museum of Antiquities and Royal Cabinet of Coins, located to the east of the city on the spacious boulevard of Narvavägen, contains a veritable mass of historical finds dating back well into the Stone Age.

Although not a museum, there is a further attraction on Djurgården— the 155-meter (508-foot) high Kaknäs Tower. The fastest elevators in Europe hurtle you up to the observation deck, from where an unparalleled view of the city and the Stockholm archipelago stretches before you.

Music and Markets

The Concert Hall, at Hötorget, is the center of Stockholm's musical life. The building, designed by Ivar Tengbom, was completed in 1926. In front is Carl Milles' huge sculptured group of Orpheus calling up the spirits. It is in this hall that the awarding of the Nobel Prizes takes place.

It's well worth your while to get to one of the market squares fairly early in the day—9:00 A.M. will do—which are masses of color whatever the season of the year. One is just in front of the Concert House, another on Öster-malm. Flowers, fresh fruits and vegetables are the principal stock in trade. Look in at the indoor markets which adjoin these squares—there you can fill your whole grocery basket from the little shops of independent dealers, and have a snack in one of the small restaurants. This is a unique aspect of Stockholm life. Incidentally, the outdoor markets operate right through the winter.

Excursions from Stockholm

Immediately outside the city limits of Stockholm proper are a number of popular attractions which you can reach within an hour by public transportation, or half an hour by car.

The sculptor Carl Milles, who was perhaps better known as an inhabitant of Cranbrook, Michigan, had his permanent home on the island of Lidingö, a Stockholm suburb, where he collected not only some of his own works, but also other outstanding pieces from several eras and countries. It was here at Millesgården that he died in September 1955, still hard at work at the age of 80, and the collection is now open to the public year-round.

The royal palace of Drottningholm is located on a little island in Lake Mälaren—the name means "Queen's Island"—a few kilometers from Stockholm. The trip is a pleasant experience, particularly by boat. If you have seen Versailles, you will be reminded of it at once when you arrive at Drottningholm, for it was clearly inspired by the French style. The palace was built by Nicodemus Tessin the Elder, and his son, Tessin the Younger, completed the gardens in the style of Le Nôtre.

Drottningholm is one of the most delightful of European palaces, embracing, as it does, all that was best in the art of living practiced by mid-18th-century royalty. In the grounds, a kind of Trianon, is the China Palace, conceived in Chinoiserie terms, a lovely little palace, hidden in the trees, where the royal family could relax and entertain their friends. Also in the grounds is the Theater. This fascinating building slumbered like the Sleeping Beauty undisturbed for well over a century, the settings and stage machinery of the 18th century in perfect condition and working order. It now houses a theater museum and delightful productions of baroque opera are once again staged in the auditorium that saw the efforts of Gustavus III to create a Swedish Golden Age. The Royal Family occupies one wing at the palace.

Haga Palace, formerly the home of the late Crown Prince Gustav Adolf, is located only a few minutes from downtown, right on the city limits of Stockholm. A more interesting building located on the same grounds is Haga Pavilion. It is a miniature summer palace built by Gustav III (late 18th century), exquisitely furnished.

The resort of Saltsjöbaden is a residential suburb the year round. During the summer it is a rendezvous for yachtsmen and motorboat enthusiasts, and the harbor is excellent. In winter there is skating, skate-sailing, ice-boating, and skiing. The modern Stockholm observatory is located here. You can reach Saltsjöbaden from Slussen on an electric train. In the same general direction, but to the north, is Gustavsberg, where the noted ceramics works may be visited in groups by previous appointment.

PRACTICAL INFORMATION FOR STOCKHOLM

GETTING TO TOWN FROM THE AIRPORT. Buses from Arlanda Airport to the city, a distance of 45 km. (28 miles) are frequent. The trip takes about 40 minutes and the bus takes you to the City Terminal above the Central Station in the center of town. The Sheraton, Royal Viking, Terminus and Continental hotels are all within two minutes' walk. The fare is approximately SEK 30, payable to the driver. You can also buy a ticket at special ticket offices at the airport and the air terminal. A scheduled bus service to Brommaplan from the airport is also available, with stops at Kista and Sundbyberg subway stations.

A taxi to the city from the airport will cost you about SEK 350. However, SAS Scandinavian Airlines operates a limousine service on a shared-taxi basis, which takes you direct to your hotel or any other address in the Greater Stockholm area for about SEK 185 or 230 according to distance. The limousine can be booked on arrival at Arlanda Airport; for the return journey ask your hotel to make a reservation well in advance—the previous day, if possible. If two or more passengers take the limousine to the same address, only the first pays the full fare; the others pay 50%.

TOURIST INFORMATION. The Tourist Center is located in the middle of the city in Sverigehuset (Sweden House), opposite the large department store *Nordiska Kompaniet*, or *N.K.*, in Kungsträdgården (789 20 00). There you will find information about interesting sights and events, one-day tours and so on and you can make bookings for sightseeing excursions. It also sells maps, postcards, books and souvenirs. The Tourist Center is open every day.

A useful publications is *Stockholm This Week* which you can get from most hotels and all tourist centers. From a kiosk on Norrmalmstorg you can buy last-minute tickets at reduced prices to concerts and theaters.

USEFUL ADDRESSES. Embassies. *American Embassy,* Strandvägen 101 (783 53 00). *British Embassy,* Skarpögatan 6–8 (667 01 40). *Canadian Embassy,* Tegelbacken 4 (near the Sheraton) (23 79 20).

Travel Agents. *American Express,* Birger Jarlsgatan 1 (23 53 30). *Wagons-Lits/Thomas Cook,* Vasagatan 22 (762 58 27).

Car Hire. *Avis,* Sveavägen 61 (34 99 10); *Hertz,* Mäster Samuelsgatan 67 (24 07 20); *Europcar,* Birger Jarlsgatan 59 (23 10 70); *Interrent,* Hotel Sheraton, Tegelbacken (21 06 50). All the major car-rental companies also have desks at Arlanda Airport.

TELEPHONE CODES. The telephone codes for Stockholm is 08. To call any number in this chapter from outside Stockholm, unless otherwise specified, this prefix must be used. Within the city, no prefix is required.

HOTELS. It is recommended that your reserve hotel rooms well in advance, especially from September to November. If you arrive in Stockholm without a reservation, consult the Hotellcentralen in the Central Station. This room-booking service is open daily 8 A.M.—9P.M. June through Sept. For the rest of the year it is open daily Mon. to Fri. 8.30–11.30 and 1–5, and, in May only, Sat. 8–5, Sun. 1–9. A charge is made for each room reserved. Most hotels have smoke-free rooms and rooms for the handicapped. Breakfast is usually included in the room rate. In general, Stockholm hotels are comfortable, but prices are fairly high.

More than 40 hotels offer the "Stockholm Package" at weekends throughout the year and daily during the summer months, with accommodations for one night costing between SEK 195 and SEK 430 per person including breakfast and a "Key to Stockholm" card, which gives free transportation within the city plus free entrance to museums and discounts on sightseeing. For details, write to Stockholm Information Service, Excursion Shop, Box 7542, S-103 93 Stockholm or phone The Hotel Center (08–24 08 80). The "Stockholm Package" is also bookable through travel agents.

Deluxe

Amaranten. Kungsholmsgatan 31 (54 10 60). 415 rooms. Contains the *Amaryllis* restaurant, the *Travellers'* piano bar and a nightclub called *Cindy*. It also boasts a Japanese-style recreation area and an "executive tower" with a roof garden and luxurious accommodations. Refurbished in 1988. (SARA). AE, DC, MC, V.

Anglais. Humlegårdsgatan 23 (24 99 00). 211 rooms. One of the leading hotels in Stockholm, conveniently situated near shopping districts and the subway. Popular restaurant, own video channel, garage. (RESO). AE, DC, MC, V.

Continental, Vasagatan (24 40 20). 250 rooms. Opposite the railway station. Currently being renovated. Special low rates available in summer. *Nike* restaurant. *Bistro Chez Charles, Cafeteria Concorde.* (RESO). AE, DC, MC, V.

Diplomat. Strandvägen 7C (663 58 00). 130 rooms. On the waterfront, within walking distance of Djurgården Park and Skansen as well as the city center. Turn-of-the-century atmosphere. Popular tea-house. AE, DC, MC, V.

Grand. Blasieholmshamnen 8 (22 10 20). 330 rooms, front rooms face the Royal Palace and the waterfront. A distinguished European deluxe hotel. Splendid ballroom, famous restaurant. *Thé dansant* on Sun. AE, DC, MC, V.

Lady Hamilton. Storkyrkobrinken 5 (23 46 80). 35 rooms. A gem of a hotel. Built in 1470 and converted to an hotel in 1980. A large collection of antiques including one of George Romney's portraits of Lady Hamilton. The Storkyrkan (the cathedral) and the Royal Palace are neighbors. Cafeteria. AE, DC, MC, V.

Lord Nelson. Västerlånggatan 22 (23 23 90). 31 small rooms. Small hotel right in the middle of the Old Town and twinned, naturally enough, with the nearby Lady Hamilton. Atmosphere throughout is decidedly nautical, even down to the cabin-sized rooms. However, standards of comfort and service are high. Sauna; no restaurant. Cafeteria. Located in rather noisy pedestrian area. AE, DC, MC, V.

Mälardrottningen (Queen of Lake Mälaren). Riddarholmen (24 36 00). 59 cabins on what was formerly American heiress—and wife of Cary Grant—Barbara Hutton's luxury yacht (built 1924). All cabins are furnished to deluxe hotel standards and the yacht has an attractive permanent berth at Riddarholmskajen, close to the Old Town. It has a restaurant and a bar on the bridge. AE, DC, MC, V.

Reisen. Skeppsbron 12–14 (22 32 60). 113 rooms. A SARA hotel built behind the facade of three 17th-century houses. Has the *Quarter Deck* restaurant and the best piano bar in town. Saunas, pool, garage. AE, DC, MC, V.

SAS Arlandia. At Arlanda Airport (0760–618 00). 300 rooms. Five minutes by bus from the airport. Restaurant, bar, nightclub, cinema, sauna, indoor pool, tennis. Close to golf and bathing. AE, DC, MC, V.

SAS Royal Viking. Vasagatan 1 (14 10 00). 340 rooms. A modern hotel of high international standard managed by SAS International Hotels. Within walking distance of the city center and shopping. Has a "sky bar" overlooking the City Hall and Old Town, a relaxation center with saunas, and a wintergarden, The *Royal*

Atrium, with a 36-meter (120-foot) high ceiling. Near airport bus, mainline trains and subway. SAS airline check-in desk. AE, DC, MC, V.

SAS Strand. Nybrokajen 9 (22 29 00). 137 rooms. Central location opposite the *Royal Dramatic Theater.* The building dates from 1912 and was completely renovated in 1984. Winter garden with a ceiling seven stories high and an outstanding gourmet restaurant. SAS airline check-in desk. AE, DC, MC, V.

Sergel Plaza. Brunkebergstorg 9 (22 66 00). 406 rooms, very central. Features trees and waterfalls in the glass-roofed lobby. It has a restaurant, saunas, solarium, bubblepool. (RESO). AE, DC, MC, V.

Sheraton-Stockholm. Tegelbacken 6 (14 26 00). 460 rooms. Near the railway station with a view of the Old Town and the City Hall. The restaurant, *Le Bistro,* is open until 1.30 A.M. Piano bar, boutiques, garage. AE, DC, MC, V.

Terminus. Vasagatan 20 (22 26 40). 155 rooms. Handy down-town location, if possibly noisy, opposite Central Station and close to airport buses. Popular restaurant, *Kasper.* AE, DC, MC.

Victory. Lilla Nygatan 5 (14 30 90). 48 rooms. In the Old Town near its sister hotels, Lady Hamilton and Lord Nelson (see above). Building dates from 1640 on site of the Lion's Tower which burnt down in 1625. Rooms with nautical decor. Restaurant on ground floor under separate management. AE, DC, MC, V.

Expensive

Birger Jarl. Tulegatan 8 (15 10 20). 252 rooms. Unlicensed. Quiet location within walking distance of Stureplan and the city center. Connected with neighboring church; has weekly services in English. Keep-fit area with a sauna and pool. Cafeteria. AE, DC, MC, V.

Bromma. Brommaplan (25 29 20). 142 rooms. 15 minutes by subway downtown, ten minutes by bus to Drottningholm Palace. Direct bus to Arlanda Airport. Restaurant, garage, small garden (RESO). AE, DC, MC, V.

Clas på Hörnet. Surbrunnsgatan 20 (16 51 30). 10 rooms. Arguably the most exclusive hotel in Stockholm, in an elegant 200-year-old town house. Excellent restaurant. AE, DC, MC, V.

Esplanade, Strandvägen 7A (663 07 40). Within walking distance of Djurgården, Skansen and the city center. A turn-of-the-century atmosphere. Breakfast only. AE, DC, MC, V.

Karelia. Birger Jarlsgatan 35 (24 76 60). 103 rooms. A few minutes' walk from Stureplan. Finnish sauna and pool. Restaurant with Finnish and Russian specialties, dancing, nightclub. A bit of Finland in the heart of Stockholm. AE, DC, MC, V.

Mornington. Nybrogatan 53 (663 12 40). 141 rooms. Near the indoor market at Östermalmstorg, within walking distance of theaters and shopping. Elegant fish restaurant. AE, DC, MC, V.

Palace, St. Eriksgatan 115 (24 12 20). 218 rooms. Sauna, garage. (RESO). AE, DC, MC, V.

Park Hotel. Karlavägen 43 (22 96 20). 202 rooms. Quiet, central location next to Humlegården Park, within walking distance of the city center. Restaurant, garden café, garage. (RESO). AE, DC, MC, V.

Moderate

Adlon. Vasagatan 42 (24 54 00). 62 rooms, all with bath. Central. AE, DC, MC, V.

August Strindberg. Tegnérgatan 38 (32 50 06). 19 rooms in a building dating from 1890. Near a park, quiet, central. No elevator. AE, MC, V.

City. Slöjdgatan 7 (22 22 40). 300 rooms. Central. Close to the Hötorget market. Many smoke-free rooms; seven rooms specially equipped for the handicapped. Run by the Salvation Army. Unlicensed. Elegant restaurant. Magnificent indoor wintergarden. AE, DC, MC, V.

Eden Terrace. Sturegatan 10 (22 31 60). 61 rooms, some with balconies. On two top floors of an office building. Breakfast room with a summer terrace overlooking Humlegården Park. Central. AE, DC, MC, V.

Flamingo. Hotellgatan 11, Solna (83 08 00). 130 rooms. Ten minutes by subway from the city. Restaurant, dancing, grillroom. Solna has a large shopping center. AE, DC, MC, V.

Flyghotellet. Brommaplan (26 26 20). 68 rooms. By subway, ten minutes from the city; by bus, ten minutes to Drottningholm Palace. Direct airport bus. AE, DC, MC, V.

Gamla Stan. Lilla Nygatan 25 (24 44 50). 51 rooms, all with bath. In the Old Town. Run by the Salvation Army. Breakfast only. No alcohol. AE, MC, V.

Kom. Döbelnsgatan 17 (23 56 30). 91 rooms. Central, quiet. Kitchenette with refrigerator in most rooms. Sauna. Breakfast only. Near the subway. AE, DC, MC, V.

Kristineberg. Hjalmar Söderbergsväg 10 (13 03 00). 98 rooms, all with bath. Near a subway station, seven minutes from the city. Free sauna. Popular restaurant suitable for motorists. AE, DC, MC.

Scandic Hotel. Järva Krog, Uppsalavägen, Solna (85 03 60). 204 rooms, of which 102 are smoke-free. North of the city on E 4. The airport bus stops here on request, and there's a regular bus service to the city. The *Rotisserie Musketör* on the 11th floor has a fine view of Brunnsviken Lake. AE, DC, MC, V.

Stockholm. Norrmalmstorg 1 (22 13 20). 92 rooms, all with baths. The hotel is on the top floor of an office building with Kungsträrden ården Park and the *N.K.* department store just around the corner. Breakfast only. AE, DC, MC, V.

Inexpensive

Alexandra. Magnus Ladulåsgatan 42 (84 03 20). 90 rooms. In the heart of Södermalm (south of Slussen). Five minutes to the city by the nearby subway. No restaurant. Renovated in 1988. AE, DC, MC, V.

Anno 1647. Mariatorget 3 (44 04 80). 42 rooms, 30 with baths. Also some higher priced and elegant rooms. Located in a centuries-old building close to Slussen. Historic surroundings. A few steps from the subway and the ferry to Skansen. Breakfast and lunch only. AE, DC, MC, V.

Domus. Körsbärsvägen 1 (16 01 95) 78 rooms. Near subway. Family apartments with pantry available. Restaurant. AE, DC, MC, V.

Jerum. Studentbacken 21 (15 50 90 and June through Aug. 63 53 80). 120 rooms, all with showers. This student hostel is only open June 1 to Aug. 31. Close to Gärdet subway station, five minutes to the city. Cafeteria. AE, DC, MC, V.

Zinken. Zinkensväg 20. (58 50 11). 28 rooms. The hotel consists of a number of pavilions near Zinkensdam subway station. Large garden with play area, access to washing machine and kitchen. Also youth hostel. Sauna. AE, DC, MC, V.

Camping

Ängby Camping. (A3) Bromma (37 04 20). West of Stockholm at Södra ängby. A 2-star camping site. Beach on Lake Mälaren. Rates approximately SEK 55 per night. Summer only.

Bredäng Camping. (A4) Skärholmen (97 70 71). A 3-star camping site at Ålgrytevägen in Sätra, ten km. (six miles) south of Stockholm. Follow the signs from E4. 500 meters (about 500 yards) to the subway, bathing, canoe rentals and so on. Rates approximately SEK 80 per night. Open all year.

Youth Hostels

af Chapman. Skeppsholmen (10 37 15). 136 beds. A 100-year-old sailing ship with the same view as the Grand Hotel in the historic heart of the city. Open Mar. to Dec. Stay limited to five nights.

Columbus Hotel. Tjärhovsgatan 11 (44 17 17). 120 beds. Open all year.

Gustaf af Klint. A ship at berth 153, at Stadsgården quay near Slussen (40 40 77). 85 beds. Open all night and all year except Christmas/New Year.

Mälaren River Boat. Söder Mälarstrand 6 (44 43 85). 28 beds. Old ship converted into a privately run hostel. Near Slussen subway station.

Skeppsholmen Hostel. Västra Brobänken (20 25 06). Behind af Chapman. 152 beds. Open all year except Christmas/New Year period.

Zinken. Zinkensväg 20 (68 57 86). 275 beds. Near Zinkensdamm subway station. Open all year.

There are also hostels at Gällnö, Möja, Arholma and Fjärdlang—all in the archipelago.

HOW TO GET AROUND. By subway and bus. The transport system is divided into zones. Tickets may be bought as coupons from ticket counters or from drivers. The basic fare is SEK 7 for journeys within one zone. Your ticket entitles you to unlimited transfers within one hour of the time your ticket was punched. Senior citizens and young people under 18 can travel for half fare.

It is cheaper to buy a special discount coupon which gives a saving of SEK 18 compared with buying separate tickets each time you travel. Alternatively, a special one-day tourist card is available at SEK 22 which gives you unlimited travel on buses and the subway within the inner city area, including the ferries to Djurgården. There is also a one-day tourist card costing SEK 40 which gives unlimited travel for the whole of the Greater Stockholm area. A similar three-day pass costs SEK 76. All these tickets are available at Pressbyrån newsstands, where you can also get maps of the bus and subway systems.

The Key to Stockholm card *("Stockholmskortet")* provides unlimited free transport on subway trains, suburban railway services and local buses throughout Greater Stockholm (except on airport bus services) and also offers free admission to 50 museums in the city plus free sightseeing trips by boat or bus. Cards valid for durations up to four days can be purchased at prices ranging from about SEK 70 to 280 (children under 18 half-price). It can be bought at a number of outlets, including the Tourist Center at Sweden House and the "Hotellcentralen" accommodations bureau at the central railway station.

By taxi. For a taxi ring 15 00 00 (15 04 00 for advance bookings). English-speaking drivers are available on request if you want to go sightseeing by taxi. You can also hail a taxi on the street—the sign *Ledig* indicates that the cab is for hire. They are not so readily available as, for example, in London, but the telephone booking service is very efficient, although it costs SEK 25 just for the taxi to get to you. Taxis are fairly expensive in Stockholm, and more so at night. Tip about 10–15%.

TOURS. A number of sightseeing tours around Stockholm are available, and the boat trips are particularly good value. A two-hour "Under the Bridges of Stockholm" trip which takes you into the fresh water of Lake Mälaren and back into the salt water of the Baltic gives you a vivid impression of the maritime influence which has dominated the city's history. Numerous boat trips take you further out into the archipelago, most leaving from the quay outside the Grand Hotel, normally at 8 A.M. Meals are often available on these trips. There is an information kiosk outside the Grand and details are also available from the tourist office. In addition, there are walking tours around the Old Town every evening from the end of May to mid-September. Authorized city guides may also be hired through the tourist office; call 789 20 00, but book well in advance.

For excursions, further afield, try Sandhamn, a yachting center reached by boat from Stockholm, where races are held during July and August. A one-hour boat trip from Stockholm will take you to Vaxholm, where an ancient fortress which is now a military museum guards the channel. A trip by boat or bus to the Gustavsberg porcelain factory might be worthwhile for reduced-price bargains. The porcelain museum is open weekdays only. A fascinating trip on Lake Mälaren can be made on the classic steamer S/S *Mariefred* (daily; approximately SEK 100). Also of interest is the university town of Uppsala, 45 minutes north of Stockholm by train. The cathedral here is the seat of the Archbishop of Sweden. Some tours combine Uppsala with a visit to Sigtuna, Sweden's oldest town, with its 11th-century fortified church ruin and other monuments of Swedish history.

MUSEUMS. The visitor to Stockholm has a wide choice of museums to see. The entrance fee is from SEK 5 to SEK 20, with children at half price or less but admission is free at most museums to holders of the Key to Stockholm card. Many museums are closed on Monday; they also tend to close earlier on Saturday and Sunday.

Armémuseum (Royal Army Museum). Located behind the Royal Dramatic Theater at Riddargatan 13. Exhibits from crossbows to automatic rifles and missiles. Equipment of the Swedish Army from many centuries. Open daily except Mon. 11–4.

Biologiska Museet (Biological Museum). Next to Skansen. An old museum showing Nordic animals against panoramic natural backgrounds. Open daily 10–4 Apr. through Sept.; 10–3 rest of the year.

Etnografiska Museet (Ethnographical Museum). Djurgårdsbrunnsvägen 34. Famous collections from Third-World cultures. A newly-built museum. Bus 69. Open Tues. to Fri. 11–4, Sat. and Sun. 12–4; closed Mon.

Hallwyl Museum. Hamngatan 4, near Norrmalmstorg. A palatial building dating from around 1900. Fine collections of painting, sculpture, furniture, ceramics, arms etc. Guided tours only, in English at 1.15 P.M. daily June 1 to Aug. 31, except Sat. Closed Mon. Sept. to May.

Historiska Museet (Museum of National Antiquities). Narvavägen 13–17. Treasures of the Vikings and their ancestors. In same building as the **Royal Cabinet of Coin**, which includes the world's largest coin. Bus 44 and 47. Open daily 11–4; closed Mon.

Leksaksmuseum (Toy Museum). Mariatorget 1C. Thousands of toys, dolls, dolls houses, tin soldiers etc. on four floors. Two large model railways are usually demonstrated on weekends. Subway Mariatorget. Open year-round Tues. to Fri. 10–4, Sat. and Sun. 12–4; closed Mon.

Liljevalchs Konsthall (Liljevalch Art Gallery). Djurgårdsvägen 60. Temporary exhibitions, mostly of Swedish contemporary art. Café Blå Porten. Bus 47. Open Tues. and Thurs. 11–9, Wed., Fri., Sat. and Sun. 11–5; closed Mon.

Livrustkammaren (Royal Armory). In the cellars of the Royal Palace with entrance at Slottsbacken. Swedish State collections of historical objects, such as costumes, arms and armory of Swedish royalty from 16th century on. Open Mon. to Fri. 10–4, Sat. and Sun. 11–4. Closed Mon., Sept. to Apr.

Medelhavsmuseet (Mediterranean Museum). Fredsgatan 2 at Gustav Adolfs Torg. 2,500 year-old terracotta sculptures of Cypriot warriors. Also a large Egyptian collection and an exhibition from the Islamic countries. Open Tues. 11–9, Wed. to Sun. 11–4; closed Mon.

Millesgården. Lidingö. Former residence of Swedish-American sculptor Carl Milles. He had his home at Lidingö in later years, where he collected not only some of his own work, but also other outstanding pieces from several eras. He died here in 1955 at the age of 80, still at work. Sparkling fountains and monuments with a view of Stockholm as a background. (The Orpheus Fountain outside the Concert House was made by Milles in 1936). Subway to Ropsten and then by bus. Open Apr. through Sept., 10–5 daily; Oct. through Mar., Tues. to Fri. 11–3, Sat. and Sun. 11–4.

Moderna Museet (Museum of Modern Art and Photography). On Skeppsholmen, behind the sailing ship youth hostel *af Chapman.* Paintings by Scandinavian artists and Picasso, Dali, Matisse, Warhol and many more. Open Tues. to Fri. 11–9, Sat. and Sun. 11–5; closed Mon.

Nationalmuseet (National Art Museum). A few steps from the Grand Hotel. Great masters from 1500 to 1900. Also prints, drawings and applied art from the Renaissance to the present day. Cafeteria and good shop. Concerts every Tues. in July and Aug. Open Tues. 10–9, Wed. to Sun. 10–5; closed Mon.

Nordiska Museet (Nordic Museum). Djurgården. Largest collection of objects showing the progress of civilization in Sweden since 1500. Magnificent specimens of rural art. Lovely collection of bridal crowns and much more. Bus 47. Open July and Aug., 10–5 daily except Mon.; rest of year 10–9 Tues., 10–5 Wed. to Sun.

Sjöhistoriska Museet (National Maritime Museum). Djurgårdsbrunnsvägen 24. Collections illustrating history of Swedish navy and merchant marine. Unique ship models. Bus 69. Open daily 10–5.

Stockholms Stadsmuseum (City Museum). At Slussen subway station. The history of Stockholm, illustrated by many archeological finds. Models of the former palaces "Tre Kronor" (Three Crowns) and "Non Pareil." Pleasant cafeteria. Open June through Aug. Mon., Fri. to Sun. 11–5, Tues. to Thurs. 11–7. Sept. through May open till 9 P.M. Tues. to Thurs.

Strindbergmuseet. Blå Tornet, Drottninggatan 85. Home of author August Strindberg. Open Tues. to Sat. 10–4, Sun. 12–5.

Tekniska Museet (Science and Technology Museum). Museivägen, on the way to the Kaknäs Tower. Models of machines illustrating developments in technical engineering and industry. Vintage aeroplanes, cars' engines; computers, telecommunications. A mine with shafts etc. Cafeteria. Bus 69 from Karlaplan. Open Mon. to Fri. 10–4, Sat. and Sun. 12–4.

Thielska Galleriet (Thiel Art Gallery). Djurgården near Blockhusudden. Private collection of Scandinavian and French art from around 1900. Beautiful surroundings. Bus 69 from Karlaplan. Open daily 12–4 (from 1 on Sun.).

Waldemarsudde. Djurgården. Former home of Prince Eugen, a great-grand uncle to the present King. He was a well-known painter and many of the Prince's own works are displayed here. Also Nordic collections. The turn-of-the-century house is surrounded by a beautiful garden on the shores of the Baltic. Cafeteria. Bus 47. Open Tues. to Sun. 11–5 and on Tues. and Thurs. evenings from 7–9. Closed Mon. Winter opening 11–4, closed Mon.; weekends only in Dec.

Wasavarvet (Wasa Museum). On Djurgården, on the way to Skansen. The salvaged 17th-century man-of-war, *Wasa*. She sank in Stockholm harbor on her maiden voyage in 1628. Rediscovered in 1956, she was raised and drydocked in 1961 and has been painstakingly restored. This is the oldest preserved warship in the world. A new museum to house *Wasa* is being built and will come into operation in June 1990. Opening times were not available at the time of going to press.

PARKS, ZOOS AND GARDENS. Djurgården (Royal Deer Park) and Skansen. A beautiful island covered in pathways, meadows and trees. Also a marina, many museums, Gröna Lund Tivoli amusement park, Skansen and its zoo, aquarium, open-air theater and various displays, and much more. Rent a bike near the bridge or take a leisurely stroll. You can also rent canoes. In summer most of the roads are closed to cars. Bus 47 or ferry from Slussen or Nybroplan (summer only).

Fjällgatan. To get a good view of the Old Town and the harbor, take the subway to Slussen and walk up on Katarina Bangatan to Fjällgatan. Most sight-seeing buses stop here for a short time.

Kungsträdgården (King's Garden). Easy to find, just across the rushing water from the Royal Palace. It contains the striking statue of King Charles XII (Karl den Tolfte) with his arm raised pointing east. On the right is the Royal Opera House, and behind that the elm trees, once threatened to make way for a new subway station, but saved by city-wide protests in 1971. The station was built elsewhere. Have a sandwich under the elms at the teahouse. The fountain in the park, built in 1873, features pictures of Nordic mythology. There are many activities in the park in summer. You can listen to music, learn to dance the Swedish *Hambo* or play chess; in winter you can skate. A meeting place for tourists and others.

Långholmsparken. Below Västerbron on the south side. Take the path to the top for the view. Some former prison buildings are still here—debate continues over the possibility of using them for a youth hostel or hotel. The little cottage is open for coffee when the flag is up. Subway Hornstull.

Skinnarviksparken. Beautiful panorama from this park. Nearest subway is Zinkensdamm. Walk towards the lake and up the mountain past some newly restored historic buildings.

HISTORIC BUILDINGS AND SITES. Drottningholm Palace. On an island in Lake Mälaren, a few kilometers from Stockholm. Reminiscent of Versailles, a magnificent 17th-century French-style building. Also in the grounds are the lovely Chinese Palace and the original court theater, with its 18th-century settings and stage machinery in perfect working order. Theater museum. Subway to Brommaplan and bus or boat from Stadshusbron. The Palace, Court Theater, and Chinese Palace are open daily May through Aug. 11–4.30 and 1–3.30 during Sept. (from 12 on Sat. and Sun.).

Gamla Stan (Old Town). Follow a lane called Storkyrkobrinken from the Great Church, past buildings that are centuries old, to a square at the base of the hill called Riddarhustorget. The two dominating buildings in the square, Riddarhuset (House of Nobility) and the white palace to its right, both date from the 17th century. The latter now houses the Supreme Court.

Haga Palace and Haga Pavilion. On the city limits of Stockholm, in Haga Park near Brunnsviken. Former home of the late Crown Prince Gustav Adolf. The Pavilion is the more interesting building—a miniature summer palace built by Gustav III in the late-18th century. Bus 515 to Haga Air Terminal. Guided tours every hour. Open mid-June through Aug., 12–4 daily except Mon.

Kaknästornet (Kaknäs Tower). Djurgården. T.V. tower, 155 meters (508 ft.) high. Indoor and outdoor platforms with breathtaking view. Cafeteria and restaurant, tourist bureau and souvenir shop. Bus 69. Open Oct. through Mar., daily 9–6; Apr. and Sept., daily 9 A.M.–10 P.M.; May to Aug., daily 9–12 midnight.

Kungliga Slottet (Royal Palace). Completed 1760. Hall of State (contains the King's silver throne), the Chapel Royal (Sunday service open to the public), the Apartments of State and of King Oscar and Queen Sophie, as well as the Guest Apartments are all open to the public daily. Also the Palace Museum (classical sculptures and antiquities), the Royal Treasury, with its collection of Crown Jewels, and the Royal Armory. All or part of the palace may be closed when state visits, royal dinners etc. are held. Changing of the guard, June through Aug., Mon. to Fri. at 12.10 P.M., Sun. at 1.10 P.M. Jan. through May, Wed., Sat. and Sun.; Sept. through Dec., Wed. and Sun. There is no band playing in the winter.

Mårten Trotzigs Gränd (Yard-wide Lane). In the Old Town, at the end of Prästgatan, leading down to Västerlånggatan. One of the narrowest thoroughfares in the world, scarcely a yard (a meter) wide.

Riddarholm Church. On Riddarholm Island. This is the Swedish Pantheon; burial place of 17 Swedish kings over about four centuries. Subway Gamla Stan. Open May through Aug., daily 10–3, Sun. 1–3; Sept., daily 12–3 except Mon. and Fri.

Stadshuset (City Hall). Completed 1923, it is the symbol of Stockholm and of considerable architectural interest. The tower, with a magnificent view, is open May through Sept., daily 10–3. Guided tours of the City Hall, Mon. to Sat. year-round at 10 A.M.; Sat., Sun. and holidays at 10 A.M. and 12 noon.

Storkyrkan (Great Church). Across the street from the south side of the Royal Palace. Believed to be the oldest building in the city, dating from about 1250. Contains Ehrenstal's *Last Judgement,* one of the world's largest paintings, and other art treasures. As Stockholm's cathedral, this is a living church with a congregation and sightseeing during services is not allowed. Occasionally there are sound and light performances.

Swedish Academy. North side of Stortorget, near the Royal Palace. Historic building, the headquarters of the Swedish Academy, which awards the Nobel Prize in literature.

SPORTS. Tennis. There are a number of indoor tennis courts as well as outdoor courts at: Hjorthagen, in Jägmästaregatan; Smedslätten, in Gustav Adolfs Park; South Ångby, in Färjestadsvägen; Enskede, Mälarhöjden, and Älvsjö sports grounds.

Golf. Golfing enthusiasts have a choice of 14 18-hole courses. Among the best are: Stockholm Golf Club, Kevinge, train from Östra Station or underground to Mörby Centrum; Djursholm Golf Club, Eddavägen Station, train from Östra Station; Drottningholm Golf Club, bus from St. Eriksgatan; Lidingö Golf Club, Sticklinge, underground to Ropsten thence bus; Saltsjöbaden Golf Club, Tattby Station, train from Saltsjöbanan Station, Slussen (change at Igelboda); on Wermdö, at Hemmestavik (bus from Slussen).

Swimming. Långholmsparken or Smedsuddsbadet. It's quite something to be able to swim in the center of a big city these days.

Fishing. You may fish free of charge from the bridges of Stockholm; the water is cleaner today than 50 years ago and salmon have been caught just in front of the Royal Palace. Up-to-date information on fishing, licenses, and equipment rental is available from the tourist office at Sweden House.

Winter sports. There are a number of ski trails in the vicinity of Stockholm and in the Södertörn and Roslagen areas. The track at Nacka is floodlit for night skiing. Both Fiskartorpet and Hammarby have slalom runs, lifts and ski jumps. For ice skating, there are the Stadium, Östermalm Sports Ground, Tennis Stadium and Johanneshov Rink at Sandstuvägen; many parks, including central Kungsträdgården, have winter rinks.

You can rent downhill skiing equipment and cross-country skis at Skid och Brädoktorn, Sturegatan 20 (63 75 75).

Spectator sports. If you want to be a spectator, call 22 18 40 and Miss Frida will tell you about the sporting events of the day in a tape recorded message.

Biking and canoeing. Bikes and canoes are available for rent at Djurgården bridge.

MUSIC, MOVIES AND THEATERS. Music. Stockholm's two musical centers are the *Royal Opera House* and the *Stockholm Concert House.* The Royal Opera, located just across the bridge from the Royal Palace, has a season running from mid-August until about June 10. The Ballet Festival is in the first week of June.

The concert season lasts from about the middle of September to about the middle of May. The Stockholm Concert Association Orchestra is in regular service at the Concert House and is fully up to international standards. But of even greater interest perhaps is the veritable parade of top international virtuosos and guest conductors, representing the cream of European, British and American talent.

Every day during the summer, concerts and other kinds of entertainment are held in the open air at *Skansen.* Also, the *Gröna Lund Tivoli* amusement park, open mid-April to mid-September, has daily open-air performances with Swedish and foreign artists. Between June 15 and the end of August, there are free concerts in the city's many parks. In the *Kungsträdgården* there are daily recorded concerts and, three evenings a week at least, free entertainment on the outdoor stage, often featuring leading variety artists.

A unique experience is to attend a concert at the *National Museum* (Art Gallery), held four times during August. Occasionally there are also concerts in the *Royal Palace.*

For information about concerts and theaters (including English-speaking theaters), call at the kiosk on Norrmalmstorg where you can also buy reduced price tickets for same-day performances.

Movies. English and American movies dominate. They are shown with Swedish sub-titles and are often released at the same time as they appear in London or New York. See the evening papers for programs. The advertisements usually mention the English as well as the Swedish title.

Theaters. Several theaters specialize in light opera—playing classics and modern musicals. It's great fun hearing and seeing a familiar perennial in a strange theater and a strange language (though many may find the language barrier insuperable). Season: Sept. to mid-June.

The *Royal Dramatic Theater*—scene of the debuts of Greta Garbo and Ingrid Bergman—actually consists of two theaters, one for major performances and a smaller one for those of more limited public interest. A number of the plays presented here and at other Stockholm theaters are hits still running in New York or London. Season: Sept. through May.

Particularly recommended is the *Court Theater* of Drottningholm Palace, a few minutes to a half-hour from downtown Stockholm by car or bus (or 50 minutes by boat). This is an 18th-century theater which was somehow lost sight of, closed up for years, and when reopened a few decades ago was found to be in its original condition. The repertoire consists almost entirely of operas and ballets contemporary with the theater: in other words, of works written for that kind of stage. Seeing a performance there is a unique theater event. Performances during May, June,

July, August and September, two to four evenings a week. Again, call at the kiosk on Norrmalmstorg for information and tickets.

SHOPPING. Shopping in Stockholm tends to be expensive, but you can be sure of the quality. You can also take advantage of the tax-free shopping system, under which a part of your sales tax will be refunded at the airport. Ask for details at the shop; you need special receipts to present at the airport, harbor or on board ship. See also "Shopping" in *Facts at Your Fingertips.* When you see the word REA, it means there's a sale in progress. The best REAs are after Christmas and mid-summer.

First shopping stop in Stockholm should be the *Nordiska Kompaniet,* known as N.K., at Hamngatan 18–20. This store is a sort of combination Neiman-Marcus and Harrods, with a few specialties of its own thrown in; you can find almost any-thing you might want to buy here. Opposite the N.K. is the *Gallerian shopping ar-cade,* where you can find shoes, clothing, books, antiques, perfume, cameras and much more. On the other side of the fountain is *Åhléns City,* a huge department store near Sergels Torg, Drottninggatan and Hötorget. Both N.K. and Åhléns are open Sundays. Here also is the *P.U.B.* department store, in buildings on both sides of Drottninggatan with a tunnel connection. P.U.B. also has an extensive range, but is less luxurious and lower-priced. It faces on to Hötorget and the Concert Hall, in an area where shops of all kinds can be found.

In Gamla Stan many specialty shops can be found on Västerlånggatan. If you walk towards Slussen and to the right on Hornsgatan, you come to a hill called Puckeln, where many small and interesting art galleries are to be found. Handicrafts are on sale at *Svensk Hemslöjd,* Sveavägen 44, the *Stockholm Handicraft Shop* at Drottninggatan 14, *Adolphson Wadle's Present* at Västerlånggatan 55 and *Brinkens Konsthantverk* at Storkyrkobrinken 1.

There are shopping malls in suburbs such as Vällingby, Kista and Skärholmen, where you can also find the huge furniture store *IKEA,* and an indoor flea market which is open on Saturdays and Sundays. Best bets for glassware include *Nordiska Kristall,* Kungsgatan 9 or *Rosenthal Studio-Haus,* Birger Jarlsgatan 6. *The Crystal Showrooms* at Drottninggatan 25 and Norrmalmstorg 4 cater mainly to U.S. visitors with all price tags in U.S. dollars.

RESTAURANTS. Since restaurants play such an important part in Stockholm life, a fairly extensive list is given here. Most have liquor licenses, though do remem-ber that alcohol is very expensive. Some of the downtown establishments close for three or four weeks during the summer. As in all big cities, there are many types of restaurant in Stockholm, such as Greek, Japanese, Chinese, Korean. All the main hotels have their own restaurants. If you are on a budget, look for bargains such as Sunday Specials, happy hours, inclusive menus etc. You'll find details in the newspapers next to the entertainments section.

Expensive

Aurora. Munkbron 11 (21 93 59). Located in a beautiful 300-year-old house in the Old Town with pleasant small rooms in vaults. Charcoal grill. Excellent food and service. AE, DC, MC, V.

Clas på Hörnet. Surbrunnsgatan 20 (16 51 36). One of the most unusual settings in Stockholm—on the ground floor of an elegant restored 200-year-old town house which is also an exclusive hotel. Excellent international and Swedish cuisine. AE, DC, MC, V.

Coq Blanc. Regeringsgatan 111 (11 61 53). Was once a theater; stage and stalls intact. Excellent food. Budget-priced lunch menu. AE, DC, MC, V.

Coq Roti. Sturegatan 19 (10 25 67). A gourmet restaurant run by professionals; French cuisine in sophisticated setting. AE, DC, MC, V.

Eriks Fisk. On quay-berth 17, Strandvägskajen (660 60 60). This former sand barge has been converted into a *de luxe* seafood restaurant. In summer enjoy the view from the deck. Choose your own fish. AE, DC, MC, V.

L'Escargot. Scheelegatan 8 (53 05 77). As the name implies, snails are a specialty of the house, but it is more popular for its daily six-course gastronomic menu. AE, DC, MC, V.

Fem Små Hus. Nygränd 10 (10 04 82). In the Old Town. Its name means "five small houses." Many small rooms in vaults. Excellent international cuisine and Swedish specialties. AE, DC, MC, V.

Garbo. Blekingegatan 32 (40 12 07). It was here that Greta Garbo was born in 1905 so the atmosphere is very movie oriented. AE, DC, MC, V.

Gourmet. Tegnérgatan 10 (31 43 98). Lives up to its name: one of the best French restaurants in town. Pleasant atmosphere. AE, DC, MC, V.

Grand Hotel. S. Blasieholmshamnen 8 (22 10 20). Excellent restaurant (terrace outside in the summer) with marvelous views of the Royal Palace and the Old Town. This is the place for *Smörgåsbord* in relaxed and sophisticated surroundings. AE, DC, MC, V.

K.B. or Konstnärshuset. Smålandsgatan 7, near Norrmalmstorg (11 02 32). Eat and drink in intimate surroundings in the heart of town. Murals by Swedish artists who paid for their drinks with paintings. AE, DC, MC, V.

Latona. Västerlånggatan 79 (11 32 60). Cavernous cellar-restaurant in the heart of the Old Town, by Järntorget. Scores for atmosphere, service and excellent food. AE, DC, MC, V.

Mälardrottningen. Riddarholmen (24 36 00). Floating restaurant and hotel on Barbara Hutton's former private yacht. Seafood specialties. Reservation essential. AE, DC, MC, V.

Operakällaren. In the Opera House facing Kungsträdgården, the waterfront and the Royal Palace (11 11 25). World-famous for international cuisine and the atmosphere. AE, DC, MC, V.

Riche and Teatergrillen. Birger Jarlsgatan 4 (10 70 22). The *Riche* side has a veranda on the street. Fine paintings create an elegant ambience. Roast beef—not perhaps one of the most obvious things to expect in Stockholm—is served from a silver trolley every day. The *Teatergrillen,* or *Theater Grill* (tel. 10 70 44) is more intimate and lives up to its name in attracting some of the theater crowd. Good for a quiet dinner. The grill is closed in July. AE, DC, MC, V.

Solliden. Skansen (660 10 55). On the heights at Stockholm's favorite pleasure grounds, ten minutes from the center of town. Open May to Aug. Wonderful view of the city and harbor. Also self-service on the ground floor and a big outdoor restaurant in summer. AE, DC, MC, V.

Stallmästargården. Norrtull (24 39 10). Historic inn with view of Brunnsviken Lake. Coffee in the courtyard, with a lovely garden, after a good meal on a summer evening is a delightful experience. AE, DC, MC, V.

Stortorgskällaren. Stortorget 7 (10 55 33). Charming medieval cellar in the Old Town near the Cathedral and the Royal Palace. Adjoining a fish restaurant with the same management. AE, DC, MC, V.

Ulriksdals Wärdshus. In a fine park near Ulriksdal Palace (85 08 15). 15 minutes by car or bus 540 from Humlegården Park. Old Swedish inn with famed *Smörgåsbord.* AE, DC, MC, V.

Moderate

Berns Salonger. Berzelii Park, next to Norrmalmstorg (24 12 80). Recently renovated restaurant with an authentic 19th-century atmosphere. AE, DC, MC, V.

Birger Bar. Birger Jarlsgatan 5 (20 72 10). Popular restaurant specializing in Italian cuisine. AE, DC, MC, V.

Cattelin. Storkyrkobrinken 9, in Old Town (20 18 18). Seafood a specialty, but there's also a bistro. Members of Parliament meet here. AE, DC, MC, V.

Colibri. Corner Drottninggatan and Adolf Fredriks Kyrkogatan (10 81 20). Plank steak.

Daily News Café. Kungsträdgården in Sverigehuset (21 56 55). Good food. Swedish and foreign newspapers to hand (but not on the menu). AE, DC, MC, V.

Gondolen. (40 22 22). Suspended under the gangway of the Katarina elevator at Slussen. View of the harbor and the Old Town. AE, DC, MC, V.

Hamngatan 1. Hamngatan 1 (20 01 36). Modern decor; open-air service on sidewalk in summer. Good food and large portions. Closed Mon. AE, DC, MC, V.

Hard Rock Café. Sveavägen 75 (16 03 50). Similar concept to its namesakes in New York and London, offering hamburgers against a rock-music background. AE, DC, MC, V.

La Grenouille. Grev Turegatan 16 (20 10 00). French-style establishment with three separate restaurants in different price brackets. AE, DC, MC, V.

Matpalatset. Hamngatan 15 (20 91 95). Was Stockholm's 1986 "Restaurant of the Year". Five small restaurants in one building. AE, DC, MC, V.

N.K. Department Store. Opposite Sverigehuset. A shoppers' favorite, with a restaurant, salad bar and coffee shop. AE, DC, MC, V.

Östergök. Kommendörsgatan 46 (61 15 07). Specializes in fish, but there's also a steakhouse and a pizzeria here. Popular. AE, DC, MC, V.

Rodolfino. Stora Nygatan 1 (11 84 97). Italian specialties, though not exclusively, in small, chic spot in the Old Town, by the Riddarhuset. Popular with the younger crowd; good food and service. AE, MC, V.

Stadshuskällaren. Stadshuset (City Hall), (50 54 54). Rustic atmosphere in the cellar of the City Hall overlooking Lake Mälaren. No meals in main restaurant during the summer. AE, DC, MC, V.

Sturehof. Stureplan 2 (14 27 50). A fairly large, unpretentious restaurant, which makes fish its business. Pub in old English style. Quieter in the back of the restaurant. Just in the middle of town. AE, DC, MC, V.

Vau-de-Ville. Hamngatan 17 (21 25 22). French-bistro atmosphere. Excellent food at reasonable prices. Chosen as Stockholm's 1986 "Restaurant of the Year." AE, DC, MC, V.

Inexpensive

Gröna Linjen. Mäster Samuelsgatan 10, second floor (11 27 90). Good for lunch. Vegetarian. No credit cards.

Tehuset (the tea house). Under the elms in Kungsträdgården Park. Lively and chic outdoor place. Have a hot sandwich there at noon and watch the Royal Guard march by. Summer only. No credit cards.

Zum Franziskaner. Skeppsbron 44 (11 83 30). German-style restaurant on the waterfront in the Old Town. Food is reasonable and service very friendly. Popular. AE, MC, V.

In the **Gallerian shopping arcade** there are several good places to eat, including *Glada Laxen* (M), a café specializing in fish, but often with lines waiting at lunchtime. Also the *Pizzeria* (I), with a salad table and other dishes besides pizza. On the balcony, you can find *Edelweiss,* with a choice of salads and cakes.

The indoor market at *Östermalmshallen* has many food shops. At this 100-year-old indoor market visit *Gerdas* fish shop, where you can get an excellent lunch at a reasonable price in unusual and noisy surroundings. In the same building, on the second floor, you can find the biggest salad table in town. It's called *Örtagården* (the Herb Garden) (I) (662 17 28).

Look out for the special lunch offers available at almost all restaurants Mon. to Fri. 10–2. A main course plus drinks, salad, bread and butter costs about SEK 30–40.

NIGHTLIFE. Stockholm has a wide range of nightspots to choose from, the names and ownership of which change fairly frequently. See the last page in the daily papers for what's on and where. There are no real nightlife bargains and you should expect a supper in one of these nightspots to cost you between SEK 200 and 300. When there is a show it could cost you more. It's also a good idea to book in advance.

Entry to a pub with live music would be about SEK 25–45. Also many restaurants have dancing a few nights a week.

Aladdin. Barnhusgatan 12 (10 09 32). Oriental decor. Big dance floor.

Atlantic. Teatergatan 3 (21 89 07). Mixed, elegant crowd.

Bacchi Wapen. Järntorgsgatan 5 (11 66 71). As well as the restaurant, there's a disco, piano bar and café.

Börsen. Jakobsgatan 6 (10 16 00). Stockholm's biggest "show restaurant," with international artists.

Café Opera. Operakajen 9 (11 00 26). Very popular, so get there as early as possible.

Club Alexandra. Birger Jarlsgatan 29 (10 46 46). Most famous nightspot in town, located in Stockholm Plaza Hotel.

Cindy's Bar. Amaranten Hotel (54 10 60).

Daily News Café. Kungsträdgården (21 56 55). Central, near the N.K. department store. Restaurant, bar and disco.

Engelen. Kornhamnstorg 59 (10 07 22). In an old pharmacy in the Old Town. Long lines and mixed crowd, but more for the younger set.

Fasching. Kungsgatan 63 (21 62 67). Stockholm's biggest jazz club.

Gamlingen. Stora Nygatan 5 (20 57 86). Again, for the younger set.

Kaos. Stora Nygatan 21 (20 58 86). In the Old Town. Wide range of music. Young, mixed crowd.

King Creole. Kungsgatan 18 (24 47 00). Some evenings features "old-time" dancing.

Melody. Birger Jarlsgatan 27 (21 21 00). Popular disco, restaurant and bar.

Stampen. Stora Nygatan 5 (20 57 93). Old Town. A pub with "trad" jazz music.

Bars

There are piano bars at the Hotel Sheraton, Amaranten, Reisen, Continental, Sergel Plaza and Malmen.

If you want something to eat after midnight, there are a few places near Norrmalmstorg such as **Collage**, Smålandsgatan 2 (10 01 95), **Café La Clé**, Hamngatan 6 (20 87 00) and **Monte Carlo**, Sveavägen 23 (11 00 25).

STOCKHOLM ENVIRONS AND GOTLAND

The Capital as an Excursion Center

Stockholm is, in a literal sense, two-faced. It turns at one and the same time to two diametrically opposed worlds which have really only one thing in common—water. To the east the world is harsh, rough, rugged, primeval and its water is the treacherous salt water of the sea. To the west the world is friendly, civilized, the cradle of an ancient culture, and its water is the sweet water shed by farmland and forest. The former is the Stockholm Archipelago, the latter the valley of the sprawling, multi-armed Lake Mälaren.

The Swedes have given the archipelago a name which is both romantic and descriptive, Skärgården, or Garden of Skerries. There are thousands of them, large and small, some wooded, some rocky, some even cultivated, separated by broad and narrow channels, indented by bays—in short, a unique seascape. The archipelago has supported a small and hardy farming and fishing population for centuries, living out quiet lives almost unnoticed until a few decades ago. Now the skerries are also a summer playground. And one of the great joys is convenience: you can get well out into the archipelago and back in a few hours.

Exploring the Stockholm Environs

Here are some of the principal summer resorts and sights, of which several are only an hour or so from Stockholm.

Sandhamn. Yachting center at the extreme eastern edge of the archipel-ago on the open Baltic Sea. Sandhamn's original importance was as a pilot station, but it is now also a popular summer resort because of its sandy beaches and good sailing facilities. The Royal Swedish Yacht Club has a clubhouse here and arranges a number of international races in the July-August regatta season. Daily boat services from Stockholm. Special pack-ages are available at an all-in price which includes the round trip to Sand-hamn by boat as well as overnight accommodations with breakfast at the comfortable Sandhamns Hotel.

Vaxholm. Characterized by an ancient fortress guarding the channel into Stockholm. (The German Field-Marshal von Moltke is said to have laughed on only two occasions in his life—one of them was at the sight of Vaxholm Fortress.) The fortress is now open as a museum showing the military defense of Stockholm over the centuries. Vaxholm is a small but progressive town with good tennis courts and bathing.

Tyresö Castle. An ancient estate southeast of Stockholm, only 40 min-utes from Ringvägen, (bus No. 10). The estate has belonged to some of Sweden's outstanding noble families since the Middle Ages. Its last owner willed it to the Nordiska Museum in 1930. Interesting art, including 18th-century French paintings.

Nynäshamn. A seaside town. Good beaches. Port of departure for steamers to the Baltic Sea island of Gotland.

Here is an important note: *Some parts of the archipelago are defense zones, closed to foreigners.* To avoid possible inconvenience, check before starting. If you put ashore at a strange point, look for the presence of a sign which might indicate that it is a prohibited area. They are posted in several languages, including English. If, for any reason, you wish to enter one of the zones—it may be quite possible that some Swedish friend or acquaintance of yours has a summer cottage within one—you can apply to the "Kustartilleri-stationen" in Vaxholm. The regulations are fairly strict, and there is no guarantee that such an application will always be approved.

Sigtuna, Skokloster and Gripsholm Castles

Sigtuna was founded about the year 1000 by Sweden's first Christian king, Olof Skötkonung, and for a time it was the chief political and reli-gious center of the country. Sigtuna is located north of Stockholm, a little more than half way to Uppsala. It is not on the main railway line; you change to a bus in Märsta. A visit to Sigtuna can suitably be combined with an outing to Uppsala. During the summer there is an excursion by boat from the City Hall bridge in Stockholm to Sigtuna, with a free guided tour of the city, continuing to Uppsala and returning by train. There is also a twice-weekly guided excursion from Stockholm by bus taking in both Uppsala and Sigtuna.

The Sigtuna sun rose rapidly and sank rapidly. Bearing witness to its brief age of glory are the ruins of the first stone edifices erected in Sweden, pre-Norman churches dedicated to St. Per, St. Olof, and St. Lars. These were also fortresses, designed as much with an eye to defense as to the glorification of God. They overlooked a thriving community for nearly 200 years, during which the first Swedish coins were minted and Anglo-Saxon missionaries pushed the conversion of the Swedes.

Despite the stone churches, the city was more or less destroyed in 1187 by Vikings from across the Baltic, but lived on, thanks partly to the Dominican Monastery. The Reformation delivered a new blow, the monasteries were closed, and Sigtuna sank into obscurity. In modern times it has begun to flourish again as an educational and religious center.

You will find Sigtuna more idyllic than exciting. Note the charm of its narrow main street—Stora Gatan—which is said to follow its original route of 950 years ago and is known as the oldest street in Sweden. The layers of earth here have furnished the archeologists with a wealth of finds, from which they have reconstructed the life of various centuries. Maria Church, once the Dominican Monastery church, was one of the first brick churches in the Lake Mälaren valley, but only a few ruins remain of the monastery itself. St. Olof's Church gives you a good idea of the military aspects of early church architecture—it dates from about 1050. The construction material was rough granite blocks, the windows are mere loopholes, and the entrance just large enough to admit one person at a time.

On the heights overlooking the city you will find the modern institutions which have given new life to Sigtuna. One is the Sigtuna Foundation, sponsored by the Swedish Church, which includes a continuation college for adults, a chapel, and a guest house—the latter popular among authors as a good place to work. The others are the Sigtuna Academy and the Humanistic Academy, both boarding schools, and the College for Laymen, for instruction in volunteer parish work. Note also the unique little 18th-century Town Hall—supposed to be the smallest in the country—and a number of rune stones. About 16 kilometers (ten miles) northeast of Sigtuna lies Skokloster Castle.

Skokloster has recently been sold to the Swedish State. It has the richest collection of art treasures from the Swedish Imperial Era, and its display of weapons is outstanding.

The castle was built between 1654 and 1679 by Carl Gustaf Wrangel, one of Gustavus Adolphus' best-known field marshals. When he died it went to a relative, Count Nils Brahe, and was passed on from one Brahe to another until the family died out about 25 years ago. It then came into the hands of a related family, the von Essens. For the most part the furniture, paintings, and tapestries antedate the Thirty Years' War. The library contains some 30,000 volumes. A motor museum is the last private owner's contribution to his forefather's collection, and there is now a hotel and vacation center in the grounds.

A pleasant place for a short excursion from Stockholm is Sturehov, 22 kilometers (14 miles) west of the city. This is an old mansion and estate belonging to the city of Stockholm and used for civic entertainment, but it is also open to the public. The mansion is an exceptionally fine example of 18th-century Swedish architecture and interior design, and contains about a dozen porcelain stoves from the famous Marieberg factory, apart from many other treasures.

Gripsholm Castle is an ideal day-excursion by boat from Stockholm. You ride three pleasant hours through the beautiful scenery of Lake Mälaren, stop in Gripsholm long enough for an inspection of the old castle and a good lunch, and get back to Stockholm by early evening. As a castle site, Gripsholm dates back to some time in the 1300s but the present towered structure was begun about 1535 on the orders of King Gustav Vasa. Fully restored, livable and well maintained—after a period as a state prison—Gripsholm today is an outstanding museum, with a large and fine collection of historical portraits.

In the castle, note particularly the little theater. It, like Drottningholm Theater, owes its existence to drama-loving King Gustav III, and has been preserved in its original condition. Although much smaller, in the opinion of many it is vastly more beautiful and full of atmosphere than its counterpart at Drottningholm. Nearby is the prison tower, where the tragic King Erik XIV (whom Strindberg made the central figure of one of his most powerful dramas) was held captive after his dethronement. The collection of portraits was begun by King Gustav Vasa himself in the 16th century, and now numbers nearly 3,000 paintings, with emphasis on Swedish royalty but with a number of royal figures from other lands.

In the courtyards note particularly the rune stones, among the best preserved to be found, and the artfully designed bronze cannons, war booty from the Swedish wars with Russia centuries ago. (Incidentally, the Soviet government has made unsuccessful efforts to get them returned to Russia. The Swedes, however, seem inclined to keep these memories of days when inferior Swedish forces often beat the tar out of the Czar's finest.)

Visby, City of Ruins and Roses

If you choose to visit Visby—the "City of Ruins and Roses" on the storied isle of Gotland in the Baltic Sea—during the off-season, say early November, you will find the short flight from Stockholm unforgettable. The sunset will provide one of those incredible displays of color that are to be found only in this part of the world.

At the Visby airport, you will be amazed to see a bed of red, red roses, in this northern corner of the world, still blooming. According to the inhabitants, roses are sometimes to be seen blooming in even December and January. Whatever the season, the red has a special brilliance resulting from the composition of the soil.

You feel something in the very atmosphere of Visby, a sense of the Middle Ages living on into the 20th century. Looping around the city is the magnificent wall, completely embracing it on all but the sea side. When you enter one of the 13th- or 14th-century gates, you find this special atmosphere among the beautiful buildings. Stepped, gabled houses date back to Visby's era of greatness. And everywhere are buildings centuries old, some of them well preserved, others, particularly the churches, in a gaunt state of disrepair that adds to their charm. Try, if you can, to see the view from the Powder Tower in the moonlight. This tower, serving as one of the main anchors of the wall, near the sea on the north side of town, is perhaps the oldest of the watch towers that rise up at intervals along the medieval wall.

The history of the island of Gotland, and the capital city Visby, goes back thousands of years, and its earth has yielded treasures speaking eloquently of contacts with the Minoan, Greek, and Roman cultures. But the Golden Age arrived in the 12th century, when Visby and Gotland dominated the trade of northern and western Europe and the town could undoubtedly be classed as one of the major cities of the world. Wealth followed wealth, and within the confines of the city wall alone, itself a magnificent structure from every standpoint, the rich merchants erected no less than 17 churches. Outside of the city, farmer-merchants built parish churches more like small cathedrals than rural houses of worship.

Trade routes shifted. War parties ravaged. The first of a series of major catastrophes took place in 1361, when the island and city fell to Danish

King Valdemar Atterdag. The decline had set in with a vengeance. The island was variously occupied by Baltic powers during the succeeding century and more, until 1645, when it was definitely sealed into the Swedish kingdom.

Exploring Gotland

Today, the island is a vacation paradise *par excellence.* There is no lack of sights in the traditional meaning. See the churches and medieval merchant palaces of Visby—St. Nicholas, St. Clemens, the Church of the Holy Spirit, St. Catarina, and a half dozen more—and the wall. *Walk* to see Visby—pick up a map and an English guidebook at the travel bureau in Burmeister House, itself a historic building near the harbor—and wander. Wherever you go, you can't go wrong. Don't miss the museum, Fornsalen, particularly the impressive picture stones, which antedate the Viking rune stones. There are other remarkable finds on display, too—coins and jewelry from many centuries, religious art (note particularly the gentle loveliness of the Öja Madonna, a medieval wood sculpture), and ancient weapons unearthed from the scenes of battles for this once flourishing island.

If you happen to be in Visby at the end of July or in early August don't miss the pageant opera "Petrus de Dacia" performed every year in the ruin of St. Nicolai Church.

Justice cannot be done to the cultural history of Visby and Gotland in anything smaller than a complete book. The names of the masters who designed and decorated these churches have been lost to history, but scientists have been able to identify and classify a few of them by characteristic features of their styles as they recur in various works. Although Visby is hilly and there are cobbled stones on the streets, you should take the time to walk leisurely around the city. Car traffic is restricted here.

The stalactite caves at Lummelunda are unique in this part of the world and are worth visiting, as is the Krusmyntagården (herb garden), north of Visby, close to the sea.

Although many tourists rent bicycles for tours of the island, there are cars for rent and there is a good network of buses. The Tourist Office arranges many day tours by bus—call and ask for details. It should be noted that the island of Farö and the northeast corner of Gotland itself are restricted areas for foreigners.

The Local Churches

On the whole island, which measures only about 48 kilometers (30 miles) by 128 kilometers (80 miles), there are approximately 100 churches still intact and in use today, dating from Gotland's great commercial area. Among them are:

Barlingbro, dating from the 13th century, with vault paintings, stained glass windows, remarkable 12th-century font.

Dalhem, one of the 16 largest rural religious edifices, construction begun about 1200 or somewhat earlier, an exquisite example of Gotland church architecture.

Gothem, one of Gotland's most impressive country churches, mainly built during the 13th century, with notable series of paintings of that period.

Grötlingbo, a 14th-century church with stone sculpture and stained glass: note the 12th century reliefs on the facade.

Tingstäde, another of the 16 largest, a puzzle of six building periods from 1169 to 1300 or so. Note the general proportions, the stained-glass windows, and murals from the 14th century.

Roma Cloister Church, the massive ruins from a Cistercian monastery founded in 1164. The ruins are sufficiently well preserved to give a good picture of the architecture and contruction.

Öja, decorated with paintings and containing a famous Holy Rood from the late 13th century.

Island Bird Refuges

There are a number of other sights well worth your time. Among them are curious rock formations along the coasts, including the "Old Man of Hoburgen" at the southern tip of the island; and two island bird refuges off the coast south of Visby, Stora and Lilla Karlsö. The bird population consists to a large extent of guillemots, which look like penguins. Visits to these refuges are permitted only in company with a recognized guide, and the easiest way to see them is to join a conducted tour from Visby.

PRACTICAL INFORMATION FOR GOTLAND

TOURIST INFORMATION. There are tourist offices at: Burmeisterska Huset, Visby (0498-109 82), open April through September, and the ferry terminal (0498–470 60).

TELEPHONE CODES. We give telephone codes in the hotel and restaurant lists that follow. These codes need only be used when calling from outside the area concerned.

HOTELS AND RESTAURANTS. Hotels. *Snäck* (L), (0498-600 00). 213 rooms. Between airport and Visby. All rooms face west. Excellent restaurant, nightclub. Beach, pool, sauna, canoes. Airport bus. AE, DC, MC, V. *Strand* (M), Strandgatan 34 (0498–126 00). 120 rooms. Breakfast only. Rooms for handicapped guests. AE, DC, MC, V. *Toftagården* (M), Tofta (0498-654 00). 78 rooms. 300 meters (about 300 yards) from beach. Restaurant, windsurfing, billiards. MC. *Villa Borgen* (M), Adelsgatan 11 (0498-71170). 18 rooms. Breakfast only. Family-run. MC. *Solhem* (I), (0498-790 70). 112 rooms. Central. On two floors. Restaurant, dancing. MC.

Restaurants. *Jacob Dubbe,* Strandgatan 16 (0495-497 22). International menu. In medieval building. Open 22 hours a day. *Rosengården,* Stora Torget (0495-181 90). Close to cloister ruin. Italian and French cuisine. Open-air service in garden. Charming. MC. *Värdshuset* (Inn), Lindgården, Strandgatan 26 (0495-187 00). In old building. Excellent food. MC

Youth Hostels. For bookings and information about youth hostels on the island of Gotland, call 0498-912 20. *Visby,* Gråboskolan (0498-169 33). Central. Open May 31 to Aug. 3.

Camping. There are many three-star sites on the island. Try *Kneippbyn* (0498-643 65). On the beach four km. (2½ miles) south of Visby. 20 cottages for rent.

HOW TO GET AROUND. One way, but not the least expensive, to see the archipelago is by chartered cruiser (Taxi-Båt). In summer scheduled water-bus services ply to most points of the archipelago from Stockholm: *embarking* at Klara Mälarstrand (near City Hall) for Gripsholm Castle and Drottningholm Castle and for Skokloster Castle; at Strömkajen (near Grand Hotel) for Sandhamn, Husarö, Möja and Vaxholm; at Slussen for Sandhamn (bus with boat connection); from Central Station by train, bus and coach to Utö.

It takes only 40 minutes to fly from Stockholm to Visby—the airport is three km. (about two miles) from the city. There are also day or night trips from the port of Nynäshamn (one hour by train, bus or car from Stockholm). You can leave Stockholm in the evening and return by midnight the next day. The boats on this run carry cars. There is also a car-ferry service from Oskarshamn as well as high-speed catamaran services, for passengers only, which operate from June through late Aug. from both Nynäshamn and Västervik.

Gotland is an ideal island for a bicycling holiday. There are over 4,000 bicycles for rent and the tourist office will sell you complete bike "packages." Gotland has a tourist office at Norrmalmstorg in Stockholm.

PLACES TO VISIT. In the archipelago. The castles at Vaxholm and Tyresö. In the valley of Lake Mälaren: Gripsholm Castle and its portrait gallery, the 17th-century castle (with its Motor Museum) of Skokloster, Sigtuna, with its rune stones and House of Antiquities.

Gotland. Fornsalen (Gotland Historical Museum). At Strandgatan 12. It features graves from the Stone, Bronze and Iron Ages. Also picture stones and hoards from Viking times, ecclesiastical art. Open Tues. to Sun 1–3; closed Mon.; May 15 to Aug 15, daily 11–5.

Krusmyntagården. Herb garden, two km. (1.2 miles) south of Lummelundagrot-torna Caves, near the sea. 300 different herbs; also herbs for sale. On Tues. and Thurs. nights, entertainers (from Gotland) and *asado* (barbecue). Open mid-June to Aug., daily 9–6. For information call 0498-701 53.

Lummelundagrottorna. 13 km. (nine miles) north of Visby. Ancient limestone caves with stalactites. 300-meter (984-foot) long cave with smaller and larger caves 6–8 meters (19–26 feet) high. Guided tours continuously. Souvenir shop and cafeteria. Open May to Sept., 9–4 daily (Jun. 21 to Aug. 9, 9–7 daily). For information call 0498-730 50.

SWEDEN'S SOUTHLAND

Breadbasket, Battlefield and Summer Playground

Southern Sweden is a world of its own, clearly distinguished from the rest of Sweden by its geography, culture, and history.

Skåne (pronounced "scorner"), the southernmost province, is known as the "granary of Sweden." It occupies a more or less rectangular area, including the almost square peninsula that forms the southern tip of the country and supports no less than one-eighth of the whole Swedish population. It is a comparatively small province of beautifully fertile plains, sand beaches, scores of castles and châteaux, thriving farms, medieval churches, and summer resorts.

East of the northern end of Skåne is the province of Blekinge, called "Sweden's garden," occupying another southern coastal reach extending to the east coast. North of the western part of Skåne, ranging along the west coast of Sweden, is the province of Halland, a rolling country of heaths and ridges rising above the beaches. Halland faces the Kattegat (the southeastern part of the North Sea), and contributed its full share of the Viking forces which once struck terror into the populations of many countries. It still produces its share of modern sea captains.

There is an old tradition that while the Lord was busy making Skåne into the fertile garden that it is today, the devil sneaked past him farther north, and made the province of Småland. The result was harsh, unyielding, unfriendly country of stone and woods. When the Lord caught up with Satan and saw what had happened he said, "All right, it's too late to do anything about the land . . . so I'm going to make the people." He did, and He made them so tough and stubborn and resilient and long-lived

400

that they carved a true civilization out of their sparse heritage. There is still a folk saying that you can deposit a son of the province of Småland on a barren stone island with only an ax in his hands and he'll manage— and have a garden going before long.

Whatever the validity of the legend, it is true that Småland is vastly different from the other three provinces of southern Sweden. It is a good deal larger and is noted particularly for its glass industries, as well as furniture and other wood products, and its great historic region with Kalmar at the center.

Skåne, Blekinge, and Halland (Halland is described in the *West Coast* chapter) also form a natural historical group of provinces; they were actually the last incorporations of territory into what constitutes the present-day Swedish kingdom. The time was 1658. These southern provinces had been part of Denmark for centuries (and thus the medieval architecture is Danish). Sweden and Denmark had been fighting intermittently for generations. Karl X (anglicized as Charles X), a king and general of parts, whatever his faults, was off in Poland on one of the many indecisive Swedish attempts for a reckoning with that country. This looked to the Danes like a perfect opportunity for a reckoning with the Swedes. But when the Danish fleet arrived at Danzig to fall on the Swedish rear, the Swedes were moving overland at top speed toward Denmark. After two bold, unprecedented marches across the ice of the sounds separating the Danish islands, the Swedish army of 12,000 battle-hardened men faced an almost undefended Copenhagen. Although Sweden was also at war with Poland and Russia, Karl X was in a position almost to name his own terms. They were so rough that one of the Danish commissioners, preparing to sign this historic Peace of Roskilde, complained, "If only I didn't know how to write!".

By virtue of that treaty Sweden achieved natural southern boundaries— the coasts of the Baltic Sea—for the first time in its history, and acquired the rich territory which now nurtures one-fourth of the population. But the marks of long association with Denmark and its Continental culture live on in the language, the architecture, the way of life and the gastronomy.

Exploring Helsingborg

Let's say that you have arrived in Helsingborg from the Danish side by ferry. In front of you stretches a long, comparatively narrow square, dominated at the far end, on the height, by a medieval tower stronghold known as Kärnan (the Keep). The surviving center tower, built to provide living quarters and defend the medieval castle of Helsingborg, is the most remarkable relic of its kind in the north. The interior, which may be visited, is divided into several floors, containing medieval kitchen fittings, a chapel, etc. From the top you have a magnificent view of the coast, the Sound, and the Danish shore.

A thousand years ago, this city was an important European capital. Today it is a thriving industrial town of some 101,000 inhabitants, the eighth largest city in Sweden. For centuries Helsingborg and its Danish neighbor across the Sound, Elsinore (Helsingør), only about five kilometers (three miles) away, controlled all shipping traffic in and out of the Baltic Sea. There is a train and ferry terminal here for services between Sweden and Denmark, with a sailing every 20 minutes.

In Södra Storgatan are St. Mary's Church, built in the 13th century and rebuilt during the 15th century, with an interesting triptych and magnificent late Renaissance pulpit, and the Town Museum, containing exhibits depicting the early history of Helsingborg. Take time to visit Fredriksdals Friluftmuseum, an 18th-century mansion set in a lovely old park around which old Skåne farmhouses and buildings have been set up to form an open-air museum. During summer there are performances in the attractive open-air theater.

About five kilometers (three miles) north of the city—bus to Pålsjöbaden, then a half-hour walk along the Sound—is Sofiero Castle, summer residence of the late King, built in 1865 in Dutch Renaissance style. The grounds are open to the public (enter by northern gate near gardener's lodge).

Golf and Tennis in Båstad

If you proceed north from Helsingborg, you come immediately into a region of summer resorts stretching along a promontory. One of the main resort towns is Mölle, near the end of the peninsula, which looks out upon the south end of the Kattegat. Proceeding back along the north shore of this peninsula, you arrive in Ängelholm, a small and charming city at least 500 years old, which has become a popular summer resort. Here you can see Sweden's oldest local prison—now a museum.

Only some of the main stops can be mentioned here. As you continue north along the coast, the next in line will be Båstad, perhaps the most fashionable of the summer resorts in this region. It is frequented throughout the summer by the international set, and ambassadors and ministers of several countries may sometimes be in residence there at the same time. The principal attractions include the natural beauty of the region (known for its flowers and fruit orchards), 18-hole golf course, and several tennis courts. International tennis tournaments are held every year at the beginning of July.

Recommended is a visit to the Norrviken Gardens, three kilometers (two miles) northwest of Båstad. They comprise a number of gardens of various styles, agreeably laid out in varied grounds and each one in character with the landscape's lines, perspectives and vistas. Just east of Båstad is Malen, with an interesting sepulchral mound from the 11th century B.C. It has been excavated and restored so that you can enter and study the stones set up in the form of a ship. Also here are a 15th-century church and many old houses in picturesque narrow winding streets.

Don't miss Torekov, a little fishing village on the point of a peninsula about nine kilometers (six miles) due west of Båstad, which has many summer visitors. Despite a too generous influx of summer folks in July and August, many of whom have built or bought their own homes, the community remains an authentic part of this coastal region. There is a tiny but interesting museum—not a few of whose treasures have been gathered from ships wrecked in the treacherous waters off the point. The days here are serene and rhythmical with the pulse of an ancient way of life, a life close to the sea. Just off the coast is an island—Hallands Väderö—a national reserve known for its flora and bird life.

Continuing north from Båstad, you cross almost at once into Halland, another of the provinces acquired by Sweden in the fantastically profitable peace of 1658. By this time you will have noticed the changing nature of the landscape, the way ridges billow up in more pronounced fashion from the coast. In back of them are broad heaths unique to this part of Sweden.

Malmö—Third-Largest City

If you start south from Helsingborg, the first coastal town of any size will be Landskrona, a modern industrial and shipping center with some 35,000 inhabitants. The 17th-century fortifications surrounding Landskrona Castle are reputed to be the best preserved relics of their kind in Europe. The citadel was built in 1549. From Landskrona there are boats to the beautiful island of Ven, between Sweden and Denmark.

Malmö, with a population of 235,000, is the small but opulent capital of a small but opulent province and a sense of well-being strikes you upon arrival. It has the friendly atmosphere normally associated with much smaller places, and its coastal location close to Denmark has given it a more cosmopolitan atmosphere than most other Swedish towns. This is reflected in its tremendous variety of restaurants—Greek, Italian and so on—and there are actually reputed to be more restaurants per head than any other Swedish city, including Stockholm. There are many reminders here of the great trading days of the Hanseatic League. The Rådhuset (Court House) dates back to the 16th century and the Malmöhus Castle, now a museum, to the 16th century. Nearby is the Malmö Technical Museum. The Lilla Torg, an attractive small cobblestoned square, has buildings from the 17th and 18th centuries, which have been restored over the past 20 years.

The impressive statue on the central square is that of Karl X—the king who acquired this part of the country for Sweden. Just off the square (look for the steeple and follow your eyes) you will find St. Peter's Church, a brick structure from shortly after 1300. It is the largest Gothic church in south Sweden.

In addition to the usual historical sights offered by most Swedish cities, Malmö distinguishes itself by having also a top-flight modern one—the City Theater. It is surprising that this comparatively small city has been able to build and maintain such an imposing stage. It was completed in 1944 and seats 1,700 persons. The city also now has an impressive 1,300-seat concert hall (Konserthuset), which has provided the Malmö Symphony Orchestra with its first permanent home in its 60-year-old history. The concert season runs between September and May. The Malmö-Card gives you free transportation and free or reduced entrance to various attractions, as well as convenient sightseeing. Buy it at the airport, railway station or tourist office.

The University City of Lund

Less than 30 kilometers (19 miles) northeast of Malmö, connected by frequent bus and train services, is Lund. Lund was once the religious capital of a region which stretched from Iceland to Finland, over which the Roman Catholic archbishop resident here held more or less absolute sway in matters of faith. The city was founded almost a thousand years ago by the Danish King Canute the Great, and during its early burst of prosperity could boast a score of churches and a half-dozen monasteries. The Reformation changed all that. But the founding of Lund University in the 1660s, after the province became part of Sweden, brought new intellectual prosperity, and the arrival of the railroads, not quite a century ago, brought industrial prosperity. The population is about 80,000, and enrollment at the university and high schools about 20,000. The most colorful students' events are Walpurgis Night, April 30, and the carnival in mid-May every four years.

The principal sight is the cathedral, consecrated in 1145, a massive structure and one of the few churches in this part of the world in Romanesque style. There are a number of medieval treasures, of which the most notable is the huge, ornate, intricate 14th-century astronomical clock that still plays daily at noon (1 P.M. on Sun.) and 3 P.M. This remarkable instrument, several yards high, will tell you practically everything about the position of the heavenly bodies and time except the date of your own birthday. The intricate mechanism and the beautifully carved figures which go into action when the clock plays make a fascinating sight. Nor should you miss Lund's Museum of Cultural History, the Archive for Decorative Art, and the Art Gallery. The Botanical Gardens have specimens of 7,000 plants from all over the world.

The Château Country

Only 32 kilometers (20 miles) from Malmö, on a tiny peninsula projecting out from the very southwest corner of Sweden, are the idyllic little twin cities of Falsterbo and Skanör, both very popular summer resorts. Ornithologists gather at Falsterbo every fall to watch the spectacular migration of hundreds of birds of prey.

Continuing on from Malmö, you can make your way to Ystad, a medieval city on the southern coast. If you are driving, you might go by way of Torup Castle, a typical example of the square fortified stronghold, built about 1550. Ystad, perhaps more than any other city on the Swedish mainland, has preserved its medieval character, with winding, narrow streets and hundreds of half-timbered houses from four or five different centuries. Perhaps the principal ancient monument is St. Maria Church, begun shortly after 1200 as a basilica in Romanesque style, but with additions from several centuries. An historical curiosity is a half-timbered house (at Stora Västergatan 6) supposed to have been occupied by King Charles VII during two brief visits in Ystad shortly before and after 1700. Do see the old Franciscan monastery and its museum.

The plains, the gently rolling hills and fields of the province of Skåne are broken every few miles by lovely castles, which have given this part of Sweden the name of the "Château Country." Usually they are surrounded by beautiful grounds, often by moats, and they add a graceful note to travels through this region. Here, perhaps more than anywhere else in Sweden, these huge estates have remained in the hands of the original families, and they date from many centuries and many architectural periods.

These hundreds of castles, châteaux, and manor houses, of every size, type, and age, constitute the great tourist attraction of Sweden's "Château Country." Among the oldest are Glimmingehus and Torup— quadrangular, thick-walled strongholds of the medieval type, built to withstand long sieges. Belonging to the great castle-building age of the 16th century are Vittskövle, Skarhult, Trolle-Ljungby, and Bosjökloster, while others, such as Trolleholm, Vrams-Gunnarstorp, and Knutstorp, bear the distinctive architectural marks of successive post-16th century reconstructions. Thousands come every year as well to visit their lovely formal gardens and parks.

Many of the châteaux are still inhabited and cannot be visited except by special arrangement, often requiring personal contact. The best way to get more than a simple exterior view is to join an organized tour. These guided tours originate in most of the major towns in Skåne during the summer season, but Malmö offers the greatest variety. However, Bosjökloster at Lake Ringsjön, Christinehof in eastern and Svaneholm in southern Skåne, Bäckaskog near Kristianstad, Snogeholm near Sjöbo and Bjärsjölagård near Hörby—with catering facilities—are regularly open to the public. Inquire at any tourist office.

On the coast here in Skåne is Kåseberga or Ales Stenar, a remarkable group of 57 stones erected in the shape of a ship. It is thought to be a memorial to a Viking chieftain.

Eastern Skåne

Turning north again, along the east coast of Skåne, you may want to have a look at Simrishamn, a charming village with a pronounced medieval atmosphere, a favorite haunt for painters because of its clear air. Still farther north you find little Kivik, center of an orchard region, boasting an ancient royal grave which the scientists say dates from 1400 B.C. The Kivik grave is a huge, rounded mound of boulders and stones, and the crypt itself contains interesting picture stones. Near Kivik is Stenshuvud, a rock rising imposingly from the Baltic and its sandy beaches. Between Brösarp and Sankt Olof you can find a vintage railway.

In Maglehem, a few kilometers farther on your route north, is to be found one of the most exquisite old churches in the whole region. It's an outstanding example of the architecture which prevailed here during the Danish era, with the massive white walls and stepped gables that you have been seeing everywhere in the province. Most of the interiors had been plastered over through the passage of the centuries, but thanks in great measure to the initiative of the local pastor, Erik Söderberg, who had devoted years to this labor of love, magnificent wall paintings have been brought out from as far back as the 14th century. There are a great many medieval churches in Sweden of which more than 150 are to be found in the province of Skåne.

The next main town on this route is Kristianstad, founded in 1614 by Danish King Christian IV as a border fortress against Sweden. The Church, the Holy Trinity, is a typical example of Christian's building style. Not far from here is Bäckaskog Castle, and from here you can proceed to Kalmar by traveling east through the province of Blekinge, then north along the Baltic coast. You can stay overnight at Bäckaskog Castle, which was originally a monastery, dating from the 13th century.

Blekinge—the Garden of Sweden

With attractive seaside resorts, forests and hills and fertile valleys, this province has earned its title as the garden of Sweden. The eastern part of the province has more hours of sunshine than any other part of the country, while the northern part gives a hint of the rocks and woods of Småland across the border. Blekinge, like Skåne and Halland, shares a long association with Denmark.

Sölvesborg, according to legend, was founded in A.D. 700 by a sea-going king named Sölve. Today it is a small port supported also by industry.

The principal sights are the old castle, which played an important part in the Swedish-Danish feuds, and the church begun in the 13th century and constructed in Gothic style.

In Listerlandet, near Hällevik, there are several picturesque fishing villages. It also boasts a small fishing museum, with relics of fishing from long ago. The ferry from Nogersund will take you to Hanö, with one of the tallest lighthouses in Northern Europe.

At the Salmon Aquarium at Mörrum you can see salmon and trout in their natural environment. The King and his guests gather at Mörrum around April 1 each year to open the salmon-fishing season. Mörrum's river has a world-wide reputation for salmon fishing. It was here that the world's biggest sea-trout was caught—32.3 lb. Salmon up to 44 lb. are not uncommon here.

Karlshamn, a port which accommodates ocean-going vessels, is an idyllic coastal town. The Kastellet, or fortress, overlooking the channel into the harbor, was started by Karl X to defend the province of Blekinge from the Danes, who had just yielded it up to him. The elevators for grains and oilseeds are said to be the largest such concentration in Europe. The emigrants' monument "Karl-Oskar and Kristina" commemorates the great Swedish exodus to America. There is a replica of this moving monument in Lindstrom Square, Minnesota. The boat trips to the Kastellet in the harbor, and from Järnavik to the beautiful island of Tjärö are to be recommended.

Ronneby was well known to vacationers of a couple of generations past for its mineral wells. The rebuilt resort hotel is set in an unusually beautiful park. The principal sight is the fortress church, Heliga Korsets Kyrka (Holy Cross Church), dating from the 12th century.

Karlskrona, a city founded in the 17th century, is built on 30 islands. It is an important naval base and acquired some notoriety a few years ago when a Soviet submarine ran aground at the entrance to the harbor after having been the victim of a "navigation error." At the Varvsmuseet (Marine Museum), there is an excellent collection of figureheads, model ships and much more. It is one of the finest marine museums in the world. Here in Karlskrona is Sweden's oldest wooden church, Amiralitetskyrkan, with its poor-box, Rosenbom, outside. Two churches here, the Holy Trinity and Fredrik's, were designed by the outstanding architect Nicodemus Tessin. The Kungsholmens Fortress, built around 1680, was erected to protect the harbor. Another fortress dating from the same time, the Drottningskärs Kastell on the island of Aspö, is still intact.

Historic Kalmar

Kalmar has the distinction of a mention on a rune stone from the 11th century. The oldest part of its famous castle dates back to the 12th century. You can see at a glance why Kalmar was once called "the Lock and Key of Sweden," and why it played an historic role in Scandinavian history before the airplane added a third dimension to warfare. The magnificent Renaissance castle—the earliest parts of which date from the 12th century—was also a mighty fortress, dominating the sound which separates the mainland from the island of Öland. When Kalmar began its age of greatness, the southern border of Sweden was only a few kilometers south—on the then Danish province of Blekinge. The long narrow island lying parallel to the mainland and thus forming a narrow channel completed the strategic picture: whoever controlled Kalmar also controlled traffic along the coast north to Stockholm.

The importance of Kalmar is reflected in the name Kalmar Union (an agreement signed here in 1397), an ill-starred attempt to unite Scandinavia under one ruler. It limped along for more than a century of intermittent civil wars before it was formally dissolved by Swedish independence under Gustav Vasa in 1523. It was this great king who made Kalmar Castle with its courts and battlements, its moat, its round towers. But even this powerful stronghold could not prevent the destruction and ravaging of the city in the recurring Danish-Swedish wars. The city was practically wiped out in the so-called Kalmar War of 1611–13. Fire again destroyed the town in 1647, and, with the Peace of Roskilde, the region lost some of its strategic importance. The decline had begun. Today Kalmar is the commercial and administrative center for southeastern Småland, a port and tourist attraction.

The principal sight is, of course, the castle. (*Note:* it closes at 4 P.M.) You get a good picture of the integrated life of a whole royal establishment as it functioned centuries ago, from the king's bedroom to the huge kitchens. Note especially the Castle Chapel, a charming little place of worship in rococo and Renaissance, which is still used for divine services (Sundays at 10 A.M.). The grim dungeon is a curiosity—it was cunningly placed below the surface level of the nearby sea—thus making attempts to tunnel out impossible. Prisoners sometimes survived for years in this dingy, damp hole. The castle also contains the extensive collections of the Kalmar Museum. One of the major attractions of the museum is the exhibition of some of the results of the salvage operation on the Swedish man-of-war *Kronan* (the Crown), which sank in battle with the Danish–Dutch fleet in June 1676, off the southeast coast of Öland with the loss of 800 lives. The wreck was discovered only in 1980 but has yielded some rich archeological finds, including valuable coins, bottles containing 300-year-old brandy and an officer's personal casket with his complete navigational outfit.

You will find the city itself rich in atmosphere and structures from the 17th and 18th centuries, when the present city was largely laid out and constructed. In particular see the cathedral (designed by Nicodemus Tessin the Elder and built about 1675). Not far from here is a smaller square (Lilla Torget), with the residence of the provincial governor, originally from 1674. The French King Louis XVIII lived here briefly in exile shortly after 1800.

Windmills and Rune Stones on Öland

The island of Öland is reached from Kalmar by a 6,070-meter (almost four miles) bridge, the longest in Europe. There are many rune stones here, dating from the Viking era. There are also relics from the Iron Age in the many graves and 16 fortifications on the island.

Gråborg Fortress, probably dating from about A.D. 500, must have been gigantic at one time, for the walls enclose an area some 229 meters (250 yards) long and 174 meters (190 yards) wide. Now only the massive stone walls, as much as eight meters (25 feet) high and eight meters (25 feet) thick, remain of this onetime stronghold.

Probably the most interesting site is at Eketorp—an excavated fortified village which has been restored to give visitors an impression of what life must have been like in a 5th-century community.

Borgholm Castle ruin is perhaps the biggest and most beautiful ruin of a castle stronghold in Sweden. It originated as a medieval fortress, was rebuilt during the 16th and 17th centuries, and ravaged by fire in 1806. It overlooks the city of Borgholm from a commanding site and is most impressive by moonlight.

Solliden is the summer residence of the royal family. The beautiful grounds around the sparkling white mansion are open from June through Aug., 12 noon–2 P.M., and are located on the outskirts of Borgholm, within easy walking distance.

The landscape of Öland is so different from the mainland that you feel almost as though you had entered another country. This, and a great profusion of old-fashioned, more or less Dutch-type windmills, give the island an unmistakable profile. With luck you may be able to count as many as 54 of the 400 windmills in a couple of hours' auto tour.

Much of Öland is covered by a huge, treeless steppe known as the Alvar, a limestone plateau with remarkable flora and unique in northern Europe. It gives a sense of peace bordering on quiet desolation. During spring and fall, this is the place to watch the migratory birds. Hundreds of species rest up here from their long flights. On the southern tip of the island, at Ottenby, is a bird station and an old lighthouse, Långe Jan (Long John), from which there is a magnificent view.

A Kingdom of Glass

In Kalmar or Växjö you are only an hour or two from some of the finest glass works in the world—Orrefors, Kosta, Boda, Strömbergshyttan. Exquisite pieces by famed designers from these factories are found in exclusive shops almost all over the world. But don't look for something that resembles an industrial region. The plants are scattered in the wooded wilderness of Småland, communities of a few hundred people built around the factory. From these isolated, unprepossessing villages go regular shipments to London and Paris, New York's Fifth Avenue, the cities of South America; special orders start on their way addressed to kings and emperors, presidents and ministers, tycoons and simple lovers of beautiful things. The glassblowers show off their skills every weekday, but they start work at 6 A.M. and finish at 3 P.M., so a morning visit is advisable. Inquire at local tourist offices to be sure of times.

You can visit most of the major plants to see the glassblowers at work and they all have large shops, some of supermarket size, where you can pick up remarkable bargains from the "seconds" on display. You'll probably be hard put to it to discover any faults on most items, but if you want to be sure of buying a "perfect" product you'll have to do your buying in a normal shop. Even so, you will probably save substantially in comparison with prices in other countries.

Orrefors is the best-known Swedish glass maker, probably produces the greatest variety, and the quality and design are, of course, unsurpassed. The community of Orrefors is located about an hour west and a little north of Kalmar (train connections). It's so unpretentious you'll pass right through it if you're not looking.

Watching the skilled craftsmen of Orrefors is almost like a slow dance—with the pieces of red hot glass being carried back and forth, passed from hand to hand, as they are blown and shaped by trained, sensitive muscles. The basic procedure and the tools are said not to have changed appreciably in 2,000 years. The designing and engraving processes are also fascinating—and the finished product is the result of unusual teamwork, from the designer to the craftsman to the finisher. (Many of the pieces get no further treatment after leaving the blower and shaper, however.) One of the special attractions of Orrefors is a magnificent display of various pieces made through the years, ranging in value up to thousands of kronor.

Other glassworks are: Johansfors, with a Crystal Museum showing a complete collection from the beginning of this century; Kosta, with a museum and exhibition hall. There are local glass museums at Lindshammar, Pukeberg, Rosdala and Skruf. The largest glass museum in Northern Europe is in Växjö, in the Småland Museum.

Tracing the Emigrants

There are about ten million Americans with Scandinavian blood. Of the Swedes, most came from Småland and the island of Öland. The emigration started in the middle of the last century and continued until the last war. On Öland, for instance, practically every household has someone who has been in America for a couple of years. Many come back, and nearly a fifth of the population, or 5,000 people, have lived and worked in America. Strangely enough, the people never traveled elsewhere to any extent. Some have seen Denmark and England en route to or from the States, others saw something of France, courtesy of the American Army in World War II. The story of the early Swedish emigrants to the U.S. has been masterfully told by a Swedish author, Vilhelm Moberg, in *The Emigrants, Unto a Good Land* and *Last Letter Home,* published, and made into a film, in English. It deals with a family from the mainland, only a few miles from Kalmar, and a look at it will give you an interesting sidelight on the histories of Sweden and America.

In Långasjö there is a small wooden house called Klasatorp open to visitors in the summer months. This was an emigrant's home, and the people here wear the costume of former days and work the farm in the traditional manner. The following tour is suggested for those who wish to see the land of their forefathers: Hovmantorp–Kosta–Ljuder–Algotsboda–Rävemåla–Linnerud–Ingelstad–Växjö. This tour covers a distance of 155 kilometers or 96 miles.

In Växjö the Emigrant Institute has an exhibition telling the story of the "American Dream" and the emigrants. There is also a research center here where the names of most emigrants are kept on file and many American visitors come here each year to trace their ancestors. In August Minnesota Day is celebrated in front of the Emigrant Institute.

PRACTICAL INFORMATION FOR
SWEDEN'S SOUTHLAND

TOURIST INFORMATION. The region's tourist offices may be found at the following places: **Ängelholm,** Storgatan 21 (0431–163 50). **Eksjö,** Österlånggatan 31 (0381–133 05). **Helsingborg,** Rådhuset (042–12 03 10). **Jönköping,** V. Storgatan 9 (036–10 50 50). **Kalmar,** Ölandshamnen 6 (0480–153 50). **Karlskrona,** S. Smedjegatan 6 (0455–834 90). **Lund,** St. Petri Kyrkogatan 4 (046–15 50 00). **Malmö,** Hamngatan 1 (040–34 12 70). **Ronneby,** Snäckebacksplan (0457–176 50). **Västervik,** Strömsholmen (0490–136 95). **Växjö,** Kronobergsgatan 8 (0470–414 10). **Ystad,** St. Knuts Torg (0411–772 78).

The **Malmö card,** costing about SEK 70 for three days and SEK 100 for a week, offers free bus transport in the Malmö area, free entrance to museums and visitor attractions, as well as discounts on boat fares, nightclub entrances, sightseeing, and car rental. Children half price.

TELEPHONE CODES. We have given telephone codes for all the towns and villages in the hotel and restaurant lists that follow. These codes need only be used when calling from outside the town or village concerned.

HOTELS AND RESTAURANTS. Because of its many tourist attractions and the popularity of its summer holiday resorts, this region is one of Sweden's best equipped from the point of view of hotel accommodations. Remember, too, that resort hotels have advantageous pension rates for stays of three days or longer.

A special hotel package is available at 18 hotels in Malmö daily from June 12 through Aug. 20, over the Christmas and Easter periods, and at weekends only for the rest of the year. Prices per person vary from about SEK 185 to SEK 350 (double occupancy) and the package includes breakfast and the Malmö card (described above). Children under 15 qualify for a 50% rebate, for which they also get breakfast and the Malmö card. The package can be booked through travel agents or direct by telephone (040–34 12 68).

For fine provincial cuisine—salmon and eel dishes are a specialty—in an authentic atmosphere, stop at some of the old country inns for a meal or two. The word for inn is *Gästgivaregård*. Here you often find *Smörgåsbords* with up to 150 dishes, such as pickled herring, shrimp, patés, home-made pies etc. To finish, ask for *spettekaka,* a delicious cake baked with eggs and plenty of sugar. Apart from those restaurants listed below, most of the region's restaurants will be found in the hotels themselves—see the listings.

Ängelholm. *Lilton* (I), Järnvägsgatan 29 (0431–824 00). 15 rooms. Central, near railway station. Breakfast only. AE, MC, V.

Bäckaskog. *Bäckaskogs Slott* (M), (044–532 50). 49 rooms. 12 km. (seven miles) from Kristianstad. Castle from 13th century, formerly a monastery. Unique atmosphere. Bus. Rowboats and bikes for rent. AE, DC, MC, V.

Båstad. *Grand Hotel Skansen* (M), Kyrkogatan 2 (0431–720 50). 52 rooms. Restaurant, sauna, rooms for disabled and those suffering from allergies. AE, DC, MC, V. *Hotel Pension Enehall* (I) (0431–750 15). 40 rooms. Pension. Restaurant, cafeteria. Sauna, outdoor pool nearby, 400 meters (440 yards) to beach. AE, DC, MC, V.

Borgholm. (On the island of **Öland**). *Halltorps Gästiveri* (Inn) (M), nine km. (five miles) south of Borgholm (0485–552 50). 10 rooms. Manor house from 17th century. Pension. Known for excellent food. Open May to Sept. and Dec. AE, DC, MC, V.

Eksjö. *Stadshotellet* (M), Stora Torget 5 (0381–130 20). 36 rooms. Central, 500 meters (546 yards) from railway station. Pension, restaurant, dancing. Also vegetarian food. Street with best-preserved 17th-century low wooden houses in the country. AE, DC, MC, V.
Youth Hostel. At Eksjö Museum, Österlånggatan 31 (0381–119 91). 50 beds. Central. Open year-round.

Gränna. *Scandic Hotel Gyllene Uttern* (M), (0390–108 00). 53 rooms. Attractive modern-style manor house with its own wedding chapel and baronial-style dining room. AE, DC, MC, V.

Helsingborg. *Grand Hotel* (E), Stortorget 8 (042–12 01 70). 130 rooms. Air terminal, 200 meters (220 yards) to railway and ferries to Denmark. Restaurant in English style, cocktail bar, sauna. AE, DC, MC, V. *Mollberg* (E), Stortorget 18 (042–12 02 70). 100 rooms. One of the oldest hotels in Sweden, recently modernized and expanded. Near ferry dock and railroad station. Piano bar; rooms for handicapped and allergy sufferers. AE, DC, MC, V.

Youth Hostel. *Villa Thalassa,* Dag Hammarskjöldsväg (042–11 03 84). 145 beds. Wonderful view of the sea. Open year-round except Christmas/New Year.

Höör. *Frostavallen* (I), (0413–220 60). 77 rooms. Cafeteria. Solarium. Canoes, bikes for rent.

Kalmar. *Slottshotellet* (E), Slottsvägen 7 (0480–882 60). 35 rooms. Elegant town house on a quiet street near the park, 500 meters (546 yards) from town center, view of the bay. Sauna. Breakfast only. AE, DC, MC, V. *Stadshotellet* (E), Stortorget 14 (0480–151 80). 140 rooms. Restaurant, sauna, rooms for disabled or allergysufferers. AE, DC, MC, V. *Witt* (E), S. Långgatan 42 (0480–152 50), 112 rooms. Restaurant, cocktail bar, pub, dancing. Sauna, pool, airport bus. AE, DC, MC, V.

Karlshamn. *Scandic* (M), Jannebergsvägen 2 (0454–166 60). 94 rooms. Motor hotel. Restaurant, sauna. AE, DC, MC, V.

Karlskrona. *Statt Hotel* (E), Ronnebygatan 37 (0455–192 50). Central. Restaurant, nightclub. AE, DC, MC, V.

Restaurants. *Krutviken* (M), Wämö, three km. (two miles) from the town center (0455–115 37). In park with a fine view of sea. Fish menu. In winter open 1–6 P.M. only. In summer open in evenings also. Closed Mon. MC, V. *Skeppet* (the Ship) (M), N. Kungsgatan 1 (0455–103 71). Marine atmosphere overlooking the main square. Fish dishes a specialty. Has pub section—*Jollen.* Closed Sat. and Sun. MC, V.

Lund. *Grand* (E), Bantorget 1 (046–11 70 10). 87 rooms. Central. Restaurant, also vegetarian menu. AE, DC, MC, V. *Sparta* (M), Tunavägen 39 (046–12 40 80). 75 rooms. Pension, restaurant, sauna. AE, MC, V.

Malmö. *SAS Royal* (L), Östergatan 10 (040–23 92 00). 221 rooms. Opened Feb. 1988. Centrally located in business and shopping district. Three restaurants. SAS airline check-in desk. AE, DC, MC, V. *Savoy* (L), Norra Vallgatan 62 (040–702 30). 100 rooms. Central. Restaurants, nightclub. AE, DC, MC, V. *Sheraton Malmö Hotel & Towers* (L), Triangeln 2 (040–740 00). 214 rooms. Opened in 1989. Central location near railroad station and airport buses. Casino, health studio, lobby bar in glass-roofed garden. Restaurant and cafeteria. AE, DC, MC, V. *Garden* (E), Baltzarsgatan 20 (040–10 40 00). 173 rooms. Central, in shopping district, close to airport bus. *Noble House* (E), Gustav Adolfstorg 47 (040–10 15 00). 128 rooms. Opened in 1986 in central but quiet location. Restaurant, rooms suitable for handicapped guests. AE, DC, MC, V. *St. Jörgen* (E), Stora Nygatan 35 (040–773 00). 286 rooms. In the heart of Malmö, five or ten minutes walk to airport bus, rail station and harbor. *Tahonga Bar,* self-service salad bar. AE, DC, MC, V. *Skyline* (E), Bisittaregatan (040–803 00). 270 rooms. Luxury accommodations at reasonable cost. Restaurant, sauna. AE, DC, MC, V. *Baltzar* (M), Södergatan 20 (040–720 05). 41 rooms. Central location, on pedestrian shopping street. AE, DC, MC, V. *Plaza* (M), S. Förstadsgatan 30 (040–771 00). 52 rooms. Centrally located. Sauna. AE, DC, MC, V. *Scandic Crown* (M), Amiralsgatan 19 (040–10 07 30). 154 rooms. Central, in same complex as concert hall. Restaurant, sauna, swimming pool, rooms for handicapped guests. AE, DC, MC, V. *Strand* (I), Strandgatan 50 (040–16 20 30). 23 rooms. Quiet, near ferry Limhamn to Dragør. Breakfast. AE, MC.

Restaurants. *Översten* (E), Regementsgatan 52A (040–91 91 00). The tallest building in the area—26 stories above Malmö. Fantastic view with the Danish coast

412 SWEDEN

on the horizon. AE, MC, V. *O'Yes* (E), Börshuset, Skeppsbron 2 (040–10 43 70). Run by top chef Victor Waldenström and named as Sweden's Restaurant of the Year in 1987. Emphasis on unconventional dishes. AE, DC, MC, V. *Pers Krog* (E), Limhamnsvägen 2 (040–70 11). One of the best restaurants in town, renowned for seafood specialties. AE, DC, MC, V. *Kockska Krogen* (E), Frans Suellsgatan 3 (040–703 20). Historic cellar restaurant, part of a building dating back to 1525. AE, DC, MC, V. *Fågel Fenix* (M), Isak Slaktaregatan 6 (040–11 10 59). Excellent vegetarian restaurant. MC. *Falstaff* (M), Baltzarsgatan 25 (040–11 40 09). Steakhouse with sauna on the premises. AE, DC, MC, V. *Rådhuskällaren* (M), Stortorget (040–790 20). Popular establishment in cellars below the City Hall. AE, DC, MC, V. *Centralens* (I), at central railway station (040–766 80). Good value for money, with popular salad buffet and special dish of the day. AE, DC, MC, V.

Youth Hostel. *Södergården,* Backavägen 18 (040–822 20). 174 beds. Bus 36 from Central Station to "Vandrarhemmet." Sauna. Open Feb. through Nov.

Camping. *Sibbarp,* Strandgatan (040–34 26 50). Located on the coast near the city. Open year-round.

Mörrum. *Walhalla* (E), Stationsvägen 24 (0454–500 44). 28 rooms. Three km. (two miles) to beach on the Baltic. Pension, restaurant. Salmon fishing. AE, MC, V.

Ronneby. *Ronneby Brunn* (M) (0457–127 50). 299 rooms. Pension, restaurant, dancing, nightclub. Sauna, heated outdoor pool in summer, tennis, minigolf. Airport bus. AE, DC, MC, V.

Toftaholm. *Toftaholm Herrgårdshotel* (M), (0370–440 55). 40 rooms. On the shore of Lake Vidöstern. Manor house dating back to 14th century, claimed to have a resident ghost. Excellent home cooking. AE, DC, MC, V.

Växjö. *Royal Corner* (E), Liedbergsgatan 11 (0470–100 00). 165 rooms. Restaurant, piano-bar, pool, sauna. Free parking. *Statt* (E), Kungsgatan 6 (0470–134 00). 130 rooms. Restaurant, dancing, *Gyllene Oxen Pub, Lucky Swede Bar,* honoring a golddigger in the Klondike. Whirlpool, sauna, solarium. Airport bus. 100 meters (110 yards) to rail station. AE, DC, MC, V.

Youth Hostel. *Evedal,* three km. (two miles) from road 23, six km. (four miles) northeast of Växjö (0470–630 70). 57 beds. Open year-round (Oct. through Apr. groups only). Direct bus to Växjö in summer.

Ystad. *Ystads Saltsjöbad* (Salt-Sea Bath) (E) (0411–136 30). 108 rooms. On the beach, one km. (two-thirds of a mile) from city center. Restaurant, dancing. Sauna, tennis, indoor pool; golf nearby. AE, DC, MC, V.

Camping

There are 125 camping sites in this area. Some are: **Hörby,** Ringsjöstrand (0415–105 67). 7 cabins. At Lake Ringsjön. Open all year; **Kalmar,** *Stenső Camping.* two km. (1.2 miles) south of Kalmar (0480–207 33). 15 cabins. Camping site open June through Aug.; **Kosta,** *Kosta Camping,* 500 meters (550 yards) southeast of Kosta Glassworks (0478–505 17). 4 cabins; **Kristianstad,** *Charlottsborgs Camping,* three km. (1.8 miles) west of town center (044–11 07 67). 9 beds. **Urshult,** *Urshults Camping,* Rävabacken (0477–202 43). At Lake Åsnen, two km. (1.2 miles) north or Urshult. 9 cabins. Open June through Aug.

HOW TO GET AROUND. By car. If you are driving from Stockholm and Helsingborg is your goal, follow Highway E4 all the way (584 km. or 363 miles). From there, Highway E6 leads into Malmö. A more scenic route to Malmö from Stockholm follows Highway E4 to Norrköping, then swings off on the mainly coastal Highway 15.

By bus and train. From Stockholm, Malmö is seven hours by train, and 10¼ hours by bus. Helsingborg is seven hours by train and nine hours by bus. There are bus services on all major roads. The express bus from Malmö to Kalmar along scenic Highway E66 takes seven hours. There is a bus service from Copenhagen International Airport to Malmö Central Station, crossing on the Dragør-Limhamn ferry, which operates almost hourly throughout the day. There is also an inter-city bus service (Line 999) which operates at frequent intervals from Copenhagen's main railway station via the Dragør-Limhamn ferry to Malmö and Lund.

By air. Malmö has its own airport at Sturup with direct services from other cities in Sweden and international flights from London, but its main airport is really Copenhagen, to which it is connected by a hovercraft service run by SAS Scandinavian Airlines. Passengers bound for Malmö check in at Copenhagen Airport in the normal way and the hovercraft runs from a ramp on the airport perimeter across the Öresund channel into Malmö harbor, where SAS has its own terminal.

By boat. Southern Sweden is linked with Denmark by boat via: Malmö to Copenhagen (1½ hours), Limhamn to Dragør (55 minutes), Helsingborg to Helsingør (25 minutes), Varberg to Grenå (4 hours), Helsingborg to Grenå (3½ hours) and Gothenburg to Frederikshavn (3¼ hours). Traffic is heavy on all runs and the ferries carry cars and, in some cases, international trains. A hydrofoil operates between Malmö and Copenhagen, with regular trips taking only 45 minutes. Catamaran-hovercraft services for passengers only have been introduced by Scanjet Ferries from Copenhagen to Malmö (journey time 30 minutes), Helsingborg (45 minutes), and Gothenburg (3 hours).

TOURS. There are daily sightseeing tours by bus leaving from Gustav Adolfs Torg in Malmö at 11 A.M. and 1 P.M. from June to Aug. Sightseeing by boat through the canals and in the harbor can be enjoyed daily from May through Aug. Tours leave from the quay opposite the Central Station in Malmö every hour between 10 A.M. and 5 P.M.

From May through Aug. there are a number of day tours to the castles, manor houses and churches in Skåne. Call at the Malmö tourist office for details.

PLACES TO VISIT. Apart from the castles, châteaux and manor houses of Skåne and Sweden's "Château Country," there are many other attractions in this region. When visiting Malmö, remember the **Malmö card,** which offers free bus transport, free admission to the museums and discounts on restaurants, sightseeing, souvenirs etc. It costs about SEK 70 for three days and SEK 100 for a week. Children half price.

Bosjökloster. 45 km. (28 miles) from Malmö on Lake Ringsjön. Founded in 1080 as Benedictine convent. Garden, exhibitions. Open May to Oct., daily 9–5.30 (0413–250 48).

Helsingborg. Fredriksdals Open-Air Museum and Botanical Garden—18th-century mansion and farmhouses and buildings from Skåne province. Open May through Sept., 10–6.

Kärnan tower (Medieval Keep). View from the ramparts of city and Danish coast. Open May through Aug., daily 9–8.

Rådhuset (Town Hall). Including tourist office.

Slottshagen (Castle Park). Beautiful park within the ramparts. Also the Tosengården with thousands of roses and a fine view of the strait.

Sofiero. A former royal summer residence. Five km. (three miles) north of Helsingborg. Beautiful garden. View of the straits. Open May through Aug., 10–6.

Höör. Frostavallen, 60 km (37 miles) from Malmö or Helsingborg, is a recreation center, hotel, youth hostel, park and zoo with Nordic animals. Also a Stone-Age village where you can stay overnight. Hides and skins are for rent, and you prepare your own Stone-Age meals. Experience how people lived 8,000 years ago. Open all year round (0413–220 60).

Kalmar. Kalmar Castle. Chapel and museum. Museum has archeological finds, weapons, furniture etc. and exhibits from the warship *Kronan.* Open May through Sept., Mon. to Sat. 10–4, with conducted tours every hour between mid-June and mid-Aug.

Karlskrona. Varvsmuseet (Marine Museum). Amiralitetsslätten. Galleon figureheads, ship models, 300 years of marine history. Open daily 12–4, (July, 12–8).

Kristianstad. Bäckaskog Castle. 10 km. (six miles) east of Kristianstad. Swedish King Charles XV's summer residence. Chapel, gardens. Open May 15 to Aug., 10–4.

Film Museum. Östra Storgatan 53. Old films (shown on request) and film equipment. Open Tues. to Fri. and Sun. 1–4; closed Mon. and Sat. Admission free.

Landskrona. Ängelholm House. Stora Norregatan 80. Built 1628, the oldest building in Landskrona.

Borstahusen. A genuine village with small houses and alleyways.

Landskrona Museum. At Slottsgatan. European and Swedish art, workshops and shops. Also prehistoric section where you can try out primitive tools. Open daily 1–5. Admission free.

Weilbullsholms flower nurseries. At southern entry to city. Open daily for inspection.

The island of Ven. Half-hour boat trip—flowers, foundations of a castle and a reconstructed observatory called **Stjärneborg** (Star Castle).

Lund. Kulturen Museet (Museum of Cultural History). Tegnérsplatsen. Open-air museum with 30 buildings from South Sweden. Exhibits of ceramics, glass, textiles, silver, weapons, and toys. Open daily 12–6.

Malmö. Malmö Museum. Malmöhusvägen in the **Malmöhus Castle,** dating from 1542. Museum shows art, natural history, history of Malmö. Outside the castle is a military museum, the **Kommendanthuset,** and the **Technical** and **Marine Museums.** Open Tues. to Sat. 12–4; Thurs. also 5–9; Sun. 12–4.30; closed Mon., except June through Aug.

Öland. Eketorp—reconstructed fortified village with small museum. 45 km. (28 miles) south of Öland Bridge near Gräsgård. Open May through Sept.; June 6 to Aug. 16, 9–6, otherwise 9–5. Guided tours; call 0485–620 23 for current times. Regular buses from Färjestaden.

Växjö. Småland Museum, behind railway station. Large collection of glass and tools, weapons, coins, 18th- and 19th-century art. Open Mon. to Fri. 9–4, Sat. 11–3, Sun 1–5.

Utvandrarnas Hus (the Emigrant Institute). Adjoining the museum (0470–201 20). Archives (research by appointment only). Permanent exhibition of "Dream of America"—the emigration of more than one million Swedes to the New World. Minnesota Day celebrated here each year on the second Sunday in Aug. Opening times as for Småland Museum, above.

Tours of Lake Helga, on the small steamer *Thor* (built 1887), depart from Kronoberg Castle. Call the tourist office for timetable.

SPORTS. There are fine sandy beaches at Falsterbo, Mölle, Tylösand, Ängelholm, Malen, Mellbystrand Skrea, Ystad, Åhus, and on the isle of Öland. Most resort hotels have **tennis** courts, and **golf** may be played at several places. 18-hole courses at Båstad, Falsterbo, Kalmar, Landskrona, Lund and Mölle.

Good salmon **fishing** in the Mörrum River, with the season from April-May until September 30. It is advisable to order fishing licenses in advance if you come during April or May. Write Hotel Walhalla, Mörrum. Sea-fishing tours are arranged from Helsingborg.

There's a good **Horseracing** track near Malmö, at Jägersro, where the Swedish Derby, usually about mid July, draws a big, international crowd.

There are many **biking** and **hiking** trails in the region.

GOTHENBURG AND THE WEST COAST

Gateway to Northern Europe

It is only proper to approach Gothenburg (or Göteborg) from the sea, for at heart it is a product of the oceans and the ships that sail them. Shipping, shipbuilding and fishing set their stamp on this region long before the age of the Vikings. You never get far from the maritime influence, and the harbor bustles (as does the city's ultra-modern airport, Landvetter).

A classic example of honesty, modesty and frankness once was found in a shipping company's guide to Gothenburg. "Gothenburg is by no means a Tourist Mecca," it read, "but it has its points." This is to certify that it does have its points, and plenty of them. Actually, Gothenburg is a gateway to the entire world, with regular freight services and frequent passenger connections to all the Seven Seas. If you come to Scandinavia with one of the Danish or Swedish lines—Scandinavian Seaways from England or with Stena Line from Germany or Denmark—Gothenburg is your first Scandinavian port of call. And the city is the ideal place to begin a round trip tour of Scandinavia, since it occupies almost the exact center of a triangle of which the capitals of Stockholm, Oslo, and Copenhagen are the points.

Exploring Gothenburg

An intangible air, perceptible enough almost to be held in your hands, distinguishes Gothenburg from Stockholm. Many attribute it to centuries

of close relations with Great Britain, birthplace of the Anglo-Saxon tradition of freedom. It has even been called "Little London." The residents
are fully conscious of this pronounced attraction westward. Others attribute it to the physical nature of the city, with its broad avenues, its huge,
sprawling harbor, its comparatively great geographical area for a city of
some 430,000 people. Finally, age has something to do with this sensation.
Gothenburg is young, officially born in 1621, when parts of Stockholm's
Old Town looked about as they do now. There is something of a friendly
rivalry between the cities.

A great Swedish king, Gustavus Adolphus, the "Lion of the North,"
gave Gothenburg its charter in 1621. He called in Dutch builders, and
the canals and architecture will show the strength of their influence. The
town soon began to play a part in history. Karl X summoned the parliament to meet there in 1659–60, in Kronhuset, the oldest building extant,
and there his son was crowned Karl XI after Karl X's death. Scotsmen
and Germans had by this time settled in the town in considerable numbers.

As early as 1699 the British community formed an association for mutu-
al support. The influx of Scots and Englishmen continued through the
18th and 19th centuries, and they and their descendants have had a decisive importance in the commercial and cultural development of the city.
Many of the finest old families of Gothenburg have typically English or
Scottish names.

At one time Gothenburg enjoyed a thriving trade with the East Indies,
as evidenced by the old factory building in the Norra Hamngatan, which
now houses the Ethnographical, Archeological, and Historical museums.
However, the city's first great commercial impetus resulted from Napoleon's continental blockade in 1806, when its port became the principal
depot of British trade with northern Europe.

The opening of the Trollhätte Canal shortly after 1800, connecting
Gothenburg by water with huge Lake Vänern and the rich forest and iron
products of the region around the lake, offered a new commercial stimulus.
Before the middle of the century the first shipbuilding yard was turning
out sailing vessels, and industrialization was under way. Today Gothenburg is the headquarters of many industries, including the world-wide
SKF ballbearing empire; AB Volvo, Scandinavia's largest maker of automobiles; hyper-modern shipyards; and the Hasselblad camera factory.
About one third of the population gets its living from industry. Incidentally, Gothenburg is one of the few remaining cities with streetcars.

Landvetter Airport provides West Sweden with access to very large aircraft with direct links to other countries. This airport has a capacity that
will meet the requirements of the regions for many years. With its location
close to Highway 40, Landvetter is easy to reach from all the towns in
West Sweden. Signposts marked with the airport symbol clearly show the
way from the roads in the vicinity.

City Highlights

You must really see the harbor to appreciate it. There are 22 kilometers
(14 miles) of quays, 200 cranes that sometimes seem to rise up like steel
forests, and the warehouse and customs sheds cover more than 1½ million
square feet. Gothenburg is the home port of 40 per cent of the Swedish
merchant fleet—better than 4 million tons of shipping—and handles a
third of the country's imports and a quarter of the exports. During the

summer there are boat tours that take you around the harbor and entrance, as well as through the city's network of canals.

Skandiahamnen is the new port for container and roll-on/roll-off traffic. Here you find the terminals of Scandinavian Seaways, Atlantic Container Line and other shipping companies.

Gothenburg's Fish Harbor, one of the largest in Scandinavia, opened in 1910. Its early morning fish auction, at which wholesalers publicly bid for cod, catfish, sole, herring, and occasionally even whale, has become something of a tourist attraction.

Trädgårdsföreningen, site of the magnificent gardens of the horticultural society, begins right across the square from the Central Station. The Palm House, erected in 1878 and completely restored recently, is an impressive example of what you can grow in a northern climate with the help of heat and glass. The new Rosarium, inaugurated in 1987, has some 10,000 roses of 3,500 different species from all over the world.

Götaplatsen is an impressive square which might be described as the cultural heart of Gothenburg. In the center is the famed "Poseidon" fountain by Milles. The columned building which rises up above the broad steps at the end of the square—and dominates it—is the Art Gallery. As you face the art museum, the building on the left is the modern City Theater, the one on the right the Concert Hall. If you climb the steps leading up to the museum, you get a fine view of the wide boulevard Kungsportsavenyen, with the profile of downtown Gothenburg in the distance. This square is notable as an expression of modern architecture, as impressive as older and better-known counterparts elsewhere in Europe.

Liseberg Amusement Park, Sweden's most popular visitor attraction, is only a few minutes from downtown by streetcar or taxi, a walk of only 15 minutes or so from the Park Avenue Hotel. This is one of the best, neatest, and best-run amusement parks in existence—partly because of beautiful gardens that you don't ordinarily find in this kind of establishment. There are several restaurants, open-air concerts, variety theater, and wide range of the usual carnival attractions.

Among other sights are the Sailor's Tower, near the Maritime Museum, a tall monument to seamen who lost their lives in World War I, from which you have an excellent view of the harbor and city; Masthugget Church, a striking modern edifice on an impressive site; Guldheden, a housing development with a pleasant central square; and the huge natural park, Slottsskogen, as well as the new Maritime Center near the city center.

There are several good museums with fine, often unique, collections. Anyone interested in shipping should by all means see the Maritime Museum between Karl Johansgatan and route E3.

Gothenburg Environs

In the neighboring industrial town of Mölndal, only a short distance away, is the delightful 18th-century mansion of Gunnebo. It is a good example of architecture and landscaping of a period that combined the best of French and English influence. The house was designed by C. W. Carlberg, who also designed the furniture in 1796. John Hall, a merchant of British origin, was the first owner of Gunnebo. It is now the property of Mölndal community. During the summer visitors are shown around in the early afternoon; there are hourly buses to Mölndal and Gunnebo from Nils Ericsonsplatsen (behind the Central Station).

Särö, a bit farther south, by bus, is known for its thriving foliage and oak trees, which grow right at the edge of the sea. On the route to Särö is the beautifully situated Hovås golf course.

To the east of Gothenburg is a large, hilly forest-and-lake area. Visit the 19th-century Nääs manor house on route E3 (32 kilometers or 20 miles from Gothenburg; hourly tours in the summer). In the outbuildings there are stables, restaurant, coffee shop and several exhibition shops selling traditional Swedish products—textiles, wood, furniture, antiques and souvenirs.

Nearby is the medieval Öijared chapel, in the middle of a 45-hole golf course. Further northeast is the Anten-Gräfsnäs vintage Railway.

The West Coast

The coast north of Gothenburg (Bohuslän province) is the beginning of fjord country, with its dozens of fishing villages and thousands of islands. Forty minutes from Gothenburg by car lies the former fishing village of Stenungsund, today Sweden's busy petrochemical center. Just outside, the mighty Tjörn bridges span the fjord—the breathtaking view will give you a strong incentive to explore.

North and slightly west of Gothenburg stretches the province of Bohuslän, a coastal and island summer playground among the most popular in Sweden—a part of the famed west coast. It was more or less discovered by the royal family. Prince Vilhelm, brother of the late king, wrote with much great feeling about Bohuslän, beginning with a visit there in the '90s with his father, King Gustav V. "So the ocean, the ships, and the rocky islands form the trinity that characterizes Bohuslän," Vilhelm writes. "A name that sounds good to all seafaring folk, for it bespeaks a coast peopled by strong men and sturdy objects, an archipelago formed of gneiss and granite and water which eternally stretches foamy arms after life."

How to Explore the Area

Proceeding north from Gothenburg, you come to Kungälv, which was a commercial center before the year 1000. It is overlooked by a hugh medieval stronghold, Bohus Fortress, built by the Norwegians in 1308. Kungälv is a sea of flowers during apple blossom time.

The island city of Marstrand was also built by the Norwegians, some time during the 13th century. This was the favorite west coast summer resort of King Oskar II, who died in 1907, and the resort hotel emits something of a turn-of-the-century air. It is still a popular summer resort. There is an interesting 17th-century fortress overlooking the city—Carlsten—used as a prison during the 18th and 19th centuries. The church is from the 15th century.

Lysekil is a popular and reasonably typical example of the villages along the west coast which have become Meccas for summer vacationers. It rests on the mouth of a long fjord, protected from sea and wind by cliffs.

On the other side of the fjord is Fiskebäckskil, another popular summering place. Farther inland, roughly northeast, is the city of Uddevalla, the biggest municipality in this region (population, over 46,000). Uddevalla as a city leaves much to be desired in its appeal to the eye, but is a good overnight halt. The principal industries are textiles, paper, wood processing, and shipbuilding.

Along the coast north of Lysekil are a whole row of villages familiar to west coast vacationers and to the painters and sailors who haunt this region in the summer time—Smögen (a singularly picturesque fishing village), Bovallstrand, Fjällbacka, Grebbestad, and many more. At the very north end of the province, just below the border to Norway, is Strömstad, the northern anchor of the Bohuslän vacation region, so to speak. The city has old traditions both as a port and military objective and as a summer resort. In addition, Strömstad offers you interesting excursions. The best from a historical point of view is to Fredriksten Fortress, just over the Norwegian border at Halden, where King Charles XII fell in 1718. This whole region was bitterly contested for centuries in the Scandinavian wars.

Just 45 minutes by boat from Strömstad are the Koster Islands, a holiday paradise for people who like boating, fishing and swimming in a car-free environment.

The west coast area of Sweden actually stretches about 400 kilometers (250 miles) south from the Norwegian border as far as Laholm. Going south from Gothenburg, you reach the town of Kungsbacka, whose square is the site of a colorful market on the first Thursday of every month. Nearby is Fjärås Bräcka, where an ice-age sand ridge divides Lake Lygnern from the sea. From the top there is a splendid view over this coastal area, as well as over the lake, which resembles those of middle or north Sweden. On the slopes are Iron Age and Viking graves. Also to be found in Fjärås are the largest horse-radish plantations in the country!

Only a few minutes away lies the impressive turn-of-the century Tjolö-holm Palace, now open to the public year-round—hourly tours every day during summer and on weekends in spring and fall—and there is also a "stable" cafeteria, a horse carriage museum, and a park. A few kilometers east of Tjolöholm is the tiny, picturesque 18th-century village of Äskhult, now an open-air museum.

Also nearby are Lerkil and Gottskär on the Onsala Peninsula, the scene of plenty of activity in the small-craft harbors. You might be able to spot some seals on skerries nearby.

South again is Varberg, an industrial center, port and holiday resort. It's only five minutes' walk from the city center to the nearest beach here. The old fortress has sections which date from the 13th century and was once the most formidable stronghold in Europe. Today it contains a unique youth hostel and a museum with the world's only known fully dressed medieval body (the Bocksten Man). Daily fishing tours are offered from Varberg with the prospect of catches of dogfish, cod and mackerel. The Getterön Reserve for migratory birds can boast more species than most similar reserves in Sweden.

Further south is the little town of Falkenberg, known for its salmon fishing and popular among vacationers. The outstanding sight is the stately bridge over the Ätran River, which dates from 1756. The Törngren Pottery, dating from 1789, is also worth a visit.

Halmstad is the center of this tourist region; a provincial capital with some 76,000 inhabitants. The town is about 600 years old and the oldest building is the church, a 14th-century Gothic structure. Miniland, near Halmstad, shows Sweden modelled in miniature (scale 1:25). Hallandsgården in Halmstad is an open-air museum with old buildings, including a school, mill and farm-house.

Other popular resorts nearby are Tylösand, Laxvik and Steninge.

PRACTICAL INFORMATION FOR

GOTHENBURG AND THE WEST COAST

TOURIST INFORMATION. The tourist office in Gothenburg has information about **Gothenburg** and all the attractions on the West Coast as far as the Norwegian border. The address is Basargatan 10 (031–10 07 40). Open daily 9–6 during the summer; Mon. to Sat. only Sept. to Apr. There is also a tourist office in the Nordstan shopping center, open year-round Mon. to Fri. 9.30–6, Sat. 9.30–3; closed Sun.

Other regional tourist offices are at: **Falkenberg,** Sandgatan-Holgersgatan (0346–174 10); **Halmstad,** Kajplan (035–10 93 45); **Kungsbacka,** Storgatan 41 (0300–346 19); **Lysekil,** S. Hamngatan 6 (0523–130 50); **Strömstad,** Norra Hamnen (0526–143 64); **Varberg,** Brunnsparken 39 (0340–887 70).

USEFUL ADDRESSES. Gothenburg. *British Consulate,* Nordstan shopping center, Götgatan 15 (031–15 13 27).

TELEPHONE CODES. We have given telephone codes for all the towns and villages in the hotel and restaurant lists that follow. These codes need only be used when calling from outside the town or village concerned.

HOTELS AND RESTAURANTS. Many new hotels have been built in Gothenburg recently, so there should be plenty of choice. If you are without a room, use the room-booking service at the tourist office. A low-cost hotel package is available daily from mid-June through mid-Aug. at 30 hotels in Gothenburg and at weekends only for the rest of the year. Rates per person per night vary from about SEK 210 to SEK 400 (double occupancy) and the package includes breakfast and the Gothenburg card (described below under "How To Get Around"). Reduced prices are available for children under 15 sharing their parents' room. The package is bookable through travel agents.

For the rest of the West Coast, accommodations are in general on the modest side. A few towns draw a more or less fashionable trade, but most of the people who come to the region in summer live in cottages or aboard their sailboats. Many resort hotels offer demi-pension rates (breakfast and dinner) and advantageous pension rates for a stay of three days or more.

The West Coast is dotted with camping sites (more than 75)—most are on beaches and all are up to a good standard. Many also have camping cabins or bungalows for rent.

Bassholmen. Youth Hostel. *Bassholmen,* near Uddevalla (0522–117 87). 38 beds. Open mid-June through mid-Aug. In the archipelago in a nature reserve.

Falkenberg. *Grand* (M), Ågatan 1 (0346–144 50). 54 rooms. Central, 300 meters (330 yards) to railway station. Restaurant, dancing, sauna; three km. (two miles) to outdoor pool. AE, DC, MC, V.

Gothenburg. *Europa* (L), Köpmansgatan 38 (Nordstan), (031–80 12 80). 480 rooms. A few steps from central station, airport bus, and Nordstan shopping center. Restaurants *Newport, Europa Garden,* and *Culinaire;* also *Jonny's Piano Bar.* Private saunas, pool, nightclub. AE, DC, MC, V. *Opalen* (L), Engelbrektsgatan 73 (031–81 03 00). 237 rooms. Smoke-free rooms. Close to *Scandinavium,* the Swedish Trade Fair Center and Liseberg. *Club Opalen* with dancing. Exotic *Tahonga* bar. Sauna. AE, DC, MC, V. *SAS Park Avenue* (L), Kungsportavenyn 36–38 (031–17 65 20). 320 rooms. One of Sweden's finest. Double rooms have balconies. Restau-

422 SWEDEN

rants *Belle Avenue* and *Harlequini*, as well as *Lorensberg* with dancing and floor show. Sauna, pool. SAS airline check-in. AE, DC, MC, V. *Sheraton Göteborg* (L), Södra Hamngatan 59–65 (031–10 16 00). 343 rooms. Central location near railway station. Built round spacious low-rise atrium lobby. Three restaurants, health center with sauna, solarium, swimming pool and gym. Piano-bar, casino and nightclub. AE, DC, MC, V.

Eggers (E), Drottningtorget (031–17 15 70). 77 rooms. Cozy 19th-century building near railway station. AE, DC, MC, V. *Ekoxen* (E), N. Hamngatan 38 (Nordstan), (031–80 50 80). 75 rooms. Very central. Whirlpool, sauna. AE, DC, MC, V. *Gothia* (E), Mässansgatan 24 (031–40 93 00). 300 rooms. View of the city. Near Liseberg and Swedish Trade Fair Center. Restaurant, piano bar on the top floor. Sauna on the 18th floor. Exercise center. AE, DC, MC, V. *Panorama* (E), Eklandagatan 51–53 (031–81 08 80). 340 rooms. Quiet, central location. Restaurant, piano bar. Sauna, pool, free parking. AE, DC, MC, V. *Poseidon* (E), Storgatan 33 (031–10 05 50). 49 rooms. Small and centrally located exclusive hotel in a tastefully renovated 19th-century building. AE, DC, MC, V. *Ramada* (E), Gamla Tingstadsgatan 1 (031–22 24 20). 121 rooms. 5 mins. from city center by car. Pool. AE, DC, MC, V. *Riverton* (E), Stora Badhusgatan 26 (031–10 12 00). 190 rooms. Restaurant, sauna, near Stena Line terminal. AE, DC, MC, V. *Rubinen* (E), Kungsportsavenyn 24 (031–81 08 00). 186 rooms. Central, on the main avenue. Restaurant and bistro. Cocktail bar and tearoom. AE, DC, MC, V. *Scandic Crown* (E), Polhemsplatsen 3 (031–80 09 00). 320 rooms (95 non-smoking). Central location near railroad station. Restaurants, sauna. AE, DC, MC, V. *Scandinavia* (E), Kustgatan 10 (031–42 70 00). 323 rooms near the Älvsborg bridge with a view of the harbor. Close to the ferry terminal for Germany. Restaurant *Oscar IV,* dancing. Cocktail bar *Langunen,* at poolside. Free garage. AE, DC, MC, V. *Windsor* (E), Kungsportsavenyn 6 (031–17 65 40). 91 rooms. Secluded British atmosphere, best location. Popular cocktail bar, restaurant. AE, DC, MC, V. *Victor's* (E), Skeppsbroplatsen 1 (031–17 41 80). 50 rooms. Most exclusive. Restaurant, bar and sauna. AE, DC, MC, V.

Carl Johan (M), Karl Johnsgatan 66–70 (031–42 00 20). 153 rooms. Close to ferries to Germany. Restaurant. AE, DC, MC, V. *Liseberg Heden* (M), Sten Sturegatan (031–20 02 80). 160 rooms. Central location near Liseberg amusement park. AE, DC, MC, V. *Lorensberg* (M), Berzeligatan 15 (031–81 06 00). 120 rooms. In the heart of the cultural center close to the *Scandinavium* arena and the Swedish Trade Fair Center. Breakfast only. AE, MC, V. *Novotel* (M), Klippan 1 (031–14 90 00). 150 rooms. Riverside location near the Älvsborg bridge and ferry terminals. Rooms for disabled travelers and allergy suffers. AE, DC, MC, V. *Ritz* (M), Burggrevegatan 25 (031–20 00 80). 100 rooms. Central, no restaurant. Run by Salvation Army. AE, DC, MC, V. *Tre Kronor* (Three Crowns) (M), N. Kustbanegatan 15 (031–80 15 00). 172 rooms. Close to the Villevi sports stadium. Restaurant, nightclub, sauna, heated garage. AE, DC, MC, V. *Vasa* (M), Viktoriagatan 6 (031–17 36 30). 44 rooms. Central, breakfast only. Buffet, sauna, solarium. AE, DC, MC, V.

Maria Eriksons Privata Rumspensionat (I), Chalmersgatan 27A (031–20 70 30). 9 rooms. No credit cards. *Kungsport* (I), Karl Gustavsgatan 21 (031–13 52 36). 6 rooms. No credit cards. *Royal* (I), Drottninggatan 67 (031–80 61 00). 80 rooms. Central. The oldest hotel in Gothenburg, refurbished in 1988. Has charm and atmosphere. On shopping street. Breakfast only. AE, DC, MC, V.

Restaurants. *Fiskekrogen* (E), Lilla Torget 1 (031–11 21 84). 30 fish dishes to choose from. Excellent for lunch. AE, DC, MC, V. *Gamle Port* (E), Östra Larmgatan 18 (031–11 07 02). Central. Fine atmosphere. Pub, nightclub. AE, DC, MC, V. *Johanna* (E), Södra Hamngatan 47 (031–11 22 50). One of the best restaurants in Sweden; French and Swedish cuisine. Closed Sun. AE, DC, MC, V. *Räkan* (the Shrimp), (E), Lorensbergsgatan 16, behind Hotel Rubinen (031–16 98 39). Direct your order to your table in small radio-controlled fishing-boats. You can also have your snapps arrive by boat. AE, DC, MC, V.

Bräutigams (M), Østra Hamngatan-Kungsgatan (031–13 60 46). Traditional *café*. Home-made pastries, sandwiches, salad bar. Also hot dishes. AE, DC, MC,

V. *Sjömagasinet* (M), Klippans Kulturreservat (031–24 65 10). Harbor location in the 200-year-old East India Company warehouse. Seafood specialties. AE, DC, MC, V. *Weise* (M), Drottninggatan 23 (031–13 14 02). A favorite meeting place for artists and poets at the turn of the century. Specializes in typical Swedish dishes like pork with brown beans. Check opening times. AE, DC, MC, V. *White Corner* (M), Vasagatan 43 (031–81 28 10). Pub in English style. Steakhouse, cafeteria, music. Open late. AE, DC, MC, V.

Annorlunda (I), Lilla Korsgatan 2 (031–13 80 26). The oldest vegetarian restaurant in Gothenburg. Open until 7 P.M. No credit cards.

In the N.K. department store there are three (M) restaurants: a café and lunch restaurant on the fourth floor and a vegetarian lunch restaurant on the ground floor. All AE, DC, MC, V.

Liseberg, the amusement park, has many excellent restaurants. You can dine in the open and watch lighted fountains and outdoor performances of various kinds. Some restaurants are open only from April to September. Worth a visit are: *Liebergs Restaurant* (M), (031–83 62 72). Classical restaurant, dancing. *Wärdshuset* (the Inn) (031–83 62 77). Includes English pub in 18th-century milieu. *Tyrolen* (031–83 62 82). A sing-along place with Tyrolean music every night except Mondays.

Youth Hostels. *Ostkupan,* Mejerigatan 2 (031–40 10 50). 219 beds. 3 km. (two miles) from city center. Bus 64 from Central Station or tram 5 to St. Sigfridsplan and then bus 62. 30 minutes' walk to Liseberg. Breakfast service, gymnasium, sauna, launderette, T.V. room. Open summer only. *Torrekulla Turiststation,* Kållered (031–95 14 95). 115 beds plus 30 in annex. Open year-round except Christmas/New Year. *Partille Vandrarhem,* åstebo, Partille (031–44 61 63). 140 beds. Open year-round except Christmas/New Year.

Camping. *Kärralund* (031–25 27 61). Three-star site, open year-round. Camping cottages available. Two pleasant sites on the coast, both open summer only, are *Askim* (031–28 62 61) and *Lilleby* (031–56 08 67).

Grebbestad. *Tanum Strand* (E), (0525–190 00). Newly-build resort hotel with a seaside location in a complex that also includes self-catering chalets and a youth hostel. Restaurant, swimming pool. AE, DC, MC, V.

Halmstad. *Grand* (E), Stationsgatan 44 (035–11 91 40). 120 rooms. Near bus and railway station, close to beaches. Restaurant, sauna. AE, MC, V.

Kungsbacka. *Halland* (M), Storgatan 35 (0300–115 30). 65 rooms. Restaurant *Mistal,* dancing, cocktail bar. AE, MC.

Restaurant. *Leksandsgården* (M), Gottskärsvägen, Onsala (0300–607 05). Ten km. (six miles) from Kungsbacka. Rustic old upper-class milieu. Specialty fish dishes. *Smörgåsbord* Sundays. AE, DC, MC, V.

Kungälv. *Fars Hatt* (M) (0303–109 70). 130 rooms. An inn here since 1684. Restaurant, dancing, sauna, heated outdoor pool. AE, DC, MC, V.

Youth Hostel. Fästningsholmen 2 (0303–189 00). 50 beds. Bus service to Gothenburg. *Båtellet,* Marstrand (0303–600 10). 98 beds. Open year-round.

Lysekil. *Fridhem* (I), Turistgatan 13 (0523–141 20). 18 rooms. On the sea, 500 meters (546 yards) from center and bus. Breakfast only. MC, V. *Lysekil* (M), Rosvikstorget 1 (0523–118 60). 50 rooms. Central, seaview. Restaurant, nightclub. *Nautic.* AE, DC, MC, V.

Smögen. *Havsbadet* (I), (0523–310 35). 25 rooms. 50 meters (164 ft.) from the sea with expensive view. Family-run hotel, restaurant, dancing. Open May through mid-Sept. AE, DC, MC, V.

Strömstad. *Laholmen* (M), opposite Societetsparken (0526–124 00). 98 rooms. Restaurant, dancing. AE, MC, V.

Youth Hostel. At Norra Kyrkogatan 12 (0526–101 93). 75 beds. Open mid-May to early Sept.

Tanumshede. *Tanums Gestgifveri* (Inn) (M), at bus stop 2.5 km. (1½ miles) east of railway station (0525–290 10). 29 rooms. The inn has been in continuous operation since 1663. Bridal suite with circular bathtub, excellent food. Famous rock carvings nearby. AE, DC, MC, V.

Tylösand. *Tylösand* (L), on the sea eight km. (five miles) from Halmstad (035–30 500). 230 rooms. Restaurant, dancing and nightclub in summer. Sauna, indoor saltwater pool. 200 meters (about 220 yards) to Sweden's most popular golfcourse (36 holes). Open all year. AE, DC, MC, V.

Uddevalla. *Bohusgården* (M), on route E6 with panoramic view of the fjord, two km. (1.2 miles) south of Uddevalla (0522–364 20). 115 rooms. Sauna, heated outdoor pool, golf nearby. MC. *Carlia* (M), Norra Drottninggatan 22 (0522–141 40). 57 rooms. Central. Piano bar, dancing. AE, MC, V.

Varberg. *Statt* (M), Kungsgatan 24 (0340–161 00). 126 rooms. 500 meters (546 yards) to beach. Restaurant, dancing, sauna. AE, MC, V.
Youth Hostel. In the fortress (0340–887 88). 101 beds. Open June through Aug. Spend a night in a guaranteed genuine prison environment.

HOW TO GET AROUND. The Gothenburg card "Göteborgskortet" is your personal key to the attractions of Gothenburg. It gives you free travel on trams and buses, sightseeing by bus and boat, entrance to all museums and the Liseberg amusement park, free trips to Fredrikshavn, Denmark and much more. The price in 1989 was SEK 70 for 24 hours, SEK 120 for 48 hours, SEK 165 for 72 hours, and SEK 200 for 96 hours. Cards for children under 15 are cheaper at SEK 35 for 24 hours, SeK 65 for 48 hours, SEK 90 for 72 hours, and SEK 110 for 96 hours. The card is obtainable at tourist offices, camping sites and Pressbyrån newspaper kiosks.

The minimum fare on a tram or bus is SEK 9. Discount coupons are available. A guided tour by bus will cost you SEK 40 for 50 minutes and SEK 65 for a longer trip.

TOURS. Regular 55-minute sightseeing tours by bus which depart from the Tourist Office at Basargatan 10 (031–10 07 40) give you a good introduction to the city. Don't miss a trip on one of the famous flat-bottomed "Paddan" sightseeing boats which depart from a quay opposite the Tourist Office on a 55-minute tour through the canals and out into the harbor.

There are many passenger boats going along the coast and from the mainland to the islands. There are also boat packages, which will give you an opportunity to get to know the waterways as well as many boat excursions from Strömstad to Norway, traveling under the Svinesund bridge.

PLACES TO VISIT. Gothenburg. Most museums in Gothenburg are open Mon. to Sat. 12–4, Sun. and holidays 11–5, Wed. evenings 6–9 except from May through September, but check opening times locally. Museums are generally closed on Mon. from Sept. to Apr.

Älvsborgs Fästning (Elfsborg Fortress). Historic island fortress dating from 1670. Regular boat trips from Stenpiren during the summer, including harbor sightseeing. Café in fortress. The island is also the center for a marine archeological expedition to uncover the remains of one of the East India Company's ships, *Götheborg,* which was wrecked at the harbor entrance in 1745 with a cargo of porcelain and silk.

Botaniska Trädgården (Botanical Garden). South of Slottsskogen Park. Rock garden, herbarium, hot houses. Open 9 A.M. to sunset.

Feskekörka (Fish Church). Rosenlundsgatan. Not a church, in fact, but built like one. It's a fascinating retail fish market where you can buy some of the delicacies trawled up by the local fishermen. Closed Mon. Nearby is the fishing harbor, where there is an auction at 7 A.M. every weekday.

Industri Museet (Industrial Museum). Åvägen 24. Articles produced by industrial concerns in and around Gothenburg; imaginative concepts of the future; exhibit of veteran cars.

Konstmusseet (Art Gallery). Götaplatsen. Excellent collections of Dutch and Italian masters, French Impressionists, Swedish paintings and sculpture from 18th century to the present. Works of Rembrandt, Rubens and Van Gogh. Closed Mon.

Kronhuset (Crown House). A block from the Gothenburg Museum. 17th-century building, cobbled courtyard, shops and cafeteria. A living handicrafts center. Closed Wed. evening.

Liseberg Amusement Park. Sweden's most popular visitor attraction, only a few minutes from downtown Gothenburg. Spectacular rides, beautiful gardens, several restaurants, variety theater, dancing, and many other attractions. Open summer only.

Maritime Center. A new visitor attraction which is being developed in the harbor near the Nordstan shopping complex. It houses a historic collection of ships, including a destroyer, lightship, trawler, and tugboats, and the number of vessels on show is still growing. Open June to Aug., daily 11–5; May and Sept. weekends only.

Ostindiska Huset (East India Company House). Norra Hamngatan 12, close to Gustav Adolfs Square. In this building you can find three museums: the **Arkeologiska Museet** (Archeological Museum). Prehistoric finds from the west coast of Sweden, such as arrow heads, fossils, etc. **Etnografiska Musset** (Ethnographical Museum). Pre-Columbia Peruvian textiles, South American Indian cultural artifacts etc. Also a Lapp section. **Historiska Museet** (the local History Museum). The development of Gothenburg from the earliest times.

Röhsska Museet (Röhss Museum of Arts and Crafts). Vasagatan 37–39, off the main avenue. Displays of Swedish and other furniture, glass, textiles, pewter etc. Oriental collection. Temporary exhibitions from around the world.

Sjöfartsmuseet (Maritime Museum). Stigbergstorget. Devoted to history of merchant shipping, fishing and Swedish Navy. Many unique models. In same building the **Aquarium** shows the aquatic life of Scandinavian coastal waters and lakes. Also the **Sjömanstornet** (Sailor's Tower), a monument to Swedish seamen who lost their lives in World War I. From the top you have an excellent view of the harbor and city. Open summer only.

Tanum. Prehistoric rock carvings. At Vitlycke, 1.5 km. (about a mile) from Tanum Church on E6. Rock-carving museum open May through mid-Aug, as well as reconstructed Bronze Age farm depicting daily life in prehistoric times. Call the tourist bureau (0525–204 00) for opening times.

Varberg. Museum at Varberg Castle. Provincial farm culture, textiles, furniture etc. The medieval Bocksten Man, with authentic clothing from that time. Open June 15 to Aug. 15, daily 10–7; rest of year, Mon. to Fri. 10–4, Sat. and Sun. 12–4.

Samfärdselmuseet (Museum of Communications). Also at the castle. A small museum with old wagons, carts, boats and bicycles. Open June 15 to Aug. 15, daily 10–7.

Varberg Castle. Guided tours every hour on the hour June 15 to Aug. 15, daily 10–5. Meet the guide at Mellersta Valvet. A small fee.

GOTHENBURG PARKS. Slottsskogen, near the Botanical Garden, is a nature reserve with a small zoo and space observatory. Huge park, cafeteria and restaurant. Open daily.

Trädgårdsföreningen, across the square from the Central Station, has acres of magnificent gardens and lawns. See the recently restored Palm House built in 1878 and the new Rosarium with 10,000 roses of 4,000 different species. Outdoor entertainments every week. Restaurant and nightclub.

SPORTS. Swimming. There are more than a dozen swimming spots around Gothenburg and in the environs of Mölndal, Kungälv and Marstrand. Valhallabadet in the city center has an indoor pool in summer, also an outdoor pool.

Golf. 18 holes—at the Gothenburg Golf Club links. Hovås, 15 minutes by bus from Linnéplatsen; also at Delsjön, Albatross and at Öijared, with two 18-hole and one 9-hole courses. Four other courses within 30 minutes by car.

Horseracing and trotting. At Åby, Mölndal, 15 minutes by tram 4.

Football, speedway, skating. At Ullevi, one of the most modern sports stadiums in the world, holding 52,000 spectators.

Athletics. Slottskogsvallen is an outdoor stadium for athletic events located near the Slottskogen park. The Scandinaviun indoor arena is also used for athletics as well as ice hockey, tennis, and horse jumping.

LAND OF LAKES AND FOLKLORE

Home of the Goths

To the north and east of Gothenburg spreads a broad region known as Sweden's lake district, containing thousands of small lakes, medium-sized lakes, and two of the largest lakes in Europe, Vättern and Vänern. The Göta Canal, a blue ribbon stretching across Sweden, combines some of them with rivers and with manmade channels and locks to create a water route from Gothenburg to Stockholm.

This part of the world, ancient home of the Goths, has been settled for some 4,000 years or more, and has a number of historic sights setting exclamation points to its variegated natural beauty. Each of the region's provinces has its own history and traditions and its own distinct character. The lake district is the cradle of Swedish culture and it is here that most Swedes live.

Västergötland

The name of Västergötland means, literally, "the western land of the Goths"—as contrasted with Östergötland, or the eastern land of the same people. The Swedish Goths apparently originated on the continent of Europe. They were thus at least distant cousins of the barbarians who overran the Roman Empire and made the name Goth a synonym for "one who is rude or uncivilized." Some investigators think this region of Sweden was the first home of the Goths. Others believe that Östergötland should have the dubious honor of having spawned all branches of this people. Certain it is, however, that Västergötland was one of the first regions of Sweden to be settled in the wake of retreating glacial ice. Giant sepulchers have been uncovered from the late Stone Age, about 2500 to 2000 B.C., and so-called gallery graves from the age following.

Geographically, the province is rich in coastline, although it can boast only the small but important piece of the ocean which includes Gothenburg. In the northwest it has some 145 kilometers (90 miles) of the shore of Lake Vänern, the largest fresh-water sea in Western Europe, and to the southeast it has Lake Vättern, not so wide but almost as long. The scenery varies from wooded mountains with rare flora, to the fertile plain around the city of Skara.

Lidköping is a city of some 35,000 people at the inner end of a bay of Lake Vänern, on the southeast shore. It is the oldest city on the lake (its charter was granted in 1446), and is proud of the Rörstrand Porcelain works where 18th-century faience and modern ceramics are made side by side. The principal sight in the city proper is the Old Courthouse, once the hunting lodge of Magnus Gabriel de la Gardie, a powerful politician, noble, and controversial figure from the time of Queen Christina, King Karl X, and his son and successor, Karl XI.

De la Gardie was responsible for an even more impressive structure, however—Läckö Castle. It lies about 24 kilometers (15 miles) north of Lidköping on a beautiful road leading to the end of Kålland peninsula. Actually, the oldest parts of the structure date from 1298, when the building was begun as the residence of the bishop of Skara. De la Gardie— during his brief period of power in the 17th century—made it largely what it is today. Few of the 200-plus rooms are now furnished, but don't miss the chapel, the Hall of Knights, and the guest room prepared for King Karl XI. By one of the ironies of history, it was this king who deprived De la Gardie not only of the Läckö earldom but of most of his other holdings, in a great program of reform reducing the property and power of the nobility. Every summer an exhibition is put on at the castle, which is always worth seeing.

Across the bay to the east from Läckö Castle you see the bold outlines of Kinnekulle, one of the unique "table mountains" of this region. To reach it you will have to retrace your route to Lidköping and move up to Kinnekulle on the eastern side of the bay. Kinnekulle (sounds approximately like "chin-eh-culeh") is notable for two things—the view from its top and the millions of years of geological history it lays open to the naked eye. The process was a complicated one—in brief, Kinnekulle and the other table mountains are masses of subsurface igneous rock which forced themselves up through fissures in the sedimentary rock when this country was still one big sea. When the sea went out and time went to work, the less resistant sedimentary rock was eaten away, but the more durable igneous rock—battered and weatherbeaten though it be—still stands. You can study the various layers and get an idea of the whole process at Kinnekulle, besides enjoying the far-flung view.

Moving south and west from Lidköping, you find yourself, after about 24 kilometers (15 miles) of travel through charming country, in the city of Skara, one of the oldest in the country. It was ravaged by war and burned several times, and the only surviving building of any real age is the cathedral. It was founded about the middle of the 11th century, and is probably the second-oldest church in Sweden (oldest—Lund Cathedral). Successive reconstructions and additions have mixed the styles—it was originally Romanesque, changed into Gothic, and its exterior is now largely a product of the last century, in traditional high Gothic style.

Skara became a religious center early in medieval times, and has been an educational center since 1641, when one of the first higher institutions of learning in Sweden was established here. Its history goes back to at least 829. If you are a bird watcher, come early in April to see the migrating cranes perform their mating dance at Hornborgasjön. Also near Skara is a newly built "sommarland" or playland for children and the young-at-heart.

Don't miss Varnhem Abbey Church, 16 kilometers (ten miles) or so east of Skara, perhaps the best preserved monastic building in Sweden. It is, furthermore, the outstanding example of the Cistercian Order's considerable building activities in Sweden (well before the Reformation, of course). The Varnhem Abbey Church, started about 1250, is notable—aside from its age and architecture—as the burial place of four medieval kings, Magnus Gabriel de la Gardie (builder of Läckö Castle), and Birger Jarl, founder of Stockholm.

Östergötland and Lake Vättern

The land of eastern Goths, or Östergötland, is a country between two coasts, as different as an imaginative nature could make them. The western coast is formed by Lake Vättern, a long, narrow inland sea around which nestle some of the nation's most treasured natural and historical sights. The east coast is on the Baltic Sea, comparatively harsh and unyielding, but just as beautiful in a bolder fashion. Between are some of the most fertile farmlands and finest estates in the entire country. Linköping, an ancient religious, administrative, and cultural center, lies in almost the exact middle of this luxuriant plain. Norrköping, sometimes inaccurately called a twin city of Linköping, is a modern industrial center forming the northeast anchor of the province on the Baltic Coast.

This whole area can be divided roughly into two regions for purposes of a visit, the east coast of Lake Vättern, ranging from Jönköping, at the southern tip, north as far as the medieval city of Vadstena, and the Linköping-Norrköping area.

Lake Vättern is the second-largest lake in Sweden, and its surface area of about 1,000 square kilomteres (750 square miles) ranks it among the major inland seas in Europe. It stretches almost due north and south for nearly a hundred miles, but its greatest width is less than 40 kilometers (25 miles). Around its shores, particularly on the eastern side, lived an ancient culture.

If you approach Lake Vättern from Gothenburg or from the south, your starting point will be Jönköping, at the very southernmost tip of the lake. Jönköping's greatest claim to fame is perhaps as the central stronghold of the Swedish Match Company, a great international enterprise. It was here, about 100 years ago, that the history of one of our most commonplace daily necessities, the safety match, began to be written. The Swedish Match Company still operates a factory and makes its headquarters in Jönköping. There is a museum in the old factory illustrating the history of manufacturing safety matches.

Jönköping is an important administrative center—besides serving as the residence of the provincial governor, it is the seat of the Göta Court of

Appeals for southern Sweden. This is the second-oldest appeals court in
Sweden, and you can see its distinguished building, from about 1650, on
the main square. Several of the other buildings, including nearby Christina
Church, are from roughly the same period.

Proceeding now along the lake shore, first east and then north, the first
main town is Huskvarna, only 6.4 kilometers (four miles) away. It is comparatively young and owes its existence principally to an arms factory
moved there shortly before 1700. The factory is still turning out weapons—in newer quarters, of course—and there are other ultramodern
plants turning out sewing machines, sporting rifles, chain saws, moped
motors, refrigerators and deep-freezers. Specially trained guides show visitors round the factory.

Gränna and Historic Visingsö Island

The next main point of interest is Gränna and, if you are spending any
time in this region, you might make this your headquarters. Stay at the
Gyllene Uttern (Golden Otter) Inn, situated about 61 meters (200 feet)
above Vättern, with a magnificent view of the lake and surroundings (including the isle of Visingsö).

Gränna is never more beautiful than when the fruit trees blossom.
You'll see signs along the road advertising *Polkagrisar*— meaning literally
"polka pigs"—a kind of red and white striped peppermint candy for which
Gränna is famous in Sweden. Do try them, fresh from the hands of the
maker.

This little community is the birthplace of a famous polar explorer, and
there are two museums devoted to his memory near the site of the house
where he was born. His name was S. A. André—and he tried to reach
the North Pole by air in 1897. He and two companions started by balloon
from an island near Spitsbergen, and disappeared silently into history.
More than three decades later the remains of the ill-fated expedition were
discovered on White Island, not far from Spitsbergen, and so well-
preserved that not only could the diaries be read but the films could be
developed.

André was buried in Stockholm with great honors, but the record of
his premature tragic death in the cause of science is to be found in the
interesting exhibits of the André and Vitö museums in Gränna. See also
the ruins of the castle built by Count Per M. Brahe some 300 years ago
on road E4. The view is magnificent.

As you look out upon Lake Vättern from Gränna you see a long, narrow
island resting peacefully 6.4 kilometers (four miles) across the water. This
island, Visingsö, played a role in history up to about 1725. Today there
are about a thousand inhabitants, mostly farmers. There is a regular boat
service (several crossings a day) to the island from Gränna, and you can
easily arrange transportation on the island to see the sights. Join one of
the horse-drawn vehicles, which take ten passengers each. The principal
sight is the ruined Visingsborg Castle, built around 1550, and last used
as a prison for captives taken in Charles XII's wars with Russia, before
it burned shortly after 1700. See also the Brahe Church, the 12th-century
Kumlaby Church (with interesting murals), the remains of the tower and
walls of the medieval castle on the southern extremity of the island. It
won't take you long to get around, the whole island is only about 16 kilometers (ten miles) long.

Proceeding north again from Gränna to Vadstena, you come first to Omberg, a national park containing Mount Omberg. There are interesting caves near the shore, but the principal attraction is the broad view from the crown of Mount Omberg, "eight cities, 30 churches, and four provinces."

Ancient Vadstena

Vadstena, the next stop, has all the natural beauties of this region plus unique historical memories. To a great extent Vadstena is the physical reflection of the long and strange life of St. Birgitta (or Bridget), high-born (shortly after 1300) daughter of the royal Folkunga dynasty, mistress of a great estate and mother of eight children, religious mystic, and founder of the Roman Catholic Birgittine Order for women. Birgitta received her instructions from God in the form of visions, which led to the founding of the order in Vadstena. About 1350 she made the strenuous journey to Rome to get the papal blessing and died there in 1373 after a pilgrimage to Jerusalem. Her remains were returned home for burial in the church she designed for Vadstena.

You can easily visit Vadstena on foot. The church is an architectural jewel, begun shortly after 1350 and requiring some 70 years in the building. Aside from the noble Catholic architecture, note particularly the triumphal crucifix, the so-called Lovely Madonna, the Maria triptych at the high altar, the Birgittine triptych showing St. Birgitta presenting her revelations to two cardinals, and—behind the high altar—the lovely coffin containing the recently authenticated relics of the saint and one of her daughters. Also behind the high altar are the confessional stalls once used by the nuns.

Ironically enough, King Gustav Vasa, whose reformation dealt a death-blow to Catholicism in Sweden, chose Vadstena for one of his great fortified castles. The castle is still framed by its protecting moat, but a massive outer wall has disappeared. Construction was begun by King Gustav Vasa about 1540 and the place was used for some time by him and his descendants, but by about 1700 had ceased to be occupied as a royal seat. Note the wedding room (so-called because Gustav Vasa took his 16-year-old bride here about 1550), the small Hall of State, and the chapel.

If you have time, take a look at the interesting old house of Mårten Skinnare (Martin the Tanner) from about 1550, located not far from the church. Theater lovers will be interested in another nearby building, the theater, opened about 1825. It is said to be the oldest provincial theater in the country, and gives you a good idea of what life on the boards was like over a century ago.

Note: Vadstena has acquired quite a reputation within Sweden for its hand-made laces. It will be worth your while at least to have a look at them in one of the shops. Not far from Vadstena are the ruins of the first monastery in Sweden, Alvastra, founded in 1143. Nearby Skänninge is a community at least 1,000 years old, which is mentioned in the text of a 10th-century rune stone. Its Church of Our Lady dates from the late 13th century.

Linköping and Norrköping

Linköping is smaller than Norrköping but vastly more interesting for a pleasure visit. It is an ancient seat of religion and learning, in the middle of a fertile agricultural region. In recent years, a growing industry (most notably aircraft and the SAAB automobile) has forced the idyllic to give ground. Even the cathedral—unhesitatingly called the most beautiful in Sweden by its highly partisan admirers—harmoniously combines both old and new.

You can't miss the cathedral. It is located a block from the central square, where you ought also to study the Milles fountain. (The sculptor Carl Milles was a well-known Swedish-American artist.) The fountain was erected to the memory of the great Folkunga dynasty of the Middle Ages (Birger Jarl, King Magnus Ladulås, St. Birgitta), and shows the progenitor, Folke Filbyter, searching for his lost grandson on a weary horse. Man and beast have traveled together for so long that the sculptor has portrayed them as one living being. The dynasty originated in this area. The oldest part of the cathedral dates from the 12th century, but was really not completed until shortly after 1500, a building period of more than 300 years. The steeple was added only about 75 years ago. Of particular interest are the truimphal crucifix and the baptismal font of the 14th and 15th centuries, the modern altar painting by Henrik Sörensen, and the modern tapestries behind. They are by Märta Afzelius, on a theme from the Creation.

If you have any interest in museums, you ought by all means to see the Provincial and City Museum in Linköping. Examine it as much for the application of modern architectural and display techniques as for the valuable collections.

11 kilometers (seven miles) from Linköping you will find Vreta Cloister, once a thriving establishment of the Cistercian Order. The cloister church, still preserved, was dedicated about 1290 by no less a personage than King Magnus Ladulås himself. The baptismal font of Gotland stone was fashioned before 1300. Several notables, from medieval times on, are buried here. The nunnery itself has fallen into ruins, but you can see fragments of the old walls. The conducted bus excursions from Linköping include both Vreta and some historic manor houses.

Norrköping, fourth-largest city in Sweden with 120,000 inhabitants, is notable principally for its industries—largely textiles and wood products. It is one of the major east coast ports. A comparatively young town, the oldest building, Hedvig's Church, is from about 1675. Incidentally Norrköping and Linköping share a full-time professional theater company of high quality, which is particularly remarkable in terms of the relatively small population of the two municipalities. Norrköping is located on a bay of the Baltic Sea, Bråviken, leading out to the archipelago. At the mouth of the bay is Arkösund, a coastal community popular with summer sailors. Kolmårdens Djurpark, 24 kilometers (15 miles) north of Norrköping on Highway E4, is a large zoo, safari park and dolphinarium with camping site, hotel, bathing beach, swimming pool and cableway. There is a regular boat service from Norrköping to the zoo, and the park is open all year round.

Building the Göta Canal

A bountiful Nature in this country of almost 100,000 lakes and rivers provided much of the route ready-made, but man had to do his full share before it was possible to travel between Stockholm and Gothenburg by water. The builders were not interested in tourists—for them the canal was a straight-out commercial freight proposition, of tremendous importance for the country's future. No less than 65 locks were required, as well as kilometers of channels to connect the lakes and rivers. The result was a waterway which tremendously facilitated the movement of freight within and across the country.

In 1800 the Trollhätte Canal connecting huge Lake Vänern with Gothenburg and the North Sea was completed and soon demonstrated its value. Then, in 1808–9, Baltzar von Platen, a military man and ranking government official, advocated the bold plan of continuing on from Lake Vänern to Lake Vättern and across to the Baltic Sea. It is a tribute to the leaders of the country in an era when the whole outlook for the future of the nation was as dismal as it had ever been, that they boldly appropriated 2,400,000 *dalers* to begin the project. It was a tremendous piece of work, and during the years of building ran into constant obstacles and required some five times the original financial appropriation. A masterful piece of hard-headed Swedish logic was applied to overcome one of them. The farmers of one region had refused to sell their land for the right of way. The representative of the canal company asked, "Did you ever see water run uphill?" Nobody could answer in the affirmative. "Well, then," he said, "when this idiot von Platen fails, too, you'll get the land back." The farmers signed. But von Platen *did* make water "run uphill", and it was been doing so in the Göta Canal ever since. Von Platen was never able to take the trip himself: he died shortly before his great dream was realized and the canal opened to traffic. You will find his grave and a statue of him in the city of Motala, on Lake Vättern, one of the cities along the route.

Some of the high points have already been described: Bohus Fortress, Trollhättan Falls, Läckö Castle, Vadstena. You can take it easy, seeing the various sights as thoroughly or superficially as suits you, enjoying the company of your 50-odd fellow passengers. You come in intimate contact with the countryside—here and there the grass alongside the narrow channel and the overhanging trees actually brush the rails and decks. You also see an almost unlimited variety of drawbridges.

You come out on the island-strewn Baltic Sea just south of Norrköping, and follow the coast north for a way before turning into the Södertälje Canal. The canal carries you into Lake Mälaren, which brings you, via the beautiful channel from the west, right to the heart of Stockholm. You tie up at Riddarholmen—rested, full of fresh air, and with a real mental image of the heart of Sweden. There are many day tours available on the canal, such as the trip between Söderköping and Arkösund, between Berg and Motala, and on the canal's western leg from Lake Vättern.

Romantic Värmland

Perhaps no other region of Sweden has been so romanticized as the province of Värmland. Sweden's greatest authoress, Selma Lagerlöf, made it a national legend in *The Saga of Gösta Berling,* and there is a widely sung, melancholy, hauntingly beautiful song titled *Song of Värmland.* It is often an anticlimax to visit a region which has been sung in song and story, Värmland will not disappoint you.

Don't be deceived by the endless woods and the idyllic nature of the landscape. The woods, the rivers, and the iron ore of the ground actually make this a leading industrial region, with ultra-modern factories dotted here and there in pleasant, comparatively small towns. The wood and iron ore industries have centuries-old traditions, and the old semi-rural culture was based to some extent on them.

Karlstad is the provincial capital and seat of the diocese, with some 74,000 inhabitants. The oldest building is the cathedral, built between 1723 and 1730. There is a comparatively large harbor on Lake Vänern which has direct connections with the ocean through the Trollhätte Canal.

The origins of Karlstad are lost in antiquity, but because of destructive fires the city hardly looks old. It has apparently been the capital of this region from the beginning of time and was formerly known as Tingvalla, after the *ting,* or meetings of the legislature, which were held here. When Duke Karl issued it a charter in 1584, he also gave it a name. Karlstad means "the city of Karl".

Värmland is cut by rivers and long narrow lakes, running roughly north to south (with a slight bias of the southern end of the axis to the east). The largest of these, and the best known, is the Fryken chain consisting of three lakes. The most popular sightseeing route is the Fryken Valley. You can rent a raft and enjoy a peaceful trip down the Klarälven River.

A tour along the following lines can be managed easily in one day by car. During the summer season, you will find guided bus tours to the principal points of interest. Take the main road north along the beautiful Klarälven River (in the spring full of timber being floated down to factories) about 40 kilometers (25 miles) to Ransäter, where you will find a rural museum, a lookout tower, and the home where Erik Gustaf Geijer, a national literary great, was born in 1783. A few kilometers farther on you come to Munkfors, site of one of the major steel plants of the Uddeholm Corporation. It will give you an idea of the highly-developed quality steel industry of this part of the world. Just north of Munkfors, turn off to the right on the road to Sunnemo. It brings you down to the narrow lake called Lidsjön. The Sunnemo church is a little known exquisite rural parish church, utterly charming in its modest expression in wood of the people's religious feeling. Note the individual carved shingles.

From here you proceed north again along Råda Lake to Uddeholm, a deceivingly peaceful village of 500 souls or so. You'd never know by looking at it, but this is the main headquarters of a huge international corporation. It is truly peaceful. But inside some of the unprepossessing buildings, direct telephone and teletype lines keep Uddeholm in constant touch with its far-flung empire, with its many plants producing iron and steel, wood products, chemicals, and paper, with its sales organization in two hemispheres. The Uddeholm Corporation descends in a direct line from a 17th-century ironworks, and today it is perhaps the largest private employer in Sweden.

Selma Lagerlöf's Home

Now, your best bet is to continue around the north end of the lake, then turn due south again and make your way back to Munkfors. But here, instead of returning directly to Karlstad, you can cut almost due west (to the right) to Sunne, which brings you into the very heart of the Selma Lagerlöf country. It's only 55 kilometers (34 miles) south of here to Mårbacka, her ancestral home, now a public museum maintained largely as she left it at the time of her death in 1940. You are better advised to go back to Sunne from Mårbacka, cross over to the west side of the Fryken Lakes, and turn south towards Karlstad again. Only a couple of kilometers below Sunne you reach famed Rottneros, the "Ekeby" of the Lagerlöf book, a truly fine example of the old culture of the landed gentry, distinguished by sculptures, flowers and a wonderful view. The buildings themselves are stately, and the grounds, overlooking the lake, are well kept. About 16 kilometers (ten miles) before you reach Karlstad, near Kil, is the Apertin Manor House. It's worth a look, but, since it is privately owned, don't expect to get inside without special arrangements. The same thing applies to Rottneros, although the public is permitted to wander freely through the grounds. There is an entrance fee. While in the area, the more adventurous might like to try a moose safari, arranged some evenings by the Sunne tourist bureau.

The city of Filipstad, about 64 kilometers (40 miles) from Karlstad, has a special interest for Americans. It is the home ground of John Ericsson, whose iron-clad ship, the *Monitor,* meant victory at sea for the North in America's Civil War. Ericsson's place in history would have been assured had he never seen America, however, for he contributed a number of major inventions to the exploding technological progress of the 19th century. Because of his contribution to American national unity, his body was delivered to Sweden in 1890 by the United States Navy, and buried with great pomp. You will find his tomb, and a memorial statue, in this idyllic little city where he grew up. The population is now something over 7,000, and there is a varied industry. The peaceful appearance of the city belies its industrial and commercial importance, however, and it is perhaps never more beautiful than in the spring, when the high waters of the Skiller River go rushing through the heart of the town, almost on a level with the sidewalks.

Dalsland and Its Canal

The province of Dalsland is for lovers of the outdoors. It is shaped in the form of a huge, irregular wedge, with Bohuslän and Norway forming the western border, Lake Vänern the eastern, and the province of Värmland the northern.

Actually, the most beautiful part of Dalsland is perhaps not the coastal regions but the deep forests and lakes of the western and northern areas. The principal tourist centers are Bengtsfors, the northwest anchor of the lovely Dalsland Canal; Ed, on the road to Norway; and Åmål, the principal city.

The Dalsland Canal, built in 1860 under the direction of Nils Ericsson, brother of John Ericsson of U.S. Civil War fame links up a 272-kilometer (169-mile) waterway with no less than 29 locks. You can travel by boat from Köpmannebro on the shores of Lake Vänern up through the whole of northern Dalsland, over the aqueduct at Håverud, and on by the way of Värmland lakes to the Norwegian border.

The Dalsland Canal is actually a system of lakes and only 9.6 kilometers (six miles) is excavated canal. Most indigenous Swedish mammals can be found in this area, including some rare creatures like the lynx and beaver, which have quite large populations here. This is real canoe country and numerous tours are offered, from one to two days up to three weeks. Many tourists also come to see the aqueduct at Håverud and its busy boat traffic. There is an exhibition there showing what the Dalsland region produces and its major sights and attractions.

Dalarna

Sweden's ancient folklore traditions are probably maintained more strongly in the province of Dalarna than in any other part of the country. Every village has its maypole—originally a pagan fertility symbol—which is ornately decorated at midsummer each year and is the focus of the annual festivities marking the longest day. The traditions are strongest in the area round Lake Siljan in the middle of Dalarna. If you visit the area at midsummer you'll see hundreds of villagers, dressed in regional costumes, arriving in their long-boats for a special service in the village church at Rättvik.

Not far from Rättvik is the village of Nusnäs, where the traditional brightly-painted Dalarna wood-carved horses are produced in vast quantities. Nearby is the small but elegant town of Mora, home of the Swedish artist Anders Zorn. A new tourist attraction in the neighborhood is Santaworld (otherwise known as Tomteland), where there are special activities for children year-round. The Grönklitt bear sanctuary near Orsa, where the animals live in a natural forest habitat, is also well worth visiting.

The main town in Dalarna is Falun, where copper has been mined for some 900 years. The best-known landmark is the "Great Pit," a huge hole in the ground which has been there since the mine caved in 300 years ago. You can put on helmet and overalls and go down into some of the old sections of the mine and see the grim conditions under which the miners used to work. It's also well worth visiting the nearby home of the well-known Swedish artist Carl Larsson in an idyllic lakeside location. His simple paintings owe much to the local folk-art tradition.

The "Bergslagen" Region

The name of this region derives from the "bergslag", co-operatives formed by the mining communities holding mineral rights. People first moved to the Örebro and Västmanland counties to work the "öres" in the early middle ages. There are still many traces of blast furnaces, blackened sites of charcoal piles and the homes and other buildings of these early miners. The iron industry is still flourishing in places like Hällefors, Karlskoga and Degerfors.

Strömsholm Castle on Lake Mälaren is a popular tourist attraction with its many horses and stables. Refreshments are served in the kitchen of the castle in summer. The Strömsholm Canal was built to transport the iron and ore of the region. These 96.5 kilometers (60 miles) of waterway and 26 locks are a popular route for smaller craft.

At Engelsberg you can see an old smelting house and relics from the Norberg mining area dating from the 14th century. From the middle of the last century until the 1920s, the power transmission system constructed by the Swedish inventor Christopher Polhem was still in use here. You can see the "Polhem Wheel" measuring 15 meters (49 feet) in diameter, well-preserved after so many years. The 400-year-old silver mine at Sala is also open to the public during the summer months.

Södermanland

South of Lake Mälaren and bordering Stockholm is Södermanland, a province of manor parks and pastoral beauty. You can take the steamer from Stockholm to Mariefred and then join a narrow-gauge vintage railway. In Mariefred is Gripsholm Castle, one of the best-known Swedish historical monuments. Mariefred also houses the national portrait collection—the largest in Europe. Strängnäs and its cathedral is nearby.

Have you ever owned a Swedish pocketknife? If you have, it was manufactured in Eskilstuna. The Rademacher Smithies here are a must to see. There's also a zoo with many rare animals, such as the panda and snow leopard. There are some 50 prehistoric sites near Eskilstuna. The best-known are the Sigurd rock carvings.

Ancient Sweden—One Hour from Stockholm

Sweden begins in Gamla Uppsala (Old Uppsala). It is here that the first Swedish kings, Aun, Egils and Adils, are buried. See the tombs and drink real Viking mead from big horns at the Odinsborg.

The magnificent Gothic cathedral in Old Uppsala is 800 years old and the seat of the Archbishop of Sweden. Nearby on a hill is the Castle with the Coronation Hall and dungeons—over 400 years old. Carl Linnaeus or Carl von Linné, the world-famous botanist and scientist, had his home here, in Hammarby. In the botanical garden in Uppsala there are still living plants dating from the days of Linnaeus. The university at Uppsala, the oldest in Scandinavia, is more than 500 years old.

This was also a mining district. In the 17th and 18th centuries Österby Bruk and Leufsta were the largest ironworks in the country. The Walloons came here to teach the Swedes how to make iron and were the origin of "Swedish" family names like De Laval, Hubinette and Gille. There are many folk festivals and music weeks at Österby Bruk.

PRACTICAL INFORMATION FOR
THE LAND OF LAKES AND FOLKLORE

TOURIST INFORMATION. The most important tourist offices, all open all year round, are at the following places: **Arvika,** Stadsparken (0570–135 60). **Borås,** Torggatan 19 (033–16 70 90). **Eskilstuna,** Fristadstorget 5 (016–10 22 50). **Falun,** Stora Torget (023–836 37). **Karlskoga,** Centralplan 1 (0586–563 48). **Karlstad,** Södra Kyrkogatan 10 (054–19 59 01). **Kolmården Zoo,** summer only (011–950 06). **Lidköping,** Gamla Rådhuset, summer only (0510–835 00). **Mariefred,** Rådhuset (0159–102 07). **Norrköping,** Drottninggatan 18 (011–15 15 00). **Örebro,** Drottninggatan 9 (019–13 07 60). **Rättvik,** Torget (0248–109 10). **Sunne,** Mejerigatan 2 (0565–135 30). **Uppsala,** Smedsgränd 7 (018–11 75 00). **Västerås,** Storatorget 5 (021–16 18 30).

TELEPHONE CODES. We have given telephone codes for all the towns and villages in the hotel and restaurant lists that follow. These codes need only be used when calling from outside the town or village concerned.

HOTELS AND RESTAURANTS. Accommodations in this region are modest on the whole. Many of the vacationers who come here stay in cottages and on sailboats.

438 SWEDEN

Alingsås. *Scandic* (M), Bankgatan 1 (0322–140 00). 67 rooms. Has Sweden's only potato-specialty restaurant to commemorate local lad Jonas Alströmer who introduced it to Sweden. AE, DC, MC, V.

Arvika. *Oscar Statt* (M), Torggatan 9 (0570–197 50). 43 rooms. AE, DC, MC, V.
Restaurant. *Stavnäsgården "Kvarnen"* (The Mill) (M), Klässbol, 15 km. (9 miles) south of Arvika. Cafeteria with home-baked bread. Don't miss the linen weaving mill. Open May to Aug., Mon to Fri. 11–6, Sat. 10–3, Sun. 11–8. AE, MC, V.

Bengtsfors. *Dalia* (I), Karlsbergsvägen 3 (0531–116 50). 45 rooms. 400 meters (440 yards) from Dalsland Canal and near Gammelgården, the homestead museum. Resort hotel, restaurant, cafeteria, sauna, golf, illuminated ski trail, ski lifts. AE, DC, MC, V.

Borås. *Hotel Borås* (E), Sandgärdsgatan 25 (033–11 70 20). 53 rooms. Member of the Romantik Hotels group. Exclusive atmosphere. AE, DC, MC, V. *Grand* (E), Hallbergsgatan 14 (033–10 82 00). 166 rooms. Excellent location in center of town overlooking the river. AE, DC, MC, V. *Gustav Adolf* (M), Andra Villagatan 5 (033–10 81 80). 37 rooms. Modern hotel in quiet but central location. AE, DC, MC, V. *Vävaren* (M), Allégatan 21 (033–10 00 20). 90 rooms. A well-run family hotel in the city center. Sauna, cafeteria. Golf and tennis in the outskirts. AE, DC, MC, V.

Borlänge. *Brage* (E), Stationsgatan 1–3 (0243–241 50). 94 rooms. Near railroad station. Sauna, rooms for handicapped travelers. AE, DC, MC, V. *Galaxen* (E), Jussi Björlings Väg (0243–800 10). 129 rooms. Sauna, rooms for handicapped guests. Restaurant. AE, DC, MC, V. *Gustaf Wasa* (M), Tunagatan 1 (0243–810 00). 76 rooms. Centrally located, near railroad station. AE, DC, MC, V.

Eskilstuna. *City* (I), Drottninggatan 15 (016–13 74 25). 60 rooms. Close to the railroad station. Breakfast only. AE, DC, MC, V.
Restaurants. *Sommarrestaurangen* (Summer Restaurant) (M), in the zoo (016–14 73 80). No credit cards. *Jernberghska Gården* (I), at the Rademacher forge museum (016–14 65 05). Also outdoor service. Closes 4 P.M. in winter and 6 P.M. in summer.

Falun. *Bergmästaren* (E), Bergskolegränd 7 (023–636 00). 89 rooms. Small cozy hotel in city center built in traditional Dalarna style with antique furnishings. Completely refurbished in 1985. Sauna and solarium. Breakfast only. AE, DC, MC, V. *Grand* (E), Trotzgatan 9 (023–187 00). 183 rooms. Modern hotel in city center, modernized in 1987. Restaurant serving international cuisine. Disco. AE, DC, MC, V.

Filipstad. *Hennickehammars Herrgård* (Manor House) (M) (0590–12 565). 57 rooms. 18th-century manor house by Lake Hemtjärn in a wonderful park. Excellent cuisine—restaurant. Sauna, tennis, fishing, ski sports, rowing boats, canoeing, 15 km. (nine miles) to golf. AE, DC, MC, V.
Restaurants. *Långbans Gästgiveri* (inn) (E), John Ericsson homestead (0590–221 69). In an old stable at the mineral-rich Långban. Fish and game specialties. *Storhöjden* (E) (0590–103 13). In an old house with a view of the city. Outdoor tables. Outlook tower. AE, MC, V.

Grythyttan. *Grythyttan Gästgivaregård* (Inn) (M), (0591–147 00). 64 rooms. Family-owned inn from 1640. Well-located by old market place. Known for good food and excellent wine cellar. Golf, fishing, etc. AE, DC, MC, V.

Jönköping. *Portalen* (E), Västra Storgatan 9 (036–11 82 00). 210 rooms. Centrally located near railroad station. Airport bus-stop outside hotel. Four restau-

rants. AE, DC, MC, V. *Ramada* (E), Strandvägen 1 (036–14 24 00). 112 rooms.
North of Huskvarna-Jönköping. Most rooms have view of Lake Vättern. Restaurant, cocktail bar. Sauna, pool, golf. AE, DC, MC, V. *City Hotel* (M), Västra Storgatan 23–25 (036–11 92 00). 70 rooms. Classic-style hotel in the city center. Refurbished five years ago. AE, DC, MC, V.

Restaurants. *Strand* (E), Huskvarnavägen 5 (036–10 05 40). Lakeside location,
with service outdoors during the summer. AE, DC, MC, V. *Svarta Börsen* (E),
Kyrkogatan 4 (036–11 22 22). Cozy restaurant in the center of town. New French
cuisine. Char from Lake Vättern; crow! AE, DC, MC, V. *Mäster Gudmunds Källare*
(M), Kapellgatan 2 (036–11 26 33). Nice atmosphere in cellar vaults. Smörgåsbord.
AE, DC, MC, V. *Warpa Skans* (M), on Lake Vättern and the E4 (036–14 21 00).
50 meters (164 ft.) from Brunstorp Inn, north of Huskvarna. *Smörgåsbord,* country-
style. Geared for bus groups. AE, MC, V.

Karlskoga. *Stadshotellet Alfred Nobel* (M), Torget 1 (0586–364 40). 73 rooms.
Nightclub, piano bar. Facilities for handicapped and non-smoking guests. AE, DC,
MC, V.

Karlstad. *Stadshotellet* (E), Kungsgatan 22 (054–11 52 20). 143 rooms. On the
Klarälven River, central, centuries of tradition. Restaurants, cocktail bar, nightclub, sauna, pool. AE, DC, MC, V. *Gösta Berling* (M), Drottninggatan 1 (054–15
01 90). 75 rooms. Genuine Värmland atmosphere in the center of Karlstad. Restaurant, cocktail bar, sauna. AE, DC, MC, V. *Winn* (M), Norra Strandgatan 9–11
(054–10 22 20). 177 rooms. Modern, centrally located hotel. AE, DC, MC, V.

Restaurants. *Inn Alstern* (E), Morgonvägen 4 (054–13 49 00). Beautifully situated with a view of Lake Alstern. Gourmet food. AE, MC, V. *Skogen-Terrassen* (E),
in Mariebergsskogen (054–15 92 03). Nicely situated in one of the leading open-air
museums and amusement parks in the country. Specializes in food from the area.
MC, V.

Kolmården. *Vildmarkshotellet* (E), (011–15 71 00). 212 rooms. Fantastic view
of Bråviken bay. Indoor pool, sauna, nightclub. Near the famous zoo and safari
park. AE, DC, MC, V.

Youth Hostel. *Kvarsebo* (011–960 46). 32 beds. Coffee, kitchen. Bus to Kolmården Zoo. Open end June to beginning Aug.

Leksand. *Korstäppan* (I), Hjorntnäsvägen 33 (0247–100 37). 34 rooms. Swimming pool, sauna. AE, DC, MC, V.

Lidköping. *Stadshotellet* (M), Gamla Stadens Torg 1 (0510–220 85). 71 rooms.
In old town, not far from Lake Vänern. Close to Rörstrand porcelain works and
museum. Restaurant. AE, DC, MC, V.

Linköping. *Ekoxen* (L), Klostergatan 68 (013–14 60 70). 194 rooms. Central,
beside a park. Restaurant, cocktail bar, sauna, pool. AE, DC, MC, V.

Restaurants. *Wärdshuset Gamla Linköping* (Old Linköping Inn) (M), Gästgi-
varegatan 1 (013–13 31 10). In house from 18th century with beautiful painted ceilings. Self-service in genuine cellar vaults. AE, MC. *Restaurang och Café MåGott*
(I), Stora Torget (013–11 06 47). In old Lagerström House. Salads and small dishes.
Also outside tables. AE, MC, V.

Youth Hostel. *Centrumgården Ryd* (013–17 64 58). 70 beds. Sauna. Buses to
center and railway station. Open June to mid-Aug.

Mariefred. *Gripsholms Värdshus* (E), Mariefred (0159–100 40). 45 rooms.
Reached by steamer from Stockholm, near the famous 14th-century castle. Claims
to be Sweden's oldest hotel, dating from 1623. AE, DC, MC, V.

Mora. *Mora Hotel* (M), Strandgatan 12 (0250–117 50). 92 rooms. On the shores
of Lake Siljan and opposite the old church. Sauna, pool. AE, DC, MC, V. *Siljan*

(I), Moragatan 6 (0250–130 00). 46 rooms. Popular, small, but modern-style establishment. Sauna, disco, restaurant. AE, DC, MC, V.

Norrköping. *Grand* (E), Tyska Torget 2 (011–19 71 00). 210 rooms. Restaurant, piano bar, wintergarden, sauna. AE, DC, MC, V. *Strand* (I), Drottninggatan 2 (011–16 99 00). 16 rooms. Breakfast only. No credit cards.
Restaurants. *Palace* (M), Gråddgatan 13 (011–18 96 00). Gourmet food, with a view of the river. MC, V. *Palace Café* has chairs outside in summer. Known for plank steak and *Caféflorett* nightclub. Music every night in café. AE, DC, MC, V. *Peter's Steakhouse* (M), Trädgårdsgatan 6B (011–18 31 30). Rustic, paintings, grouped sofas. Closed July; Sun. AE, DC, MC, V.

Örebro. *Grand* (E), Fabriksgatan 23 (019–15 02 00). 228 rooms. Central location. Some "VIP" rooms. Sauna, bubble-pool. AE, DC, MC, V. *City* (M), Kungsgatan 24 (019–10 02 00). 113 rooms. Modern city-center hotel opened in 1986. Facilities for disabled guests. Restaurant specializes in "home cooking." AE, DC, MC, V.
Restaurants. *Gyllene Drotten* (Golden Ruler) (M), Drottninggatan 15 (019–11 77 82). Central, cellar vaults. AE, DC, MC, V. *Två Krögare* (Two Innkeepers) (M), Rudbecksgatan 18 (019–11 13 67). Central. Good food in pleasant surroundings. AE, MC, V.

Orsa. *Orsa Hotel* (M), Järnvägsgatan 4 (0250–409 40). 25 rooms. Adjoins railroad station. Sauna, restaurant. AE, DC, MC, V.

Söderköping. *Söderköpings* Brunn (Spa) (M), Skönbergagatan 35 (0121–109 00). In large wooded park on the Göta Canal. 108 rooms. Historic spa hotel from 1774. Entertainment in park, dancing, sauna. AE, DC, MC, V.

Sunne. *Selma Lagerlöf* (M), (0565–130 80). 156 rooms. New hotel built in old Värmland manor-house style. AE, DC, MC, V.

Svartå. *Svartå Herrgård* (I), (0585–500 03). 40 rooms. Late 18th century manor house in a rambling garden, near Kilsbergen mountain range. AE, DC, MC.

Tällberg. *Åkerblads* (E) (0247–508 00). 64 rooms. Typical Dalarna farmstead dating back to the early 17th century that has been a hotel since 1910 and is now run by the 14th and 15th generations of the Åkerblad family. DC, MC, V. *Green* (M), (0247–502 50). 100 rooms. Timber building, dating from 1917. Wonderful view of Lake Siljan. Some rooms with open fireplaces. Unique art collection. Staff dressed in folk costumes. Restaurant, cocktail bar. Five saunas, golf, tennis, outdoor and indoor pools, dancing on Sat. AE, DC, MC, V. *Tällbergsgården* (M), (0247–500 26). 50 rooms. Family atmosphere, fine view of Lake Siljan. Restaurant, cocktail bar, cafeteria. Sauna, golf, tennis, bikes, skis. *Smörgåsbord* served every day. Folk fiddlers entertain on Sun. AE, DC, MC, V.

Uppsala. *Sara Gillet* (E), Dragarbrunnsgatan 23 (018–15 53 60). 169 rooms. Located in the city center. Recently modernized. Sauna and gourmet restaurant. AE, DC, MC, V.
Restaurants. *Slottskällan* (Castle Springs) (E), Sjukhusvägen 3 (018–11 15 10). In house dating from 18th century, below the castle at the swan pond. AE, MC, V. *Domtrappkällaren* (M), St. Eriksgränd 15 (018–13 09 55). In a 14th-century cellar near the Cathedral (Domkyrkan). Restaurant established 1939. Good Swedish and French food, also coffee with home-baked bread, ice cream. AE, DC, MC, V.
Youth Hostels. *Sunnersta Herrgård* (Manor House), about six km. (four miles) south of the center (018–32 42 20). 88 beds. Open May through Aug. *Interrail Point,* Tunet (018–18 85 66). Two km. (just over one mile) north of city (bus 7 from Stora Torget). 40 beds. Open early July through mid-Aug.

Vadstena. *Klostergården* (I), Lasarettsgatan (0143–115 30). 25 rooms. Breakfast only. Closed Christmas/New Year. AE, DC, MC, V.

Restaurants. *Munkklostret* (the Monastery) (M), (0143–130 00). Medieval atmosphere. Fish from Lake Vättern is specialty. AE, DC, MC, V. *Värdshuset Kungs Starby* (M), near the south entrance to Vadstena from road 50. 75-year-old building, outdoor service in summer, large park. *Smörgåsbord* every day. AE, DC, MC, V.

Youth Hostel. *Vadstena Vandrarhem,* Skänningegatan 20 (0143–103 02). 65 beds. Walking distance to sights. Tåkern bird sanctuary, eight km. (five miles) away. Bike rental. Open June through Aug. (groups only rest of year).

Västerås. *Park Hotel* (E), Gunnilbogatan 2 (021–11 01 20). 139 rooms. Restaurant, nightclub, dancing, sauna. AE, DC, MC, V. *Traffic Hotel* (M), Hallstagårdsgatan 1 (021–30 04 00). 91 rooms. On route E18 just outside city. Restaurant, 24-hour cafeteria, sauna, bubble pool. AE, DC, MC, V.

Restaurants. *Bacchus Källare* (M), (021–11 56 40). In a building dating from 17th century. Near the Svartå River. Central. AE, MC, V. *Johannes* (M), Stora Torget (021–13 06 63). Central. Well-known restaurant with excellent food. Outdoor service in summer. AE, DC, MC, V.

Campsites. The following campsites have bungalows or rooms to rent. It is advisable to book a few days in advance. *Dals-Långed,* Laxsjön (0531–300 10); *Lidköping,* Framnäs (0510–268 04); *Mora,* Mora Camping (0250–265 95); *Norrköping,* Himmelstalund (011–17 11 90); *Rättvik,* Siljansbadet (0248–116 91); *Sunne,* Kolsnäsudden (0565–113 12); *Tärnsjö,* Osta (0292–430 04); *Vadstena,* Vätterviksbadet (0143–127 30).

HOW TO GET AROUND. By car or train. The best way to see a lot of this region is to take the main highway or the train from Gothenburg to Stockholm, or from Stockholm to Karlstad. The section of road between Vadstena and Jönköping is one of the most spectacular, with the road winding along the eastern shore of Lake Vättern.

Karlstad is easily reached by car or train from Gothenburg or Stockholm. If you go from Gothenburg, you will pass the lakes and forest of Dalsland and should plan to stop at Håverud to see the locks of the Dalsland Canal.

Linköping and Norrköping are respectively 217 km. (135 miles) annd 145 km. (90 miles) from Stockholm and are close enough for a day excursion. There are frequent bus tours to Kolmården Zoo.

By air. The area is well served by air. From Stockholm there are up to nine flights a day to Borlänge/Falun, 10 to Karlstad, nine to Jönköping and six to Norrköping.

By boat. You can see this region with graceful ease by boat on the Göta Canal, a waterway which is more than 100 years old. Several boats ply the Göta Canal, offering tours of varying length. There are boats that go from Söderköping to Arkösund, from Norsholm to Söderköping, and from Karlsborg to Töreboda. If you are at Trollhättan, you can take the *Strömkarlen* on a canal tour. For schedules call 0141–100 50 or call at the nearest tourist bureau.

The traditional tour to take on the canal is the three-day trip between Gothenburg and Stockholm on the *Diana, Juno,* or *Wilhelm Tham.* They operate between the middle of May and the beginning of September. You can book this tour through your travel agency before you leave for Sweden. You can also rent your own boat by phoning *Boatco* (0431–340 93).

Boats also operate on the big lakes such as Fryken in Värmland, Siljan in Dalarna, Vänern and Vättern.

By bicycle. There are many bicycle trails in this region and maps for them are available in book shops or at the tourist bureaux. In particular, look for maps of a marked trail called "Mälardalsleden." There is also a biking or hiking trail along the Göta Canal, where oxen once drew barges.

You can rent bicycles in Söderköping (0121–134 75). Borensberg (0141–400 60), Töreboda (0506–104 96), or in Sjötorp (0501–510 03).

PLACES TO VISIT. In addition to the veritable inland seas of Lake Vänern and Vättern and the Göta Canal which wends its scenic way from Stockholm to Gothenburg, there are many other distinctive glimpses of past and present in this region.

Eskilstuna. Djurgården Museum and Sörmlandsgården. At Carlaägen-Djurgårdsvägen. Open-air museum showing local history. Sörmlandsgården is an early 19th-century farm complete with stables, hay barn etc. Open May through Sept., daily 11–4.

Rademacher Smedjorna. The Rademacher Smithies, built in 1658 and now an open-air homestead museum. Demonstrations in the copper and iron smithies; a hatter making hats and tin soldiers being made in the tin foundry. Also an industrial and armory museum nearby (closed Mon.). Daily performances at the Rademacher in Jul. Cafeteria. Open daily 10–4; Jul. through Aug., Mon. to Fri. 10–6, Sat. and Sun. 10–4. Admission free.

Gränna. Andrée Museet. Pictures and memorabilia of S.A. Andrée's unsuccessful attempt to reach the North Pole by balloon in 1987. Open mid-May through Aug., daily 10–5; daily 12–4 rest of year. Open till 8 on Wednesdays during July.

Jönköping. County Museum. A museum for the whole family, with art gallery, displays of modern porcelain, and exhibits depicting the industrialization of Småland. Cafeteria. Admission free. Open Mon., Wed. and Fri. 11–4, Tues. and Thurs. 11–8, Sat. 11–3, and Sun. 1–5.

Riddersberg Manor. In Rogbergs, 10 km. (six miles) east of Jönköping. Huge wooden sculptures in a park, such as the 103-meter (338-ft.) high *Indian Rope Trick* and the *Bounty* (a ship on land). *The Giant Vist,* another sculpture by the same artist, Calle Örnemark, is visible from the road at Huskvarna. The artist lives on the premises and sometimes conducts guided tours himself. Open daily 10–6 (often till 8 in summer). Admission free.

Tändsticksmuseet (Match Museum). Storgatan 18 (036–10 55 43). Match manufacturing started here in Jönköping in the middle of the last century and made the city famous. Here in the original factory are machines and exhibits showing the development of the match industry. 13-minute film *The Match.* Large collection of matchbox labels. Open May 19 to Sept. 12 Mon. to Fri. 9–7, Sat. 10–12, Sun. 3–5 (limited opening times rest of year).

Karlskoga. Nobelmuseet. Björkborn. The Alfred Nobel residence, including library, study and laboratory with original equipment. Open June through Aug., daily 10–4, Tues. and Thurs. also 7–9 P.M. On request at other times. Call 0586–818 94.

Katrineholm. Julita Gård. On Lake Öljar, 25 km. (16 miles) north of Katrineholm. Typical turn-of-the-century manor house with parks and gardens. A homestead museum, dairy museum and the Skansen church. Museums open mid-May to mid-Aug., daily 11–4. Main building, guided tours only. For information call 0150–912 90 or 08–22 41 20.

Malmköping. Musiespårväg. Vintage tramway. 75-year-old tram on which you can take a half-hour trip. Tram museum, road museum. Open mid-June to mid-Aug., daily 11–5; May and Sept. on Sat. and Sun. only.

Mariefred. Gripsholm Castle. Castle was begun in 1370s. Among the many interesting things in an 18th-century theater. National portrait collection is here, one of largest in Europe. Modern portraits are in school building nearby. Boats from Stockholm. Open May through Aug., daily 10–4; check locally for opening times rest of year. For information call 0159–101 94.

Östra Södermanlands Järnväg. Veteran railway operating between Mariefred and Läggesta during summer months. Call 0159–110 06 for timetable.

Mora. Zorn Museum. Vasagatan 36. Original paintings, sketches and sculptures of Swedish artist Anders Zorn. Open June 15 to Aug. 15, Mon. to Sat. 9–5; Sun. 11–5.

Zorngården. Adjoining museum. Zorn's home 1896–1920. In unchanged condition with silver collection, art, furniture etc. Guided tours every half-hour. Open year-round Mon. to Sat. 9–5, Sun. 11–5 (closed Mon. in winter).

Örebro. Wadköping. In Stadsparken, 1.5 km. (a mile) from the center of town. Open-air museum. Old Town of Örebro with old wooden houses, streets and squares, handicrafts, workshops, exhibitions. Cafeteria. Open daily 12–5.

Sunne. Mårbacka. Östra Ämtervik, 10 km. (six miles) south of Sunne. The home of Nobel prize winner (1909) Selma Lagerlöf. (Most of her books are available in English and German). Manor house in unchanged condition. Cafeteria. Guided tours—for information call 0565–310 27. Open May to Aug. daily 9–6; Sept., Sat. and Sun. only 9–6.

Rottneros Manor. 3 km. (two miles) south of Sunne. One of Sweden's most beautiful gardens with flowers, herb garden, sculptures and a wonderful view of Lake Fryken. Open May to Sept. daily 9–6; July, daily 8–7.

NORRLAND AND LAPLAND

Europe's Last Wilderness

The Swedish highlands, ranging from central Sweden up beyond the Arctic Circle for a distance of 800 kilometers (500 miles) or more, offer you vacations quite unlike any others anywhere; this is truly Europe's last wilderness. The region has been settled for centuries, its natural resources are among the most important in northern Europe, yet it is a country of open spaces, virgin wilderness, and a combination of natural beauties not to be found anywhere else in the world.

Norrland—as the entire region of northern Sweden is called—occupies half of Sweden's territory but holds only 17 per cent of its population. Modern industry already has put its stamp on parts of Norrland, with its vast resources of timber, iron ore, and water power. But the traditional peasant culture of the river valleys and coastal areas, deep-rooted in the Middle Ages, and the ageless civilization of the independent, nomadic Lapps have remained virtually unchanged.

This area has its charm at all seasons of the year and offers a variety of delights to lovers of the outdoors. From Christmas to May skiing predominates. If the winters are long, the summers are brilliant—the countryside bursts into bloom, temperatures of 80–85°F (27–29°C) are not unusual, and the "sunlit nights" merge day into day with only a few hours of twilight between. In the far north, the Midnight Sun sees to it that there is no night at all from May 25 to July 15.

Härjedalen

Sandwiched between Norway in the west, Jämtland in the north, the coastal provinces in the east, and Dalarna in the south, Härjedalen possesses only one center of any size—Sveg, with a little over 4,000 inhabitants. Because of this—or in spite of it—Härjedalen was the first mountain province to attract visitors in the days when both tourism and skiing were in their infancy. One reason for its continued popularity with skiers is the great variety of terrain it offers, from the gentle rounded southern mountains to the originally volcanic Helag Mountains in the north. Fjällnäs, Funäsdalen, Bruksvallarna and Vemdalskalet all offer comfortable lodging and are both summer and winter resorts.

Across the Flatruet plateau in the western part of the province runs the highest road in Sweden (914 meters or 3,000 feet), offering a breathtaking view from its summit. On one of the cliff walls are rock paintings, almost 4,000 years old, depicting animal and human figures. Another curiosity is the "frozen sea" of the Rogen area, with its striated and pitted Ice Age boulders.

Jämtland

Östersund is on the railroad line that crosses the Scandinavian peninsula from Sundsvall, industrial center on the east coast of Sweden, to Trondheim on Norway's Atlantic coast, a fact which accounts for much of its growth in recent years. Despite its northerly clime, however, the region around Storsjön, or the Great Lake, has been settled since heathen times. The ancient capital of this region was Frösön, an island in the lake just off what is now Östersund. It was the site of a heathen sacrificial temple and the place where the *ting,* or popular council, met. The strange Viking alphabet also penetrated here, and the northernmost rune stone in Sweden is to be found on Frösön near the bridge. It was erected there by one Östman Gudfastsson about the year 1050. From the heights of Frösön you have unbelievably distant views—of the lake, the cultivated areas around the shores, and, in the west, the mountains reaching above the timberline.

Today Östersund has taken over Frösön's role as capital of the province, and has grown into a city of 56,000 inhabitants, with several industries. It is a good starting point for motor tours within the province or into Norway—the joint Swedish-Norwegian "Trondheimsleden" highway leads via Enafors and Storlien to Trondheim.

Here are some of the principal resorts in the region stretching west of Östersund:

Åre, site of a former World Ski Championship, and located in the beautiful Åre valley at the foot of the Åreskutan mountain, is popular both winter and summer. It is the largest resort in this region and also boasts a church dating from the 12th or 13th century.

There are a dozen or so other resorts or mountain hotels, among them Duved, Undersåker, Hålland, Ånn, Bydalen, and Anjan, all with good terrain. Farther north, in even more isolated country, are Gäddede and Jormlien. You're really in the wilderness here—observe reasonable precautions before taking off from your hotel. There are expert guides. The requirement that you notify the management of your intended route when you go out any distance is a simple precaution for your own safety. Don't laugh at it. Even if you're in perfect safety, which is likely, you'll feel awfully silly if half the population drops its other pursuits to come out looking for you.

Gästrikland and Hälsingland

Going north along the coast you reach the regions of Gästrikland and Hälsingland. The provincial capital is Gävle, a town with a busy harbor on the Baltic. Gävle's "old section" still has the small wooden houses of former times, and a castle built in 1613. Further on, 80 kilometers (50 miles) from Gävle, is the veteran Jädraas-Tallas railway. Here the traveler can enjoy a landscape of forest and lake, and a coastline dotted with bays, inlets and islands.

Hälsingland is known throughout Sweden for the world's largest folk dancing competition, with 1,500 couples competing. It is held in July in Hårga, Bollnäs, Arbrå and Järvsö. A visit to Järvsö should also be relished for the magnificence of its scenery. The manor houses to be seen in this area are generally large and memorable. Characterized by folklore and handicraft products, this country's culinary specialty is smoked Baltic herring, called "böckling."

Medelpad and Ångermanland

Here, in a region also known as Västernorrland, you are right in the middle of Sweden: Flataklackarna at Torpshammar is actually the geographical center. You will encounter stretches of coast here that are quite different from the rest of the country. On the Höga Kusten, or High Coast, at Nordingrå, steep hills rise straight out of the sea and the inlets would be better described as fjords.

The rivers are also distinctive features of the landscape, with the Indal and Ångerman Rivers being the most impressive. On the Indal there is a 72-kilometer (45-mile) long channel for canoeing with rustic overnight cabins. There are many hiking trails in this area. An important beaver colony can be found near Ramsele.

Near Sundsvall is Alnön, known for its unusual geological features. From neighbouring Härnösand, a pleasant town with old-world charms, and Örnsköldsvik you can take a boat trip to Trysunda and Ulvön, which is known as the "Pearl of the Baltic." The view from the 350-meter (1,150-foot) high "Skuleberget" is fantastic. A chair lift operates from Docksta.

Västerbotten—the Gateway to Lapland

The road from Umeå is called Blå Vägen, or the Blue Route (E79). This beautiful road goes all the way to the Atlantic. Other parallel routes have names like the Silver Road, the Saga Road and the Road of the Seven Rivers. The Stekenjokk Road goes from Vilhelmina over bare mountains to the province of Jämtland.

Along the coast at Lövånger are more than a hundred timber cottages dating from the 17th century. They are now renovated and available for tourists to stay in. At Lycksele on the Blue Route there is a large zoo featuring Nordic animals. Also Gammelplatsen—an outdoor museum—and a pretty 18th-century church.

Lapland

There is nothing more dramatic in all of Scandinavia than this region north of the Arctic Circle. It seems terribly far north, terribly distant, and it is at about the same latitude as northern Alaska. Yet it is a remarkably accessible place. You climb aboard an express train in Stockholm one afternoon, sleep soundly in a comfortable sleeper, eat in the diner, and by noon the next day you have arrived in a strange and wonderful world. (The flight from Stockholm to Kiruna takes 95 minutes.)

These contradictions never fail to fascinate the visitor. The region is huge—the province of Lapland covers about one fourth of Sweden's total area, but is only sparsely settled, of course. And its great beauty as a vacation region is the ease and comfort with which you reach it, without strain, special clothes or equipment, or much traveling time.

If you travel by train, the main line proceeds on or near the eastern coast, along the Gulf of Bothnia, all the way to the city of Boden. You pass through a huge industrial region—largely forest products—and magnificent natural scenery. Since this is a night train you will sleep through most of it, but the coastal cities, such as Gävle, a major port; Sundsvall, a paper and pulp center; Umeå, the cultural capital of northern Sweden; and Luleå, with a museum featuring Lapp collections and a 15th-century church, are of more than passing interest. Outside Luleå there is an archipelago of 300 islands.

The whole of northern Sweden is a region of forests and huge rivers. The rivers cut eastward across country from the mountain range along the Norwegian border to the east coast of Sweden, and are used both to float logs to factories on the Baltic coast and for hydro-electric power. A trip through this region shows you why Sweden is one of the world's great producers of paper, woodpulp, and other wood products—the forests seem endless. At Boden, a northern military and industrial hub, the line makes a junction with the line going diagonally across Norrland, from Luleå on the Swedish coast to Narvik, Norway. It was built around the turn of the century to exploit the huge finds of iron ore (up to 70 per cent pure) at Gällivare and Kiruna. Narvik, an ice-free port, has become the principal shipping point, and Luleå ranks second. Up to 16,000,000 tons of ore are taken out and shipped annually via this line, and the ore trains run day and night.

The coast at Piteå is called the Riviera of the North; there is a lot of sun here in summer and the water is sometimes as warm as the water in the Mediterranean. This is a favorite vacation spot for Norwegians from northern Norway, since the water in the Atlantic is much colder.

North of the Arctic Circle

Keep your eyes open after you leave Boden. About 97 kilometers (60 miles) north—and a little west—you will see a line of white stones cutting squarely across the railroad tracks and a sign "Arctic Circle" in two or three languages, including English. You're now in the land of the Midnight Sun, near the legendary home of Santa Claus.

The sun never sets from the end of May until the middle of July, and if you have looked at pictures of it making its way across the horizon, let us assure you at once they are misleading. The apparent darkness in the photos, giving more of an impression of moonlight than sunlight, is caused by the filters used when shooting directly at the sun. Actually, the Midnight Sun is as bright as it is anywhere an hour or so before sunset. The whole thing has a mystical, unreal, ethereal quality—you sometimes find yourself feeling almost light headed. But well before the date when the sun actually stays above the horizon all night and well afterwards, the nights are light all night long. So if your visit must take place a week or two before or after the specific dates given, you will still enjoy the "sunlit nights" that give you approximately the same sensation.

64 kilometers (40 miles) north of Boden you arrive in Gällivare, center of a mining region with ore reserves estimated at 400,000,000 tons. The principal mine is Malmberget, about four miles out of town. From here you can take an interesting side trip, the railway to Porjus and then by a new road to Vietas, not far from the Saltoluokta Tourist Station, and from there a motorboat trip in Sjöfallsleden, "Lapland's Blue Ribbon", the source lakes of the Big Lule River. Combined with some 19 kilometers (12 miles) walking you will, by this westbound route, finally reach the Atlantic. At Gällivare you will get the first glimpse of the Lapland mountains. Dundret (Thunder Mountain), 760 meters (2,500 feet), has a convenient chair lift to its summit, and the view is well worth the trip. The midnight sun is visible in this neighborhood from June 1 to July 12.

Kiruna

Another 80 kilometers (50 miles) or so north on the main railway line is Kiruna, the world's biggest city in terms of area. Kiruna became big enough to accommodate, shall we say, London, New York, and a few dozen other cities by incorporating the whole province within the municipality some years ago. It covers no less than 4,800 square kilometers (1,850 square miles), about the same size as the province of Skåne. The mining town proper had a population of some 21,000, but only picked up an additional 6,000 or so people by this huge extension of its borders. The people, including the Lapps, were quick to react to the knowledge that they were living in the world's biggest city. A man we know was trying to get hold of a Lapp friend of his by telephone to a remote village. He finally succeeded in locating the man's wife, who said her husband wasn't at home: "He's out in the city with the reindeer herd."

Kiruna lies on a slope between two ore-bearing mountains with the jaw-cracking names of Kirunavaara and Luossavaara. The ore reserves are estimated at 500,000,000 tons. Mining operations are going more and more underground, but during the past decades most ore has been taken out by the open-cast method. You should try to see the biggest pit—if possible when blasting is going on. Tons of dynamite go off at one time in a huge manifestation of explosive power. From high points around Kiruna you get beautiful views—on clear days you can see the irregular contours of Kebnekaise, Sweden's highest mountain, about 80 kilometers (50 miles) away. And here in Kiruna you may see the blue and red costumes of the Lapps for the first time.

Meeting the Lapps

For a long time the Lapps were believed to be of Mongolian origin, but the latest theory now supposes they stem from somewhere in central Europe. Presumably they came to northern Scandinavia more than 1,000 years ago. They number about 8,000 in Sweden (of whom only 2,000 are nomads deriving a living from the breeding of reindeer), 20,000 in Norway, 2,500 in Finland, and perhaps less than 2,000 in the Soviet Union.

The reindeer is the bone, sinew, and marrow of the economy of the nomadic Lapps of this area. (There are also forest Lapps and fishing Lapps.) Reindeer is the only domestic animal which can feed itself on the meager vegetation here beyond the Arctic Circle. The Lapps are nomads perhaps less from a restless desire to keep on the move than from the necessity of following their reindeer herds from one grazing ground to another. In the winter they move down to the protected forests, east and south of the mountains, but in the spring they travel in the opposite direction for the grazing on the high slopes. The total number of reindeer in the Swedish herds has been estimated at something like 200,000.

The Lapp culture is not as primitive as many have chosen to believe—rather, it is a highly developed culture perfectly adapted to perhaps the only way of life which will mean independent survival in these northern wastes. Take just the matter of languages, for example: practically all of the Lapps are at least bi-lingual and many are fluent in three or four tongues—their own language, Swedish, Norwegian, Finnish, and possibly others. Their handicrafts make use of the horns and skins of reindeer, and their distinctive costumes, largely in red, yellow, and blue, are as functional as they are ornamental. During the war they performed invaluable services to the Allied cause by helping Norwegians and other prisoners of the Nazis escape from Norway through the mountains to Sweden.

The Lapps, as they follow their herds, live in a special type of tepee, or hut, which is called a *kåta*. They eat reindeer meat—some reindeer are milked—and about the only things a Lapp family needs from the outside world are coffee and salt. They, like other people in the North, are devoted to coffee. Some of the larger reindeer owners are wealthy. Many now move to and from the summer camps by helicopter, leaving only the young men to accompany the herds. But don't ask a Lapp how many reindeer he has. It is the measure of his wealth, and is about as rude and nosy a question as asking an acquaintance how much money he has.

The Lapps have equal status with other Swedes under the law, and some special privileges. The government provides special schools for their education, and attendance is compulsory, as it is for all the other groups. There is a special inn for Lapps in Kiruna, and you may see them on the streets. Or you may meet them on the train carrying knapsacks. Don't be patronizing—they're not "simple" people. They have produced at least one great primitive artist and some university professors. But whatever their talents, whatever their education, most of them prefer their own way of life. You may get some idea of the traditional Lapp way of life by visiting the "Lappstaden" at Arvidsjaur, an old village of 70 cone-shaped Lapp huts which are still used for church visits at festival times.

Jukkasjärvi

Almost due east of Kiruna, about 15 to 25 kilometers (ten or 15 miles), is Jukkasjärvi, a little village. This is a sort of semi-permanent Lapp headquarters, with a modern school, an equally modern home for aged Lapps, and an appealing old church. The structure dates from 1726, was built on the site of a previous church (1611) which was the second one in all of Lapland. Note the remarkable architecture. At the times of the great religious holidays, Lapps gather here in huge crowds, and a Lapp wedding may be a tremendous event.

To get to Jukkasjärvi you must cross the mighty Torne River. These rushing waters make a magnificent sight, and beneath the turbulent surface there are fighting game fish—including salmon, trout, and grayling.

At Kaitum, 24 kilometers (15 miles) south of Kiruna is the Kaitum Chapel consecrated in 1964 as an ecclesiastical center for Laplanders but also as a memorial to Dag Hammarskjöld, the Swedish-born Secretary General of the United Nations.

Mount Kebnekajse, 2,111 meters (6,926 feet) above sea level, the highest mountain in Sweden, is an excursion point best reached from Kiruna. It is really in the wilderness, about 32 kilometers (20 miles) by bus, 40 (25 miles) by motorboat, and the last 24 (15 miles) on foot. (In the winter it's bus and skis; sometimes sleighs are available.) Here you literally get away from it all, but the trip is recommended only for those who are in good physical condition. From Kebnekaise the sun is visible round the clock from May 23 to July 22.

An hour or so north of Kiruna on the main railway line you approach the southern shore of Lake Torneträsk, a long, narrow body of water which extends for miles almost to the Norwegian border. This is the real wilderness, but modern communications put it right outside your window. The railroad and the new road follow the southern shore, and at the eastern end you come to one of the most popular resort regions in Lapland.

The first resort, and the best known, that you reach is Abisko. There are regular motorboat tours on Lake Torneträsk, mountain excursions during the summer season and skiing during the spring. The sun is visible round the clock from June 12 to July 4. Björkliden is a few kilometers farther along, also on the railway line, located near Lake Torneträsk. About eight kilometers (five miles) away is Laktatjakko.

The very last resort before you cross into Norway is Riksgränsen (the frontier). The little railway station also serves as the customs house. Here you can enjoy skiing by the light of the Midnight Sun, which shines from May 26 to July 18.

PRACTICAL INFORMATION FOR THE NORTH

TOURIST INFORMATION. There are tourist offices in the following places: **Åre,** Torget (0647–512 20). **Bräcke** (0693–100 00). **Dorotea,** Torget (0942–112 06). **Funäsdalen** (0684–21420). **Gäddede** (0672–105 00). **Gävle,** Norra Strandgatan 11–13 (026–10 16 00). **Hammarstrand** (0696–102 73). **Hede** (0684–110 80). **Kiruna,** Bus Station (0980–188 80). **Luleå,** Rådstugatan 9 (0920–937 46). **Östersund,** Rådhusgatan 44 (063–14 40 01). **Skellefteå,** Storgatan 46 (0910–588 80). **Sollefteå,** Storgatan 59 (0620–143 67). **Sundsvall,** Torget (060–11 42 35). **Sveg** (0680–107 75). **Tärnaby,** Västra Strandvägen 11 (0954–104 50). **Umeå,** Renmarkstorget (090–16 16 16). **Vemdalen** (0684–302 70).

TELEPHONE CODES. We have given telephone codes for all the towns and villages in the hotel and restaurant lists that follow. These codes need only be used when calling from outside the town or village concerned.

HOTELS AND RESTAURANTS. North, south and west of Östersund, the mountain resorts of Jämtland are concentrated. These are not generally luxury establishments: they are designed principally for people who like the outdoors, and the rates are reasonable. In Lapland, you will find both modest hotels and modern, comfortable tourist hotels.

Åre. *Diplomat-Åre* (E), (0647–502 65). 41 rooms; open Nov. to May. *Åre Fjällby* (M), (0647–504 50). 147 flats. 800 meters (880 yards) to railway station. Sauna, pool, gym, restaurants, dancing. Near ski lifts. Open year-round. AE, DC, MC, V. *Åregården* (M), (0647–502 65). 84 rooms. 400 meters (1,312 ft.) above sea level. 100 meters (328 ft.) to cable lift and railway station. Sauna, pool, dancing. Sports equipment for rent. Open year-round. AE, MC, V. *Sunwing Åre* (M) (0647–504 30). 79 rooms, 143 flats. Restaurant, dancing, nightclub, cafeteria. Sauna, pool, ski lift. AE, DC, MC, V.

Arvidsjaur. *Laponia* (M), (0960–108 80). 115 rooms. Restaurant, nightclub, saunas, pool. AE, DC, MC, V.

Björkliden. *Hotel Fjället* (I) (0980–400 40). 66 rooms. On railway and road to Swedish border. 500 meters (1,640 ft.) above sea level. Overlooking majestic mountain and Lake Torneträsk. Midnight Sun May 31 to July 16. Pension. Restaurant, dancing. Saunas, ski lifts. Excursions summer and winter. Open Feb. to middle Sept. (bookings 08–24 83 60). AE, MC, V.

Borgafjäll, S. Lappland. *Hotel Borgafjäll* (I) (0942–420 16). 30 chalet-type rooms. 540 meters (1,772 ft.) above sea level. Bus to Dorotea. Restaurant, sauna, slalom, fishing. Also self-service cottages. Open Feb. 15 to Apr. 30 and middle June through Sept. AE, MC, V.

Bruksvallarna, Härjedalen. *Ramundberget* (I) (0684–270 10). 58 rooms. Nine km. (five miles) to Bruksvallarna. 750 meters (2,460 ft.) above sea level. Restaurant, dancing. Sauna, indoor pool, ski lifts, excursions, fishing. Open Jan. to beginning May and July through Dec. MC, V.

Dorotea. *Hotel Dorotea* (I), (0942–10810). 29 rooms. Excellent cuisine. Try *Hubbes Horrible Hash,* mountain lake char *à la Raukasjö.* AE, DC, MC.

Gävle. *Grand Central* (E), Nygatan 45 (026–12 90 60). 232 rooms. Central. Restaurants *Trägårn* and *Skeppet* with marine atmosphere. Dancing, nightclub. AE, DC, MC, V. *Hotel Sara Gävle* (E), Norra Slottsgatan 9 (026–17 70 00). 200 rooms. Pleasant atmosphere. Café artist restaurant. Piano bar. AE, DC, MC, V.
Restaurants. *Skeppet* (the Ship) (M), Nygatan 45 (026–12 90 60). In 100-year-old cellar vaults. Fresh *strömming* (Baltic herring) in all variations. MC, V. *Strandgården* (M), at Bönan fishing village, 13 km. (eight miles) north of Gävle (026–992 80). View of the sea. Fish, especially *strömming.* MC, V.

Hammarstrand. *Gullbacken* (I), (0696–107 80). 30 rooms, 22 cabins. Pool, sauna, restaurant. Open year-round. MC.

Hemavan, Lappland. *Hemavan Högfjällshotellet* (Mountain Resort Hotel) (0954–301 50). 52 rooms. 500 meters (1,640 ft.) above sea level. Pension. Restaurant, sauna. Ski lifts, helicopter lift, marked trails, canoes etc. Dec. to early May and mid-June to early Oct. AE, DC, MC, V.

Kiruna. *Ferrum* (E), Lars Janssonsgatan 15 (0980–186 00). 170 rooms. 510 meters (1,673 ft.) above sea level. Restaurant, cocktail bar, saunas. Also 90 flats at *Ripan.* AE, DC, MC, V.

Youth Hostel. Strandstigen (0980–171 95). 90 beds. 500 meters (546 yards) from bus stop and railway station. Open June 15 through Aug.

Luleå. *SAS Luleå* (L), Storgatan 17 (0920–940 00). 212 rooms. SAS check-in, airport bus. Restaurant *Cook's Krog,* nightclub, sauna, solarium. AE, DC, MC, V. *Scandic* (M), Mjölkudden (0920–283 60). 158 rooms. Restaurant, sauna, solarium, airport bus. AE, DC, MC, V.

Östersund. *Hotel Östersund* (E), Kyrkgatan 70 (063–11 76 40). 129 rooms. Central. Sauna, restaurant, dancing, nightclub. AE, DC, MC, V. *Winn* (E), Prästgatan 16 (063–12 77 40). 177 rooms. Central, airport bus. Restaurant *Stadshuskällaren,* dancing, sauna. AE, MC, V.

Youth Hostel. Tingsgatan 12 (063–12 85 61). 100 beds. Open mid-June to beginning Aug.

Stora Blåsjön. *Blåsjöns Fjällhotel* (I), (0672–210 40). 32 rooms and flats and 16 cabins. Sauna, restaurant, outdoor activities, near ski lifts. Open July to Sept., Nov. to early Jan., early Feb. to May. AE, MC, V.

Storlien. *Storliens Högfjällshotel* (I), (0647–701 70). 192 rooms, 34 cabins. Sauna, pool, restaurant, dancing, near ski lifts. Open year-round except May to June. AE, DC, MC, V.

Sundsvall. *Sundsvall.* (M), Esplanaden 29 (060–17 16 00). 201 rooms. Restaurant, dancing, sauna. AE, DC, MC, V.

Restaurants. *Oskar* (M), Vängåvan (060–12 98 11). Central. French cuisine and Nordic fare. MC, V. *Turistpaviljongen* (I), Norra Stadsberget (060–11 42 22). On a mountain-top with an excellent view of the city. Three km. (two miles) from the center. MC, V.

Youth Hostel. Gaffelbyn (060–11 21 19). 150 beds. 2.5 km. (1.6 miles) from center of town, on hill. Open all year.

Tänndalen. *Hotel Tänndalen (I), (0684–220 00). 65 rooms. Indoor swimming pool, sauna. AE, DC, MC, V.*

Umeå. *Blå Aveny* (E), Rådhusesplanaden 14 (090–13 23 00). 165 rooms. Central. Restaurant, cocktail bar, dancing, pub. Sauna, peaceful atmosphere. AE, DC, MC, V. *Blå Dragonen* (Blue Dragon) (M), Norrlandsgatan 5 (090–13 23 80). 71 rooms. Central. Steakhouse *Ryttmästaren* (Cavalry Captain) and restaurant *Blå Dragonen.* Dancing, sauna, heated outdoor pool, sun terrace. AE, DC, MC, V.

Restaurants. *Sävargården* (E), at the open-air museum Gammlia, five minutes by car from center (090–11 02 22). Dates from 18th century. Headquarters of the Russian General Kamenski for a time during the 1808–9 war. *Smörgåsbord,* with food from Västerbotten. AE, MC, V. *Cajsa Warg* (I), Kungsgatan 52 (090-12 44 22). Central. Steakhouse. Specialties from area. During day self-service, at night table service. AE, MC, V.

Youth Hostel. Åliden (090–19 43 00). 100 beds. Three km. (two miles) from railway station. Bus 8. Open June to mid-August.

Camping

There are over 200 camping sites in this area. Many of them have log cabins and chalets for rent and most of them can be reached by bus or train: **Bollnäs,** Orbaden, Vallsta (0278-455 63). 24 chalets. On Lake Orsjön. Bus 500 meters (546 yards). Near ski lifts. Bike, canoe rentals. Open all year. **Delsbo,** *Delsbo Camping,* west of Delsbo on road 84 (0653-163 03). 4 chalets. On lake, 500 meters (546 yards) from bus stop. Canoes for rent. Open June 15 to Aug. 15. **Haparanda,** Kukkolaforsen (0922-310 00). 20 chalets. On route 99, 15 km. (nine miles) north of Haparanda. Restaurant, fishing, canoe safaris. Open all year. **Hede,** *Hede Camping* (0684-110

20). 15 chalets. On lake, excursions, boats, canoe rentals. Open all year. **Jokkmokk,** Kuossinjarka, Vaihijaur (097-310 13). 50 chalets. Bus stop, 12 km. (7.4 miles) from center. On lake. Bike, boat, canoe rentals. Open June to Aug. **Lycksele,** Ansia (0950-100 83). 38 chalets. On road 90 on east side of Umeå River, 1.5 km. (a mile) from town center. Bus 200 meters (200 yards). Canoe and bike rentals. Open June through Aug. **Luleå,** *Luleå Camping* at Skogsvallen (0920-932 64). 26 chalets. Central, bus stop, bike and canoe rentals. Open June to Aug. **Nordingrå,** Norrfällsviken, 30 km. (19 miles) from E4 (0613-213 82). 20 chalets. Canoes for rent. Open June 18 through Aug. **Östersund,** *Östersunds Camping,* Odenslingan 831, on E75 (063-11 37 06). 112 cabins. Central. Open all year. **Skellefteå,** *Skellefteå Camping,* on E4 (0910-188 55). 34 chalets. 14 km. (8.6 miles) north of town center. Sauna, ski lift; bikes for rent. Open all year. **Storuman,** *Storuman Camping,* 200 meters (220 yards) south of Blue Route (0951-106 96). 22 cabins. On lake. Sauna; boats and canoes for rent. Open June through Aug. **Sundsvall/Härnösand,** Bye Rast, Söråker, on E4 (060-450 55). 20 chalets. 38 km. (24 miles) north of Sundsvall. Canoes and boats for rent. Open all year. **Undersåker,** Ristafallet, on Indal River (0647-311 10). 8 cabins. 400 meters (440 yards) south of E75 and seven km. (4.3 miles) west of Järpen. Waterfall. Open June through Aug.

HOW TO GET AROUND. By car. The most important route to northern Sweden, Highway E4, continues from Stockholm to Haparanda on the Finnish border—1,134 km. (705 miles). The main routes to the interior highlands branch off this highway at Hudiksvall: road 84 via Sveg to Funäsdalen—322 km. (200 miles); Sundsvall: E75 via Östersund to Åre—300 km. (186 miles) and Storlien, so further into Norway to Trondheim; at Umeå: roads 92, 93 and 361—the very scenic Blå Vägen—through Storuman to Tärnaby and Hemavan, and on to Mo i Rana, below the Arctic Circle; at Luleå: roads 97 and 98 via Jokkmokk and Gällivare to Kiruna—381 km. (237 miles).

The new "Norgevägen" (Norway Route) from Kiruna to Narvik is now open. It passes through upland marshes and gently-rolling hills which rise up gradually to the mountains near the Norwegian border at Riksgränsen, from which the road makes a quick descent to the coast. Another route leading into Norway goes from Vilhelmina along the beautiful Lake Vojmsjön to Dikanäs and Kittelfjäll and via the frontier village of Skalmodal to Mosjöen in Norway—400 km. (248 miles).

Note that it is forbidden to take photographs near the defense areas of Sundsvall and Kalix on Highway E4, and Boden on Highway 97.

By train. Two main rail lines traverse Sweden in a south-north direction: from Stockholm near the coast to the Finnish border, and the Inlandsbanan (inland railway) from Dalarna province through the interior to Gällivare. The Inlandsbanan runs for more than 1,120 km. (696 miles) from Kristinehamn via Mora and Östersund to Gällivare. Part of the run is by bus. During the summer a discount ticket is offered for two or three weeks' unlimited travel on the line. Among other sites, the train stops at the Arctic Circle south of Jokkmokk. An Arctic Circle or *Polcirkel* certificate is sold at the tourist office in Jokkmokk. The Sundsvall-Trondheim and Luleå-Narvik lines cross it in an east-west direction. Secondary lines and postal buses, fanning out from the railroad stations, supplement this network and make even remote districts conveniently accessible. From Stockholm it is 6¼ hours to Östersund by express train, 9 to Storlien, 15 to Luleå, 18 to Kiruna and 20 to Abisko.

By bus. Long-distance buses link Stockholm and Gothenburg with Funäsdalen and Sundsvall with Luleå. Swedish State Railways also offers nine-day guided bus tours of the North Cape twice weekly from mid-June to mid-August, starting at Luleå and ending at Narvik in Norway.

By air. There are airports at Gävle, Östersund, Sundsvall, Kramfors, Skellefteå, Umeå, Luleå, Gällivare and Kiruna. You can fly from Stockholm to Sundsvall in 50 minutes, to Umeå in 60 minutes, to Luleå in 75 minutes, to Östersund in 60 minutes, to Kiruna in 95 minutes.

By ferry. If your preference is for a more leisurely route, there is a car ferry service from Vaasa in Finland to Sundsvall (8½ hours) and Umeå (5hours), and from Pietarsaari in Finland to Skellefteå (5 hours).

454 SWEDEN

PLACES TO VISIT. Wilderness, forests and mountains are not the whole story. Among the other sights at the far north of Sweden are:

Arjeplog. Silvermuseet. Storgatan 20. Large collection of Lapp handicrafts and silver; 600-year-old tools and fireplaces, and much more. Open Mon. to Fri. 11–3, Sat. and Sun. 12–3. In summer, longer opening hours. Adm. free.

Härnösand. Murberget Homestead Museum. 1.5 km. (a mile) from center of town. Old farmhouses from the area; church, shop, school from 19th century. Tour every day. Demonstrations of spinning, weaving etc. weekly—for information on tours call 0611-232 40. Open June to Aug. 15, daily 10–4. Admission free.

Länsmuseet (Provincial Museum). Near Murberget. Has archeological finds, handicrafts etc. and is open same times as Homestead Museum.

Jokkmokk. Jokkmokk Museum. Kyrkogatan. Also called the "Arctic Circle Museum." Lapp handicrafts and silver. Exhibits showing the frontier life of settlers. Animals of the north. Open Mon. to Fri. 12–3, Sat. and Sun. 1–4; June through Aug., Mon. to Fri. 10–7, Sat. and Sun. 12–6.

Jukkasjärvi. Jukkasjärvi Homestead Museum. 17 km. (11 miles) south of Kiruna. Old farm, log cabins and many types of Lapp *kåta* (huts) and sheds. Beautiful altar painting in nearby wooden church. Cafeteria. Tour four times daily—call 0980-211 90 for times. Open June through Aug., daily 10–9.

Östersund. Jamtli Open-Air Museum. Centrally placed. 18th-century manor house, Lapp *kåta* (huts), town houses, market place etc. Mid-summer to Aug. there are activities in many of the buildings, daily 10–6. Park open all year. Small admission fee.

Jämtlands Läns Museum. Provincial museum close to Jamtli. Rich collections of folk art, paintings etc. Temporary exhibitions. Open Mon. to Fri. 10–4, Sat. and Sun. 12–5. Admission free.

Storforsen. Skogsbruksmuseet (Forestry Museum). At Storforsen River, 40 km. (25 miles) west of Älvsbyn. Permanent exhibition of forestry and timber-floating through the ages. Charcoal and tar are occasionally made here in the traditional way. Tour three times daily—call 0929-310 91 for times of tours. Open June through Aug., daily 10–4. Admission free.

Sundsvall. Norra Berget (North Hill) Homestead Museum. Two km. (1.2 miles) from center of city (uphill). Buildings from the 19th century. Open Mon. to Fri. 10–4, Sat and Sun. 11–4; June through Aug., daily 9–7. Admission free.

Sundsvall Museum. Storgatan 29. Sawmill and city history. Finds from Iron Age, paintings etc. Temporary exhibitions. Open Mon. to Thurs. 11–8, Fri. to Sun. 11–4; summer, daily 11–4. Admission free.

SPORTS. Many well-marked trails for **hiking** and **climbing** criss-cross the entire mountain area. Most spectacular of these is the "King's Trail" (Kungsleden) leading from Jäckvik through the Sarek district north to Abisko. Kvikkjokk is the starting point for tours up the beautiful Tarra valley and can be conveniently reached from Jokkmokk. From Kiruna you can reach Nikkaluokta at the foot of 2,111-meter (6,926-ft) Mount Kebnekaise, Sweden's highest mountain, but experience of tough mountaineering, including snow and ice climbing, is essential. The "Jämtland Triangle", a large block of mountains to the west towards the Norwegian border, is a popular area for hiking. Storsylen reaches a height of 1,762 meters (5,780 ft.) and Sylarna is a jagged range with three small glaciers. An extensive network of mountain huts is maintained by the Swedish Touring Club, and expeditions with guides start regularly from the various tourist stations.

Fine possibilities for trout **fishing** exist throughout the region; also char, grayling, and salmon. Among the waterways, try the Dalälven, Ljungan, Indal, Ljusnan, and

Torne rivers, and the "Ströms vattudal", nine connecting lakes stretching northwest from Strömsund to Frostviken. Other excellent fishing centers are Saxnäs, Tärnaby, Ammarnäs, and Arvidsjaur. Fishing license fees are low; for fishing in Jämtland waters write to the Tourist Office, Rådhusplan, S-83182 Östersund, and for fishing in Lapland to Norrbotten Tourist Board, S-951 84 Luleå, or to Västerbotten Länsturistnämnd, S-90107 Umeå.

Forests abound in game for the **hunter,** especially moose, particularly plentiful in Jämtland; open season: four days, usually starting the second Monday of September. Special permits are required for the import and export of rifles and ammunition, and expeditions are arranged for hunters from abroad; write to the Tourist Office, Rådhusplan, S-83182 Östersund.

WINTER SPORTS. The northland is **skiing** country—slalom and cross-country. The Swedes are specialists in cross-country, with a string of Olympic titles to prove the point. Härjedalen: Smallest of Sweden's four skiing provinces, also the highest; not quite as accessible as the others but very good skiing facilities, ski lifts in most resorts, and many good hotels; season in Fjällnäs district runs from January to mid-April. Jämtland: Sweden's most frequented winter resort area, thanks to its accessibility, facilities, and fine accommodations along Stockholm-Östersund-Trondheim railway; "snow weasels" are a feature, also torchlight sleigh rides, fishing through the ice, curling; season in Åre-Storlien district from January to mid-April. Lapland: Only distance from the capital and the lateness with which its season starts prevent this area from nosing out Jämtland as Sweden's top skiing region; this is purely skiing country—no ice sports or sleighing parties; the tree line is low, so there are plenty of open slopes; latitude is the greatest asset here and spring skiing the greatest delight—this is where you enjoy the sensation of skiing in the Midnight Sun; season in the Tärna district runs from March to early May, in Abisko district from March through May.

Informality is the keynote of Swedish winter resort life. There is no shortage of *après ski* activities in the larger resorts like Åre, but in general the accent is on good companionship, relaxing before open fires, and the opportunity of acquiring a midwinter tan. A word of caution with respect to the latter: the late winter-spring sun here has an unsuspected power—take good sun-glasses and be careful generally about over-exposing your face and body. Here is a brief survey of the provinces with their resorts and facilities.

Härjedalen is sleigh-ride and cross-country skiing territory, with marked trails and sleeping huts enticing skiers to two or three-day excursions. Its chief resorts are all clustered together, on a U-shaped road starting on the Norwegian border at *Fjällnäs* (732 meters or 2,400 ft.) and then paralleling the Tännan River southeastward through *Hamrafjället* (732 meters or 2,400 ft.) and *Tänndalen* (695 meters or 2,280 ft.), after which it swings around northeastward, with *Funäsdalen* (663 meters or 2,175 ft.) in the center of the bottom of the U and then turns northwest, with the last of the principal resorts, *Bruksvallarna* (778 meters or 2,550 ft.) falling at about the middle of the upper line of the U. *Vemdalsskalet,* finally, lies a little apart farther eastwards and just on the border to Jämtland province. Ski lifts at Fjällnäs, Hamrafjället, Bruksvallarna, Tänndalen, Tännäs, Funäsdalen, Sveg, Lofsdalen, Messlingen, and Vemdalsskalet.

Jämtland offers a bewildering richness of resorts. Its transportation key is *Östersund,* the main station on the Stockholm-Trondheim line, which, while not strictly a resort, can be used as a center from which to sally forth to skiing slopes in the vicinity. It has excellent skating rinks. The most easily accessible resorts are those on this rail line, which, starting from Östersund, are *Hålland* and *Undersåker,* both with ski lifts; *Åre,* the chief winter sports center of Jämtland, with an overhead cable railway, several ski lifts and skating and curling rinks; *Duved* with new chair lift; *Ånn;* and *Storlien,* the second-largest resort, which has a jump, ski lifts, slalom runs, one of which drops 235 meters (770 ft.) in a distance of 999 meters (3,280 ft.), ski schools for adults and children and skating rinks.

Another important area hugs the frontier south of Storlien, which gets you into some fairly high altitudes. First comes *Blåhammarstugan* (1,084 meters or 3,560 ft.). Southeast lies *Storulvåstugan* (730 meters or 2,395 ft.), south of that *Sylstugorna* (951 meters or 3,120 ft.), with a ski camp built another 91 meters (300 ft.) above it; and a little more than a few kilometers more to the south is the province's highest peak, *Mount Sylarna* (2,066 meters or 6,780 ft.). Of these resorts, Storulvåstugan has slalom runs and ski instructors on hand.

A few other resorts south of the main railway, between the border and Östersund, are worth mentioning. Farthest west, reached by road from Undersåker (on the rail line) is *Vålådalen,* a small popular resort with slalom and downhill runs, ski lift, a practice jump and a skating rink. Vålådalen is known as a training center for Sweden's Olympic cross-country skiers. About halfway between here and Östersund, and just about as far south of the railway, is *Bydalen,* with ski lift, and about as much farther south again, *Arådalen.* At *Hammarstrand,* some 97 km. (60 miles) east of Östersund, is a winter sports center with bobsleigh track, slalom run, ski lifts.

Lapland's most popular section is its farthest north, above the Arctic Circle. The entrance to this region is the iron-ore center of *Kiruna,* 200 km. (124 miles) north of the Arctic Circle. Kiruna is not itself a resort, but the nearby mountains provide slopes of all degrees of difficulty within easy reach, and by continuing through it on the Stockholm-Narvik railway or by road you pass in rapid succession through the three big winter sports centers of northern Lapland, all of which have slalom slopes, lifts, ski instructors and guides for the long excursions.

The first one reached from Kiruna is *Abisko* (310 meters or 1,020 ft.). A chair lift takes you up to the summit of Mount Nuolja with Midnight Sun from May 31 to July 16. Next comes *Björkliden,* which has a ski lift. Last station on the line, practically on the Norwegian border is *Riksgränsen,* also with a ski lift; the great attraction here is not simply sliding downhill from the top of the lift, but making excursions across the spectacular broad snowfields high up in the Riksgränsen mountains under the Midnight Sun.

There is also a winter sports center in southern Lapland around the resorts of Hemavan and Kittelfjäll. Ski lifts and good accommodations, but a little awkward to reach: direct train with sleepers from Stockholm to Storuman, then by bus.

Index

Index

The letter H indicates Hotel and other accommodations.
The letter R indicates Restaurants.

GENERAL INFORMATION

(See also Practical Information sections for each country and
Practical Information at the end of each chapter.)

Denmark
Practical Information

Geographical

Finland
Practical Information

Iceland
Practical Information

Geographical

Norway
Practical Information

Geographical

Sweden
Practical Information

Geographical

Fodor's Travel Guides

U.S. Guides

Alaska
Arizona
Atlantic City & the
  New Jersey Shore
Boston
California
Cape Cod
Carolinas & the
  Georgia Coast
The Chesapeake Region
Chicago
Colorado
Dallas & Fort
  Worth

Disney World & the
  Orlando Area
Florida
Hawaii
Houston &
  Galveston
Las Vegas
Los Angeles, Orange
  County, Palm Springs
Maui
Miami, Fort Lauderdale,
  Palm Beach
Michigan, Wisconsin,
  Minnesota

New England
New Mexico
New Orleans
New Orleans (Pocket
  Guide)
New York City
New York City (Pocket
  Guide)
New York State
Pacific North Coast
Philadelphia
The Rockies
San Diego
San Francisco

San Francisco (Pocket
  Guide)
The South
Texas
USA
Virgin Islands
Virginia
Waikiki
Washington, DC
Williamsburg

Foreign Guides

Acapulco
Amsterdam
Australia, New Zealand,
  The South Pacific
Austria
Bahamas
Bahamas (Pocket
  Guide)
Baja & the Pacific
  Coast Resorts
Barbados
Beijing, Guangzhou &
  Shanghai
Belgium &
  Luxembourg
Bermuda
Brazil
Britain (Great Travel
  Values)
Budget Europe
Canada
Canada (Great Travel
  Values)
Canada's Atlantic
  Provinces
Cancun, Cozumel,
  Yucatan Peninsula

Caribbean
Caribbean (Great
  Travel Values)
Central America
Eastern Europe
Egypt
Europe
Europe's Great
  Cities
Florence & Venice
France
France (Great Travel
  Values)
Germany
Germany (Great Travel
  Values)
Great Britain
Greece
The Himalayan
  Countries
Holland
Hong Kong
Hungary
India, including Nepal
Ireland
Israel
Italy

Italy (Great Travel
  Values)
Jamaica
Japan
Japan (Great Travel
  Values)
Jordan & the
  Holy Land
Kenya, Tanzania,
  the Seychelles
Korea
Lisbon
Loire Valley
London
London (Great
  Travel Values)
London (Pocket Guide)
Madrid & Barcelona
Mexico
Mexico City
Montreal &
  Quebec City
Munich
New Zealand
North Africa
Paris
Paris (Pocket Guide)

People's Republic of
  China
Portugal
Rio de Janeiro
The Riviera (Fun on)
Rome
Saint Martin &
  Sint Maarten
Scandinavia
Scandinavian Cities
Scotland
Singapore
South America
South Pacific
Southeast Asia
Soviet Union
Spain
Spain (Great Travel
  Values)
Sweden
Switzerland
Sydney
Tokyo
Toronto
Turkey
Vienna
Yugoslavia

Special-Interest Guides

Health & Fitness
  Vacations
Royalty Watching

Selected Hotels of
  Europe

Selected Resorts and
  Hotels of the U.S.
Shopping in Europe

Skiing in North Amer
Sunday in New York